Brief Contents

Contents

Human Rights
under the

$^{+}$
n

n

George Williams

OXFORD
UNIVERSITY PRESS

OXFORD

UNIVERSITY PRESS

253 Normanby Road, South Melbourne, Victoria 3205, Australia

Oxford University Press is a department of the University of Oxford.
It furthers the University's objective of excellence in research, scholarship,
and education by publishing worldwide in

Oxford New York

Auckland Bangkok Buenos Aires Cape Town Chennai
Dar es Salaam Delhi Hong Kong Istanbul Karachi Kolkata
Kuala Lumpur Madrid Melbourne Mexico City Mumbai Nairobi
São Paulo Shanghai Singapore Taipei Tokyo Toronto

with an associated company in Berlin

OXFORD is a trade mark of Oxford University Press
in the UK and in certain other countries

National Library of Australia

Cataloguing-in-Publication data:

Williams, George, 1969–

Human rights under the Australian Constitution.

Bibliography.
Includes index.
ISBN 019 554111 1.

1. Constitutional law—Australia. 2. Human rights—
Australia. 3. Civil rights—Australia. I. Title.
342.94085

Edited by Michele Sabto
Indexed by PTO Indexing Services
Cover designed by Steve Randles
Typeset by Desktop Concepts Pty Ltd, Melbourne
Printed by Craftprint, Singapore

Foreword

George Williams has shown great sagacity in selecting the title to this book. If it had been titled *Human Rights in the Australian Constitution* it would have been a slimmer volume and would have contained much less information.

For those readers who wish to obtain a panoramic perspective of how the Australian Constitution engages with human rights, this book will be invaluable. The author has explored all the ways in which the Constitution can be said to have a bearing on human rights.

Of all the books that have been published on the Constitution, this, more than any other, may disturb the long and peaceful slumber of the delegates to the constitutional Conventions at the end of the nineteenth century. On the one hand, they would be surprised to learn that they brought into existence an instrument that is now hailed as making a significant, albeit far from comprehensive, contribution to the protection of human rights, a concept that played an exiguous part in the jurisprudence with which they were familiar. On the other hand, they might be embarrassed to discover that, in the modern world, their desire to preserve a freedom to pursue policies now seen as discriminatory is regarded as unacceptable.

And what would they make of the principle of constitutional interpretation expounded by Kirby J in *Newcrest Mining v. Commonwealth* (1997) 147 ALR 42 at 147–51 and applied in his Honour's dissenting judgment in *Kartinyeri v. Commonwealth* (1998) 152 ALR 540 at 599: 'Where the Constitution is ambiguous, this court should adopt that meaning which conforms to the principles of universal and fundamental rights rather than an interpretation which would involve a departure from such rights'? What would have been the reaction of Sir Samuel Griffith, Sir Edmund Barton, and Sir Richard O'Connor to a submission inviting them to accept a proposition expressed in these terms?

What would have astonished the Justices almost a century ago may not seem astonishing today. As Mr Alfred Deakin foresaw so clearly in his second-reading speech on the Judiciary Bill of 1903, the Constitution evolves over time as the High Court elucidates its meaning in constantly changing conditions and circumstances. Whether it will evolve to the point that Justice Kirby's principle is accepted is one of the important unresolved constitutional questions of this time.

This question apart, a book giving a human rights perspective on the Australian Constitution is long overdue. The lack of such a perspective may have contributed to some of the criticism of High Court decisions that have been seen as implying rights in the Constitution, limited though these rights have been. Lack of understanding of the Court and of its role is seen as a problem that must be overcome. This book certainly fills the gaps. As well as answering a need, it contains much in the way of interesting discussion and comment on the Constitution by an author who has already become a well-known commentator on that enigmatic instrument.

The Hon. Sir Anthony Mason AC KBE

Preface

Much has already been written about constitutional rights in Australia. In this book I have set out to produce the first comprehensive text on human rights and the Australian Constitution. Decisions of the High Court over the last decade have made this project worthwhile. My aim has been to write a book that is accessible to students, academics, and practitioners. This book explores the decisions of the High Court on express and implied constitutional rights, as well as some of the underlying themes, and charts the possibilities of an Australian Bill of Rights.

In general, my method has been to adopt a case-based approach to the subject matter. I have learnt much from Peter Hogg's *Constitutional Law of Canada*[1] and Leslie Zines's *The High Court and the Constitution*.[2] Within a primarily case-based approach, I have striven to achieve a small measure of the clarity and analysis that these works are renowned for. Constitutional theory has its place in several of the chapters in this book, although the focus of the work remains on the decisions of the High Court. This reflects my belief that an understanding of this area must begin with the work of that institution. As a result, significant parts of this book are necessarily descriptive. However, as Chapter 9 demonstrates, this reveals much about the interpretation of rights generally, and illustrates several themes. On many occasions I have only been able to touch on these deeper issues. In such areas I hope that this book provides a springboard to further scholarship and inquiry.

This book is the product of several years work. It had its beginnings in 1992, when the High Court handed down its decisions in *Nationwide News Pty Ltd v. Wills* (1992) 177 CLR 1 and *Australian Capital Television Pty Ltd v. Commonwealth* (1992) 177 CLR 106, in which it held that the Constitution contains an implied freedom of political communication. At that time I was fortunate to be working as associate to Justice

---

1   P. Hogg, *Constitutional Law of Canada*, 4th edn, Carswell, 1997.
2   L. Zines, *The High Court and the Constitution*, 4th edn, Butterworths, 1997.

McHugh of the High Court. These decisions fired my interest in the Constitution as a document capable of protecting fundamental rights and were the subject of much of my initial writing. Some of the chapters of this book reflect my earlier writings, occasionally even reproducing passages. In other areas I have developed my views to the extent that I have departed from my earlier conclusions.

My colleagues at the Australian National University and elsewhere have been invaluable in assisting me to develop and deepen my ideas. I owe a considerable debt to the scholars whose arguments and analysis have inspired many of the thoughts and ideas expressed in this book. Some colleagues have kindly read and commented on earlier versions of various chapters. For this I thank John Braithwaite, Peter Cain, Hilary Charlesworth, Annemarie Devereux, John McMillan, Adrienne Stone, and Leslie Zines. The very helpful comments of the anonymous referees provided by Oxford University Press also deserve acknowledgment. More generally, I owe a great intellectual debt to Tony Blackshield, Michael Coper, and George Winterton, with whom I have had many discussions about these topics, and who have been unfailingly generous in regard to my endeavours in this field. Tony Blackshield deserves a further mention. As a teacher he sparked my interest in constitutional law and, as his co-author on *Australian Constitutional Law and Theory: Commentary and Materials*,[3] I was again privileged to be exposed to his ideas and methodology. Significant parts of this book reflect that collaboration.

This book has been supported by a grant from the Australian Research Council, which enabled me to travel to both the USA and Canada to conduct research. Geraldine Chin, Matthew Darke, Gim Del Villar, Amelia Simpson, and Kerrie-Ann Smith assisted with the collection of materials and proofreading. Permission was kindly given by LBC Information Services to reproduce some material. I have benefited greatly from my time in the Law Program at the Research School of Social Sciences in the Australian National University, where most of this book was completed. Finally, deep appreciation goes to Emma Armson, without whose support this book would remain as yet unwritten. This book is dedicated to the memory of my father, John Williams.

This book states the law to the end of September 1998.

George Williams

---

3   A. R. Blackshield and G. Williams, *Australian Constitutional Law and Theory: Commentary and Materials*, 2nd edn, Federation Press, 1998.

Table of Legislation

1. AUSTRALIA

Commonwealth

Table of Cases

ONE

Human Rights in Australia

Introduction

The High Court's approach to guarantees of individual liberty in the Australian Constitution continues to be replete with contradictions and uncertainty. The current period of development began with the decision of the High Court in *Street v. Queensland Bar Association* (1989) 168 CLR 461, in which the Court gave a substantive interpretation to the protection offered to out-of-state residents by s. 117 of the Constitution (see Chapter 5). However, while the express civil and political rights in the Constitution appeared to offer much at this point in time, they have as yet delivered little. On the other hand, freedoms implied from the system of representative government created by the Constitution rose, faltered, and rose again in a different guise (see Chapter 7). Over the same period, the Court has more quietly developed potentially far-reaching freedoms from the separation of judicial power brought about by the Constitution (see Chapter 8). Freedoms from this latter source, including any right to due process, might ultimately allow the High Court to constitutionalise key aspects of criminal procedure.

The year 1989 marked the point at which the High Court shifted from being a disinterested interpreter of constitutional rights to seeking to robustly construe such rights.[1] The work of the Court today reflects this change, with the energy of its judges now focused on questions of rights rather than on its traditional case-load of Commonwealth powers and Australian federalism. This shift has not been without controversy. Some members of the Court have reacted by embracing the conservatism of past decades, complete with pleas for a return to 'neutral' judicial decision-making. Although the High Court has been active in protecting rights via constitutional means, this does not make the Court 'activist' compared to comparable judicial bodies (see Chapter 7).[2] It is just that the Court's new determination to give effect to the rights in the Australian

---

1   An earlier indication of this shift was given in *Davis v. Commonwealth* (1988) 166 CLR 79 (see Chapter 4).
2   Compare, for example, the Hungarian Constitutional Court: see S. Zifcak, 'Hungary's Remarkable, Radical, Constitutional Court' (1996) 3 *Journal of Constitutional Law in Eastern and Central Europe* 1.

Constitution is in startling contrast to the unduly narrow approach to the construction of civil and political rights that it has taken over many decades.

The modern High Court's interpretation of the rights in the Australian Constitution is bereft of an essential feature. With the possible exception of Murphy J (see Chapter 7), no judge has articulated a vision of the role that constitutional rights should play in Australian democracy. Consequently, while recent decisions have revitalised the place of constitutional rights in Australia, this has been without a coherent theoretical or methodological underpinning (see Chapter 9). This is demonstrated by an apparent lack of direction in some decisions, and judicial and academic uncertainty as to where the development of constitutional freedoms will ultimately lead. It is also apparent in the High Court's ad hoc use of decisions from the courts of other countries. The result is that the generous interpretation of some rights may rest on a weak foundation.

While this book is primarily concerned with the protection of human rights under the Australian Constitution, that instrument cannot be considered independently of its context. Myriad other influences, such as international law, impact on constitutional interpretation in Australia and assist in locating the subject of constitutional rights within a broader legal and social framework. This is an essential feature of any understanding of the constitutional protection of rights in Australia. The wider perspective demonstrates the limitations of any approach to human rights based solely on constitutional law (see Chapter 3).[3]

What are human rights?

Conceptions of human rights are affected by a person's social, economic, and cultural background.[4] For example, some African cultures may approach human rights as obligations and duties rather than as rights.[5] Similarly, perceptions of human rights may differ between Australian men and women, as well as between Australians above and below the poverty line. Context is important. The international community has, however, sought to entrench the notion that certain human rights are universal: that is, that some interests should be regarded as human rights regardless of context. The process of determining human rights in the international sphere began after the Second World War with the *Universal Declaration of Human Rights 1948* (the *Declaration*) and has continued apace with a growing number of international instruments that witness the commitment of nations to various fundamental freedoms. While in the past Australian lawyers turned to English constitutional documents such as the *Magna Carta 1215* or the *Bill of*

---

3   See S. Bronitt and G. Williams, 'Political Freedom as an Outlaw: Republican Theory and Political Protest' (1996) 18 *Adelaide Law Review* 289, where this argument is developed in respect of the right to engage in political protest.

4   *Gerhardy v. Brown* (1985) 159 CLR 70 at 126 per Brennan J: 'an attempt to define human rights and fundamental freedoms exhaustively is bound to fail, for the respective religious, cultural and political systems of the world would attribute differing contents to the notions of freedom and dignity and would perceive at least some differences in the rights and freedoms that are conducive to their attainment'.

5   A. Devereux, 'Should "Duties" Play a Larger Role in Human Rights? A Critique of Western Liberal and African Human Rights Jurisprudence' (1995) 18 *University of New South Wales Law Journal* 464.

Rights 1688 (I Will & Mary, Sess 2 c 2) to found basic rights,[6] they increasingly turn today to international instruments for the same purpose.

The *Declaration* was adopted by the General Assembly of the United Nations on 10 December 1948. Since 1948, it has become a powerful authority for, and symbol of, the protection of human rights. In its 30 articles, the *Declaration* lists a broad range of rights, including:

- Everyone has the right to life, liberty and security of person. (Article 3)
- No one shall be arbitrarily deprived of his property. (Article 17(2))
- Everyone has the right to freedom of opinion and expression; this right includes freedom to hold opinions without interference and to seek, receive and impart information and ideas through any media and regardless of frontiers. (Article 19)
- Everyone has the right to rest and leisure, including reasonable limitation of working hours and periodic holidays with pay. (Article 24)

The preamble to the *Declaration* states that these rights are 'fundamental human rights'. In other words, they derive generally from the dignity and worth of the human person rather than from a particular social, cultural, or other context.[7] As such, the preamble states that these rights are 'a common standard of achievement for all peoples and all nations'.

The *Declaration* was subsequently bolstered by the *International Covenant on Civil and Political Rights 1966* (ICCPR) and the *International Covenant on Economic, Social and Cultural Rights 1966* (ICESCR). These treaties were ratified by Australia in 1980 and 1976 respectively. Unlike the *Declaration*, these covenants distinguish between civil and political rights on the one hand, and economic, social, and cultural rights on the other. The distinction between the two types of rights has been described as follows:

> If civil and political rights can be defined as the rights which enable individuals to operate freely within the political system and to be protected from arbitrary action in the administration of the law, including particularly the criminal law, then economic, social and cultural rights can be described as allowing people to own property, to work in fair conditions and to be guaranteed an adequate standard of living and facilities for education and the enjoyment of life and of the culture in which they live or have been brought up.[8]

The ICCPR recognises rights such as the following:

- No one shall be subjected to torture or to cruel, inhuman or degrading treatment or punishment. In particular, no one shall be subjected without his free consent to medical or scientific experimentation. (Article 7)
- Anyone who is arrested shall be informed, at the time of arrest, of the reasons for his arrest and shall be promptly informed of any charges against him. (Article 9(2))
- Everyone lawfully within the territory of a State shall, within that territory, have the right to liberty of movement and freedom to choose his residence. (Article 12(1))

---

6   In *Re Cusack* (1985) 60 ALJR 302 at 303–4, Wilson J held that neither the *Magna Carta* nor the *Bill of Rights* is capable of rendering inconsistent Commonwealth legislation invalid. See also *Jago v. District Court (NSW)* (1989) 168 CLR 23.

7   Article 1 of the *Declaration* states that 'All human beings are born free and equal in dignity and rights'.

8   P. Bailey, *Human Rights: Australia in an International Context*, Butterworths, 1990, p. 12.

- The right of men and women of marriageable age to marry and to found a family shall be recognised. (Article 23(2))

The ICESCR recognises rights such as the following:

- The State Parties to the present Covenant undertake to ensure … the right of everyone to form trade unions and join the trade union of his choice, subject only to the rules of the organization concerned, for the promotion and protection of his economic and social interests. (Article 8(1)(a))
- The State Parties to the present Covenant recognize the right of everyone to social security, including social insurance. (Article 9)
- The State Parties to the present Covenant recognize the right of everyone to an adequate standard of living for himself and his family, including adequate food, clothing and housing, and to the continuous improvement of living conditions. (Article 11(1))
- The State Parties to the present Covenant recognize the right of everyone to the enjoyment of the highest attainable standard of physical and mental health. (Article 12(1))
- The State Parties to the present Covenant recognize the right of everyone to education. (Article 13(1))

The rights created by the ICCPR are sometimes referred to as 'first generation' rights, while those recognised by the ICESCR are called 'second generation' rights. 'Third generation' rights refer to collective, or group, rights, such as the right to development or to self-determination.

A distinction sometimes drawn between civil and political rights, and economic, social and cultural rights is that the former can be regarded as legal rights (that is, they are enforceable at law), whereas the latter cannot be so easily regarded as legal rights, as they are more akin to aspirations.[9] This is reinforced by the fact that while the (first) *Optional Protocol of the International Covenant of Civil and Political Rights 1966* establishes enforcement mechanisms for the ICCPR, there is no similar instrument for enforcing obligations imposed by the ICESCR. The fact that these rights are sometimes regarded as aspirations rather than legal rights is also apparent in the obligations that each instrument places on its signatories. Article 2(2) of the ICCPR requires that each of the 'state parties' to the Covenant 'undertakes *to take the necessary steps*, in accordance with its constitutional processes and with the provisions of the present Covenant, to adopt such legislative or other measures as may be necessary *to give effect* to the rights recognized in the present Covenant' (emphasis added). Article 2(3) further provides that each of the state parties undertakes 'to ensure that any person whose rights or freedoms as herein recognized are violated shall have an effective remedy' and 'to ensure that the competent authorities shall enforce such remedies when granted'. In contrast, Article 2(1) of the ICESCR merely requires that each of the state parties to the Covenant 'undertakes *to take steps*, individually and through international assistance and co-operation, especially economic and technical, *to the maximum of its available resources*, with a view to *achieving progressively* the full realization of the rights recognized in the present Covenant by all appropriate means, including particularly the adoption of legislative measures' (emphasis added). The ICESCR makes no mention of remedies.

---

9   Bailey, pp. 11–20.

A similar distinction is embodied in the Bill of Rights in the South African Constitution (in force since 7 February 1997). While the civil and political rights of this Bill are generally expressed in mandatory language, many of its economic, social, and cultural rights are expressed in a manner less susceptible to judicial enforcement. For example, while s. 18 provides that 'Everyone has the right to freedom of association', the right to 'access to adequate housing' in s. 26(1) is qualified by s. 26(2): 'The state must take reasonable legislative and other measures, within its available resources, to achieve the progressive realisation of this right'. The South African Constitution also demonstrates the problems in drawing a line between the two categories of rights. The rights to a 'basic education' in s. 29(1)(a), and to a clean, healthy and sustainable environment in s. 24, both of which might be regarded as a economic, social, and cultural rights, are given unqualified protection.

The differences perceived between, on the one hand, civil and political rights, and on the other, economic, social, and cultural rights stem also from the distinction that is sometimes drawn between negative and positive rights (see Chapter 3).[10] The notion of positive and negative rights is illustrated by the scheme developed by Wesley Hohfeld.[11] Hohfeld noted that the legal use of the term 'right' denotes at least four distinct conceptions. Each of these concepts defines a relationship between the right-bearer and at least one other person:

1 **claim-right**—A claim-right involves an affirmative claim as against another person. Correlatively, the other person owes a 'duty' to the right-bearer (for example, X has a claim-right not to be assaulted, thus Y has a duty not to assault X). The opposite concept to a claim-right is where there is an absence of duty by the other person.

2 **privilege** (or 'liberty')—When a person is entitled to the benefit of a privilege, he or she is free from the claim, or right, of another. There is an absence of a duty *not* to do the act in question.

3 **power**—A power is the ability to alter legal rights and duties, or legal relations generally. The person whose legal relations are altered by the exercise of the power is said to be under a 'liability'. A 'power' is different to a claim-right because there is no correlative duty imposed on another person.

4 **immunity**—When a person is entitled to the benefit of an immunity, he or she is not under a liability to have his or her legal relations altered by another. Correlatively, the person who lacks the power to alter the immunity holder's legal relations is said to be under a 'disability'.

While claim-rights and powers can be seen as positive rights (the right to …), privileges and immunities are best viewed as negative rights (a freedom from …). Under Hohfeld's scheme, the civil and political rights in the Australian legal system would normally operate as negative rights: that is, as privileges (as in the case of the common law) or as immunities (as in the case of constitutional rights). This latter distinction results from the fact that while Australian parliaments are able to abrogate common law rights

---

10 See I. Berlin, *Two Concepts of Liberty*, Oxford University Press, 1958; and C. Sampford, 'The Four Dimensions of Rights', in B. Galligan and C. Sampford (eds), *Rethinking Human Rights*, Federation Press, 1997, p. 50.

11 W. N. Hohfeld, *Fundamental Legal Conceptions as Applied in Judicial Reasoning*, Greenwood Press, 1919. See also N. E. Simmonds, *Central Issues in Jurisprudence: Justice, Law and Rights*, Sweet & Maxwell, 1986, ch. 8.

(see pp. 15–17), they are unable to do the same to rights recognised by the Australian Constitution. However, if economic, social, and cultural rights are to be protected by law, they cannot, generally, be understood as negative rights (in the form of privileges or immunities). Economic, social, and cultural rights frequently require State action for their fulfilment, and thus they must be in a different form if they are to be enforceable by the right holder. This is not to say that such rights are not rights at all, or that they are 'second-class rights'.[12] After all, each set of rights has the same basic concern: the 'integrity, freedom and equality of all human beings'.[13] It is more a matter of recognising the differences between rights, and the conclusions that follow from this as to how the law should be structured in order to best attain each type.

In many instances, it is appropriate to talk of *realising* economic, social, and cultural rights, rather than of *protecting* them. For example, it makes no sense to categorise the right to the highest attainable standard of physical and mental health as a privilege, or immunity, when such a right is dependent on State action. Accordingly, if economic, social, and cultural rights are to be given legal effect they would generally need to be expressed as positive rights in the form of claim-rights, with the right-holder possessing the claim-right, and another person (or the government) being under a duty (for example, a duty to provide adequate health services). Thus far, rights have not been categorised as claim-rights in Australia. This is because Anglo–Australian law has, traditionally, derived much from the concept of liberalism, especially liberalism's focus on the individual's freedom from government action. It has not been concerned with placing obligations on others to protect or realise human rights. The law, including Australian constitutional law, has operated to protect individuals whose rights might otherwise be infringed, but it has not placed obligations on government, or others, to ensure that certain rights are fulfilled. In *Dietrich v. The Queen* (1992) 177 CLR 292, a majority of the High Court found that the power of a court to order a stay where an unfair trial would result may be exercised where an accused is charged with a serious offence and, through no fault of his or her own, is unable to obtain legal representation. Although the Court recognised a person's right to legal representation in some cases, it did not construct this right as an obligation on government to provide representation, but rather as a limitation on the power of courts to proceed with an unfair trial.

Even though it is apparent that some rights possess different characteristics to other rights in the way that they might be attained, this divide does not neatly separate civil and political rights from economic, social, and cultural rights. Some civil and political rights cannot be characterised as merely privileges or immunities. For example, the right to a fair trial, or more particularly the right to counsel, requires State action and not merely a zone of non-interference in order to be attained. The stay of an unfair trial provided for

---

12 There is an ongoing debate about the place of economic, social, and cultural rights in the international framework of rights protection. For example, Maurice Cranston argues that the rights named in the ICESCR 'are not universal human rights at all' (M. Cranston, *What are Human Rights?*, Bodley Head, 1973, p. 66). See also M. C. R. Craven, *The International Covenant on Economic, Social and Cultural Rights: A Perspective on its Development*, Clarendon Press, 1995, pp. 7–16; A. Eide, C. Krause, and A. Rosas (eds), *Economic, Social and Cultural Rights: A Textbook*, Martinus Nijhoff, 1995, pp. 15–62; and G. J. H. van Hoof, 'The Legal Nature of Economic, Social and Cultural Rights: A Rebuttal of Some Traditional Views', in P. Alston and K. Tomasevski (eds), *The Right to Food*, Martinus Nijhoff, 1984, p. 97.

13 A. Eide, 'Economic, Social and Cultural Rights as Human Rights', in Eide et al., p. 22.

by *Dietrich v. The Queen* is not the same as guaranteeing a fair trial. The division between, on the one hand, civil and political rights, and on the other, economic, social, and cultural rights is problematic given the lack of a clear dividing line between the two. The boundary can obviously be blurred and quite arbitrary. For example, the right to self-determination recognised in Article 1(1) of the ICCPR[14] contains elements of economic, social, and cultural rights, and is also found in Article 1(1) of the ICESCR; the right to found a family in Article 23(2) of the ICCPR might similarly be located in the ICESCR; and the right to join a trade union in Article 8(1) of the ICESCR is also listed in Article 22(1) of the ICCPR, in the context of 'freedom of association'. Moreover, while some economic, social, and cultural rights, such as the right to adequate housing,[15] might be regarded by some as more of an aspiration than a legal right, it is not clear why this need be so.

Republican theory challenges the traditional conception of human rights as merely privileges or immunities. It supports an agenda different from the non-interference of liberalism, and provides scope for greater governmental action, including the legal enforcement of economic, social, and cultural rights. Liberalism proposes an *asocial* concept of individual freedom, in which interference by others must be minimised or eliminated. On the other hand, republican theory adopts a very different perspective. John Braithwaite has described a concept of freedom called 'dominion' as follows:

> Dominion is a republican conception of liberty. Whereas the liberal conception of freedom is the freedom of an isolated atomistic individual, the republican conception of liberty is the freedom of a social world. Liberal freedom is objective and individualistic. Negative freedom for the liberal means the objective fact of individuals' being left alone by others. For the republican, however, freedom is defined socially and relationally. You only enjoy republican freedom—dominion—when you live in a social world that provides you with an intersubjective set of assurances of liberty. You must subjectively believe that you enjoy these assurances, and so must others believe. As a social, relational conception of liberty, by definition it also has a comparative dimension. To fully enjoy liberty, you must have equality-of-liberty with other persons. If this is difficult to grasp, think of dominion as a conception of freedom that, by definition, incorporates the notions of *liberté, égalité,* and *fraternité*; then you have the basic idea.[16]

Philip Pettit has coalesced this republican vision of liberty into the concept of 'freedom as non-domination'.[17] This is based on the idea that a person is only truly free when he or she is not under the arbitrary sway of another, or subject to the arbitrary interference of another. This approach has implications for the structure of government and for the doctrine of parliamentary sovereignty (see Chapter 9).

Republican theory suggests that liberalism does not go far enough in seeking to secure fundamental freedoms. It also challenges the conception of rights as promoting either positive or negative liberty.[18] The individual must be accorded more than a

---

14　'All peoples have the right of self-determination. By virtue of that right they freely determine their political status and freely pursue their economic, social and cultural development'.

15　See A. Devereux, 'Australia and the Right to Adequate Housing' (1992) 20 *Federal Law Review* 223.

16　J. Braithwaite, 'Inequality and Republican Criminology', in J. Hagan and R. D. Peterson (eds), *Crime and Inequality*, Stanford University Press, 1995, p. 279. See also J. Braithwaite and P. Pettit, *Not Just Deserts: A Republican Theory of Criminal Justice*, Clarendon Press, 1990.

17　P. Pettit, *Republicanism: A Theory of Freedom and Government*, Oxford University Press, 1997, p. 51.

18　Pettit, ch. 1.

negative freedom or an immunity from conduct that breaches his or her human rights. A person must be accorded a position in society whereby he or she is not potentially subjected to the domination of another. This is because liberty can be lost without actual interference, but due to the domination of another. Liberty can therefore only be achieved by establishing a system under which a person possesses a level of means or legal protection that grants him or her independence from such influences. In many cases, this independence will only be gained by the enforcement, by government (or others), of a person's economic, social, and cultural rights. Such rights must be enforceable against government so that government is placed under a corresponding liability to fulfil the particular right. In other words, they must be claim-rights. Republican theory suggests that unless this occurs, individuals will not be truly free or in possession of their basic human rights.

The protection of human rights under Australian law

Human rights are protected by law in Australia at many levels.[19] This book focuses on the protection of rights under the Australian Constitution. Nevertheless, it is important not to neglect the other avenues of fostering civil liberties. In many instances, these other avenues do not suffer from the limitations of rights protected under the Constitution (see Chapter 3), and therefore offer a better alternative to litigants. The protection of rights under Australian law, other than under the federal Constitution, is examined below.

The state constitutions and the territory self-government Acts

While it has been proposed that the constitutions of the Australian states and the self-government Acts of the territories should incorporate bills of rights,[20] they remain today largely barren of provisions that are explicitly rights orientated. There are some exceptions. Both the *Northern Territory (Self-Government) Act 1978* (Cth) (s. 50) and the *Australian Capital Territory (Self-Government) Act 1988* (Cth) (s. 23) provide that the respective parliaments cannot legislate for 'the acquisition of property otherwise than on just terms'. This replicates the limitation on Commonwealth power found in s. 51(xxxi) of the Australian Constitution (see Chapter 6). None of the state constitutions contains a like provision. Another exception is found in s. 46 of the Tasmanian Constitution (*Constitution Act 1934* (Tas)), which provides for the freedoms of conscience and religion:

---

19 See generally P. Bailey (ed.), *Laws of Australia*, vol. 21, *Human Rights*, LBC, 1995.

20 Australian Capital Territory Attorney-General's Department, *A Bill of Rights for the ACT?*, Australian Capital Territory, 1993, see especially pp. 91–3; Constitutional Committee of the Victorian Parliament, *Report on the Desirability or Otherwise of Legislation Defining and Protecting Human Rights*, Victorian Government Printer, 1987; Electoral and Administrative Review Commission (Qld), *Report on Review of the Preservation and Enhancement of Individuals' Rights and Freedoms*, Electoral and Administrative Review Commission (Qld), August 1993; S. Gibb and K. Eastman, 'Why are we Talking About a Bill of Rights?'(1995) 33(7) *Law Society Journal* 49; and Sessional Committee on Constitutional Development (Northern Territory), *Final Draft Constitution for the Northern Territory*, Legislative Assembly of the Northern Territory, August 1996.

(1) Freedom of conscience and the free profession and practice of religion are, subject to public order and morality, guaranteed to every citizen.

(2) No person shall be subject to any disability, or be required to take any oath on account of his religion or religious belief and no religious test shall be imposed in respect of the appointment to or holding of any public office.

However, s. 46 is not entrenched, meaning that the Tasmanian Parliament can amend it merely by passing an ordinary law that amends or repeals the provision.[21] Thus, to abridge freedom of conscience and the free profession and practice of religion, the Tasmanian Parliament need only pass a law to that effect. Because such a law would be enacted after s. 46 came into effect, it would override the guarantee in s. 46. The amending law need not even express an intention to amend s. 46: it can do so impliedly.[22] Accordingly, s. 46 offers no protection against an Act that infringes any of the listed rights. At best, it offers a political impediment to any such law. No other state constitution or territory self-government Act contains even a provision of such limited effect as s. 46, and they are similarly silent on other rights: for example, those relating to free speech and jury trial.

In 1992, the High Court found that the Australian Constitution embodies an implied freedom of political communication (see Chapter 7).[23] Two years later in *Stephens v. West Australian Newspapers Ltd* (1994) 182 CLR 211, the Court recognised that a similar freedom could be derived from the Western Australian Constitution, the *Constitution Act 1889* (WA). Like the federal implication, this was held to be derived from the system of representative democracy created by the relevant instrument. In 1978, s. 73(2) was inserted into the Western Australian Constitution. Section 73(2) entrenches laws of Western Australia, including the Constitution Act, that would be affected by bills of the several kinds specified in the provision[24] (including, in s. 73(2)(c), a bill that 'expressly or impliedly provides that the Legislative Council or the Legislative Assembly shall be composed of members other than members chosen directly by the people'). In *Stephens*, Brennan J stated (at p. 236) that s. 73(2)(c):

> entrenches in the *Constitution Act* the requirement that the Legislative Council and the Legislative Assembly be composed of members chosen directly by the people. This requirement is drawn in terms similar to those found in ss 7 and 24 of the Commonwealth Constitution from which the implication that effects a constitutional freedom to discuss government, governmental institutions and political matters is substantially derived. By parity of reasoning, a similar implication can be drawn from the *Constitution Act* with respect to the system of government of Western Australia therein prescribed.

---

21 Section 41A is the only entrenching provision in the Tasmanian Constitution Act. However, it does not entrench s. 46 and is not itself entrenched. Thus, while s. 41A currently requires that certain amendments be supported by a special majority, s. 41A may itself be amended or repealed by an ordinary Act of parliament and the entrenchment removed. On entrenchment generally, see A. R. Blackshield and G. Williams, *Australian Constitutional Law and Theory: Commentary and Materials*, 2nd edn, Federation Press, 1998, ch. 9.

22 *McCawley v. The King* [1920] AC 691.

23 *Nationwide News Pty Ltd v. Wills* (1992) 177 CLR 1; *Australian Capital Television Pty Ltd v. Commonwealth* (1992) 177 CLR 106.

24 Under sections 73(2)(f) and (g), such bills must be passed by an absolute majority of both houses of the Parliament and be approved by the electors of the state at a referendum.

Entrenched provisions in other state constitutions and territory self-government Acts that establish a system of representative democracy or require that members of parliament be chosen by the people may also give rise to an implied freedom of political communication that will limit the powers of the respective parliament. In addition to the Constitution of Western Australia, it has been suggested that a freedom of political communication might be derived from the constitutions and self-government Acts of the Australian Capital Territory, New South Wales, the Northern Territory, and South Australia,[25] but that such a freedom may not be apparent in the constitutions of Queensland, Tasmania, and Victoria, due to a lack of entrenchment.[26] Like s. 46 of the Tasmanian Constitution, this implied freedom of political communication will only be effective in limiting the power of a state parliament to the extent to which the provisions from which it is implied are entrenched against legislative repeal. If there is no entrenchment, an implied freedom in a state constitution could be abrogated by repealing the provisions giving rise to the implication, or by amending the state constitution to provide that no such implication may be derived.

Some state constitutions and territory self-government Acts also enshrine provisions that respect political rights by mandating a level of voter equality, or 'one-vote one-value'. For example, s. 77 of the South Australian Constitution requires that whenever an electoral redistribution is made for the South Australian Parliament, the redistribution is to be made by applying the principle that the number of electors in any electorate should not deviate by more than 10 per cent from the electoral quota (that is, the figure derived by dividing the number of electors by the number of electoral districts). Section 77 is entrenched by s. 88(2), which requires that any Bill to amend s. 77 be approved by the electors of South Australia at a referendum. The self-government Act of the Australian Capital Territory and the Constitution of New South Wales also establish a 10 per cent margin, while the self-government Act of the Northern Territory establishes a 20 per cent tolerance.[27]

Statute law: a de facto Bill of Rights?

There are many statutes at both the Commonwealth and state level that protect human rights.[28] Significantly, such statutes commonly deal with conduct beyond the scope of

---

25 Australian Capital Territory (Self-Government) Act, sections 66B, 67A, 67B, 67C; *Constitution Act 1902* (NSW), sections 11B, 26, 27, 28, 29, Sch. 7; Northern Territory (Self-Government) Act, sections 13, 14; *Constitution Act 1934* (SA), sections 4, 11, 14, 19, 27, 28, 32, 64A, Part 5. *Muldowney v. South Australia* (1996) 186 CLR 352 raised the issue of whether an implied freedom of political communication could be derived from the Constitution of South Australia. However, the Solicitor-General of South Australia conceded in argument (at p. 367) that the South Australian Constitution contains a constitutionally entrenched limitation on state legislative power that 'precluded interference by an ordinary law with freedom of discussion about political affairs'. See also *Cameron v. Becker* (1995) 64 SASR 238.

26 S. Lloyd, 'Constitutional Guarantees of Rights', in *Laws of Australia*, vol. 19, *Government*, LBC, 1995, subtitle 19.6, p. 62.

27 Australian Capital Territory (Self-Government) Act, s. 67D; Constitution Act (NSW), s. 28; Northern Territory (Self-Government) Act, s. 13.

28 See H. Charlesworth, 'The Australian Reluctance about Rights', in P. Alston (ed.), *Towards an Australian Bill of Rights*, Centre for International and Public Law, Australian National University, 1994, pp. 34–40. On the other hand, legislation may do little more than hamper the free exercise of certain rights, such as the ability to protest: see, for example, *Unlawful Assemblies and Processions Act 1958* (Vic), sections 3, 4; and *Peaceful Assembly Act 1992* (Qld). See also Bronitt and Williams.

constitutional rights. While constitutional rights are generally only concerned with imposing limitations on governmental action, human rights legislation frequently also establishes rights and obligations as between private individuals, such as between employer and employee, or between landlord and tenant. This means that the enactment of the Canadian Charter of Rights and Freedoms, or even the *New Zealand Bill of Rights Act 1990*, has not diminished the importance of statute law in either Canada[29] or New Zealand.[30] Human rights legislation may thus play a separate complementary role even where a constitution contains significant protection of individual liberty.

A detailed treatment of human rights legislation in Australia is beyond the scope of this book, but has received treatment elsewhere.[31] The most significant of the rights-orientated legislation lies in the area of anti-discrimination legislation.[32] Commonwealth legislation includes the *Racial Discrimination Act 1975* (Cth), the *Sex Discrimination Act 1984* (Cth)[33] and the *Disability Discrimination Act 1992* (Cth). These Acts operate throughout Australia and are enforced, to the extent possible given the separation of powers in the Australian Constitution,[34] by the Human Rights and Equal Opportunity Commission.[35] The scope of this legislation is very broad. For example, s. 9(1) of the Racial Discrimination Act provides:

> It is unlawful for any person to do any act involving a distinction, exclusion, restriction or preference based on race, colour, descent or national or ethnic origin which has the purpose or effect of nullifying or impairing the recognition, enjoyment or exercise, on an equal footing, of any human right or fundamental freedom in the political, economic, social, cultural or any other field of public life.[36]

The validity of federal anti-discrimination legislation depends on the Commonwealth's power to legislate with respect to 'external affairs' under s. 51(xxix) of the Constitution. In *Commonwealth v. Tasmania (Tasmanian Dam Case)* (1983) 158 CLR 1, and in subsequent decisions,[37] the High Court held that this power enables the federal Parliament to pass legislation to implement obligations that it has incurred by becoming a party to international instruments such as treaties and covenants. It may implement such instruments to the extent that its laws are 'capable of being reasonably considered to be appropriate and adapted' to meeting the treaty obligation.[38] If there is not sufficient conformity, or proportionality, between the law and the obligation, the law will be invalid. Parliament is not bound to meet all of its obligations in a treaty, nor must it

---

29   P. Hogg, *Constitutional Law of Canada*, 4th edn, Carswell, 1997, p. 779.

30   See *Human Rights Act 1993* (NZ).

31   Bailey, *Human Rights: Australia in an International Context*; N. O'Neill and R. Handley, *Retreat from Injustice: Human Rights in Australian Law*, Federation Press, 1994.

32   Bailey, *Human Rights: Australia in an International Context*, chs 6, 7; O'Neill and Handley, ch. 17. See also *Privacy Act 1988* (Cth).

33   See also *Affirmative Action (Equal Employment Opportunity for Women) Act 1986* (Cth); *Equal Employment Opportunity (Commonwealth Authorities) Act 1987* (Cth); and *Public Service Act 1922* (Cth).

34   *Brandy v. Human Rights and Equal Opportunity Commission* (1995) 183 CLR 245 (see Chapter 8).

35   *Human Rights and Equal Opportunity Commission Act 1986* (Cth). See Bailey, *Human Rights: Australia in an International Context*, ch. 5.

36   See also s. 10 of this Act.

37   *Richardson v. Forestry Commission* (1988) 164 CLR 261; *Queensland v. Commonwealth (Tropical Rainforests Case)* (1989) 167 CLR 232; *Victoria v. Commonwealth (Industrial Relations Act Case)* (1996) 187 CLR 416.

38   *Tasmanian Dam Case* at 259 per Deane J.

meet any particular obligation fully or exactly.[39] The Court has shown flexibility in leaving the scope and means of implementation to Parliament. The Racial Discrimination Act relies on the *International Convention on the Elimination of All Forms of Racial Discrimination*;[40] the Sex Discrimination Act on the *Convention on the Elimination of All Forms of Discrimination Against Women*; and the *Disability Discrimination Act* on the *International Labour Organisation Convention 111—Discrimination (Employment and Occupation) Convention*, the ICCPR, and the ICESCR.

Commonwealth anti-discrimination legislation has another significant constitutional dimension. Where federal legislation is inconsistent with state legislation, it renders the state legislation 'invalid' in accordance with s. 109 of the Constitution.[41] 'Invalid' in this context means 'inoperative' rather than void, meaning that inconsistent state legislation is revived if the overriding Commonwealth legislation is repealed.[42] Under the tests for inconsistency developed by the High Court, state legislation will be 'inconsistent', and thus inoperative:[43]

1   if it is impossible to obey both laws (one law requires that you must do X, the other that you must not do X)[44]

2   if one law purports to confer a legal right, privilege or entitlement that the other law purports to take away or diminish (one law says that you can do X, the other that you cannot do X)[45]

3   if the Commonwealth law evinces a legislative intention to 'cover the field'. In such a case there need not be any direct contradiction between the two enactments. It may even happen that both require the same conduct, or both pursue the same legislative purpose. What is imputed to the Commonwealth Parliament is a legislative intention that its law shall be all the law there is on that topic. In that event, what is inconsistent with the Commonwealth law is the existence of any state law at all on that topic.[46]

---

39   Compare *Industrial Relations Act Case* at 488 per Brennan CJ, Toohey, Gaudron, McHugh, and Gummow JJ.

40   *Koowarta v. Bjelke-Petersen* (1982) 153 CLR 168.

41   *Viskauskas v. Niland* (1983) 153 CLR 280; *University of Wollongong v. Metwally* (1984) 158 CLR 447. The Australian Capital Territory (Self-Government) Act, s. 28, has a similar effect as s. 109, as between federal and Australian Capital Territory legislation. Northern Territory legislation may also be invalid for inconsistency with Commonwealth legislation even though the Northern Territory Self-Government Act is silent on the issue. See *Attorney-General (NT) v. Minister for Aboriginal Affairs* (1989) 90 ALR 59 at 75 per Lockhart J: 'It is beyond the power of the Northern Territory of Australia to make laws repugnant to or inconsistent with laws of the Commonwealth or to exercise powers conferred by Northern Territory laws in a manner inconsistent with, or repugnant to laws of the Commonwealth. It is not a question of inconsistency between the two sets of laws which may otherwise be valid, rather it is a question going to the competency of the subordinate legislature to enact laws or to cause laws to operate in a manner inconsistent with or repugnant to laws of the paramount legislature'. See also *Federal Capital Commission v. Laristan Building and Investment Co. Pty Ltd* (1929) 42 CLR 582 at 588 per Dixon J; *Webster v. McIntosh* (1980) 32 ALR 603 at 605–6 per Brennan J; *R. v. Kearney; Ex parte Japanangka* (1984) 158 CLR 395 at 417–19 per Brennan J.

42   *Carter v. Egg and Egg Pulp Marketing Board (Vic)* (1942) 66 CLR 557 at 573 per Latham CJ.

43   The following list has been adapted from Blackshield and Williams, *Australian Constitutional Law and Theory: Commentary and Materials*, pp. 302–3.

44   *R v. Brisbane Licensing Court; Ex parte Daniell* (1920) 28 CLR 23. See L. Katz, '*Ex parte Daniell* and the Operation of Inoperative Laws' (1976) 7 *Federal Law Review* 66.

45   *Colvin v. Bradley Brothers Pty Ltd* (1943) 68 CLR 151.

46   *Clyde Engineering Co. Ltd v. Cowburn* (1926) 37 CLR 466 per Isaacs J; *Ex parte McLean* (1930) 43 CLR 472 per Dixon J.

Tests 1 and 2 are often referred to as 'direct' tests of inconsistency. Test 3 involves a more indirect form of inconsistency and makes s. 109 a more powerful instrument for ensuring the supremacy of Commonwealth legislation.

In addition, because the 'cover the field' test operates according to the intention of the Commonwealth in enacting a law, the Commonwealth can indicate an intention that its law is not to 'cover the field' with respect to state and territory laws. While this would eliminate most cases in which state and territory laws would be held inconsistent under s. 109 of the Constitution, it would not prevent s. 109 operating on direct inconsistency between state and federal laws.[47] By indicating an intention not to 'cover the field', the Commonwealth has provided scope in its anti-discrimination legislation for the operation of similar state legislation.[48] For example, s. 6A(1) of the Racial Discrimination Act (Cth) states: 'This Act is not intended, and shall be deemed never to have been intended, to exclude or limit the operation of a law of a State or Territory that furthers the objects of the Convention and is capable of operating concurrently with this Act'. Such provisions have meant that each of the states, the Australian Capital Territory, and the Northern Territory have been able to pass anti-discrimination legislation.[49] Of course, other Commonwealth enactments lacking a clause such as s. 6A(1) are still capable of overriding state anti-discrimination legislation under the 'cover the field' test.[50]

The wide operation of the Commonwealth's anti-discrimination legislation combined with the broad interpretation given to s. 109 of the Constitution by the High Court means that there is great scope for such legislation to protect human rights. Sir Harry Gibbs, a former Chief Justice of the High Court, commented that in s. 9 of the Commonwealth Racial Discrimination Act 'we may already have what appears to be a bill of rights, limited it is true in scope, which is effectively [sic] entrenched against the States'.[51] This has proved correct in the field of native title, where inconsistency with the Commonwealth Racial Discrimination Act has rendered inoperative legislative attempts by the Queensland and Western Australian governments to extinguish or limit the native title held by indigenous peoples in their state.[52] It is also true of the *Human Rights (Sexual Conduct) Act 1994* (Cth), which has been effective in overriding Tasmanian statute law that prohibited homosexual sexual activity between consenting adult males in that state (see pp. 19–20).

---

47 *R v. Credit Tribunal; Ex parte General Motors Acceptance Corporation* (1977) 137 CLR 545 at 563 per Mason J: 'a provision in a Commonwealth statute evincing an intention that the statute is not intended to cover the field cannot avoid or eliminate a case of direct inconsistency or collision, of the kind which arises, for example, when Commonwealth and State laws make contradictory provision upon the same topic, making it impossible for both laws to be obeyed'. See Blackshield and Williams, pp. 302–3, 319–20.

48 Racial Discrimination Act (Cth), s. 6A; Sex Discrimination Act (Cth), sections 10(3), 10(4); Disability Discrimination Act (Cth), s 13.

49 See *Anti-Discrimination Act 1977* (NSW); *Anti-Discrimination Act 1991* (Qld); *Anti-Discrimination Act 1992* (NT); *Discrimination Act 1991* (ACT); *Equal Opportunity Act 1984* (Vic); *Equal Opportunity Act 1984* (SA); *Equal Opportunity Act 1984* (WA); *Sex Discrimination Act 1996* (Tas).

50 For example, in *Australian Mutual Provident Society v. Goulden* (1986) 160 CLR 330, the High Court unanimously held that the New South Wales Anti-Discrimination Act was inconsistent with the Commonwealth *Life Insurance Act 1945*. See also *Ansett Transport Industries (Operations) Pty Ltd v. Wardley* (1980) 142 CLR 237.

51 H. Gibbs, 'The Constitutional Protection of Human Rights' (1982) 9 *Monash University Law Review* 1 at 13.

52 *Mabo v. Queensland (No 1)* (1988) 166 CLR 186; *Western Australia v. Commonwealth (Native Title Act Case)* (1995) 183 CLR 373.

At the Commonwealth level, except where an appropriate 'manner and form' provision has been enacted (see Chapter 10),[53] it is difficult to see how such legislation can restrict the power of the Commonwealth Parliament to abrogate human rights. This can be compared to the approach taken by the Supreme Court of Canada. In *Insurance Corporation of British Columbia v. Heerspink* [1982] 2 SCR 145 at 158,[54] Lamer J argued that a provincial human rights code was 'not to be treated as another ordinary law of general application. It should be recognized for what it is, a fundamental law'. This was taken further by the Supreme Court in *Winnipeg School Division No 1 v. Craton* [1985] 2 SCR 150. In that case, it was held that a federal human rights statute could prevail over a subsequent inconsistent federal statute. McIntyre J, speaking for the Court, stated at p. 156:

> Human rights legislation is of a special nature and declares public policy regarding matters of general concern. I[t] is not constitutional in nature in the sense that it may not be altered, amended, or repealed by the Legislature. It is, however, of such nature that it may not be altered, amended, or repealed, nor may exceptions be created to its provisions, save by clear legislative pronouncement.[55]

Despite some support for this line of reasoning from New Zealand judges,[56] a leading Canadian commentator has argued that this 'reasoning is dubious'.[57] Certainly, it is difficult to see the approach outlined in *Winnipeg School Division No 1 v. Craton* being adopted in Australia given its apparent inconsistency with the doctrine of parliamentary sovereignty (see Chapter 9). The doctrine of parliamentary sovereignty is, essentially, the notion expressed by A. V. Dicey that a parliament has 'the right to make or unmake any law whatever',[58] including a law of a predecessor parliament. However, the Canadian approach does not mean that an earlier human rights statute cannot be amended, just that the parliament must be express and clear in seeking to achieve this. An Australian court might find that the doctrine of parliamentary sovereignty is able to encompass the notion that legislation is only effective in abrogating a fundamental right already recognised by statute where the intent of the parliament to do so is clear and unambiguous. This would place fundamental rights protected by statute in the same position as fundamental rights recognised by the common law (see p. 17). There is evidence of such an approach in the judgment of Lord Scarman of the House of Lords in *R v. Cain* [1985] 1 AC 46 at 55–6. In any event, even in the absence of a legal limitation, legisla-

---

53 See G. Winterton, 'Can the Commonwealth Parliament Enact Manner and Form Legislation?' (1980) 11 *Federal Law Review* 167.

54 See also *Ontario Human Rights Commission v. Simpson-Sears Ltd* [1985] 2 SCR 536 at 547 per McIntyre J: 'Legislation of this type is of a special nature, not quite constitutional but certainly more than the ordinary—and it is for the courts to seek out its purpose and give it effect'.

55 See the similar argument put by B. J. Shaw QC in *Chu Kheng Lim v. Minister for Immigration, Local Government and Ethnic Affairs* (1992) 176 CLR 1 at 6.

56 *Coburn v. Human Rights Commission* [1994] 3 NZLR 323 at 334 per Thorp J; *New Zealand Van Lines Ltd v. Proceedings Commissioner* [1995] 1 NZLR 100 at 104 per Smellie J.

57 Hogg, p. 318, fn. 51.

58 A. V. Dicey, *Introduction to the Study of the Law of the Constitution*, 10th edn [1st edn, 1885], Macmillan, 1959, p. 40. See *R v. Public Vehicles Licensing Appeal Tribunal (Tas); Ex parte Australian National Airways Pty Ltd* (1964) 113 CLR 207 at 226 per the Court: 'The will of a Parliament is expressed in a statute or Act of Parliament and it is the general conception of law that what Parliament may enact it may repeal'. See also *Kartinyeri v. Commonwealth* (1998) 152 ALR 540.

tion such as the Commonwealth Racial Discrimination Act may prove an important political obstacle to the restriction of rights. For example, the need to amend the Racial Discrimination Act has acted as a barrier to the extinguishment or modification of the native title rights of Australian Aborigines by the federal Parliament.

The common law

The common law represents a vibrant and rich source of human rights. As a 'work in progress' encompassing the concerns and values of many generations, it is open to continual development and the input of judicial imagination. Thus, for example, in *Dietrich v. The Queen* (1992) 177 CLR 292, the High Court developed the common law to recognise that, in certain circumstances, a person has a right to counsel when accused of a serious crime. However, the common law is limited in the rights or interests that it has thus far recognised or protected. For example, in *Victoria Park Racing and Recreation Grounds Co. Ltd v. Taylor* (1937) 58 CLR 479, the High Court refused to recognise a common law right to privacy.[59] In that case, the defendant sought to construct a tower on his land, from which he proposed to broadcast descriptions of races held on the property of the Victoria Park Racing and Recreation Grounds Co. Ltd. Victoria Park Racing sought an injunction. The High Court refused to grant the order, finding that no legal interest of Victoria Park Racing had been breached. Latham CJ, a member of the majority, commented (at p. 494): 'Any person is entitled to look over the plaintiff's fences and to see what goes on in the plaintiff's land. If the plaintiff desires to prevent this, the plaintiff can erect a higher fence'.

A more serious limitation on the ability of the common law to foster the protection of human rights is that it falls away in the face of inconsistent legislation.[60] In *Dr Bonham's Case* (1610) 8 Co Rep 107a [77 ER 638] at 118a, Coke CJ held:

> And it appears in our books, that in many cases, the common law will controul Acts of Parliament, and sometimes adjudge them to be utterly void: for when an Act of Parliament is against common right and reason, or repugnant, or impossible to be performed, the common law will controul it, and adjudge such Act to be void.[61]

However, the power expressed here to hold legislation void has not been exercised by an English,[62] let alone an Australian, court. In 1885, Dicey was able to deal with *Dr Bonham's Case* in a footnote. He declared the idea that a judge might declare legislation 'void' for being 'against common right and reason' as being 'obsolete'.[63] Similarly, the power expressed in the case has, at least to the present day, been accurately described as 'empty phrases'.[64]

---

59   See Bailey, *Human Rights: Australia in an International Context*, ch. 10. In *Police v. Carbone* (1997) 68 SASR 200, an argument that a right of privacy could be implied from the Commonwealth Constitution also failed.

60   See generally G. Winterton, 'Constitutionally Entrenched Common Law Rights: Sacrificing Means to Ends?', in C. Sampford and K. Preston (eds), *Interpreting Constitutions: Theories, Principles and Institutions*, Federation Press, 1996, p. 121.

61   See D. A. Smallbone, 'Recent Suggestions of an Implied "Bill of Rights" in the Constitution, Considered as Part of a General Trend in Constitution Interpretation' (1993) 21 *Federal Law Review* 254.

62   Compare *Day v. Savadge* [1614] Hob 85 at 87 [80 ER 235]; *City of London v. Wood* (1701) 12 Mod 669 at 687–8 [88 ER 1592].

63   Dicey, pp. 61–2, fn. 2.

64   S. de Smith and R. Brazier, *Constitutional and Administrative Law*, 7th edn, Penguin, 1994, p. 76.

The common law in Australia today accordingly affords bare protection to the fundamental freedoms of the Australian people where they have been abrogated by legislation.[65] Where the common law and the will of the Parliament, as expressed in legislation, clash, parliamentary sovereignty (which Dicey regarded as the 'dominant characteristic of our political institutions'[66]) holds sway. There is no scope for the common law to, as Coke put it in *Dr Bonham's Case*, 'adjudge such Act to be void'. This function is instead left to the Australian Constitution. Lord Reid recognised this in *British Railways Board v. Pickin* [1974] AC 765 at 782, when he stated that the common law does not contain rights that run so deep that Parliaments lack the capacity to destroy them. In *Building Construction Employees & Builders' Labourers Federation of NSW v. Minister for Industrial Relations* (1986) 7 NSWLR 372 at 405, Kirby P agreed with this conclusion, doing so 'in recognition of years of unbroken constitutional law and tradition in Australia and, beforehand, in the United Kingdom'.[67] Martin CJ and Mildren J applied this approach in *Wake v. Northern Territory* (1996) 109 NTR 1, to reject the application of a 'right to life' to override the Northern Territory's voluntary euthanasia legislation.[68] They stated (at p. 8) that 'absent authoritative guidance, the exercise of legislative power is not constrained in this case by reference "to rights deeply rooted in our democratic system of government and the common law"'. On this analysis, fundamental common law freedoms in Australia are residual: that is, they can be exercised until revoked by law.[69] In the classification system devised by Hohfeld (see p. 5), common law rights are merely 'privileges', meaning that 'everyone is free to do whatever the law does not prohibit'.[70]

Interestingly, the High Court has left a faint possibility of the common law playing a larger role in protecting human rights against abrogation by statute. Sir Robin Cooke, a former President of the New Zealand Court of Appeal, has argued that certain rights lie so deep that they are incapable of legislative repeal.[71] He stated in *Taylor v. New Zealand Poultry Board* [1984] 1 NZLR 394 at 398: 'I do not think that literal compulsion, by torture for instance, would be within the lawful powers of Parliament. Some common law rights presumably lie so deep that even Parliament could not override

---

65 But see J. Toohey, 'A Government of Laws, and Not of Men?' (1993) 4 *Public Law Review* 158. See also Winterton, 'Constitutionally Entrenched Common Law Rights', pp. 132–5.

66 Dicey, p. 39.

67 See N. O'Neill, 'Blue-eyed Babies May be Murdered: Dicey's First Principle Upheld in the Court of Appeal' (1987) 12 *Legal Service Bulletin* 2; G. Winterton, 'Extra-Constitutional Notions in Australian Constitutional Law' (1986) 16 *Federal Law Review* 223 at 231–5.

68 *Rights of the Terminally Ill Act 1995* (NT). See G. Williams and M. Darke, 'Euthanasia Laws and the Australian Constitution' (1997) 20 *University of New South Wales Law Journal* 647.

69 This is true even where a court might describe a fundamental freedom, such as freedom of speech, as a 'right'. See, for example, *Bonnard v. Perryman* [1891] 2 Ch 269 at 284; *R v. Metropolitan Police Commissioner; Ex parte Blackburn (No 2)* [1968] 2 All ER 319 at 320, 320–1. But compare T. R. S. Allan, 'The Common Law as Constitution: Fundamental Rights and First Principles', in C. Saunders (ed.), *Courts of Final Jurisdiction: The Mason Court in Australia*, Federation Press, 1996, p. 148.

70 E. Barendt, 'Dicey and Civil Liberties' [1985] *Public Law* 596 at 606.

71 *L v. M* [1979] 2 NZLR 519 at 527; *Brader v. Ministry of Transport* [1981] 1 NZLR 73 at 78; *New Zealand Drivers Association v. New Zealand Carriers* [1982] 1 NZLR 374 at 390; *Fraser v. State Services Commission* [1984] 1 NZLR 116 at 121. See Lord Irvine of Lairg, 'Judges and Decision-Makers: The Theory and Practice of Wednesbury Review' [1996] *Public Law* 59 at 76–8; Winterton, G, 'Constitutionally Entrenched Common Law Rights: Sacrificing Means to Ends?', pp. 139–40.

them'. In *Union Steamship Co. of Australia Pty Ltd v. The King* (1988) 166 CLR 1 at 10, the Court cited decisions of Cooke J, stating:

> Whether the exercise of … legislative power is subject to some restraints by reference to rights deeply rooted in our democratic system of government and the common law … a view which Lord Reid firmly rejected in *Pickin v. British Railways Board*, is another question which we need not explore.[72]

The common law does have some scope to protect civil liberties against statute law. Though essentially residual, the common law can play a practical and important role in protecting human rights from legislative interference.[73] Common law rules of statutory interpretation have been developed under which parliament must be 'unmistakably clear' in its intent to restrict a fundamental freedom, lest a court recast the legislation in a way that does not involve such interference.[74] This reflects a presumption against the invasion of common law rights by the legislature.[75] According to Mason CJ, Brennan, Gaudron and McHugh JJ in *Coco v. The Queen* (1994) 179 CLR 427 at 437:

> The insistence on express authorization of an abrogation or curtailment of a fundamental right, freedom or immunity must be understood as a requirement for some manifestation or indication that the legislature has not only directed its attention to the question of the abrogation or curtailment of such basic rights, freedoms or immunities but has also determined upon abrogation or curtailment of them. The courts should not impute to the legislature an intention to interfere with fundamental rights. Such an intention must be clearly manifested by unmistakable and unambiguous language. General words will rarely be sufficient for that purpose if they do not specifically deal with the question because, in the context in which they appear, they will often be ambiguous on the aspect of interference with fundamental rights.[76]

Thus, 'a statute or statutory instrument which purports to impair a right to personal liberty is interpreted, if possible, so as to respect that right'.[77]

Members of the Court have also been active in translating the common law into effect through constitutional interpretation.[78] In *Leeth v. Commonwealth* (1992) 174

---

72 See *Polyukhovich v. Commonwealth (War Crimes Act Case)* (1991) 172 CLR 501 at 636 per Dawson J. Compare *Kable v. Director of Public Prosecutions (NSW)* (1996) 189 CLR 51 at 66 per Brennan CJ, at 71–6 per Dawson J, at 90–1 per Toohey J.

73 See J. J. Doyle, 'Common Law Rights and Democratic Rights' in P. D. Finn, (ed.), *Essays on Law and Government*, vol. 1, *Principles and Values*, LBC, 1995, p. 144.

74 *Re Bolton; Ex parte Beane* (1987) 162 CLR 514 at 523 per Brennan J.

75 D. C. Pearce and R. S. Geddes, *Statutory Interpretation in Australia*, 4th edn, Butterworths, 1996, pp. 145–6.

76 See also *Nationwide News Pty Ltd v. Wills* (1992) 177 CLR 1 at 43 per Brennan J: 'A court will interpret laws of the Parliament in the light of a presumption that the Parliament does not intend to abrogate human rights and fundamental freedoms but the court cannot deny the validity of an exercise of a legislative power expressly granted merely on the ground that the law abrogates human rights and fundamental freedoms or trenches upon political rights which, in the court's opinion, should be preserved'; *Sargood Bros v. Commonwealth* (1910) 11 CLR 258 at 279 per O'Connor J; *Pyneboard Pty Ltd v. Trade Practices Commission* (1983) 152 CLR 328 at 341 per Mason ACJ, Wilson and Dawson JJ; S. Kenny, 'Principles of Statutory Interpretation Relating to Government', in Finn, *Essays on Law and Government*, vol. 2, *The Citizen and the State in the Courts*, pp. 233–7.

77 *Re Bolton; Ex parte Beane* (1987) 162 CLR 514 at 523 per Brennan J. See *Balog v. Independent Commission Against Corruption* (1990) 169 CLR 625 at 635–6 per the Court.

78 See Winterton, 'Constitutionally Entrenched Common Law Rights', p. 121.

CLR 455 at 487, Deane and Toohey JJ argued that a right of equality under the law could be discerned in the Constitution (see Chapter 8). In finding this, they stated:

> [O]nce it is appreciated that it is the ordinary approach of the Constitution not to spell out the fundamental common law principles upon which it is structured, the existence of a number of specific provisions which reflect the doctrine of legal equality serves to make manifest rather than undermine the status of that doctrine as an underlying principle of the Constitution as a whole.[79]

International law[80]

International law has come to concern more than the relations between States and questions of sovereignty. It has come to involve issues of how nations treat their own citizens. This concern began with the *Charter of the United Nations 1945*, which states: 'We the peoples of the United Nations determined ... to reaffirm faith in fundamental human rights, in the dignity and worth of the human person, in the equal rights of men and women'. This was spelt out more fully in the *Universal Declaration of Human Rights 1948*, in which the General Assembly of the United Nations proclaimed 'as a common standard of achievement for all peoples and all nations' a list of human rights contained in thirty articles (see pp. 2–3).

Today, there is a plethora of international instruments to which Australia is a party that protect or foster human rights.[81] The most important of these are the ICCPR and the ICESCR. However, the impact of these instruments on domestic Australian law is limited. The orthodox position was stated by Gibbs CJ in *Kioa v. West* (1985) 159 CLR 550 at 570: 'treaties do not have the force of law unless they are given that effect by statute'. Thus, in *Dietrich v. The Queen* (1992) 177 CLR 292, Mason CJ and McHugh J found that the effect of the ICCPR on Australian law is as follows: 'Ratification of the ICCPR as an executive act has no direct legal effect on domestic law; the rights and obligations contained in the ICCPR are not incorporated into Australian law unless and until specific legislation is passed implementing the provisions'.

As discussed at pp.11–12, the Commonwealth is able to give effect to its treaty obligations under its power over 'external affairs' in s. 51(xxix) of the Constitution. The Commonwealth has relied on this power to implement a range of treaties that seek to protect human rights. The various Commonwealth anti-discrimination acts fall into this category,[82] as does Commonwealth legislation that protects the right to engage in sex-

---

79 See *Nationwide News Pty Ltd v. Wills* (1992) 177 CLR 1 at 69 per Deane and Toohey JJ.
80 See generally S. Donaghue, 'Balancing Sovereignty and International Law: The Domestic Impact of International Law in Australia' (1995) 17 *Adelaide Law Review* 213; A. Mason, 'International Law as a Source of Domestic Law', in B. R. Opeskin and D. R. Rothwell (eds), *International Law and Australian Federalism*, Melbourne University Press, 1997, p. 210; P. Mathew, 'International Law and the Protection of Human Rights in Australia: Recent Trends' (1995) 17 *Sydney Law Review* 177.
81 At a recent count Australia had entered into 920 substantive treaties: Senate Legal and Constitutional References Committee, *Treaties and the External Affairs Power*, Discussion Paper, AGPS, March 1995, p. 12. For a list of the major multilateral human rights instruments to which Australia is, and is not, a party, see H. Charlesworth, 'Human Rights', in H. Reicher (ed.), *Australian International Law: Cases and Materials*, LBC, 1995, pp. 629–30. See D. de Stoop, 'Australia's Approach to International Treaties on Human Rights' (1970–73) 5 *Australian Yearbook of International Law* 27.
82 Racial Discrimination Act (Cth); Sex Discrimination Act (Cth); Disability Discrimination Act (Cth).

ual conduct in private[83] and economic rights, such as freedom from unfair dismissal.[84] These Acts are merely a small example of what the Commonwealth might achieve under its 'external affairs' power. The power is wide enough to mean that if it wished to, the federal Parliament would be able to legislate to enact a statutory Bill of Rights by implementing its obligations under the ICCPR and the ICESCR (see Chapter 10).

Despite the apparent need for formal implementation of international human rights instruments into Australian law, international law is playing an increasingly important role in the protection of human rights in Australia.[85] Even when not incorporated by enactment, international treaties are increasingly being given informal status by Australian courts.[86] These developments have been spurred on by a series of international judicial colloquia, beginning in Bangalore in 1988, that have dealt with the application of international human rights norms within domestic legal systems.[87]

In the absence of incorporation, treaties may affect human rights in Australia in three main ways:

1 by providing alternative forms of relief where rights under the ICCPR have been abrogated

The (first) *Optional Protocol of the International Covenant of Civil and Political Rights* came into force in Australia in 1991.[88] Under article 5(2)(b) of the *Optional Protocol*, anyone within Australian jurisdiction may, after they have 'exhausted all available domestic remedies', make a complaint to the Human Rights Committee[89] that their rights under the ICCPR have been breached. This occurred when Nicholas Toonen, an activist for homosexual rights in Tasmania, complained to the Human Rights Committee that his rights were infringed by the now repealed[90] sections 122 and 123 of the *Criminal Code Act 1924* (Tas).[91] Section 122 of Chapter XIV ('Crimes Against Morality') of the Code made homosexual sexual activity between consenting adult males a crime by establishing the offence, punishable by jail, of having 'carnal knowledge of any person against the order of nature'. The Human Rights Committee upheld Toonen's claim that the

---

83 Human Rights (Sexual Conduct) Act (Cth).

84 *Industrial Relations Reform Act 1993* (Cth). See *Victoria v. Commonwealth (Industrial Relations Act Case)* (1996) 187 CLR 416.

85 M. Kirby, 'The Role of the Judge in Advancing Human Rights by Reference to International Human Rights Norms' (1988) 62 *Australian Law Journal* 514; A. Mason, 'The Influence of International and Transnational Law on Australian Municipal Law' (1996) 7 *Public Law Review* 20.

86 P. Bayne, 'Administrative Law, Human Rights and International Humanitarian Law' (1990) 64 *Australian Law Journal* 203.

87 M. Kirby, 'The Australian Use of International Human Rights Norms: From Bangalore to Balliol—A View from the Antipodes' (1993) 16 *University of New South Wales Law Journal* 363; M. Kirby, 'The Role of International Standards in Australian Courts', in P. Alston and M. Chiam (eds), *Treaty-Making and Australia: Globalisation Versus Sovereignty*, Federation Press, 1995, p. 81; Lord Lester of Herne Hill, 'The Georgetown Conclusions on the Effective Protection of Human Rights Through Law' [1996] *Public Law* 562.

88 See C. Caleo, 'Implications of Australia's Accession to the First Optional Protocol to the ICCPR' (1993) 4 *Public Law Review* 175; H. Charlesworth, 'Australia's Accession to the First Optional Protocol to the International Covenant on Civil and Political Rights' (1991) 18 *Melbourne University Law Review* 428.

89 The Human Rights Committee is an international body established under Article 28 of the ICCPR.

90 *Criminal Code Amendment Act 1997* (Tas), sections 4, 5.

91 See A. Funder, 'The Toonen Case' (1994) 5 *Public Law Review* 156; W. Morgan, 'Sexuality and Human Rights: The First Communication by an Australian to the Human Rights Committee Under the Optional Protocol to the International Covenant on Civil and Political Rights' (1992) 14 *Australian Yearbook of International Law* 277; I. Shearer, 'United Nations: Human Rights Committee: The Toonen Case' (1995) 69 *Australian Law Journal* 600.

law was inconsistent with the right to privacy set out in Article 17 of the ICCPR.[92] The Commonwealth responded by passing the *Human Rights (Sexual Conduct) Act 1994* (Cth).[93] Section 4(1) of that Act provides that 'Sexual conduct involving only consenting adults acting in private is not to be subject, by or under any law of the Commonwealth, a State or a Territory, to any arbitrary interference with privacy within the meaning of Article 17 of the International Covenant on Civil and Political Rights'. This provision was clearly designed to override, under s. 109 of the Constitution, the Tasmanian legislation. A matter was brought before the High Court to test whether the Commonwealth law was effective in achieving this.[94] The main difficulty faced by this challenge was that although two activists had publicly stated that they had breached the Tasmanian law, they had not been prosecuted by the Tasmanian authorities. In resisting the attempt to invoke s. 109 of the Constitution, the Tasmanian government argued that as no proceedings had been brought or threatened against the plaintiffs, there was no 'matter' within the meaning of that term in s. 76 of the Constitution and s. 30 of the *Judiciary Act 1903* (Cth) that could be judicially determined. However, this argument was rejected by the High Court, which unanimously held that the issue could be brought before it. Gaudron, McHugh, and Gummow JJ found that: 'The conduct by the plaintiffs of their personal lives in significant respects is overshadowed by the presence of ss 122 and 123 of the Code. The policy of the law which animates the operation of the Australian legal system includes the encouragement, and indeed the requirement, of observance of the law'.[95] In the wake of this finding, Tasmania conceded that sections 122 and 123 of the *Criminal Code Act* had been overridden by the Commonwealth Act.

2 indirectly, through Australia's treaty obligations impacting on administrative law

In *Minister for Immigration and Ethnic Affairs v. Teoh* (1995) 183 CLR 273,[96] the High Court held that Commonwealth decision-makers may need to take account of international treaties ratified by Australia but not implemented by legislation. In the absence of any statutory or executive indications to the contrary, a treaty may give rise to a 'legitimate expectation' by a person affected by a decision that the decision will conform to the terms of the treaty. However, the impact of *Teoh* has been blunted by two Joint Statements, the first by the Minister for Foreign Affairs, Senator Gareth Evans, and the Attorney-General, Michael Lavarch, dated 10 May 1995, and the second, which replaced the first, by the Minister for Foreign Affairs, Alexander Downer, and the

---

92 Human Rights Committee, Communication No. 488/1992, UN Doc. CCPR/C/50/D/488/1992, 8 April 1994. See also *A (name deleted) v. Australia*, Human Rights Committee, Communication No. 560/1993, UN Doc. CCPR/C/59/D/560/1993, 30 April 1997, in which the Committee held that Australia had breached Article 2(3) and Articles 9(1) and (4) of the ICCPR in its detentions of a Cambodian citizen seeking refugee status.

93 See S. Bronitt, 'The Right to Sexual Privacy, Sado-masochism and the *Human Rights (Sexual Conduct) Act 1994* (Cth)' (1995) 2 *Australian Journal of Human Rights* 59.

94 *Croome v. Tasmania* No H004 of 1995.

95 *Croome v. Tasmania* (1997) 142 ALR 397 at 410.

96 See M. Allars, 'One Small Step for Legal Doctrine, One Giant Leap Towards Integrity in Government: *Teoh's* Case and the Internationalisation of Administrative Law' (1995) 17 *Sydney Law Review* 204; R. Piotrowicz, 'Unincorporated Treaties in Australian Law' [1996] *Public Law* 190; A. Twomey, '*Minister for Immigration and Ethnic Affairs v. Teoh*' (1995) 23 *Federal Law Review* 348; K. Walker, 'Treaties and the Internationalisation of Australian Law', in Saunders, pp. 218–27. See, in the New Zealand context, *Tavita v. Minister of Immigration* [1994] 2 NZLR 257.

Attorney-General, Daryl Williams, dated 25 February 1997.[97] These Statements have provided an executive indication, and foreshadowed a legislative indication, that 'the act of entering into a treaty does not give rise to legitimate expectations in administrative law'.[98] A legislative indication would have been provided by the Administrative Decisions (Effect of International Instruments) Bill 1995 (Cth), which lapsed with the March 1996 federal election. A second attempt to provide a legislative indication was the Administrative Decisions (Effect of International Instruments) Bill 1997 (Cth), which passed the House of Representatives, but met difficulties in the Senate, and lapsed with the October 1998 election.[99] The South Australian Parliament provided a legislative indication in the *Administrative Decisions (Effect of International Instruments) Act 1995* (SA).

3 indirectly, by shaping the development of the common law and the interpretation of statutes and the Constitution.[100]

International human rights norms have had a significant influence on the development of the Australian common law.[101] In *Mabo v. Queensland (No 2) (1992) 175 CLR 1* at 42, in the context of recognising the continuance of 'traditional native title', Brennan J stated:

> The opening up of international remedies to individuals pursuant to Australia's accession to the Optional Protocol to the International Covenant on Civil and Political Rights brings to bear on the common law the powerful influence of the Covenant and the international standards it imports. The common law does not necessarily conform with international law, but international law is a legitimate and important influence on the development of the common law, especially when international law declares the existence of universal human rights. A common law doctrine founded on unjust discrimination in the enjoyment of civil and political rights demands reconsideration. It is contrary both to international standards and to the fundamental values of our common law to entrench a discriminatory rule which, because of the supposed position on the scale of social organization of the indigenous inhabitants of a settled colony, denies them a right to occupy their traditional lands.

Mason CJ and McHugh J agreed with Brennan J. In other cases, while reaffirming the approach of Brennan J in *Mabo (No 2),* the High Court has made more cautious use of international law in the development of the common law.[102] In *Dietrich v. The Queen (1992) 177 CLR 292,* Mason CJ and McHugh J argued that the use of international law is only legitimate when the common law is ambiguous or uncertain.[103] In that case,

---

97 'International Treaties and the High Court Decision in Teoh', *Ministerial Document Service*, No. 179/94-95, 11 May 1995, at 6228–30; 'The Effect of Treaties in Administrative Decision-Making', *Commonwealth of Australia Gazette*, No. S 69, 26 February 1997.

98 'The Effect of Treaties in Ministerial Decision-Making'. Doubt has been expressed about the effectiveness of these Statements. See *Department of Immigration and Ethnic Affairs v. Ram* (1996) 69 FCR 431 at 437–8 per Hill J; *Re Yad Ram and Department of Immigration and Ethnic Affairs* (1995) 22 AAR 372 at 377–8 per the Tribunal; *Fang v. Minister for Immigration and Ethnic Affairs* (1996) 135 ALR 583 at 604 per Carr J; *Davey Browne v Minister for Immigration and Multicultural Affairs* [1998] 566 FCA (unreported, 29 May 1998) per Wilcox J.

99 See Senate Legal and Constitutional Legislation Committee, *Consideration of Legislation Referred to the Committee—Administrative Decisions (Effect of International Instruments) Bill 1997*, Senate Printing Unit, October 1997.

100 See Walker, pp. 209–18.

101 See, for example, *Jago v. District Court of New South Wales* (1988) 12 NSWLR 558.

102 See, for example, *Environment Protection Authority v. Caltex Refining Co. Pty Ltd* (1993) 178 CLR 477 at 499 per Mason CJ and Toohey J; *Minister for Immigration and Ethnic Affairs v. Teoh* (1995) 183 CLR 273 at 288 per Mason CJ and Deane J, at 315 per McHugh J.

103 Compare this finding with Walker, pp. 213–14.

at p. 306, Mason CJ and McHugh J were not prepared to apply international norms to support a right (the right of an accused to counsel at public expense) 'which has hitherto never been recognised'.

There has also been increasing recognition that international law may play a role in the interpretation of statutes. This recognition builds on s. 15AB(2) of the *Acts Interpretation Act 1901* (Cth), inserted in 1984, which, in defined circumstances, permits reference to 'any treaty or other international agreement that is referred to in the Act' for the purpose of construing that Act. Courts have gone further than s. 15AB(2) in providing a role for international law in the interpretation of statutes generally.[104] Thus, Brennan, Deane and Dawson JJ stated in *Chu Kheng Lim v. Minister for Immigration* (1992) 176 CLR 1 at 38: 'We accept the proposition that the courts should, in a case of ambiguity, favour a construction of a Commonwealth statute which accords with the obligations of Australia under an international treaty'.[105] Mason CJ and Deane J endorsed this approach in *Minister for Immigration and Ethnic Affairs v. Teoh* (1995) 183 CLR 273 at 287, as did Gummow and Hayne JJ in *Kartinyeri v. Commonwealth* (1998) 152 ALR 540 at 571. This does not mean that rules of international law are capable of overriding statutes. Where there is inconsistency, it is clear that the latter will prevail. Thus, a person will be bound by a statute even where that statute breaches a rule of international law.[106]

In the *Engineers Case* (1920) 28 CLR 129, Knox CJ, Isaacs, Rich, and Starke JJ at 148–50 and Higgins J at 161–2[107] stated that the Constitution, an Act of the British Parliament (see Chapter 2), should be interpreted according to the ordinary rules of statutory construction. It might be argued that if international law can play a role in the interpretation of statutes, it can also assist in the interpretation of the Constitution. International law has a prominent role to play in the interpretation of the Bill of Rights in the South African Constitution. Section 39(1) of that Constitution states that: 'When interpreting the Bill of Rights, a court, tribunal or forum … (b) must consider international law'. In Australia, the use of international law in constitutional interpretation has yet to gain the same acceptance as has its use in construing the common law and statute law. Nevertheless, it has an enormous unrealised potential for the construction of express and implied rights in the Australian Constitution. An important part of the application of constitutional rights is the search for appropriate norms to underpin the development of the particular right or to assist with the balancing of a right as against other community interests. The development of human rights guarantees in international law since the Second World War is an appropriate source of such guidance.

In *Newcrest Mining (WA) Ltd v. Commonwealth* (1997) 147 ALR 42 at 148, Kirby J argued that:

---

104 See D. C. Pearce and R. S. Geddes, *Statutory Interpretation in Australia*, 4th edn, Butterworths, 1996, p. 53.
105 See *Derbyshire County Council v. Times Newspapers* [1992] QB 770 at 830 per Butler-Sloss LJ.
106 *Polites v. Commonwealth* (1945) 70 CLR 60; *Horta v. Commonwealth* (1994) 181 CLR 183 at 195 per the Court.
107 Compare *Victoria v. Commonwealth (Payroll Tax Case)* (1971) 122 CLR 353 at 394–5 per Windeyer J.

international law is a legitimate and important influence on the development of the common law and constitutional law, especially when international law declares the existence of universal and fundamental rights. To the full extent that its text permits, Australia's Constitution, as the fundamental law of government in this country, accommodates itself to international law, including insofar as that law expresses basic rights. The reason for this is that the Constitution not only speaks to the people of Australia who made it and accept it for their governance. It also speaks to the international community as the basic law of the Australian nation, which is a member of that community.

Kirby J then applied this approach to support his conclusion that s. 51(xxxi) of the Constitution, which requires that the Commonwealth provide 'just terms' in any 'acquisition of property' (see Chapter 6), applies to laws passed by the Commonwealth for the territories under s. 122. He adopted a similar approach in his dissent in *Kartinyeri v. Commonwealth* (1998) 152 ALR 540 at 598–9. In that case, reference (at p. 593) to international law supported his conclusion that the Commonwealth's races power in s. 51(xxvi) 'does not extend to the enactment of laws detrimental to, or discriminatory against, the people of any race (including the Aboriginal race) by reference to their race'. Kirby J's willingness to apply international law in this way has yet to be embraced by the other members of the High Court.[108] Indeed, it may be some time, if at all, before his approach achieves an accepted status. His vision of the Constitution as a document that 'speaks to the international community' is a novel one in Australian constitutional law because it challenges the traditional insular focus on the Constitution as an instrument concerned only with Australian governance. Kirby J's approach is consistent with developments in international law, but is some time ahead of similar developments in Australia.

Conclusion

In Australia, human rights are protected at a number of different levels. This loose and sometimes overlapping web of protection offers significant support for civil liberties and may act as an important legal and political barrier to a government wishing to breach fundamental rights. However, the regime outlined above is inadequate. The protection offered is ad hoc and of limited scope. Brian Burdekin, a former Australian Human Rights Commissioner, commented in 1994 that: 'It is beyond question that our current legal system is seriously inadequate in protecting many of the rights of the most vulnerable and disadvantaged groups in our community'.[109]

The scheme of protection is also unsatisfactory because it is largely unknown.[110] There is little knowledge among Australians of their legal rights. Such rights are not readily accessible and thus fail to serve the important educative or symbolic function

---

108 Compare the use made of international law by Gummow and Hayne JJ in *Kartinyeri v. Commonwealth* at 571–3.

109 B. Burdekin, 'Foreword', in Alston, p. v.

110 Australians possess an appalling lack of knowledge about their system of government. See Civics Expert Group, *Whereas the People: Civics and Citizenship Education*, AGPS, 1994.

that should underlie their operation. Ultimately, they do not effectively protect fundamental freedoms from being abrogated by Australian parliaments. Although an approach based on liberalism might suggest that Australians have largely been free, republican theory suggests otherwise. Australians remain subject to the dominion of their parliaments because, at any time, their representatives could choose to arbitrarily interfere with individual liberty. The Australian people are subjugated by this potential. There is a need for greater protection entrenched in a statutory or constitutional Bill of Rights (see Chapter 10).

TWO

Human Rights and the Drafting of the Australian Constitution

Introduction

In *Australian Capital Television Pty Ltd v. Commonwealth* (1992) 177 CLR 106 at 136, Mason CJ sought to foreclose the possibility of an implied Bill of Rights in the Australian Constitution. He stated:

> it is difficult, if not impossible, to establish a foundation for the implication of general guarantees of fundamental rights and freedoms. To make such an implication would run counter to the prevailing sentiment of the framers that there was no need to incorporate a comprehensive Bill of Rights in order to protect the rights and freedoms of citizens. That sentiment was one of the unexpressed assumptions on which the Constitution was drafted.

Here, Mason CJ was expressing a widely held view. Many argue that while the framers of the Australian Constitution contemplated the inclusion of a Bill of Rights, they eventually rejected the idea and concluded that rights were adequately protected by other means. People were to be protected by the common law and the good sense of elected representatives, as constrained by the doctrine of responsible government. This view is grounded on a fallacy. It is based on the premise that the framers were generally sympathetic to the need to protect the rights of minorities. It also assumes that the framers actually debated whether or not to include a comprehensive Bill of Rights. In fact, they merely debated a few ad hoc rights provisions.

The orthodox reasons given for the absence of a Bill of Rights in the Australian Constitution ignore the real motivations of the drafters. The prevailing sentiment of the framers was that the Constitution should not incorporate rights-orientated provisions. This was not due to a belief that rights across the community were generally well protected. While it was certain that the rights and interests of the framers themselves would be protected under the new federal system, they sought to establish the means by which the rights of other sections of the community could be abrogated. In this respect the framers were driven by a desire to maintain race-based distinctions, which today would undoubtedly be regarded as racism. They considered a Bill of Rights undesirable because it might protect, as citizens, 'Chinamen, Japanese, Hindoos, and other barbarians' in the context of such areas as employment.[1] This should not be surprising. By today's standards, the mores of the time were racist and discriminatory.[2] After all, one of the first pieces of legislation passed by the new federal Parliament was the *Immigration Restriction Act 1901* (Cth), s. 3(a) of which prohibited the immigration into Australia of any person who, when asked by an officer, was unable to 'write out at dictation and sign in the presence of the officer a passage of fifty words in length in an European language directed by the officer'.[3] This was the means by which the White Australia policy was implemented.[4]

The motivations behind the drafting of the Australian Constitution were complex and varied. The process was driven by factors such as the need for a greater defence preparedness, a desire for free trade, and a sentimental attachment to nationhood. Despite being drafted by popularly elected representatives, the Australian Constitution was not written primarily as a people's constitution. Instead, it was a compact between the Australian colonies that was designed to meet, amongst other things, the needs of trade and commerce.[5] Consequently, the Constitution says more about the marriage of the colonies and the powers of their progeny, the Commonwealth, than it does about the relationship between Australians and their government. The document does not expressly embody the fundamental rights or aspirations of the Australian people. Nor is there expressed any spirit of reconciliation with Australia's indigenous peoples. While the new South African Constitution has its own song, 'One Law for One Nation',[6] one could not imagine any such thing for the Australian Constitution, which has eight chapters, including one on 'Finance and Trade', but only a few provisions that are explicitly rights-orientated. According to Lois O'Donoghue, former Chairperson of the Aboriginal and Torres Strait Islander Commission: 'It says very little about what it is to be Australian. It says practically nothing about how we find ourselves here—save being an amalgamation of former colonies. It says nothing of how we should behave towards each other as human beings and as Australians'.[7]

This chapter examines the place of human rights in the drafting of the Australian Constitution. It accounts for the influence of other constitutional models, including their effect on the decision of the framers not to insert provisions that might have pro-

---

1   *Official Record of the Debates of the Australasian Federal Convention: 1891–1898* [hereafter *Convention Debates*], vol. 5, *Melbourne 1898*, Legal Books, 1986, p. 1784 per Dr Quick. See also *Convention Debates*, vol. 5, *Melbourne 1898*, p. 1752 per Dr Quick, where he refers to 'people of any undesirable race or of undesirable antecedents'.

2   See, for example, the following debates on the exclusion of Aboriginal people from the federal franchise: Australia, House of Representatives 1902, *Debates*, vol. 9, 24 April, pp. 11975–80; and, Australia, Senate 1902, *Debates*, vol. 10, 29 May 1902, pp. 13002–11.

3   See *Potter v. Minahan* (1908) 7 CLR 277; *R v. Wilson; Ex parte Kisch* (1934) 52 CLR 234.

4   See A. C. Palfreeman, *The Administration of the White Australia Policy*, Melbourne University Press, 1967.

5   See, for example, Constitution, s. 92. As Manning Clark has argued, the Constitution was written by drafters who 'wanted a Constitution that would make capitalist society hum': M. Clark, 'The People and the Constitution', in S. Encel, D. Horne, and E. Thompson (eds), *Change the Rules! Towards a Democratic Constitution*, Penguin, 1977, p. 18.

6   The text of 'One Law for One Nation' can be found on the Internet at <http://www.constitution. org.za/onelaw.htm>.

7   F. Brennan, *Securing a Bountiful Place for Aborigines and Torres Strait Islanders in a Modern, Free and Tolerant Australia*, Constitutional Centenary Foundation, 1994, p. 18.

tected basic freedoms. The focus is on the drafting of the major civil and political rights in the Constitution: sections 41, 80, 116, and 117 (see Chapter 5). Other provisions that have since been interpreted to offer some protection of rights, such as s. 51(xxxi), are not examined because the drafters themselves did not see such provisions as raising human rights issues.[8]

The concept of human rights emerged after the Second World War, largely as a consequence of international instruments such as the *Universal Declaration of Human Rights 1948* (the *Declaration*).[9] Any analysis of the 1890s Conventions that drafted the Australian Constitution must be understood in this light, lest the analysis produce a distorted picture. However, this is not to say that the idea of protecting basic freedoms in a constitution was alien to the Australian drafters. They had before them the United States Bill of Rights, which had been in operation for a century by the time of the 1891 Convention. It is thus appropriate to examine the extent to which the framers viewed the Australian Constitution as an instrument designed to protect basic liberties.

The making of the Australian Constitution

The Australian Constitution was drafted at two constitutional Conventions.[10] These Conventions were preceded by the 1890 Federation Conference in Melbourne.[11] The main issues at the Conventions were the financial and trade issues arising from federation, and how best to weigh the interests of the small states against those of the more populous states in the new federal Parliament.[12] Customs duties, tariffs, and the capacity of the upper house of the federal Parliament to veto money bills were of far greater concern to the Convention delegates than the protection of human rights. After all, 'the Constitution was mainly conceived by its framers as a treaty between States'.[13]

The first Convention was held in Sydney in 1891 and was attended by representatives of the colonial parliaments. The Convention did not include any women (the first woman elected to an Australian parliament was Edith Cowan, who was elected to the Western Australian Legislative Assembly in 1921), or any representatives of Australia's indigenous peoples or ethnic communities. Andrew Inglis Clark,[14] the Tasmanian

---

8   Note, however, that Sir George Turner objected to the use of the words 'just terms' in s. 51(xxxi), stating that 'they are not proper words to put into the Constitution. We assume that the Federal Parliament will act strictly on the lines of justice': *Convention Debates*, vol. 4, *Melbourne 1898*, p. 153.

9   See Chapter 1 for a discussion of the *Declaration*.

10 See generally on the making of the Australian Constitution: J. A. La Nauze, *The Making of the Australian Constitution*, Melbourne University Press, 1972; J. Quick and R. Garran, *The Annotated Constitution of the Australian Commonwealth*, 1901 edn, Legal Books, 1995.

11 See R. Sharwood, 'The Australasian Federation Conference of 1890', in G. Craven (ed.), *The Convention Debates 1891–1898: Commentaries, Indices and Guide*, vol. 6, Legal Books, 1986, p. 41.

12 For summaries of the issues addressed at the Conventions, see Quick and Garran, pp. 123–43 (Sydney 1891), 165–82 (Adelaide 1897), 187–94 (Sydney 1897), 194–206 (Melbourne 1898).

13 La Nauze, p. 190.

14 See M. Haward and J. Warden (eds), *An Australian Democrat: The Life, Work, and Consequences of Andrew Inglis Clark*, Centre for Tasmanian Historical Studies, University of Tasmania, 1995. A copy of Clark's draft constitution bill is contained, as an appendix, in J. Reynolds, 'A.I. Clark's American Sympathies and his Influence on Australian Federation' (1958) 32 *Australian Law Journal* 62. See also J. M. Williams, '"With Eyes Open": Andrew Inglis Clark and our Republican Tradition' (1995) 23 *Federal Law Review* 149 at 171–8.

Attorney-General and a member of the Convention, had prepared a draft constitution after the 1890 Federation Conference. In 1891, this draft provided an important starting point. Clark's draft constitution contained several provisions that sought to protect human rights, and it also contained many of the checks and balances that characterise the United States Constitution. For example, the draft provided for the separate vesting of legislative, executive, and judicial power; for an independent and entrenched High Court; and for freedom of religion and trial by jury. This draft had a profound impact both on the shape of the draft constitution that emerged from the 1891 Convention, where all but eight clauses of the 96 clauses of Clark's draft were adopted in some form, and on the Australian Constitution as finally enacted, where all but ten clauses of Clark's draft appeared or had a recognisable counterpart.[15] The draft constitution adopted by the 1891 Convention was to be put to a referendum in each colony, with a view to it then being enacted for Australia by the British Parliament. The proposal faltered when it lapsed in New South Wales without having gone to a referendum.

The Convention process began afresh in 1895. The premiers of the colonies agreed to establish a popularly elected Convention to produce a further draft constitution to be put to the people in each colony at a referendum. This Convention met in Adelaide and Sydney in 1897, and in Melbourne in 1898. Popularly elected representatives were sent by New South Wales, South Australia, Tasmania, and Victoria. Queensland was not represented at the Convention, and Western Australia sent parliamentary representatives rather than popularly elected delegates.

There was a low turnout for the election of the delegates to this second Convention, with 139 850 people out of 260 000 enrolled electors voting in New South Wales, and 99 108 out of 238 000 enrolled electors voting in Victoria.[16] William Trenwith, a member of the Victorian Parliament and former bootmaker and trade union organiser, was the only representative of the Labour movement at the Convention. As in 1891 there were no female[17] or Aboriginal delegates: 'It was for the most part the big men of the established political and economic order, the men of property or their trusted allies, who moulded the federal Constitution Bill'.[18] However, women did play a role in the making of the Constitution. They participated in grassroots political organisations such as the Woman's Christian Temperance Union, which petitioned the Conventions in support of federation and equal voting rights, and the Women's Federal League, which lobbied men seeking their support for federation.[19]

Rather than making a fresh start, the delegates to the 1897–98 Convention revised the draft constitution endorsed by the 1891 Convention. Under the leadership of Edmund Barton, later Australia's first Prime Minister and one of the first members of the High Court, the Convention refined the document to incorporate later compro-

---

15 J. M. Neasey, 'Andrew Inglis Clark Senior and Australian Federation' (1969) 15(2) *Australian Journal of Politics and History* 1 at 7–8. See also La Nauze, pp. 74–6.

16 Quick and Garran, p. 164. See K. Dermody 'The 1897 Federal Convention Election: A Success or Failure?', in *Papers on Parliament*, Department of the Senate, Parliament House, No. 30, November 1997, p. 93.

17 Catherine Helen Spence stood for election as a South Australian delegate to the 1897–1898 Convention. She was unsuccessful: see D. Headon, 'No Weak-Kneed Sister: Catherine Helen Spence and "Pure Democracy"', in H. Irving (ed.), *A Woman's Constitution?*, Hale & Iremonger, 1996, p. 42; and S. Magarey, *Unbridling the Tongues of Women—A Biography of Catherine Helen Spence*, Hale & Iremonger, 1985.

18 L. F. Crisp, *Australian National Government*, 4th edn, Longman Cheshire, 1978, p. 14.

19 H. Irving, 'Fair Federalists and Founding Mothers', in Irving, p. 1.

mises. This revised draft constitution was put to the people of New South Wales, South Australia, Tasmania, and Victoria. No referendum was held in Queensland or Western Australia. The draft constitution received majority support in each of the four colonies holding referendums, but was nevertheless unsuccessful in New South Wales because the number of people that voted for the draft did not reach the 80 000 required by the New South Wales Parliament. The results of the 1898 referendums were as follows:[20]

Colony	Votes for	Votes against	Majority of votes
New South Wales	71 595 (52%)	66 228 (48%)	5367 (4%)
Victoria	100 520 (82%)	22 099 (18%)	78 421 (64%)
South Australia	35 800 (67%)	17 320 (33%)	18 480 (35%)
Tasmania	11 797 (81%)	2716 (19%)	9081 (63%)
Total	219 712 (67%)	108 363 (33%)	111 349 (34%)

The draft constitution was then amended at an 1899 conference attended by the Premiers of all six colonies. In 1899 and 1900 it was again put to the voters in the colonies, this time also in Queensland and Western Australia:[21]

Colony	Votes for	Votes against	Majority of votes
New South Wales (1899)	107 420 (56%)	82 741 (44%)	24 679 (13%)
Victoria (1899)	152 653 (94%)	9805 (6%)	142 848 (88%)
South Australia (1899)	65 990 (79%)	17 053 (21%)	48 937 (59%)
Tasmania (1899)	13 437 (94%)	791 (6%)	12 646 (89%)
Queensland (1899)	38 488 (55%)	30 996 (45%)	7492 (11%)
Western Australia (1900)	44 800 (69%)	19 691 (31%)	25 109 (39%)
Total	422 788 (72%)	161 077 (28%)	261 711 (45%)

At the referendums of 1899 and 1900 the draft constitution was supported by a majority of voters in each colony. Voting was voluntary, with only 60% of the people eligible to vote at the referendums doing so.[22] Large sections of the community were also excluded from voting, including most women and many of Australia's Aboriginal peoples.[23] Women were only able to vote for or against the draft constitution in South Australia and Western Australia; and Aboriginal people were only able to vote in New South Wales, South Australia, Tasmania, and Victoria. Overall, only a small percentage of Australians actually cast a vote in favour of the draft constitution. In New South Wales, Queensland, and Tasmania the figure was below 10%.[24]

After the referendums of 1899 and 1900, a delegation representing the Australian colonies was sent to London to have the draft constitution enacted by the British Parliament. In the absence of revolution or other severing of ties with Britain, the Imperial

---

20   Source: Quick and Garran, p. 213.
21   Source: Quick and Garran, pp. 225, 250.
22   Crisp, p. 12. For a breakdown by colony, see Twomey, A, *The Constitution—19th Century Colonial Office Document or a People's Constitution?*, Parliamentary Research Service, Commonwealth Parliament, 1994, Background Paper No. 15, at 30.
23   Brennan, p. 6.
24   Twomey, p. 31.

Parliament still exercised ultimate power over the Australian colonies. Thus, it was the source of power to which colonists naturally turned to bring about the new Australian federation. However, the British Colonial Office and the Secretary of State for the Colonies, Joseph Chamberlain, were not prepared to have the Imperial Parliament pass the draft constitution in the form presented by the Australian colonies. Concern centred on clause 74, which restricted appeals from the proposed High Court to the Privy Council. Following Colonial Office changes, a Bill containing the draft constitution was introduced into the House of Commons. Clause 74 had been amended to allow greater scope for appeal to the Privy Council from the High Court.[25] The Bill completed its passage through the Imperial Parliament on 5 July 1900, was assented to by the Queen on 9 July 1900, and came into force on 1 January 1901. Entitled the *Commonwealth of Australia Constitution Act 1900* (63 & 64 Vict. Ch. 12), s. 9 of the Act reads 'The Constitution of the Commonwealth shall be as follows', and thereafter contains the entire text of the Australian Constitution.

The making of the Australian Constitution was neither representative nor inclusive of the Australian people generally.[26] It was drafted by a small, privileged, section of society. Whole sections of the community were excluded from the Conventions or from voting for the draft constitution. Of the eligible voters, less than half actually cast a vote in favour of the Constitution. Even then, the Constitution did not become law until it was further altered to meet the objections of the British Colonial Office. However, these factors do not rule out the Constitution being considered an instrument of the Australian people. As Helen Irving points out, to require an endorsement at the polls of a very large majority of a population 'positively rules out probably most historical claims to a mandate'.[27] She argues that 'what matters is less the statistics, and more the mechanism'.[28] While the mechanism was certainly flawed in that it excluded the direct participation of many Australians, it did create a field of public debate and a climate in which the Australian people could move towards federation under a Constitution that had their acquiescence, if not their direct support.

The influence of comparative models

The framers of the Australian Constitution were deeply influenced by their British heritage and assumed that the Australian federation would be steeped in the Westminster tradition of responsible government. Responsible government was understood to mean that the executive would be responsible to, rather than independent of, the parliament. However, the Westminster tradition was inadequate as a model for an Australian federal government that was to be based on a written constitution. The drafters were accordingly forced to look more widely afield.

---

25 For the full list of amendments made to the draft constitution endorsed in Australia, see Quick and Garran, p. 242.
26 Compare the experience of the 1998 Constitutional Convention. See G. Williams, 'The Peoples' Convention?' (1998) 23 *Alternative Law Journal* 2.
27 H. Irving, 'The People and their Conventions', in M. Coper and G. Williams (eds), *Power, Parliament and the People*, Federation Press, 1997, p. 122.
28 Irving, 'The People and their Conventions', p. 122.

In the 1890s, the obvious comparative models to which the Australian drafters might turn were the written constitutions of Switzerland, Canada, and the USA.[29] Neither the Swiss nor the Canadian models were as compelling as that of the USA. Switzerland, which had become a federation in 1848 and had revised its Constitution in 1874, possessed a language and political traditions alien to the Australian drafters.[30] The Canadian Constitution might at first have appeared to be the appropriate model given its creation of a federal structure under the British Crown. However, the Canadian Constitution was rejected because it was believed to give too much power to the central government. The provinces received only some specified powers, while the central government was bestowed with some specific powers and all residual power.[31] Of course, there is a great irony in the fact that the Canadian Constitution has since been interpreted in a manner that has brought about a greater degree of decentralisation and provincial power than exists in either Australia or the USA.

The primacy given to the United States Constitution owes much to Clark and his 1891 draft constitution. Clark was a republican who according to a contemporary 'was more American than the Americans in his admiration of American institutions'.[32] Clark's republican vision revolved around the idea that government should embody both the rule of law and the rule of check and balance.[33] Hence Clark proposed that the Australian Constitution incorporate a separation of powers and entrench the position of the High Court. Even for those drafters who did not share Clark's republican vision, the United States Constitution best approximated their federal desires. This was not due to any deep appreciation or knowledge by the framers of the United States system; in fact 'with a few exceptions—Inglis Clark in 1891, Isaacs in 1897–8—their knowledge of the actual judgments of the US Supreme Court was apparently not profound'.[34] Barton, for example, was unfamiliar with the foundational decision of the United States Supreme Court in *Marbury v. Madison* 5 US (1 Cranch) 137 (1803).[35] Although the United States model was not sufficiently influential to bring about a Bill of Rights in the Australian Constitution (the Australian framers not being guided by the same desire to protect liberty by limiting governmental power), it nevertheless had a profound impact. The instrument was especially useful in terms of how it provided for the continuing power of the colonies (once they had achieved statehood) and how it balanced the relative powers of the smaller and larger states. Thus, the Australian Constitution creates a Senate in which the states are equally represented, and provides for specific powers to be vested in the federal government with the states having all residual power.

---

29 Quick and Garran, p. 130.
30 The amendment formula in s. 128 of the Australian Constitution is based on an equivalent provision in the Swiss Constitution. See Quick and Garran, p. 986.
31 See H. Charlesworth, A Constitutional Bill of Rights: North American Experience and Australian Prospect, SJD thesis, Harvard University, 1985, pp. 104–6.
32 B. R. Wise, *The Making of the Australian Commonwealth 1889–1900*, Longmans, Green & Co, 1913, p. 74. See Reynolds; Williams, '"With Eyes Open"'.
33 By rule of check and balance it is meant that 'the authorities who hold power under the law are institutionally constrained so that they cannot easily abuse their position': P. Pettit, 'Republican Themes' (1992) 6(2) *Legislative Studies* 29 at 29.
34 La Nauze, p. 232. See Neasey, at 2.
35 See J. A. Thomson, 'Constitutional Authority for Judicial Review: A Contribution from the Framers of the Australian Constitution', in Craven, p. 179; Williams, '"With Eyes Open"' at 169.

The Australian Constitution is a creature of both the United States and the United Kingdom models. While its United States heritage is obvious on the face of the Constitution, its United Kingdom heritage is less clear. Its British origins are reflected in s. 64, which provides that 'no Minister of State shall hold office for a longer period than three months unless he is or becomes a senator or a member of the House of Representatives'. Here, responsible government won out over the United States model. This was highlighted by Lord Haldane in the motion for leave to introduce the *Commonwealth of Australia Constitution Act* into the British House of Commons:

> The difference between the Constitution which this bill proposes to set up and the Constitution of the United States is enormous and fundamental. This bill is permeated through and through with the spirit of the greatest institution which exists in the Empire, and which pertains to every Constitution established within the Empire—I mean the institution of responsible government, a government under which the Executive is directly responsible to—nay, is almost the creature of—the Legislature. This is not so in America, but it is so with all the Constitutions we have granted to our self-governing colonies. On this occasion we establish a Constitution modelled on our own model, pregnant with the same spirit, and permeated with the principle of responsible government. Therefore, what you have here is nothing akin to the Constitution of the United States except in its most superficial features.[36]

This passage was quoted by the High Court in *Amalgamated Society of Engineers v. Adelaide Steamship Co Ltd (Engineers Case)* (1920) 28 CLR 129 at 147, where it was applied by Knox CJ, Isaacs, Rich, and Starke JJ to reject the use of United States authorities in the interpretation of the Australian Constitution (see Chapter 4). While Lord Haldane overstated the differences between the Australian and United States models, he did identify the essential difference between the two, that is, that the Australian executive is a parliamentary executive, while the United States executive is independent of the legislature. This provides some explanation for why a Bill of Rights in the American mould might have been thought unnecessary. While the United States executive needed to be constrained by a Bill of Rights, as it was independent of Congress, this did not hold true in Australia where the executive was to be responsible and accountable to the Parliament.

As might have been expected, Clark took a different view from that of Lord Haldane on the influence of the American model on the Australian Constitution. Writing in 1901, he argued that the Australian Constitution 'so closely resembles the Constitution of the United States of America that it may be not improperly described as an adaptation of that Constitution'.[37] He also argued that 'the authors of its American prototype may be fitly regarded as being also the primary authors of the Constitution of the Commonwealth of Australia'.[38] Clark clearly also overstated the comparison. The

---

36 United Kingdom, House of Commons, 1900, *Parliamentary Debates*, vol. 83 (4th Series), pp. 98–9. See O. Dixon, *Jesting Pilate*, LBC, 1965, p. 101. Compare the approaches in both these sources with *Attorney-General (Commonwealth) v. Colonial Sugar Refining Co. Ltd* (1913) 17 CLR 644 at 652 per Lord Haldane.

37 A. I. Clark, *Studies in Australian Constitutional Law*, 1901 edn, Legal Books, 1997, p. 358. See Dixon, p. 102, who describes the Australian Constitution as 'roughly speaking … a redraft of the American Constitution of 1787 with modifications found suitable for the more characteristic British institutions and for Australian conditions'. See also Dixon pp. 44, 113, 166–7.

38 Clark, *Studies in Australian Constitutional Law*, p. 358.

Australian Constitution was drafted in circumstances that were very different from those surrounding the drafting of the United States Constitution, and by people with very different ideals. The Australian colonies had not emerged from revolution against a tyrannous Crown and were less inspired by notions of individual freedom and republican ideology.[39] Nor was the Australian Constitution drafted with the same spirit of civic virtue and public good that permeated the American experience.[40] While the Australian colonies did come together partly out of concerns for collective security arising from German activity in New Guinea, this was hardly the inspirational material of the American revolution. It was certainly not enough to fire the enthusiasm of delegates to introduce a Bill of Rights into the new structure of government.

The Australian drafters sought an appropriate financial arrangement between the colonies rather than a declaration of independence from the United Kingdom. They were not prepared to seriously consider an Australian republic with an Australian head of State. In 1891, George Dibbs, a former Premier of New South Wales who possessed 'a slight tinge of republican notions',[41] described 'the republic of Australia' as 'the inevitable destiny of the people of this great country'.[42] Sir Henry Parkes, then the Premier of New South Wales, replied 'I have no time to talk of this question of republicanism which has been so ungraciously launched amongst us'.[43] Alfred Deakin, subsequently Prime Minister of Australia, in rejecting the notion that the Governor-General of Australia should be popularly elected, stated that 'the office of Governor-General is not one to which a democrat will aspire'.[44] The motion for a popularly elected Governor-General was defeated 35 votes to 3.[45] In its place, s. 2 of the Australian Constitution provides that the Governor-General shall be 'appointed by the Queen'.

Human rights at the constitutional Conventions

The 1891 and 1897–98 Conventions were largely unconcerned with the protection of human rights.[46] The drafters were more interested in rights of a different kind; namely, the rights of the colonies, once they became states, to retain their powers and to maintain racially discriminatory laws. This interest is reflected in the text of the Constitution and is offset to only a small extent by the few explicitly rights-oriented provisions that Clark was able to introduce into the instrument. Clark's achievement, although limited,

---

39 M. McKenna, *The Captive Republic: A History of Republicanism in Australia 1788–1996*, Cambridge University Press, 1996, ch. 9. See G. A. Davies, 'A Brief History of Australian Republicanism', in G. Winterton (ed.), *We, the People: Australian Republican Government*, Allen & Unwin, 1994, p. 49; J. Warden, 'The Fettered Republic: The Anglo-American Commonwealth and the Traditions of Australian Political Thought' (1993) 28 *Australian Journal of Political Science* 83; G. Williams, 'A Republican Tradition for Australia?' (1995) 23 *Federal Law Review* 133.

40 See C. R. Sunstein, 'Interest Groups in American Public Law' (1985) 38 *Stanford Law Review* 29 at 44; G. S. Wood, *The Creation of the American Republic 1776–1787*, University of North Carolina Press, 1969.

41 *Convention Debates*, vol. 1, Sydney 1891, p. 185.

42 *Convention Debates*, vol. 1, Sydney 1891, p. 186.

43 *Convention Debates*, vol. 1, Sydney 1891, p. 323.

44 *Convention Debates*, vol. 1, Sydney 1891, p. 571.

45 *Convention Debates*, vol. 1, Sydney 1891, p. 573.

46 See G. Kennett, 'Individual Rights, the High Court and the Constitution' (1994) 19 *Melbourne University Law Review* 581 at 581–3.

is shown by contrasting the few rights in the Australian Constitution against the even fewer rights in the Canadian Constitution (as enacted in 1867).[47] Significantly, the Canadian Constitution, as enacted, lacked rights protecting religion, inter-state residence and trial by jury.

It is a mistake to overestimate the level or quality of debate at the Conventions, just as it is a mistake to believe that the records of the debates present the whole picture.[48] Debate on fundamental constitutional concepts was unsophisticated and showed a lack of understanding by many speakers. This must be taken into account in seeking guidance from the Convention debates, lest a modern view of the Constitution betray the same ignorance. An illustrative example is the debate on the extent to which the Australian Constitution should incorporate the separation of powers doctrine, a doctrine that has subsequently been robustly applied by the High Court.[49] According to Fiona Wheeler, the separation of powers doctrine was:

> accorded scant attention by the founding fathers … the introduction of an Antipodean version of the doctrine of separation of powers appears to have been, at best, a somewhat hazy consideration in the establishment of the Commonwealth. For the most part, delegates appear not to have turned their minds to the issue, or, if their attention was so directed, not to have apprehended its significance.[50]

Care must also be taken when the views of the drafters are inconsistent with the subsequent interpretation of the Constitution by the High Court. To give one example, Barton, amongst others, argued that the Constitution should not guarantee freedom of religion in regard to federal law, as such protection was unnecessary because the Commonwealth would lack the power to legislate on religious matters.[51] Barton's argument did not predict that although the Commonwealth does not have an express power to legislate with respect to 'religion', it nevertheless has the power to restrict religious freedom incidentally in legislating for a number of its other powers, such as that over defence in s. 51(vi) of the Constitution.[52]

---

47 See *Constitution Act 1867* (30 & 31 Vict. Ch. 3), sections 93, 121, and 133.

48 *Convention Debates*, vol. 1, *Sydney 1891*, p. 914 per Mr Deakin: 'There is much unstated in that record, because the delegates to this Convention have practically lived together for six weeks in private and well as in public intercourse, and from the natural action and reaction of mind upon mind have been gradually shaping their thoughts upon this great question. The bill which we present is the result of a far more intricate, intellectual process than is exhibited in our debates; unless the atmosphere in which we have lived as well as worked is taken into consideration, the measure as it stands will not be fully understood'.

49 See, for example, *R v. Kirby; Ex parte Boilermakers' Society of Australia (Boilermakers Case)* (1956) 94 CLR 254; *Brandy v. Human Rights and Equal Opportunity Commission* (1995) 183 CLR 245 (see Chapter 8).

50 F. Wheeler 'Original Intent and the Doctrine of the Separation of Powers in Australia' (1996) 7 *Public Law Review* 96 at 99.

51 *Convention Debates*, vol. 4, *Melbourne 1898*, p. 661 (see also pp. 658–9 per Mr O'Connor); *Convention Debates*, vol. 5, *Melbourne 1898*, p. 1778 per Mr O'Connor. Samuel Griffith, subsequently the first Chief Justice of the High Court, apparently shared this belief: see Charlesworth, p. 115. This conception is perhaps consistent with the 'reserved state powers' doctrine applied by the early High Court of Griffith CJ, Barton, and O'Connor JJ (see Chapter 4).

52 See *Krygger v. Williams* (1912) 15 CLR 366; *Adelaide Company of Jehovah's Witnesses Inc v. Commonwealth (Jehovah's Witnesses Case)* (1943) 67 CLR 116 (see Chapter 5). Barton's argument for the inclusion of s. 51(xxxi) of the Constitution—that is, so as to enable the Commonwealth to acquire property—has been similarly overtaken by subsequent High Court reasoning (see Chapter 6). See *Convention Debates*, vol. 4, *Melbourne 1898*, pp. 151–4.

Clark's draft constitution

While the delegates to the 1891 and 1897–98 Conventions did not debate whether the Australian Constitution should contain a Bill of Rights, they did debate several rights-orientated provisions proposed by Clark. Although Clark did not realise all of his aims, several of his ideas did filter through into the Constitution. Without these scattered provisions, the Constitution would otherwise have been devoid of express rights. Clark's choice of rights in his draft constitution was idiosyncratic. For example, he included a clause respecting freedom of religion, but nothing that would protect freedom of speech or association. The rights he included in his 1891 draft were:

- The Federal Parliament shall not make any law for the establishment or support of any religion, or for the purpose of giving any preferential recognition to any religion, or for prohibiting the free exercise of any religion. (clause 46)[53]
- The trial of all crimes cognisable by any Court established under the authority of this Act shall be by Jury, and every such trial shall be held in the Province where the crime has been committed and when not committed within any Province the trial shall be held at such place or places as the Federal Parliament may by law direct. (clause 65)
- No Province shall make any law prohibiting the free exercise of any religion. (clause 81)

Clauses 46 and 65 emerged in the Constitution as sections 116 and 80 respectively, although clause 65 was diminished by being restricted to offences against Commonwealth, but not state, laws. Clause 81 has no equivalent in the Australian Constitution.[54]

Clauses 46 and 81: freedom of religion[55]

Clark was not a delegate at the 1897–98 Convention.[56] At the 1898 Melbourne session, Henry Higgins, later a justice of the High Court, proposed a clause similar to Clark's clause 81. Higgins did not support the clause in order to protect human rights, but out of a desire to placate 'a number of people whose votes we should like to secure for the Constitution' who might have voted against the draft constitution due to fears that the reference to 'Almighty God' in its preamble meant that the Commonwealth could legislate on matters of religion.[57] Higgins's proposal was defeated: the delegates voted not to place such a restriction on the states.

Higgins subsequently proposed a clause similar to Clark's clause 46 (that became s. 116 of the Constitution). Clause 46, like s. 116, prevented only the Commonwealth from making certain laws on the subject of religion. The final placement of s. 116 in 'Chapter V—The States' of the Constitution is perhaps explained by the fact that freedom of religion was first considered in the context of Clark's clause 81, which only restricted the power of each 'Province' (or by the fact that s. 116 came to be accepted

---

53   See R. Ely, 'Andrew Inglis Clark and the Church-State Separation' (1975) 8 *Journal of Religious History* 271.
54   A proposal was put to the Australian people in 1988 to amend the Constitution to extend the guarantee of freedom of religion to the states. The proposal failed (see Chapter 10).
55   See generally R. Ely, *Unto God and Caesar: Religious Issues in the Emerging Commonwealth, 1891–1906*, Melbourne University Press, 1976.
56   Clark was apparently unable to attend due to illness and a trip to the United States: La Nauze, p. 93.
57   *Convention Debates*, vol. 4, *Melbourne 1898*, p. 654 per Mr Higgins (see also pp. 656 and 663 per Mr Higgins).

primarily as a device by which to ensure that the states retained legislative control over religious matters). This revised clause found acceptance with the delegates, not so much to protect rights, but to, in the words of Higgins:

> make it clear beyond doubt that the powers which the states individually have of making such laws as they like with regard to religion shall remain undisturbed and unbroken, and to make it clear that in framing this Constitution there is no intention whatever to give to the Federal Parliament the power to interfere in these matters.[58]

What was to be protected was the freedom of the states to legislate on religious matters, including the freedom to derogate from religious liberty. Higgins made this even clearer in stating 'I simply want to leave things as they are. I do not want to interfere with any right the state has'.[59] Even so, the proposal had its opponents. For example, Simon Fraser of Victoria spoke against the clause because it might facilitate religious diversity, arguing that 'we are now a homogeneous people, and the safer plan is to leave us so'.[60] Josiah Symon QC, a former Attorney-General of South Australia, responded by referring to Higgins's earlier point, and stated that, despite the 'great force' in Fraser's argument, he would support the clause in the hope of 'securing every vote possible for this Bill'.[61] In a last ditch stand, Fraser argued that the clause would allow an 'infinitesimal minority' to come to Australia to 'indulge in extraordinary practices', with the result that 'we may have all the theatres and all the music halls in Australia open on Sunday'.[62] The clause was carried by 25 votes to 16.

Clause 65: trial by jury

A similar desire to demarcate legislative power rather than protect individual rights is demonstrated by the delegates' adoption of s. 80 of the Constitution, a more limited version of Clark's clause 65. Higgins, this time speaking against the provision, argued, 'I feel very strongly that, no matter how much we may value trial by jury as a piece of machinery, it is not a matter for this Constitution at all'.[63] Richard O'Connor, one of the first justices of the High Court, then contributed that such a provision was not needed as Parliament could be trusted not to increase the number of offences not triable by jury.[64] On the other hand, Bernhard Wise of New South Wales argued that s. 80 'is a necessary safeguard to the individual liberty of the subject in every State'.[65] He also

---

58 *Convention Debates*, vol. 5, *Melbourne 1898*, p. 1769.
59 *Convention Debates*, vol. 5, *Melbourne 1898*, p. 1769.
60 *Convention Debates*, vol. 5, *Melbourne 1898*, p. 1775. Compare this with Bernhard Wise of New South Wales who argued for the clause on the basis of protecting the religious rights of minorities (pp. 1773–4). However Wise also suggested that the clause was merely concerned to deprive the Commonwealth of power and to leave the states to do as they pleased (p. 1778).
61 *Convention Debates*, vol. 5, *Melbourne 1898*, p. 1776.
62 *Convention Debates*, vol. 5, *Melbourne 1898*, p. 1779. A further concern was that Seventh Day Adventists, 'a very powerful body in America' who recognised Saturday as the Sabbath, might undermine Sunday as a uniform day of rest by working on Sunday (*Convention Debates*, vol. 4, *Melbourne 1898*, p. 664 per Sir Joseph Abbott).
63 *Convention Debates*, vol. 4, *Melbourne 1898*, p. 350. See *Convention Debates*, vol. 3, *Adelaide 1897*, pp. 990–1 per Mr Higgins.
64 *Convention Debates*, vol. 4, *Melbourne 1898*, pp. 352–3.
65 *Convention Debates*, vol. 4, *Melbourne 1898*, p. 350 (see also p. 351, where Wise is reported as calling s. 80 'a safeguard of liberty').

spoke against a proposal that the draft clause be amended to allow the federal Parliament to move a trial from the state where the offence was committed, stating that a requirement that the trial take place in the state where the offence was committed 'is a measure of protection to the states and to the citizens of the states'.[66] Section 80 was finally adopted after being amended to refer only to indictable offences against Commonwealth law (see Chapter 5). Moreover, it was amended so that it would arguably allow the Commonwealth itself to determine whether an offence was indictable, and thus whether its trial would be by jury. Isaac Isaacs, later Chief Justice of the High Court and Australia's first Australian Governor-General, suggested that the provision, as agreed to by the Convention, would not have 'any real effect at all', and that the federal Parliament could 'say that murder was not to be an indictable offence, and therefore the right to try a person accused of murder would not necessarily be by jury'.[67]

Equal protection of the laws, and due process of law[68]

Clark's attempt to include provisions in the Constitution that would protect rights was not limited to the provisions contained in his 1891 draft constitution. At the 1891 Convention, Clark sought to include the following clause: 'A State shall not make or enforce any law abridging any privilege or immunity of citizens of other States of the Commonwealth, nor shall a State deny to any person, within its jurisdiction, the equal protection of the laws'. This clause was not in Clark's original draft bill, but was added when he and other members of the drafting sub-committee of the 1891 Convention cruised the Hawkesbury River on the SS *Lucinda* on the Easter weekend of 1891.[69] The clause was obviously based on the Fourteenth Amendment to the United States Constitution. That Amendment, inserted after the United States Civil War, provides in part:

> No State shall make or enforce any law which shall abridge the privileges or immunities of citizens of the United States; nor shall any State deprive any person of life, liberty, or property, without due process of law; nor deny to any person within its jurisdiction the equal protection of the laws.

Clark's provision was incorporated as clause 17 of the draft constitution adopted by the 1891 Convention. It remained unamended until the 1898 session in Melbourne. By 1898, Clark had become convinced that the provision needed to be bolstered to better protect rights. He proposed, through the Tasmanian Parliament, that the Convention delete clause 17 and insert a new clause 110:

> The citizens of each state, and all other persons owing allegiance to the Queen and residing in any territory of the Commonwealth, shall be citizens of the Commonwealth, and shall be entitled to all privileges and immunities of citizens of the Commonwealth in the several

---

66 *Convention Debates*, vol. 4, *Melbourne 1898*, p. 354.
67 *Convention Debates*, vol. 5, *Melbourne 1898*, p. 1895.
68 See C. Pannam, 'Discrimination on the Basis of State Residence in Australia and the United States' (1967) 6 *Melbourne University Law Review* 105 at 106–16; J. M. Williams, 'Race, Citizenship and the Formation of the Australian Constitution: Andrew Inglis Clark and the "14th Amendment"' (1996) 42 *Australian Journal of Politics and History* 10.
69 La Nauze, pp. 229–30. Clark was ill with influenza and was unable to join the SS *Lucinda* until the Sunday of the weekend. This meant that, with the exception of this new clause, he arrived 'too late to have had any considerable share in the revisions': La Nauze, p. 68.

states; and a state shall not make or enforce any law abridging any privilege or immunity of citizens of the Commonwealth, nor shall a state deprive any person of life, liberty, or property without due process of law, or deny to any person within its jurisdiction the equal protection of its laws.[70]

Clark argued for the revision by quoting Justice Cooley of Michigan: 'the security of individual rights, it has often been observed, cannot be too frequently declared, nor in too many forms of words; nor is it possible to guard too vigilantly against the encroachments of power'.[71]

If Clark had been successful in inserting clause 110 into the Australian Constitution, the instrument may have been a very different document. None of the rights provisions that emerged in the Australian Constitution bore the potential scope of clause 110. This might have had a significant impact on the interpretation of the Constitution generally, in that it could have undermined the extremely restrictive interpretation subsequently given by the High Court to the other express civil and political rights in the instrument (see Chapter 5). Alternatively, the Court has proved itself extremely adept at restricting the rights provisions incorporated in the Constitution. Why would clause 110 have been any different? On balance, this latter argument seems the more likely.

Clause 110 did not survive in the form Clark had proposed. Amendments were put forward by New South Wales, Victoria, and Tasmania, in part because of difficulties of comprehension.[72] This led to the deletion from the clause of the words 'make or enforce any law abridging any privilege or immunity of citizens of other States of the Commonwealth', leaving the clause with the nonsensical phrase 'a State shall not: nor shall a State deny to any person'. The delegates then agreed to dispense with clause 110 entirely. The Convention subsequently agreed to insert a new provision into the draft constitution, which became s. 117 of the Constitution, a mere shadow of Clark's original vision.

The framers, human rights, and clause 110

The framers' approach to Clark's clause 110 illustrates their attitude to human rights and their limited vision for the Australian Constitution. Clause 110 was rejected by the 1897–98 Convention for two main reasons. First, the delegates did not share Clark's republican outlook. Many delegates believed that, as a matter of practice, the entrenched rights provisions suggested by Clark were unnecessary. Some delegates believed that a federal system incorporating the institution of responsible government[73] would adequately protect those rights that ought to be protected. Second, the delegates sought to ensure that the Australian states would have the power to continue laws of the colonies that discriminated against people in employment, or in other contexts, on the basis of their race.[74]

---

70   *Convention Debates*, vol. 4, *Melbourne 1898*, p. 667.
71   'Proposed Amendments to the Draft of a Bill to Constitute the Commonwealth of Australia', quoted in Williams, '"With Eyes Open"', p. 177.
72   See *Convention Debates*, vol. 4, *Melbourne 1898*, pp. 666–7 per Mr Carruthers.
73   See Dixon, pp. 101–2; R. Menzies, *Central Power in the Australian Commonwealth*, Cassell & Co, 1967, pp. 52–4.
74   La Nauze, pp. 231–2; R. C. L. Moffat, 'Philosophical Foundations of the Australian Constitutional Tradition' (1965) 5 *Sydney Law Review* 59 at 86; Williams, 'Race, Citizenship and the Formation of the Australian Constitution'.

Responsible, not republican, government

Clark's republican vision was inconsistent with the view that the Australian Constitution should be founded on a system of responsible government in which there would be little or no role for provisions that explicitly protected human rights. As early as the 1891 Convention, Clark publicly stated, 'I do not expect my ideals to be realised in the federal constitution about to be framed'.[75] Indeed, the fact that the Constitution bears any explicitly rights-orientated provisions was a testament to the energy and enthusiasm of Clark rather than the aims and desires of a majority of the delegates.[76]

Many of the framers were clearly influenced by the works of two nineteenth-century English constitutional commentators, J. Bryce (*The American Commonwealth*) and A.V. Dicey (*Introduction to the Study of the Law of the Constitution*)[77]. Both authors were sceptical of the need to expressly guarantee rights in written constitutions.[78] Writing within a scheme of responsible government, Dicey argued that civil liberties can be adequately protected through the common law and political processes without the incorporation of guarantees of rights in a written constitution.[79] He saw this as one aspect of the rule of law. The failure to include a Bill of Rights in the Australian Constitution was consistent with the Diceyean notion of parliamentary sovereignty, which Dicey described as the 'dominant characteristic of our political institutions'.[80] By parliamentary sovereignty, Dicey meant 'that Parliament ... has ... the right to make or unmake any law whatever; and, further, that no person or body is recognised by the law of England as having a right to override or set aside the legislation of Parliament'.[81] This found expression in a diluted form in the Australian Constitution, in the grant of plenary power to the Commonwealth in the specified areas listed mainly in sections 51 and 52, but subject to the adoption of the United States notion of judicial review, under which the High Court can invalidate legislation inconsistent with the Constitution (see Chapter 8).[82] Parliamentary sovereignty found clearer expression in the unwillingness of the Convention delegates to place fetters on the power of the new federal and state Parliaments to abrogate human rights.[83]

The desire of the delegates that the Australian Constitution reflect their British inheritance was clearly manifested in the Convention debates. Several delegates suggested that the Australian Constitution did not need to incorporate express rights as the rule of law would provide adequate protection: 'Like anyone else within the English tradition, they must have felt that the protections to individual rights provided by the traditions of acting as honourable men were quite sufficient for a civilised society'.[84]

---

75 *Convention Debates*, vol. 1, *Sydney 1891*, p. 242.
76 Sir Owen Dixon described s. 116 of the Constitution as a 'probably unnecessary exception' to the decision of the framers not to include a Bill of Rights: Dixon, p. 102.
77 J. Bryce, *The American Constitution*, 3rd edn [1st edn, 1888], Macmillan, 1912; A.V. Dicey, *Introduction to the Study of the Law of the Constitution*, 10th edn [1st edn, 1885], Macmillan, 1959.
78 H. Patapan, 'The Dead Hands of the Founders? Original Intent and the Constitutional Protection of Rights and Freedoms in Australia' (1997) 25 *Federal Law Review* 211 at 217–19.
79 Dicey, pp. 195–202. Compare this with E. Barendt, 'Dicey and Civil Liberties' [1985] *Public Law* 596; W. I. Jennings, *The Law and the Constitution*, 5th edn, University of London Press, 1959.
80 Dicey, p. 39.
81 Dicey, pp. 39–40.
82 Thomson, p. 173.
83 See Dixon, pp. 101–2.
84 Moffat, pp. 85–6. See *Convention Debates*, vol. 5, *Melbourne 1898*, p. 1761 per Mr Trenwith: 'it seems to me to be utterly impossible to conceive that such a Parliament will proceed to infringe any of the liberties of the citizens'.

Thus, in Melbourne in 1898, in the debate over Clark's clause 110, Dr Alexander Cockburn, former Premier of South Australia, argued that it would 'be a reflection on our civilization' if the Australian Constitution protected Australians from laws that would 'deprive any person of life, liberty, or property without due process of law'.[85] He argued that such constitutional protection would mean that 'People would say—"Pretty things these States of Australia; they have to be prevented by a provision in the Constitution from doing the grossest injustice"'.[86] Here, in the words of Sir Owen Dixon, former Chief Justice of the High Court, Cockburn was asking why 'should doubt be thrown on the wisdom and safety of entrusting to the chosen representatives of the people … all legislative power, substantially without fetter or restriction?'[87]

This position did not go entirely unchallenged. O'Connor replied strongly that protection was needed as a right attaching to the citizenship of the Australian people:

> We are making a Constitution which is to endure, practically speaking, for all time. We do not know when some wave of popular feeling may lead a majority in the Parliament of a state to commit an injustice by passing a law that would deprive citizens of life, liberty, or property without due process of law.[88]

After interjections by Isaacs and Cockburn, and a suggestion by John Gordon of South Australia that 'might you not as well say that the states should not legalize murder',[89] O'Connor continued: 'We need not go far back in history to find cases in which the community, seized with a sort of madness with regard to particular offences, have set aside all principles of justice'.[90] O'Connor's argument failed on the floor of the Convention. Nevertheless, his foresight was proved accurate by the failed attempt to ban communism in Australia in the early 1950s, when legislation sought to abrogate basic freedoms such as the rights to association and free speech.[91] After Sir Edward Braddon of Tasmania pointed out that the clause 'is calculated to do harm rather than good'[92] and would also interfere with the 'rights of the several states',[93] the guarantee that no person be deprived of life, liberty, or property except with due process of law was rejected by 23 votes to 19. The delegates were perhaps repelled by the 'distinctly republican flavour' of rights based on citizenship.[94] They also struggled unsuccessfully with the concepts of state and Commonwealth citizenship. Thus, s. 117 of the Constitution, which came to replace Clark's clause 110, confers protection on 'a Subject of the Queen, resident in any State', rather than on the 'citizens of each State' and the 'citizens of the Commonwealth'.[95]

---

85 *Convention Debates*, vol. 4, *Melbourne 1898*, p. 688.
86 *Convention Debates*, vol. 4, *Melbourne 1898*, p. 688.
87 Dixon, p. 102.
88 *Convention Debates*, vol. 4, *Melbourne 1898*, p. 688.
89 *Convention Debates*, vol. 4, *Melbourne 1898*, p. 689.
90 *Convention Debates*, vol. 4, *Melbourne 1898*, p. 689.
91 See *Australian Communist Party v. Commonwealth* (1951) 83 CLR 1 (see Chapter 8).
92 *Convention Debates*, vol. 4, *Melbourne 1898*, p. 689.
93 *Convention Debates*, vol. 4, *Melbourne 1898*, p. 690.
94 *Street v. Queensland Bar Association* (1989) 168 CLR 461 at 553 per Toohey J.
95 See *Australasian Temperance and General Mutual Life Assurance Society Ltd v. Howe* (1922) 31 CLR 290 at 327 per Higgins J.

Maintaining discriminatory laws

Clause 110 was also rejected because the delegates were concerned to maintain the power of colonies, once they became the Australian states, to discriminate between people on the ground of their race. Cockburn argued that the Fourteenth Amendment to the United States Constitution had been inserted 'to inflict the grossest outrage which could be inflicted on the Southern planters, by saying—"You shall not forbid the negro inhabitants to vote. We insist on their being placed on an equal footing in regard to the exercise of the franchise with yourselves"'.[96] Cockburn's position is clear from his focus on the 'outrage' committed on the southern American states rather than on any prior abrogation of the rights of black Americans. In Cockburn's view, there was no need for clause 110 because 'We are not going to have a civil war here over a racial question'.[97]

The debate on clause 110 undermined any pretence that the framers were generally concerned to foster human rights or that they viewed responsible government as being appropriate because of its scope to protect minority rights. Their intention was in fact the opposite: to ensure that the Australian Constitution did not prevent the colonies, once they became states, from continuing to enact racially discriminatory legislation. After Isaacs had pointed out that clause 110 would prevent the colonies discriminating against people on the basis of their race, Higgins interjected: 'It protects Chinamen too, I suppose, as well as negroes?'[98] Isaacs answered this by arguing that clause 110 should be deleted because it might otherwise override racially discriminatory factory legislation in the colonies. He supported this by reference to the decision of the United States Supreme Court in *Yik Wo v. Hopkins* 118 US 356 (1886). That case, on the Fourteenth Amendment to the United States Constitution, showed, Isaacs said, how that amendment operated 'in several cases in a way quite unexpected'.[99] The result in *Yik Wo v. Hopkins* was that a 'Chinese established his right in spite of the state legislation to have the same laundry licence as the Caucasians have'.[100] Clause 110 might thus have made it more difficult to gain the support of the 'workers of this colony [Victoria] or of any other colony'.[101]

There were also concerns that clause 110 would override Western Australian laws under which 'no Asiatic or African alien can get a miner's right or go mining on a goldfield'.[102] Sir John Forrest, Premier of Western Australia, summed up the mood of the 1897–98 Convention when he stated:

> It is of no use for us to shut our eyes to the fact that there is a great feeling all over Australia against the introduction of coloured persons. It goes without saying that we do not like to

---

96 *Convention Debates*, vol. 4, *Melbourne 1898*, p. 685 (see also p. 668 per Mr Isaacs, who stated that 'this Article 14 had to be rammed down the throats of the Southern States').

97 *Convention Debates*, vol. 4, *Melbourne 1898*, p. 685.

98 *Convention Debates*, vol. 4, *Melbourne 1898*, p. 687.

99 *Convention Debates*, vol. 4, *Melbourne 1898*, p. 669.

100 *Convention Debates*, vol. 4, *Melbourne 1898*, p. 669.

101 *Convention Debates*, vol. 4, *Melbourne 1898*, p. 687 (see also p. 666 per Sir John Forrest and Mr Reid, and pp. 690 and 669 per Mr Isaacs). The attitude of Mr Trenwith, the only representative of the Labour movement at the Conventions, must have reinforced this (see *Convention Debates*, vol. 5, *Melbourne 1898*, p. 1792).

102 *Convention Debates*, vol. 4, *Melbourne 1898*, p. 665 per Sir John Forrest. See *Goldfields Act 1895* (WA), sections 14, 92; *Goldfields Act (Amendment) Act 1898* (WA), s. 4.

talk about it, but still it is so. I do not want this clause to pass in a shape which would undo what is about to be done in most of the colonies, and what has already been done in Western Australia, in regard to that class of persons.[103]

In formulating the words of s. 117 of the Constitution, which replaced Clark's clause 110, Higgins argued that that the new provision 'would allow Sir John Forrest ... to have his law with regard to Asiatics not being able to obtain miners' rights in Western Australia. There is no discrimination there based on residence or citizenship; it is simply based on colour and race'.[104]

The issue of race in other clauses

Some clauses inserted into the Constitution were drafted specifically to impinge on the liberty and rights of some sections of the Australian community, particularly Asian migrants and indigenous peoples. The drafting of provisions concerning Australia's indigenous peoples conformed to the pattern set by the framers' rejection of Clark's clause 110. As enacted, s. 51(xxvi) of the Constitution provided that the federal Parliament could legislate with respect to 'the people of any race, other than the aboriginal race in any State, for whom it is deemed necessary to make special laws',[105] while s. 127 stated that 'In reckoning the numbers of the people of the Common-wealth, or of a State or other part of the Commonwealth, aboriginal natives shall not be counted'.[106]

Barton made it clear that s. 51(xxvi) was necessary to enable the Commonwealth to 'regulate the affairs of the people of coloured or inferior races who are in the Com-monwealth'.[107] In summarising the effect of s. 51(xxvi), John Quick and Robert Gar-ran, writing in 1901, stated that:

> It enables the Parliament to deal with the people of any alien race after they have entered the Commonwealth; to localise them within defined areas, to restrict their migration, to confine them to certain occupations, or to give them special protection and secure their return after a certain period to the country whence they came.[108]

There were delegates who spoke strongly against the use of legislative power in this way. For example, Symon argued: 'It is monstrous to put a brand on these people when you admit them. It is degrading to us and our citizenship to do such a thing. If we say

---

103 *Convention Debates*, vol. 4, *Melbourne 1898*, p. 666.
104 *Convention Debates*, vol. 5, *Melbourne 1898*, p. 1801.
105 See, on the drafting of s. 51(xxvi), M. J. Detmold, 'Original Intentions and the Race Power' (1997) 8 *Public Law Review* 244; J. Williams and J. Bradsen, 'The Perils of Inclusion: The Constitution and the Race Power' (1997) 19 *Adelaide Law Review* 95.
106 See, on the evolution of s. 127, La Nauze, pp. 67–8; G. Sawer, 'The Australian Constitution and the Aus-tralian Aborigine' (1966) 2 *Federal Law Review* 17. Compare s. 25 of the Constitution, which was appar-ently intended to replicate s. 2 of the Fourteenth Amendment to the United States Constitution. See Constitutional Commission, *Final Report of the Constitutional Commission*, vol. 1, AGPS, 1988, pp. 156–7; Quick and Garran, pp. 455–6. The Constitutional Committee of the 1891 Sydney Convention proposed to discriminate against 'Asiatics' and 'Polynesians' by not counting these people in determining the 'free population' of a state and thus the number of seats each state was entitled to in the House of Represen-tatives. See La Nauze, p. 301.
107 *Convention Debates*, vol. 4, *Melbourne 1898*, pp. 228–9.
108 Quick and Garran, p. 622.

they are fit to be admitted amongst us, we ought not to degrade them by putting on them a brand of inferiority'.[109] However, lest it be thought that the Constitution might contain a provision similar to the Fourteenth Amendment to the United States Constitution, and thus produce a result like *Yik Wo v. Hopkins* 118 US 356 (1886) preventing racial discrimination, Quick and Garran continued: 'On the contrary, it would seem that by sub-sec xxvi the Federal Parliament will have power to pass special and discriminating laws relating to "the people of any race," and that such laws could not be challenged on the ground of unconstitutionality'.[110]

In a 1967 referendum, Australian voters chose to strike out the words 'other than the aboriginal race in any State' in s. 51(xxvi) and to delete s. 127 entirely (see Chapter 10).

The rights of women in the Australian Constitution

While women did not take a direct role in the Conventions, they did participate through lobby groups and other organisations.[111] The objective was frequently to secure rights for Australian women, such as the right to vote.[112] At the Adelaide session of the 1897–98 Convention, Frederick Holder, the Treasurer of South Australia, proposed that the draft constitution contain the following clause: 'Every man and woman of the full age of twenty-one years, whose name has been registered as an elector for at least six months, shall be an elector'.[113] By this provision, Holder sought to extend, at least in regard to federal elections, the right to vote enjoyed by South Australian women since 1894. As with other rights clauses, this attempt foundered on the fact that, for the framers, ensuring the legislative autonomy of the states took precedence over protecting individual rights. For example, Adye Douglas, the President of the Legislative Council of Tasmania, protested 'I do not see why it should be forced on people who do not want it, simply because South Australia has got it'[114] and also stated that 'I have not found a single women yet who is anxious for this franchise'.[115] The proposal was defeated by 23 votes to 12.[116]

In the wake of this defeat, Holder suggested a compromise that would allow women who were qualified to vote under the law of their state to also be able to vote for the new federal Parliament. This preserved the ability of each state to determine its own franchise for federal elections, at least until the federal Parliament enacted a uniform franchise. Holder's compromise was approved by 18 votes to 15[117] and is expressed in s. 41 of the Constitution (see Chapter 5). Section 41 received strong support from organisations such as the Womanhood Suffrage League of New South Wales. It was also a reaction to threats made by South Australian delegates to the 1897–98 Convention that South Australians would reject federation if South Australian women were unable to vote in federal elections.[118] The compromise expressed in s. 41 received some strong

---

109 *Convention Debates*, vol. 4, *Melbourne 1898*, p. 250.
110 Quick and Garran, p. 623. See *Convention Debates*, vol. 4, *Melbourne 1898*, pp. 672–3.
111 See Irving, *A Woman's Constitution?*
112 See S. Tarrant, 'The Woman Suffrage Movements in the United States and Australia: Concepts of Suffrage, Citizenship and Race' (1996) 18 *Adelaide Law Review* 47.
113 *Convention Debates*, vol. 3, *Adelaide 1897*, p. 715.
114 *Convention Debates*, vol. 3, *Adelaide 1897*, p. 725.
115 *Convention Debates*, vol. 3, *Adelaide 1897*, p. 724.
116 *Convention Debates*, vol. 3, *Adelaide 1897*, p. 725.
117 *Convention Debates*, vol. 3, *Adelaide 1897*, p. 732.
118 *Convention Debates*, vol. 3, *Adelaide 1897*, p. 132 per Mr Symon; p. 150 per Mr Holder.

reactions, in part because it was still viewed with suspicion as being an attempt to bring about universal adult suffrage Australia-wide. At the Melbourne session of the 1897–98 Convention, a Tasmanian delegate and member of the Tasmanian Parliament, Henry Dobson, addressed the following remark to the South Australian delegates: 'I ask them to leave the women of Tasmania to do as they like in the matter. May I point out to them that in the United States the movement in favour of the extension of the franchise to women is dying out'.[119] Isaacs followed this by suggesting that South Australian pressure for other States to adopt its franchise would be 'a bait to the women of Tasmania'.[120]

Instead of providing for universal adult suffrage, the drafters came only a small part of the way. Section 41 requires that where a person has the right to vote for the more numerous House of the Parliament of a state, he or she shall, while the right continues, be guaranteed the right to vote at elections for the federal Parliament. This meant that women were guaranteed the right to vote at Commonwealth elections only where they were given the right by their own state. Thus, in 1901 only women in South Australia and Western Australia were able to vote in federal elections. In 1902, a uniform federal franchise was enacted[121] that extended the right to vote at federal elections equally to men and women.

Conclusion

Harrison Moore, writing in 1902, stated that the 'great underlying principle' of the Constitution is 'that the rights of individuals are sufficiently secured by ensuring, as far as possible, to each a share, and an equal share, in political power'.[122] For its time, the Australian Constitution was one of the most democratic in the world. However, as seen through modern eyes, Moore was blind to the position of many Australians, particularly ethnic minorities, indigenous peoples, and women. In fact, the Constitution was predicated on ensuring that these people, by virtue of state legislation or otherwise, would be unable to access the rights that might give them political and economic power. For some of these people, the 'great underlying principle' of the Australian Constitution was not equality, but the framers' desire to enable each state to 'preserve the cultural and racial homogeneity of their societies'[123] and to ensure their exclusion from the political process. This was evident both in the drafting of the Constitution and in the referendums that endorsed it.

This perspective of the drafting of the Australian Constitution does not sit well with contemporary versions of the place of human rights in the Constitution. For example, Mason CJ, Toohey, and Gaudron JJ in *Theophanous v. Herald & Weekly Times Ltd* (1994) 182 CLR 104 at 128 stated that: 'The framers of the Constitution … no

---

119 *Convention Debates*, vol. 5, *Melbourne 1898*, p. 1852.
120 *Convention Debates*, vol. 5, *Melbourne 1898*, p. 1852.
121 *Commonwealth Franchise Act 1902* (Cth). See A. Brooks, 'A Paragon of Democratic Virtues? The Development of the Commonwealth Franchise' (1993) 12 *University of Tasmania Law Review* 208. At the same time as conferring the right to vote upon women, the Act denied that right to Aboriginal people.
122 W. H. Moore, *The Constitution of the Commonwealth of Australia*, Murray, 1902, p. 329.
123 Charlesworth, H, A Constitutional Bill of Rights: North American Experience and Australian Prospect (unpublished SJD thesis, Harvard University, 1985) at 101.

doubt considered that the ultimate protection of freedom of expression, along with other important rights, might be found in the common law and in … the legislatures'. However, instead of seeking to establish the Constitution as a catalyst for the protection of the civil liberties, the framers sought to infuse the Constitution with responsible government in a way that would enable some fundamental rights to be abrogated by a sovereign parliament even where such rights might have been recognised by the common law. Where the framers felt that there were rights worth protecting, these were not the rights of those in need or of minorities, but the rights of those already with a share of power. In any event, those people with political power were already capable of exerting influence through the political process to safeguard their rights, thereby justifying the faith of the framers that the doctrine of responsible government would, in practice, respect such interests.

The Convention debates are a significant impediment to the robust protection of rights under the Australian Constitution. Since the decision of the High Court in *Cole v. Whitfield* (1988) 165 CLR 360, greater use has been made of material from the Convention debates, and this raises the potential for the derogation of human rights in the debates to spill over into the contemporary interpretation of the Constitution (see Chapter 4). This should be avoided. On questions of human rights, the usefulness of seeking guidance from the attitudes and intentions that shaped the Constitution is undermined by the inconsistency of such attitudes and intentions with the values and aspirations of Australians today. The views of the drafters on issues of human rights and race no longer provide an appropriate blueprint for the interpretation of the Constitution.

Where does this leave the Australian Constitution? Its text, structure, and few rights-orientated provisions owe much to Clark, a republican influenced by the United States experiment. However, the instrument was adopted by Convention delegates steeped in the Westminster tradition of responsible government and parliamentary sovereignty, who did not share his vision, and accepted provisions such as sections 80 and 116 for reasons that had little to do with the protection of human rights. It is not possible to produce a coherent vision of the Constitution by reconciling the position of Clark with that of delegates such as Cockburn. At the heart of the conflict between these positions lies the decision of the 1897–98 Convention to reject Clark's clause 110. The Constitution created a strong and stable federal structure premised on the operation of representative government. Otherwise, Australia possesses a hybrid Constitution that is republican in structure, with some checks and balances but few express rights, set within a framework of responsible government. Does this leave such constitutional ambiguity that the instrument lacks any consistent and coherent theoretical underpinning? Is the Constitution incapable of offering real protection to fundamental freedoms? The members of the High Court, the ultimate interpreters of the Constitution, can provide the answers to these questions. It is thus understandable that the Constitution exerts a powerful force on each generation of judges to seek their own meaning in the instrument.

THREE

Human Rights in the Australian Constitution

Introduction

The idea that the Constitution does not have a role to play in protecting human rights is incorrect. It is also damaging. It misstates the situation and undermines the legitimacy of the High Court in applying constitutional rights. Unfortunately, this view has been orthodox for most of this century. Although recently challenged, it still has a firm hold in Australian law. The origins of this idea derive from the fact that the Constitution was drafted to incorporate only meagre protection for human rights (see Chapter 2). This Chapter proceeds from a different perspective. It is based on the premise that the Constitution does have an important role to play in the protection of human rights, and that the Constitution should be interpreted, within the limits of its text and structure, to realise this potential.

The absence of an express Bill of Rights in the Constitution can be misleading. As Deane J stated in *Street v. Queensland Bar Association* (1989) 168 CLR 461 at 521–2:

> It is often said that the Australian Constitution contains no bill of rights. Statements to that effect, while literally true, are superficial and potentially misleading. The Constitution contains a significant number of express or implied guarantees of rights and immunities … All of those guarantees of rights or immunities are of fundamental importance in that they serve the function of advancing protecting the liberty, the dignity or the equality of the citizen under the Constitution. Some of them, such as ss 71, 90, 92, 109 and 118, are also integral parts of the very structure of the federation.

The Constitution was designed so that the structures and doctrines on which it rests, such as the principle of responsible government, would respect and protect certain freedoms. This means that the Constitution already has a foundation on which to base a rights jurisprudence. This foundation is capable of supporting a new awareness of rights without fracturing the essential nature of the instrument. This capability is strengthened by the High Court's recent recognition that the sovereignty of the Constitution now rests with the Australian people rather than with the British Parliament (see Chapter 4). What is needed is a willingness on the part of Australian judges and the other participants in the constitutional system to recognise and make effective the protection already provided. The best way to initiate this process is through a re-exploration of the Australian Constitution and by refining existing interpretative methods (see Chapter 4). Of course, to undertake such a process is not to admit that the protection of rights provided by the constitutional is adequate (see Chapter 10), just that much can be achieved with the rights already there.

The central aim of this Chapter is to outline the rights that can be found in the Australian Constitution. It does this by examining the express provisions of the Constitution, as well as the structures and doctrines embodied in the document. Another aim is to outline the limitations of constitutional rights. Although the Constitution may harbour important rights protection, such rights suffer from significant weaknesses that undermine their ability to meet the needs of the community.

Human rights and the text of the Australian Constitution

For many years the Australian Constitution was not viewed as being sympathetic to human rights. This stemmed from the summary treatment given to human rights at the 1890s Conventions at which the Constitution was drafted (see Chapter 2), and it has had a major impact on the level of protection that the document has actually afforded. Expectation has had a way of foreshadowing reality. In the murky field of constitutional interpretation, judicial perceptions of the legitimate scope of High Court decision-making can have a very real impact on High Court decisions.

When commentators have listed the protection afforded to civil liberties by the Constitution they have normally listed only the explicitly rights-orientated provisions in the Constitution, namely:

- s. 41—right to vote
- s. 51(xxxi)—Commonwealth not to acquire property except on just terms
- s. 80—trial by jury
- s. 92—'trade, commerce, and intercourse among the States, whether by means of internal carriage or ocean navigation, shall be absolutely free'
- s. 116—freedom of religion
- s. 117—freedom from disabilities or discrimination on the basis of state residence.

Some commentators have been a little more adventurous in also listing:

- s. 51(ii)—Commonwealth not to discriminate between states or parts of states in legislating with respect to taxation
- s. 51(xxxiiiA)—Commonwealth can legislate to provide medical or dental services, 'but not so as to authorise any form of civil conscription'
- s. 99—Commonwealth not, by any law or regulation of trade, commerce, or revenue, to give preference to any one state or part of state over another state or part of state.

Even when the lists are combined, the relevant provisions are indeed sparse and the protection offered apparently minimal.

Peter Bailey has gone further in arguing that the Constitution contains twenty-seven provisions that respect rights.[1] In addition to the provisions mentioned above, Bailey listed sections such as:

- s. 31—'Until the Parliament otherwise provides, but subject to this Constitution, the laws in force in each State for the time being relating to elections for the more numerous House of the Parliament of the State shall, as nearly as practicable, apply to elections in the State of members of the House of Representatives'
- s. 75—original jurisdiction of High Court to include matters 'in which a writ of Mandamus or prohibition or an injunction is sought against an officer of the Commonwealth'
- s. 84—public servants transferred from a state to the Commonwealth public service not to lose any of their existing or accruing employment entitlements
- s. 113—states to have the power to regulate 'fermented, distilled, or other intoxicating liquids' passing through or remaining in that state.

Many of the provisions listed by Bailey, such as s. 113, have only a tenuous connection with the protection of rights. Bailey divided these provisions into political rights (nine sections),[2] civil and legal process rights (five sections),[3] economic and equality rights (11 sections)[4] and social rights (two sections).[5] Such attempts to list rights demonstrate that there is little logic or order in the protection of rights under the Constitution. The sections listed show an ad hoc scheme in search of the coherence that might be provided by a Bill of Rights. Rights such as trial by jury and those of transferred public servants receive protection, while freedom of expression and conscience are ignored, yet the Constitution provides no rationale for the privileging of one interest over another.

Almost any provision in the Constitution can be viewed as having a role to play in the protection of human rights. Sections 90 and 109 are provisions that might be thought to have nothing to do with the protection of rights. Section 90 guarantees the exclusive power to the Commonwealth to levy excise duties, while s. 109 provides that in cases of inconsistency between Commonwealth and state laws the former will prevail. Two cases show that even these provisions can play a role in fostering rights.[6] *Capital Duplicators Pty Ltd v. Australian Capital Territory (No 1)* (1992) 177 CLR 248 concerned the scope of s. 90. At issue was whether s. 90, which clearly prevents the states from levying excise duties, also prevents the territories from doing so. The question was complicated by the fact that the territory in issue, the Australian Capital Territory, derives its law-making power from an Act of the Commonwealth Parliament.[7] Argument in the case addressed the question of whether, by legislating under s. 122 of

1   P. Bailey, *Human Rights: Australia in an International Context*, Butterworths, 1990, pp. 84–105.
2   Constitution, sections 8, 16, 24, 30, 31, 41, 34, 109, 128. Bailey does not list s. 7 of the Constitution which, like s. 24 in respect of the House of Representatives, requires that the members of the Senate be 'directly chosen by the people'. Recent High Court decisions, such as *Australian Capital Television Pty Ltd v. Commonwealth* (1992) 177 CLR 106 (see Chapter 7), indicate that s. 7 should now be included in any such list.
3   Constitution, sections 51(xxxiiiA), 75, 80, 92, 116.
4   Constitution, sections 51(ii), 51(xxxi), 84, 88, 90, 92, 99, 100, 102, 104, 117. Bailey might also have listed s. 51(iii), which is a provision of a similar type to sections 51(ii) and 99.
5   Constitution, sections 113, 119.
6   See G. Kennett, 'Individual Rights, the High Court and the Constitution' (1994) 19 *Melbourne University Law Review* 581 at 587–9.
7   *Australian Capital Territory (Self-Government) Act 1988* (Cth).

the Constitution to grant limited powers of self-government, the Commonwealth Parliament had delegated to that territory its own exclusive power to levy duties of excise under s. 90. A majority of the High Court —Brennan, Deane, Toohey, and Gaudron JJ—rejected this. One of the bases on which Brennan, Deane, and Toohey JJ reached this conclusion was their construction of s. 90 as a provision respecting the rights of the Australian people. They viewed s. 90 as being 'not for the protection of the Parliament but for the protection of the people of the Commonwealth'.[8]

The second case, concerning s. 109, is *University of Wollongong v. Metwally* (1984) 158 CLR 447.[9] In the earlier case of *Viskauskas v. Niland* (1983) 153 CLR 280, the High Court held that the racial discrimination provisions in the *Anti-Discrimination Act 1977* (NSW) were 'invalid' under s. 109 because they were inconsistent with like provisions in the *Racial Discrimination Act 1975* (Cth). The Commonwealth had not intended that the Racial Discrimination Act should exclude similar state legislation.[10] One month after *Viskauskas*, the Commonwealth amended the Racial Discrimination Act to make it clear that the Commonwealth law was intended to operate concurrently with state and territory legislation.[11] The amendment also sought to retrospectively overcome the *Viskauskas* decision and thereby to revive the racial discrimination provisions of the New South Wales Anti-Discrimination Act. It was the retrospective aspect of the amendment that was challenged in *Metwally*.[12] The Court, by 4 to 3, found that the amendment was invalid in seeking to retrospectively revive the state racial discrimination law. It was held that a Commonwealth statute could not reverse what had been achieved by s. 109, as 'Commonwealth statutes cannot prevail over the Constitution'.[13] Deane J, part of the majority, took a slightly different approach. He argued that the amendment was invalid because it infringed the human rights protected by s. 109. He stated, at pp. 476–7:

> the Australian federation was and is a union of people and … whatever may be their immediate operation, the provisions of the Constitution should properly be viewed as ultimately concerned with the governance and protection of the people from whom the artificial entities called Commonwealth and States derive their authority. So viewed, s. 109 is not concerned merely to resolve disputes between the Commonwealth and a State as to the validity of their competing claims to govern the conduct of individuals in a particular area of legislative power. It serves the equally important function of protecting the individual from the injustice of being subjected to the requirements of valid and inconsistent laws of Commonwealth and State Parliaments on the same subject.[14]

Mason J, in dissent, at p. 463, attacked Deane J's characterisation of s. 109 as a guarantee of civil liberties:

---

8 *Capital Duplicators* at 279.
9 See L. Zines, *The High Court and the Constitution*, 4th edn, Butterworths, 1997, pp. 411–13.
10 M. Coper, *Encounters with the Australian Constitution*, CCH, 1988, p. 22.
11 Racial Discrimination Act, s. 6A(1): 'This Act is not intended, and shall be deemed never to have been intended, to exclude or limit the operation of a law of a State or Territory that furthers the objects of the Convention and is capable of operating concurrently with this Act'.
12 For the facts of the case, and the particular injustice to which Mr Metwally was subjected, see Coper, pp. 19–24.
13 *University of Wollongong v. Metwally* at 457 per Gibbs CJ.
14 See also Gibbs CJ at 458.

[Section 109] is not a source of individual rights and immunities except in so far as individual rights and immunities are necessarily affected because the section renders inoperative a State law which is inconsistent with a Commonwealth law. Nor is the section a source of protection to the individual against the unfairness and injustice of a retrospective law. That is a matter which lies quite outside the focus of the provision. In these circumstances to distil from s. 109 an unexpressed fetter on Commonwealth legislative power is to twist the section from its true meaning and stand it on its head.[15]

The approach of Deane J in *Metwally* demonstrates how provisions of the Constitution can be interpreted in a way that reveals a connection with, or a sympathy for, human rights. Mason J was correct in that human rights do lie 'outside the focus of the provision', but argued this on the basis of the 'true meaning' of s. 109. Surely no provision of the Constitution has a 'true meaning' capable of denying the relevance of that provision to human rights. Each provision can only be interpreted in light of what is revealed by its application to the facts of a case. In some cases, such as *Metwally*, a concern for civil liberties can assist to reveal the content of a provision and how it should be applied. This does not necessarily mean that Deane J's interpretation of s. 109 in *Metwally* was correct, but merely that provisions such as s. 109 can be construed so as to be rights protecting, particularly in the grey areas of constitutional interpretation.

Human rights and the constitutional framework

The Australian Constitution can be conceptualised as a document that fosters and protects fundamental freedoms. Of course, whether or not such a course should be taken depends on one's perspective of the role of the Constitution in the protection of basic liberties. Nevertheless, it is possible to re-examine the doctrines and provisions of the instrument from the vantage point of human rights, rather than from the more traditional perspective of ascertaining the scope of Commonwealth and state power. By this process, even in the absence of a Bill of Rights, the structures and doctrines inhering in the Constitution, such as federalism, can provide a foundation for the protection of rights. Such a foundation may enable the implication of rights or provide a framework within which rights can be given effect. Rights are meaningless unless they are articulated within an appropriate constitutional and political framework. After all, the Chinese Constitution has a Bill of Rights, as did the 1936 USSR Constitution at the height of the great purges initiated by Joseph Stalin.

What then is the foundation or the doctrines on which the Australian Constitution is based? According to Deane and Toohey JJ in *Nationwide News Pty Ltd v. Wills* (1992) 177 CLR at 69–70:

There are at least three main general doctrines of government which underlie the Constitution and are implemented by its provisions. One of them is the doctrine or concept of a federal system under which the content of legislative, executive and judicial powers is divided between a central (or Commonwealth) government and regional (or State) governments.

---

15   Leslie Zines has expressed a similar view. See L. Zines, 'Constitutionally Protected Individual Rights', in P. D. Finn (ed.), *Essays on Law and Government*, vol. 2, *The Citizen and the State in the Courts*, LBC, 1996, p. 137.

Another is the doctrine of a separation of legislative, executive and judicial powers ... the third of those general doctrines of government which underlie the Constitution and form part of its structure ... can conveniently be described as the doctrine of representative government, that is to say, of government by representatives directly or indirectly elected or appointed by, and ultimately responsible to, the people of the Commonwealth. The rational basis of that doctrine is the thesis that all powers of government ultimately belong to, and are derived from, the governed.

They subsequently stated (although only in a footnote): 'The doctrine of responsible government embodied in the Cabinet or Westminster system can arguably be seen as a fourth main general doctrine underlying the Constitution as a whole'.[16] It is ironic that the doctrine of responsible government, which was of greater concern to the framers of the Constitution than the doctrine of representative government or perhaps even than the separation of powers, should be viewed by Deane and Toohey JJ as being of lesser significance. These four doctrines are examined below in the context of their role in guaranteeing fundamental freedoms.

Federalism

The federal system created by the Australian Constitution is spelt out in several key provisions.[17] The preamble to the Constitution begins: 'WHEREAS the people of New South Wales, Victoria, South Australia, Queensland, and Tasmania, humbly relying on the blessing of Almighty God, have agreed to unite in one indissoluble Federal Commonwealth'. Section 107 recognises the continuing plenary power of the new state Parliaments, while other sections, notably s. 51, vest power in the federal Parliament. Commonwealth laws override inconsistent state laws under s. 109. Section 7 requires the equal representation of the original states in the upper house of the federal Parliament, the Senate, while s. 24 requires that each original state have at least five seats in the lower house, the House of Representatives. Sections 51(ii) and 99 prevent the Commonwealth from discriminating between states or parts of states, while other provisions, most importantly s. 92, show that the federal structure conceived by the framers rests on free trade between the states. The Australian federal structure is not underpinned by express protection for human rights. Section 117 is an aberration in this regard in providing that: 'A subject of the Queen, resident in any State, shall not be subject in any other State to any disability or discrimination which would not be equally applicable to him if he were a subject of the Queen resident in such other State' (see Chapter 5).

In the USA federalism is seen as making an important contribution to the protection of rights. Alexander Hamilton wrote in *The Federalist Papers* that the United States Constitution, including the federal system created and the checks and balances imposed, 'is itself, in every rational sense, and to every useful purpose, A BILL OF RIGHTS'.[18] This has been a continuing theme in United States constitutional law. For example, Kennedy J recently stated that federalism is designed to secure 'the liberties that derive from a diffusion of sovereign power'.[19] Australian judges have not viewed federalism in the same

---

16 *Nationwide News* at 75 fn. 25.
17 See Constitutional Commission, *Final Report of the Constitutional Commission*, vol. 1, AGPS, 1988, pp. 53–4.
18 J. Madison, A. Hamilton, and J. Jay, *The Federalist Papers*, Penguin Books, 1987, p. 477 (No. 84).
19 *United States v. Lopez* 131 L Ed 2d 626 at 648–9 (1995), quoting *Coleman v. Thompson* 501 US 722 at 759 (1991).

way,[20] despite federalism being just as central to the Australian Constitution. Political scientists in Australia have, however, developed the argument, although with a twist. Brian Galligan, Rainer Knopff, and John Uhr have argued that attempts to bring about a Bill of Rights in Australia have, in part, failed because federalism is such a significant protector of human rights that it *removes* the need for an Australian Bill of Rights.[21]

The conception of United States federalism as intimately concerned with rights suggests that the Australian federal system can also be viewed this way. After all, Australian federalism is based on the United States model (see Chapter 2). Implicitly or inadvertently, the founders of the Australian Constitution drew from the republican sentiments that underpin the drafting of the United States Constitution.[22] Republicanism reinforces the idea that the federal system is an important safeguard for civil liberties. A federal system distributes power among governments and thus acts as a safeguard against any one government being able to assume oppressive powers.[23] Thus, in Canada, restrictions on freedom of expression enacted by provinces have been struck down by members of the Canadian Supreme Court on the basis that the power to enact such statues lies instead with the federal Parliament (see Chapter 7).[24]

Federalism reduces the concentration of power and thereby the scope for a government to act arbitrarily.[25] It conforms with the pluralist notion that appropriate results may be achieved by the competing actions of a number of actors. Harold Laski has developed this in arguing that: 'There can be no servility in a State that divides its effective governance. The necessity of balancing interests, the need for combining opinions, results in a wealth of political thought such as no state where the real authority is single can attain'.[26] Hence, drawing on *The Federalist Papers*, Brian Galligan and Cliff Walsh have argued the case for Australian federalism as follows:

> The case for federalism follows directly from the key attributes of federal theory. These are: that federalism provides a robust constitutional system that anchors pluralist democracy, and that it enhances democratic participation through providing dual citizenship in a compound republic. If one values these two things, one ought to favour federalism.[27]

While federalism can be viewed as establishing institutional processes important to the protection of civil liberties, it need not be limited to this role. In some areas the

---

20 But see *Victoria v. Commonwealth (Industrial Relations Act Case)* (1996) 187 CLR 416 at 568–9 per Dawson J.

21 B. Galligan, R. Knopff, and J. Uhr, 'Australian Federalism and the Debate over a Bill of Rights' (1990) 20(4) *Publius* 53. But compare J. Gillespie, 'New Federalisms', in J. Brett, J. Gillespie, and M. Goot (eds), *Developments in Australian Politics*, Macmillan, 1994, pp. 70–1.

22 See P. P. Craig, *Public Law and Democracy in the United Kingdom and the United States of America*, Clarendon Press, 1990, p. 329; G. S. Wood, *The Creation of the American Republic 1776–1787*, University of North Carolina Press, 1969; G. Williams, 'A Republican Tradition for Australia?' (1995) 23 *Federal Law Review* 133.

23 P. Pettit, *Republicanism: A Theory of Freedom and Government*, Oxford University Press, 1997, pp. 178–9.

24 *Reference re Alberta Statutes* [1938] SCR 100; *Switzman v. Elbling* [1957] SCR 285.

25 Gillespie, pp. 69–70.

26 H. J. Laski, *Studies in the Problem of Sovereignty*, Yale University Press, 1917, pp. 273–4. See G. V. Portus (ed.), *Studies in the Australian Constitution*, Angus & Robertson, 1933, pp. 14–15.

27 B. Galligan and C. Walsh, 'Australian Federalism Yes or No?', in G. Craven (ed.), *Australian Federation*, Melbourne University Press, 1992, p. 196. Galligan and Walsh (p. 196) comment that: 'Surprisingly this definitive exposition of federalism by its United States inventors was not well known to the Australian founders, and only in recent times has become a primary source for exposition of Australian federalism that was largely copied from the United States model'.

doctrine might be applied to produce or bolster interpretations of the Constitution that are consistent with the protection of rights. This is not to suggest that considerations of human rights will influence the characterisation process by which federal laws are squared with heads of Commonwealth power.[28] Instead, federalism might be a source of implied constitutional rights. Like other foundational constitutional concepts, such as the separation of powers and representative government, federalism has been a source of constitutional implications. Both before and after *Amalgamated Society of Engineers v. Adelaide Steamship Co. Ltd (Engineers Case)* (1920) 28 CLR 129 (see Chapter 4), federalism has been vigorously applied to protect the Commonwealth and the states from the impact of each other's laws. Indeed, it was in this context that Dixon J stated in *West v. Commissioner of Taxation (NSW)* (1937) 56 CLR 657 at 681–2:

> Since the *Engineers' Case* a notion seems to have gained currency that in interpreting the Constitution no implications can be made. Such a method of construction would defeat the intention of any instrument, but of all instruments a written constitution seems the last to which it could be applied. I do not think that the judgment of the majority of the court in the *Engineers' Case* meant to propound such a doctrine.

Thus, in *Melbourne Corporation v. Commonwealth* (1947) 74 CLR 31 the High Court held that a Commonwealth law that compelled the states and their authorities, including local government authorities, to bank with the Commonwealth Bank was invalid. Dixon J stated, at p. 83, that:

> the considerations on which the States' title to protection from Commonwealth control depends arise not from the character of the powers retained by the States but from their position as separate governments in the system exercising independent functions. But, to my mind, the efficacy of the system logically demands that, unless a given legislative power appears from its content, context or subject matter so to intend, it should not be understood as authorizing the Commonwealth to make a law aimed at the restriction or control of a State in the exercise of its executive authority. In whatever way it may be expressed an intention of this sort is, in my opinion, to be plainly seen in the very frame of the Constitution.[29]

In subsequent cases, this implied immunity has been applied such that: (1) a Commonwealth law may not discriminate against a state; and (2) a Commonwealth law may not inhibit or impair a state's continued existence or capacity to function.[30] Conversely, federal concepts have underpinned the even greater protection afforded to the Commonwealth from state laws.[31]

Federalism can also support results protective of human rights. This is demonstrated by the High Court's decision in *R v. Smithers; Ex parte Benson* (1912) 16 CLR 99. Section 3 of the *Influx of Criminals Prevention Act 1903* (NSW) provided:

> If any person (other than a person who has been resident in New South Wales at or prior to the commencement of this Act), has before or after such commencement, been convicted in

---

28 See Zines, 'Constitutionally Protected Individual Rights', p. 139.

29 See *Victoria v. Commonwealth (Payroll Tax Case)* (1971) 122 CLR 353; *Queensland Electricity Commission v. Commonwealth* (1985) 159 CLR 192; *Re Australian Education Union; Ex parte Victoria* (1995) 184 CLR 188.

30 *Queensland Electricity Commission v. Commonwealth* (1985) 159 CLR 192 at 217 per Mason J.

31 *Commonwealth v. Cigamatic Pty Ltd (In Liquidation)* (1962) 108 CLR 372; *Re Residential Tenancies Tribunal (NSW); Ex parte Defence Housing Authority (Henderson's Case)* (1997) 190 CLR 410.

any other State … of an offence for which in such State he was liable to suffer death, or to be imprisoned for one year or longer; and if before the lapse of three years after the termination of any imprisonment by him in respect of any such offence, such person comes into New South Wales, he shall be guilty of an offence against this Act.

John Benson was convicted in Victoria of having unlawful means of support and was sentenced to imprisonment for twelve months. Shortly after being released from prison he went to New South Wales to obtain work. He was arrested there and was convicted under s. 3 and sentenced to a further twelve months imprisonment. Benson appealed to the High Court, arguing that s. 3 contravened the Australian Constitution and was thereby beyond the competence of the New South Wales Parliament.

The High Court, consisting of Griffith CJ, Barton, Isaacs, and Higgins JJ, unanimously found s. 3 to be invalid. Isaacs and Higgins JJ did so by applying the s. 92 requirement that 'intercourse among the States … shall be absolutely free' (see Chapter 6). Griffith CJ and Barton J applied a different approach. They held that the Constitution recognises an implied freedom of movement between states and of access to government and to the seat of government. Reliance was placed on the decisions of the United States Supreme Court in *Crandall v. Nevada* 73 US 35 (1867) and the *Slaughterhouse Cases* 83 US 36 (1872). Griffith CJ quoted the following passage from the judgment of Miller J in *Crandall v. State of Nevada* at 44:

> the citizen also has correlative rights. He has the right to come to the seat of government to assert any claim he may have on that government, or to transact any business he may have with it; to seek its protection, to share its offices, to engage in administering its functions.

Barton J also quoted this passage, and stated, at p. 109, that the reasoning of the United States Supreme Court 'is as cogent in relation to the Constitution of this Commonwealth, as it was when applied to the Constitution of the United States'. Accordingly, he found, at pp. 109–10, that:

> the creation of a federal union with one government and one legislature in respect of national affairs assures to every free citizen the right of access to the institutions, and of due participation in the activities of the nation. In my opinion the reasons for the decision are conclusive as to all parts of Australia.[32]

This freedom operated 'entirely irrespective of the provisions of sections 92 and 117'.[33] Griffith CJ also found, at p. 109, that 'the former power of the States to exclude any persons whom they might think undesirable inhabitants is cut down to some extent by the mere fact of federation'. The implied freedom recognised by Griffith CJ and Barton J is clearly not just a freedom of access to government and to governmental institutions, but a general freedom of movement between the states. The provision struck down by the freedom, s. 3 of the *Influx of Criminals Prevention Act*, did not hinder access to government but instead restricted entry into New South Wales from other states. The

---

32 See *Pioneer Express Pty Ltd v. Hotchkiss* (1958) 101 CLR 536 at 550 per Dixon CJ: 'No one would wish to deny that the constitutional place of the [Australian] Capital Territory in the federal system of government and the provision in the Constitution relating to it necessarily imply the most complete immunity from State interference with all that is involved in its existence as the centre of national government, and certainly that means an absence of State legislative power to forbid restrain or impede access to it'.

33 *R v. Smithers* at 109 per Griffith CJ.

approach taken by Griffith CJ and Barton J did not mean that the power of the states to exclude people was totally overridden. It could still be exercised for a narrow range of reasons, such as to exclude persons 'who are or may be dangerous to its domestic order, its health, or its morals'.[34]

The implied freedom of movement developed by Griffith CJ and Barton J in *R v. Smithers* has been referred to in other decisions,[35] and might support the drawing of other implications from federalism to protect human rights. Militating against the use of this approach today would be that it draws on a style of reasoning reminiscent of the 'reserved state powers' doctrine exploded by the *Engineers Case*[36] (see Chapter 4). It does so in that both the judgments of Griffith CJ and Barton J and the doctrine of 'reserved state powers' depart from a literal reading of the text and draw on wider sources and notions about the Australian Constitution. Despite this, the advent of various implied rights, and the drawing of implications from the concept of representative government in particular (see Chapter 7), has meant that the approach of Griffith CJ and Barton J has found favour with the modern High Court. For example, in *Nationwide News Pty Ltd v. Wills*[37] and *Australian Capital Television Pty Ltd v. Commonwealth*,[38] several judges made reference to *R v. Smithers*, apparently with approval. In *Australian Capital Television*, Brennan J stated, at p. 60, that the freedom recognised in *R v. Smithers* 'is implied from the reposing of power in the central government of a representative democracy. It is implied by the necessity of providing access by the governed to the government'.

Arguably, the federal system created by the Constitution supports an implication that the people of Australia possess an individual freedom of movement in and about the Commonwealth of Australia. This is implicit in the system of free trade and the protection of inter-state residents achieved by the Constitution, as well as in the very fact of federation. This freedom might also be based on s. 92 of the Constitution (see Chapter 6)[39] or implied from the system of representative government created by the Constitution (see Chapter 7). One of the key aspects of federalism, at least as it is understood in the USA, is that it grants individuals the ability to live in the legal system of their choice and, consequently, the ability to move from one legal system to another. Robert Bork, in writing of the United States Constitution, declared federalism to be 'the only constitutional protection of liberty that is neutral'.[40] It is neutral in that it does not specify which freedoms are to be protected:

> But if another state allows the liberty you value, you can move there, and the choice of what freedom you value is yours alone, not dependent on those who made the Constitution. In

---

34   *R. v. Smithers* at 110 per Barton J.
35   For example, *Cunliffe v. Commonwealth* (1994) 182 CLR 272 at 307–8 per Mason CJ.
36   An early indication of the *Engineers* approach can be found in *R v. Smithers*, where Isaacs J (the architect of the *Engineers* decision) quoted, at p. 112, 'the invaluable canon of constitutional construction' of Lord Selborne in *R v. Burah* (1878) 3 App Cas 889 at 904–5: 'If what has been done is legislation, within the general scope of the affirmative words which give the power, and if it violates no express condition or restriction by which that power is limited … it is not for any Court of justice to inquire further, or to enlarge constructively these conditions and restrictions'. Hence, Isaacs J, at p. 111, found s. 92 to be the 'only section that I find it necessary to deal with'.
37   (1992) 177 CLR 1 at 60 per Brennan J, at 73–4 per Deane and Toohey JJ.
38   (1992) 177 CLR 106 at 192–4 per Dawson, at 213–14 per Gaudron J, at 232 per McHugh J.
39   See *Gratwick v. Johnson* (1945) 70 CLR 1.
40   R. H. Bork, *The Tempting of America: The Political Seduction of the Law*, Macmillan, 1990, p. 53.

this sense, federalism is the constitutional guarantee most protective of the individual's freedom to make his own choices.[41]

This view of federalism would be undermined if Australians were unable to move freely from one part of the federal structure to another: that is, between states.

Of course, a freedom of movement will be ineffective if a person is incapable of moving from one state to another. Bork gives an example of how federalism protects individual liberty, pointing out that 'Blacks engaged in great migrations to Northern states at a time when Southern states blatantly discriminated'.[42] This assumes that black people had a choice to move states to escape systemic discrimination. While some did, many, for economic or other reasons, were unable to. The protection of human rights offered by this approach to federalism is accordingly limited and needs support from other basic freedoms. Rather than removing the need for a Bill of Rights or a framework of protective legislation, the usefulness of federalism in protecting civil liberties is dependent on basic rights being fostered in individual states. A freedom of movement founded on federalism offers little to individuals or groups, such as indigenous peoples, if the rights they seek are infringed in every state to which they have the right of moving or if the particular right they are seeking to vindicte, such as a right to land, can only be made out in a particular state.

If a freedom of movement can be implied from the Constitution, in addition to any freedom based on s. 92, the federal structures embodied in the document form the most appropriate foundation. Despite this, in *Kruger v. Commonwealth* (1997) 190 CLR 1, the Court, in considering whether such a freedom could be implied, did so by asking whether it could be seen as an incident of the freedom of political communication implied from sections 7 and 24 of the Constitution (see Chapter 7). Naturally, scepticism was expressed as to whether a freedom of movement could be derived from such a foundation. Sections 7 and 24 respectively provide that the members of the Senate and the House of Representatives 'shall be composed of members directly chosen by the people'. They thereby found the basis for the system of representative democracy created by the Constitution. However, the sections are not the appropriate basis for an implied freedom of movement. The requirement that the members of the Federal Parliament be directly elected by the Australian people does not necessary imply that the Australian people possess the freedom to travel about Australia.

The separation of powers

The Constitution clearly reflects the separation of legislative, executive, and judicial power. Section 1 of Chapter I vests legislative power in the Parliament; s. 61 of Chapter II vests executive power in the Queen; and s. 71 of Chapter III vests judicial power in the High Court and in such other federal courts as the federal Parliament decides to create or invest with federal jurisdiction. The separation between legislative and executive power is not strictly maintained in the Constitution. In providing for a system of responsible government, s. 64 states that federal ministers—that is, members of the executive—must sit in the Parliament. One result of this has been that the High Court has allowed leeway for the interaction of the legislative and executive arms of government by, for example, allow-

---

41 Bork, p. 53.
42 Bork, p. 52.

ing the executive to be invested with the power to make delegated legislation such as regulations.[43] On the other hand, the separation of the judiciary from both the legislature and the executive has been strictly enforced by the High Court. It is the separation of judicial power that offers the most scope for the protection of human rights.

One implication of the separation of judicial power is that only courts created under Chapter III of the Constitution can exercise federal judicial power. Thus, in *New South Wales v. Commonwealth (Wheat Case)* (1915) 20 CLR 54, the High Court held that the Inter-State Commission established under s. 101 of the Constitution was not a Chapter III court and could therefore not exercise judicial power. The Court held this despite s. 101 of the Constitution, which states that 'There shall be an Inter-State Commission, with such *powers of adjudication* and administration as the Parliament deems necessary' (emphasis added). More recently, in *Brandy v. Human Rights and Equal Opportunity Commission* (1995) 183 CLR 245, the Court invalidated provisions of the Commonwealth Racial Discrimination Act that gave the effect of a judicial order to the determinations of a non-judicial body, the Human Rights and Equal Opportunity Commission. The converse to the implication that only courts created under Chapter III of the Constitution can exercise federal judicial power is that a Chapter III court cannot exercise non-judicial power. Thus, in *R v. Kirby; Ex parte Boilermakers' Society of Australia (Boilermakers Case)* (1956) 94 CLR 254[44] the High Court held that the vesting of judicial power in the Arbitration Court, which also exercised arbitral (that is, non-judicial) power, was unconstitutional.

Implications drawn from Chapter III of the Constitution might support rights such as a right of equality under the law[45] or a freedom from retrospective criminal laws.[46] These might be implied from the fact that the separation of judicial power requires that courts established under the Constitution may only exercise judicial power in certain ways. In *Street v. Queensland Bar Association* (1989) 168 CLR 461 at 521, Deane J, in the context of listing a number of rights contained in the Constitution, commented: 'The most important of them is the guarantee that the citizen can be subjected to the exercise of Commonwealth judicial power only by the "courts" designated by Ch III (s 71)'. Similarly, in *Re Tracey; Ex parte Ryan* (1989) 166 CLR 518 at 580, Deane J suggested that the separation of judicial power effected by the Constitution is 'the Constitution's only general guarantee of due process'.[47] These issues are examined in Chapter 8.

Representative government

The Constitution creates a system of representative government: that is, government of the people by their elected representatives.[48] This is established by the text of the Constitution, particularly sections 7 and 24. Sections 7 and 24, respectively, provide that the members of the Senate and the House of Representatives 'shall be composed of members directly chosen by the people'. Sections 7, 8, 25 and 41 show that even though

---

43 *Victorian Stevedoring and General Contracting Co. Pty Ltd and Meakes v. Dignan (1931)* 46 CLR 73.
44 See, on appeal, *Attorney-General of the Commonwealth of Australia v. The Queen* [1957] AC 288.
45 *Leeth v. Commonwealth* (1992) 174 CLR 455.
46 *Polyukhovich v. Commonwealth (War Crimes Act Case)* (1991) 172 CLR 501.
47 See *Re Tyler; Ex parte Foley* (1994) 181 CLR 18 at 34 per Deane J.
48 See Zines, *The High Court and the Constitution*, ch. 15.

s. 24 (unlike s. 7) does not mention 'voting', such a system of selection was clearly intended.[49] Other sections in the Constitution are also consistent with the creation of a system of representative government. Sections 8 and 30 speak of the qualifications of electors for the Senate and House of Representatives, respectively, while s. 41 states that 'no adult person who has or acquires a right to vote at elections for the more numerous House of the Parliament of a State' can be denied the right to vote at elections for the Commonwealth Parliament (see Chapter 5).

In recent years, the High Court has found that implications can be drawn from the system of representative government created by the Constitution, or at least from the constitutional text giving rise to that system. Thus, in *Australian Capital Television*, a majority of the Court held that a freedom to discuss political matters can be derived from the Constitution. This was based on the finding that, in providing for members of Parliament to be 'directly chosen' by electors, sections 7 and 24 necessarily require that electors not be unduly hindered in their ability to discuss the fitness for office of candidates and their policies. In later cases, the implied freedom of political communication has been extended to reshape the common law of defamation as it applies to political figures,[50] but not so as to give rise to a guarantee of voter equality, or 'one vote one value'.[51] Other freedoms, such as a freedom of association, have also been canvassed.[52] These issues are examined in Chapter 7.

Responsible government

The doctrine of responsible government permeates the operation of government in Australia. This has been consistently recognised by the High Court.[53] According to Isaacs J in *Commonwealth v. Kreglinger & Fernau Ltd and Bardsley* (1926) 37 CLR 393 at 413: 'It is part of the fabric on which the written words of the Constitution are superimposed'. The doctrine has been defined as being:

> whereby the ministers are individually and collectively answerable to the Parliament and can retain office only while they have the 'confidence' of the lower House, that is, the House of Representatives in the case of the Commonwealth and the Legislative Assembly or House of Assembly in the case of the States.[54]

Sir Robert Menzies, a former Australian Prime Minister, regarded the doctrine of responsible government as being the 'ultimate guarantee of justice and individual rights' in Australia.[55] In fact, he argued that the doctrine meant that Australia had no need of the 'formality and definition'[56] of rights in the United States Constitution: that is, of a Bill of Rights.

---

49 *Australian Capital Television Pty Ltd v. Commonwealth* (1992) 177 CLR 106 at 137 per Mason CJ.
50 *Theophanous v. Herald and Weekly Times Ltd* (1994) 182 CLR 104; *Lange v. Australian Broadcasting Corporation* (1997) 189 CLR 520.
51 *Attorney-General (Cth), Ex rel McKinlay v. Commonwealth* (1975) 135 CLR 1; *McGinty v. Western Australia* (1996) 186 CLR 140.
52 *Kruger v. Commonwealth* (1997) 190 CLR 1.
53 See, for example, *Lange v. Australian Broadcasting Corporation* (1997) 189 CLR 520 at 557 per the Court.
54 Constitutional Commission, p. 84. See G. Lindell, 'Responsible Government', in Finn, vol. I, *Principles and Values* pp. 76–9.
55 R. Menzies, *Central Power in the Australian Commonwealth*, Cassell, 1967, p. 54.
56 Menzies, p. 54.

Responsible government is reflected in the express terms of the Constitution and in conventions and traditions inherited from the Westminster system of government—that is, the 'unwritten maxims of the Constitution'.[57] Under the Constitution, executive power is vested by s. 61 in the Queen, whose representative at the federal level is the Governor-General (s. 2). Executive power is exercised by ministers appointed by the Governor-General, who by convention, act on the advice of the Prime Minister. Such ministers are required to be members of Parliament under s. 64 of the Constitution. They are responsible to the Parliament for the exercise of their executive powers, both individually and collectively (as members of the body of ministers called the Cabinet).[58] In recent times, the doctrine of responsible government has failed to have the impact of doctrines such as representative government, in part as a result of the executive's dominance of the lower house of the federal Parliament and Parliament's apparent inability to act as an effective check on executive power.[59]

The joint judgment of Knox CJ, Isaacs, Rich, and Starke JJ in the *Engineers Case* gave special prominence to the doctrine of responsible government (see Chapter 4). They did this in the context of dismissing the relevance of United States authority for the interpretation of the Australian Constitution. Despite laying down an approach to constitutional interpretation that focused on the text of the instrument to the neglect of other values and influences,[60] the judgment stated, at p. 146, that:

> For the proper construction of the Australian Constitution it is essential to bear in mind two cardinal features of our political system which are interwoven in its texture and, notwithstanding considerable similarity of structural design, including the depositary of the residual powers, radically distinguish it from the American Constitution. Pervading the instrument, they must be taken into account in determining the meaning of its language. One is the common sovereignty of all parts of the British Empire; the other is the principle of responsible government.

The joint judgment, at p. 147, also accepted the words of Lord Haldane that the Constitution is 'modelled on our own [English] model, pregnant with the same spirit, and permeated with the principle of responsible government' (see Chapter 2).

The role of responsible government in informing the process of constitutional interpretation might make the doctrine a potentially useful tool in constructing an instrument sympathetic to human rights. Like federalism, responsible government acts to check the exercise of arbitrary power. It is an institutional process by which those exercising executive power must answer to a body consisting of the people's representatives. Responsible government is different from federalism and representative government in that it focuses on the executive. In general the express rights in the Australian Constitution are expressed as limitations on legislative power.[61] In acting on the

---

57   J. S. Mill, *Utilitarianism, Liberty, Representative Government*, JM Dent & Sons, 1972, p. 228.

58   See *FAI Insurances Ltd v. Winneke* (1982) 151 CLR 342 at 364 per Mason J.

59   Lindell, pp. 93–7; K. Turner, 'Parliament', in R. Smith, (ed.), *Politics in Australia*, 2nd edn, Allen & Unwin, 1993, p. 78.

60   See R. T. E. Latham, 'The Law and the Commonwealth', in W. K. Hancock, *Survey of British Commonwealth Affairs*, vol. 1, *Problems of Nationality 1918–1936*, Oxford University Press, 1949 (first published 1939), pp. 563–4.

61   But see Constitution, s. 117. The implied freedom of political communication has been expressed to operate as a limitation upon both legislation and executive power. See, for example, *Theophanous v. Herald and Weekly Times Ltd* (1994) 182 CLR 104 at 147 per Brennan J.

executive, responsible government, like the other building blocks of Australian constitutionalism, has the capacity to inform the development of constitutional jurisprudence. It might also be a source of constitutionally implied limitations. For example, it might be argued that the doctrine acts as a check on the executive by shaping or constitutionally entrenching aspects of administrative law. Ministers might be required to act in accordance with the rules of natural justice, and thus to provide adequate reasons for their actions. Alternatively, ministers might be prevented from making decisions for improper purposes, or on bad faith, or based on irrelevant considerations. Conversely, the doctrine might constitutionally entrench certain interests potentially inimical to individual rights, such as cabinet secrecy.[62]

However, it may not be possible to gain the necessary foundation for such implications. Implications from responsible government are more difficult to derive than implications from other sources. Although the Constitution is clearly premised on the operation of a system of responsible government, this is not evident in the text or structure of the Constitution to the same extent as federalism, the separation of powers, or representative government. Some textual support for responsible government is found in s. 64, perhaps bolstered by s. 75(v), which grants the High Court original jurisdiction in matters 'in which a writ of Mandamus or prohibition or an injunction is sought against an officer of the Commonwealth'. Otherwise, the application of responsible government in Australia depends on the operation of conventions. Conventions do not impose legally enforceable limits on the exercise of legislative or executive power. Instead, they act as an ethical constraint on the participants in the constitutional process. As Martland, Ritchie, Dickson, Beetz, Chouinard, and Lamer JJ of the Canadian Supreme Court stated in *Re Constitution of Canada* (1982) 125 DLR (3d) 1 at 84,[63] 'In contradistinction to the laws of the Constitution, they are not enforced by the Courts ... unlike common-law rules, conventions are not judge-made rules'. Similarly, A. V. Dicey saw constitutional conventions as 'conventions, understandings, habits, or practices which, though they may regulate the conduct of the several members of the sovereign power, of the Ministry, or of other officials, are not in reality laws at all since they are not enforced by the courts'.[64] The fact that the system of responsible government in Australia is largely determined by conventions rather than the text or structure of the Constitution suggests that the task of deriving enforceable implications from this source will be very difficult.

The limitations of constitutional rights

The protection of human rights under the Australian Constitution suffers from a number of limitations. Some of these limitations can be met by protecting rights by other legal means (see Chapter 1). On the other hand, some of these limitations are symptomatic of the legal protection of rights generally.

---

62 Lindell, pp. 86–8.
63 See also Laskin CJC, Estey, and McIntyre JJ at 111. Nevertheless, constitutional conventions can be influential in shaping the law. See, for example, *Copyright Owners Reproduction Society Ltd v. EMI (Australia) Pty Ltd* (1958) 100 CLR 597 at 612 per Dixon CJ. See also C Sampford, '"Recognise and Declare": An Australian Experiment in Codifying Constitutional Conventions' (1987) 7 *Oxford Journal of Legal Studies* 369.
64 A. V. Dicey, *An Introduction to the Study of the Law of the Constitution*, 10th edn [1st edn, 1885], Macmillan, 1962, p. 24. Compare I. Jennings, *The Law and the Constitution*, 5th edn, University of London Press, 1959, p. 74.

The range of rights protected

Even a generous conception of the rights protected under the Australia Constitution reveals gaping holes. This is obvious from a quick cross-reference between the Australian Constitution and international instruments, such as the *International Covenant on Civil and Political Rights 1966* and the *International Covenant on Economic, Social and Cultural Rights 1966*, or comparative instruments, such as the United States Bill of Rights or the Canadian Charter of Rights and Freedoms. Simply put, the Australian Constitution was not framed to contain a Bill of Rights (see Chapter 2). The result is that some very basic rights apparently receive no constitutional protection. The Australian Constitution does not reveal anything amounting to a freedom from discrimination on the basis of sex,[65] a right to marry and to found a family, and a freedom from torture. Although the Constitution has been interpreted to reveal a freedom of political communication,[66] it lacks a more general right of free speech. The inadequate coverage of the Constitution was illustrated by the High Court's decision in *Kruger v. Commonwealth* (1997) 190 CLR 1. In that case it was found that the Constitution did not strike down a law that enabled Aboriginal children ('the stolen generation') to be forcibly removed from their families and communities.[67]

In addition to the Constitution not protecting certain basic rights, not all Australians are entitled to the protection of the rights that are entrenched. There are gaps in the coverage of the rights in the Constitution, largely due to High Court interpretation. The most important gap is that certain rights do not extend to the territories, and thus to Australians living in those areas. For example, it has been held that the guarantee of trial by jury in s. 80 does not extend to the territories,[68] and it is unclear whether the guarantee of religious freedom in s. 116 does so (see Chapter 5). The High Court has recently been reexamining the place of the territories in the Australian federation. For example, in *Newcrest Mining (WA) Ltd v. Commonwealth* (1997) 147 ALR 42, a majority of the High Court found that the requirement in s. 51(xxxi) that in acquiring property the Commonwealth must do so on 'just terms', is capable of applying in the Northern Territory (see Chapter 6). Non-citizens are also afforded only limited protection by the rights in the Constitution. This was a key factor in the High Court upholding, in *Chu Kheng Lim v. Minister for Immigration, Local Government and Ethnic Affairs* (1992) 176 CLR 1 (see Chapter 8),[69] the validity of Commonwealth legislation that authorised the forced detention of Cambodian 'boat people'.

The rights in the Australian Constitution also offer no protection from the action or inaction of private individuals. For example, s. 116 of the Constitution, which aims to protect freedom of religion, has nothing to say where an employer refuses to hire a person because of that person's religious beliefs. Where rights need to be protected not

---

65 Compare *Ansett Transport Industries (Operations) Pty Ltd v. Wardley* (1980) 142 CLR 237 at 267 per Murphy J: 'The Constitution makes no discrimination between the sexes. It may be that an implication should be drawn from its terms that the Parliament's legislative powers do not extend to authorizing arbitrary discrimination between the sexes'.

66 *Australian Capital Television Pty Ltd v. Commonwealth* (1992) 177 CLR 106 (see Chapter 7).

67 See M. Byers, 'The Kruger Case' (1997) 8 *Public Law Review* 224 (see Chapters 5, 7 and 8).

68 *R v. Bernasconi* (1915) 19 CLR 629.

69 See *Cunliffe v. Commonwealth* (1994) 182 CLR 272, discussed in Chapter 7; B. Wells, 'Aliens: The Outsiders in the Constitution' (1996) 19 *University of Queensland Law Journal* 45.

from government but from other private actors, statute law can be particularly important in complementing any constitutional protection (see Chapter 1).

Rights or freedoms?

Guarantees of human rights in the Constitution are sometimes referred to as 'freedoms' rather than 'rights' (this book uses both expressions).[70] This is because such guarantees have been interpreted by the High Court to impose limitations on governmental power—hence, 'a freedom from ... ' or 'a freedom of ... '. On the other hand, they have not been interpreted so as to confer positive rights—hence, they are not 'rights to ... '.[71] Consequently, while guarantees derived from the Australian Constitution might be applied to strike down a law or to modify the operation of the common law, they cannot require a person or government to adopt a certain policy or to initiate specified action. Such guarantees operate as a shield rather than as a sword: that is, they are negative rather than positive. They offer no equality of opportunity, merely a zone of protection against government transgressions. They may thus be categorised, using Wesley Hohfeld's terminology, as 'immunities', but not as 'claim-rights' (see Chapter 1). Even then, with the exception of s. 117 (see Chapter 5),[72] they do not gain this status of their own accord, but as a correlative of the fact that the Constitution places the legislature and the executive under a 'disability' with respect to such rights. However, at least as 'immunities' they are not subject, as is the common law, to abridgment by the legislature.

The language of the express rights in the Constitution generally lends them to being constructed as 'immunities' from legislative power. For example, s. 116, in providing for freedom of religion, begins: 'The Commonwealth shall not make any law'. However, not all express guarantees of human rights in the Constitution are constructed in this way. Section 117, in protecting the rights of inter-state residents, includes the wording 'resident in any state, shall not be subject', and might therefore allow wider scope than the mere striking down of laws that infringe the rights of such residents. The implied freedom of political communication might also be interpreted more broadly, at least as a restriction on the common law (see Chapter 7). Where a right is not expressly a restriction on governmental power, it might instead be limited by something akin to the United States 'state action doctrine',[73] which could, in any event, have the effect of limiting the applicability of constitutional rights to government and governmental actors.[74] The question of whether the implied freedom of political communication 'could also conceivably constitute a source of positive rights' was left open by Mason CJ, Toohey, and Gaudron JJ in *Theophanous v. Herald and Weekly Times Ltd* (1994) 182 CLR 104 at 125.[75] However, the High Court's subsequent decision in

---

70   See S. Gageler, 'Implied Rights', in M. Coper and G. Williams (eds), *The Cauldron of Constitutional Change*, Centre for International and Public Law, Australian National University, 1997, pp. 85–6.

71   See, on the distinction between positive and negative rights, I. Berlin, *Two Concepts of Liberty*, Oxford University Press, 1958.

72   *Street v. Queensland Bar Association* (1989) 168 CLR 461 at 503 per Brennan J: 'Section 117 is a singular provision. It does not purport to limit the grant of legislative power to the Commonwealth, to restrict the scope of any power of a State ... It is not in terms directed either to the Commonwealth or the States'. See also Brennan J at p. 504: 'Uniquely in the Constitution, s. 117 carves out an area of personal immunity which cannot be breached by law, executive action or judicial order'.

73   *Civil Rights Cases* 109 US 3 (1883).

74   See generally G. Gunther, *Constitutional Law*, 12th edn, Foundation Press, 1991, pp. 889–941.

75   See *Nationwide News Pty Ltd v. Wills* (1992) 177 CLR 1 at 50–1 per Brennan J, at 76 per Deane and Toohey JJ.

McGinty v. Western Australia (1996) 186 CLR 140, where a narrow approach was taken to the implied freedom, suggested that the wider construction was unlikely. This was confirmed in *Lange v. Australian Broadcasting Commission* (1997) 189 CLR 520, where the joint unanimous judgment of the Court, at p. 560, made the following statement about sections 7 and 24 of the Constitution, the provisions giving rise to the implied freedom of political communication: 'Those sections do not confer personal rights on individuals. Rather they preclude the curtailment of the protected freedom by the exercise of legislative or executive power'. This confirmed Brennan J's description, in *Australian Capital Television* (1992) 177 CLR 106 at 150, of the implied freedom as 'an immunity consequent on a limitation of legislative power'.

The categorisation of constitutional rights as 'immunities' is supported by the approach to constitutional rights in the USA,[76] where the Supreme Court has not imposed a duty on governments to effectuate rights.[77] In *DeShaney v. Winnebago County Department of Social Services* 489 US 189 at 195 (1989), Rehnquist J, delivering the opinion of the Court, found that:

> nothing in the language of the Due Process Clause itself requires the State to protect the life, liberty, and property of its citizens against invasion by private actors. The Clause is phrased as a limitation on the State's power to act, not as a guarantee of certain minimal levels of safety and security.

In this case, Brennan J stated, at 204: 'The Court's baseline is the absence of positive rights in the Constitution and a concomitant suspicion of any claim that seems to depend on such rights'.

The distinction between positive and negative rights has not been rigidly maintained by the United States Supreme Court.[78] For example, in applying the due process clause in the Fourteenth Amendment to the United States Constitution, the Court has held that government may have a duty to assume some responsibility for the care and well-being of a person in the custody of the state. Thus, in *Youngberg v. Romeo* 457 US 307 (1982) the Court held that a duty was imposed on government by the Constitution to provide certain services and care to an intellectually disabled person who had been involuntarily committed to a state institution. However, this did not mean that government was under a duty to protect a child from the physical abuse of a parent when a complaint had been made to the relevant authority.[79] The Court also arguably crossed the line between positive and negative rights in *Brown v. Board of Education* 347 US 483 (1954). In that case the Court held, at p. 495, that 'separate educational

---

76 D. P. Currie, 'Positive and Negative Rights' (1986) 53 *University of Chicago Law Review* 864.

77 *San Antonio Independent School District v. Rodriguez* 411 US 1 (1973). Powell J, at p. 36, delivering the opinion of the Court, stated: 'The Court has long afforded zealous protection against unjustifiable governmental interference with the individual's rights to speak and vote. Yet we have never presumed to possess either the ability or the authority to guarantee to the citizenry the most *effective* speech or the most *informed* electoral choice. That these may be desirable goals of a system of freedom of expression and of a representative form of government is not to be doubted. These are indeed goals to be pursued by a people whose thoughts and beliefs are freed from governmental interference. But they are not values to be implemented by judicial intrusion into otherwise legitimate state activities' (emphasis in original).

78 The distinction has also been blurred by the Canadian Supreme Court in the context of applying the equality guarantee in s. 15 of the Canadian Charter of Rights and Freedoms. See *Eldridge v. British Columbia (Attorney General)* [1997] 3 SCR 624.

79 *DeShaney v. Winnebago County Department of Social Services* 489 US 189 (1989).

facilities are inherently unequal' and thus that laws requiring or permitting racial segregation of schools violated the 'equal protection of the laws' required by the Fourteenth Amendment to the United States Constitution. The Court ordered desegregation, and in doing so, found that schools were under an 'affirmative duty to take whatever steps might be necessary to convert to a unitary system in which racial discrimination would be eliminated root and branch'.[80]

The classification of constitutional rights in Australia as 'immunities' is a significant limitation on the ability of such guarantees to protect human rights. As a limitation on power, it offers protection against governmental action but cannot assist human rights by protecting individuals from governmental inaction. In many areas, this is exactly what is needed. It is government inaction, not government action, that leads to many human rights not being realised, particularly economic, social, and cultural rights—such as the right to education or adequate housing. As Brennan J of the United States Supreme Court has stated, 'inaction can be every bit as abusive of power as action'.[81] To take another example, consider the distinction between a constitutionally guaranteed freedom to vote and a positive right to vote. The former would invalidate laws restricting the ability to vote, such as a franchise that excluded women or imposed a property qualification. However, it would not, unlike a positive right to vote, require parliament to provide ballot boxes to indigenous peoples in isolated areas. Constitutional law may thus satisfy a liberal agenda in protecting certain freedoms from erosion, but it cannot meet the need for wider protection of human rights. The Constitution may offer protection for civil and political rights, but it offers little or nothing to people in the most economic need, or to people or groups who are culturally alienated within society. To such people, constitutional rights are no substitute for political action.

Remedies

Many constitutions offer a range of remedies, including damages, for breaches of constitutional rights: for example, s. 24(1) of the Canadian Charter of Rights and Freedoms ('Anyone whose rights or freedoms, as guaranteed by this Charter, have been infringed or denied may apply to a court of competent jurisdiction to obtain such remedy as the court considers appropriate and just in the circumstances') and s. 38 of the South African Constitution in force from 7 February 1997 ('Anyone listed in this section has the right to approach a competent court, alleging that a right in the Bill of Rights has been infringed or threatened, and the court may grant appropriate relief'). The Canadian Supreme Court has creatively developed a range of remedies to counter breaches of the Canadian Charter of Rights and Freedoms. For example, in *Reference Re Manitoba Language Rights* [1985] 1 SCR 721 the Court held that unconstitutional laws were to be given temporary validity so as to provide the legislature with time to pass corrective legislation. In *Miron v. Trudel* [1995] 2 SCR 418 and *Vriend v. Alberta* [1998] 1 SCR 493 the remedy of 'reading in' was applied, whereby words were inserted into a statute to cure a constitutional defect.

---

80 *Green v. County School Board of New Kent County* 391 US 430 at 437–8 (1968) per Brennan J (delivering the opinion of the Court).
81 *DeShaney v. Winnebago County Department of Social Services* at 212.

Even in the absence of an express provision, the United States Constitution has been held to confer a right to damages. In *Bivens v. Six Unknown Named Agents of the Federal Bureau of Narcotics* 403 US 388 (1971), the United States Supreme Court held that damages could be awarded to an individual whose home and person had been searched in contravention of the guarantee in the Fourth Amendment to the United States Constitution against 'unreasonable searches and seizures'. The majority held that the plaintiff was able to seek damages not merely under the law of tort but also as a function of the breach of the Constitution. Bivens was reaffirmed in *Butz v. Economou* 438 US 487 at 504 (1978) as standing for the principle that damages are available to 'a citizen suffering compensable injury to a constitutionally protected interest'. The *New Zealand Bill of Rights Act 1990* (NZ), which does not expressly confer any remedies, has also been interpreted to provide for the recovery of damages on the basis that it must be implied that effective remedies would be available for a breach of the Act.[82]

By contrast, the Australian Constitution has been interpreted to offer little in the way of remedies when there has been a breach of a constitutionally protected right.[83] The conception of constitutional rights as merely limitations on government power has had an important impact. A successful challenge based on a constitutional right will normally only entitle the successful party to a declaration that the relevant law is invalid or void *ab initio*,[84] and to whatever consequences flow from this, rather than to compensation for the effects of the unconstitutional action. In *James v. Commonwealth* (1939) 62 CLR 339 Dixon J, sitting alone, clarified how s. 92 of the Constitution (see Chapter 6) protects individuals. Frederick James, who was in the dried fruits business, had his product seized by the Commonwealth for being in breach of legislation that sought to control the dried fruits trade. James successfully challenged the validity of the Commonwealth statute that authorised the seizure, and had it declared invalid under s. 92 of the Constitution. However, Dixon J denied that unconstitutional interference with James's business had given rise to any cause of action for damages. There was no remedy in damages for the breach of s. 92. Nevertheless, on each occasion on which the Commonwealth had seized James's property the seizure itself was tortious. The legislation authorising the seizures would normally have acted as a defence against this tort, but when s. 92 operated to invalidate the legislation, it deprived the Commonwealth of its defence, enabling James to claim damages at common law. The claim to damages depended on the fact that an action in tort could not be defended by pleading statutory authority.[85] According to Dixon J, at p. 362:

> Prima facie a constitution is concerned with the powers and functions of government and the restraints on their exercise. There is, in my opinion, no sufficient reason to regard s. 92 as including among its purposes the creation of private rights sounding in damages. It gives to all an immunity from the exercise of governmental power. But to find whether a governmental act be wrongful the general law must be applied. Sec 92 will do no more than nullify

---

82 *Simpson v. Attorney-General (Baigent's Case)* [1994] 3 NZLR 667.
83 See E. Campbell, 'Unconstitutionality and its Consequences', in G. Lindell (ed.), *Future Directions in Australian Constitutional Law*, Federation Press, 1994, p. 90.
84 *South Australia v. Commonwealth* (1942) 65 CLR 373 at 409 per Latham CJ.
85 See, for example, *James v. Cowan* (193) 43 CLR 386 at 393.

an alleged justification. The plaintiff cannot, therefore, recover damages under s. 92 independently of any tort by the Commonwealth.[86]

In *Lange v. Australian Broadcasting Corporation* (1997) 189 CLR 520, the High Court established that Dixon J's approach in *James v. Commonwealth* is not limited to s. 92, but applies to all constitutional restrictions on legislative and executive power. This was reaffirmed in *Kruger v. Commonwealth* (1997) 190 CLR 1 by Brennan CJ, Toohey, and Gaudron JJ, who, with support from Gummow J, held that even if a provision authorising the forced removal of Aboriginal children from their parents were unconstitutional, there would not be any entitlement to damages other than such damages that might be obtained under the common law. For example, Brennan CJ, at p. 142, found that 'the Constitution creates no private rights enforceable directly by an action for damages'.

When a constitutional right has been breached, the remedies to which a person is entitled are limited. As in *James v. Commonwealth*, successfully pleading a breach of the Constitution might be used to undermine a defence of the Commonwealth, or otherwise to defend an action brought under an unconstitutional provision. However, this is a very circuitous method of protecting rights, possibly involving more than one action by the successful party. Together with the enormous cost of bringing an action in the High Court, this factor limits the protection afforded by constitutional rights. The protection is even weaker if damage has been suffered during the course of a breach that cannot be claimed by way of any action under the common law. For example, although in *Street v. Queensland Bar Association* (1989) 168 CLR 461 the plaintiff was successful in having a Queensland law that prevented him from practising in that state declared inapplicable to him under s. 117 of the Constitution (see Chapter 5), he was not eligible for any damages for the income he lost while the law was in operation.[87] In some circumstances, damages for a breach of the Constitution will be the only way of redressing the harm suffered by someone affected by unconstitutional action.[88] This might be because the governmental agency otherwise liable in tort cannot be made to pay damages, as it is protected by crown immunity.[89] This was the case in *Bivens* 403 US 388 (1971), where Harlan J stated, at p. 410, that for 'people in Bivens' shoes, it is damages or nothing'.

Critique of rights debate

By what measure should the effectiveness of rights protection be assessed? Does the legal protection of rights improve the conditions, and access to justice, of the politically and economically oppressed and of ordinary members of the community? Perhaps debate over whether rights should be entrenched in the Constitution merely shifts attention from other more pragmatic and effective approaches. The critique of rights debate has exposed many of the inadequacies of protecting civil liberties by the constitutional entrenchment of rights.[90] Jenny Morgan has summarised the argument as follows:

---

86   See *Arthur Yates & Co. Pty Ltd v. Vegetable Seeds Committee* (1945) 72 CLR 37 at 64 per Latham CJ.
87   Compare *Davis v. Passman* 442 US 487 (1979), where a plaintiff was awarded damages after her employment was terminated in breach of the Fifth Amendment to the United States Constitution.
88   See M. Pilkington, 'Damages as a Remedy for Infringement of the Canadian Charter of Rights and Freedoms' (1984) 62 *Canadian Bar Review* 517.
89   In Australia, the Commonwealth has waived its immunity by statute (see *Judiciary Act 1903* (Cth), s. 64).
90   See, for example, M. Tushnet, 'An Essay on Rights' (1984) 62 *Texas Law Review* 1363.

'"Rights" are indeterminate, abstract and decontexualised, alienating, obfuscate political claims, can be constantly set off against one another, and Bills of Rights pass power from the political arena to the judicial'.[91] It has also been argued that 'prevailing understandings of human rights are gendered and privilege particular male life patterns'.[92]

Constitutional rights, or, indeed, the legal protection of rights generally, are inadequate to meet social needs. For example, a constitutional right to equality will not remove the outstanding inequities between men and women in Australia. Likewise, a guarantee of freedom from racial discrimination will not change the racist attitudes of some Australians. The entrenchment of certain rights, or a certain perspective on rights, may also narrow debate to the exclusion of other interests and needs. It may shift political, social and economic issues from the legislative to the judicial sphere,[93] thereby politicising the judiciary without assisting in the resolution of such problems.[94] Constitutional rights are also of little practical use to even those who may have a claim to their protection. The costs of seeking such protection in the High Court are prohibitive,[95] and the time taken can be measured in months and years. In addition, like the United States Supreme Court,[96] the High Court has developed a sophisticated jurisprudence that it applies to exclude some actions, for example, when it considers a matter non-justiciable or when a party lacks sufficient standing to raise the issue.[97]

These limitations do not mean that there should be no rights entrenched in the Australian Constitution, just that the weaknesses of such rights should be recognised. Despite their inadequacies, constitutional rights do have a role to play. Perhaps one of the most important contributions of constitutional rights is not the resolution or benefit they bring to the small number of litigants that succeed in invoking them, but the rights–culture that they nourish (see Chapter 10). As Hilary Charlesworth has suggested: 'The assertion of rights can have great symbolic force for oppressed groups within a society offering a significant vocabulary to formulate political and social grievances which is recognised by the powerful'.[98]

---

91 J. Morgan, 'Equality Rights in the Australian Context: A Feminist Assessment', in P. Alston (ed.), *Towards an Australian Bill of Rights*, Centre for International and Public Law, Australian National University, 1994, p. 123. See H. Charlesworth, 'The Australian Reluctance about Rights', in Alston, pp. 15 51; S. Pritchard, 'The Jurisprudence of Human Rights: Some Critical Thought and Developments in Practice' (1995) 2 *Australian Journal of Human Rights* 3. For further references on the critique of rights debate, see J. Thomson, 'An Australian Bill of Rights: Glorious Promises, Concealed Dangers' (1994) 19 *Melbourne University Law Review* 1020 at 1060, fn. 263.

92 H. Charlesworth, 'Taking the Gender of Rights Seriously', in B. Galligan and C. Sampford (eds), *Rethinking Human Rights*, Federation Press, 1997, p. 31.

93 See P. Hanks, 'Moving Towards the Legalisation of Politics' (1988) 6 *Law in Context* 80 at 93.

94 See J. G. Ison, 'The Sovereignty of the Judiciary' (1986) 10 *Adelaide Law Review* 1.

95 See High Court Of Australia (Fees) Regulations. On 15 May 1997, regulations were tabled in the Federal Parliament to significantly increase the fees payable. Under the new fee structure, a one day civil appeal in the High Court would have led to Court fees of $20 000 for an individual (up from $4250) and $40 000 for a corporation (up from $8500). These fee increases were disallowed by the Senate on 19 June 1997. See C. J. L. Pullin 'High Court Fees', *Australian Bar Gazette*, No. 3, July 1997, 2.

96 H. J. Abraham, *The Judicial Process*, 6th edn, Oxford University Press, 1993, pp. 348–370. See L. Henkin, *The Age of Rights*, Columbia University Press, 1990, p. 148.

97 A. R. Blackshield and G. Williams, *Australian Constitutional Law and Theory: Commentary and Materials*, 2nd edn, Federation Press, 1998, pp. 483–95, 499–505.

98 H. Charlesworth, 'The Australian Reluctance about Rights', p. 49. See P. J. Williams, 'Alchemical Votes: Reconstructing Ideals from Deconstructed Rights' (1987) 22 *Harvard Civil Rights – Civil Liberties Law Review* 401 at 416.

It must also be remembered that constitutionally entrenched rights can have an extra-legal impact. Like the guarantee of 'freedom of speech' in the First Amendment to the United States Constitution, freedoms in the Australian Constitution have the potential to act beyond their legal bounds. Such rights can shape attitudes and promote tolerance through their social and political force. Like the First Amendment, they have the potential to be invoked outside the legal regime as cultural symbols with a 'persuasive power despite the legalities'.[99] Constitutional freedoms can support minorities and social diversity by ameliorating the social pressures that drive individuals and groups towards conformity. Of course, the difficulty is that if Australians are unaware of their rights under the Australian Constitution—and there is much to suggest that this is true in regard to most Australians[100]—the cultural impact of such rights will be minimal.

Conclusion

There is considerable scope for the protection of human rights under the Australian Constitution. This emerges when the text and doctrinal foundations of the Constitution are examined from a rights perspective rather than merely with the intent of delineating Commonwealth power and exploring the issues raised by Australian federalism. Many of the avenues opened up by this analysis remain unexplored by the High Court but hold potential for litigants and judges faced with choices that affect human rights.

However, even given the significant opportunities for the protection of human rights under the Constitution, it is important to recognise that the protection offered has very significant limitations. The range of rights protected is lacking in many crucial areas, the protection offered is only a limitation on governmental power and not a source of positive rights, and the remedies provided for a successful challenge may not redress the harm suffered. There is thus doubt about the capacity of rights to meet the needs of the average Australian, let alone the needs of the disadvantaged and oppressed in the community. Nevertheless, constitutional rights do fulfil an important role in Australian law. As part of the Constitution, they bind governments and cannot be overridden except by the consent of the people expressed under s. 128 of the Constitution (see Chapter 10). They are thus the final line of defence where a government seeks, with or without the support of a majority of the community, to abrogate fundamental freedoms.

---

99 S. Shiffrin, *The First Amendment, Democracy, and Romance,* Harvard University Press, 1990, p. 88. See L. Bollinger, *The Tolerant Society: Freedom of Speech and Extremist Speech in America,* Oxford University Press, 1986.

100 See Civics Expert Group, *Whereas the People: Civics and Citizenship Education,* AGPS, 1994.

Constitutional Interpretation and Human Rights

Introduction

The High Court exercises a tremendous power in interpreting the Australian Constitution. As Sir John Downer stated at the 1898 Convention in Melbourne:

> With [the judges of the High Court] rest the vast powers of judicial decision … With them rest the interpretation of intentions which we have in our minds, but which have not occurred to us at the present time. With them rests the obligation of finding out principles which are in the minds of this Convention in framing this Bill and applying them to cases which have never occurred before, and which are very little thought of by any of us.[1]

Yet interpretation of the Australian Constitution is in a state of flux. There is no dominant or accepted method of interpretation, only competing views as to what are suitable approaches. In recent years, interpretative methodology has been debated in the context of determining which rights can be implied from the Constitution (see Chapters 7–9). A focus of the debate has been the continuing relevance of the literalist method of interpretation laid down by the Court in *Amalgamated Society of Engineers v. Adelaide Steamship Co. Ltd (Engineers Case)* (1920) 28 CLR 129, and whether contemporary decisions that have identified implied rights have contravened the methodology there outlined. Deep divisions and sharp words have divided members of the Court.

This Chapter does not seek to develop a free-standing theory of interpretation, nor does it even suggest that such a theory is attainable. Instead, the aim is to highlight and expose the High Court's approach to constitutional interpretation as it has been applied to human rights issues. If any approach to constitutional interpretation underpins the analysis in this Chapter, it is a modest one that is in keeping with traditional methods of interpretation. It does, however, recognise the value choices open to judges, and directs such choices towards the protection of rights. This interpretative approach might proceed

---

1   *Official Record of the Debates of the Australasian Federal Convention: 1891–1898* [hereafter *Convention Debates*], vol. 4, *Melbourne 1898*, Legal Books, 1986, p. 275.

in three stages. First, a judge should derive meaning from the text and structure of the Constitution, as informed by precedent, constitutional principle such as the doctrine of responsible government (see Chapter 3), and history. Second, it should be recognised that step one will frequently not determine a result but will leave open a range of choices for the judge. Third, where such indeterminacy exists, interpretations of the Constitution that are consistent with protecting fundamental freedoms (as identified by Australian and international norms and the common law—see Chapter 1) should be preferred over interpretations that do not. Kirby J of the High Court has adopted this approach, stating in *Newcrest Mining (WA) Ltd v. Commonwealth* (1997) 147 ALR 42 at 147: 'There is one final consideration which reinforces the view to which I am driven by the foregoing reasons. Where the Constitution is ambiguous, this Court should adopt that meaning which conforms to the principles of fundamental rights rather than an interpretation which would involve a departure from such rights'. Murphy J adopted a similar approach in some of his decisions, such as in *R v. Pearson; Ex parte Sipka* (1983) 152 CLR 254 at 268 and 274, as did Gaudron J in *Kruger v. Commonwealth* (1997) 190 CLR 1 at 123 and 131. In *Tavita v. Minister of Immigration* [1994] 2 NZLR 257 at 266, Cooke P of the New Zealand Court of Appeal gave some support to a similar approach, as did the Supreme Court of Canada in *Attorney-General (Quebec) v. Blaikie* [1979] 2 SCR 1016 at 1039–30 (a decision handed down before the enactment of the Canadian Charter of Rights and Freedoms) and *Hunter v. Southam* [1984] 2 SCR 145 (a decision handed down in respect of the Charter). In *Hunter v. Southam*, the Supreme Court, at p. 156, quoted Lord Wilberforce in *Minister of Home Affairs v. Fisher* [1980] AC 319 at 328, to the effect that constitutional rights require 'a generous interpretation avoiding what has been called the "austerity of tabulated legalism," suitable to give to individuals the full measure of the fundamental rights and freedoms referred to'. Such an approach does not deny the doctrine of parliamentary sovereignty, but takes account of the fact that in nations such as Australia, Canada, and the USA, a written Constitution embodying fundamental rights acts as a significant qualification of that doctrine.

The third step is no more 'political' or problematic than the approach put forward by O'Connor J in *Jumbunna Coal Mine NL v. Victorian Coal Miners' Association* (1908) 6 CLR 309 and repeatedly endorsed by other judges in later cases.[2] In *Jumbunna Coal Mine*, O'Connor J argued, at pp. 367–8, that:

> it must always be remembered that we are interpreting a Constitution broad and general in its terms, intended to apply to the varying conditions which the development of our community must involve.
>
> For that reason, where the question is whether the Constitution has used an expression in the wider or in the narrower sense, the Court should, in my opinion, always lean to the broader interpretation unless there is something in the context or in the rest of the Constitution to indicate that the narrower interpretation will best carry out its object and purpose.

---

2   See, for example, *Bank of New South Wales v. Commonwealth (Bank Nationalisation Case)* (1948) 76 CLR 1 at 332–3 per Dixon J; *R v. Public Vehicles Licensing Appeal Tribunal (Tas), Ex parte Australian National Airways Pty Ltd* (1964) 113 CLR 207 at 225–6 per the Court; *Worthing v. Rowell and Muston Pty Ltd* (1970) 123 CLR 89 at 96 per Barwick CJ; *Koowarta v. Bjelke-Petersen* (1982) 153 CLR 168 at 227–8 per Mason J; *R v. Coldham; Ex parte Australian Social Welfare Union* (1983) 153 CLR 297 at 313–14 per the Court.

This statement tilts the Constitution in favour of an expansive reading of Commonwealth power, while the interpretative method outlined above achieves the same—but in favour of individual liberty. This latter shift might be buttressed by recent High Court moves to base the sovereignty of the Constitution not in the Imperial Parliament but in the Australian people.

This Chapter outlines some central themes in constitutional interpretation in Australia and how they have impacted on rights in the Australian Constitution. The topic is further developed in Chapters 9 and 10. The subject of constitutional interpretation is a deep and complex one that continues to perplex judges and commentators alike. The themes explored below have been chosen because of their importance to the scope of constitutional rights protection in Australia.

Literalism and the *Engineers Case*

The Engineers Case

The orthodox starting point for the interpretation of the Australian Constitution is the High Court's decision in 1920 in the *Engineers Case* (1920) 28 CLR 129.[3] The decision reflected the view that, twenty years after federation, and only a few years after the close of the First World War, 'Australians were now one people and Australia one country and that national laws might meet national needs'.[4] The decision overturned the methodology of the first judges of the High Court: Griffith CJ, Barton, and O'Connor JJ. Their approach had been to protect the powers and role of the states, as against the Commonwealth, by developing the 'implied immunity of instrumentalities' and 'reserved state powers' doctrines.[5] The former doctrine meant that the states and the Commonwealth were normally immune from each other's laws, while the latter meant that the specific grants of Commonwealth power were to be interpreted to achieve minimal encroachment on the 'residual' powers of the states. Neither doctrine found expression in the text of the Constitution, but was implied from understandings of what the Constitution had been drafted to achieve. In fact, rather than being derived from the text of the Constitution, these doctrines were in opposition to the logical consequences of its words. The effect of the text was to bring about a central government pre-eminent over the states. For example, s. 109 provides that in the case of inconsistency between a Commonwealth and a state law, the Commonwealth law prevails.

The lack of a textual basis for the doctrines developed by the early High Court was exposed by the majority in the *Engineers Case*. The judgment of Knox CJ, Isaacs, Rich, and Starke JJ commented, at pp. 141–2, on the earlier decisions of the Court as follows:

---

3 See M. Coper and G. Williams (eds), *How Many Cheers for Engineers?*, Federation Press, 1997; L. Zines, *The High Court and the Constitution*, 4th edn, Butterworths, 1997, pp. 7–16.

4 *Victoria v. Commonwealth (Payroll Tax Case)* (1971) 122 CLR 353 at 396 per Windeyer J.

5 See A. R. Blackshield, 'Damadam to Infinities! The Tourneyold of the Wattarfalls', in M. Sornarajah (ed), *The South West Dam Dispute: The Legal and Political Issues*, University of Tasmania, 1983, p. 37. Geoffrey Sawer has criticised the joint judgment in the *Engineers Case* as being 'one of the worst written and organized in Australian judicial history. Isaacs was given to rhetoric and repetition, and here he gave those habits full rein': G. Sawer, *Australian Federalism in the Courts*, Melbourne University Press, 1967, p. 130. According to Leslie Zines: 'The joint judgment is in large part very loosely reasoned and badly organised. It is written with more fervour than clarity' (Zines, p. 10).

The more the decisions are examined, and compared with each other and with the Constitution itself, the more evident it becomes that no clear principle can account for them. They are sometimes at variance with the natural meaning of the text of the Constitution; some are irreconcilable with others, and some are individually rested on reasons not founded on the words of the Constitution or on any recognized principle of the common law underlying the expressed terms of the Constitution, but on implication drawn from what is called the principle of 'necessity,' that being itself referable to no more definite standard than the personal opinion of the Judge who declares it. The attempt to deduce any consistent rule from them has not only failed, but has disclosed an increasing entanglement and uncertainty, and a conflict both with the text of the Constitution and with distinct and clear declarations of law by the Privy Council.[6]

In overturning the approach of the early High Court, the *Engineers Case* set the Court and the Constitution on a very different path. In a reaction to the early High Court decisions, Knox CJ, Isaacs, Rich, and Starke JJ advocated an approach based on strict adherence to the text of the Constitution. They argued, at p. 142, 'It is therefore, in the circumstances, the manifest duty of this Court to turn its earnest attention to the provisions of the Constitution itself'.

In constructing an approach based squarely on the text of the Constitution, the majority naturally turned to English decisions on statutory interpretation. After all, the Australian Constitution is a statute of the British Parliament (see Chapter 2). The joint judgment in the *Engineers Case* quoted, at pp. 142–3, Lord Macnaghten in *Vacher & Sons Ltd v. London Society of Compositors* [1913] AC 107 at 118: 'a judicial tribunal has nothing to do with the policy of any Act which it may be called on to interpret. That may be a matter for private judgment. The duty of the Court, and its only duty, is to expound the language of the Act in accordance with the settled rules of construction'. By the 'settled rules of construction' the majority meant literalism or an approach based on the plain meaning of the text. They illustrated this, at p. 149, with a further quote from *Vacher's Case*, this time from Lord Haldane at p. 113:

> I propose, therefore, to exclude consideration of everything excepting the state of the law as it was when the statute was passed, and the light to be got by reading it as a whole, before attempting to construe any particular section. Subject to this consideration, I think that the only safe course is to read the language of the statute in what seems to be its natural sense.

The majority also quoted, at p. 149, Lord Selborne in *R v. Burah* (1873) 3 App Cas 889 at 904–5, to undermine the 'implied immunity of instrumentalities' and 'reserved state powers' doctrines:

> The established Courts of Justice, when a question arises whether the prescribed limits have been exceeded, must of necessity determine that question; and the only way in which they can properly do so, is by looking to the terms of the instrument by which, affirmatively, the legislative powers were created, and by which, negatively, they are restricted. If what has been done is legislation, within the general scope of the affirmative words which give the power, and if it violates no express condition or restriction by which that power is limited (in which category would, of course, be included any Act of the Imperial Parliament at variance with

---

6   See also *Engineers Case* at 145 per Knox CJ, Isaacs, Rich, and Starke JJ.

it), it is not for any Court of Justice to inquire further, or to enlarge constructively those conditions and restrictions.

By referring to these passages, Knox CJ, Isaacs, Rich, and Starke JJ built an approach to constitutional interpretation that centred on the text of the instrument and sought to exclude non-textual material. This approach has been termed literalism.

Literalism, legalism, and human rights

Literalism should be distinguished from legalism. The former, adopted by the majority in the *Engineers Case*, refers to a process of interpretation based on the language of the Constitution, while the latter represents a more general approach to judicial decision-making, perhaps including a reliance on literalism. Greg Craven has described literalism as 'comprising the view that the Constitution is to be interpreted by reading its words according to their natural sense and in documentary context, and then giving to them their full effect'.[7] Legalism, at its most general, suggests a 'close adherence to legal reasoning', and in practice, a reliance on technical legal solutions rather than considerations of policy.[8] Stephen Gageler has defined legalism as:

> based on the belief that the Constitution sets definite substantive limits on government power and that it is possible for the judiciary to determine those substantive limits simply by a process of interpretative judgment based on the letter and spirit of the constitutional text. It has involved the belief that the Court can and must draw lines to contain government power and that adherence to the strict analytical and conceptual techniques of formal legal argument provides the only sure method of approaching what is necessarily a sensitive political function.[9]

Legalism has played an important part in maintaining the legitimacy of the High Court in the face of its role of making decisions about intensely political matters—hence Sir Owen Dixon's statement on becoming Chief Justice of the High Court in 1952 that 'There is no other safe guide to judicial decisions in great conflicts than a strict and complete legalism'.[10] Brian Galligan has argued that legalism 'has enabled the dignity and independence of the law to be maintained while allowing the Australian High Court to perform a delicate political function in a society that has been divided over important aspects of political ideology and political economy'.[11] Or, as put more bluntly by Sir Gerard Brennan, a former Chief Justice of the High Court, 'The rhetoric based on strict and complete legalism masked the truth of the judicial method'.[12]

Dixon himself did not strictly adhere to the legalism he preached. As Leslie Zines has shown, in reaching his decisions Dixon frequently took account of extra-legal

---

7 G. Craven, 'The Crisis of Constitutional Literalism in Australia', in H. P. Lee and G. Winterton (eds), *Australian Constitutional Perspectives*, LBC, 1992, p. 2.

8 'Swearing in of Sir Owen Dixon as Chief Justice' (1952) 85 CLR xi at xiv. See G. Evans, 'The High Court and the Constitution in a Changing Society', in D. Hambly and J. Goldring (eds), *Australian Lawyers and Social Change*, LBC, 1976, p. 45; Zines, pp. 424–6.

9 S. Gageler, 'Foundations of Australian Federalism and the Role of Judicial Review' (1987) 17 *Federal Law Review* 162 at 176.

10 'Swearing in of Sir Owen Dixon as Chief Justice' (1952) 85 CLR xi at xiv. See *Attorney-General (Cth); Ex parte McKinlay v. Commonwealth* (1975) 135 CLR 1 at 17 per Barwick CJ.

11 B. Galligan, *Politics of the High Court*, University of Queensland Press, 1987, p. 40.

12 G. Brennan, 'A Critique of Criticism' (1993) 19 *Monash University Law Review* 213 at 213.

factors, including considerations of social and political policy and value judgment.[13] His successor as Chief Justice, Sir Garfield Barwick, did the same.[14] More recently, Chief Justice Sir Anthony Mason differed from Dixon and Barwick, not in the sense that he was prepared to apply policy considerations and value judgment but in his willingness to *admit* to doing so. By explicitly having reference to policy factors, Mason departed from the strictly legalistic approach advocated by his predecessors. The approach of Dixon and Barwick to constitutional interpretation in decision-making was a response to the conundrum put by Lord Porter in *Commonwealth v. Bank of NSW (Bank National-isation Case)* (1949) 79 CLR 497 at 639, as to s. 92 of the Constitution (see Chapter 6): 'The problem to be solved will often be not so much legal as political, social or economic. Yet it must be solved by a court of law'. This has become more apparent in recent years. In part, this is a consequence of the Court's move away from legalism, particularly during the latter period of Mason's tenure as Chief Justice. It is no coincidence that, during this period, decision-making by the Court became increasingly controversial and the legitimacy of the Court was increasingly subject to challenge.

The 'settled rules of construction', the literalist approach adopted by the majority in the *Engineers Case*, was applied in that decision to overrule the doctrines devised by the early High Court to protect the states. A consequence of this was that the rhetoric of the *Engineers Case* has also made it more difficult to derive other implications from the Constitution, including implied rights. Literalism and implications might be seen as incompatible, one focusing on the language of the Constitution, the other concerned with the political structures created by the instrument. However, this delineation is superficial. No text can stand in isolation. The text of an instrument such as the Constitution is always capable of giving rise to further meaning by implication. Indeed, in some cases the text may only be understood by also recognising what is implied by it. This has been acknowledged in decisions since the *Engineers Case*, particularly as regards Australia's federal structure (see Chapter 3). According to Dixon J in *Australian National Airways Pty Ltd v. Commonwealth* (1945) 71 CLR 29 at 85, 'We should avoid pedantic and narrow constructions in dealing with an instrument of government and I do not see why we should be fearful about making implications'.[15] This was supported by Mason CJ in *Australian Capital Television Pty Ltd v. Commonwealth* (1992) 177 CLR 106, when he stated, at p. 134, that the *Engineers Case* should not be taken to stand for such a 'Draconian and unthinking approach to constitutional interpretation'.[16] While the *Engineers Case* could not negate the possibility of deriving constitutional implications, including those that might protect human rights, the literalist method of interpretation laid down by that decision inhibited the drawing of such implications, particularly in the area of human rights, for many decades.

Literalism is not naturally inconsistent with a robust interpretation of the express human rights provisions in the Constitution. Just as it has been applied to reach broad interpretations of the Commonwealth powers listed in s. 51 of the Constitution, it

---

13 Zines, pp. 429–30.
14 Zines, pp. 430–2.
15 See *West v. Commissioner of Taxation (NSW)* (1937) 56 CLR 657 at 681–2 per Dixon J; *Victoria v. Common-wealth (Payroll Tax Case)* (1971) 122 CLR 353 at 401–2 per Windeyer J.
16 Compare *Australian Capital Television* at 186 per Dawson J.

might be used to give a wide operation to express provisions respecting civil liberties, such as the guarantee in s. 117 against the imposition of any disability or discrimination on the basis of state residence (see Chapter 5). This would simply be a matter of applying the 'settled rules of construction' endorsed by the *Engineers Case*. However, the interpretation of the Constitution by the High Court did not proceed in this way. Instead, in the decades following the *Engineers Case*, the Court developed broad interpretations of s. 51 powers, while simultaneously reaching narrow constructions of provisions protecting civil and political rights (see Chapter 9). This preference cannot be explained by the literalist method laid down by the *Engineers Case*, as there is nothing in the text of the Constitution to support such a distinction. The dictum of O'Connor J in *Jumbunna Coal Mine* (see p. 70) offers a better explanation. At best, the *Engineers* methodology would support a bias against the derivation of rights implications from broad concepts such as federalism or representative government.

There is a possible hint in the *Engineers Case* of a policy preference that might support the subsequent non-literalist interpretations of the Court. The majority argued that any abuse or misuse of power by the Commonwealth must be guarded against by the people and not by the courts. They stated, at pp. 151–2:

> The ordinary meaning of the terms employed in one place may be restricted by terms used elsewhere: that is pure legal construction. But, once their true meaning is so ascertained, they cannot be further limited by the fear of abuse. The non-granting of powers, the expressed qualifications of powers granted, the expressed retention of powers, are all to be taken into account by a Court. But the extravagant use of the granted powers in the actual working of the Constitution is a matter to be guarded against by the constituencies and not by the Courts. When the people of Australia, to use the words of the Constitution itself, 'united in a Federal Commonwealth,' they took power to control by ordinary constitutional means any attempt on the part of the national Parliament to misuse its powers. If it be conceivable that the representatives of the people of Australia as a whole would ever proceed to use their national powers to injure the people of Australia considered sectionally, it is certainly within the power of the people themselves to resent and reverse what may be done. No protection of this Court in such a case is necessary or proper.

This might be taken to provide some support for the giving of full literal effect to provisions granting Commonwealth power, but not to provisions limiting that power in order to protect human rights. However, this passage is a weak basis for this conclusion. The passage recognises that the 'ordinary meaning of the terms employed in one place may be restricted by terms used elsewhere' and then goes on to state that 'once their true meaning is so ascertained, they cannot be further limited by the fear of abuse'. This suggests that the passage does not support a narrow construction of the express rights listed in the Constitution, but merely warns against the Court discovering further implied limitations to safeguard against 'the fear of abuse'.

An aspect of the *Engineers Case* that did come to undermine the ability of the Constitution to protect rights was its rejection of the use of United States authority. Particularly in the latter part of the twentieth century, decisions of the United States Supreme Court may have provided an alternative source of legal reasoning permeated with the object of protecting individual liberty from arbitrary governmental action. In the first two decades after federation, judges of the High Court frequently relied on United

States authorities in interpreting the Australian Constitution. For example, in *R v. Smithers; Ex parte Benson* (1912) 16 CLR 99, Griffith CJ and Barton J applied United States decisions to find that the Constitution recognises an implied freedom of movement between states and of access to government and to the seat of government (see Chapter 3). Despite the lack of a Bill of Rights in the Australian Constitution, such reliance on United States decisions was understandable given the considerable influence of the United States model on the drafting of the Constitution (see Chapter 2).

Nevertheless, the majority in the *Engineers Case* rejected the relevance of United States decisions, stating, at p. 146, that 'we conceive that American authorities, however illustrious the tribunals may be, are not a secure basis on which to build fundamentally with respect to our own Constitution'. This conclusion was based on their view, expressed at p. 146, that 'two cardinal features of our political system … radically distinguish it from the American Constitution … One is the common sovereignty of all parts of the British Empire; the other is the principle of responsible government'. Significantly, despite emphasising the need to strictly construe the text of the Constitution, the majority here relied on two concepts that are nowhere to be found in the text of the Constitution. The majority made the same 'error' it had accused the early High Court of committing.[17] This meant that the *Engineers* majority itself interpreted the text of the Constitution within a wider scheme, albeit a different scheme to that of the first members of the High Court. Subsequently, the role of non-textual factors in constitutional interpretation was recognised even by a member of the *Engineers* majority. The central architect of the *Engineers* decision, Isaacs J, argued in *Commonwealth v. Kreglinger & Fernau Ltd & Bardsley* (1926) 37 CLR 393 at 413:[18]

> Constitutions made, not for a single occasion, but for the continued life and progress of the community may and, indeed, must be affected in their general meaning and effect by what Lord Watson in *Cooper v. Stuart* calls 'the silent operation of constitutional principles.' 'Responsible government,' … is part of the fabric on which the written words of the Constitution are superimposed.

Challenges to the Engineers Case

The *Engineers Case* has exerted a powerful influence over the High Court's approach to constitutional interpretation. Yet it seems that literalism is now in decline, perhaps 'because it has substantially achieved the purpose for which it was designed … the goal of centralising power in the Australian Federation has largely been attained'.[19] The *Engineers Case* retains its adherents, even though in more recent times it has come under steady fire. The attack has not always been an explicit one. It has been waged through decisions of the High Court, which although they have not expressly undermined the *Engineers Case*, have nevertheless achieved this through the logic of their reasoning. For example, the methodology applied by Deane and Toohey JJ in *Leeth v. Commonwealth*

---

17 R. T. E. Latham, 'The Law and the Commonwealth', in W. K. Hancock, *Survey of British Commonwealth Affairs*, vol. 1, *Problems of Nationality 1918–1936*, Oxford University Press, 1949 (first published 1937), pp. 563–4.
18 See also *Australasian Temperance and General Mutual Life Assurance Society Ltd v. Howe* (1922) 31 CLR 290 at 306 per Isaacs J.
19 Craven, p. 14.

(1992) 174 CLR 455 to discern an implied right to equality under the Constitution is obviously not in keeping with the approach demanded by the *Engineers Case* (see Chapters 8 and 10). Recent debate has centred on whether the *Engineers Case* is consistent with the freedom of political communication derived by implication from the Constitution (see Chapter 7).[20]

The supporters of the *Engineers Case* have not been silent. Dawson and McHugh JJ, particularly, have sought to highlight departures from the case. McHugh J, for example, in *Theophanous v. Herald & Weekly Times* (1994) 182 CLR 104, stated at p. 202:

> With great respect, it seems to me that those judgments in *Australian Capital Television* and *Nationwide News Pty Ltd v. Wills* that hold that the institution of representative government is part of the Constitution independently of the terms of certain sections of the Constitution unintentionally depart from the method of constitutional interpretation that has existed in this country since the time of the *Engineers' Case*.[21]

One of the factors that has undermined literalism and has led to a move away from the *Engineers Case* has been recognition of the necessary role played in interpretation by extrinsic factors. One such factor has been recourse to a judge's sense of community values. A key proponent of this has been Sir Anthony Mason, Chief Justice of the High Court from 1987 to 1995. He has argued that judges may have 'reference to values which they perceive to be desirable, accepted community values'.[22] Furthermore:

> it is impossible to interpret any instrument, let alone a constitution, divorced from values. To the extent they are taken into account, they should be acknowledged and should be accepted community values rather than mere personal values. The ever present danger is that 'strict and complete legalism' will be a cloak for undisclosed and unidentified policy values.[23]

Nowhere is this use of community values more evident, or more controversial, than in its use by Deane J. In *Theophanous* Deane J argued, at p. 173, that the Constitution should be interpreted as a 'living force'.[24] He took this to heart in construing the implied freedom of political communication in that case, finding, at p. 185, that 'the effect of the constitutional implication is to preclude completely the application of State defamation laws to impose liability in damages on the citizen for the publication of statements about the official conduct or suitability of a member of the Parliament or other holder of high Commonwealth office'. This result gave more protection to political speech in defamation proceedings brought by political figures than the United States Supreme Court had been prepared to give in *New York Times v. Sullivan* 376 US 254 (1964) in working from the express guarantee of free speech in the First Amendment to the United States Constitution. One basis of Deane J's finding was 'a widespread public perception that such proceedings represent a valued source of tax-free profit for the

---

20   G. Williams, *'Engineers is Dead, Long Live the Engineers!'* (1995) 17 *Sydney Law Review* 62.

21   See *McGinty v. Western Australia* (1996) 186 CLR 140 at 232 per McHugh J.

22   G. Sturgess and P. Chubb, *Judging the World: Law and Politics in the World's Leading Courts*, Butterworths, 1988, p. 345.

23   A. Mason, 'The Role of a Constitutional Court in a Federation: A Comparison of the Australian and the United States Experience' (1986) 16 *Federal Law Review* 1 at 5.

24   This conception was adopted by Toohey J in *McGinty v. Western Australia* (1996) 186 CLR 140 at 200.

holder of high public office who is defamed and an effective way to "stop" political criticism, particularly at election times'.[25]

The move to incorporate extrinsic factors such as community values into interpretation is part of a wider shift away from legalism, or legal formalism.[26] The development of purposive constructions of the Constitution, particularly the doctrine of proportionality, is also indicative of this. It has seen the High Court move away from the doctrine of legalism to, in the words of Mason, 'a species of legal realism'.[27]

Literalism has also been challenged because it has not been consistently applied. The majority in the *Engineers Case* did not provide a basis for the distinctions, subsequently drawn by the Court, between the Commonwealth's s. 51 powers and express civil and political rights, and between express civil and political rights and express economic rights (see Chapter 9). A purely literalist approach would not support such double standards, as there is nothing in the text of the Constitution to support them. Such distinctions make it clear that in construing Commonwealth power, the Court has not always felt constrained by literalism. It has frequently applied the dicta of O'Connor J in *Jumbunna Coal Mine* (see p. 70) to the effect that, where there is doubt, the interpreter should lean to the broader rather than the narrower interpretation of a Commonwealth power. This influenced Mason J in the *Commonwealth v. Tasmania (Tasmanian Dam Case)* (1983) 158 CLR 1 at 127–8 to find that powers vested in the Commonwealth by s. 51 of the Constitution should be 'construed with all the generality which the words used admit'.[28]

The High Court has recognised that the Commonwealth possesses an implied nationhood power derived not from the text of the Constitution, but by obvious inference from the existence of the Australian nation. According to Mason CJ, Deane, and Gaudron JJ in *Davis v. Commonwealth* (1988) 166 CLR 79 at 93: 'the legislative powers of the Commonwealth extend beyond the specific powers conferred on the Parliament by the Constitution and include such powers as may be deduced from the establishment and nature of the Commonwealth as a polity'.[29] On the other hand, literalism has been strictly applied to reach an extremely narrow interpretation of the express civil and political rights in the Constitution (see Chapter 5).[30] For example, in *Henry v. Boehm* (1973) 128 CLR 482 at 487 Barwick CJ stated of s. 117 of the Constitution:

> Whilst it might have been thought that such a provision in the Constitution as s. 117 would be a substantial aid to the unity of citizenship throughout Australia, it is expressed in precise

25 *Theophanous* at 174.

26 A. Mason, 'Future Directions in Australian Law' (1987) 13 *Monash University Law Review* 149 at 155–63; Zines, pp. 444–8.

27 A. Mason, 'The Role of the Courts at the Turn of the Century' (1993) 3 *Journal of Judicial Administration* 156 at 164.

28 The quote originally appeared at *R v. Public Vehicles Licensing Appeal Tribunal (Tas); Ex parte Australian National Airways Pty Ltd* (1964) 113 CLR 207 at 225 per the Court.

29 See *State Chamber of Commerce and Industry v. Commonwealth (Second Fringe Benefits Tax Case)* (1987) 163 CLR 329 at 357 per Mason CJ, Wilson, Dawson, Toohey, and Gaudron JJ. Compare *Davis v. Commonwealth* (1988) 166 CLR 79 at 101–4 per Wilson and Dawson JJ, and at 117–19 per Toohey J, who argued against any notion of an implied nationhood power on the basis that any such power is textually based in a combination of the executive power in s. 61 and the incidental power in s. 51(xxxix).

30 See H. Charlesworth, 'Individual Rights and the Australian High Court' (1986) 4 *Law in Context* 52 at 65–6.

and narrow terms representing a compromise of competing views amongst those responsible for the drafting of the Constitution ... We are here concerned only with the application of the actual words of the Constitution properly construed as in an organic instrument.

The net result has been an expansion of Commonwealth power at the expense of constitutionally guaranteed liberties.

The High Court's 'reading down' of express constitutional freedoms is consistent with the doctrine of parliamentary sovereignty (see Chapter 9), itself a non-literal doctrine that found expression in the *Engineers Case*. According to Sir Anthony Mason, there has been a 'willingness to read down constitutional prohibitions in conformity with a belief in the virtues of parliamentary supremacy'.[31] Such a willingness is rarely explicit. The judgments of Gibbs, Mason, and Wilson JJ in *Attorney-General (Vict); Ex rel Black v. Commonwealth* (1981) 146 CLR 559 on s. 116 of the Constitution are an exception (see Chapter 5). Wilson J stated, at pp. 652–3:

> The plaintiffs' plea for a broad construction overlooks the fact that we are dealing with a clause which does not grant power, but denies it. While it is true that a constitutional grant of plenary legislative power should be construed with all the generality which the words used will admit, carrying with it whatever is incidental to the subject-matter of the power, the same is not true of a provision which proscribes power.

Although this approach did not find favour with Barwick CJ,[32] it did express a general theme that can be found in many cases dealing with the clash of constitutional rights and Commonwealth power, a theme that is hard to characterise as one of the 'settled rules of construction'.

History and constitutional interpretation

The Convention debates as an aid to interpretation

The first justices of the High Court, Griffith CJ, Barton, and O'Connor JJ, were appointed in 1903. In 1904, in *Municipal Council of Sydney v. Commonwealth* (1904) 1 CLR 208 at 213–14, Griffith CJ rejected the use of the debates of the 1891 and 1897–98 Conventions that drafted the Australian Constitution (see Chapter 2) as an aid to interpretation except 'for the purpose of seeing what was the subject-matter of discussion, what was the evil to be remedied, and so forth'.[33] Over time, this exception had little impact in the face of a general reluctance by members of the Court to make use of the Convention debates. Having actively participated in the Conventions, the first justices of the High Court, as well as Isaacs and Higgins JJ (who were appointed in 1906), in any event possessed an intimate knowledge of the intended scope of the Constitution. This led the first justices of the High Court to interpret the Constitution to achieve a model of balanced or coordinate federalism sympathetic to the continuing power of the states as against the Commonwealth. With the composition of the Court changing over the years this first-hand knowledge of the Conventions dissipated and

---

31 Mason, 'The Role of a Constitutional Court in a Federation', p. 11.
32 *Attorney-General (Vict); Ex rel Black v. Commonwealth* at 577.
33 See *Tasmania v. Commonwealth* (1904) 1 CLR 329 at 333 per Griffith CJ (in argument); *Stephens v. Abrahams (No 2)* (1903) 29 VLR 229 at 239, 241 per Williams J (in argument).

the debates at the Conventions came to exert less of an influence. This culminated in the decision of the Court in the *Engineers Case*, which acted as a catalyst for the expansion of federal power at the expense of the states.

In the wake of the *Engineers Case*, the High Court continued to reject the use of the Convention debates in the interpretation of the Constitution.[34] However, this did not preclude the Court from referring to events that occurred prior to federation. According to Barwick CJ in *Attorney-General (Cth); Ex Rel McKinlay v. Commonwealth* (1975) 135 CLR 1 at 17:

> In case of ambiguity or lack of certainty, resort can be had to the history of the colonies, particularly in the period of and immediately preceding the development of the terms of the Constitution. But it is settled doctrine in Australia that the records of the discussions in the Conventions and in the legislatures of the colonies will not be used as an aid to the construction of the Constitution.[35]

Thus, although the Convention debates were shunned, the Court was prepared to refer to draft versions of the Constitution[36] and to the evolution of specific provisions of the Constitution.[37] More anomalous was the High Court's preparedness to refer to John Quick and Robert Garran's *The Annotated Constitution of the Australian Commonwealth*,[38] a commentary on the Constitution, published in 1901, that makes use of material from the Convention debates.[39] Use of Quick and Garran rather than the debates themselves shows that the Court was prepared to use secondary material, the accuracy of which has been seriously questioned in some areas,[40] but not the primary material on which the secondary material itself relied.

---

34 *Attorney-General (Cth); Ex Rel McKinlay v. Commonwealth* (1975) 135 CLR 1 at 17 per Barwick CJ, at 47 per Gibbs J; *Attorney-General (Cth) v. T & G Mutual Life Society Ltd* (1978) 144 CLR 161 at 187 per Aickin J; *Attorney-General (Vict); Ex rel Black v. Commonwealth* (1981) 146 CLR 559 at 577–8 per Barwick CJ, at 603 per Gibbs J. See P. Brazil, 'Legislative History and the Sure and True Interpretation of Statutes in General and the Constitution in Particular' (1961) 4 *University of Queensland Law Journal* at 16–21; J. A. Thomson, 'Constitutional Interpretation: History and the High Court: A Bibliographical Survey' (1982) 5 *University of New South Wales Law Journal* 309. Compare *Municipal Council of Sydney v. Commonwealth* (1904) 1 CLR 208 at 213–14 per Griffith CJ (in argument); *Deputy Federal Commissioner of Taxation (NSW) v. W R Moran Pty Ltd* (1939) 61 CLR 735 at 794 per Evatt J.

35 Compare *In Re Webster* (1975) 132 CLR 270 at 279 per Barwick CJ.

36 See, for example, *Tasmania v. Commonwealth* (1904) 1 CLR 329 at 333 per Griffith CJ (in argument), at 350–1 per Barton J, at 359–60 per O'Connor J; *Baxter v. Commissioners of Taxation (NSW)* (1907) 4 CLR 1087 at 1115 per Griffith CJ, Barton, and O'Connor JJ; *Attorney-General (Cth) v. T & G Mutual Life Society Ltd* (1978) 144 CLR 161 at 176 and 180–1 per Stephen J, at 186–7 and 192–3 per Aickin J; *Seamen's Union of Australia v. Utah Development Co.* (1978) 144 CLR 120 at 142–4 per Stephen J.

37 See, for example, *Tasmania v. Commonwealth* (1904) 1 CLR 329 at 351–5 per Barton J; *Victoria v. Commonwealth (Second Uniform Tax Case)* (1957) 99 CLR 575 at 603–4 per Dixon CJ; *Seamen's Union of Australia v. Utah Development Co.* (1978) 144 CLR 120 at 142–4 per Stephen J. See also P. H. Lane, *The Australian Federal System*, 2nd edn, LBC, 1979, pp. 1109–12.

38 J. Quick and R. Garran, *The Annotated Constitution of the Australian Commonwealth*, 1901 edn, Legal Books, 1995. See C. McCamish, 'The Use of Historical Materials in Interpreting the Commonwealth Constitution' (1996) 70 *Australian Law Journal* 638 at 641–2; G. Sawer, 'Foreword', in Quick and Garran, p. v.

39 See, for example, *Pirrie v. McFarlane* (1925) 36 CLR 170 at 196 per Isaacs J; *R v. Federal Court of Bankruptcy; Ex parte Lowenstein* (1938) 59 CLR 556 at 570 per Latham CJ; *Worthing v. Rowell and Muston Pty Ltd* (1970) 123 CLR 89 at 109 per Kitto J; *Attorney-General (Vic); Ex rel Black v. Commonwealth (DOGS Case)* (1981) 146 CLR 559 at 608 per Stephen J, at 612 per Mason J.

40 See, on the accuracy of the work in regard to s. 116 of the Constitution, R. Ely, *Unto God and Caesar: Religious Issues in the Emerging Commonwealth, 1891–1906*, Melbourne University Press, 1976, ch. 12. In regard to federalism and the Senate, see B. Galligan, 'Senate Committees: Can They Halt the Decline of Parliament?', in *Papers on Parliament*, No. 12, Department of the Senate, September 1991, p. 84.

The Court revised its approach to the Convention debates in its unanimous decision in *Cole v. Whitfield* (1988) 165 CLR 360.[41] Although not adverting to any change of policy, the Court reinterpreted s. 92 of the Constitution by making detailed reference to the debates. The Court had come to rely on the Convention debates nearly a century after the first Convention in 1891, long after the passing of the social context in which the debates had taken place. In taking this course, the Court set out a problematic[42] distinction between when regard could and could not be had to the Convention debates. Reference was acceptable 'for the purpose of identifying the contemporary meaning of language used, the subject to which that language was directed and the nature and objectives of the movement toward federation from which the compact of the Constitution finally emerged'.[43] On the other hand, the debates could not be referred to 'for the purpose of substituting for the meaning of the words used the scope and effect—if such could be established—which the founding fathers subjectively intended the section to have'.[44] Arguably, the now permissible use of the Convention debates fell within the exception put forward by Griffith CJ in *Municipal Council of Sydney v. Commonwealth* in 1904. The approach taken to the Convention debates in *Cole v. Whitfield* was reaffirmed by the High Court in *Port MacDonnell Professional Fishermen's Assn Inc. v. South Australia* (1989) 168 CLR 340 at 375–7. In that case, the Court quoted significant portions of the debates to assist in ascertaining the subject of s. 51(xxxviii) of the Constitution. Similarly, in *New South Wales v. Commonwealth (Incorporation Case)* (1990) 169 CLR 482, a majority of the Court examined the debates 'to establish the subject to which [s 51(xx)] was directed'.[45]

The use of the Convention Debates by the High Court since 1988 has been strongly criticised. The reasoning in the *Incorporation Case* has been particularly attacked.[46] That decision prevented the Commonwealth from legislating for a national corporations and securities regime. The Court held, with Deane J dissenting, that s. 51(xx) does not enable the Commonwealth to regulate the process of incorporation because the text of the Constitution limits the Commonwealth's power by reference to 'trading and financial corporations *formed* within the limits of the Commonwealth' (emphasis added), that is, to corporations 'which have been formed'.[47] The majority examined drafts of s. 51(xx) and quoted a passage from Sir Samuel Griffith at the 1891 Convention[48] to support their conclusion. In dissent, Deane J argued, at p. 511, against the use of the Convention debates by the majority:

---

41 See *Brown v. The Queen* (1986) 160 CLR 171 at 189 per Wilson J, at 214 per Dawson J. See G. Craven, 'Original Intent and the Australian Constitution: Coming Soon to a Court Near You?' (1990) 1 *Public Law Review* 166; D. Dawson, 'Intention and the Constitution: Whose Intent?' (1990) 6 *Australian Bar Review* 93.

42 P. Schoff, 'The High Court and History: It Still Hasn't Found(ed) What It's Looking For' (1994) 5 *Public Law Review* 253.

43 *Cole v. Whitfield* at 385.

44 *Cole v. Whitfield* at 385.

45 *Incorporation Case* at 501 per Mason CJ, Brennan, Dawson, Toohey, Gaudron, and McHugh JJ.

46 S. Corcoran, 'Corporate Law and the Australian Constitution: A History of Section 51(xx) of the Australian Constitution' (1994) 15 *Journal of Legal History* 131 at 151–6; G. Kennett, 'Constitutional Interpretation in the *Corporations* Case' (1990) 19 *Federal Law Review* 223 at 237–42; R. McQueen, 'Why High Court Judges Make Poor Historians: The Corporations Act Case and Early Attempts to Establish a National System of Company Regulation in Australia' (1990) 19 *Federal Law Review* 245.

47 *Incorporation Case* at 502 per Mason CJ, Brennan, Dawson, Toohey, Gaudron, and McHugh JJ.

48 *Convention Debates*, vol. 1, *Sydney 1891*, p. 686.

The first answer to that argument is that the few brief references in the Convention Debates are far from compelling (see, e.g., *Convention Debates* (Adelaide 1897) vol III, p. 439) and one can point to contrary statements in early authority (see W. Harrison Moore, *Constitution of the Commonwealth of Australia* (1902), p. 148). The second answer is a more fundamental one … It is that it is not permissible to constrict the effect of the words which were adopted by the people as the compact of a nation by reference to the intentions or understanding of those who participated in or observed the Convention Debates.[49]

Limiting constitutional rights by use of the Convention debates

The delegates to the 1891 and 1897–98 Conventions, who drafted the Australian Constitution, were generally unsympathetic to the incorporation of express rights (see Chapter 2). The framers were more concerned to implement a system of responsible government and to allow the states to continue to enact racially discriminatory laws than to foster the rights of migrants, indigenous peoples, and women. It is thus not surprising that since the decision in *Cole v. Whitfield* the Convention debates have been relied on by members of the High Court to limit the scope for the protection of human rights under the Australian Constitution. This has occurred in two ways. First, judges have relied on the drafters' failure to include a Bill of Rights in the Constitution as a basis for restricting the implication of rights from the instrument. Second, reference to the drafting of particular provisions, such as s. 80 (see Chapter 5), has been applied (expressly or implicitly) to restrict the operation of such provisions. This latter use of the Convention debates is analysed, where applicable, in Chapter 5 in dealing with the interpretation of specific rights.

Dawson J has been prominent in invoking the framers to restrict the implication of constitutional rights. In his dissenting judgment in *Australian Capital Television Pty Ltd v. Commonwealth* (1992) 177 CLR 106, he stated, at p. 186: 'those responsible for the drafting of the Constitution saw constitutional guarantees of freedoms as exhibiting a distrust of the democratic process. They preferred to place their trust in Parliament to preserve the nature of our society and regarded as undemocratic guarantees which fettered its powers'.[50] He further argued, at p. 182, that the decision by the framers not to include a Bill of Rights 'was deliberate and based on a faith in the democratic process to protect Australian citizens against unwarranted incursions on the freedoms which they enjoy'.[51] As has been shown in Chapter 2, this argument is not entirely consistent with the Convention debates. The delegates did not exhibit 'faith in the democratic process' to protect the rights of *all* Australians, particularly minorities, and in some areas instead demonstrated a desire to maximise the power of the states to abrogate certain rights. Dawson J himself also recognised in a later decision, *Kruger v. Commonwealth* (1997) 190 CLR 1 at 67, that the process by which the Constitution was endorsed lacked a 'degree of equality' given the exclusion of 'most women and many Aboriginals' from the 1898–1900 referendums (see Chapter 2).

Deane J has been a vocal critic of the use of the Convention debates to restrict the scope for rights in the Australian Constitution. In *Theophanous v. Herald & Weekly Times*

---

49   See *Breavington v. Godleman* (1988) 169 CLR 41 at 132–3 per Deane J.
50   See also *Australian Capital Television* at 136 per Mason CJ.
51   See also *Australian Capital Television* at 228–9 per McHugh J.

Ltd (1994) 182 CLR 104, he sought to discredit what he called, at p. 171, the 'dead hands theory' of constitutional interpretation: that is, the argument that the decision of the framers not to include a Bill of Rights in the Constitution restricts the scope for the High Court to subsequently derive implied rights from the instrument. He stated, at pp. 167–8:

> With due respect to those who see the matter differently, the argument seems to me to be flawed at every step it takes beyond the obvious facts that our Constitution does not incorporate a 'Bill of Rights' of the type contained in the United States model and that the framers of our Constitution had confidence in the common law. For one thing, the argument reverses ordinary principles of construction. For another, it imputes to the framers of our Constitution an intention which it would seem they did not have. Most important, the argument seems to me to adopt a theory of construction of the Constitution which unjustifiably devitalizes its provisions by effectively treating its long dead framers rather than the living people as the source of its legitimacy …
>
> To the extent that the views of the framers of the Constitution can be gleaned from the largely ex tempore and sometimes ill-informed speeches and comments of participants in the Convention debates, they lend no real support for the proposition that the absence of an express bill of constitutional rights was intended by the framers to preclude the implication of such rights.

Deane J's last sentence does not take full account of the deliberations of the 1897–98 Convention in rejecting Clark's clause 110 (see Chapter 2). That debate showed the desire of many of the framers to allow the states to abrogate the rights of sections of the community on racial grounds. Undoubtedly, these delegates believed that a clause frustrating this aim should not be implied from the Constitution. However, this belief was merely an unexpressed assumption of the framers, as was any more general belief that their failure to include a Bill of Rights meant that the High Court should not subsequently imply rights from the Constitution. Deane J is correct in arguing that the framers' failure to include a Bill of Rights offers 'no real support' to the argument that judges should not imply rights from the Constitution. According to Mason CJ in *Australian Capital Television* at 135,[52] an unexpressed assumption of the framers 'stands outside the instrument'. Dixon J made the same point in *Australian National Airways Pty Ltd v. Commonwealth* (1945) 71 CLR 29 at 81.

In *Theophanous*, Deane J took his argument further, finding, at p. 171, that:

> even if it could be established that it was the unexpressed intention of the framers of the Constitution that the failure to follow the United States model should preclude or impede the implication of constitutional rights, their intention in that regard would be simply irrelevant to the construction of provisions whose legitimacy lay in their acceptance by the people. Moreover, to construe the Constitution on the basis that the dead hands of those who framed it reached from their graves to negate or constrict the natural implications of its express provisions or fundamental doctrines would deprive what was intended to be a living instrument of its vitality and its adaptability to serve succeeding generations.

---

52 See G. Williams, 'Civil Liberties and the Constitution—A Question of Interpretation' (1994) 5 *Public Law Review* 82 at 100–1.

Interestingly, he then went on to support this, at pp. 171–2, with a quote from *Studies in Australian Constitutional Law* by Andrew Inglis Clark.[53] Central to this second limb of the attack by Deane J on the use of the debates to limit the protection of rights under the Constitution was his belief that the sovereignty of the Constitution now lies with the Australian people.[54] This second limb goes to the heart of the legitimacy of using the Convention debates to restrict the implication of constitutional rights.

Deane J's argument is a strong one. The failure of the delegates to the 1891 and 1897–98 Conventions to include a Bill of Rights is not an adequate reason to deny the existence of implied rights in the Constitution. The Convention debates themselves provide a hint that the modern High Court should move beyond the attitudes of the 1890s. As Isaac Isaacs, later Chief Justice of the High Court and Australia's first Australian Governor-General, remarked in the Melbourne session of the 1897–98 Convention:

> We are taking infinite trouble to express what we mean in this Constitution; but as in America so it will be here, that the makers of the Constitution were not merely the Conventions who sat, and the states who ratified their conclusions, but the judges of the Supreme Court. Marshall, Jay, Storey [sic], and all the rest of the renowned Judges who have pronounced on the Constitution, have had just as much to do in shaping it as the men who sat in the original Conventions.[55]

Current judicial use of the debates is flawed in that it does not accurately reflect the designs and motivations of the framers. Ultimately, the High Court must recognise that the attitudes of the framers were inimical to the fundamental freedoms of minorities. The framers believed in the capacity of the institution of responsible government and the Constitution, as drafted, to both protect their own interests and to allow the states to pass racially discriminatory laws to override the rights of others. The Court will need to reconcile the use that may be made of the Convention debates since *Cole v. Whitfield* with the fact that the attitudes of the framers in the area of human rights are not only inconsistent with but are opposed to the core values and beliefs of contemporary Australians,[56] and hence to modern 'community values' (see pp. 77–8). No Australian legislature today would claim a mandate to pass racially discriminatory laws, although it is arguable that certain laws recently passed do fall into this category.[57] The debates may be useful in interpreting the financial settlement embodied in the Constitution but are inappropriate for use in the area of basic freedoms. It may be that in any event the Constitution cannot support wide human rights protection and that many basic rights can find no foundation in the instrument. If this is so, it should not be because of the framers' attitudes, but because such rights cannot be supported by the text and structure of the Constitution as given meaning by the modern High Court.

---

53   A. I. Clark, *Studies in Australian Constitutional Law*, 1901 edn, Legal Books, 1997, pp. 21–2.
54   See *Theophanous* at 171. At p. 128, Mason CJ, Toohey, and Gaudron JJ adopted a more moderate line: 'The beliefs of the founders at the end of the last century as to the sufficiency of protections conferred by statute and common law cannot limit the content of an implication to be drawn from the Constitution, particularly if it transpires that the effect of the common law and statute law as it now stands is to interfere unduly with the relevant freedom of communication'.
55   *Convention Debates*, vol. 4, *Melbourne 1898*, p. 283. See Clark, pp. 21–2. Compare *Convention Debates*, vol. 5, *Melbourne 1898*, pp. 1381 per Mr Gordon.
56   See J. Braithwaite, 'Community Values and Australian Jurisprudence' (1995) 17 *Sydney Law Review* 351.
57   For example, *Queensland Coast Islands Declaratory Act 1985* (Qld); *Land (Titles and Traditional Usage) Act 1993* (WA); *Native Title Amendment Act 1998* (Cth).

The doctrine of proportionality

Members of the High Court have increasingly applied the concept of proportionality to assist in the process of constitutional interpretation.[58] It is a useful tool when the Court needs to balance rights against other community interests. The doctrine is reflected in earlier High Court cases, such as *R v. Burgess; Ex parte Henry* (1936) 55 CLR 608. In that decision, Starke J found, at pp. 659–60, that the Commonwealth's power over external affairs in s. 51(xxix) of the Constitution allowed it to legislate for 'all means which are appropriate, and are adapted to the enforcement of' the international convention or treaty. Distinctions might be drawn between the concept of proportionality and the 'appropriate and adapted' test.[59] However, any such distinction has not been developed by the High Court. Indeed, in *Lange v. Australian Broadcasting Corporation* (1997) 189 CLR 520, in the context of determining the scope of a limitation on Commonwealth power, the joint unanimous judgment found, at p. 562, that 'there is no need to distinguish these concepts'. 'For ease of expression', the judgment used 'the formulation of reasonably appropriate and adapted'.[60]

The modern development of the proportionality test in Australian constitutional law derives from the European Court of Human Rights in its construction of the *European Convention for the Protection of Human Rights and Fundamental Freedoms*, and from the European Court of Justice.[61] In that jurisdiction, proportionality has been applied because 'inherent in the whole of the Convention is a search for a fair balance between the demands of the general interest of the community and the requirements of the protection of the individual's fundamental rights'.[62]

The concept of proportionality was applied by the High Court in the *Tasmanian Dam Case* (1983) 158 CLR 1[63] in the context of the Commonwealth's power over external affairs in s. 51(xxix) of the Constitution. Since that case, the doctrine has been expressed in different forms and has been applied to assist in determining whether a federal law falls within a head of power,[64] and in determining whether a federal law breaches a constitutional limitation, including sections 92[65] and 117[66] of the Constitution.[67] In this latter context, Bradley Selway has summarised the operation of the test as follows:

> Where there is a constitutional guarantee, immunity or limitation on power and a balance needs to be struck to ascertain whether a relevant law falls within the guarantee, immunity or limitation or not, the test is whether the law is reasonably capable of being seen as

---

58   For a critique of the application of the doctrine in Australia, see J. Kirk, 'Constitutional Guarantees, Characterisation and the Concept of Proportionality' (1997) 21 *Melbourne University Law Review* 1.
59   *Levy v. Victoria* (1997) 189 CLR 579 at 645–6 per Kirby J.
60   *Lange v. Australian Broadcasting Corporation* at 562.
61   *Leask v. Commonwealth* (1996) 187 CLR 579 at 594–5 per Brennan CJ, at 600–1 per Dawson J, at 615 per Toohey J; *Minister for Resources v. Dover Fisheries Pty Ltd* (1993) 116 ALR 54 at 64 per Gummow J.
62   *Soering v. United Kingdom* (1989) 11 EHRR 439 at 468.
63   *Tasmanian Dam Case* at 172 per Murphy J, and at 259–61 and 278 per Deane J. See *Richardson v. Forestry Commission* (1988) 164 CLR 261.
64   *Davis v. Commonwealth* (1988) 166 CLR 79 at 100; *Polyukhovich v. Commonwealth (War Crimes Act Case)* (1991) 172 CLR 501 at 592–3.
65   *Castlemaine Tooheys Ltd v. South Australia* (1990) 169 CLR 436 at, for example, 473–4.
66   *Street v. Queensland Bar Association* (1989) 168 CLR 461 at, for example, 573–4.
67   Zines, pp. 44–8.

appropriate and adapted to achieving a legitimate purpose and the impairment of the constitutional guarantee, immunity or limitation is merely incidental to that purpose. However, it may be that some judges would apply a broader test of whether the law is appropriate or adapted to a legitimate purpose. [68]

Deane J in *Cunliffe v. Commonwealth* (1994) 182 CLR 272 at 337 stated that the outcome of the proportionality test 'will ultimately depend on an assessment of the character (including purpose), operation and effect of the particular law'.

For most of the heads of power in s. 51 of the Constitution, a law will be valid where it can be shown to be with respect to the *subject matter* of the power. For example, a law will be valid under s. 51(vii) where it is on the subject matter of 'Lighthouses, lightships, beacons and buoys'. For some powers it is necessary to show that the law is enacted to fulfil the *purpose* expressed by that power. For example, the defence power in s. 51(vi) of the Constitution 'seems rather to treat defence or war as the purpose to which the legislation must be addressed'.[69] Similarly, the power to implement treaty obligations under the external affairs power has been characterised as being a purposive power. Where a head of Commonwealth power is purposive, the proportionality doctrine may be relevant to the process of determining whether a law has been validly passed under that power.

Where the proportionality test is applied in determining whether a law is valid under a purposive head of power, there may be a role for human rights concerns. In ascertaining whether a law is 'reasonably and appropriately adapted to achieve the ends that lie within the limits of constitutional power',[70] the Court may take into account the effect of the legislation on fundamental freedoms recognised in the Constitution or at common law. This may require the High Court, as in *Nationwide News Pty Ltd v. Wills* (1992) 177 CLR 1, to scrutinise an Act that has been passed under a purposive power to determine whether it should be impugned due to a disproportionate adverse impact on freedom of expression.

The Commonwealth's implied nationhood power, a power 'inherent in its existence or in the fact of Australian nationhood and international personality',[71] has been viewed as a purposive power. Using this power, the Commonwealth sought to enact the *Australian Bicentennial Authority Act 1980* (Cth), which regulated aspects of the 1988 Australian Bicentenary. In *Davis v. Commonwealth* (1988) 166 CLR 79, the High Court considered the validity of this legislation. The plaintiff, Lou Davis, was an indigenous Australian who wished to market Bicentennial T-shirts bearing messages such as '200 Years of Suppression and Depression'. He was barred from doing so because sections 22 and 23 of the Act restricted the use of any symbol or logo associated with the Bicentenary, as well as any use, in conjunction with '1788' or '1988', of words including 'Bicentenary', 'Bicentennial', 'Sydney', 'Melbourne', 'First Settlement', and '200 years'. The Court unanimously held these provisions invalid, although the final order was limited to the words '200 years' as only these words were directly in issue.

---

68 B. Selway, 'The Rise and Rise of the Reasonable Proportionality Test in Public Law' (1996) 7 *Public Law Review* 212 at 217.

69 *Stenhouse v. Coleman* (1944) 69 CLR 457 at 471 per Dixon J.

70 *Davis v. Commonwealth* (1988) 166 CLR 79 at 100 per Mason CJ, Deane, and Gaudron JJ.

71 *Tasmanian Dam Case* (1983) at 252 per Deane J.

Mason CJ, Deane, and Gaudron JJ held the provisions invalid by applying the doctrine of proportionality. The doctrine enabled them to assess whether the legislation was disproportionate to its purpose because it abrogated fundamental freedoms. After finding that the Act would restrict the use of phrases such as 'Family Law Conference Melbourne 1988', they continued, at pp. 99–100:

> the effect of the provisions is to give the Authority an extraordinary power to regulate the use of expressions in everyday use in this country, though the circumstances of that use in countless situations could not conceivably prejudice the commemoration of the Bicentenary or the attainment by the Authority of its objects. In arming the Authority with this extraordinary power the Act provides for a regime of protection which is grossly disproportionate to the need to protect the commemoration and the Authority ... Here the framework of regulation created by s. 22(1)(a) with s. 22(6)(d)(i) and (ii) reaches far beyond the legitimate objects sought to be achieved and impinges on freedom of expression by enabling the Authority to regulate the use of common expressions and by making unauthorized use a criminal offence. Although the statutory regime may be related to a constitutionally legitimate end, the provisions in question reach too far. This extraordinary intrusion into freedom of expression is not reasonably and appropriately adapted to achieve the ends that lie within the limits of constitutional power.

Similar reasoning was employed by Brennan J in *Polyukhovich v. Commonwealth (War Crimes Act Case)* (1991) 172 CLR 501. Ivan Polyukhovich, who was eventually acquitted by a jury, was the first person to be tried in Australia under the *War Crimes Amendment Act 1988* (Cth). The Act permitted the prosecution and trial in Australia of Australian residents alleged to have committed war crimes in Europe during the Second World War. The High Court, with Brennan J in dissent, held that the Act was within the Commonwealth's legislative power with respect to external affairs. Having held that the law could not be upheld as one with respect to external affairs, Brennan J turned to the defence power in s. 51(vi) of the Constitution, a purposive power. Brennan J, with whom Toohey J agreed, found that the validity of the law depended on whether the imposition of a retrospective criminal sanction was proportionate to the defence interest to be served. He held, at p. 593, that the measure was invalid because it abrogated 'a principle which is of the highest importance in a free society, namely, that criminal laws should not operate retrospectively'.[72]

Nationwide News, *Davis v. Commonwealth* and the *War Crimes Act Case* demonstrate that proportionality has enabled human rights concerns to be factored into the assessment of the validity of federal legislation under certain heads of Commonwealth power. By impinging on a fundamental freedom, a law enacted under a purposive power may be disproportionate to its object and therefore invalid. The fundamental freedoms thus protected include freedoms not mentioned explicitly in the Constitution. However, one of the weaknesses of the approach may be the limited number of rights that it recognises. While it may take account of civil and political rights long recognised by the common law as fundamental,[73] such as the rights of speech,

---

72   See *Re Tracey; Ex parte Ryan* (1989) 166 CLR 518 at 596–7.
73   J. J. Doyle, 'Common Law Rights and Democratic Rights' in P. D. Finn (ed.), *Essays on Law and Government*, vol. 1, *Principles and Values*, LBC, 1995, p. 161.

association, and trial by jury, it seems less likely that a proportionality approach would protect rights not recognised by the common law, such as any right to privacy,[74] let alone any social, economic and cultural rights, such as the right to adequate housing.[75]

The scope for proportionality to protect civil liberties was widened by the decision of Mason CJ in *Nationwide News Pty Ltd*. He argued that a purposive element is present not only in purposive powers such as the defence power but also in the incidental aspect attaching to every power listed in s. 51. By the incidental aspect of a power, Mason CJ was referring to where the Commonwealth has legislated not on the core aspects of a power but in relation to matters incidental thereto. According to Dixon CJ, McTiernan, Webb, and Kitto JJ in *Grannall v. Marrickville Margarine Pty Ltd* (1955) 93 CLR 55 at 77: 'every legislative power carries with it authority to legislate in relation to acts, matters and things the control of which is found necessary to effectuate its main purpose, and thus carries with it power to make laws governing or affecting many matters that are incidental'. Mason CJ's argument that the proportionality test may be applied to the incidental aspect of every Commonwealth power in s. 51 was developed in *Cunliffe v. Commonwealth* (1994) 182 CLR 272. However, after his retirement, the Court re-examined the issue in *Leask v. Commonwealth* (1996) 187 CLR 579. While that decision did not strictly raise the issue of the incidental power,[76] it did mark that the expansion of the proportionality test proposed by Mason CJ is unlikely to be accepted by a majority of the Court.

The concept of proportionality has an additional dimension that is significant for the protection of human rights. It has been applied by the High Court to assist with the application of express and implied constitutional rights. Such freedoms cannot be absolute and must be weighed against other community interests. This is true even of the rights set out in the United States Constitution, which are expressed with no textual limitation. The First Amendment to the United States Constitution, for example, simply states that 'Congress shall make no law … abridging the freedom of speech'. Yet, it could not be true that this provision overrides laws that penalise criminal conspiracy or make it an offence to shout 'fire' in a crowded theatre to cause panic.[77]

The process of determining whether a law breaches a constitutional right is normally a two-stage one. The clearest exposition of this process was the unanimous decision of the High Court in *Lange v. Australian Broadcasting Corporation* (1997) 189 CLR 520, where the Court set out, at pp. 567–8, the questions to be answered in determining whether a law has breached the implied freedom of political communication (see Chapter 7):

> When a law of a State or federal Parliament or a Territory legislature is alleged to infringe the requirement of freedom of communication imposed by ss 7, 24, 64 or 128 of the Constitution, two questions must be answered before the validity of the law can be determined. First,

---

74 *Victoria Park Racing and Recreation Grounds Co. Ltd v. Taylor* (1937) 58 CLR 479.
75 A. Devereux, 'Australia and the Right to Adequate Housing' (1992) 20 *Federal Law Review* 223 at 230–1.
76 *Leask v. Commonwealth* at 624 per Gummow J: 'No recourse to ancillary or incidental legislative power is necessary to sustain validity.'
77 *Schenck v. United States* 249 US 47 at 52 (1919) per Holmes J. Compare Black J, with whom Douglas J joined, in *New York Times v. Sullivan* 376 US 254 at 297 (1964), who argued that in certain respects the First Amendment guarantee is 'unconditional'.

does the law effectively burden freedom of communication about government or political matters either in its terms, operation or effect? Second, if the law effectively burdens that freedom, is the law reasonably appropriate and adapted to serve a legitimate end the fulfilment of which is compatible with the maintenance of the constitutionally prescribed system of representative and responsible government and the procedure prescribed by s. 128 for submitting a proposed amendment of the Constitution to the informed decision of the people … If the first question is answered 'yes' and the second is answered 'no', the law is invalid.

The proportionality test applied by the High Court to determine whether a law is invalid for infringing on a constitutional right is still being developed and lacks the sophistication of the similar test applied by the Canadian Supreme Court in respect of the Canadian Charter of Rights and Freedoms. Section 1 of the Charter provides: 'The Canadian Charter of Rights and Freedoms guarantees the rights and freedoms set out in it subject only to such reasonable limits prescribed by law as can be demonstrably justified in a free and democratic society'.[78] In *R v. Oakes* [1986] 1 SCR 103, Dickson CJ of the Canadian Supreme Court set out the universal[79] test to be applied under s. 1. The test laid down was a more elaborate version of the balancing test set out in *Lange*. Dickson CJ stated, at pp. 138–9 of the *Oakes* judgment:

> To establish that a limit is reasonable and demonstrably justified in a free and democratic society, two central criteria must be satisfied. First, the objective, which the measures responsible for a limit on a *Charter* right or freedom are designed to serve, must be 'of sufficient importance to warrant overriding a constitutionally protected right or freedom' … It is necessary, at a minimum, that an objective relate to concerns which are pressing and substantial in a free and democratic society before it can be characterized as sufficiently important.
>
> Second once a sufficiently significant objective is recognized, then the party invoking s. 1 must show that the means chosen are reasonable and demonstrably justified. This 'involves a form of proportionality test'.

Dickson CJ then outlined, at p. 139, the components of the 'proportionality test':

> First, the measures adopted must be carefully designed to achieve the objective in question. They must not be arbitrary, unfair or based on irrational considerations. In short, they must be rationally connected to the objective. Second, the means, even if rationally connected to the objective in this first sense, should impair 'as little as possible' the right or freedom in question … Third, there must be a proportionality between the effects of the measures which are responsible for limiting the Charter right or freedom, and the objective which has been identified as of 'sufficient importance'.

The proportionality test laid down in *Oakes* is seemingly of greater sophistication than that set out in *Lange*.[80] However, the difference may be more apparent than real. At their

---

78 See also the equivalent test in s. 36 of the South African Constitution in force from 7 February 1997, which, with the words 'the relation between the limitation and its purpose' specifically incorporates a proportionality criterion into the balancing test to be undertaken by a court.

79 Compare *Andrews v. Law Society of British Columbia* [1989] 1 SCR 143 as to whether the *Oakes* test applies to infringements of the equality guarantee in s. 15 of the Canadian Charter of Rights and Freedoms.

80 See generally the commentary in P. Hogg, *Constitutional Law of Canada*, 4th edn, Carswell, 1997, pp. 867–98.

core, both tests establish a process by which a limitation on power may be set against the policy objective behind the impugned law. In addition, each limb of the Canadian formulation has not been independently applied. Instead, the experience of the Canadian Supreme Court has been that certain of the elements in the *Oakes* formulation have coalesced (notably the requirements of proportionate effect and that the law pursue an objective that is sufficiently important to justify infringing a Charter right[81]). Subsequent decisions have shown that 'the heart and soul of s. 1 justification'[82] has turned out to be the least-drastic-means requirement: that is, that the law 'should "impair as little as possible" the right or freedom in question'. In the United States context, the same work is done by the 'overbreadth doctrine'.[83] As Harlan J stated in *NAACP v. Alabama* 377 US 288 at 307 (1964), 'a governmental purpose to control or prevent activities constitutionally subject to state regulation may not be achieved by means which sweep unnecessarily broadly and thereby invade the area of protected freedoms'.

In *Levy v. Victoria* (1997) 189 CLR 579 at 589, Brennan CJ found that 'Under our Constitution, the courts do not assume the power to determine that some more limited restriction than that imposed by an impugned law could suffice to achieve a legitimate purpose'.[84] Despite this, the least-drastic-means requirement can be seen in the use of proportionality by the High Court. For example, in the *Tasmanian Dam Case* (1983) 158 CLR 1 at 260, Deane J outlined an example of the operation of the proportionality test. He argued that a law would fail the test if, in meeting the obligation to 'safeguard against the spread of some obscure sheep disease which had been detected in sheep in a foreign country and which had not reached these shores', the law required 'that all sheep in Australia be slaughtered'. The fact that the law pursued 'an extreme course' was one factor in this conclusion.[85] To say that a law adopts 'an extreme course' is another way of saying that a law might have achieved its object by less drastic means. As in Canada, it is possible that the least-drastic-means component of the proportionality test will become a more significant, perhaps even the most significant aspect, of the proportionality test as applied by the High Court. This may be for no better reason than that the least-drastic-means approach offers an apparently higher degree of objectivity, or a greater degree of certainty, that the mere requirement that a law be reasonably 'appropriate and adapted' to its legislative purpose. However, the least-drastic-means approach could not be strictly applied. If it were, the mere fact of some other conceivable way of achieving the same objective with a smaller infringement on the right or freedom would lead to invalidity, and as Blackmun J of the United States Supreme Court stated in *Illinois Elections Bd v. Socialist Workers' Party* 440 US 173 at 188–9 (1979): 'A judge would be unimaginative indeed if he could not come up with any something a little less "drastic" or a little less "restrictive" in almost any situation, and thereby enable himself to vote to strike legislation down'. Accordingly, some leeway of choice must be given to the Parliament.

---

81 Hogg, at p. 700, argues that 'an affirmative answer to the first step—sufficiently important objective—will always yield an affirmative answer to the fourth step—proportionate effect. If this is so, then the fourth step has no work to do, and can safely be ignored'.
82 Hogg, p. 694.
83 See generally G. Gunther, *Constitutional Law*, 12th edn, Foundation Press, 1991, pp. 1191–202.
84 See also pp. 627–8 per McHugh J.
85 *Tasmanian Dam Case* at 261.

In cases dealing with the implied freedom of political communication in Australia, Brennan J applied a 'margin of appreciation'[86] in determining whether Parliament had infringed the constitutional right. This concept is derived from the European Court of Human Rights,[87] and has also been applied by the Canadian Supreme Court.[88] If the High Court sharpened its proportionality test to apply a least-drastic-means requirement, it would be appropriate to apply a concept like the 'margin of appreciation' test to build in a suitable level of deference to the democratically elected legislature.[89] However, the 'margin of appreciation' doctrine could not be simply uplifted with its European roots and transplanted into Australian constitutionalism. As decisions of the European Court of Human Rights such as that in *Handyside v. United Kingdom* (1976) 1 EHRR 737 at 759 make clear, the doctrine is applied by that Court because it is necessary to recognise legitimate differences between states that are parties to the *European Convention for the Protection of Human Rights and Fundamental Freedoms* and because a national government's laws are entitled to a significant degree of deference from an international court less familiar with local circumstances.[90] If an Australian 'margin of appreciation' doctrine is to develop, it must be indigenous to Australian constitutional law.

Popular sovereignty

The Australian Constitution is set out in s. 9 of the *Commonwealth of Australia Constitution Act 1900* (63 & 64 Vict. Ch. 12), an Act of the British Parliament. When enacted, the source of the Constitution's status as higher law was thought to derive from the British Parliament and not from the Australian people. In other words, the instrument was sovereign because of its enactment in Britain, not because of its acceptance by the Australian people at referendums held between 1898 and 1900 (see Chapter 2). According to Sir Owen Dixon:

> It is not a supreme law purporting to obtain its force from the direct expression of a people's inherent authority to constitute a government. It is a statute of the British Parliament enacted in the exercise of its legal sovereignty over the law everywhere in the King's Dominions.[91]

Decades after its enactment, understandings of the Australian Constitution have changed. There is a growing awareness that the Constitution now derives its efficacy and sovereignty from the Australian people. The preamble to the Australian

---

86   For example, *Australian Capital Television* at 159.
87   See, for example, *The Observer and the Guardian v. United Kingdom* (1991) 14 EHRR 153 at 178. See generally H. C. Yourow, *The Margin of Appreciation Doctrine in the Dynamics of European Human Rights Jurisprudence*, Kluwer Law International, 1996.
88   See, for example, *Irwin Toy v. Que* [1989] 1 SCR 927 at 999.
89   Kirk, pp. 53–63.
90   M. Janis, R. Kay, and A. Bradley, *European Human Rights Law: Text and Materials*, Clarendon Press, 1995, p. 167.
91   O. Dixon, 'The Law and the Constitution' (1935) 51 *Law Quarterly Review* 590 at 597. See *Kirmani v. Captain Cook Cruises Pty Ltd (No 1)* (1985) 159 CLR 351 at 458 per Dawson J; J. G. Latham, 'Interpretation of the Constitution', in R. Else-Mitchell (ed.), *Essays on the Australian Constitution*, 2nd edn, LBC, 1961, p. 5; Quick and Garran, p. 300; J. A. Thomson, 'The Australian Constitution: Statute, Fundamental Document or Compact?' (1985) 59 *Law Institute Journal* 1199 at 1199.

Constitution provides some support for this. Although not as stirring as the opening words of the United States Constitution ('We the people of the United States … do ordain and establish this Constitution for the United States of America'), the preamble to the Commonwealth of Australia Constitution Act begins:'WHEREAS the people of New South Wales, Victoria, South Australia, Queensland, and Tasmania … have agreed to unite in one indissoluble Federal Commonwealth under the Crown of the United Kingdom of Great Britain and Ireland, and under the Constitution hereby established'. The preamble does not mention the people of Western Australia, despite referring to the people of the other states.[92] Further mixed support for popular sovereignty is provided by s. 128 of the Constitution. Section 128 provides for amendment of the Constitution by the Australian people voting at a referendum. However, constitutional change cannot be initiated by popular will, as such power rests exclusively with the Commonwealth Parliament.[93]

The notion of popular sovereignty in Australia has been supported by several judges of the High Court. In *Bistricic v. Rokov* (1976) 135 CLR 552 at 566, Murphy J stated that:'The original authority for our Constitution was the United Kingdom Parliament, but the existing authority is its continuing acceptance by the Australian people'. He went on to find, at p. 567, that 'Australia's independence and freedom from United Kingdom legislative authority should be taken as dating from 1901'.[94] This approach was consistent with Murphy J's finding in *Attorney-General (Cth); Ex rel McKinlay v. Commonwealth* (1975) 135 CLR 1 at 70 that s. 24 of the Constitution, which requires that the members of the House of Representatives be 'directly chosen by the people', entails as a 'standard of equality the alternatives of equal numbers of people and equal numbers of electors' (see Chapter 7). Murphy J's acceptance of the sovereignty of the Australian people was not based on a concept of gradually evolving Australian independence. He believed that Australian legal independence had arrived, explosively, with the creation of the Australian nation on 1 January 1901.[95] Dixon J stated in *In re Foreman & Sons Pty Ltd; Uther v. Federal Commissioner of Taxation* (1947) 74 CLR 508 at 530:'Like the goddess of wisdom the Commonwealth *uno ictu* sprang from the brain of its begetters armed and of full stature'. Murphy J took this to its logical extreme, arguing that, as a polity 'of full stature', the Commonwealth was legally independent and its people sovereign from its birth.

Murphy J's approach anticipated later judicial opinion. While he was a member of the Court, his view of popular sovereignty was shared by Deane J in *University of Wollongong v. Metwally* (1984) 158 CLR 447 at 476–7. In an article published in 1986 Geoffrey Lindell argued that:

> the Constitution now enjoys its character as a higher law because of the will and authority of the people. Such an explanation more closely conforms to the present social and political

---

92   This is explained by the fact that Western Australia was a late, almost last-minute, entrant into the Commonwealth of Australia. This is reflected in the recognition of the people of Western Australia in covering clause 3.

93   See *McGinty v. Western Australia* (1996) 186 CLR 140 at 274–5 per Gummow J; G. Winterton, 'Popular Sovereignty and Constitutional Continuity' (1998) 26 *Federal Law Review* 1 at 8.

94   See *China Ocean Shipping Co. v. South Australia* (1979) 145 CLR 172 per Murphy J.

95   *Kirmani v. Captain Cook Cruises Pty Ltd (No 1)* (1985) 159 CLR 351 at 383:'On the inauguration of the Commonwealth on 1 January 1901, British hegemony over the Australian colonies ended and the Commonwealth of Australia emerged as an independent sovereign nation in the community of nations'.

reality and has the advantage of ensuring that the legal explanation for the binding character of the Constitution coincides with popular understanding.[96]

This conclusion was based on the evolution of Australian independence in the international community and the legal changes brought about by the *Statute of Westminster 1931* (UK)[97] and the *Australia Act* 1986 (Cth). The final step in the process would occur if Australia became a republic.

The concept of popular sovereignty has gained wide acceptance[98] as the High Court has moved inexorably toward recognising that the sovereignty of the Australian Constitution derives from the Australian people and not from the British Parliament.[99] Mason CJ, citing Lindell, stated in *Australian Capital Television* (1992) 177 CLR 106 at 138 that the Australia Act 'marked the end of the legal sovereignty of the Imperial Parliament and recognised that ultimate sovereignty resided in the Australian people'. Similarly, Deane J argued in *Theophanous* (1994) 182 CLR 104 at 171 that the present legitimacy of the Constitution 'lies exclusively in the original adoption (by referendums) and subsequent maintenance (by acquiescence) of its provisions by the people'. More recently, in *McGinty v. Western Australia* (1996) 186 CLR 140 at 230, McHugh J found that 'Since the passing of the Australia Act (UK) in 1986, notwithstanding some considerable theoretical difficulties, the political and legal sovereignty of Australia now resides in the people of Australia'.[100]

The consequences of recognising that ultimate sovereignty in Australia lies with the people have yet to be fully explored. It might be that it is a purely symbolic development that has little effect on the interpretation of the Constitution.[101] After all, it merely means that legal recognition has been given to the political reality. Nevertheless, it seems that this shift will have an important impact on how members of the High Court approach the task of constitutional interpretation (see Chapter 9).[102]

---

96 G. Lindell, 'Why is Australia's Constitution Binding?: The Reasons in 1900 and Now, and the Effect of Independence' (1986) 16 *Federal Law Review* 29 at 37.

97 See *Statute of Westminster Adoption Act 1942* (Cth).

98 F. Brennan, 'The Indigenous People', in Finn, pp. 33–9; Constitutional Commission, *Final Report of the Constitutional Commission*, vol. 1, AGPS, 1988, p. 123; S. Donaghue, 'The Clamour of Silent Constitutional Principles' (1996) 24 *Federal Law Review* 133 at 144–7; Finn, 'A Sovereign People, A Public Trust', in Finn, pp. 2–5; M. Kirby, 'Introduction' (1996) 20 *Melbourne University Law Review* 949 at 949–50; M. J. Detmold, *The Australian Commonwealth*, LBC, 1985, ch. 6; H. A. Finlay, 'In Search of the Unstated Premise: an Essay in Constitutional Interpretation' (1982) 56 *Australian Law Journal* 465 at 472; K. Mason, 'Citizenship', in C. Saunders (ed.), *Courts of Final Jurisdiction: The Mason Court in Australia*, Federation Press, 1996, p. 35; J. A. Thomson, 'American and Australian Constitutions: Continuing Adventures in Comparative Constitutional Law' (1997) 30 *John Marshall Law Review* 627 at 644–9; K. C. Wheare, *The Constitutional Structure of the Commonwealth*, Oxford University Press, 1960, p. 108; G. Williams, 'The High Court and the People', in H. Selby (ed.), *Tomorrow's Law*, Federation Press, 1995, p. 271; Winterton, pp. 7–8; Zines, pp. 393–7, 415–16; Zines, 'The Sovereignty of the People', in M. Coper and G. Williams, (eds), *Power, Parliament and the People*, Federation Press, 1997, p. 91.

99 See, for example, *Leeth v. Commonwealth* (1992) 174 CLR 455 at 486 per Deane and Toohey JJ; *Ridgeway v. The Queen* (1995) 184 CLR 19 at 91 per McHugh J.

100 See also *McGinty v. Western Australia* at 274–5 per Gummow J.

101 Zines, *The High Court and the Constitution*, p. 396.

102 M. Kirby, 'Deakin: Popular Sovereignty and the True Foundation of the Australian Constitution' (1996) 3 *Deakin Law Review* 129 at 143; Thomson, 'American and Australian Constitutions: Continuing Adventures in Comparative Constitutional Law' at 648–9. Compare the conclusions reached by Lindell, pp. 43–9 and H. G. A. Wright, 'Sovereignty of the People: The New Constitutional *Grundnorm*?' (1998) 26 *Federal Law Review* 165.

Popular sovereignty has the potential to strengthen and widen the operation of rights under the Australian Constitution. Once it is recognised that constitutional power ultimately resides in and is derived from the Australian people, it is arguable that the product of that power, the Constitution, should be construed in a manner that is sympathetic to the rights of the Australian people, particularly so as to enhance popular participation in government. One consequence of this approach would be to enhance the power of the judiciary over the legislature. This underlies what the High Court has achieved in recognising that the Constitution contains an implied freedom of political communication (see Chapter 7). In this context, popular sovereignty has been linked to the system of representative government created by the Constitution. According to Deane and Toohey JJ:

> the doctrine of representative government which the Constitution incorporates is not concerned merely with electoral processes. As has been said, the central thesis of the doctrine is that the powers of government belong to, and are derived from, the governed, that is to say, the people of the Commonwealth. The repositories of governmental power under the Constitution hold them as representatives of the people under a relationship, between representatives and represented, which is a continuing one. The doctrine presupposes an ability of represented and representatives to communicate information, needs, views, explanations and advice.[103]

Popular sovereignty might even underpin an approach to constitutional interpretation based on the idea that the Parliament holds its power on trust for the people and that breaches of this trust might be remedied by courts. Paul Finn, now a judge of the Federal Court, has suggested that:

> Because the people, not the parliament, are sovereign the implication seems necessarily to be that it is beyond the competence of the parliament as a donee of power: (a) at the least, to reconstitute the general scheme of government in a way that denies its fundamental character (as least without the express authorisation of the people so to do); and (b) at the contentious most, in serving the people, to exercise its powers in a way that unduly interferes with such 'inherent rights' as the people may have despite or because of their union in our polity.[104]

Keith Mason, now President of the New South Wales Court of Appeal, has spelt out the link between popular sovereignty and rights discourse similarly as follows:

> Major premise—all public authority is derived from the people
> Minor premise—the people would not have been silly enough to arm government with power to do X
> Result—the Executive cannot do X, nor (if the limitation can find a toehold in the Constitution) can Parliament authorise it.[105]

On the other hand, popular sovereignty need not foster the expansion of constitutional rights, but might instead underpin judicial restraint. This approach could be based on the notion that if the people are sovereign, and given that the Constitution provides

---

103 *Nationwide News Pty Ltd v. Wills* (1992) 177 CLR 1 at 72.
104 Finn, 'A Sovereign People, A Public Trust', pp. 20–1. See P. D. Finn, 'The Abuse of Public Power in Australia: Making Our Governors Our Servants' (1994) 5 *Public Law Review* 43; J. Toohey, 'A Government of Laws, and Not of Men?' (1993) 4 *Public Law Review* 158 at 170.
105 Mason, 'Citizenship', p. 45.

a means for the people to alter the Constitution under s. 128 (even though this can only be initiated by the federal Parliament), it is inappropriate for judges of the High Court to shape the Constitution by implying new rights as this would be to usurp the role of the people to themselves amend the instrument. This argument was foreshadowed by McHugh J in *McGinty v. Western Australia* in his reference to and use of prior referendums under s. 128.[106] In that case McHugh J bolstered his conclusion that the Constitution did not contain an implied guarantee of voter equality (or 'one vote, one value') with the fact that a proposal to insert such a provision into the Constitution had twice been rejected by the Australian people, once on 18 May 1974 and again on 3 September 1988.[107] McHugh J put this argument after finding that the sovereignty of the Constitution lies with the Australian people.

Conclusion

There are many strands to the interpretation of the Australian Constitution. What is lacking is a coherent expression of the Constitution's role in shaping the relationship between the Australian people and their elected parliaments. There is no articulated vision for constitutional rights in Australia. This is due in part to the complex range of personalities, and the inherent preferences and biases of each, that have impacted on the Constitution. It is not surprising that the creative and diverse approaches of High Court judges ranging from Isaacs to Murphy and from Dixon to Mason have failed to develop a clear picture of the role of rights in the Australian Constitution. The incoherence of constitutional rights (see Chapter 9) is also a consequence of the literalist approach championed by the *Engineers Case*, an approach that was not rigorously applied in the *Engineers Case* itself.

The Constitution has been interpreted with an unarticulated tendency to defer to the doctrine of parliamentary sovereignty by selectively applying a literal approach to the Constitution. This approach is no less political than one that would seek to foster human rights, it is simply an approach with different objectives. The *Engineers Case*, in espousing a focus on the text of the Constitution combined with a tendency to privilege Commonwealth power over restrictions imposed by implied constitutional rights, has undermined any notion of a rights-orientated Constitution. Recently, the influence of the *Engineers Case* has been eroded by greater recognition of the role of implications in interpretation, by the introduction of new purposive approaches to the construction of federal powers and by visions of the Constitution as a document of the Australian people and not of the British legislature. The impact of these changes in this post-legalist era is slowly being felt (see Chapter 10).

---

106 *McGinty v. Western Australia* at 356–7, 358. See M. Coper, 'The People and the Judges: Constitutional Referendums and Judicial Interpretation', in G. Lindell (ed.), *Future Directions in Australian Constitutional Law*, Federation Press, 1994, p. 73.

107 *McGinty v. Western Australia* at 245–6. See also p. 180, fn. 196 per Dawson J. For the referendum results, see A. R. Blackshield and G. Williams, *Australian Constitutional Law and Theory: Commentary and Materials*, 2nd edn, Federation Press, 1998, pp. 1187, 1188. Compare *Newcrest Mining (WA) Ltd v. Commonwealth* (1997) 147 ALR 42 at 139 per Kirby J: 'The notion that the court should stay its hand because of the rejection of the constitutional referendum in 1988 is the least convincing reason of all. There were several connected proposals any one of which could have explained the failure to pass the constitutional alteration concerning State and Territory acquisitions of property'.

FIVE

Express Rights: Civil and Political

Introduction

Civil and political rights have been defined as 'the rights which enable individuals to operate freely within the political system and to be protected from arbitrary action in the administration of the law, including particularly the criminal law'[1] (see Chapter 1). There are many provisions in the Australian Constitution that have the potential to foster such rights. This Chapter focuses on the most important of these. The aim is to explain and analyse those sections that are explicitly rights-orientated, rather than those provisions that have the potential to be interpreted to foster civil liberties. Thus, for example, s. 80, which guarantees trial by jury is discussed, whereas s. 109, which gives supremacy to Commonwealth over state laws (see Chapter 3), is not.

A right to vote?

Section 41 of the Constitution is the closest that the Constitution comes to expressly conferring a right to vote in federal elections. Even then, any right conferred is not direct, but derivative. The provision does not bestow an unqualified right to vote on specified people or groups, but on an 'adult person who has or acquires a right to vote at elections for the more numerous House of the Parliament of a State'. Accordingly, s. 41 only operates where a state law already allows a person to vote. Moreover, the section does not actually confer a right. Section 41 is worded as a restriction on the power of the Commonwealth to pass certain laws. It does not vest any individual entitlement.[2]

The limited scope of s. 41 is explained by its origins. It was conceived by the framers of the Constitution as a way of ensuring that South Australian women, who

---

1   P. Bailey, *Human Rights: Australia in an International Context*, Butterworths, 1990, p. 12.
2   *Muldowney v. Australian Electoral Commission* (1993) 178 CLR 34 at 38–9 per Brennan J; *Snowdon v. Dondas* (1996) 139 ALR 475 at 483 per the Court.

were entitled to vote in South Australian elections from 1894, were not denied the ability to vote in federal elections (see Chapter 2). It was not intended to extend the franchise to women generally or to provide for universal adult suffrage.

The language of s. 41 is prone to ambiguity. This is compounded by its history. Particular difficulty is associated with the words 'who has or acquires a right to vote at elections for the more numerous House of the Parliament of a State'. At least four main interpretations are possible; namely, that s. 41 guarantees the right to vote in federal elections:

1   to any person who is entitled to vote for the more numerous house of the state parliament

2   to that class of persons who had acquired the entitlement to vote for the more numerous house of the state parliament before the enactment of a uniform federal franchise

3   to any person who had acquired the entitlement to vote for the more numerous house of the state parliament before the enactment of a uniform federal franchise

4   to any person who had acquired the entitlement to vote for the more numerous house of the state parliament at the time of federation.

The first option offers the widest guarantee. While it has less support from the drafting history of s. 41 than the other options, it is the reading most consistent with a literal wording of the section.[3] The third option is more narrow. Unlike the second option, it would not entitle to vote South Australian women coming of age after the federal franchise had come into effect, but would only apply to those individual women who had acquired the vote prior to that date. The Commonwealth provided for a uniform federal franchise shortly after federation in the *Commonwealth Franchise Act 1902* (Cth). This Act came into force on 12 June 1902. If the third option were correct, s. 41 would have no further work to do once all those people who had acquired a right to vote in a state as at 12 June 1902 had died. On the other hand, if the fourth option were correct, s. 41 would be spent when those people who had acquired a right to vote in a state up until 1 January 1901 had died.

There is support for each of these options in the early works on the Australian Constitution. Writing in 1901, John Quick and Robert Garran tentatively argued for the third option, finding that s. 41 was merely a transitional provision designed to preserve the voting rights of South Australian women until the new Commonwealth Parliament could enact a uniform federal franchise.[4] They based their support for the third option, as opposed to the second, on the fact that s. 41, in acting on an 'adult person', concerns individuals and not classes of people. Although Quick and Garran found that the word 'acquires' in s. 41 should be taken to mean 'acquires before the framing [of] the federal franchise', they weakened this conclusion by stating that 'it may certainly be argued that "acquires" is not expressly limited in point of time'.[5]

---

3   A. Brooks argues for this option in 'A Paragon of Democratic Virtues? The Development of the Commonwealth Franchise' (1993) 12 *University of Tasmania Law Review* 208.

4   J. Quick, and R. Garran, *The Annotated Constitution of the Australian Commonwealth*, 1901 edn, Legal Books, 1995, pp. 483–7. Garran also supported this view as Secretary to the federal Attorney-General's Department in an advice given on 27 July 1914. See *Opinions of Attorneys-General of the Commonwealth of Australia*, vol. 1, AGPS, 1981, p. 695.

5   Quick and Garran, p. 487.

In the first edition of his book *The Constitution of the Commonwealth of Australia*, written in 1902, Harrison Moore argued that s. 41 should be given a meaning corresponding to either the second or the fourth option. According to Moore, the correct meaning depended on that given to s. 30 of the Constitution, which provides: 'Until the Parliament otherwise provides, the qualification of electors of members of the House of Representatives shall be in each State that which is prescribed by the law of the State as the qualification of electors of the more numerous House of Parliament of the State'. If s. 30 referred to the 'law in force in each State at the establishment of the Commonwealth', then the fourth option should be preferred.[6] On the other hand, if s. 30 'means laws enacted by the State Parliament at any time before the establishment of a federal franchise by the Commonwealth Parliament', s. 41 would 'probably' accord to the second interpretation.[7] Moore did not develop his argument further and suggest which option he considered to be the correct construction.[8] However, he did reject the interpretation offered by Quick and Garran: that is, the third option. Moore said of this option, 'But such an operation of the law would be so partial and anomalous as to constitute a strong reason for rejecting altogether the limitation of time'.[9]

The Convention debates are of some assistance in setting out the intentions of the framers as regards s. 41. At the 1897–98 Convention, Frederick Holder, the South Australian Treasurer and author of s. 41, intended that s. 41 be limited by the enactment of a federal franchise.[10] For example, he stated: 'What I wish is that these rights should be preserved which have been acquired up to the time that the Commonwealth makes its franchise'.[11] Quick and Garran suggested that Holder 'probably intended that South Australian women should be entitled to vote, whether actually qualified before or after the federal law':[12] that is, the second option. However, Holder is not recorded at the Convention as clearly differentiating between the second and third options.

The contribution of other views at the Convention debates is also inconclusive.[13] However, it was clearly a concern of the 1897–98 Convention that s. 41 might operate to enable the states to modify the federal franchise. Edmund Barton, subsequently Australia's first Prime Minister and one of the first members of the High Court, argued that: 'To give a state the power, after the Federal Parliament is established, of altering the composition and character of the Legislature and the legislation of the

---

6   W. H. Moore, *The Constitution of the Commonwealth of Australia*, 1st edn, Murray, 1902, p. 109. Moore's interpretation is actually wider than that set out in option 4. He argued that s. 41 would confer the right to vote in federal elections on those people who had such a right at the state level at the time of federation, 'or who at any time afterwards acquires a right under that law' (Moore, p. 109).

7   Moore, p. 109.

8   Nor did he develop this further in the second edition of his book. In the second edition, in 1910, he had removed the material on s. 41, stating in a footnote that s. 41 'might have been important if the Commonwealth had adopted a franchise narrower than the states. The wide franchise adopted, however, makes it unnecessary to recur to the matters discussed in the first edition of this book at pp. 107–109, and in *Quick and Garran*, 483–7' (Moore, 2nd edn [1910], Legal Books, 1997, p. 126, fn. 2).

9   Moore, 1st edn, p. 109, fn. 1.

10   *Official Record of the Debates of the Australasian Federal Convention: 1891–1898* [hereafter *Convention Debates*], vol. 3, *Adelaide 1897*, Legal Books, 1986, p. 1195; *Convention Debates*, vol. 5, *Melbourne 1898*, p. 1843.

11   *Convention Debates*, vol. 3, *Adelaide 1897*, p. 732; *Convention Debates*, vol. 5, *Melbourne 1898*, p. 1195.

12   Quick and Garran, pp. 486–7.

13   See, for example, *Convention Debates*, vol. 5, *Melbourne 1898*, p. 1853 per Mr Barton. Compare A. Twomey, 'Book Review' (1997) 25 *Federal Law Review* 205 at 209.

Commonwealth certainly would be unwise'.[14] Isaac Isaacs, later Chief Justice of the High Court and Australia's first Australian Governor-General, suggested that the clause should be amended to make clear that this was not the intention by altering the clause to begin: 'Any elector who has, at the establishment of the Commonwealth, or who afterwards, and before the Parliament prescribes the qualification of electors for the Houses of Parliament, acquired a right to vote'.[15] This amendment was not adopted.[16]

Despite its open-ended wording, it seems likely that s. 41 was intended to be limited in the way set out in either the second or third option: that is, by the enactment of a uniform federal franchise. Despite this, in the 1902 debate in the federal Parliament over the Bill that introduced the federal franchise there is not only support for these options, but also for the first option.[17] Section 4 of the Commonwealth Franchise Act provided that Australia's Aboriginal peoples could not vote at federal elections. In the debate over s. 4 in the federal Parliament, the issue arose of how s. 4 might be affected by s. 41 if a state were to subsequently give Aboriginal peoples the right to vote in state elections. Ironically, s. 41 was not seen by some speakers as being limited by the Bill then under consideration. In the House of Representatives, Isaacs stated: 'If it is ever desired by one or more of the States to invest the aboriginals within their territory with the franchise for the more numerous State House, they will come under s. 41 of the Constitution, which then gives them the right to vote for the Federal Parliament'.[18] Subsequently, in the Senate, Sir John Downer, a member of the 1891 and 1897–98 Conventions, was even firmer in supporting the first option:

> The laws, as they exist now in the States, defining the right to vote shall continue, though in each State they may be divergent, and laws in future passed by each State deciding who shall vote shall also prevail, notwithstanding any law we may pass to the contrary. So that any law that we may pass now on this matter will be subject to the existing or future law of any State.[19]

The historical evidence is inconclusive on the ambit of s. 41. There is support in contemporary materials and by persons who participated in the drafting of s. 41 for each of the four interpretations outlined above. It is clear that the section was designed to give recognition in federal elections to state electoral qualifications. However, there was no commonly held view as to who might be entitled to this recognition and for what time. In any event, the intended purpose of s. 41 must be reconciled with the literal meaning of the section, which does not suggest any limitation of the type set out in the second, third or fourth options.

---

14 *Convention Debates*, vol. 5, *Melbourne 1898*, p. 1841.
15 *Convention Debates*, vol. 5, *Melbourne 1898*, p. 1851.
16 See *R v. Pearson; Ex parte Sipka* (1983) 152 CLR 254 at 272 per Murphy J.
17 Brooks, pp. 236–8.
18 Australia, House of Representatives 24 April 1902, *Debates*, vol. 9, p. 11 979.
19 Australia, Senate, 29 May 1902, *Debates*, vol. 10, p. 13 006. See also p. 13 005 per Major Gould: 'There is, also, a further power under the Constitution for the enfranchisement of aboriginal inhabitants in the future, if the State in which they reside thinks fit to enfranchise them. Section 41 of the Constitution provides that … So it appears that under the Constitution Act there is an opportunity for the enfranchisement of the aboriginal inhabitants of any State where they are not enfranchised at the present time'.

The High Court has had the opportunity to grapple with s. 41 on only a few occasions. The first opportunity[20] came in *Muramats v. Commonwealth Electoral Officer (WA)* (1923) 32 CLR 500. Jiro Muramats was born in Japan and naturalised in Australia. His application to be enrolled to vote in federal elections was rejected on the basis that he was disqualified under s. 39(5) of the *Commonwealth Electoral Act 1918* for being an 'aboriginal native of … Asia'. He took the matter to the High Court, where he argued that because he was entitled to be enrolled in Western Australia under s. 17 of the *Electoral Act 1907* (WA), s. 41 protected his right to vote in federal elections. This argument failed, but not because of a narrow reading of s. 41. Instead, it was held that s. 41 did not apply because Muramats was not even entitled to be enrolled in Western Australia. Section 18 of the Western Australian *Electoral Act*, like the Commonwealth provision, disqualified anyone who was an 'aboriginal native of … Asia'. As obiter, Higgins J gave some support for a broad interpretation of s. 41, stating, at p. 504, that if Muramats had not been disqualified under s. 18, 'his right to vote at elections for the [Western Australian] Assembly, and therefore to be enrolled on the Commonwealth roll, would seem to be clear'.

The next time s. 41 came before the High Court was in *King v. Jones* (1972) 128 CLR 221. At the time of federation, and for many years afterwards, the voting age across Australia was set at 21 years. Under the *Constitution Act Amendment Act (No 2) 1970* (SA), the South Australian Parliament, like the New South Wales and Western Australia Parliaments before it, reduced the voting age for state elections from 21 to 18 years. Until 1973, it remained a requirement that a person be at least 21 years old to vote in federal elections.[21] Three South Australians aged between 18 and 21 years applied to be placed on the Commonwealth electoral roll. Their applications were rejected. It was argued in the High Court that, as they were qualified to vote for the more numerous House of the South Australian Parliament, s. 41 applied to also allow them to vote in federal elections. The Court unanimously rejected this argument. It did so on the ground that the plaintiffs could not be considered to be 'adult person[s]' under s. 41.

The Court interpreted 'adult' by giving it the 'commonly accepted meaning' that it held at the time of federation: that is, a person who had attained 21 years.[22] The Court was not prepared to allow the word a widening denotation so that 'adult' might have come to encompass people aged between 18 and 21. The argument that 'adult' means the attainment of a certain level of maturity,[23] which in the 1970s may have been met by a person aged 18 years, was rejected. A central concern was that the Court may have

---

20 In *Cameron v. Fysh* (1904) I CLR 314, two men were refused the vote in a federal election because their names were on the state electoral roll and not on the Commonwealth electoral roll. While not citing s. 41, Griffith CJ stated, at p. 319: 'As to the objection that voters on the State roll, and not on the Commonwealth roll, were not allowed to vote, I am not inclined to encourage the idea that they had any right to vote'.

21 *Commonwealth Electoral Act 1973* (Cth), s. 39.

22 *King v. Jones* at 234 per Barwick CJ.

23 In argument before the High Court Lionel Murphy QC proposed, at p. 224, 'to call as a witness a professor of sociology who is an expert on the subject of the development of persons to maturity'. Barwick CJ responded: 'The Court will not receive evidence at this point. It will first decide the construction of the Constitution. When argument is finished we will reserve our view on that and whether we resume the hearing'.

had to 'gauge the degree of physical or mental maturity of persons of a certain age'.[24] The Court also rejected the argument that 'adult' meant a person who had attained his or her majority, and that, as the *Age of Majority (Reduction) Act 1971* (SA) had reduced this from 21 to 18 years, people between the age of 18 and 21 in South Australia could be considered 'adults'.

The Court's finding that the plaintiffs were not 'adult persons' under s. 41 meant that the Court did not need to address wider issues, including the four options outlined above. However, some judges commented as obiter on these issues. Barwick CJ described the 'precise intent' of s. 41 as 'obscure', before stating, at p. 231, that only the definition of 'adult person' needed to be determined to answer the matter at hand. Walsh J, at p. 251, and Stephen J, at p. 267, were prepared to assume a wide operation for s. 41, but did not state a considered view. On the other hand, Menzies J gave unqualified support to an interpretation of s. 41 which was not limited in time: that is, the first option. He stated at p. 246:

> The character of s. 41 is that of a permanent constitutional provision. It is not a provision to make temporary arrangements for the period between the establishment of the Constitution and the making of Commonwealth laws. It applies to a person, who, in 1901, had or who, in the future, acquires particular voting rights by the laws of a State.

Gibbs J gave the question the most detailed treatment. He examined the positions of Quick and Garran, and Moore. He went on to reject the theory put forward by Moore that s. 41 only applies to persons whose right to vote at state elections was acquired under a law passed before the establishment of the Commonwealth, and stated, at p. 259, that 'The view of Quick and Garran … is far from clearly correct, but I find it unnecessary to express a final opinion on it'.

The issue of whether s. 41 is limited by the enactment of the federal franchise arose in *R v. Pearson; Ex parte Sipka* (1983) 152 CLR 254. Late in the afternoon of 3 February 1983, Prime Minister Malcolm Fraser called a snap federal election for 5 March 1983. The next day, 4 February 1983, proclamations were made to the effect that the writs for the election would be issued later that day. This meant that, under s. 45(a) of the Commonwealth Electoral Act, persons who had not yet enrolled had until 6 p.m. that day, instead of the normal several days, if they wished to be able to vote in the election. The four plaintiffs sought enrolment after that time and were placed on the electoral roll for New South Wales. However, they were refused enrolment for the federal election due to s. 45(a). They brought an action in the High Court claiming that they were entitled to vote in the federal election due to s. 41. Their action was heard on 16 and 17 February 1983, with the Court handing down its decision on 24 February 1983.[25]

Despite the obiter expressed in *King v. Jones*, the High Court found, with Murphy J dissenting, that s. 41 was merely a transitional provision. It was held that it should be given the meaning set out in the third option, that is, that 's 41 preserves only those rights which were in existence before the passing of the *Commonwealth Franchise Act 1902*'.[26] The majority consisted of two joint judgments, each made up of three judges.

---

24 *King v. Jones* at 262 per Gibbs J. See also pp. 271–2 per Stephen J.
25 As to the logistics of bringing the matter on such short notice, see Australian Legal Workers Group (NSW), 'The High Court Misses the Vote' (1993) 8 *Legal Service Bulletin* 69 at 70.
26 *R v. Pearson; Ex parte Sipka* at 264 per Gibbs CJ, Mason, and Wilson JJ.

Gibbs CJ, Mason, and Wilson JJ recognised that their conclusion involved giving s. 41 a narrow construction. However, they found, at p. 261, that 'this construction of the section is supported not only by obvious considerations of policy, but also by the history of the section'. The policy they referred to was that if s. 41 were not limited in time it would stand as a continuing barrier to the Commonwealth being able to maintain a uniform franchise. A state could unilaterally amend that franchise, perhaps to the benefit of its own residents, and 'It is impossible to suppose that results of this kind were intended'.[27] As to the history of s. 41, regard was had to the views of Quick and Garran, and Moore, but not to the Convention debates (which at that time were still an impermissible source of guidance—see Chapter 4). Brennan, Deane, and Dawson JJ delivered a judgment to the same effect, but with greater reliance on the policy basis for the narrow view rather than the historical materials. They recognised, at p. 280, that:

> It follows, of course, that the practical effect of s. 41 is spent. Most of the electors who acquired a right to vote at federal elections under ss 30 and 8 of the Constitution would have died. Since 12 June 1902, when the *Commonwealth Franchise Act* came into force, no person has acquired a right to vote the exercise of which is protected by s. 41.

Murphy J dissented in arguing for a wide construction of s. 41 corresponding to that set out in the first option.[28] His approach was very different from that of the other judges. He characterised the provision as 'one of the few guarantees of the rights of persons in the Australian Constitution'.[29] As such, it 'should not be read narrowly. A right to vote is so precious that it should not read out of the Constitution by implication. Rather every reasonable presumption and interpretation should be adopted which favours the right of people to participate in the elections of those who represent them'.[30] He then went on to interpret s. 41 according to its literal 'plain meaning', that is, as 'a constitutional guarantee that every adult person who has a right to vote at State elections shall not be prevented by any Commonwealth law from voting at federal elections'.[31] Murphy also examined the historical materials. He criticised the restrictive interpretation favoured by Quick and Garran, on the basis that they had not fully examined the material from the Convention debates. Murphy J also based his conclusion on policy considerations. He argued that s. 41 had been effective in guaranteeing Aboriginal people the vote in federal elections, which had been denied by the Commonwealth Franchise Act and subsequent legislation until 1962. He argued at pp. 270–1:

> Until then, the only right of Australian Aboriginals to vote in federal elections was derived from the guarantee in s. 41 … It guaranteed the right to vote to Aborigines in New South Wales, Victoria, South Australia and Tasmania. The history of discrimination against Aborigi-

---

27 *R v. Pearson; Ex parte Sipka* at 261.
28 Murphy J also dissented in his view of *King v. Jones*. He had been one of the unsuccessful advocates in that case. In *R v. Pearson; Ex parte Sipka*, one of the plaintiffs was aged 18, and was thus not an 'adult person' according to *King v. Jones*. In *R v. Pearson; Ex parte Sipka* at 274 Murphy J held that the eighteen year old plaintiff should be entitled to the benefit of s. 41 and that *King v. Jones* should be overruled as being 'inconsistent with general principles of constitutional interpretation which would give such words an ambulatory operation'.
29 *R v. Pearson; Ex parte Sipka* at 268.
30 *R v. Pearson; Ex parte Sipka* at 268.
31 *R v. Pearson; Ex parte Sipka* at 268.

nal voting rights repudiates the argument that giving the s. 41 guarantee the full scope of its plain meaning would be an undesirable departure from the allegedly 'Uniform Federal Franchise' introduced in 1902.

Murphy J was, however, wrong on this point.[32] The view of s. 41 applied at the administrative level was the narrow definition in the third option. Moreover, even where Aboriginal people might have been entitled to vote under this option, they were denied the vote in contravention of s. 41.

Writing in 1988 in *Encounters with the Australian Constitution*,[33] Michael Coper examined s. 41 under the heading 'The Right to Vote: Centenarians Rejoice'. Today, it would seem likely that there is no one alive who could claim the benefit of s. 41 on the interpretation reached by the High Court in *R v. Pearson; Ex parte Sipka*. In 1988, the Constitutional Commission described s. 41 as a 'dead letter' and recommended that it be removed from the Constitution.[34] Nevertheless, s. 41 has still had some work to do. Despite *R v. Pearson; Ex parte Sipka*, s. 41 has been a source of protection for rights. Along with other sections of the Constitution, it has been cited as providing a foundation for the notion that the Constitution prescribes a system of representative government and thus that it guarantees freedom of political communication (see Chapter 7).[35]

R v. Pearson; Ex parte Sipka means that s. 41 no longer has any role to play in guaranteeing the right to vote in federal elections to people entitled to vote in state elections. Unless there is some other relevant implied protection, perhaps in part based on s. 41, the Court's interpretation leaves the federal franchise in the hands of the Commonwealth parliament. The literal meaning of the text of s. 41 and the confused and uncertain history of the provision left scope for the Court to reach a broader interpretation. Murphy J exposed this in his dissent in *R v. Pearson; Ex parte Sipka*. He made it clear that the Court had a choice between s. 41 as a guarantee of human rights and s. 41 as a mere transitional provision. He alone chose the former option. In any event, while the strong policy arguments for enabling the Commonwealth to enact a uniform federal franchise tell against the first option, this is not the case in respect of the second option, which is a feasible interpretation that perhaps best meets the intentions of the drafters of the provision.

Trial by jury

Section 80 is based on Article III, s. 2 of the United States Constitution. It is the weaker guarantee in that, while the United States provision begins 'The Trial of all Crimes, except in Cases of Impeachment, shall be by Jury',[36] the Australian section states 'The trial on indictment of any offence against any law of the Commonwealth shall be by jury'. The notion of a 'trial on indictment' in s. 80 has proved crucial. The High Court

---

32 A. R. Blackshield and G. Williams, *Australian Constitutional Law and Theory: Commentary and Materials*, 2nd edn, Federation Press, 1998, pp. 160–1. See also P. Stretton and C. Finnimore, 'Black Fellow Citizens: Aborigines and the Commonwealth Franchise' (1993) 25 *Australian Historical Studies* 521.

33 M. Coper, *Encounters with the Australian Constitution*, CCH, 1988, p. 309.

34 Constitutional Commission, *Final Report of the Constitutional Commission*, vol. 1, AGPS, 1988, p. 144.

35 *Australian Capital Television Pty Ltd v. Commonwealth* (1992) 177 CLR 106 at 229 per McHugh J.

36 See also United States Constitution, Sixth Amendment.

has interpreted these words to allow the federal Parliament to itself determine whether a trial is to be on indictment, and thus whether there need be a jury trial. This interpretation has transformed s. 80 into a provision that provides no meaningful guarantee or restriction on Commonwealth power. It is simply the valve by which the Commonwealth can choose whether an offence shall be tried by jury. Geoffrey Sawer's comment in 1967 that the guarantee of trial by jury in s. 80 of the Constitution 'has been in practice worthless'[37] remains correct today.

The High Court's interpretation of s. 80 comes as no surprise when the history of s. 80 is examined (see Chapter 2). The first draft of s. 80 prepared by Andrew Inglis Clark provided for the trial by jury of 'all crimes cognisable by any' federal court. Sir Samuel Griffith then changed this to 'all indictable offences cognisable by any' federal court,[38] which was the version accepted in this or a similar form, until the 1898 Melbourne Convention. At the 1898 Melbourne Convention, concerns were expressed about the draft and its impact on Commonwealth power. Barton successfully proposed that the words 'of all indictable offences' be struck out and replaced with the words that now appear in s. 80: 'on indictment of any offence'.[39] He was concerned that the original wording would mean that numerous minor Commonwealth offences would need to be tried by jury, 'a cumbrous thing'.[40] The purpose of the successful amendment was to allow the Commonwealth to itself determine whether an offence was to lead to a 'trial on indictment', and thus whether it was to give rise to a jury trial. Isaacs suggested that the provision as amended and agreed to by the Convention would not have 'any real effect at all' and that the federal Parliament could 'say that murder was not to be an indictable offence, and therefore the right to try a person accused of murder would not necessarily be by jury'.[41] Isaacs was of the view that s. 80 did not act as 'any safeguard at all'.[42] The Convention debates clearly indicate that it was not intended that s. 80 limit the choice of the Commonwealth as to which offences be tried by jury. Nevertheless, if the framers agreed with Isaacs, why did they vote for a provision that would be of no real effect? Why did they bother inserting s. 80 into the Constitution?[43]

Most attempts at construction of s. 80 by the High Court have rendered illusory whatever protection the section might have conferred, thus confirming the prediction of Isaacs. The first case on s. 80 raised the issue of whether it limited the Commonwealth's power to legislate for Australian territories under s. 122 of the Constitution. In *R v. Bernasconi* (1915) 19 CLR 629, the High Court heard a matter on appeal from the Central Court of Papua, then an Australian territory. The accused had been tried and convicted without a jury for an assault occasioning actual bodily harm and was sentenced to two months imprisonment. He appealed to the High Court, arguing that s. 80 had been infringed. The Court held that the territories power, exercised directly by

---

37 G. Sawer, *Australian Federalism in the Courts*, Melbourne University Press, 1967, p. 19.
38 *Convention Debates*, vol. 1, Sydney 1891, p. 958.
39 *Convention Debates*, vol. 5, Melbourne 1898, p. 1894.
40 *Convention Debates*, vol. 5, Melbourne 1898, p. 1895, per Mr Barton.
41 *Convention Debates*, vol. 5, Melbourne 1898, p. 1895. This view is shared by Quick and Garran, p. 808.
42 *Convention Debates*, vol. 4, Melbourne 1898, p. 352.
43 C. L. Pannam, 'Trial by Jury and Section 80 of the Australian Constitution' (1968) 6 *Sydney Law Review* 1 at 24 suggests that, together with s. 116 of the Constitution, s. 80 'represents the high water mark of uncritical and seemingly senseless copying of inappropriate American precedent'.

the Commonwealth or by a subordinate legislature, was not limited by Chapter III of the Constitution, including s. 80, and thus that the Commonwealth could legislate for Papua to establish an indictable offence triable otherwise than by jury. It may have been intended that this finding only apply to external territories, and not to internal territories such as the Northern Territory. Isaacs J drew a distinction between territories that are 'constituent parts of the self-governing body' and territories, such as the one in question, 'annexed to the Commonwealth and subordinate to it'.[44] While it was not necessary to comment on the meaning of 'trial on indictment' in s. 80, Isaacs J did so, finding, unsurprisingly, that 'If a given offence is not made triable on indictment at all, then sec 80 does not apply'.[45]

This last finding by Isaacs J was referred to with approval by a majority in *R v. Archdall & Roskruge; Ex parte Carrigan and Brown* (1928) 41 CLR 128. Knox CJ, Isaacs, Gavan Duffy, and Powers JJ gave extremely short shrift to the notion that s. 80 might be anything other than a mere procedural device by which the Commonwealth could determine which trials would be by jury. Without further elaboration, they stated, at p. 136, 'The suggestion that the Parliament, by reason of sec 80 of the Constitution, could not validly make the offence punishable summarily has no foundation and its rejection needs no exposition'. The shortness of the rejection of any substantive operation for s. 80 means that it is only possible to guess at the reasons underlying this conclusion. Higgins J reached the same conclusion, again without explanation. He paraphrased the effect of s. 80, at pp. 139–40, as follows: 'if there be an indictment, there must be a jury; but there is nothing to compel procedure by indictment'. Only Starke J did not express a narrow view of the scope of s. 80, and that was because he did not mention s. 80 at all.

Section 80 was discussed in obiter, although it was not argued by counsel, in *R v. Federal Court of Bankruptcy; Ex parte Lowenstein* (1938) 59 CLR 556. Latham CJ and McTiernan JJ stated that *R v. Archdall* was good authority and should be followed. On the other hand, Dixon and Evatt JJ joined in a famous dissent. Quoting the paraphrase of s. 80 by Higgins J in *R v. Archdall*, they continued, at pp. 581–2:

> It is a queer intention to ascribe to a Constitution; for it supposes that the concern of the framers of the provision was not to ensure that no one should be held guilty of a serious offence against the laws of the Commonwealth except by the verdict of a jury, but to prevent a procedural solecism, namely, the use of an indictment in cases where the legislature might think fit to authorize the court itself to pass on guilt or innocence of the prisoner. There is high authority for the proposition that 'the Constitution is not to be mocked.' A cynic might, perhaps, suggest the possibility that sec 80 was drafted in mockery; that its language was carefully chosen so that the guarantee it appeared on the surface to give should be in truth illusory. No court could countenance such a suggestion.[46]

This passage, particularly the charge that a 'cynic might ... suggest ... that sec 80 was drafted in mockery' resonates throughout the case law on express and implied rights. It

---

44 *R v. Bernasconi* at 637.
45 *R v. Bernasconi* at 637. Compare the importance attached to s. 80 by Isaacs J in *New South Wales v. Commonwealth (Wheat Case)* (1915) 20 CLR 54 at 90.
46 Compare Pannam at 6: 'With the greatest of respect to their Honours it might be said that one need not be a cynic but merely an historian to observe that the phrase "the trial on indictment" was inserted in s. 80 for the very purpose of producing the result they regarded as a "mockery" '.

has been powerfully evoked by judges such as Murphy and Deane JJ.[47] It may have its origins in the judgment of Gavan Duffy and Rich JJ in *R v. Snow* (1915) 20 CLR 315 at 365, where they suggested that if s. 80 left to the Court 'the right to control at its pleasure the verdict of the jury', s. 80 would indeed be a '"mockery, a delusion and a snare"'.

Dixon and Evatt JJ went on to argue that s. 80 should be given a substantive meaning. It should guarantee the right to trial by jury where there is a 'trial on indictment', with this being a constitutional issue to be determined by the High Court rather than a matter for manipulation by the federal Parliament. They found that a 'trial on indictment' has two elements: first, at p. 583, 'that some authority constituted under the law to represent the public interest for the purpose took the responsibility of the step which put the accused on his trial';[48] second, at p. 583, that the offender be liable 'to a term of imprisonment or to some graver form of punishment'.

The narrow interpretation of s. 80 expressed in *R v. Archdall* and *Ex parte Lowenstein* has held good ever since. In *Zarb v. Kennedy* (1968) 121 CLR 283, a person sentenced to two years imprisonment for refusing to present himself for military service, without the benefit of a jury trial, was unsuccessful in invoking s. 80 to overturn his conviction. The seven-member Court unanimously affirmed the interpretation of s. 80 laid down in *R v. Archdall* and *Ex parte Lowenstein*. Barwick CJ confirmed the prediction of Isaacs J that under s. 80 even someone charged with murder could be tried without a jury, stating at p. 294, 'in my opinion, the proposition that the Parliament is unable to provide that any offence shall be tried summarily is untenable'. Barwick CJ, like the other members of the Court, regarded the interpretation of s. 80 as being 'long settled'.[49]

In *Zarb v. Kennedy*, and in other decisions such as *Sachter v. Attorney-General (Cth)* (1954) 94 CLR 86, *Li Chia Hsing v. Rankin* (1978) 141 CLR 182, and *Kingswell v. The Queen* (1985) 159 CLR 264,[50] a majority of the High Court endorsed the idea that s. 80 allows the Commonwealth to itself determine which offences shall be tried by jury. Accordingly, in the words of Barwick CJ in *Spratt v. Hermes* (1965) 114 CLR 226 at 244, 'What might have been thought to be a great constitutional guarantee has been discovered to be a mere procedural provision'. However, the course of decisions on s. 80 has not been without its opponents. Drawing heavily from the dissent of Dixon and Evatt JJ in *Ex parte Lowenstein*, Murphy and Deane JJ have sharply criticised the interpretation adopted by the High Court.

In *Li Chia Hsing v. Rankin*, while a majority of the Court affirmed the narrow reading of s. 80 that made it largely redundant, Murphy J argued, at p. 198, that the section should be read as 'a guarantee of a fundamental right to trial by jury in criminal cases (at least in serious ones)'.[51] By this he meant that where the accused is charged with an offence that carries a term of imprisonment, Dixon and Evatt JJ's interpretation of s. 80 entitles the accused to the benefit of a trial by jury.

---

47   See, for example, *Attorney-General (Vic); Ex rel Black v. Commonwealth (DOGS Case)* (1981) 146 CLR 559 at 633 per Murphy J; *Polyukhovich v. Commonwealth (War Crimes Act Case)* (1991) 172 CLR 501 at 607 per Deane J.

48   *R v. Archdall* at 583.

49   *Zarb v. Kennedy* at 294.

50   The issues litigated in this decision are discussed in J. Willis, 'To What Extent is s. 235 of the Customs Act 1901–1975 (Cth) Invalid as Contravening s 80 of the Constitution?' (1978) 52 *Australian Law Journal* 502.

51   See also *Beckwith v. The Queen* (1976) 135 CLR 569 at 585 per Murphy J.

While a majority of the Court in *Kingswell v. The Queen* again regarded the interpretation of s. 80 as being settled, Deane J dissented. In a detailed and lengthy judgment, he argued that s. 80 should be given a substantive interpretation reflecting the status of trial by jury as a fundamental component of the justice system in Australia at least since the inception of the Constitution, and indeed in England since the fourteenth century. With one qualification, Deane J adopted the interpretation of s. 80 proposed by Dixon and Evatt JJ in *Ex parte Lowenstein*. While they had argued that s. 80 applies wherever an offence carries a term of imprisonment, Deane J argued that the section only applies where the offence carries a term of imprisonment of more than 12 months. He justified this difference on the basis that, at the time of federation, legislation in force in England and the Australian colonies commonly enabled less serious offences carrying terms of imprisonment of not more than one year to be tried summarily. In reaching a substantive interpretation of s. 80, Deane J distinguished the results in earlier cases, either on the basis that they had concerned offences carrying periods of imprisonment of not more than one year, or on other grounds. Brennan J also dissented in *Kingswell v. The Queen*, although on a different basis that did not deny the findings in *R v. Archdall* and *Ex parte Lowenstein*. He held that s. 80 invalidates a law that establishes, for an offence prosecuted on indictment, liability to a greater maximum penalty according to findings of fact by a judge.

The current interpretation of s. 80 as a 'mere procedural provision' is far from satisfactory. The interpretation does not rest on a considered view of s. 80, but on the authority of *R v. Archdall* and *Ex parte Lowenstein*. In *R v. Archdall*, a conclusion as to the effect of s. 80 was stated without any reasons being given, and in *Ex parte Lowenstein* any discussion was obiter and was evenly balanced between Latham CJ and McTiernan J, on one hand, and Dixon and Evatt JJ on the other.[52] In any event, the conclusion stated by Latham CJ and McTiernan J in *Ex parte Lowenstein* rested on the authority of the first case. The current view of s. 80, while apparently being the settled interpretation, lacks a reasoned basis. Even if the current interpretation proves to be the better approach, and, despite the history of the provision, this has yet to be shown, the law on s. 80 should be amenable to reexamination. In *Street v. Queensland Bar Association* (1989) 168 CLR 461, the High Court recast the law on s. 117 and in doing so overruled earlier authority. Mason CJ stated at p. 489:

> The earlier decisions do not rest on a principle gradually worked out in a significant succession of cases. And the decisions have not been independently acted on in a manner or to an extent that works against reconsideration of them. Furthermore, there is in the present case an additional factor. The question at issue relates to an important provision in the Constitution dealing with individual rights central to federation. The earlier decisions placed an incorrect interpretation on it. The Court has a responsibility to set the matter right.[53]

The same could be said of s. 80.

---

52   In *Ex parte Lowenstein* at 573, Rich J stated 'I agree that the questions submitted by the special case should be answered in the manner stated by the Chief Justice'. He did not state that he agreed with the obiter expressed by Latham CJ on a point not argued or arising out of the questions needing to be answered.

53   See also *Street* at 588 per McHugh J.

The narrow interpretation of s. 80 has been accepted by a majority of the High Court for several decades. It might have been thought that this would preclude s. 80 from acting as a significant restriction on governmental power. As Gibbs CJ, Wilson, and Dawson JJ stated in *Kingswell v. The Queen*, at p. 276, 'The fact that s. 80 has been given an interpretation which deprives it of much substantial effect provides a reason for refusing to import into the section restrictions on the legislative power which it does not express'. However, this has not proved to be the case. While the Court has allowed the Commonwealth to pick and choose when an accused may receive a jury trial, the Court has laid down stringent guidelines for those circumstances when a jury trial is set down. The little leeway given to the Commonwealth to shape the concept of the jury trial sits in contrast to the fact that the Court's interpretation allows the Commonwealth to freely abrogate a person's ability to be judged by his or her peers.

The development of the concept of 'trial by jury' in s. 80 has its roots in a decision handed down at the time of *R v. Bernasconi* (1915) 19 CLR 629, which was the first High Court decision to indicate that s. 80 was to be construed as a 'mere procedural provision'. In *R v. Snow* (1915) 20 CLR 315, three of the six judges hearing the matter, Griffith CJ, Gavan Duffy, and Rich JJ, suggested that where a trial is held under s. 80, the provision prevents a court from setting aside on appeal a verdict of not guilty, even where that verdict was at the direction of the trial judge. Gavan Duffy and Rich JJ stated, at p. 365, that in providing for trial by jury, s. 80 requires that 'persons tried shall have all the benefits incidental to a trial by jury'. Griffith CJ argued in the same vein, stating, at p. 323, that s. 80 'ought *primá facie* to be construed as an adoption of the institution of "trial by jury" with all that was connoted by the phrase in constitutional law and in the common law of England'.

In *Brown v. The Queen* (1986) 160 CLR 171, the Court considered s. 7 of the *Juries Act 1927* (SA), which allowed an accused to elect to be tried without a jury for certain offences. The provision applied to offences under Commonwealth law due to s. 68 of the *Judiciary Act 1903* (Cth). Brennan, Deane, and Dawson JJ, with Gibbs CJ and Wilson J dissenting, held that s. 7 was inapplicable to Commonwealth indictable offences, as it contravened s. 80. In finding that the jury trial specified by s. 80 could not be waived by an accused, Brennan, Deane, and Dawson JJ emphasised the mandatory language of s. 80 in its requirement that a jury trial be held for indictable offences. Their conclusion rested on a characterisation of s. 80 as being 'for the benefit of the community as a whole as well as for the benefit of the particular accused'[54] and part of 'the community's guarantee of sound administration of criminal justice'.[55] In dissent, Gibbs CJ and Wilson J viewed the guarantee of a jury trial under s. 80 as being 'directed to effectively securing to an accused person presented for trial on indictment the right to have the general issue between him and the Crown determined by the verdict of a jury'.[56] Applying authority to the effect that a statutory right can be waived by the person for whose benefit it is granted, they found that an accused could be given the ability to waive his or her right to a jury trial without contravening s. 80. Gibbs CJ and Wilson J were fortified in their dissent by decisions of the United States Supreme Court that the guarantee of trial by

---

54 *Brown v. The Queen* at 201 per Deane J.
55 *Brown v. The Queen* at 197 per Brennan J.
56 *Brown v. The Queen* at 190 per Wilson J.

jury in Article III, s. 2 of the United States Constitution could be waived by an accused.[57] They found that to deny the accused the right to waive the right to a jury trial under s. 80 would be, in the words of Frankfurter J of the United States Supreme Court, 'to imprison a man in his privileges and call it the Constitution'.[58]

The High Court again adopted a rigid view of the requirements of a jury trial held under s. 80 in *Cheatle v. The Queen* (1993) 177 CLR 541. Section 57(1) of the South Australian Juries Act enabled a judge to accept a majority verdict: that is, the verdict of 10, or 11, out of 12 jurors. In a joint unanimous judgment, the Court held that unanimity is an essential element of a jury trial held under s. 80[59] and thus that the provision could not apply to trials on indictment for Commonwealth offences. Citing *R v. Snow*, the joint judgment found that the essential features of 'trial by jury' in s. 80 could be derived from the common law, and, at p. 550, that 'the common law has, since the fourteenth century, consistently and unequivocally insisted on the requirement of unanimity'. The requirement for unanimity was also supported by decisions in England, the USA, and Australia, and by considerations of principle, most importantly, 'a fundamental thesis of our criminal law, namely, that a person accused of a crime should be given the benefit of any reasonable doubt'.[60]

Interestingly, the Court took care to reject the notion that 'trial by jury' under s. 80 incorporates the common law aspects by which, in 1900, women and unpropertied persons were excluded from jury service.[61] The judgment stated, at p. 560, that it would be 'absurd' to require, by parity of reasoning, that women and unpropertied persons be similarly excluded today from a jury trial held under s. 80. In fact, the Court stated, without further elaboration, at p. 561, 'To the contrary, in contemporary Australia, the exclusion of females and unpropertied persons would itself be inconsistent with such a requirement'.

Other Courts have heard arguments similar to that in *Brown* and *Cheatle* as to the essential requirements of a 'trial by jury' held under s. 80. In *Brownlee v. The Queen* (1997) 142 ALR 590, the New South Wales Court of Criminal Appeal found that a jury constituted under s. 80 could consist of 10, rather than 12 members. Similarly, in *Ah Poh Wai v. The Queen* (1995) 132 ALR 708, the Western Australian Court of Criminal Appeal held that the use of a reserve juror to replace another juror after a trial had begun did not conflict with an essential element of the jury trial. In *R v. Su* [1997] 1 VR 1 at 20, the Court of Appeal of the Supreme Court of Victoria held that the right to a trial by jury under s. 80 incorporates the notion that 'the jury should be representative of the wider community and randomly selected'. The Court found that the practice of police providing the prosecution with a list of potential jurors with 'non-disqualifying convictions' for use in the jury selection process did not breach s. 80.

---

57 *Patton v. United States* 281 US 276 (1930); *Adams v. US; Ex rel McCann* 317 US 269 (1942); *Singer v. United States* 380 US 24 (1965).
58 *Adams v. United States; Ex rel McCann* at 280.
59 This was also the view adopted by H.V. Evatt, 'The Jury System in Australia' (1936) 10 (Supplement) *Australian Law Journal* 49 at 64.
60 *Cheatle v. The Queen* at 553.
61 See the criticism levied at this approach by J. Goldsworthy, 'Originalism in Constitutional Interpretation' (1997) 25 *Federal Law Review* 1.

Decisions that constitutionalise aspects of trial by jury under s. 80 hold greater scope to protect civil liberties than yet realised. It might be that a jury trial under s. 80 imports not only requirements as to the makeup and operation of the jury itself but can also extend into other aspects of the trial process.[62] For example, if a trial by jury under s. 80 requires that an accused receive a 'fair trial', this may preclude the admission of certain evidence or require that an accused have adequate representation.[63] Acting against the expansion of s. 80 in this direction is the decision of the High Court in *Sorby v. Commonwealth* (1983) 152 CLR 281. In that case, a majority of the Court applied *Huddart, Parker & Co. Pty Ltd v. Moorehead* (1909) 8 CLR 330 to hold that the privilege against self-incrimination is not a necessary part of a jury trial held under s. 80.[64] Gibbs CJ went further in obiter, stating, at p. 298, 'The Parliament can, in relation to a trial by jury, alter the rules of evidence, or the rules relating to the onus of proof'. In any event, even if the Court were to expand on this aspect of s. 80, the Parliament would have the power to negate this by providing that trials were to be tried by judge alone, unless such limitations could be based in an independent implication arising from Chapter III of the Constitution (see Chapter 8).

Freedom of religion

Section 116 of the Constitution provides that Commonwealth laws are unable to abrogate certain religious freedoms. It is not expressed to limit the power of the states. Here lies a hint as to the purpose of the provision (see Chapter 2), and perhaps also to the placement of s. 116, a provision restricting Commonwealth and not state power, in 'Chapter V—The States' of the Constitution. Section 116 was inserted to ensure that the power to legislate about religious matters remained with the state Parliaments. This reflected fears expressed at the 1897–98 Convention that the reference to 'Almighty God' in the preamble to the Constitution might enable the Commonwealth to legislate on matters of religion.[65] Accordingly, the primary object of s. 116 was not to protect human rights. Indeed, at the Convention debates, concern was expressed that the provision might allow people, such as Seventh Day Adventists, to 'indulge in extraordinary practices', so that 'we may have all the theatres and all the music halls in Australia open on Sunday'.[66] Despite its drafting history, High Court interpretation of s. 116, unlike that of sections 41 and 80 of the Constitution, has not been carefully narrowed in accordance with the perceived intentions of the framers. However, this has not meant that s. 116 has been given a robust interpretation. There have simply been other factors at work that have meant that s. 116 has been given little work to do.

The guarantee of religious freedom in s. 116 is modelled on equivalent provisions in the United States Constitution. Article VI of that instrument states that 'no religious

---

62 *Polyukhovich v. Commonwealth (War Crimes Act Case)* (1991) 172 CLR 501 at 615 per Deane J.
63 See *Dietrich v. The Queen* (1992) 177 CLR 292.
64 Compare *Sorby v. Commonwealth* at 313 per Murphy J; *Hammond v. Commonwealth* (1982) 152 CLR 188 at 201 per Murphy J. See also *Yager v. The Queen* (1977) 139 CLR 28 at 51–2 per Murphy J.
65 *Convention Debates*, vol. 4, *Melbourne 1898*, pp. 654, 656, 663 per Mr Higgins.
66 *Convention Debates*, vol. 5, *Melbourne 1898*, p. 1779. See also *Convention Debates*, vol. 4, *Melbourne 1898*, p. 664 per Sir Joseph Abbott.

Test shall ever be required as a Qualification to any Office or public Trust under the United States', while the First Amendment provides, 'Congress shall make no law respecting an establishment of religion, or prohibiting the free exercise thereof'. The main difference between these provisions and s. 116 is that s. 116 contains an extra guarantee, that relating to 'religious observance'. Section 116 thus embodies four distinct guarantees. However, neither individually nor collectively do these limitations on Commonwealth power amount to a requirement of separation of Church and State. The first three guarantees prohibit the Commonwealth from making any law 'for establishing any religion', 'for imposing any religious observance' or 'for prohibiting the free exercise of any religion'. The fourth guarantee states that 'no religious test shall be required as a qualification for any office or public trust under the Commonwealth'. There have been very few decisions of the High Court on s. 116. The decisions to date have dealt only with the first and third[67] guarantees. Section 116 has never been successfully invoked to strike down a law.[68] Each time the High Court has considered an argument based on s. 116, the argument has failed.

The first decision of the High Court to deal with s. 116 was *Krygger v. Williams* (1912) 15 CLR 366. The *Defence Act 1903* (Cth) introduced a system of compulsory peacetime military training. Under s. 135 'every person who in any year, without lawful excuse, evades or fails to render the personal service required by this Part shall be guilty of an offence.' Edgar Krygger was charged with failure to render service under s. 135. In a hearing before a magistrate, Krygger stated at pp. 367–88:

> I decline to render military service because it is opposed to the word of God … Attendance at drill is against my conscience and the will of God … I put military training on the same footing as gambling. To me it is as much a sin in the sight of God as gambling, racing, or any other sin … If I went to military training I would be prohibited from the free exercise of my religion … Sixty-four hours drill a year would prohibit the free exercise of my religion.

When the matter came before the High Court consisting of Griffith CJ and Barton J, the argument that s. 135 of the Defence Act breached s. 116 was given short shrift. Griffith CJ found, at p. 369, that 'To require a man to do a thing which has nothing at all to do with religion is not prohibiting him from a free exercise of religion'.[69] The key factor in the decision was that the law did not target religious expression but was a law of general application. Griffith CJ continued, at p. 369: 'It may be that a law requiring a man to do an act which his religion forbids would be objectionable on moral grounds, but it does not come within the prohibition of sec 116'. The fact that s. 143(3) of the Defence Act also provided an exception whereby 'all persons liable to be trained … who are forbidden by the doctrines of their religion to bear arms shall so far as possible

---

67   In *R v. Winneke; Ex parte Gallagher* (1982) 152 CLR 211 at 227–9, Murphy J suggested that the *Royal Commissions Act 1902* (Cth) breached the third guarantee in its provision for the taking of an oath or affirmation.

68   The provision has, however, been applied in disputes involving the custody of a child. See, for example, *Evers v. Evers* (1972) 19 FLR 296 at 302–3.

69   Compare the obiter statement of Higgins J in *Judd v. McKeon* (1926) 38 CLR 380 at 387: 'I might add that, in my opinion, if abstention from voting were part of the elector's religious duty, as it appeared to the mind of the elector, this would be a valid and sufficient reason for his failure to vote (sec 116 of the Constitution)'. It is not clear that this statement can be reconciled with the approach of Griffith CJ and Barton J in *Krygger*.

be allotted to non-combatant duties' reinforced this conclusion. Barton J reached the same conclusion, stating, at p. 373, that 'this objection is as thin as anything of the kind that has come before us'.

The next decision on s. 116 was *Adelaide Company of Jehovah's Witnesses Inc v. Commonwealth (Jehovah's Witnesses Case)* (1943) 67 CLR 116, which was heard by five members of the High Court. Regulation 3 of the National Security (Subversive Associations) Regulations 1940 (Cth) provided that: 'Any body corporate or unincorporate, the existence of which the Governor-General … declares to be in his opinion, prejudicial to the defence of the Commonwealth or the efficient prosecution of the war, is hereby declared to be unlawful'. Once an association was declared unlawful, it was dissolved under the Regulations and could have its property occupied and forfeited. The Regulations were described by Starke J, at p. 154, as being 'arbitrary, capricious and oppressive'. On 17 January 1941, the Governor-General made a declaration under reg. 3 in relation to the Adelaide Company of Jehovah's Witnesses Inc. That day, a Commonwealth officer attempted to occupy the Jehovah's Witnesses' Kingdom Hall in Adelaide. While the Regulations were held invalid by the High Court as being beyond the scope of the Commonwealth's defence power in s. 51(vi) of the Constitution, in part because of the impact of the Regulations on religious freedom,[70] the challenge based on s. 116 unanimously failed.

According to Rich J, at p. 148, 'In one sense the provision is very wide and in another narrow'. This accurately summed up the Court's approach to s. 116. While 'religion' for the purposes of s. 116 was construed to be extremely inclusive, the protection afforded to such 'religions' was minimal. Indeed, the latter conclusion flowed naturally from the former. In the leading judgment of the Court, Latham CJ set out some of the practices that during periods of human history have been regarded as religious, including the 'essentially evil and wicked', such as 'human sacrifice or animal sacrifice'.[71] By including such practices within the scope of s. 116, he was able to point out that the protection offered by s. 116 to the 'free exercise of any religion' could not be absolute. This was particularly true where the free exercise of religious belief would threaten ordered government under the Constitution.

Latham CJ supported his findings as to the limited protection afforded by s. 116 by reference to United States authorities. After stating, at p. 127, that the First Amendment to the United States Constitution is 'very similar' to s. 116, Latham CJ established that the interpretation of the First Amendment had not produced an absolute freedom of religious expression, and that this had been established by the United States Supreme Court by the time that the Australian Constitution had come into effect. He then went on to accept as applicable to s. 116 a test that he derived from the United States case law. Under this approach, a law would infringe s. 116 if a court is able to determine that 'freedom of religion has been *unduly* infringed by some particular legislative provision'.[72] Under this test, the 'exercise of any religion' would not be excepted from laws of general application such as 'the criminal law dealing with the conduct of citizens generally'.[73] While the criminal law was a clear case of a law that did not infringe s. 116,

---

70 *Jehovah's Witnesses Case* at 165 per Williams J.
71 *Jehovah's Witnesses Case* at 125.
72 *Jehovah's Witnesses Case* at 131 (emphasis in original).
73 *Jehovah's Witnesses Case* at 131.

Latham CJ did not explore the more difficult position of other laws of general application, such as, for example, a law forbidding any person from wearing a turban. In any event, Latham, CJ did not need to apply the test derived from the United States authorities. Taking into account the apparent purpose of the Regulations, he found, at p. 132, that the Regulations could be characterised as 'a law to protect the existence of the community' rather than 'a law for prohibiting the free exercise of any religion'.[74] For the other members of the Court, the fact that s. 116 could not be an absolute guarantee meant that the provision was not infringed by a law which enabled the Commonwealth to suppress persons and bodies prejudicial to the defence of the Commonwealth, or, in the words of Rich J, at p. 150, 'dangerous to the common weal'.[75]

It will only be in very rare cases, and indeed there have not been any since the decision in the *Jehovah's Witnesses Case* in 1943, that the test devised by Latham CJ might be applied to strike down a law for breaching the free exercise of religion guarantee in s. 116. This is because legislation that specifically targets and penalises religious practice is extremely rare, particularly when the Parliament may be able to achieve the same result by enacting a law that is apparently of general application. It will be difficult to demonstrate a breach of s. 116 in any case where the relevant law is a law of general application. A law of general application does not, at least on its face, target the exercise of religion, and thus will be unlikely to be a law 'unduly' trenching on the freedom. This is reflected in the approach recently developed by the United States Supreme Court in *Employment Div, Dept of Human Resources of Ore v. Smith* 494 US 872 (1990), in which it was held that the First Amendment does not relieve an individual of the obligation to comply with a law that incidentally forbids the performance of an act that his religious belief requires if the law is not specifically directed to religious practice and is otherwise constitutional when applied to others who engage in the act for non-religious reasons. This approach is clearly designed to uphold neutral laws of general application that may have the incidental effect of interfering with the exercise of religion. It may be that under the test put forward by Latham CJ a law of general application will only breach the s. 116 guarantee if it is clear that it is nevertheless directed, as a matter of its substantive operation, at particular religious practices. This would depend on a court being willing to examine the substance rather than merely the form of a law, a course which the High Court recently adopted as to other guarantees in *Cole v. Whitfield* (1988) 165 CLR 360 (as to s. 92—see Chapter 6), and *Street v. Queensland Bar Association* (1989) 168 CLR 461 (as to s. 117).

An impediment to a robust application of the 'free exercise' clause in s. 116 is the broad interpretation given to the meaning of 'religion' for the purposes of that section. While 'evil and wicked' practices are regarded as 'religious', this will need to be taken into account in interpreting s. 116 so as to ensure that such practices are not given constitutional authority. In *Church of The New Faith v. Commissioner of Pay-Roll Tax (Vic)* (1983) 154 CLR 120, the High Court reaffirmed a wide understanding of what

---

74 This use of either/or characterisation has overtones of the similar approach subsequently applied by Latham CJ in *Melbourne Corporation v. Commonwealth* (1947) 74 CLR 31 at 60–2. This approach has now been discredited. See, for example, *Murphyores Incorporated Pty Ltd v. Commonwealth* (1976) 136 CLR 1.

75 See also p. 155 per Starke J ('The constitution provision does not protect unsociable actions or actions subversive of the community itself.'), at 157 per McTiernan J, and at 159–61 per Williams J.

constitutes 'religion'. Although the case raised the issue of whether Scientology, or the Church of New Faith, was a religion for the purposes of the *Pay-roll Tax Act* 1971 (Vic), and thus whether it could claim an exemption from pay-roll tax, the issues were obviously relevant to interpretation of s. 116. Indeed, despite the wide definition adopted for the purposes of the Pay-roll Tax Act, Wilson and Deane JJ suggested, at p. 173, that there might be grounds 'for attributing a wider meaning to the word "religion" in the context of a constitutional guarantee'.

The Court unanimously held that Scientology was a religion. In doing so, the Court gave 'religion' an extremely wide definition. Mason ACJ and Brennan J, at p. 136, identified two criteria:

first, belief in a supernatural Being, Thing or Principle; and second, the acceptance of canons of conduct in order to give effect to that belief, though canons of conduct which offend against the ordinary laws are outside the area of any immunity, privilege or right conferred on the grounds of religion.

Wilson and Deane JJ set out five indicia, at p. 174, none of which was necessarily determinative:

One of the more important indicia of 'a religion' is that the particular collection of ideas and/or practices involves belief in the supernatural, that is to say, belief that reality extends beyond that which is capable of perception by the senses. If that be absent, it is unlikely that one has 'a religion'. Another is that the ideas relate to man's nature and place in the universe and his relation to things supernatural. A third is that the ideas are accepted by adherents as requiring or encouraging them to observe particular standards or codes of conduct or to participate in specific practices having supernatural significance. A fourth is that, however loosely knit and varying in beliefs and practices adherents may be, they constitute an identifiable group or identifiable groups. A fifth, and perhaps more controversial, indicium … is that the adherents themselves see the collection of ideas and/or practices as constituting a religion.

On the other hand, Murphy J did not attempt to define 'religion', finding, at p. 150, that, while Scientology was a 'religion', 'to determine what religion is … poses a threat to religious freedom'.[76]

Krygger v. Williams and the *Jehovah's Witnesses Case* concerned the third guarantee in s. 116 relating to the 'free exercise of any religion'. *Attorney-General (Vic); Ex rel Black v. Commonwealth (DOGS Case)* (1981) 146 CLR 559 instead dealt with the first guarantee by which the Commonwealth cannot 'make any law for establishing any religion'. The members of the Defence of Government Schools organisation sued through the Attorney-General of Victoria seeking a finding that federal funding to church schools breached s. 116. They argued that s. 116 prevented the Commonwealth from making any law providing recognition, aid, or support to a particular religion or religions generally. Alternatively, it was argued that s. 116 prevented the Commonwealth from giving preference to one religion over another. While it was held that grants made to the states by the Commonwealth under s. 96 of the Constitution are subject to s. 116, the argument that s. 116 was breached was rejected. Murphy J dissented in applying United States authorities to find, at p. 624, that s. 116 prohibits the Commonwealth

---

76 Murphy J reached a similar conclusion in *Attorney-General (NSW) v. Grant* (1976) 135 CLR 587 at 612.

from 'non-preferential sponsoring of or aiding religion'. He argued, at p. 632, that an 'essential condition of religious liberty is that religion be unaided by the Commonwealth'.

The plaintiffs relied heavily on decisions on the 'establishment clause' in the First Amendment to the United States Constitution, particularly the decision of Black J, delivering the opinion of the United States Supreme Court, in *Everson v. Board of Education* 330 US 1 at 15–16 (1947):[77]

> The 'establishment of religion' clause of the First Amendment means at least this: Neither a state nor the Federal Government can set up a church. Neither can pass laws which aid one religion, aid all religions, or prefer one religion over another. Neither can force nor influence a person to go to or to remain away from church against his will or force him to profess a belief or disbelief in any religion. No person can be punished for entertaining or professing religious beliefs or disbeliefs, for church attendance or non-attendance. No tax in any amount, large or small, can be levied to support any religious activities or institutions, whatever they may be called, or whatever form they may adopt to teach or practice religion. Neither a state nor the Federal Government can, openly or secretly, participate in the affairs of any religious organizations or groups and vice versa. In the words of Jefferson, the clause against establishment of religion by law was intended to erect 'a wall of separation between Church and State'.

However, the majority in the *DOGS Case* found, in contrast to the approach of Latham CJ in the *Jehovah's Witnesses Case*, that United States authorities provided little, if any, assistance. The reason lay in the differences the majority identified between s. 116 and the First Amendment. Although the latter provision differed from s. 116 in context and history (the former provision not being located within a Bill of Rights or within the same historical tradition), the more significant problem was differences in wording. While s. 116 prohibits the Commonwealth from making any law '*for* establishing any religion', the First Amendment prohibits Congress from making any law '*respecting* an establishment of religion'. This led Barwick CJ to comment, at p. 579, on the 'radically different' language of the provisions. 'For' was seen as providing a significantly lesser operation than 'respecting', meaning that s. 116 was to be interpreted more narrowly than the First Amendment, even though s. 116 referred to '*establishing any* religion' rather than merely '*an establishment of* religion'.

Consistent with this approach, and on the basis of historical analysis,[78] the majority gave a narrow definition to 'establishing' in s. 116. Barwick CJ found, at p. 582, that 'establishing a religion involves its adoption as an institution of the Commonwealth, part of the Commonwealth "establishment"'. Gibbs J found, at p. 604, that the phrase meant to confer on 'a particular religion or religious body the position of a state (or national) religion or church'. Mason and Wilson JJ both found that 'establishing' entitled recognition of a religion 'as a national institution' of the state'.[79] Aickin J agreed

---

77 See N. O'Neill, 'Constitutional Human Rights in Australia' (1987) 17 *Federal Law Review* 85 at 104–8.

78 Compare R. Ely, 'The View from the Statute: Statutory Establishments of Religion in England Ca 1300 to Ca 1900' (1986) 8 *University of Tasmania Law Review* 225, who argues that the answers reached by most of the members of the High Court in the *DOGS Case* are historically flawed.

79 *DOGS Case* at 612 per Mason J, at 653 per Wilson J.

with Gibbs and Mason JJ. Stephen J took a slightly wider view in arguing, at p. 610, that the guarantee would be breached by setting up a national church or by 'the favouring of one church over another'. These definitions meant that s. 116 was not breached by a federal law that provided financial assistance to church schools.

The Court gave some hints as to how s. 116 might be interpreted more generally. These hints provided little encouragement for a wide operation of the provision. It was found that the use of 'for' before the first three guarantees in s. 116 indicated that s. 116 invalidated laws having the prohibited purpose.[80] However, Barwick CJ argued, at p. 579, that for a law to breach s. 116 it must have the prohibited purpose as 'its express and, as I think, single purpose'. This purpose was to be gleaned from the law at the time of its making, and not from the operation or administration of the law. In these circumstances, a challenge to a law would need to show that the express words, or form of the law, as opposed to the substantive operation of the law, infringed one of the first three guarantees in s. 116. Under this approach, it would be almost impossible for s. 116 to invalidate a law of general application, the impact of such laws being only ascertainable by examining how the law has operated in practice.

The *DOGS Case* raised an issue of general importance to the interpretation of constitutional rights. While decisions of the High Court, such as that of O'Connor J in *Jumbunna Coal Mine NL v. Victorian Coal Miners' Association* (1908) 6 CLR 309 at 367–8 (see Chapter 4), have established that the Court should be generous in its construction of Commonwealth power, such decisions have rarely been applied to broadly interpret restrictions on Commonwealth power. Indeed, as the provisions dealt with in this Chapter show, the experience has been to treat such provisions in the converse way, that is, to construe them narrowly (see Chapter 9). This distinction between provisions conferring power and those restraining it was not made explicit in the many cases in which limitations have been narrowly interpreted. The *DOGS Case* is different in that members of the majority made clear their view that, as a rule, limitations on power should be treated differently from provisions conferring power. Wilson J stated, at pp. 652–3:

> The plaintiffs' plea for a broad construction overlooks the fact that we are dealing with a clause which does not grant power, but denies it. While it is true that a constitutional grant of plenary legislative power should be construed with all the generality which the words used will admit, carrying with it whatever is incidental to the subject matter of the power, the same is not true of a provision which proscribes power.

Mason J stated, at p. 615, that while a grant of legislative power might be applied over time to new things and events, the same was not true of limitations. These, he argued, must be applied according to their meaning as at 1900, as there was 'no reason for enlarging its scope of operation beyond the mischief to which it was directed'. Gibbs J reasoned in a similar manner. In response to the argument that s. 116 should be liberally construed, Gibbs J found that the language of the provision could not bear an expanded interpretation. He went on to say, at p. 603:

> In any case, the establishment clause imposes a fetter on legislative power, and unlike the words which forbid the making of any law prohibiting the free exercise of any religion, does

---

80   For an example of how this approach can lead to s. 116 being narrowly applied, see *Minister for Immigration and Ethnic Affairs v. Lebanese Moslem Association* (1987) 17 FCR 373.

not do so for the purpose of protecting a fundamental human right; indeed, the purpose for which it was inserted in the Constitution remains obscure.[81]

The *DOGS Case* demonstrated the willingness of the High Court to narrowly construe limitations on Commonwealth power that might protect rights. This was true even in the judgment of Barwick CJ, who had argued, at p. 577, that he could

> find no reason why the words of the Constitution should not be given their full effect, whether they be expressed in a facultative or prohibitory provision. In particular, in this case, the emphatic universality of the language of s. 116 seems to me to brook no restraint sought to be imposed by any such doctrine as the submission propounds.

Despite rejecting Wilson J's approach, Barwick CJ still adopted the same pedantic construction of the guarantee as Wilson J, an interpretation that did not sit well with the broad scope Barwick CJ had given to Commonwealth powers in other decisions.[82] Moreover, Barwick CJ achieved this result by overstating the textual differences between the Australian and United States position. While Murphy J went too far in describing, at p. 632, these differences as 'trifles' and 'hair-splitting'—it being more onerous to show that a law is 'for' a particular object than that it 'respects' that same object—Barwick CJ went too far in the opposite direction in arguing, at p. 579, that the guarantees were 'radically different'.[83] Overall, whether it was explicit in the judgments or not, the majority in the *DOGS Case* made it clear that the policy of the Court was to reach for a wide construction of federal power, while simultaneously searching within the Court's traditional methods of constitutional interpretation for ways to narrowly construe provisions limiting that power.[84]

Kruger v. Commonwealth (1997) 190 CLR 1 involved a challenge to the *Aboriginals Ordinance 1918* (NT). This Ordinance authorised the forced removal of Aboriginal children in the Northern Territory from their families and tribal culture, to be brought up by adoptive or foster parents or in institutional homes. It was argued that the Ordinance was invalid under s. 116 because it was a law 'for prohibiting the free exercise of any religion'. This argument was unsuccessful. Two difficulties faced the plaintiffs. First, it was not clear that s. 116 limited the Commonwealth's territories power in s. 122 of the Constitution.[85] While Dixon CJ stated in *Lamshed v. Lake* (1958) 99 CLR 132 at 143 that he could not see any reason 'why s. 116 should not apply to laws made under s. 122', Gibbs J reached the opposite conclusion in the *DOGS Case*, at pp. 593–4.

---

81   See also p. 609 of the judgment, per Stephen J.

82   See, for example, Barwick CJ's interpretation of s. 51(xx), the Commonwealth's corporations power, in *Strickland v. Rocla Concrete Pipes Ltd (Concrete Pipes Case)* (1971) 124 CLR 468.

83   Compare C. L. Pannam, 'Travelling Section 116 with a US Road Map' (1963) 4 *Melbourne University Law Review* 41 at 41, who describes s. 116 as a 'fairly blatant piece of transcription' and as representing 'the ultimate of completely senseless copying'. However, at p. 81, Pannam recognises that there are 'significant differences' between the Australian and United States establishment clauses, though he particularly focuses upon the use of 'any religion' in s. 116 and 'of religion' in the First Amendment.

84   See S. McLeish, 'Making Sense of Religion and the Constitution: A Fresh Start for Section 116' (1992) 18 *Monash University Law Review* 207.

85   See F. D. Cumbrae-Stewart, 'Section 116 of the Constitution' (1946) 20 *Australian Law Journal* 207; H. T. Gibbs, 'Section 116 of the Constitution and the Territories of the Commonwealth' (1947) 20 *Australian Law Journal* 375; C. L. Pannam, 'Section 116 and the Federal Territories' (1961) 35 *Australian Law Journal* 209.

Kruger did not resolve the issue. Gaudron J found that s. 116 does limit territory laws, although she qualified this by stating, at p. 123, that 's 116 is directed to laws made by the Commonwealth, not laws enacted by the legislature of a self-governing territory'. While Toohey and Gummow JJ were strongly inclined to reach the same conclusion, Dawson J, with whom McHugh J agreed, found that s. 122 is not limited by s. 116. Dawson J based his conclusion on *R v. Bernasconi* (1915) 19 CLR 629, which found that s. 80 of the Constitution does not restrict s. 122. He stated, at p. 60: 'I do not think that it is possible while *R v. Bernasconi* stands to hold that s. 116 restricts s. 122. Nor do I think that the reasoning in *Lamshed v. Lake* is necessarily to be preferred to that in *R v. Bernasconi*'.

The second difficulty facing the plaintiffs was that the challenged provisions were expressed to be protective of aboriginal people. For example, s. 6(1) of the Ordinance provided:

> The Chief Protector shall be entitled at any time to undertake the care, custody, or control of any aboriginal or half-caste, if, in his opinion it is necessary or desirable in the interests of the aboriginal or half-caste for him to do so, and for that purpose may enter any premises where the aboriginal or half-caste is or is supposed to be, and may take him into his custody.

Moreover, the challenge was restricted to whether such provisions, on their face, infringed s. 116. The matter had not been the subject of findings of fact, nor were there agreed facts. The Court was thus left with the question of whether such provisions breached s. 116 in providing a power to be exercised in the 'interests' of Aboriginal people. It was not suprising that the Court was unable to conclude that s. 116 had been infringed.

In reaching this conclusion, members of the Court adopted the test developed in the *DOGS Case*: that is, 'To attract invalidity under s. 116, a law must have the purpose of achieving an object which s. 116 forbids'.[86] By 'purpose' was meant the object of the legislation rather than the underlying motive. In the absence of any evidence to the contrary, and in light of the expressed purpose of the law, the Ordinance was held to be valid. This conclusion was carefully constructed in that s. 116 was held not to have been breached 'as the matter has come before the Court'.[87]

Gaudron J was the only judge not prepared to find that s. 116 had not been breached. She instead found, at p. 132, that this could not 'presently be determined' as it was not possible on the evidence before her to ascertain whether the Ordinance was in breach of s. 116. She also went further than any other member of the Court in seeking to give s. 116 significant effect. This flowed from her view, at p. 131, in contrast to that expressed in the *DOGS Case* by Wilson J, of the 'need to construe constitutional guarantees liberally, even limited guarantees of the kind effected by s. 116'. She argued that s. 116 should be given a substantive interpretation whereby the provision would not merely strike down laws that on their face expressed a purpose of restricting religious expression, but also laws that operated to prevent the free exercise of religion. This meant that s. 116 might invalidate laws that were apparently neutral laws of general application.[88] Gaudron J also recognised, in contrast to the approach of Barwick CJ in

---

86 *Kruger* at 40 per Brennan CJ.
87 *Kruger* at 87 per Toohey J.
88 See also *Kruger* at 160 per Gummow J.

the *DOGS Case*, that a law could have more than one purpose, and that a law would infringe s. 116 where any one of its purposes was to limit the free exercise of religion.

On this latter point Gaudron J must surely be correct. The suggestion of Barwick CJ in the *DOGS Case* that a law might have a single purpose in breach of s. 116 mirrored his insistence in *Victoria v. Commonwealth (Payroll Tax Case)* (1971) 122 CLR 353 that a law would infringe the implied immunity of the states from Commonwealth laws if, on its true characterisation, 'the subject matter of the law is in substance the States or their powers or functions of government'.[89] This depended on his view that: 'The law must be on one or other of the subjects. It cannot be on both'.[90] The notion that a law might have a single identifiable character is reflected in other areas of the High Court's constitutional jurisprudence, such as in *R v. Barger* (1908) 6 CLR 41 and Latham CJ's decision in *Melbourne Corporation v. Commonwealth* (1947) 74 CLR 31. Such views have now been soundly rejected by the High Court in decisions such as *Fairfax v. Federal Commissioner of Taxation* (1965) 114 CLR 1, *Murphyores Incorporated Pty Ltd v. Commonwealth* (1976) 136 CLR 1, and *Northern Suburbs General Cemetery Reserve Trust v. Commonwealth* (1993) 176 CLR 555. As Stephen J recognised in *Actors and Announcers Equity Association v. Fontana Films Pty Ltd* (1982) 150 CLR 169 at 192, 'a law may possess a number of quite disparate characters'. Any search for the 'single character' or 'single purpose' of a law is flawed in that it will be an unusual case that a law can be characterised in this way.

The failure of the challenge based on s. 116 in the *Kruger* did not mean that the plaintiff's attempts to gain redress in respect of acts done under the Ordinance were at an end. Brennan CJ described the power conferred by s. 6 of the Ordinance as being 'a power which in terms is conferred to serve the interests of those whose care, custody or control might be undertaken. It is not a power to be exercised adversely to those individual interests'.[91] This meant that acts purportedly done under the Ordinance would be *ultra vires* if they were not consistent with the protective purpose expressed by the Ordinance. This was consistent with the view of Barwick CJ in the *DOGS Case*, though not of Gaudron J in *Kruger*, that s. 116 is directed to 'the *making* of law' and not 'the administration of a law'.[92]

Rights of out-of-state residents

At the 1890s Convention debates, Andrew Inglis Clark supported a provision that would have enshrined 'due process of law' as well as 'equal protection of [the] laws' in the Constitution. Ultimately, this proposal failed, and s. 117 was inserted in its place (see Chapter 2). Both s. 117 and the original proposal were drafted to protect rights attaching to Australian citizenship. As conceived in the 1890s, a citizen meant a 'subject of the Queen'. Although s. 117 'recognizes in express terms a common citizenship amongst the States',[93] it clearly lacks the vision or scope that motivated the original proposal.

---

89 *Payroll Tax Case* at 372.
90 *Payroll Tax Case* 373.
91 *Kruger* at 35–6.
92 *DOGS Case* at 580–1 (emphasis in original).
93 *Davies and Jones v. Western Australia* (1904) 2 CLR 29 at 52 per O'Connor J.

Section 117 is unlike the other express rights in the Constitution in that it does not have a close correlation with a right in the United States Constitution. The provision in the United States Constitution that comes closest, and which likewise fosters a coherent federal structure, is Article IV, s. 2, which provides: 'The Citizens of each State shall be entitled to all Privileges and Immunities of Citizens in the several States'.

The object of s. 117 is clear. It prohibits a state from imposing any disability or discrimination on a person on the basis of that person being resident in another state. It should be read with sections 51(ii) and 99. Section 51(ii) allows the Commonwealth to legislate with respect to 'Taxation; but so as not to discriminate between States or parts of States', [94] while s. 99 states that the Commonwealth 'shall not, by any law or regulation of trade, commerce, or revenue, give preference to one State or any part thereof over another State or any part thereof'. There is an important textual difference between s. 117 and these provisions. While sections 51(ii) and 99 are expressed to limit the Commonwealth's law-making power, s. 117 is not so limited. Indeed, in contrast to each of the express rights examined above (ss 41, 80, and 116), s. 117 directly confers a right on individuals. It does not mention laws of the Commonwealth or of the states, but grants to a 'subject of the Queen, resident in any State' the immunity then outlined. It is thus clear that s. 117 applies not only to Commonwealth laws, but also to state laws, and may have an unexplored effect on the common law should any rule of the common law infringe the guarantee. This last possibility is made clear by the High Court's decisions in *Theophanous v. Herald & Weekly Times Ltd* (1994) 182 CLR 104 and *Lange v. Australian Broadcasting Corporation* (1997) 189 CLR 520, where it was held that the Constitution is capable of overriding, or reshaping, inconsistent common law rules (see Chapter 7).

The unequivocal textual basis of s. 117 has not meant that the provision has been able to escape the restrictive interpretations given to other, less textually secure, constitutional rights. Like provisions such as s. 80, s. 117 was successfully euthanised by the High Court. However, unlike s. 80, the High Court has since recanted in favour of giving s. 117 a significant and meaningful operation.

The early decisions on s. 117 were not promising. In *Davies and Jones v. Western Australia* (1904) 2 CLR 29, the provision was interpreted in an extremely narrow and legalistic fashion. Edward Davies, a resident of Western Australia, died, leaving his possessions to his son, Alfred Davies, who was resident and domiciled in Queensland. Tax was payable on the 'real and personal estate of the deceased' under s. 86 of the *Administration Act 1903* (WA). However, s. 86 also provided that 'in so far as beneficial interests pass to persons *boná fide* residents of and domiciled in Western Australia … duty shall be calculated so as to charge only one half of the percentage on the property acquired by such person'. Section 86, in providing a privilege to 'persons *boná fide* residents of and domiciled in Western Australia', also subjected persons not falling into this category to discrimination, in that they were liable to pay double the rate of tax. It was argued in the High Court that this breached s. 117. This submission was unanimously rejected by Griffith CJ, Barton, and O'Connor JJ. While it was held that the granting of a privilege to a resident of a state and not to residents of other states would infringe s. 117,[95] s. 117

---

94 See also the Australian Constitution, s. 51(iii).
95 Compare *Henry v. Boehm* (1973) 128 CLR 482 at 488 per Barwick CJ, at 495–6 per Gibbs J.

nevertheless did not apply in this case. The Court found that s. 117 applied where the criterion for discrimination was residence, but that it did not apply where the criterion was not just residence, but residence *and* domicile. As O'Connor J stated, at p. 49, s. 117 does not apply where the discrimination 'arises from residence accompanied by some superadded condition'. This meant that s. 117 could be avoided by a state 'conferring special privileges on those of its own people who, in addition to residence within the State, fulfil some other substantial condition or requirement'.[96] Despite this legalistic approach, Griffith CJ did adopt a broad view of 'resident' in s. 117, stating, at p. 39, that it 'must be construed distributively, as applying to any kind of residence which a state may attempt to make a basis of discrimination'.

Davies and Jones was underpinned by the legal differences that were identified between the concepts of residence and domicile. These differences were emphasised to the extent that the significant overlap in fact between the concepts was obscured. Writing in 1906, two years after *Davies and Jones* was handed down, F. L. Stow argued:

> Now the bulk of the residents of a State are in fact domiciled there ... The effect, therefore, of the decision is that section 117 is practically abrogated. Any State legislature can work what discrimination it likes. It can simply say that persons domiciled in the other States shall be subject to any special disabilities it pleases, and this disability will attach, in spite of section 117, to the great bulk of the residents in the other States. The section is gone.[97]

Stow then commented that it was to be hoped 'that lovers of the Constitution' would seek to have the decision appealed to the Privy Council, where it would be determined whether 'section 117 is a real protection or is a mere delusion and sham'.[98]

In *Lee Fay v. Vincent* (1908) 7 CLR 389, the High Court again rejected an argument based on s. 117. Section 46 of the *Factories Act 1904* (WA) provided that 'no person of the Chinese or other Asiatic race' could be employed in a factory unless such a person was so employed on or immediately before 1 November 1903. Lee Fay, a Chinese factory owner resident in Western Australia, employed another Chinese man, Lee New. On 1 November 1903, Lee New had been employed in a factory in Victoria, where he had been resident at that time. Lee Fay was convicted under s. 46. He appealed to the High Court, where he argued that he was protected from prosecution by s. 117. Griffith CJ delivered the judgment of himself, Barton, and O'Connor JJ. The reliance on s. 117 was rejected, at p. 392, in three sentences:

> That section only applies to a person who, being resident in one State, is seeking to assert rights in another. In the present case the person in respect of whom the rights are asserted is a resident in Western Australia, not in another State, and the rights are asserted in Western Australia. The section has therefore no application.

This finding meant that s. 117 did not apply (1) where discrimination is based on past residence in another state, and (2) where a person is subject to a penalty because of a connection between that person and another person who is an interstate resident. Both conclusions are arguably supported by a literal reading of the text of s. 117,

---

96 *Davies and Jones v. Western Australia* at 53 per O'Connor J.
97 F. L. Stow, 'Section 117 of the Constitution' (1906) 3 *Commonwealth Law Review* 97 at 99.
98 Stow, pp. 105–6.

although both are ignorant of any underlying policy objective of the provision. More-over, this strict interpretation frustrates any substantive operation for s. 117. By way of example, consider the following scenario. In hard economic times, the New South Wales government wishes to limit new employment in the steel industry to residents of that state. A law that made it an offence for an interstate resident to apply for work in the industry would infringe s. 117. However, if the law instead stated that it was an offence for an employer to hire someone who was not a resident of New South Wales, it would not breach s. 117. Nonetheless, the laws are equivalent in that they both involve discriminatory employment practices in the steel industry in New South Wales based on a person's residence in another state.

It took several decades for s. 117 to be raised again in the High Court. *Henry v. Boehm* (1973) 128 CLR 482 concerned the Rules of Court Regulating the Admission of Practitioners (SA). Rule 27(1) provided that 'An applicant previously admitted else-where shall reside for at least three calendar months in the State continuously and immediately preceding the filing of his notice of application for admission', while under rule 28(1) 'An applicant previously admitted elsewhere shall, in the first place, be admitted conditionally only for a period of one year'. Under rule 28(2), even after the one year probation, the applicant could only gain 'absolute admission if he satisfies the Court by affidavit that since his conditional admission, and until the date of the applica-tion for the order absolute, he has continuously resided in the State'. A solicitor residing in Victoria seeking admission in South Australia brought a challenge based on s. 117. Despite what might have been regarded as a blatant contravention of the principle expressed by s. 117 that a person should not be discriminated against on the basis of their residence in a state, the Court, with Stephen J dissenting, found that there had been no breach of the Constitution.

The leading judgment was delivered by Barwick CJ, with whom McTiernan J agreed. The reasoning of Menzies and Gibbs JJ was substantially similar to that of Bar-wick CJ. Barwick CJ, in a comment reminiscent of his rejection of s. 80 as a 'great con-stitutional guarantee',[99] stated, at p. 487:

> Whilst it might have been thought that such a provision in the Constitution as s. 117 would be a substantial aid to the unity of citizenship throughout Australia, it is expressed in precise and narrow terms representing a compromise of competing views amongst those responsible for the drafting of the Constitution.

From this beginning, Barwick CJ constructed s. 117 in a way that ensured that it would have no application in the case at hand, nor any likely application in the future. The key to his approach was the interpretation of s. 117 as a provision that had no application to laws that, on their face, applied equally to residents of the legislating state and residents of other states. Thus, there was no breach of s. 117 by rules 27(1) and 28(2) because 'the plaintiff, being a resident of Victoria within the meaning of s. 117, would be liable to observe in South Australia exactly the same provisions as he would if he were a resident of South Australia'.[100] In addition, it was held that the rules did not require the plaintiff to give up his residence in Victoria, and thus that his residence in that state was not

---

impeded. By finding that 'resident in any State' under s. 117 entails a degree of permanence and is not displaced by a temporary absence, and in thus rejecting the broad definition suggested by Griffith CJ in *Davies and Jones*, it was found that the plaintiff would not cease to be a resident of Victoria for the purposes of s. 117 if he resided in South Australia in compliance with rules 27(1) and 28(2).

In dissent, Stephen J foreshadowed the approach that the High Court was to take to s. 117 some years later. While the majority adopted a legalistic approach that examined the form of rules 27(1) and 28(2), Stephen J argued that s. 117 applied to the rules because of their real or practical effect of requiring an interstate practitioner to give up his or her practice in that other state in order to be admitted in South Australia. He found that s. 117 had been breached because, in applying the comparison required by the text of s. 117— whereby the plaintiff's actual situation was contrasted with a hypothetical one in which it was assumed that he was a resident of South Australia—a disability or discrimination was evident: 'were he resident in South Australia the disability involved in lengthy residence away from Victoria would either be wholly absent or be substantially mitigated'.[101]

The effect of *Henry v. Boehm*, in combination with *Davies and Jones* and *Lee Fay v. Vincent*, was disturbing. A provision that, on its face, was clearly directed towards the elimination of discrimination on the basis of state residence had almost been interpreted out of existence. Section 117 expressed ideals necessary for a robust and coherent Australian federation, but had proved unable to meet this task, despite its general language and apparent scope. Nevertheless, even after *Henry v. Boehm*, s. 117 was applied by state Supreme Courts. In *Re Loubie* [1986] 1 Qd R 272 and *Ex parte Veltmeyer* [1989] 1 Qd R 462, the Queensland Supreme Court held that s. 16(3)(b) of the *Bail Act 1980* (Qld) infringed s. 117. That section required a court to refuse bail where a defendant was not ordinarily resident in Queensland, unless the defendant could show cause why detention in custody was not justified. Section 117 was also applied by the New South Wales Supreme Court in *Australian Building Construction Employees' & Builders' Labourers' Federation v. Commonwealth Trading Bank* [1976] 2 NSWLR 371 to strike down a provision in the Supreme Court Rules of New South Wales that allowed the Court to order a plaintiff to give security for costs where 'a plaintiff is ordinarily resident outside the State'.

The interpretation of s. 117 took a dramatic U-turn in *Street v. Queensland Bar Association* (1989) 168 CLR 461, when the majority decision in *Henry v. Boehm* was overruled and the dissenting judgment of Stephen J adopted. Although a majority of the Court did not feel the need to also overrule *Davies and Jones*, there must now be considerable doubt as to whether that decision is good law.[102] *Street* again raised the issue of whether admission requirements breached s. 117. Under rule 15(4) of the Rules of the Supreme Court (Qld), barristers from other Australian states could be admitted in Queensland. However, by rule 38(d) any such applicant had to make an affidavit as set out in Form 10, stating in para (6): 'That I ceased to practise as a barrister in *(here set forth the dates when the applicant ceased to practise in the various courts to which he has been admitted, and the nature of his employment hereafter.)*'. In para (7), the applicant was to state

---

101 *Henry v. Boehm* at 507.
102 *Street* at 486 per Mason CJ, at 533 per Deane J, at 549 per Dawson J, at 561 per Toohey J, at 569–70 per Gaudron J, at 588–9 per McHugh J.

the day on which he or she 'arrived' in Queensland. On 2 July 1987, the Queensland admission rules were amended. Paragraphs (6) and (7) of Form 10 were deleted, and a new para (6) required an applicant to state that: 'It is my intention to practise principally in the State of Queensland commencing on *(here set forth any relevant date)*'. A new Rule 15B also imposed a one-year period of conditional admission on out-of-state applicants, during which the applicant had to show that 'he has practised principally in Queensland'. A New South Wales barrister wishing to practise in Queensland while continuing to practise in New South Wales challenged these rules. The High Court unanimously upheld his claim, finding that the rules both in their original form and as amended infringed s. 117.

The judgments in *Street* provide a powerful contrast to the reasoning in the earlier decisions on s. 117, and indeed to the course of decisions on sections 41, 80, and 116. No longer was s. 117 characterised as a narrow provision seemingly incapable of a substantive operation. Instead, it was conceived by Mason CJ, at p. 485, as 'one of the comparatively few provisions in the Constitution which was designed to enhance national unity and a real sense of national identity by eliminating disability or discrimination on account of residence in another State'. Indeed, the provision was seen as being born out of a federation which aimed 'to bring into existence one nation and one people'.[103] How the language and tone of the Court had shifted since *Henry v. Boehm*! It was not surprising that *Street* was viewed by some as heralding the beginning of a fresh approach to other express rights, such as s. 80.

This change of heart in *Street* also had an impact at the doctrinal level. Where Wilson J in the *DOGS Case* (1981) 146 CLR 559 at 652–3 had argued that limitations on power should be narrowly construed, the opposite emerged from *Street*, where s. 117 was broadly construed because it was a limitation on power protective of individual liberty. In doing so, Deane and Toohey JJ cited decisions such as *Jumbunna Coal Mine NL v. Victorian Coal Miners' Association* (1908) 6 CLR 309[104] and *R v. Public Vehicles Licensing Appeal Tribunal (Tas); Ex parte Australian National Airways Pty Ltd* (1964) 113 CLR 207,[105] two decisions that have often been applied to achieve a broad interpretation for powers granted to the Commonwealth by s. 51 of the Constitution (see Chapter 4).

This led to a new approach to s. 117. The narrow definition of 'resident' for the purposes of s. 117 adopted in *Henry v. Boehm* was rejected and the broad definition proposed by Griffith CJ in *Davies and Jones* endorsed. It was held that 'resident' should be given a wider meaning that did not require some element of permanence, the aim being to 'guarantee to the individual a right to non-discriminatory treatment in relation to all aspects of residence'.[106] In *Street*, the test of whether s. 117 had been breached was that which had been put forward by Stephen J in *Henry v. Boehm*. Mason CJ set out the test as follows, at p. 488:

> It seems to me that for s. 117 to apply it must appear that, were the person a resident of the legislating State, that different circumstance would of itself either effectively remove the

---

103 *Street* at 485.
104 *Jumbunna* at 367–8 per O'Connor J.
105 *R v. Public Vehicles Licensing Appeal Tribunal* at 225 per the Court.
106 *Street* at 485 per Mason CJ.

disability or discrimination or, for practical purposes in all the circumstances, mitigate its effect to the point where it would be rendered illusory.

This involves, as the text of s. 117 requires, imagining the hypothetical position that the plaintiff would be in if he or she were actually a resident of the legislating state.[107]

It was found that a law that reveals a disability or discrimination when channelled through this test does not necessarily contravene s. 117. The provision, like other constitutional rights and guarantees, could not be absolute. According to Mason CJ, at pp. 491–2:

> To allow the section an unlimited scope would give it a reach extending beyond the object which it was designed to serve by trenching on the autonomy of the States to a far-reaching degree. Accordingly, there may be cases where the need to preserve that autonomy leads to a recognition that a particular disability or discrimination is not prohibited … The preservation of the autonomy of the States demands that the exclusion of out-of-State residents from the enjoyment of rights naturally and exclusively associated with residence in a State must be recognized as standing outside the operation of s. 117.

It was recognised by the Court that some laws must be able to discriminate according to state residence: 'some subject-matters are the concern only of the people of each State'.[108] It was incontrovertible, for example, that a state could limit the right to vote for the parliament of that state to its own residents. Less obviously, a state might be able to limit its hospital or other similar services to residents of the state, whose taxes had paid for the service. There were various attempts to examine when such differential treatment, or discrimination, might be permissible under s. 117. For example, Deane J found, at p. 528, that a disability flowing 'naturally from the structure of the particular State, the limited scope of its legislative powers or the nature of the particular right, privilege, immunity or other advantage or power to which it relates' lies outside s. 117, while Brennan J referred, at p. 513, to the 'necessity to preserve the institutions of government and their ability to function'. In a later case, Dawson and Toohey JJ described the various dicta of the members of the Court as 'probably a difference in approach rather than principle'.[109]

It was unanimously held that the Queensland admission rules, both in their original form and as amended, breached s. 117. Even though the amended rules removed the need to reside in Queensland, the requirement that a person 'practise principally' in that state in order to be admitted would be 'substantially deprived of its onerous nature' were the plaintiff, hypothetically, to reside in Queensland.[110] Under s. 117, the requirement to 'practise principally' in Queensland could be equated with a requirement to reside in that state, and thus to give up residence in the original state of residence. As Mason CJ put it at p. 489, 'A disability or discrimination based on grounds apart from residence is effectively removed if those grounds relate to characteristics which are in the circumstances concomitants of the individual's notionally changed residence'. Discrimination on the basis of state residence was clearly imposed by the admission rules,

---

107 *Street* at 506 per Brennan J.
108 *Street* at 583 per McHugh J.
109 *Goryl v. Greyhound Australia Pty Ltd* (1994) 179 CLR 463 at 485.
110 *Street* at 495 per Mason CJ.

and it could not be found that such discrimination was something that lay outside the ambit of s. 117. Various methods were put forward to suggest when 'discrimination' might be present under s. 117.[111] Brennan J argued, at p. 510, that:

> The absence of discrimination consists as much in the unequal treatment of unequals as in the equal treatment of equals … However, a difference in treatment on a ground which is rationally connected with an unrelated objective will nevertheless be discriminatory if the difference is not proportionate to the relevant inequality.

This meant that s. 117 might apply to 'the discriminatory imposition of a disadvantage by a law of general application'.[112] Gaudron J also found, at p. 574, that 'the issue may be expressed as whether the different treatment is reasonably capable of being seen as appropriate and adapted to a relevant difference'. On the other hand, McHugh J, while recognising that discrimination 'frequently involves the notion of unjustified differentiation', found that 'in s. 117, however, "discrimination" seems to mean the act of distinguishing or treating differently irrespective of whether the distinction or different treatment can be justified'.[113]

In *Street*, the Court adopted a substantive approach to s. 117, one that made it clear that s. 117 'extends beyond a law, administrative policy or judicial practice of general application to the actual impact which a law, policy or practice produces on the persons to whom it is directed'.[114] Section 117 clearly applies to laws that use residence in a state as the criterion with which to discriminate between persons. It thus overrides a state law that restricts entry into a profession to persons residing in that state. However, would s. 117 strike down a law that restricted entry into a profession to people who have graduated from a university located in that state, or to people born in that state? The answer is less clear. If, as a matter of substance, residence in a state can be equated with the criterion, or if that criterion can be seen as a normal concomitant of residence in a state, then s. 117 should apply. Such judgments pose difficult questions of fact and degree that have yet to be explored by the High Court. Nevertheless, if the Court is to avoid the result in *Davies and Jones*, the Court must adopt an interpretation that looks beyond mere residence. This the Court did in *Street*, when it equated the requirement to 'practise principally' in Queensland with residence in that state. Such an approach will also be necessary if the problems that have beset the interpretation of sections 51(ii) and 99 are to be avoided. The limitations in those sections against discrimination and preference 'between States or parts of States' can be avoided by drafting a law to select an area not because it is a state or part of a state, but on some other basis, such as population, that in effect selects the same region.[115]

Section 117 only confers a right on a 'subject of the Queen'. In *Street*, Toohey J explained, at p. 553, that these words were chosen so as to avoid using the word

---

111 See J. Morgan, 'Equality Rights in the Australian Context: A Feminist Assessment' in P. Alston (ed), *Towards an Australian Bill of Rights*, Centre for International and Public Law, Australian National University, 1994, pp. 141–2.
112 *Street* at 518 per Brennan J.
113 *Street* at 582.
114 *Street* at 508 per Brennan J.
115 *Elliott v. Commonwealth* (1935) 54 CLR 657.

'citizen', which carried a 'distinctly republican flavour'. He concluded, citing *Nolan v. Minister for Immigration and Ethnic Affairs* (1988) 165 CLR 178 at 186, that:

> 'Subject of the Queen' is now to be understood as referring to the Queen in right of Australia ... Whether a person living in Australia, but not a natural born or naturalized Australian citizen, is entitled to the protection accorded by s. 117 is a matter to be considered when the occasion arises.[116]

Deane and Dawson JJ also relied on *Nolan* to conclude that s. 117 extends to any Australian citizen. Brennan J discussed but did not decide the issue.

Street was applied in *Goryl v. Greyhound Australia Pty Ltd* (1994) 179 CLR 463. A resident of New South Wales was injured in a bus accident in New South Wales, while on a bus travelling from Brisbane. She sued the bus owner in Queensland for damages. Section 20 of the *Motor Vehicles Insurance Act 1936* (Qld) limited her, as a New South Wales resident, to the damages she could have recovered under New South Wales law, which were less than the damages that she could have recovered under Queensland law. A resident of Queensland would have been entitled to claim the higher damages under Queensland law. The test set out in *Street* was applied and found to have been breached. The Court unanimously held that s. 20 contravened s. 117, and therefore that s. 20 could not be applied to limit the amount of damages.

The order of the Court in *Street* and *Goryl* was that the relevant laws were 'inapplicable' to the plaintiffs. Unlike the normal situation where a law that contravenes a constitutional guarantee is found to be invalid, or void, the effect of this order was that the laws were unable to apply. One reason for this might be that s. 117, unlike provisions such as sections 80 and 116, is not expressed in the form 'The Commonwealth (and the States) shall make no law'. However, s. 92 (see Chapter 6) is not expressed in this way either, and it has always been seen to render inconsistent laws invalid rather than inapplicable. Rather, the reason lies in the fact that s. 117, unlike s. 92, is expressed to confer a personal immunity. Hence, where the Court finds that s. 117 has been breached, the effect is to recognise this personal immunity by declaring the law to be inapplicable to that person, rather than finding that the relevant legislature lacked the power to pass the law. Thus: 'A law which imposes an impermissible disability or discrimination on a protected person is not invalid; it remains in full force and, except in relation to protected persons, in full effect'.[117] However, it has been suggested, but never pursued, that 'an enactment might be rendered wholly invalid by s. 117 if it depended for its operation on the imposition of a prohibited form of disability or discrimination'.[118]

Conclusion

The year 1989 was the first time that a plaintiff was successfully able to invoke an express guarantee of a civil and political right in the High Court. For almost all of the twentieth century, such rights in the Constitution have been interpreted so as to be

---

116 *Street* at 554. See p. 572 per Gaudron J.
117 *Street* at 504 per Brennan J.
118 *Street* at 486 per Mason CJ.

ineffective. It is hard to avoid the conclusion that until 1989 judges of the High Court have selectively used whatever tool was available, particularly literalism and historical materials, to construe sections 41, 80, 116, and 117 as empty guarantees (see Chapter 9). Thus, while literalism was applied to limit the operation of s. 80, it was not applied to s. 41 where it would have suggested a wide operation. Even more uncanny was the fact that the interpretations of sections 41 and 80 matched the limited vision of these provisions in the Convention debates, yet such debates were not permissible sources of interpretative meaning until the decision of *Cole v. Whitfield* (1988) 165 CLR 360 (see Chapter 4). When policy factors did come to the fore, as in the interpretation of s. 41, they were applied to support a narrow reading. By contrast, the policy factors that would have clearly supported a broad interpretation of s. 117 were ignored.

There has been only one exception to this pattern. In 1989, s. 117 was reinterpreted in *Street* to provide real protection against discrimination on the basis of out-of-state residence. Moreover, it seemed that the unanimous Court in *Street* had signalled a reinterpretation of other rights that, like s. 117, had been give an artificial and legalistic construction. This promise has not yet been realised. Section 117 of the Constitution remains the only express civil and political right that has been given a substantive interpretation. In part, this is because few cases have come before the Court that would have enabled as significant a shift as in *Street*. Judicial energy has instead been directed to developing protection in the form of implied rights (see Chapters 7 and 8). Nevertheless, *Kruger* did give the Court the opportunity to revisit its approach to s. 116, an opportunity that, apart from the judgment of Gaudron J, was not taken.

Express Rights: Economic

Introduction

At the international level, economic rights have been grouped with social and cultural rights, at least for the purposes of the *International Covenant on Economic, Social and Cultural Rights 1966*. In this context, it has been said that 'economic, social and cultural rights can be described as allowing people to own property, to work in fair conditions and to be guaranteed an adequate standard of living and facilities for education and the enjoyment of life and of the culture in which they live or have been brought up'.[1] The Australian Constitution protects economic rights, but lacks the social and cultural rights that characterise many new constitutions, such as the South African Constitution in force from 7 February 1997.[2]

Even in protecting economic rights, the Australian Constitution has a very narrow focus. The economic rights in the instrument are not part of any Bill of Rights, but are scattered throughout the document. The rights discussed in this Chapter are given expression in two different ways. They may be freestanding guarantees, as in the case of s. 92, which guarantees that 'trade, commerce, and intercourse among the States … shall be absolutely free'. Or, they may not be drafted as rights at all but as grants of legislative power with an attaching guarantee, as in the case of s. 51(xxiiiA), which limits the Commonwealth's ability to bring about 'civil conscription' in legislating with respect to 'The provision of … medical and dental services', and s. 51(xxxi), which allows the Commonwealth to legislate with respect to 'The acquisition of property on just terms from any State or person for any purpose in respect of which the Parliament has power to make laws'.

---

1 P. Bailey, *Human Rights: Australia in an International Context*, Butterworths, 1990, p. 12.
2 See, for example, South African Constitution, sections 30 ('Everyone has the right to use the language and to participate in the cultural life of their choice, but no one exercising these rights may do so in a manner inconsistent with any provision of the Bill of Rights.'), and 31.

Sections 51(ii) and 99 of the Constitution are not dealt with in this Chapter, despite having sometimes been seen as guarantees of economic rights.[3] Section 51(ii) allows the Commonwealth to pass laws on the subject of 'Taxation; but so as not to discriminate between States or parts of States',[4] while under s. 99 'The Commonwealth shall not, by any law or regulation of trade, commerce, or revenue, give preference to one State or any part thereof over another State or any part thereof'. These sections, along with provisions such as s. 117 (see Chapter 5), which guarantees the rights of out-of-state residents, seek to eliminate discrimination between states and between the people of the states and to bring about an integrated national economy. However, while s. 117 is clearly an individual right, sections 51(ii) and 99 are best viewed as part of the federal fabric created by the Constitution, and like s. 109, which deals with inconsistency between Commonwealth and State laws (see Chapter 3), not as rights-orientated provisions.[5] Section 92 might also have been viewed this way. As one commentator has remarked, 'the words of s. 92 and s. 99 are both general in expression and both alike originated in the realm of politics and economics rather than that of individual juristic rights'.[6] However, while sections 51(ii) and 99 have not been characterised by the High Court as individual rights, s. 92 has confounded its framing and has been shaped by the High Court, at least for most of this century, into the most potent individual right in the Australian Constitution.

Freedom of interstate trade, commerce, and intercourse

Section 92 has been applied many times to strike down federal and state legislation. A crucial plank in Australian federation, s. 92 secures freedom of interstate 'trade, commerce, and intercourse'. By 1988, the number of cases in the High Court and the Privy Council relating to s. 92 was estimated at around 140 to 150. The conflicting strands of interpretation arising from the struggle to explain how the content of s. 92 could be 'absolutely free' yet subject to regulation were replaced with a single new approach by the unanimous decision in *Cole v. Whitfield* (1988) 165 CLR 360. This Chapter is not about that story, which has been told elsewhere.[7] Instead, this Chapter focuses on the characterisation of s. 92 as a guarantee of human rights.

In *Miller v. TCN Channel Nine Pty Ltd* (1986) 161 CLR 556 at 618 Deane J argued that as a result of High Court decisions s. 92 'has been converted into a form of consti-

---

3   P. Hanks, 'Constitutional Guarantees', in H. P. Lee and G. Winterton (eds), *Australian Constitutional Perspectives*, LBC, 1992, pp. 116–23.
4   See also the Australian Constitution, s. 51(iii).
5   L. Zines and G. J. Lindell, 'Form and Substance: "Discrimination" in Modern Constitutional Law' (1992) 21 *Federal Law Review* 136 at 148.
6   P. D. Phillips, 'Trade, Commerce and Intercourse Part II—Preferences and Freedoms in Interstate Trade', in R. Else-Mitchell (ed.), *Essays on the Australian Constitution*, LBC, 1952, p. 241.
7   A. R. Blackshield and G. Williams, *Australian Constitutional Law and Theory: Commentary and Materials*, 2nd edn, Federation Press, 1998, ch. 23; M. Coper, *Encounters with the Australian Constitution*, CCH, 1988, ch. 7; M. Coper, *Freedom of Interstate Trade under the Australian Constitution*, Butterworths, 1983; M. Coper, 'Section 92 of the Australian Constitution Since *Cole v. Whitfield*', in Lee and Winterton p. 129; L. Zines, *The High Court and the Constitution*, 4th edn, Butterworths, 1997, chs 6–8.

tutional guarantee of the economics of laissez-faire and the politics of "small government"'. This observation summed up several decades of interpretation of s. 92 in which
the 'individual rights' view of the section commanded considerable support in the High
Court, though there were periods when it came under strong challenge, such as during
the 1930s when the countervailing view of Evatt J largely held sway.[8] Isaacs J was the
first champion of the 'individual rights' theory of s. 92. For example, in *James v. Cowan*
(1930) 43 CLR 386 at 418, in referring to the taking of goods by a state, he found: 'The
question is, how has the personal right of trading inter-State by the former owner been
interfered with? That is a personal right, not a property right'. He also stated, at p. 418,
that 'The right of inter-State trade and commerce protected by sec 92 from State interference and regulation is *a personal right attaching to the individual and not attaching to the
goods*' (emphasis in original). For Isaacs J, it was clear that s. 92 was not merely a limit on
legislative power, but was also a guarantee of an individual right. On appeal in the Privy
Council, his approach was described by Lord Atkin as 'convincing'.[9]

The approach of Isaacs J to s. 92 was taken up and refined by Dixon J after Isaacs J
had left the Court. However, the core of the Isaacs approach remained intact. Dixon J,
like his predecessor, saw s. 92 as being a guarantee of the economic rights of the interstate trader. For example, in *O Gilpin Ltd v. Commissioner for Road Transport and Tramways
(NSW)* (1935) 52 CLR 189 at 211, Dixon J said, 'Trade, commerce and intercourse
among the States is an expression which describes the activities of individuals. The
object of sec 92 is to enable individuals to conduct their commercial dealings and their
personal intercourse with one another independently of State boundaries'. The 'individual rights' theory was upheld in the Privy Council in *James v. Commonwealth* [1936]
AC 578 at 614, where Lord Wright found that s. 92 is 'a constitutional guarantee of
rights, analogous to the guarantee of religious freedom in s. 116, or of equal right[s] of
all residents in all States in s. 117'. Section 92 had come to be grouped with other rights
in the Constitution, although, unlike rights such as sections 116 and 117 (see Chapter
5), it was proving effective as a check on legislative power.

The high point of the 'individual rights' theory of s. 92 came in the decisions of the
High Court[10] and the Privy Council[11] in the *Bank Nationalisation Case*. The Chifley
Government's attempt to nationalise Australian banking was held invalid on grounds
that included a breach of s. 92. Part VII of the *Banking Act 1947* (Cth) enabled the progressive prohibition 'of the carrying on of banking business by private banks'. In the
High Court, it was held by 4:2, Latham CJ and McTiernan J dissenting, that this was
inconsistent with the 'freedom' to conduct interstate trade under s. 92. The Privy
Council affirmed this conclusion, and also the 'individual rights' approach to s. 92
expressed in the High Court by judges such as Dixon J. Rich and Williams JJ, for example, described 'the freedom guaranteed by s. 92' as 'a personal right attaching to the
individual'.[12] It was in the period after the *Bank Nationalisation Case* that Julius Stone
was able to state, 'under the Australian Constitution, the "freedom" of trade, commerce

---

8   See, for example, *Milk Board (NSW) v. Metropolitan Cream Pty Ltd* (1939) 62 CLR 116. Evatt J outlined his
    approach to s. 92 most clearly in *R v. Vizzard; Ex parte Hill* (1933) 50 CLR 30.
9   *James v. Cowan* [1932] AC 542 at 561.
10 *Bank of NSW v. Commonwealth* (1948) 76 CLR 1.
11 *Commonwealth v. Bank of New South Wales* [1950] AC 235.
12 *Bank of NSW v. Commonwealth* at 283.

and intercourse guaranteed under sec 92 is coming to be interpreted to include tacitly within itself a guarantee of individual freedom of contract and choice of vocation of persons operating within the field of inter-State commerce'.[13]

For Barwick CJ, s. 92 was a provision that guaranteed to individuals the right to engage in interstate trade free of regulation. Like Isaacs J before him, Barwick CJ found very little room for the Commonwealth to interfere with that 'right'.[14] Moreover, he found that s. 92 constitutionally entrenched a *laissez faire* economy, or at least *laissez faire* interstate trade. Although his interpretation of s. 92 did not achieve the acceptance that characterised the views of Isaacs J and Dixon J, Barwick CJ shared with them the view that s. 92 guaranteed individual rights. During his time on the High Court, Barwick CJ sought, with mixed success, to extend the reach of s. 92 beyond that accepted by the Dixon Court. For example, while the Dixon Court held in *Wragg v. New South Wales* (1953) 88 CLR 353[15] that 'the first sale across the border' was not part of interstate trade, Barwick CJ sought, successfully,[16] to extend the effect of s. 92 to exactly this activity. He was also influential in arguing that the Court should look beyond the legal effect of a law to its real and practical effect on interstate trade.

The 'individual rights' interpretation of s. 92 meant that the provision, in its impact on interstate trade, expressed some of the substantive protection of economic matters, such as freedom of contract, that was also evident in decisions of the United States Supreme Court in the first part of the twentieth century.[17] At the close of the nineteenth century, the United States Supreme Court declared in *Allgeyer v. Louisiana* 165 US 578 at 589 (1897) that the Fourteenth Amendment to the United States Constitution, in guaranteeing that a person could not be deprived of his or her 'liberty' without 'due process of law', included the right:

> to be free in the enjoyment of all his faculties; to be free to use them in all lawful ways; to live and work where he will; to earn his livelihood by any lawful calling; to pursue any livelihood or avocation, and for that purpose to enter into all contracts which may be proper, necessary, and essential to his carrying out to a successful conclusion the purposes above mentioned.

This was applied in the notorious decision of *Lochner v. New York* 198 US 45 (1905). In that case a New York law prohibiting employment in bakeries for more than 60 hours a week was found to be invalid because it infringed the freedom to contract impliedly expressed in the Fifth and Fourteenth Amendments to the United States Constitution. Peckham J, who delivered the opinion of the Court, upheld, at p. 54, 'the right of the individual to labor for such time as he may choose'. He found that attempts to regulate working conditions infringed the concept of 'substantive due process', under which the Court scrutinised the content or subject matter of the law, because they were 'mere

---

13 J. A. Stone, 'A Government of Laws and Yet of Men' (1948–1950) 1 *University of Western Australia Annual Law Review* 461 at 511.

14 *North Eastern Dairy Co. Ltd v. Dairy Industry Authority of NSW* (1976) 134 CLR 559 at 581–2.

15 See *Grannall v. Marrickville Margarine Pty Ltd* (1955) 93 CLR 55, where it was held that acts 'preparatory or antecedent' to interstate trade were not protected by s. 92.

16 *SOS (Mowbray) Pty Ltd v. Mead* (1972) 124 CLR 529; *North Eastern Dairy Co. Ltd v. Dairy Industry Authority of NSW* (1975) 134 CLR 559.

17 See Blackshield and Williams, pp. 990–3; L. H. Tribe, *American Constitutional Law*, 2nd edn, Foundation Press, 1988, ch. 8.

meddlesome interferences with the rights of the individual'.[18] The concept of 'substantive due process' was also applied in *Adkins v. Children's Hospital* 261 US 525 (1923), where a law prescribing minimum wages for women was found to be invalid. In other cases, it was applied to find invalid laws providing minimum labour conditions or setting health and safety standards.

In *Lochner*, Holmes J delivered a famous dissent that powerfully demonstrated that the concept of 'substantive due process' was a means whereby the Court had sought to impose its own political view of economics, or what he called, at p. 76, the 'inarticulate major premise', over the views of elected legislatures. He stated, at p. 75, that 'The Fourteenth Amendment does not enact Mr Herbert Spencer's Social Statics ... [A] constitution is not intended to embody a particular economic theory, whether of paternalism and the organic relation of the citizen to the State or of *laissez faire*'. The perils of the Court finding legislation invalid because it breached 'substantive due process' became apparent in the 1930s, during which the Supreme Court struck down legislation that was a part of President Roosevelt's 'New Deal' to revitalise the United States economy. The Court had come to champion one particular brand of economic theory, that of *laissez faire* economics, at the expense of the economic policies of the elected government. After President Roosevelt threatened to 'pack' the Court with new appointments to increase its size from nine judges to fifteen judges, the Court changed its mind. In *West Coast Hotel Co. v. Parrish* 300 US 379 (1937) ('the switch in time that saved nine') the Court overruled *Lochner* and *Adkins v. Children's Hospital*.

The *Lochner* period has cast a long shadow. Since 1937, the United States Supreme Court has been reluctant to review economic regulation.[19] In Canada, it meant that in drafting s. 7 of the Canadian Charter of Rights and Freedoms ('Everyone has the right to life, liberty and security of the person and the right not to be deprived thereof except in accordance with the principles of fundamental justice') the framers omitted any reference to property and did not include a guarantee of freedom of contract.[20] The result is that s. 7 has been interpreted to exclude any protection of economic liberty[21] and does not extend to corporations.[22] The only express guarantee of economic rights in the Charter is s. 6, which in protecting mobility rights, includes the right 'to pursue the gaining of a livelihood in any province'. The shadow cast by *Lochner* took longer to reach Australia. At least until 1988, the High Court applied its own version of 'substantive due process' in its interpretation of s. 92. Both *Lochner* and the interpretation of s. 92, particularly the approach of Barwick CJ, relied on constitutional implementation of a *laissez faire* view of the economy. In the case of s. 92, this was limited to that section of the economy that involved interstate trade. Nevertheless, s. 92 stood as a potent force

---

18   *Lochner v. New York* at 61.
19   Compare R. A. Epstein 'Property, Speech, and the Politics of Distrust', in G. R. Stone, R. A. Epstein, and C. R. Sunstein, *The Bill of Rights in the Modern State*, University of Chicago Press, 1992, p. 41; D. A. Schultz and C. E. Smith, *The Jurisprudential Vision of Justice Antonin Scalia*, Rowman & Littlefield, 1996, ch. 1.
20   *Re BC Motor Vehicle Act* [1985] 2 SCR 486 at 504–5 per Lamer J; P. Hogg, *Constitutional Law of Canada*, 4th edn, Carswell, 1997, pp. 1070–1. The *International Covenant on Civil and Political Rights* 1966 also fails to protect property rights in this way (see, for example, Article 9). Compare *Canadian Bill of Rights* 1960, sections 1(a) and 2(e).
21   *Reference re Criminal Code (Man)* [1990] 1 SCR 1123 at 1163–6, 1173 per Lamer J.
22   *Irwin Toy v. Quebec* [1989] 1 SCR 927 at 1002–4 per Dickson CJ, Lamer, and Wilson JJ; *Dywidag Systems v. Zutphen Brothers Construction* [1990] 1 SCR 705 at 709 per Cory J.

against any other vision of the national economy that a federal government might wish to implement. This was evident in the failed attempt of the Chifley government to bring about the nationalisation of Australian banking in the late 1940s. It was also apparent in the earlier decision of the High Court in *Australian National Airways Pty Ltd v. Commonwealth* (1945) 71 CLR 29 to strike down the Chifley government's *Australian National Airlines Act 1945* (Cth) in so far as it granted a monopoly over interstate airline movements to the Australian National Airlines Commission, a newly established government-owned, and run, body. To the extent that the Chifley government sought to pursue a 'socialist' agenda in its nationalisation of certain industries, s. 92 proved an impenetrable barrier to such policies.

Such decisions showed that the High Court had not heeded the warnings of Chief Commissioner Piddington of the Inter-State Commission[23] in *The Seizure of Wheat Case*.[24] Piddington rejected the suggestion that s. 92 embodies a particular theory of economic regulation, and that such a theory prevents the federal government from pursuing some other approach to the economic regulation of interstate trade. Writing less than a decade after *Lochner* had been handed down, Piddington stated 'The Constitution of Australia is distinguished from that of the United States of America by the very fact that no attempt has been made anywhere to bind the electors to any prescribed course of economic action'.[25] He went on:

> If ever any Legislature in Australia, whether it is the Parliament of the Commonwealth for national purposes, or the Parliament of a State for the residue of self-government confided to it by the Constitution, adopts in its legislation the policy of 'Socialism in our time', I do not believe it will be incumbent on the Courts to point to section 92 as saying 'Never, in this Commonwealth'.[26]

Murphy J developed a similar argument in a series of judgments, the first of which was *Buck v. Bavone* (1976) 135 CLR 110. In that case, he rejected the 'individual rights' approach to s. 92, arguing, at p. 133, that the Court should withdraw from 'a legislative role' that 'has caused a substantial and serious inroad into the spheres of State and Federal legislatures'. He continued this theme in *McGraw-Hinds (Aust) Pty Ltd v. Smith* (1978) 144 CLR 633 and *Uebergang v. Australian Wheat Board* (1980) 145 CLR 266. In the latter case, at p. 309, he narrowly construed s. 92 to avoid the Court taking on 'a super-legislative role' as regards interstate trade. This was backed by his view, expressed at p. 308, that those members of the Court adopting a broader interpretation of s. 92 'are being forced to assume a supervisory role over the national economy'. He found, at p. 309, that although 'the Constitution did not entrench nineteenth century economic ideas … for most of its history, s. 92 has been construed as if it guaranteed that nineteenth century notions of laissez-faire would prevail'.[27] Murphy J showed that in its

---

23   See M. Coper, 'The Second Coming of the Fourth Arm: The Role and Functions of the Inter-State Commission' (1989) 63 *Australian Law Journal* 731.
24   Australia, Parliament 1914–15, Parl. Paper 69, *Session 1914–17*, vol. 2.
25   Australia, Parliament 1914–15, Parl. Paper 69, p. 29.
26   Australia, Parliament 1914–15, Parl. Paper 69, p. 29.
27   See Lord Wright, 'Section 92—A Problem Piece' (1954) 1 *Sydney Law Review* 145 at 156–7.

interpretation of s. 92 the High Court had made the same errors that characterised the application of 'substantive due process' by the *Lochner* Court.

The 'individual rights' theory of s. 92—the edifice constructed by judges such as Isaacs J, Dixon J, and Barwick CJ—came crashing down in *Cole v. Whitfield* (1988) 165 CLR 360. In that case, a unanimous High Court fundamentally reinterpreted s. 92. It developed a new test, at p. 394, under which s. 92 was found to be infringed if a Commonwealth or State law imposes 'discriminatory burdens of a protectionist kind' or if its effect is 'discriminatory against interstate trade and commerce in that protectionist sense'. This new test was based on the Court's view of the intentions of the 1890s drafters in framing s. 92 (see Chapter 4). The reasoning of many of the cases decided by the Court prior to *Cole v. Whitfield* was now to be regarded as wrong. In particular, the 'individual rights' theory, as expressed in decisions such as the *Bank Nationalisation Case*, was swept away, leaving a more modest operation for s. 92.

Cole v. Whitfield dampened the interpretation of s. 92 as a guarantee of the rights of the interstate trader. However, it left room for s. 92 to protect individual rights in its requirement that 'intercourse among the States … shall be absolutely free'. While the Court established a new test of discriminatory protectionism in respect of s. 92's application to 'trade' and 'commerce', the Court was careful to indicate that this test did not apply to 'intercourse'. It stated at p. 393:

> The two elements in s. 92 which provide an arguable foundation for giving the section a wider operation with respect to trade and commerce than that foreshadowed by its history are the reference to 'intercourse' and the emphatic words 'absolutely free'. A constitutional guarantee of freedom of interstate intercourse, if it is to have substantial content, extends to a guarantee of personal freedom 'to pass to and fro among the States without burden, hindrance or restriction': *Gratwick v. Johnson* [(1945) 70 CLR 1 at 17] … It is not necessary now to consider the content of the guarantee of freedom of various forms of interstate intercourse. Much will depend on the form and circumstance of the intercourse involved. But it is clear that some forms of intercourse are so immune from legislative or executive interference that, if a like immunity were accorded to trade and commerce, anarchy would result.

Significantly, the Court recognised that s. 92 has a wider operation in respect of 'intercourse' than in respect of 'trade' and 'commerce' and that 'intercourse' is not limited to commercial intercourse.[28]

The guarantee of free interstate 'intercourse' in s. 92 supports freedom of movement. The Court in *Cole v. Whitfield* recognised, at p. 393, that s. 92 means that 'personal movement across a border cannot, generally speaking, be impeded'. Of course, the guarantee of movement in s. 92 is only a guarantee of interstate movement (presumably along with any movement preparatory to such movement). A more comprehensive freedom of movement, including movement intrastate and perhaps from Australia to overseas might be implied from the federal system (see Chapter 3) or the system of representative government (see Chapter 7) created by the Constitution. Indeed, in *Buck v. Bavone* (1976) 135 CLR 110 at 137, Murphy J suggested that freedom of movement was 'so fundamental that it is not likely it would be hidden away in s. 92'.

---

28   *Cole v. Whitfield* at 394: 'there is no reason in logic or commonsense for insisting on a strict correspondence between the freedom guaranteed to interstate trade and commerce and that guaranteed to interstate intercourse'.

An interpretation of s. 92 as a guarantee of freedom of interstate movement was given by Quick and Garran, writing in 1901, who stated, 'absolute freedom of trade, commerce, and intercourse may be defined as the right to introduce goods, wares, and merchandise from one State into another, the right to sell the same, *and the right to travel unburdened by State restrictions, regulations or obstructions*' (emphasis added).[29] This aspect of s. 92 was recognised in two decisions prior to *Cole v. Whitfield*, both of which remain good law.[30] *R v. Smithers; Ex parte Benson* (1912) 16 CLR 99 was a challenge to s. 3 of the *Influx of Criminals Prevention Act 1903* (NSW). Section 3 provided that a person could not enter New South Wales if he or she had 'been convicted in any other State … of an offence for which in such State he was liable to suffer death, or to be imprisoned for one year or longer' and three years had not yet elapsed since that imprisonment. John Benson was convicted in Victoria of having unlawful means of support and was sentenced to imprisonment for twelve months. Shortly after being released from prison he went to New South Wales to obtain work. He was arrested there, convicted under s. 3 and sentenced to a further twelve months imprisonment. The High Court unanimously found s. 3 to be invalid. Griffith CJ and Barton J did so by applying an implied freedom of movement derived from the federal structure created by the Constitution (see Chapter 3). Isaacs and Higgins JJ applied the s. 92 requirement that 'intercourse among the States … shall be absolutely free'. It was found by Isaacs J, at p. 117, that s. 92 contains 'an absolute prohibition on the Commonwealth and States alike to regard State borders as in themselves possible barriers to intercourse between Australians'.

In *Gratwick v. Johnson* (1945) 70 CLR 1, the High Court heard a challenge to the Restriction of Interstate Passenger Transport Order, made under the National Security (Land Transport) Regulations 1944 (Cth). The Order sought to restrict travel throughout Australia during the Second World War. Dulcie Johnson sought a permit under the order to travel from Sydney to Perth to visit her fiance. Her request was refused. However, she undertook the travel in any event in October 1944 and was charged with an offence. In the High Court she argued that the Order infringed s. 92 and was therefore invalid. The Court unanimously accepted this submission, finding a clear breach of the requirement in s. 92 that interstate 'intercourse' be 'absolutely free'. In the words of Dixon J, at p. 19, the Order had been drafted with 'an indifference to, if not a disdain of, the terms of s. 92'.

Since *Cole v. Whitfield* other judges have dealt with the guarantee of free interstate 'intercourse', but without any resolution of the scope of the guarantee. In *Nationwide News Pty Ltd v. Wills* (1992) 177 CLR 1, the publishers of the *Australian* newspaper challenged the validity of s. 299(1)(d)(ii) of the *Industrial Relations Act 1988* (Cth), which restricted public criticism of the Industrial Relations Commission. The High Court unanimously held the provision to be invalid either because in applying a proportionality test it was 'beyond power' (see Chapter 4) or because it infringed the implied guarantee of freedom of political communication (see Chapter 7). The plaintiffs also invoked s. 92. Only Brennan J gave an answer to this argument, and he found, at p. 56, that s. 92 did not apply, as the law imposed no discriminatory burden on any

---

29   J. Quick and R. Garran, *The Annotated Constitution of the Australian Commonwealth*, 1901 edn, Legal Books, 1995, pp. 845
30   See also *Miller v. TCN Channel Nine Pty Ltd* (1986) 161 CLR 556.

interstate communication. This was because to attract s. 92 'it is essential that something (or some person) be moved'. He stated at p. 56 that, moreover, 'Ideas cannot be moved. They have no geographical location'. Section 92 could not be invoked as s. 299(1)(d)(ii) outlawed an idea or argument rather than interstate movement. There were also arguments as to the scope of freedom of interstate 'intercourse' in *Australian Capital Television Pty Ltd v. Commonwealth* (1992) 177 CLR 106 and *Cunliffe v. Commonwealth* (1994) 182 CLR 272. As in *Nationwide News* the issue was only dealt with by a few judges, and then in a way that revealed little. However, the judgments in *Cunliffe* did reveal that a proportionality-like test (see Chapter 4) is to be applied in determining whether a law breaches the protection of interstate 'intercourse'. According to Deane J at p. 346:

> The freedom of intercourse which the section demands is freedom within an ordered community and a law which incidentally and non-discriminately affects inter-State intercourse in the course of regulating some general activity, such as the carrying on of a profession, business or commercial activity, will not contravene s. 92 if its incidental effect on interstate intercourse does not go beyond what is necessary or appropriate and adapted for the preservation of an ordered society or the protection or vindication of the legitimate claims of individuals in such a society.[31]

One other thing is clear from these decisions, the word 'intercourse' in s. 92 entails more than movement. 'Intercourse' suggests a wide variety of activities or interaction between persons or organisations. It suggests the exchange of something. An obvious contemporary example of interstate 'intercourse' is the Internet. It would be likely that internet traffic would be protected by s. 92. Given that the Internet encompasses both intrastate and interstate communication simultaneously, any attempt to regulate the transmission of information via the Internet must be examined in the context of s. 92. As Brennan J stated in *Nationwide News* at pp. 55–6:

> The protection of s. 92 is given to the movement of people, the transport of goods, the transmission of communications, the passage of signals of any kind and any other means by which 'interchange, converse and dealings between States in the affairs of life' are carried on across State boundaries … The means of movement will vary with what is moved; it is not essential that the means of movement be physically perceptible.

In the same case, Deane and Toohey JJ found, at p. 83, that 'intercourse' 'encompasses all of the modern forms of interstate communication'.

Powers that are also rights

Section 51 of the Constitution lists 40 subject matters on which the Commonwealth can legislate. The reasoning in *Amalgamated Society of Engineers v. Adelaide Steamship Co. Ltd (Engineers Case)* (1920) 28 CLR 129 suggests that each of these powers is to be interpreted independently, and that one power should not be interpreted as being subject to any other power.[32] For example, a narrow view of a power should not be

---

31 See also p. 308 per Mason CJ, p. 366 per Dawson J, pp. 395–6 per McHugh J.
32 See Blackshield and Williams, pp. 564–5.

adopted because a broad reading would render another power otiose.[33] Similarly, a distinction maintained by one power—say in s. 51(i) between interstate and intrastate trade—should not be imposed on other powers. Thus, in *Pidoto v. Victoria* (1943) 68 CLR 87, the High Court found that s. 51(xxxv), the Commonwealth's power over interstate industrial disputes, does not place limits on the Commonwealth's use of its defence power under s. 51(vi) to regulate intrastate industrial disputes.

Nevertheless, in some cases the High Court has found that the words of one power may limit the scope of another. According to Leslie Zines, this may occur 'where the wording of a particular power expressly extracts from or restricts what otherwise might be included within it'.[34] An example of such a power is s. 51(xiii), which enables the Commonwealth to legislate with respect to 'Banking, other than State banking'. In *Bourke v. State Bank of New South Wales* (1990) 170 CLR 276, the High Court held that the words 'other than State banking' not only limit s. 51(xiii), but also other heads of power. The words 'other than State banking' in s. 51(xiii) limit the other heads of power in s. 51 because they are expressed as an exception. On the other hand, the finding in *Pidoto v. Victoria* was based on the fact that s. 51(xxxv) contains no such exception.

Two of the powers listed in s. 51 have been found to contain an exception protective of human rights that limits not only the particular power containing the exception but the other s. 51 powers as well. The first is s. 51(xxiiiA), which, in enabling the Commonwealth to provide 'medical and dental services', states 'but not so as to authorize any form of civil conscription'. The second is s. 51(xxxi), which states that the Commonwealth can legislate for 'The acquisition of property on just terms from any State or person for any purpose in respect of which the Parliament has power to make laws'.

The words 'on just terms' are not prefaced by clear language, such as words like 'other than' (as in s. 51(xiii)) or 'but not' (as in s. 51(xxiiiA)), indicating that they are to operate as an exception not only on s. 51(xxxi) but on the other powers listed in s. 51 as well. Indeed, the subject matter of s. 51(xxxi) would appear to have more in common with powers that do not contain an exception—such as s. 51(i) ('Trade and commerce with other countries, and among the States') and s. 51(xxxv)—than with powers such as s. 51(xiii). This would also be consistent with the apparent intention of the framers of s. 51(xxxi).[35] At the 1897 Convention in Adelaide, Bernhard Wise of New South Wales doubted whether the new federal government would possess the power to take over public works within a state.[36] This perhaps led to the provision which became s. 51(xxxi) being introduced and discussed at the 1898 Convention in Melbourne. There, it was clear that the provision was inserted not in order to ensure that all acquisitions by the Commonwealth were 'on just terms'—although, if they thought the provision necessary because no other provision enabled such acquisitions, the drafters may have believed that this was the effect of the Constitution—but to ensure that the Common-

---

33 See *New South Wales v. Commonwealth (Seas and Submerged Lands Case)* (1975) 135 CLR 337 at 471 per Mason J, at 497 per Jacobs J.

34 Zines, p. 24.

35 See R. L. Hamilton 'Some Aspects of the Acquisition Power of the Commonwealth' (1973) 5 *Federal Law Review* 265 at 266–7.

36 *Official Record of the Debates of the Australasian Federal Convention: 1891–1898* [hereafter *Convention Debates*], vol. 3, Adelaide 1897, Legal Books, 1986, p. 1199.

wealth possessed the power to compulsorily acquire property.[37] Despite this, the High Court has held that acquisitions of property under a s. 51 head of power must provide the 'just terms' required by s. 51(xxxi). In *Attorney-General (Cth) v. Schmidt* (1961) 105 CLR 361, Dixon CJ, with the support of the other members of the Court, explained the situation in the following way, at pp. 371–2:

> It is hardly necessary to say that when you have, as you do in par (xxxi), an express power, subject to a safeguard, restriction or qualification, to legislate on a particular subject or to a particular effect, it is in accordance with the soundest principles of interpretation to treat that as inconsistent with any construction of other powers conferred in the context which would mean that they included the same subject or produced the same effect and so authorized the same kind of legislation but without the safeguard, restriction or qualification.

A further reason given in the *Bank Nationalisation Case* (1948) 76 CLR 1 at 349 by Dixon J was that the Court will not permit the adoption of 'a circuitous device to acquire indirectly the substance of a proprietary interest without at once providing the just terms guaranteed by s. 51(xxxi) of the Constitution when that is done'. Such statements in these and other decisions[38] establish that s. 51(xxxi) is capable of limiting the other s. 51 powers. However, it does not satisfactorily explain why the words 'acquisition of property on just terms' contain a qualification while the words in other powers do not. It seems likely that s. 51(xxxi) has been interpreted in this way because the Court has viewed it as guaranteeing an important economic freedom. As Gibbs CJ, Mason, Wilson, Brennan, Deane, and Dawson JJ stated in *Clunies-Ross v. Commonwealth* (1984) 155 CLR 193 at 201–2, s. 51(xxxi) 'is to be given the liberal construction appropriate to such a constitutional provision'.[39]

Not all s. 51 powers are limited by s. 51(xxxi). Some powers exhibit an intention that they should not be bound by the requirement to give 'just terms' in the 'acquisition of property'. For example, in *Attorney-General (Cth) v. Schmidt* Dixon CJ found that, despite s. 51(xxxi), the Commonwealth's power over 'Bankruptcy' in s. 51(xvii) could support legislation under which the property of a bankrupt was sequestrated. However, this did not mean that all laws passed under s. 51(xvii) would be unaffected by the requirement regarding 'just terms'. Dixon CJ was careful to point out, at p. 372, that 'if a law was made under which a piece of land was acquired for a Bankruptcy Office, s. 51(xxxi) would govern the legislation and not s. 51(xvii)'. There are other powers like s. 51(xvii). The most obvious is the Commonwealth's power over taxation in s. 51(ii). The

---

37 *Convention Debates*, vol. 4, *Melbourne 1898*, pp. 151–4; *Convention Debates*, vol. 5, *Melbourne 1898*, p. 1874. Compare Quick and Garran, p. 641.

38 See, for example, *Johnston Fear & Kingham & The Offset Printing Co. Pty Ltd v. Commonwealth* (1943) 67 CLR 314 at 318 per Latham CJ, at 325 per Starke J; *WH Blakeley & Co. Pty Ltd v. Commonwealth* (1953) 87 CLR 501 at 521 per the Court; *Trade Practices Commission v. Tooth and Co. Ltd* (1979) 142 CLR 397 at 403 per Barwick CJ, at 407 per Gibbs J, at 427 per Mason J, at 445–8 per Aickin J; *Australian Tape Manufacturers Association Ltd v. Commonwealth* (1993) 176 CLR 480 at 526 per Dawson and Toohey JJ; *Health Insurance Commission v. Peverill* (1994) 179 CLR 226 at 259 per McHugh J; *Nintendo Co. Ltd v. Centronics Systems Pty Ltd* (1994) 181 CLR 134 at 160 per Mason CJ, Brennan, Deane, Toohey, Gaudron, and McHugh JJ.

39 See *Minister of State for the Army v. Dalziel* (1944) 68 CLR 261 at 276 per Latham CJ; *Australian Tape Manufacturers Association Ltd v. Commonwealth* (1993) 176 CLR 480 at 509 per Mason CJ, Brennan, Deane, and Gaudron JJ; *Re Director of Public Prosecutions; Ex parte Lawler* (1994) 179 CLR 270 at 285 per Deane and Gaudron JJ; *Commonwealth v. WMC Resources Ltd* (1998) 152 ALR 1 at 25 per Gaudron J, at 70 per Kirby J. Compare *Commonwealth v. WMC Resources* at 35–6, 43 per McHugh J.

very notion of such a power is inconsistent with the idea that it could only be exercised to take property if 'just terms' are given. This was one basis of Mason CJ's conclusion in *Mutual Pools & Staff Pty Ltd v. Commonwealth* (1994) 179 CLR 155 at 174–5[40] that 'a law with respect to taxation which regulates competing claims and interests is not a law for the acquisition of property'. A further example was given in *Nintendo Co. Ltd v. Centronics Systems Pty Ltd* (1994) 181 CLR 134, where Mason CJ, Brennan, Deane, Toohey, Gaudron, and McHugh JJ reiterated, at p. 160, that the operation of s. 51(xxxi) on other grants of power 'is subject to a contrary intention either expressed or made manifest in those other grants', and thus that the requirement that an 'acquisition of property' be on 'just terms' cannot apply where 'the other grant of legislative power manifests a contrary intention which precludes the abstraction from it of the legislative power to make such a law'. It was found that the Commonwealth's power in s. 51(xviii) over 'Copyrights, patents of inventions and designs, and trade marks' was such a power.

Civil conscription

In 1946, as a result of a successful referendum held under s. 128 (see Chapter 10), the Constitution was amended to insert a new s. 51(xxiiiA), which gave the Commonwealth the power to pass laws with respect to 'the provision of' specified pensions, benefits, services, and allowances. The power to provide for 'medical and dental services' was qualified by the words 'but not so as to authorize any form of civil conscription'.[41] In *British Medical Association v. Commonwealth* (1949) 79 CLR 201, it was held that this qualification applies only to the provision of 'medical and dental services', and not to any of the other matters in the power.[42] However, the qualification applies whenever 'medical and dental services' are provided, 'whether as services exclusively or in the course of providing some other benefit', such as pharmaceutical benefits.[43]

In *British Medical Association v. Commonwealth*, the High Court examined the prohibition against civil conscription in the context of s. 7A of the *Pharmaceutical Benefits Act 1947* (Cth). Section 7A required medical practitioners to use a Commonwealth form in writing out prescriptions for certain medicines. A majority held that s. 7A breached s. 51(xxiiiA). Latham CJ reached this conclusion on the basis that the prohibition against 'any form of civil conscription' extended not only to legal compulsion to engage in medical practice, but also to a requirement that a medical practitioner practise his or her profession in a specified manner. Dixon and McTiernan JJ dissented, Dixon J finding that while compulsion to render a medical or dental service would amount to

---

40   See also p. 187 per Deane and Gaudron JJ.
41   In *General Practitioners Society v. Commonwealth* (1980) 145 CLR 532 at 565, Murphy J suggested that a freedom from civil conscription might also be implied from the Constitution: 'The Constitution makes no reference to different classes of society and its terms are inconsistent with slavery, serfdom or similar vestiges of a feudal society. It contains an implication of a free society which limits Parliament's authority to impose civil conscription'.
42   *British Medical Association v. Commonwealth* at 254–5 per Rich J, at 261 per Dixon J, at 281–2 per McTiernan J, and at 286–7 per Williams J. See *General Practitioners Society v. Commonwealth* (1980) 145 CLR 532 at 548 per Gibbs J and at 563–4 per Stephen J; *Alexandra Private Geriatric Hospital Pty Ltd v. Commonwealth* (1987) 162 CLR 271 at 279 per the Court. Compare *British Medical Association v. Commonwealth* at 250–1 per Latham CJ.
43   *British Medical Association v. Commonwealth* at 287 per Williams J. See also p. 277 per Dixon J; *General Practitioners Society v. Commonwealth* (1980) 145 CLR 532 at 549 per Gibbs J, at 563–4 per Stephen J; *Alexandra Private Geriatric Hospital Pty Ltd v. Commonwealth* (1987) 162 CLR 271 at 279–80 per the Court.

civil conscription, regulation of the provision of the service did not. The majority adopted a very broad view of 'civil conscription' in finding invalid a law that required no more than that a medical practitioner use a government form. While the term 'conscription' has been applied in the context of military, and similar service, as meaning compulsory enlistment, it had come to mean much more when inserted as 'civil conscription' into s. 51(xxiiiA).[44]

General Practitioners Society v. Commonwealth (1980) 145 CLR 532 concerned the validity of sections 16A, 16B, and 16C of the *Health Insurance Act 1973* (Cth). These provisions placed conditions on the entitlement to benefits in respect of the provision of pathology services. Obligations, such as the need to become an approved pathology practitioner, were placed on medical practitioners providing pathology services so as to deter excessive servicing. The Court held that the provisions did not breach the limitation in s. 51(xxiiiA). A majority agreed with the finding in *British Medical Association v. Commonwealth* that practical, in addition to legal, compulsion may amount to civil conscription, but found that the provisions did not amount to practical compulsion. Gibbs J distinguished *British Medical Association v. Commonwealth*, finding, at p. 557, that 'any form of civil conscription':

> refers to any sort of compulsion to engage in practice as a doctor or a dentist or to perform particular medical or dental services. However, in its natural meaning it does not refer to compulsion to do, in a particular way, some act in the course of carrying on practice or performing a service, when there is no compulsion to carry on the practice or perform the service.

General Practitioners Society v. Commonwealth sits uncomfortably with the decision in *British Medical Association v. Commonwealth*. Gibbs J's attempt to distinguish the earlier case is unconvincing. His dicta are difficult to reconcile with the result in *British Medical Association v. Commonwealth* because it is hard to see a requirement that a medical practitioner use a government form as anything other than 'compulsion to do, in a particular way, some act in the course of carrying on practice or performing a service'. In light of this, if *British Medical Association v. Commonwealth* were to be reexamined by the Court, there is a strong possibility that Court would favour the dissenting approach of Dixon J.

Acquisition of property on just terms

While the guarantee in s. 51(xxxi) is drafted as a grant of power, the equivalent provision in the United States Constitution is set out as a limitation on power. The Fifth Amendment to the United States Constitution states 'No person shall be ... deprived of ... property, without due process of law; nor shall private property be taken for public use, without just compensation'.[45] The words of s. 51(xxxi) must be viewed and applied as a whole. However, they can also be broken down into three important elements for the purpose of analysis: the Commonwealth can effect an *acquisition* of *property* on *just terms*. The words 'from any State or person' add little except to indicate that

---

44 For criticism of the majority finding, see J. H. Kennan, 'The Possible Constitutional Powers of the Commonwealth as to National Health Insurance' (1975) 49 *Australian Law Journal* 261 at 263–4; R. Sackville, 'Social Welfare in Australia: The Constitutional Framework' (1973) 5 *Federal Law Review* 248 at 261–2.

45 See *Newcrest Mining (WA) Ltd v. Commonwealth* (1997) 147 ALR 42 at 148–50 per Kirby J for discussion of similar guarantees in international instruments and other constitutions.

the states are not free from the coercive aspect of the power. The final phrase 'for any purpose in respect of which the Parliament has power to make laws' has received some attention. In *WH Blakeley & Co. Pty Ltd v. Commonwealth* (1953) 87 CLR 501, a unanimous High Court stated, at pp. 518–19:

> It seems to be plain enough that the Constitution, in using the word 'purpose', is speaking of the object for which the land is needed. The word itself does not refer to any power or powers defined in the various paragraphs of ss 51 or 52 of the Constitution or elsewhere conferred; it is referring to the object for which the land is acquired. That object, however, must be one falling within the Commonwealth's power to make laws. It does not matter, however, from which of the paragraphs the power to make a law covering that object is derived.

In *Attorney-General (Cth) v. Schmidt* (1961) 105 CLR 361 at 372, Dixon CJ, with the support of the other members of the Court, added that the expression 'covers laws with respect to the acquisition of real or personal property for the intended use of any department or officer of the Executive Government of the Commonwealth in the course of administering laws made by the Parliament in the exercise of its legislative power'. He then went on to say that it had yet to be settled whether the expression 'for any purpose' might have a wider meaning. Any wider meaning remains to be fully explored.[46]

There must be an 'acquisition' for s. 51(xxxi) to apply. 'Acquisition' refers to a compulsory acquisition under a law of the Commonwealth, not a voluntary acquisition by agreement.[47] In contrast to the Fifth Amendment to the United States Constitution, an 'acquisition' involves more than the 'taking' of property; someone else must also have acquired something. However, the benefit flowing to another person need not be the same as the thing that was taken away. One thing can be taken away from one person which causes a different thing to be acquired by someone else. For example, in *Georgiadis v. Australian and Overseas Telecommunications Corporation* (1994) 179 CLR 297, it was held that the extinguishment of a cause of action brought against the Commonwealth amounted to an 'acquisition' because, although the Commonwealth did not itself acquire a cause of action—that is, what was taken away—it did acquire a direct benefit or financial gain in the form of a release from liability for damages.[48]

Even though an 'acquisition' does not require that someone acquire the same thing that has been taken away, it does require that something actually be acquired. It is not enough that a law extinguishes or modifies a person's property. This was the basis of the finding of three judges in *Commonwealth v. Tasmania (Tasmanian Dam Case)* (1983) 158 CLR 1 that there had not been an 'acquisition' of property. In that case, the *World Heritage Properties Conservation Act 1983* (Cth) prevented the use of land for specific purposes. The Act did not vest any possessory or proprietary rights. Mason, Murphy, and Brennan JJ found that there had been no 'acquisition' as the Commonwealth had not acquired an interest in any 'property'. According to Mason J, at p. 145:

---

46 See *Trade Practices Commission v. Tooth and Co. Ltd* (1979) 142 CLR 397 at 422–5 per Stephen J; *Clunies-Ross v. Commonwealth* (1984) 155 CLR 193 at 200–1 per Gibbs CJ, Mason, Wilson, Brennan, Deane, and Dawson JJ; *Nintendo Co. Ltd v. Centronics Systems Pty Ltd* (1994) 181 CLR 134 at 165–7 per Dawson J.

47 *Trade Practices Commission v. Tooth and Co. Ltd* (1979) 142 CLR 397 at 416–17 per Stephen J.

48 For a further example of where one thing was taken away and a different thing acquired by someone else, see *Newcrest Mining (WA) Ltd v. Commonwealth* (1997) 147 ALR 42.

The emphasis in s. 51(xxxi) is not on a 'taking' of private property but on the *acquisition* of property for purposes of the Commonwealth. To bring the constitutional provision into play it is not enough that legislation adversely affects or terminates a pre-existing right that an owner enjoys in relation to his property; there must be an acquisition whereby the Commonwealth or another acquires an interest in property, however slight or insubstantial it may be.[49]

While Deane J recognised, at p. 283, that 'The mere extinguishment or deprivation of rights in relation to property does not involve acquisition', he found, at p. 287, that a benefit flowed to the Commonwealth in the form of 'a prohibition, which the Commonwealth alone can lift, of the doing of the specified acts on the … land'. This was enough for him to conclude that there had been an 'acquisition'.

Section 51(xxxi) states that there must be an 'acquisition', but it does not require that there be an 'acquisition' by the Commonwealth. It is enough that a statute can be characterised as being a law with respect to an 'acquisition' of property, whether that 'acquisition' be by the Commonwealth, a state, an organisation, or a person. In *PJ Magennis Pty Ltd v. Commonwealth* (1949) 80 CLR 382, a majority of the High Court found that the *War Service Land Settlement Agreements Act 1945* (Cth) was invalid under s. 51(xxxi) in providing for the acquisition of property, without just terms, by a state government. Williams J found, at p. 423, that 'It is immaterial whether the acquisition is to be made by the Commonwealth or some body authorized to acquire property by the Commonwealth or by a State by agreement with the Commonwealth'.[50] One basis for this conclusion was that if s. 51(xxxi) only applied to acquisitions by the Commonwealth, there would be a 'serious gap in the constitutional safeguard'.[51]

In *Nintendo Co. Ltd v. Centronics Systems Pty Ltd* (1994) 181 CLR 134, the High Court found that certain of the powers in s. 51 manifest an intention that they not be subject to s. 51(xxxi). It was also found that, irrespective of which power they are passed under, certain types of laws are also incapable of being subject to s. 51(xxxi). This is because they cannot be characterised as effecting an 'acquisition' of property. An obvious example is a law that imposes a penalty by way of punishment for a criminal offence.[52] More generally, Mason CJ, Brennan, Deane, Toohey, Gaudron, and McHugh JJ stated that s. 51(xxxi) does not apply to 'a law which is not directed towards the acquisition of property as such but which is concerned with the adjustment of the competing rights, claims or obligations of persons in a particular relationship or area of activity'.[53] The law in that case was such a law because it was 'a law for the adjustment and regulation of the competing claims, rights and liabilities of the designers or first

---

49 (emphasis in original). See *Australian Tape Manufacturers Association Ltd v. Commonwealth* (1993) 176 CLR 480 at 499–500 per Mason CJ, Brennan, Deane and Gaudron JJ; *Australian Capital Television* (1992) 177 CLR 106 at 165–6 per Brennan J.

50 See *Jenkins v. Commonwealth* (1947) 74 CLR 400 at 406 per Williams J; *McClintock v. Commonwealth* (1947) 75 CLR 1 at 23 per Starke J, at 36 per Williams J; *Trade Practices Commission v. Tooth and Co Ltd* (1979) 142 CLR 397 at 427 per Mason J, at 451–2 per Aickin J; *Australian Tape Manufacturers Association Ltd v. Commonwealth* (1993) 176 CLR 480 at 510–11 per Mason CJ, Brennan, Deane, and Gaudron JJ, at 526 per Dawson and Toohey JJ.

51 *Trade Practices Commission v. Tooth and Co. Ltd* (1979) 142 CLR 397 at 452 per Aickin J.

52 *R v. Smithers; Ex parte McMillan* (1982) 152 CLR 477 at 487 per the Court; *Re Director of Public Prosecutions; Ex parte Lawler* (1994) 179 CLR 270.

53 *Nintendo* at 161.

makers of original circuit layouts and those who take advantage of, or benefit from, their work'.[54]

The finding that certain laws do not effect an 'acquisition' of property because they are really concerned with adjusting competing rights was an important aspect of the decision of the High Court in *Mutual Pools & Staff Pty Ltd v. Commonwealth* (1994) 179 CLR 155. An earlier decision of the Court had held that a statute levying a tax on swimming pools constructed inground breached s. 55 of the Constitution and was therefore invalid. While that litigation was pending, the Swimming Pool and Spa Association of Australia, an association of pool suppliers, made an agreement with the Commissioner of Taxation. This agreement provided that the Association's members would continue to pay the tax, but that if the High Court action was successful, a refund with interest would be paid. After losing the High Court action, the Commonwealth, by the *Swimming Pools Tax Refund Act 1992* (Cth), sought to override the agreement and to distribute the invalidly collected taxes in a different manner. The Act provided that the tax paid would be refunded to a pool supplier if it had not been passed on to the purchaser or if the purchaser had later received a refund from the supplier. On the other hand, where a purchaser had borne the tax, the Act enabled that person to claim the refund. It was held that the Act did not breach s. 51(xxxi). This was because there had been no 'acquisition of property' on which s. 51(xxxi) could operate. In an important judgment, Deane and Gaudron JJ found, at p. 187, that just as some powers, such as that over 'taxation' in s. 51(ii), could not be subject to s. 51(xxxi), so certain types of acquisitions 'are of their nature antithetical to the notion of just terms but … were plainly intended to be permissible under laws made pursuant to one or more of the grants of power contained in s. 51'. They gave as examples, at pp. 187–8, 'the compulsory forfeiture to the Commonwealth of money or specific property as punishment for breach of some general rule of conduct prescribed by a valid law of the Commonwealth' or 'the forfeiture of illegally imported goods in the hands of an innocent third party'.[55] They then set out, at pp. 189–90, in general terms two categories of laws that, although effecting an acquisition of property, could not be required to provide 'just terms':

> One such category consists of laws which provide for the creation, modification, extinguishment or transfer of rights and liabilities as an incident of, or a means for enforcing, some general regulation of the conduct, rights and obligations of citizens in relationships or areas which need to be regulated in the common interest. Another category consists of laws defining and altering rights and liabilities under a government scheme involving the expenditure of government funds to provide social security benefits or for other public purposes.

This attempt to synthesise the acquisitions that are not subject to s. 51(xxxi) has yet to be adopted by the High Court. However, it does represent a very useful start that is consistent with the general approach that the Court has been taking toward why s. 51(xxxi) does not operate on certain acquisitions.

A further example of what does not amount to an 'acquisition' of property came in *Health Insurance Commission v. Peverill* (1994) 179 CLR 226. Section 20A of the *Health*

---

54   *Nintendo* at 161.
55   See *Burton v. Honan* (1952) 86 CLR 169 at 180–1 per Dixon CJ; *Re Director of Public Prosecutions; Ex parte Lawler* (1994) 179 CLR 270.

Insurance Act 1973 (Cth) provided that a patient entitled to Medicare benefits may assign that entitlement to a doctor or pathologist if the latter will 'bulk bill': that is, accept the assignment of Medicare benefits as payment in full. Dr Richard Peverill 'bulk billed' in respect of testing for rubella by Enzyme-Linked Immunosorbent Assay (the ELISA test). For each test he claimed a fee of $34.50 under Item 1345 of the Schedule to the Health Insurance Act. However, the Health Insurance Commission ruled that the test came under Item 2294, which set a fee of $4.60. Dr Peverill successfully challenged that ruling in the Federal Court. The Parliament responded by enacting the *Health Insurance (Pathology Services) Amendment Act 1991* (Cth), which retrospectively excluded the ELISA test from Item 1345 and included it under new Items 2294 and 2295. The Amendment Act was challenged in the High Court, where it was unanimously held that it did not infringe s. 51(xxxi). One reason was that there had been no 'acquisition' of property to which s. 51(xxxi) could relate. This was due to the nature of the entitlement affected by the Amendment Act. Mason CJ, Deane, and Gaudron JJ found, at p. 237, that 'the rights that have been terminated or diminished are statutory entitlements to receive payments from consolidated revenue which were not based on antecedent proprietary rights recognized by the general law. Rights of that kind are rights which, as a general rule, are inherently susceptible of variation'. Such rights include 'the nature and quantum of welfare benefits', where it is 'expected that the level of benefits will change from time to time'.[56] This finding does not mean that all statutory rights may be altered without giving 'just terms'. Many statutory rights, such as certain mining interests,[57] are not 'inherently susceptible of variation' and may only be acquired where just terms are given.[58]

The High Court could have given a narrow technical meaning to the word 'property' in s. 51(xxxi). Instead, its interpretation has been a generous one, reflecting the fact that the term is 'the most comprehensive term that can be used'.[59] Regulation 54 of the National Security (General) Regulations (Cth), which were made during the Second World War, enabled the Commonwealth, in the interests of 'public safety, the defence of the Commonwealth, or the efficient prosecution of the war or for maintaining supplies and services essential to the life of the community', to take possession of land for an indefinite period. The Commonwealth, relying on reg. 54, took possession of vacant land in Sydney being used by a weekly tenant, Arthur Dalziel, as a commercial car park. The matter was taken to the High Court, where the Court was called on to decide whether there had been an acquisition of 'property' under s. 51(xxxi). In *Minister of State for the Army v. Dalziel* (1944) 68 CLR 261, the Court, with Latham CJ dissenting, held that there had been. This conclusion rested on a broad definition of 'property'. In contrast to the narrow and legalistic approach taken to the express civil and political rights in the

---

56 *Health Insurance Commission v. Peverill* at 237.
57 See *Newcrest Mining (WA) Ltd v. Commonwealth* (1997) 147 ALR 42.
58 The Commonwealth may be able to create statutory rights that can be subsequently modified or extinguished without attracting the need for compensation under s. 51(xxxi). According to McHugh J in *Commonwealth v. WMC Resources Ltd* (1998) 152 ALR 1 at 37: 'to avoid "contravening" s. 51(xxxi) it would seem that the parliament need ensure only that the legislation creating the property right contains words to the following effect: "any property interest created by this Act endures only until varied or extinguished by subsequent federal legislation"'.
59 *Commonwealth v. New South Wales* (1923) 33 CLR 1 at 20–1 per Knox CJ and Starke J.

Constitution (see Chapter 5), Rich J found, at p. 285, that s. 51(xxxi) should be construed in accordance with its 'fundamental character designed to protect citizens from being deprived of their property by the Sovereign State except on just terms'. According to Starke J, at p. 290, 'Property ... extends to every species of valuable right and interest including real and personal property, incorporeal hereditaments such as rents and services, rights of way, rights of profit or use in land of another, and choses in action'. McTiernan J took a similar broad view, at p. 295: 'It means any tangible or intangible thing which the law protects under the name of property. The acquisition of the possession of land is an instance of the acquisition of property'.

It has not been doubted since that 'property' in s. 51(xxxi) should be broadly interpreted. It has thus been found to include 'money and the right to receive a payment of money'[60] as well as intellectual property[61] and native title.[62] Soon after the decision in *Minister of State for the Army v. Dalziel*, in the *Bank Nationalisation Case* (1948) 76 CLR 1, it was found that the *Banking Act 1947* (Cth), which allowed the Commonwealth to take over control of a private bank by appointing directors in lieu of those elected by shareholders, breached s. 51(xxxi). In the words of Dixon J, at p. 349, shareholders were to be 'stripped of the possession and control of the entire undertaking', although they remained entitled to any dividends declared by the directors. The crucial finding was that the Act involved an acquisition of 'property'. Dixon J took *Minister of State for the Army v. Dalziel* to mean that 'property':

> is not to be confined pedantically to the taking of title by the Commonwealth to some specific estate or interest in land recognized at law or in equity and to some specific form of property in a chattel or chose in action similarly recognized, but that it extends to innominate and anomalous interests and includes the assumption and indefinite continuance of exclusive possession and control for the purposes of the Commonwealth of any subject of property.[63]

In *Minister of State for the Army v. Dalziel*, Starke J suggested that 'property' under s. 51(xxxi) includes a chose in action. This was tested in *Georgiadis v. Australian and Overseas Telecommunications Corporation* (1994) 179 CLR 297. Constantinos Georgiadis sought to sue the Commonwealth in respect of back injuries sustained in 1985 and 1986 while he was an employee of the Commonwealth. The *Compensation (Commonwealth Government Employees) Act 1971* (Cth) had given Georgiadis the option of claiming workers' compensation or of pursuing a common law action for damages. However, s. 44 of the *Commonwealth Employees' Rehabilitation and Compensation Act 1988* (Cth) (since renamed the *Safety, Rehabilitation and Compensation Act 1988* (Cth)) extinguished

---

60　*Australian Tape Manufacturers Association Ltd v. Commonwealth* (1993) 176 CLR 480 at 509 per Mason CJ, Brennan, Deane, and Gaudron JJ.

61　*Australian Tape Manufacturers* at 527 per Dawson and Toohey JJ; *Trade Practices Commission v. Tooth and Co. Ltd* (1979) 142 CLR 397 at 434 per Murphy J; *Smith Kline & French Laboratories (Australia) Ltd v. Secretary, Department of Community Services and Health* (1990) 95 ALR 87 at 134–6 per Gummow J. In *Trade Practices Commission v. Tooth* at 434 Murphy J also suggested that 'property' includes 'the right to vote'. He cited *Amalgamated Society of Engineers v. Smith* (1913) 16 CLR 537 at 553 per Barton ACJ to support this.

62　*Mabo v. Queensland (No 2)* (1992) 175 CLR 1 at 110–12 per Deane and Gaudron JJ. See J. Behrendt, 'So Long, and Thanks for all the Fish ... ' (1995) 3(72) *Aboriginal Law Bulletin* 11; A. Turello, 'Extinguishment of Native Title and the Constitutional Requirement of Just Terms' (1993) 3(62) *Aboriginal Law Bulletin* 11.

63　*Bank Nationalisation Case* at 349.

any claim Georgiadis might have had to common law damages. Mason CJ, Deane, and Gaudron JJ, with Brennan J concurring, found that s. 44 effected an 'acquisition of property', and as it did not provide 'just terms', it was invalid. The majority conclusion rested on two findings. First, it was found that there had been an 'acquisition' because, although Georgiadis' cause of action was not 'acquired' by anyone, the Commonwealth did acquire a direct benefit or financial gain in the form of a release from liability for damages. Second, it was held that a chose in action amounted to 'property'. Mason CJ, Deane, and Gaudron JJ suggested at p. 307 that the finding that s. 44 was invalid was 'finely balanced'. If s. 44 had established a compensation scheme applying to employers and employees generally, as opposed to just Commonwealth employees, it might have been characterised as a law regulating competing claims and interests and thus not subject to s. 51(xxxi).

Dawson, Toohey, and McHugh JJ dissented. Dawson and Toohey JJ held, as they had in *Mutual Pools* and *Health Insurance Commission v. Peverill*, that a mere claim to money or financial benefits is not 'property' and therefore that a release from liability to such a claim is not an 'acquisition' of property. McHugh J found that a chose in action is 'property' and that there had been an 'acquisition'. Nevertheless, he found, at p. 325, that s. 51(xxxi) did not apply:

> because the right of the plaintiff to bring his action was dependent on federal law and was always liable to be revoked by federal law. A right which can be extinguished by a federal law enacted under a power other than s. 51(xxxi) is not a law which falls within the terms of that paragraph.

In *Commonwealth v. Mewett* (1997) 146 ALR 299, the High Court was asked by the Commonwealth to reassess its decision in *Georgiadis*. The result was that *Georgiadis* was reaffirmed. Three former members of the Royal Australian Navy, the respondents, commenced actions against the Commonwealth in 1994. The actions sought damages under the common law of contract and tort for injuries sustained in 1979 (by the first respondent) and 1985 (by the second and third respondents). However, the Commonwealth argued that each of the proceedings should be struck out as a result of s. 44 of the Safety, Rehabilitation and Compensation Act. As in *Georgiadis*, this was met by the argument that s. 44 was in contravention of s. 51(xxxi).

The Commonwealth sought to convince the Court that McHugh J had reached the correct conclusion in his dissent in *Georgiadis*. It was argued that, because the respondents' claims against the Commonwealth arose under a Commonwealth statute, the *Judiciary Act 1903* (Cth), those rights, like the rights considered in *Peverill*, were inherently susceptible of modification or extinguishment. This raised the issue of the source of the Commonwealth's liability. Dawson J found, at p. 309, that 'the preferable view and the view that accords most with the trend of recent authority ... is that s. 64 [of the Judiciary Act] is the provision which removes Crown immunity from suit and allows a citizen to proceed against the Commonwealth (or a State, for that matter) within federal jurisdiction'.[64] However, even though the ability to bring a common

---

64   Section 64 of the Judiciary Act provides, 'In any suit to which the Commonwealth or a State is a party, the rights of parties shall be as nearly as possible be the same, and judgment may be given and costs awarded on either side, as in a suit between subject and subject'.

law action against the Commonwealth depended on s. 64, this did not prevent s. 51(xxxi) applying to strike down s. 44. Although s. 64 allowed the action against the Commonwealth to proceed, s. 64 did not create the cause of action of the respondents against the Commonwealth. The chose in action in each case was a creature of the common law of contract and tort, and could not be equated with a statutory right. Gummow and Kirby JJ agreed with the view that the actions were not statutory rights, but differed in finding that the source of liability lay in Chapter III of the Constitution and not in the Judiciary Act.

A second issue in *Mewett* was whether s. 44 had acquired 'property'. Under the relevant state legislation, the actions brought by the respondents were statute-barred unless they could gain an extension of time. The Commonwealth argued that as the actions were statute-barred, they could not be 'property' for the purposes of s. 51(xxxi). This was rejected. It was found that, although they were statute-barred (which limited the remedies available), the actions were not extinguished by the limitations legislation, and that the possibility of an extension of time not being granted merely went to the value of the causes of action.

'Just terms' must be given where a law can be characterised as providing for an 'acquisition of property' under s. 51(xxxi). By contrast, the Fifth Amendment to the United States Constitution requires 'just compensation'. Whereas 'just compensation' implies market value, 'just terms' suggests a requirement of 'fairness'.[65] In *Grace Brothers Pty Ltd v. Commonwealth* (1946) 72 CLR 269, the Court rejected an argument that 'just terms' can be equated with the exact money value of the property taken or with the money value of the property to the person from whom it had been acquired.[66] Dixon J found, at p. 290, that the question was 'whether the law amounts to a true attempt to provide fair and just standards of compensating or rehabilitating the individual considered as an owner of property, fair and just as between him and the government of the country'. He made it clear, at p. 291, that in answering this question the Court must 'examine the justice of the terms provided' and should not 'disregard the interests of the public or of the Commonwealth'.[67] Moreover, according to McTiernan J at p. 295, the Court was not to ask whether 'just terms' had been provided, but whether 'the terms enacted by Parliament *might reasonably be regarded* as just terms' (emphasis added). Latham CJ likewise suggested, at p. 280, that the terms provided would be valid 'unless it is such that a reasonable man could not regard the terms of acquisitions as being just'.[68] The Parliament is thus accorded some discretion in setting compensation. This discretion might be exercised by setting up a scheme under which persons are compensated on the recommendation of a minister or by a board or committee, although, as Dixon J found in *Nelurgaloo Pty Ltd v. Commonwealth* (1948) 75 CLR 495 at 567, legislation cannot authorise a decision-maker to make a decision that would lead to unjust compensation.

If 'just terms' are required by s. 51(xxxi), a just process must be as well. For example, it would be difficult, if not impossible, to find that 'just terms' had been given if a person could only gain recompense after a 30-year waiting period, or if the procedures by

---

65   *Nelungaloo Pty Ltd v. Commonwealth* (1948) 75 CLR 495 at 569 per Dixon J.
66   Compare *McClintock v. Commonwealth* (1947) 75 CLR 1 at 38 per Williams J.
67   See also p. 280 per Latham CJ: 'Justice involves consideration of the interests of the community as well as of the person whose property is acquired'.
68   See also p. 285 per Starke J; *McClintock v. Commonwealth* (1947) 75 CLR 1 at 24, 26 per Starke J.

which a person could claim compensation were manifestly unfair.[69] Deane J recognised this in the *Tasmanian Dam Case* (1983) 158 CLR 1, where he was the only member of the Court to find that the Act effected an 'acquisition of property', and therefore was the only judge to discuss whether 'just terms' had been provided. Section 17 of the *World Heritage Properties Conservation Act 1983* (Cth) established a scheme for fixing compensation. Claims under $5 000 000 were to be heard by the Federal Court, while for claims over $5 000 000 there was to be a six-month waiting period, during which compensation might be agreed to, followed by a Commission of Inquiry that was to recommend, within 12 months of its formation, 'fair and just' compensation. Deane J stated, at p. 290:

> where the Parliament does not specify the amount of compensation but provides a procedure for determining what is fair and just, the Court will examine the nature and extent of the entitlement of a claimant under the procedure established and the nature of the procedure itself in deciding whether the acquisition for which the law provides is 'on just terms'.

He then proceeded to do just this. He found that s. 17 did not provide 'just terms'. This was because there was:

> something intrinsically unfair in a procedure which, in effect, ensures that, unless a claimant agrees to accept the terms which the Commonwealth is prepared to offer, he will be forced to wait years before he is allowed even access to a court, tribunal or other body which can authoritatively determine the amount of the compensation which the Commonwealth must pay.[70]

This conclusion was reinforced by another aspect of s. 17, the fact that it did not provide for the payment of interest over the period in which the compensation was being worked out.

In *Pye v. Renshaw* (1951) 84 CLR 58, the High Court held that a grant made to New South Wales by the Commonwealth under s. 96 of the Constitution that enabled the state to acquire land was not subject to s. 51(xxxi). It was held that the grant did not amount to an 'acquisition of property' by the Commonwealth. This means that the Commonwealth can avoid the requirement to pay 'just terms' under s. 51(xxxi) by granting money to a state under s. 96 on condition that the state itself acquire the property and then make use of that property in accordance with a specified Commonwealth policy objective. Hence, the use of s. 96 by the Commonwealth, as upheld in *Pye v. Renshaw*, enabled the Commonwealth to circumvent the High Court's holding in *PJ Magennis Pty Ltd v. Commonwealth* (1949) 80 CLR 382 that legislation to a similar effect breached s. 51(xxxi) by not providing 'just terms'.

More difficult questions have arisen in regard to the Commonwealth's plenary power to legislate for the Australian territories under s. 122 of the Constitution. Under s. 122, the federal Parliament 'may make laws for the government of any territory'. While it is clear that s. 51(xxxi) is capable of applying to the Commonwealth's other powers in s. 51, which are expressed to be 'subject to this Constitution', it is less clear

---

69 See *Australian Apple and Pear Marketing Board v. Tonking* (1942) 66 CLR 77 at 109 per Rich J; *Johnston Fear & Kingham & The Offset Printing Co. Pty Ltd v. Commonwealth* (1943) 67 CLR 314 at 332–3 per Williams J.

70 *Tasmanian Dams Case* at 291.

that it can apply to s. 122, which contains no such qualification. In *Teori Tau v. Common-wealth* (1969) 119 CLR 564, the Court held that laws passed pursuant to s. 122 are not subject to s. 51(xxxi). Barwick CJ spoke for the Court at p. 570: 'The grant of legislative power by s. 122 is plenary in quality and unlimited and unqualified in point of subject matter. In particular, it is not limited or qualified by s. 51(xxxi) or, for that matter, by any other paragraph of that section'.

Teori Tau was reassessed in *Newcrest Mining (WA) Ltd v. Commonwealth* (1997) 147 ALR 42. In 1989, the federal Cabinet decided that stage three of the Kakadu National Park in the Northern Territory should be increased to include the Coronation Hill area. In 1989 and 1991, Proclamations were made to this effect under the *National Parks and Wildlife Conservation Act 1975* (Cth). Newcrest Mining (WA) Ltd held 25 mining tenements in that area. Under s. 10(1A) of the Act, as amended by the *National Parks and Wildlife Conservation Amendment Act 1987* (Cth), 'No operations for the recovery of minerals shall be carried on in Kakadu National Park'. The result was to prohibit New-crest from exploiting the tenements. Section 7 of the National Parks and Wildlife Con-servation Amendment Act further provided that 'Notwithstanding any law of the Commonwealth or of the Northern Territory, the Commonwealth is not liable to pay compensation to any person by reason of the enactment of this Act'. Newcrest brought an action in the High Court claiming that the 1989 and 1991 Proclamations breached s. 51(xxxi) of the Constitution.

Four judges, Toohey, Gaudron, Gummow, and Kirby JJ, found that there was an 'acquisition of property' for the purposes of s. 51(xxxi) and that s. 51(xxxi) applied because (regardless of the position under s. 122) there was an acquisition for Com-monwealth purposes under s. 51. Specifically, the National Parks and Wildlife Conser-vation Act could be characterised as a valid law under the Commonwealth's external affairs power in s. 51(xxix). The reasoning supporting this approach was expressed by Gaudron J, at p. 77:

> It is one thing to read down s. 51(xxxi) so that it does not apply to a law enacted pursuant to s. 122 of the Constitution. It is another to treat it as not applying to a law which has two pur-poses, one of which falls within the terms of s. 51(xxxi) and the other of which is for the government of a Territory. That is to rewrite the terms of s. 51(xxxi), not to read them down. Neither course is permissible. Rather, the proper approach is to construe constitutional guar-antees as liberally as their terms will allow.

According to Toohey J at p. 71, 'it seems almost inevitable that any acquisition of prop-erty by the Commonwealth will now attract the operation of s. 51(xxxi) because it will be in pursuit of a purpose in respect of which the parliament has power to make laws, even if that acquisition takes place within a Territory'.[71]

The reasoning of Gaudron J was novel. Arguably, it is inconsistent with the Court's approach to characterisation. Under the long-standing theory of 'dual characterisation' developed in cases such as *Fairfax v. Federal Commissioner of Taxation* (1965) 114 CLR 1, *Murphyores Incorporated Pty Ltd v. Commonwealth* (1976) 136 CLR 1 and *Northern Suburbs General Cemetery Reserve Trust v. Commonwealth* (1993) 176 CLR 555, a statute will be

---

71 *Newcrest Mining* at 71.

valid if it can be seen to be a law with respect to a subject matter within Commonwealth power, even if it also deals with matters that lie outside such power. This might have been applied in *Newcrest* to find that if a statute could be characterised as a law under s. 122 (and thus not subject to s. 51(xxxi)), the statute would be valid, even if it could also be characterised as a law under s. 51(xxix) (which is subject to s. 51(xxxi)).[72] The fact that s. 122 is not subject to s. 51(xxxi) distinguishes the situation set out in *Bourke v. State Bank of New South Wales* (1990) 170 CLR 276, whereby a limitation in a s. 51 power may be capable of limiting the exercise of other s. 51 powers.

Three of the majority judges—Gaudron, Gummow, and Kirby JJ—were in any event prepared to go further and to hold that s. 51(xxxi) applies to laws made under s. 122, and hence generally to acquisitions of property in the territories. These three judges were prepared to overrule *Teori Tau*. Kirby J examined the property rights conferred by the *Universal Declaration of Human Rights*; the Magna Carta; the French Declaration of the Rights of Man and of the Citizen 1789; and the constitutions of the USA, India, Malaysia, Japan, and South Africa. He reinforced his conclusion, at p. 147, by developing another novel tenet of interpretation. He stated, 'Where the Constitution is ambiguous, this court should adopt that meaning which conforms to the principles of fundamental rights rather than an interpretation which would involve a departure from such rights'. Over time, this sentence might come to assume the same importance for the protection of constitutional rights as has the statement by O'Connor J in *Jumbunna Coal Mine NL v. Victorian Coal Miners' Association* (1908) 6 CLR 309 at 367–8 that in construing Commonwealth power the High Court should, in the case of ambiguity, 'always lean to the broader interpretation' (see Chapter 4).

The 25 mining tenements were granted under the *Mining Ordinance 1939* (NT) and subsequently recognised by the *Mining Act 1980* (NT). Nevertheless, it was found that the tenements were not mere statutory rights and that the decision in *Health Insurance Commission v. Peverill* could be distinguished to find that the tenements amounted to 'property'. It was also found that there had been an 'acquisition'. According to Gummow J at p. 129, the effect of the Proclamations was that the Commonwealth and the Director of National Parks and Wildlife:

> acquired identifiable and measurable advantages. In the case of the Director, those advantages were the acquisition of the land freed from the rights of Newcrest to occupy and conduct mining operations thereon and, in the case of the Commonwealth, the minerals freed from the rights of Newcrest to mine them.

Brennan CJ, Dawson, and McHugh JJ dissented. Although Brennan CJ found, and Dawson J assumed, that there was an 'acquisition of property', they applied *Teori Tau* to hold that s. 51(xxxi) does not bind the territories. McHugh J also applied *Teori Tau*, but was in lone dissent in finding that there was no 'acquisition of property'. He found, at p. 81, that 'The effect of the proclamations was merely to impinge on Newcrest's rights to exploit those interests. But even if there was effectively a diminution or extinguishment of all or part of Newcrest's interests, there was no gain by the Commonwealth'.

---

72   See *Newcrest Mining* at 51 per Brennan CJ.

McHugh J's reasoning highlighted the difficulty in reconciling the majority conclusion in *Newcrest* with the finding of Mason, Murphy, and Brennan JJ in the *Tasmanian Dam Case* that legislation that prevents the use of land for specific purposes, and does not vest any possessory or proprietary rights, does not amount to an 'acquisition of property'.[73]

Shortly after deciding *Newcrest*, the High Court handed down its decision in *Commonwealth v. WMC Resources Ltd* (1998) 152 ALR. In both cases it was argued that the modification or extinguishment of a statutory permit amounted to an 'acquisition of property' under s. 51(xxxi). While this argument succeeded in *Newcrest*, it failed in *WMC Resources*. Given that 'The mere extinction or diminution of a proprietary right residing in one person does not necessarily result in the acquisition of a proprietary right by another',[74] *Newcrest* demonstrated a willingness on the part of the High Court to be creative in locating a benefit or identifiable interest acquired by the Commonwealth. *WMC Resources* showed that this willingness has its limits.

WMC Resources held an interest in an exploration permit issued under the *Petroleum (Submerged Lands) Act 1967* (Cth). The permit covered an area within the Timor Gap that, under s. 28, the permit holder was authorised 'to explore for petroleum, and to carry on such operations and execute such works as are necessary for that purpose'. Several million dollars was expended to this end and there were prospects of discovering petroleum deposits capable of exploitation. At the time the permit was issued, Australia and Indonesia each claimed sovereign rights to explore and to exploit the natural resources of the Timor Gap. Australia and Indonesia subsequently entered into a treaty by which they agreed to create a zone of cooperation divided into areas designated A, B, and C. Some of the area covered by the permit fell within area A. The Treaty was carried into effect in Australia by the *Petroleum (Australia-Indonesia Zone of Cooperation) Act 1990* (Cth) and the *Petroleum (Australia-Indonesia Zone of Cooperation) (Consequential Provisions) Act 1990* (Cth). The former Act established that petroleum exploration and exploitation could only be carried out in area A with the approval of the joint authority established under the treaty, while the effect of the latter Act was to reduce the area covered by the permit so that it no longer extended to area A. WMC Resources brought an action in which it argued that these Acts effected an 'acquisition of property' under s. 51(xxxi).[75]

The Full Court of the Federal Court had decided that the exploration permit was 'property' for the purposes of s. 51(xxxi),[76] and this was not contested by the Commonwealth in the High Court. Argument in the High Court accordingly centred on

---

73 Brennan CJ, the only judge common to both findings, did not seek to distinguish his earlier decision in the *Tasmanian Dam Case* in reaching his conclusion in *Newcrest*.

74 *Australian Tape Manufacturers Association Ltd v. Commonwealth* (1993) 176 CLR 480 at 528 per Dawson and Toohey JJ.

75 If this argument had been successful, the Commonwealth legislation would not have been invalid, as s. 24(2) of the Petroleum (Australia-Indonesia Zone of Cooperation) (Consequential Provisions) Act stated that 'Where, but for this section, the operation of the amendments made by this Part would result in the acquisition of property from a person otherwise than on just terms, the Commonwealth is liable to pay compensation of a reasonable amount to the person in respect of the acquisition'. Hence, WMC Resources sought 'just terms' compensation under s. 24(2) rather than the invalidity of the Act. Safety-net provisions of this type have become common in federal legislation to guard against s. 51(xxxi) rendering an Act invalid. See, for example, *Native Title Act 1993* (Cth), sections 18, 53; *Olympic Insignia Protection Act 1987* (Cth), s. 21.

76 *Commonwealth v. Western Mining Corporation Ltd* (1996) 136 ALR 353 at 359–63 per Black CJ, at 383–4 per Beaumont J, at 397 per Cooper J. See *WMC Resources* at 7 per Brennan CJ, at 68–9 per Kirby J.

whether there had been an 'acquisition'. A majority consisting of Brennan CJ, Gaudron, McHugh, and Gummow JJ, with Toohey and Kirby JJ dissenting, found that there had not been an 'acquisition of property' for the purposes of s. 51(xxxi), and thus that there was no requirement on the part of the Commonwealth to provide 'just terms'. Brennan CJ found, at p. 10, that 'Where a law of the Commonwealth creates or authorises the creation of a right, a statutory modification or extinguishment of the right effects its acquisition if, but only if, it modifies or extinguishes a reciprocal liability to which the party acquiring the right was subject'. In *Newcrest*, the National Parks and Wildlife Conservation Act had extinguished the liability of the Commonwealth to have minerals extracted from its land, thereby enhancing its interest in that land. The situation in *WMC Resources* was distinguishable because, unlike the Northern Territory land considered in *Newcrest*, the Commonwealth has no property interest at common law in the Timor Gap continental shelf. In the language of Gaudron J, at p. 27, 'the Consequential Provisions Act simply modified a statutory right which had no basis in the general law and which was inherently susceptible to that course'. Hence, like the entitlement to Medicare benefits considered in *Health Insurance Commission v. Peverill*, the permit rights could be modified or extinguished without infringing s. 51(xxxi). In dissent, Toohey and Kirby JJ held that the Commonwealth had acquired a real and identifiable benefit. Toohey J stated, at p. 21, that the effect of the Commonwealth legislation was that:

> the sovereign right to explore resources within the excised area was revested in the Commonwealth. In turn this freed the Commonwealth to deal with this right. It also enabled the Commonwealth to enter into treaty arrangements to its financial benefit and towards the resolution of the ongoing dispute with Indonesia as to sovereign rights in the Timor Gap.

The case law on s. 51(xxxi) reveals a fractured jurisprudence. On one hand, there is general acceptance that s. 51(xxxi) cannot apply to certain types of laws, such as taxation laws, laws that impose a penalty, and laws defining and altering rights and liabilities under a government scheme. On the other hand, there is a lack of doctrinal clarity or commonality between the judges of the High Court as to how such exceptions should be determined and applied. The struggle to achieve a common standard is evident in many of the judgments of the Court, such as the judgment of Deane and Gaudron JJ in *Mutual Pools*. The resistance of s. 51(xxxi) to clear guiding principles prevents its application from achieving an acceptable degree of certainty. The number of cases being litigated in the Federal Court and High Court on s. 51(xxxi) suggests that the intricate rules of interpretation developing around the section do not provide clear answers to new problems. This is apparent even for problems that depart in only a small way from a fact situation already litigated. It may be that the complex web of legal relationships to which s. 51(xxxi) must apply, combined with the dual nature of s. 51(xxxi) as both a power and a guarantee, make it nearly impossible to achieve a definitive set of guiding rules for the section.

Conclusion

In its interpretation of the economic rights in the Constitution, the High Court has been faced with many choices. These choices have determined whether economic rights were to emerge as real limitations on legislative power, and thus as real guarantees of rights, or whether they were to play a minor role in Australian constitutionalism. On most occasions the High Court has chosen to be generous in its interpretation of economic guarantees. Whereas it was not until 1989 that a plaintiff was able to invoke a civil and political right to strike down a law (see Chapter 5), each of the economic rights discussed in this Chapter has been applied in this way. In the case of sections 51(xxxi) and 92, laws have been found to be inconsistent with the guarantee, and thus invalid, on many occasions.

It can be expected that economic rights will continue to loom large in the protection of human rights under the Constitution. While the reinterpretation of s. 92 in *Cole v. Whitfield* meant the end of that provision as a guarantee of the 'individual rights' of the interstate trader, it still has considerable work to do in fostering rights. That provision's scope to protect interstate 'intercourse' will be a significant impediment to the regulation of emerging forms of communication, such as the Internet, and will hamper any attempt to restrict interstate movement. Section 51(xxxi) will also continue to generate a large volume of work for the High Court and will be a source of irritation to federal attempts to regulate property, such as native title. Incremental developments have seen s. 51(xxxi) jurisprudence deepen in complexity without the emergence of any unifying vision. Nevertheless, the ambit of s. 51(xxxi) has continued to expand to new areas, such as to causes of action, despite several cases in which it has been found that there has been no 'acquisition' under s. 51(xxxi). The judgments of Gaudron and Kirby JJ in *Newcrest* show that s. 51(xxxi) may one day act as a catalyst for change in the interpretation of rights generally. If nothing more, *Newcrest* may spur recognition that constitutional rights should apply to Commonwealth laws passed for the territories.

Implications from Representative Government

Introduction

The Australian Constitution lacks a Bill of Rights, and those express civil and political rights that it does contain have been, with one recent exception, interpreted almost out of existence (see Chapter 5). It is not surprising, therefore, that in the context of ever increasing international recognition of human rights (see Chapter 1), the High Court has looked to other avenues to foster civil liberties. One such avenue is the notion of deriving implications from the Constitution. Despite the rhetoric of *Amalgamated Society of Engineers v. Adelaide Steamship Co. Ltd (Engineers Case)* (1920) 28 CLR 129, there is a long history of the High Court deriving implications from the Constitution (see Chapter 4). As Dixon J argued in *Melbourne Corporation v. Commonwealth* (1947) 74 CLR 31 at 83, the 'efficacy of the system logically demands' that certain implications be given recognition. In that case Dixon J recognised an implied immunity of the states from Commonwealth laws. If an implication could provide the states with some immunity from Commonwealth laws, the very thing that the decision in the *Engineers Case* had railed against, it might be possible to use a similar approach to discover implications of human rights. As Mason CJ argued in one decision, 'there is no reason to limit the process of constitutional implication to that particular source'.[1] Cases such as *Melbourne Corporation* provided the High Court of the 1990s with the methodology to underpin its foray into implied rights. The debt owed to decisions such as *Melbourne Corporation* is clear.

The implied freedoms developed in the 1990s to protect human rights have a different foundation to the implied immunity of the states from Commonwealth laws. In *Melbourne Corporation*, Dixon J stated that the 'efficacy of the system logically demands', but which system? The 'system' he was referring to in *Melbourne Corporation* was the federal system created by the Constitution (see Chapter 3), which gave rise to an

---

1   *Australian Capital Television Pty Ltd v. Commonwealth* (1992) 177 CLR 106 at 134.

implied immunity that could be 'plainly seen in the very frame of the Constitution'.[2] On the other hand, the implied freedom of political communication developed by the Court in more recent times is derived from the system of representative government enshrined in the Constitution. Other freedoms, such as any implied freedom from retrospective criminal laws, arise from the separation of judicial power achieved by Chapter III of the Constitution (see Chapter 8).

The 1990s was not the first time members of the High Court discovered that rights could be implied from the Constitution. Even before the *Engineers Case*, Griffith CJ and Barton J in *R v. Smithers; Ex parte Benson* (1912) 16 CLR 99 argued for an implied freedom of movement between states and of access to government and to the seat of government (see Chapter 3). Several decades later, Murphy J was a lone voice in arguing for a broader range of implied freedoms.

The Murphy supernova[3]

Murphy J[4] was a passionate believer in the protection of human rights by legal means. As Attorney-General in the Whitlam government, he introduced the Human Rights Bill 1973 (Cth) into the federal Parliament (see Chapter 10). This Bill sought to implement the *International Covenant on Civil and Political Rights 1966* (see Chapter 1) in Australia, but was never enacted. Soon after, he was appointed to the High Court, a position he held until his death in 1986. As a judge, he handed down a series of decisions that sought to give life to the rights he perceived in the Australian Constitution. He did so by broadly interpreting the express rights contained in the instrument, namely sections 41,[5] 80,[6] and 116[7] (see Chapter 5), and by discovering a number of other rights by implication.[8] These judgments were undoubtedly the most explicitly rights-orientated decisions ever handed down by a member of the High Court.

In charting the rights contained in the Australian Constitution, Murphy J found what almost amounted to an implied Bill of Rights. The first case in which Murphy J suggested that the Constitution embodies implied freedoms was *R v. Director-General of Social Welfare (Vic); Ex parte Henry* (1975) 133 CLR 369. There he found, at p. 388, that 'It would not be constitutionally permissible for the Parliament of Australia or any of the States to create or authorize slavery or serfdom'.[9] He justified this conclu-

---

2 *Melbourne Corporation* at 83 per Dixon J.
3 A supernova was named after Murphy J in 1977. This was only the third time that a supernova was named after a person. See M. Coper, *Encounters with the Australian Constitution*, deluxe edn, CCH, 1987, p. 356.
4 See generally A. R. Blackshield, D. Brown, M. Coper, and R. Krever (eds), *The Judgments of Justice Lionel Murphy*, Primavera Press, 1986; M. Coper and G. Williams (eds), *Justice Lionel Murphy: Influential or Merely Prescient?*, Federation Press, 1997; J. A. Scutt, (ed.), *Lionel Murphy: A Radical Judge*, McCulloch, 1987.
5 *R v. Pearson; Ex parte Sipka* (1983) 152 CLR 254.
6 *Li Chia Hsing v. Rankin* (1978) 141 CLR 182.
7 *Attorney-General (Vic); Ex rel Black v. Commonwealth (DOGS Case)* (1981) 146 CLR 559.
8 See generally G. Williams, 'Lionel Murphy and Democracy and Rights' in M. Coper and G. Williams, p. 50; J. M. Williams, 'Revitalising the Republic: Lionel Murphy and the Protection of Individual Rights' (1997) 8 *Public Law Review* 27; L. Zines, *The High Court and the Constitution*, 4th edn, Butterworths, 1997, pp. 416–18.
9 See *General Practitioners Society v. Commonwealth* (1980) 145 CLR 532 at 565 per Murphy J: 'The Constitution makes no reference to different classes of society and its terms are inconsistent with slavery, serfdom or similar vestiges of a feudal society. It contains an implication of a free society which limits Parliament's authority to impose civil conscription.'

sion in two sentences, at p. 388: 'The reason lies in the nature of our Constitution. It is a Constitution for a free society'.[10] As this quote suggests, Murphy J was not afraid to venture beyond orthodox understandings of the Constitution, or even the text of the instrument itself, into the realm of 'silent constitutional principles ... not mentioned in the Constitution'.[11] Murphy J located such principles in 'the democratic theme of the Constitution'.[12]

Murphy J subsequently discovered other rights. In *Attorney-General (Cth); Ex rel McKinlay v. Commonwealth* (1975) 135 CLR 1, he found that s. 24 of the Constitution, which requires that the members of the House of Representatives be 'directly chosen by the people', entails as a 'standard of equality the alternatives of equal numbers of people and equal numbers of electors'.[13] In other cases he implied freedoms of movement and communication,[14] a right to be heard before being subject to an adverse order,[15] and a freedom from 'cruel and unusual punishment'.[16] In *Ansett Transport Industries (Operations) Pty Ltd v. Wardley* (1980) 142 CLR 237 at 267, he even argued that 'It may be that an implication should be drawn from its terms that the Parliament's legislative powers do not extend to authorizing arbitrary discrimination between the sexes'. This conclusion was based on the fact that 'The Constitution makes no discrimination between the sexes'.[17]

In some cases, Murphy J sought to develop in greater detail the source from which he drew constitutional rights, particularly the system of representative government created by the Constitution. In *Ansett Transport Industries (Operations) Pty Ltd v. Commonwealth* (1977) 139 CLR 54 at 88, he stated:

> Elections of federal Parliament provided for in the Constitution require freedom of movement, speech and other communication, not only between the States, but in and between every part of the Commonwealth. The proper operation of the system of representative government requires the same freedoms between elections. These are also necessary for the proper operation of the Constitutions of the States (which now derive their authority from Ch V of the Constitution[)]. From these provisions and from the concept of the Commonwealth arises an implication of a constitutional guarantee of such freedoms, freedoms so elementary that it was not necessary to mention them in the Constitution.

Murphy J also sought to develop a foundation based on a system of representative democracy in *Miller v. TCN Channel Nine Pty Ltd* (1986) 161 CLR 556 at 581–2. This basis was clearly a more persuasive foundation than the unhelpful 'It is a Constitution

---

10 See *Seamen's Union of Australia v. Utah Development Co.* (1978) 144 CLR 120 at 157 per Murphy J: 'The Constitution is a framework for a free society'.

11 *Victoria v. Australian Building Construction Employees' and Builders Labourers' Federation* (1982) 152 CLR 25 at 108 per Murphy J.

12 *Attorney-General (NSW); Ex rel McKellar v. Commonwealth* (1977) 139 CLR 527 at 569 per Murphy J.

13 *McKinlay* at 70.

14 *Buck v. Bavone* (1976) 135 CLR 110 at 137; *McGraw-Hinds (Aust) Pty Ltd v. Smith* (1979) 144 CLR 633 at 670; *Ansett Transport Industries (Operations) Pty Ltd v. Commonwealth* (1977) 139 CLR 54 at 88; *Uebergang v. Australian Wheat Board* (1980) 145 CLR 266 at 312; *Koowarta v. Bjelke-Petersen* (1982) 153 CLR 168 at 240; *Gallagher v. Durack* (1983) 152 CLR 238 at 248; *Miller v. TCN Channel Nine Pty Ltd* (1986) 161 CLR 556 at 581–2.

15 *Taylor v. Taylor* (1979) 143 CLR 1 at 20.

16 *Sillery v. The Queen* (1981) 180 CLR 353 at 362.

17 *Ansett Transport Industries (Operations) Pty Ltd v. Wardley* at 267.

for a free society' relied on in *R v. Director-General of Social Welfare (Vic); Ex parte Henry* (1975) 133 CLR 369 at 388.

Murphy J's views on implied rights found no favour with the other members of the High Court. In *Miller v. TCN Channel Nine Pty Ltd*, a case dealing with s. 92 of the Constitution that was handed down on 21 October 1986 an hour before Murphy J died, he referred to 'guarantees of freedom of speech and other communications and freedom of movement not only between the States and the States and the Territories but in and between every part of the Commonwealth'. This drew a series of stinging rebukes from the other members of the Court, including from Mason J, at p. 579:

> There was an alternative argument put by the defendant, based on the judgment of Murphy J in *Buck v. Bavone*, that there is to be implied in the Constitution a new set of freedoms which include a guarantee of freedom of communication. It is sufficient to say that I cannot find any basis for implying a new s. 92A into the Constitution.[18]

'Directly chosen by the people'

Murphy J discovered a range of implied rights, sometimes apparently from little more than his own vision of what the Constitution ought to contain. The central challenge facing judges who subsequently sought to imply rights was to develop a more secure foundation. This involved moving beyond the approach developed by Murphy J. This is perhaps one reason why Murphy J has been so rarely cited in later implied rights decisions, despite some similarities between his approach in cases such as *Ansett Transport Industries (Operations) Pty Ltd v. Commonwealth* and the reasoning of later judges.[19]

One source of implication turned to in the 1990s was the system of representative government created by the Constitution. Section 1 of the Constitution creates the federal Parliament, consisting of the Queen, the Senate (the upper house), and the House of Representatives (the lower house). Other sections establish the link between the Parliament and the Australian people, and thereby the representative nature of the body. Most importantly, sections 7 and 24 require, respectively, that the members of the Senate and the House of Representatives be 'directly chosen by the people'. This imperative recognises a system of government based on democratic elections; parliamentarians are to be 'chosen'—that is, elected—by the 'people'. Sections 7, 8, 25, and 41 establish that this is to occur by 'voting' in an 'election', and sections 5, 13, and 28 establish that elections are to be held at least approximately every three years.

The words 'directly chosen by the people' in sections 7 and 24 harbour many implications. 'Great rights are often expressed in simple phrases', as Murphy J said of these words in one case.[20] The word 'directly' indicates that electors are to cast their choice for candidates without any intervening stage, such as an electoral college.[21] The word

---

18 For further criticism, see P. Bickovskii, 'No Deliberate Innovators: Mr Justice Murphy and the Australian Constitution' (1977) 8 *Federal Law Review* 460; G. Winterton, 'Extra-Constitutional Notions in Australian Constitutional Law' (1986) 16 *Federal Law Review* 223.

19 G. Williams, 'Lionel Murphy and Democracy and Rights', p. 61.

20 *Attorney-General (Cth); Ex rel McKinlay v. Commonwealth* (1975) 135 CLR 1 at 65.

21 *Australian Capital Television Pty Ltd v. Commonwealth* (1992) 177 CLR 106 at 227 per McHugh J.

'chosen' is more significant. The 'choice' mandated by sections 7 and 24 would be frustrated by any law that provided that there could only be one candidate per electorate, or indeed a limited number of candidates per electorate. It would also be inconsistent with a law that limited eligibility to stand for office to members of a particular political party, or indeed a law that provided that members of a certain organisation could not stand for election. A 'choice' implies, if nothing more, a free and 'genuine choice',[22] perhaps even an informed choice.

Section 245(1) of the *Commonwealth Electoral Act 1918* (Cth) states, 'It shall be the duty of every elector to vote at each election'. The section then goes on to establish a penalty for electors who fail to vote in federal elections. Might it be argued that the 'choice', or 'genuine choice', required by sections 7 and 24 includes the right not to make a choice? In *Adelaide Company of Jehovah's Witnesses Inc v. Commonwealth* (1943) 67 CLR 116 at 123, Latham CJ argued 'The prohibition in s. 116 operates not only to protect the freedom of religion, but also to protect the right of a man to have no religion'. It may be that s. 245 does not force a person to make a choice, and that while it requires attendance at the polling booth and the depositing of the voting paper in the ballot box, the voter need not mark the ballot paper.[23] Nevertheless, it might be argued that the system of compulsory voting established by s. 245 is unconstitutional.[24]

The result in *Langer v. Commonwealth* (1996) 186 CLR 302 suggests that compulsory voting is not inconsistent with the 'choice' required by sections 7 and 24. McHugh J concluded in that case that 'this Court has held that compulsory voting in federal elections is within the power of the Parliament'.[25] Section 240 of the Commonwealth Electoral Act stated that 'In a House of Representatives election a person shall mark his or her vote' by numbering every square '1, 2, 3, 4 … '. Under s. 270, a ballot paper 'shall not be informal' if it includes a sequence of consecutive numbers beginning with '1', even if numbers are duplicated and even if one square is blank. Thus a paper numbered '1, 2, 3, 3 … ' will be counted as indicating a preference for candidates '1' and '2'. Under s. 329A it was an offence, attracting up to 6 months' imprisonment, to 'print, publish or distribute … any matter or thing with the intention of encouraging persons … to fill in a ballot paper otherwise than in accordance with' s. 240.

At the 1993 federal election Albert Langer urged electors to vote '1, 2, 3, 3 … ', with the major parties being placed equal last.[26] Advertising by the Electoral Commission countered that a formal vote must number every square using consecutive numbers. Langer sued in the High Court for an injunction, arguing that the Commission's advertising was 'misleading and intimidating', and would 'have an effect … [on] the Election such that it will no longer be free or fair'. He argued that sections 240 and 329A were invalid because they were inconsistent with the requirement in s. 24 of the Constitution that representatives be 'directly chosen by the people', and the people, if choosing freely, must be free not to choose. Langer also maintained in his written,

---

22 *Langer v. Commonwealth* (1996) 186 CLR 302 at 325 per Dawson J.

23 A. Twomey, 'Free to Choose or Compelled to Lie?—The Rights of Voters After *Langer v. The Commonwealth*' (1996) 24 *Federal Law Review* 201 at 208–10.

24 Compare *Judd v. McKeon* (1926) 38 CLR 380, where the High Court upheld compulsory voting.

25 *Langer* at 340, referring to *Judd v. McKeon* (1926) 38 CLR 380. Compare Twomey at 211.

26 See C. Field, '"Tweedledum and Tweedledee 1,2,3,3"—The Albert Langer Story', Parliamentary Research Service, Commonwealth Parliament, *Current Issues Brief No. 14*, 1995–96.

though not in his oral, argument that s. 329A infringed the implied freedom of political communication (see p. 183).

The High Court unanimously held that s. 240 was valid. The Court, with Dawson J dissenting, held that s. 329A was also valid.[27] Underpinning these conclusions was the view that the Constitution, in sections 31 and 51(xxxvi), gives the Commonwealth Parliament a broad role in selecting, and protecting, the means by which the members of the federal Parliament are elected. According to Brennan CJ at p. 317, s. 240 was valid as it could 'reasonably be regarded as prescribing a method of freely choosing members of the House of Representatives', while s. 329A was valid as 'a law which is appropriate and adapted to prevent the subversion of that method'. Section 270 was characterised not as establishing an alternate method of voting, but as being a mere saving provision designed to enable the counting of the vote of persons who had not filled in a ballot paper in accordance with s. 240. This meant that s. 329A did not breach any implied freedom of political communication.

Dawson J delivered a strong dissent. He argued, at p. 325, that s. 24 requires that voters be given a 'genuine choice', meaning that 'those eligible to vote must have available to them the information necessary to exercise such a choice'. After characterising s. 270 not as mere saving provision but as establishing an alternate means of expressing a valid choice, Dawson found, at p. 325, that s. 329A was invalid because:

> It is a law which is designed to keep from voters information which is required by them to enable them to exercise an informed choice. It can hardly be said that a choice is an informed choice if it is made in ignorance of a means of making the choice which is available and which a voter, if he or she knows of it, may wish to use in order to achieve a particular result.

The High Court applied the same reasoning in *Muldowney v. South Australia* (1996) 186 CLR 352.[28] Section 76 of the *Electoral Act* 1985 (SA), like s. 240 of the Commonwealth Electoral Act, required that electors mark their ballot paper by numbering the boxes '1, 2, 3, 4 … '. However, although s. 76 stated that electors 'shall mark' their papers in this fashion, sections 61(2) and 85(2), in expressly allowing an elector to leave his or her paper unmarked, showed that this was not an enforceable obligation but merely rendered a ballot paper informal. Sections 126(1)(b) and (c) of the Act made it an offence for a person to 'publicly advocate that a person who is entitled to vote at an election should abstain from voting at the election' or that 'a voter should refrain from marking a ballot paper issued to the voter for the purpose of voting'.

Patrick Muldowney sought a declaration in the High Court that sections 76 and 126 were invalid. His challenge failed. The High Court unanimously held that the provisions were consistent with the implied freedom of political communication derived from sections 7 and 24 of the Constitution. Gaudron J stated that the implied freedom 'does not operate to strike down a law which curtails freedom of communication in

---

27 In the aftermath of this decision, in its *Report of the Inquiry into all Aspects of the Conduct of the 1996 Federal Election and Matters Related Thereto* (AGPS, June 1997, p. 32), the Joint Standing Committee on Electoral Matters recommended that s. 329A be repealed and that s. 240 be amended to include the words 'consecutive numbers, without the repetition of any number'. These recommendations are implemented by the *Electoral and Referendum Amendment Act 1998* (Cth).

28 The author appeared in this case as counsel for the plaintiff.

those limited circumstances where that curtailment is reasonably capable of being viewed as appropriate and adapted to furthering or enhancing the democratic processes of the states'.[29]

Langer and *Muldowney* show that compulsory voting, or at least requiring a person to attend the polling booth and deposit a voting paper in the ballot box, is consistent with sections 7 and 24 of the Constitution. The High Court has given the Parliament considerable leeway to shape and determine the electoral process. While sections 7 and 24 require that a 'choice' be made, it is up to the Parliament to determine how that 'choice' is to be made, including whether attendance to make such a 'choice' is compulsory. Moreover, the Parliament may protect the system it has created by limiting the information provided to electors about how electors may cast an effective vote.

Do the words 'directly chosen by the people' in sections 7 and 24 confer a right to vote? Even though the High Court held in *R v. Pearson; Ex parte Sipka* (1983) 152 CLR 254 that such a right is not conferred by s. 41 of the Constitution (see Chapter 5), this does not preclude sections 7 and 24 supporting an implied right to vote. After all, these provisions require a 'choice' by the 'people'. McHugh J stated in *Australian Capital Television Pty Ltd v. Commonwealth* (1992) 177 CLR 106 at 227, 'the proper conclusion to be drawn from the terms of sections 7 and 24 of the Constitution is that the people of Australia have constitutional rights of freedom of participation, association and communication in relation to federal elections'. If these rights are guaranteed, how could the right to vote not be?

Decisions on sections 7 and 24 have not addressed the question whether each Australian is vested with a constitutionally guaranteed right to vote. The issue has never arisen for decision in this way. It might arise if a disenfranchised person, say a person excluded under s. 93(8)(b) of the Commonwealth Electoral Act because he or she is serving a sentence of five years or longer for an offence against the law of the Commonwealth or of a state or territory,[30] were to seek a declaration as to his or her entitlement to cast a vote. *Obiter dicta* in several cases has approached the question from the converse, but equivalent, perspective of whether sections 7 and 24 limit the Commonwealth's power to restrict the federal franchise as provided for by s. 93 of the Commonwealth Electoral Act. The universal adult franchise recognised by several members of the High Court, in obiter, as entrenched by sections 7 and 24 may make the question of a separate implied right to vote obsolete. Whether a personal right to vote, or at least an immunity from legislative and executive interference with that right, can be implied from the Constitution may be irrelevant when the Commonwealth lacks the power to legislate other than for universal adult suffrage.

In *Attorney-General (Cth); Ex rel McKinlay v. Commonwealth* (1975) 135 CLR 1 at 36, McTiernan and Jacobs JJ stated, 'the long established universal adult suffrage may now be recognized as a fact and as a result it is doubtful whether, subject to the particular provision in s. 30, anything less than this could now be described as a choice by the people'. In *McGinty v. Western Australia* (1996) 186 CLR 140 at 201, Toohey J argued that 'according to today's standards, a system which denied universal adult franchise would

---

29 *Muldowney* at 376.
30 See G. Orr, 'Ballotless and Behind Bars: The Denial of the Franchise to Prisoners' (1998) 2 *Federal Law Review* 55.

fall short of a basic requirement of representative democracy'. Gaudron[31] and Gummow JJ[32] also supported the notion that universal adult suffrage is now entrenched in the Australian Constitution. Only Dawson J rejected this.[33] In *Langer*, McHugh J supported entrenchment of the franchise by stating, at p. 342, that 'it would not now be possible to find that the members of the House of Representatives were "chosen by the people" if women were excluded from voting or if electors had to have property qualifications before they could vote'.[34] According to these judges, the right to vote of, say, Australian women or indigenous peoples could not now be abrogated. This would be inconsistent with the requirement that the federal Parliament is to be 'directly chosen by the *people*'. This conclusion depends on a view of the Constitution as an evolving document, one that, at the end of the twentieth century, embraces a notion of 'the people' very different from that held at the beginning.[35] After all, the uniform federal franchise, as enacted by the *Commonwealth Franchise Act 1902* (Cth), extended the vote to women, but, in s. 4, denied it to any 'aboriginal native of Australia'.[36]

While the above dicta point strongly to the conclusion that the Constitution prevents the Commonwealth from limiting the federal franchise, there are also contrary dicta. In *Muldowney v. Australian Electoral Commission* (1993) 178 CLR 34 at 39, Brennan ACJ outlined the effect of *R v. Pearson; Ex parte Sipka* on the interpretation of s. 41 of the Constitution, and concluded: 'Thus a right to vote in an election for the Senate or the House of Representatives now depends entirely on the [Commonwealth Electoral] Act'. More recently, in *Snowdon v. Dondas* (1996) 139 ALR 475 at 483, five members of the High Court, sitting as the Court of Disputed Returns for the Northern Territory, unanimously reaffirmed the conclusion of Brennan ACJ. However, this was again in the context of the limited effect of s. 41. These dicta are best explained not as being contradictory to dicta in decisions such as *McGinty*, but as standing for the narrower proposition that s. 41 does not restrict the Commonwealth's ability to set the federal franchise.

Even though sections 7 and 24 might constitutionally entrench universal adult suffrage, they have not been interpreted to entrench equality in voting power, or the idea of 'one-vote, one-value'. This issue arose in *McKinlay*, where it was argued that the election of 18 May 1974 for the House of Representatives had not been in accordance with s. 24 because the electorates had not been of equal population size. Provisions of the Commonwealth Electoral Act and the *Representation Act 1905* (Cth) were accordingly said to be invalid. The High Court, with Murphy J dissenting, held that s. 24 of the Australian Constitution does not imply a constitutional requirement of as near as practicable equal numbers of people per electoral division for the House of Representatives.

In dissent, Murphy J found, at p. 70, that s. 24 requires as a 'standard of equality the alternatives of equal numbers of people and equal numbers of electors'. He based this

---

31 *McGinty v. Western Australia* at 221–2: 'Notwithstanding the limited nature of the franchise in 1901, present circumstances would not, in my view, permit senators and members of the House of Representatives to be described as "chosen by the people" within the meaning of those words in sections 7 and 24 of the Constitution if the franchise were to be denied to women or to members of a racial minority or to be made subject to a property or educational qualification.'.

32 *McGinty v. Western Australia* at 287.

33 *McGinty v. Western Australia* at 183.

34 Compare *McGinty v. Western Australia* (1996) 186 CLR 140 at 243 per McHugh J.

35 See J. Goldsworthy, 'Originalism in Constitutional Interpretation' (1997) 25 *Federal Law Review* 1.

36 For the debate in the federal Parliament on this point, see Australia, House of Representatives, 24 April 1902, *Debates*, vol. 9, pp. 11975–80; Australia, Senate, 29 May 1902, *Debates*, vol. 10, pp. 13002–11.

conclusion on an analysis of the United States authorities, particularly *Wesberry v. Sanders* 376 US 1 (1964). On the other hand, the majority in *McKinlay* held that a requirement of equality of voting power could not be implied from sections 7 and 24. Stephen J acknowledged, at p. 57, that representative democracy 'has finite limits and in a particular instance there may be absent some quality which is regarded as so essential to representative democracy as to place that instance outside those limits altogether'. Thus, an electoral system might lack some quality such that any representatives elected under the system would not have been 'directly chosen by the people' pursuant to sections 7 and 24 of the Constitution. However, 'one-vote, one-value' was not such a 'quality'. In finding this, the majority rejected any analogy with the words 'directly chosen by the people' in Article I of the United States Constitution, or with the interpretation of those words by the United States Supreme Court in cases such as *Baker v. Carr* 369 US 186 (1962) and *Wesberry v. Sanders*. Barwick CJ distinguished the context within which the provisions operated. He found, at pp. 23–4, that in 'high contradistinction' to the United States model, 'the Australian Constitution was developed not in antagonism to British methods of government but in co-operation with and, to a great extent, with the encouragement of the British Government'. This, and the presence of a Bill of Rights in the United States Constitution, meant that, as expressed at p. 24, 'in the case of the American Constitution, restriction on legislative power is sought and readily implied whereas, where confidence in the parliament prevails [as in the Australian context], express words are regarded as necessary to warrant a limitation of otherwise plenary powers'.

The majority did not totally reject the notion that s. 24 requires some form of equality. *Obiter dicta* suggested that, in some situations, there might be such a degree of malapportionment between electoral divisions as to bring into question whether the Parliament had been 'directly chosen by the people'. For example, Mason J stated, at p. 39:

> It is perhaps conceivable that variations in the numbers of electors or people in single member electorates could become so grossly disproportionate as to raise a question whether an election held on boundaries so drawn would produce a House of Representatives composed of members directly chosen by the people of the Commonwealth.

McTiernan and Jacobs JJ, in a joint judgment at pp. 36–7, and Stephen J in a separate judgment at p. 57 voiced similar views.

Since *McKinlay*, electoral malapportionment has continued to be an important political issue at the state level. In Western Australia, the number of voters per electoral district differs markedly between districts. At the 1993 Western Australian election, the most populous electorate in the Legislative Assembly was Wanneroo, which had 26 580 enrolled voters, while the least populous electorate was Ashburton, which had only 9135 enrolled voters. There were even greater differences (up to 376 per cent) between the quotients for members of the Legislative Council.

The plaintiffs in *McGinty* challenged the legislation giving rise to these differences in voting power.[37] It was argued that a system of representative government was created

---

37   The distribution of voters to electorates for the Legislative Assembly and the Legislative Council of Western Australia is achieved by the *Constitution Acts Amendment Act 1899* (WA) and the *Electoral Districts Act 1947* (WA), as amended by the *Acts Amendment (Electoral Reform) Act 1987* (WA).

by the Australian Constitution, which was breached by the electoral boundaries in Western Australia. Dawson, McHugh, and Gummow JJ reaffirmed the decision in *McKinlay* and found, in the words of Dawson J at p. 185, that 'electorates of equal numerical size are not a necessary characteristic of representative government'. The six-judge Court was not decisive on whether the Australian Constitution contains a guarantee of voter equality, as Brennan CJ expressed no final opinion and Toohey and Gaudron JJ dissented. However, all six judges held that, even if there were such a requirement at the Commonwealth level, it could not extend to state electoral systems. It was found that in significant ways the Australian Constitution is inconsistent with any notion of equality in voting in state elections. For example, under s. 128 of the Constitution the aggregate of votes of persons living in one of the less populous states is given the same weight as the aggregate of votes of persons living in one of the more populous states for the purposes of achieving a majority of votes in a majority of states. It was also relevant that under s. 7 there is equal representation of Original States, rather than people, in the Senate, as well as the fact that each of the Original States is guaranteed at least five seats in the House of Representatives under s. 24 of the Constitution. As Brennan CJ stated at p. 175, 'Far from containing an implication affecting State disparities, the text of Pts II and III of Ch I of the Australian Constitution and the structure of the Constitution as a whole are inconsistent with such an implication'. Accordingly, no implication arose from the Australian Constitution that could bind, by virtue of s. 106 of the Constitution or otherwise, state legislatures to achieve equality of voting power.

In 1978, s. 73(2) was inserted into the Western Australian Constitution. Section 73(2)(c) entrenches Western Australian laws, including the Western Australian Constitution itself, against a Bill that 'expressly or impliedly provides that the Legislative Council or the Legislative Assembly shall be composed of members other than members chosen directly by the people'. In *McGinty*, it was also argued that s. 73(2)(c) supports a requirement of equality of voting power in Western Australian state elections. A majority, with Toohey and Gaudron JJ dissenting, held that there was no such implication. Brennan CJ pointed out, at p. 178, that to discover such an implication 'would be to find a legislative intention destructive of the means by which the enacting Parliament was elected'.

In the earlier decision of *Stephens v. West Australian Newspapers Ltd* (1994) 182 CLR 211, it had been held that s. 73(2)(c) could support an implied freedom of political communication (see pp. 179–80). Nevertheless, in *McGinty*, a differently constituted majority found that no guarantee of voter equality could be implied. This finding rested on a value judgment as to the minimum content of the system of representative government created by the Western Australian Constitution. The judgment was made in light of evolving notions and perceptions of Australian democracy. A pertinent factor was that while freedom of communication has generally been an integral and accepted part of the process whereby the Australian people choose their representatives, equality of voting power has not enjoyed the same acceptance either in the Australian states or in some other nations.[38] As Dawson J put it at p. 184, 'the matter of electoral systems,

---

38 See *Dixon v. British Columbia (Attorney-General)* (1989) 59 DLR (4th) 247 and *Reference re Prov. Electoral Boundaries (Sask)* [1991] 2 SCR 158, where a concept of equality of voting power similar to that argued for in *McGinty* was rejected, and the United States position in cases like *Baker v. Carr* 369 US 186 (1962), *Wesberry v. Sanders* 376 US 1 (1964) and *Reynolds v. Sims* 377 US 533 (1964) was distinguished.

including the size of electoral divisions, and indeed whether to have divisional representation at all, is left to the parliament'.

The majority paid little attention to the further question of whether the Western
Australian electoral districts might be unconstitutional due to malapportionment.
Although such a question could not arise in regard to the Australian Constitution,
which had nothing to say about equality of voting power in state elections, it could
arise in regard to the Western Australian Constitution if *McKinlay* were to operate by
parity of reasoning. This issue was not addressed explicitly by Brennan CJ, McHugh or
Gummow JJ. Dawson J briefly stated at p. 189 that the 'extreme situations' considered in
McKinlay were 'markedly different from that which exists under the relevant Western
Australian legislation'. It was on this point that Toohey and Gaudron JJ dissented. They
found that the level of malapportionment meant that 'persons elected under a system
involving significant disparity in voting value, could not ... now be described as "chosen by the people"'.[39]

The decisions discussed above show that the High Court has yet to develop a
coherent jurisprudence in its interpretation of sections 7 and 24. It is not clear why the
malapportionment considered in *McGinty* was not sufficient to trigger the consequences set out in obiter in *McKinlay*. More fundamentally, it is unclear why the franchise (that is, who can vote) should have become entrenched over time while the
concept of equality of voting power (that is, that each vote should be of relatively equal
weight) has not. It is not that the two cannot be distinguished, but that the High Court
has so far failed to do so adequately. This is problematic because the High Court has
indicated that it will require Commonwealth laws to comply with the minimum
requirements of representative government as entrenched by sections 7 and 24. State
parliaments will also be restricted in the same way if they have equivalent provisions in
their Constitution. However, it is not certain what the minimum requirements of representative government are or how they will be determined. This is likely to be a focal
point of future High Court litigation.

Freedom of political communication

Foundations of the implied freedom of political communication

In two cases handed down on 30 September 1992, *Nationwide News Pty Ltd v. Wills*
(1992) 177 CLR 1 and *Australian Capital Television* (1992) 177 CLR 106, six members
of the High Court found that the system of representative government created by the
Constitution, or at least the text of sections 7 and 24, necessarily requires for its efficacy
that the Australian people be free to discuss matters relating to Australian government.[40]

---

39 *McGinty* at 222 per Gaudron J.
40 *Nationwide News* at 50–1 per Brennan J ('freedom to discuss governments and governmental institutions
    and political matters'), at 72–3 per Deane and Toohey JJ ('freedom of communication of information and
    opinions about matters relating to the government of the Commonwealth'), at 94–5 per Gaudron J
    ('freedom of political discourse'); *Australian Capital Television* at 139 per Mason CJ ('Freedom of communi-
    cation in relation to public affairs and political discussion'), at 149 per Brennan J ('freedom of discussion of
    political and economic matters'), at 168 per Deane and Toohey JJ ('freedom within the Commonwealth of
    communication about matters relating to the government of the Commonwealth'), at 212 per Gaudron J
    ('freedom of political discourse'), at 233 per McHugh J ('right of the people to participate in the federal
    election process').

Although Dawson J was the only judge who found that there was no freedom of political communication, McHugh J also construed any such freedom narrowly in finding that it was limited to a freedom to communication about political matters during election periods. Dawson J accepted that sections 7 and 24 require that the people be given a 'true choice'[41] in electing their representatives, but held that this did not amount to a freedom of political communication. The majority findings in both decisions were given support by the emerging notion that the source of the sovereignty of the Constitution has shifted from the British Parliament to the Australian people (see Chapter 4).[42] Although it was not necessary in either case to determine whether the implication also extended to state political matters, Mason CJ, Deane, and Toohey suggested that it did.[43]

The freedom of political communication implied from the Constitution by the High Court can be contrasted with the express guarantees of expression in other constitutions. In some respects, such as in its application to non-verbal or symbolic communication (see pp. 192–3), the implied freedom may be of wider scope than the guarantee of 'freedom of speech' in the First Amendment to the United States Constitution. However, in other respects the Australian guarantee is more limited. The central reason for this is that the Australian guarantee is derived from, and thereby limited by, the concept of representative government. On the other hand, free-standing express guarantees of expression in other constitutions may have a broader conceptual basis.[44] In Canada, the guarantee of 'freedom of … expression' in s. 2(b) of the Canadian Charter of Rights and Freedoms has been interpreted widely. Initially, there were suggestions that the guarantee might be confined to political expression.[45] However, these were rejected when s. 2(b) was found to apply to labour picketing.[46] In *Irwin Toy v. Quebec (Attorney-General)* [1989] 1 SCR 927 at 976, Dickson CJ, Lamer, and Wilson JJ set out the principles and values underlying the guarantee as follows:

> (1) seeking and attaining the truth is an inherently good activity; (2) participation in social and political decision-making is to be fostered and encouraged; and (3) the diversity in forms of individual self-fulfillment and human flourishing ought to be cultivated in an essentially tolerant, indeed welcoming, environment not only for the sake of those who convey a meaning, but also for the sake of those to whom it is conveyed.

---

41 *Australian Capital Television* at 187.
42 See, for example, *Australian Capital Television* at 138 per Mason CJ: 'the *Australia Act 1986* (UK) marked the end of the legal sovereignty of the Imperial Parliament and recognized that ultimate sovereignty resided in the Australian people'.
43 *Australian Capital Television* at 142 per Mason CJ: 'Public affairs and political discussion are indivisible and cannot be subdivided into compartments that correspond with, or relate to, the various tiers of government in Australia'; *Nationwide News* at 75 per Deane and Toohey JJ: 'there is obviously much to be said for the view that the Constitution's implication of freedom of discussion extends to all political matters, including matters relating to other levels of government within the national system which exists under the Constitution'.
44 See generally on rationales for freedom of expression: E. Barendt, *Freedom of Speech*, Clarendon Press, 1985, ch. 1; T. Campbell, 'Rationales for Freedom of Communication', in T. Campbell and W. Sadurski (eds), *Freedom of Communication*, Dartmouth, 1994, p. 17; T. I. Emerson, 'Towards a General Theory of the First Amendment' (1963) 72 *Yale Law Journal* 877; K. Greenawalt, 'Free Speech Justifications' (1989) 89 *Columbia Law Review* 119; F. Schauer, *Free Speech: A Philosophical Enquiry*, Cambridge University Press, 1982.
45 See, for example, *Re Klein and Law Society of Upper Canada; Re Dvorak and Law Society of Upper Canada* (1985) 50 OR (2d) 118.
46 *RWDSU v. Dolphin Delivery Ltd* [1986] 2 SCR 573. See *Ford v. Quebec (Attorney-General)* [1988] 2 SCR 712 at 764 per the Court.

This broad vision has meant that 'expression' in s. 2(b) has been widely construed. Dickson CJ, Lamer, and Wilson JJ stated, at p. 968, that 'Activity is expressive if it attempts to convey meaning', excluding only expression that is 'purely physical and does not convey or attempt to convey meaning'. Moreover, s. 2(b) operates to protect all expression irrespective of its content: 'the content of a statement cannot deprive it of the protection accorded by s. 2(b) no matter how offensive it may be'.[47] Section 2(b) has been applied to protect expression such as tobacco advertising[48] and the promotion of hatred of minority groups.[49] This content-neutral approach to s. 2(b) does not mean that all expression is constitutionally protected from legislative interference, but that, under s. 1 of the Charter, the government must show, in respect of such expression, that it has imposed a reasonable limit that can be 'demonstrably justified in a free and democratic society' (see Chapter 4). Of course, a wide view of 'expression' has placed strains on the test required by s. 1.[50]

The foundations of 'freedom of speech' in the First Amendment to the United States Constitution[51] and also the guarantee of 'freedom of expression' in Article 10(1) of the *European Convention for the Protection of Human Rights and Fundamental Freedoms*[52] have also been widely construed. However, in the case of the First Amendment, there have been suggestions that the guarantee is primarily an instrument of self-government, with consequent limitations on the freedom. In *Mills v. Alabama* 384 US 214 at 218 (1966), Black J stated, 'Whatever differences may exist about interpretations of the First Amendment, there is practically universal agreement that a major purpose of that Amendment was to protect the free discussion of governmental affairs'. Similarly, in *Garrison v. Louisiana* 379 US 64 at 74–5 (1964), Brennan J stated that 'For speech concerning public affairs is more than self-expression, it is the essence of self-government'. Alexander Meiklejohn argued that freedom of speech is only protected where it is on issues relating to the political process, and does not extend to private speech on topics not related to the choice to be made by voters.[53] He also argued that even in the absence of the First Amendment, a guarantee of freedom of political speech could be implied.[54] Nevertheless, the United States Supreme Court has now established that the First Amendment has a broader basis (including a truth-discovery justification and a

---

47 *R v. Keegstra* [1990] 3 SCR 697 at 828 per McLachlin J. See *Irwin Toy v. Quebec (Attorney-General)* at 986 per Dickson CJ, Lamer, and Wilson JJ.

48 *RJR-MacDonald Inc v. Canada (Attorney General)* [1995] 3 SCR 199.

49 *R v. Keegstra* [1990] 3 SCR 697.

50 J. Cameron, 'The Past, Present, and Future of Expressive Freedom under the *Charter*' (1997) 35 *Osgoode Hall Law Journal* 1.

51 See K. Greenawalt, 'Free Speech in the United States and Canada' (1992) 55 *Law and Contemporary Problems* 5.

52 *Lingens v. Austria* (1986) 8 EHRR 407 at 418: 'freedom of expression … constitutes one of the essential foundations of a democratic society and one of the basic conditions for its progress and for each individual's self-fulfilment'.

53 A. Meiklejohn, *Political Freedom: The Constitutional Powers of People*, Harper & Brothers, 1960. See V. Blasi, 'The Checking Value in First Amendment Theory' (1977) *American Bar Foundation Research Journal* 521. Compare Z. Chafee, 'Book Review: Alexander Meiklejohn's Free Speech: And its Relation to Self Government' (1949) 62 *Harvard Law Review* 891.

54 A. Meiklejohn, 'The First Amendment is an Absolute' [1961] *Supreme Court Review* 245 at 253–4; Meiklejohn, *Political Freedom: The Constitutional Powers of People*, p. 84. See R. Bork, 'Neutral Principles and Some First Amendment Problems' (1971) 47 *Indiana Law Journal* 1 at 23: 'Freedom for political speech could and should be inferred even if there were no first amendment'.

role in the development of personal autonomy and self-fulfilment) and accordingly that it is not limited to speech involving the political process. Meiklejohn himself came to recognise this, if only because a wider range of speech than mere political speech has a role to play in contributing to governance.[55] Like the Canadian guarantee, the First Amendment has been applied beyond the political process to areas such as commercial speech, including advertising.[56]

By comparison,[57] the freedom of political communication implied from the Australian Constitution is far more limited in its scope. It has an institutional rather than an individual foundation in that it is designed to facilitate the operation of representative government and not, except incidentally, to promote the general welfare of the individual. This has led to an unwillingness on the part of Australian judges to engage in dialogue about possible wider underpinnings of the implication.[58] The implied freedom only applies to certain types of communication. Fundamentally, it extends only to political communication, and is not a general guarantee of freedom of expression (although on occasion it has been questioned whether it might ultimately extend this far[59]). The narrow scope of the implied freedom is a consequence of the source from which it is derived. Other bases, such as those set out in *Irwin Toy v. Quebec (Attorney-General)*, do not form part of the foundation of the Australian guarantee and thus cannot act to bring about broader protection. To do so would be to give the guarantee life beyond what the Constitution enables.

In *Nationwide News* (1992) 177 CLR 1, the publisher of the *Australian* newspaper was prosecuted under s. 299(1)(d)(ii) of the *Industrial Relations Act 1988* (Cth). That section provided: 'A person shall not ... by writing or speech use words calculated ... to bring a member of the [Industrial Relations] Commission or the Commission into disrepute'. The prosecution related to an article published in the *Australian* that sharply criticised the Commission and referred to its members as 'corrupt labour "judges"'. In an action brought in the High Court, it was argued that s. 299(1)(d)(ii) was invalid. This argument was unanimously upheld. There were two alternate routes by which this conclusion was reached. Mason CJ, Dawson, and McHugh JJ held that the provision was invalid because, in applying a test of proportionality (see Chapter 4), it was not within the scope of the implied incidental power attaching to the Commonwealth's industrial relations power in s. 51(xxxv) of the Constitution. As the law did not fall within a head of power, they did not need to address the issue of whether the law breached an implied freedom of political communication. On the other hand, Brennan, Deane, Toohey, and Gaudron JJ held that even if s. 299(1)(d)(ii) was within a head of power, it was nevertheless invalid as infringing an implied freedom of political communication. It was found by Brennan J, at p. 53, that the provi-

---

55 Meiklejohn, 'The First Amendment is an Absolute'.

56 *Bigelow v. Virginia* 421 US 809 (1975); *Virginia Board of Pharmacy v. Virginia Citizens Consumer Council* 425 US 748 (1976); *44 Liquormart, Inc v. Rhode Island* 134 Law Ed 2d 711 (1996).

57 See *Brown v. Classification Review Board* (1998) 154 ALR 67 at 79 per French J, at 84 per Heerey J; D. S. Bogen, 'Telling the Truth and Paying for It: A Comparison of Two Cases: Restrictions on Political Speech in Australia and Commercial Speech in the United States' (1996) 7 *Indiana International and Comparative Law Review* 111.

58 See D. Z. Cass, 'Through the Looking Glass: The High Court and the Right to Speech' (1993) 4 *Public Law Review* 229.

59 See, for example, *Australian Capital Television* (1992) 177 CLR 106 at 212 per Gaudron J.

sion 'purports impermissibly to prevent public discussion about an important agency of social regulation'.

Australian Capital Television (1992) 177 CLR 106 involved a challenge to the *Political Broadcasts and Political Disclosures Act 1991* (Cth), which added a new Part IIID dealing with 'Political Broadcasts' to the *Broadcasting Act 1942* (Cth). Section 95B imposed a blanket prohibition on political advertisements on radio or television during federal election periods. There were similar bans for Territory elections under s. 95C and for state and local-government elections under s. 95D. Exceptions to the ban were made for policy launches, news and current affairs items, talkback radio programs, and advertisements for charities that did not 'explicitly advocate' a vote for one candidate or party. Division 3 of Part IIID established a scheme of 'free time' for political advertising. Of the total time available, 90 per cent was reserved for parties represented in the previous Parliament who were fielding a minimum number of candidates. Units of 'free time' could be used for a two-minute telecast or one-minute radio broadcast by a single speaker ('without dramatic enactment or impersonation') accompanied in a telecast by a picture of the speaker's head and shoulders.

Part IIID clearly fell within the Commonwealth's power over broadcasting in s. 51(v) of the Constitution, or under the Commonwealth's power with respect to federal elections. The question before the Court was therefore whether Part IIID was invalid because it infringed a constitutionally guaranteed freedom of political communication. The Court, with Dawson J dissenting, found that such an implication could be found in the Constitution. Mason CJ, Deane, Toohey, and Gaudron JJ held that Part IIID was wholly invalid. McHugh J found that Part IIID was invalid except in relation to s. 95C, which concerned territory elections. Brennan J found that Part IIID was not invalid as it could be reconciled with the implied freedom as a reasonable restriction on political communication. The reasoning of Mason CJ was typical of the majority. He found, at p. 132, that the Act would favour 'the established political parties and their candidates without securing compensating advantages or benefits for others who wish to participate in the electoral process or in the political debate which is an integral part of that process'.[60] In determining that the relevant legislation was invalid, the majority judges gave little weight to the views of the Parliament, which had determined that the Act was a necessary response to problems perceived in the political process, such as corruption.[61]

In *Nationwide News* and *Australian Capital Television* it was held that an implied freedom of political communication could be located in the system of representative government created by the Constitution. Reliance on this concept meant that the implication was cast narrowly to protect only political communication, as opposed to expression generally. According to Brennan J in *Nationwide News* at pp. 48–9, 'Once it is recognized that a representative democracy is constitutionally prescribed, the freedom of discussion which is essential to sustain it is as firmly entrenched in the Constitution as the system of government which the Constitution expressly ordains'. The absence of

---

60 Compare this with the findings of G. N. Rosenberg and J. M. Williams, 'Do Not Go Gently into that Good Right: The First Amendment in the High Court of Australia' (1997) 11 *Supreme Court Review* 439.
61 See Joint Standing Committee on Electoral Matters, *Who Pays the Piper Calls the Tune: Joint Standing Committee on Electoral Matters*, Report No. 4, AGPS, June 1989.

political expression was seen to be 'a threat to the very existence of such a society'.[62] The reasoning applied to reach this conclusion mirrored that applied in cases such as *Melbourne Corporation* (1947) 74 CLR 31 at 83, where Dixon J, speaking of Australian federalism, stated that the 'efficacy of the system logically demands' an implied immunity of the states from Commonwealth laws. This lineage was made particularly clear in the judgment of Mason CJ in *Australian Capital Television*, where his Honour accepted the tradition of *Melbourne Corporation* over that of the *Engineers Case* (see Chapter 4).

The application of such reasoning to the text and structure of the Constitution, particularly sections 7 and 24, was a firm basis from which to imply a freedom of political communication. The approach is certainly far less daring, and far more based in the text and context of the Australian Constitution, than, for example, the deeply controversial finding of a right to privacy in the United States Constitution. Douglas J, delivering the judgment of the Supreme Court of the United States in *Griswold v. Connecticut* 381 US 479 at 484–5 (1965), found that a right of privacy in the marital relationship could be implied as follows:

> specific guarantees in the Bill of Rights have penumbras, formed by emanations from those guarantees that help give them life and substance … Various guarantees create zones of privacy. The right of association contained in the penumbra of the First Amendment is one … The Third Amendment in its prohibition against the quartering of soldiers 'in any house' in time of peace without the consent of the owner is another facet of that privacy. The Fourth Amendment explicitly affirms the 'right of the people to be secure in their persons, houses, papers, and effects, against unreasonable searches and seizures.' The Fifth Amendment in its Self-Incrimination Clause enables the citizen to create a zone of privacy which government may not force him to surrender to his detriment. The Ninth Amendment provides: 'The enumeration in the Constitution, of certain rights, shall not be construed to deny or disparage others retained by the people.' … We have had many controversies over these penumbral rights of 'privacy and repose.' … These cases bear witness that the right of privacy which presses for recognition here is a legitimate one.[63]

Other courts have been even bolder, taking, as did Murphy J of the Australian High Court, great leaps from the text of the Constitution to discover a range of implied rights. The rights discovered by the Supreme Court of Israel,[64] by the Constitutional Court of Hungary[65] or in the Irish Constitution are good examples. In addition to the rights listed in the Irish Constitution, many unenumerated rights have been implied from article 40.3, which guarantees 'the personal rights of the citizen', and then goes on to state 'in particular, … the life, person, good name, and property rights of every citizen'. In a line of decisions beginning with that of Kenny J in *Ryan v. Attorney General* [1965] IR 294, it has been found that the words 'in particular', in article 40.3, show that the rights listed are not exhaustive and that it is the role of the courts to determine

---

62 *Nationwide News* at 79 per Deane and Toohey JJ.
63 See *Roe v. Wade* 410 US 113 (1973).
64 See A. Maoz, 'Defending Civil Liberties Without a Constitution: The Israeli Experience' (1988) 16 *Melbourne University Law Review* 815; A. Zysblat, 'Protecting Fundamental Rights in Israel without a Written Constitution', in I. Zamir and A. Zysblat (eds), *Public Law in Israel*. Clarendon Press, 1996, p. 47.
65 See S. Zifcak, 'Hungary's Remarkable, Radical, Constitutional Court' (1996) 3 *Journal of Constitutional Law in Eastern and Central Europe* 1.

which other rights are protected. By this means, Irish courts have protected a wide range of rights, such as the rights to strike, to privacy, to travel, to marry and found a family, and rights of communication.[66]

Judgments in *Nationwide News* and *Australian Capital Television* relied to a significant degree on Canadian authority. Prior to the enactment of the Canadian Charter of Rights and Freedoms, the Canadian Constitution (the *Constitution Act 1867* (30 & 31 Vict. ch. 3)) did not expressly protect freedom of expression. Nevertheless, the Canadian Supreme Court was able to afford some protection by means of constitutional implication. This was based, in part, on the system of representative government created by the instrument, although it emerged as a limitation on the power of the provinces, not on the central legislature. Indeed, the implication owed more to the division of powers achieved by the Constitution than to the system of representative government. The Constitution Act specified one list of legislative powers to be exercised by the central legislature (s. 91) and another list to be exercised by the provinces (s. 92). When the implication emerged, it was not so much a guarantee of freedom of political expression as a finding that a law restricting political expression did not lie within the list of powers granted to the provinces under s. 92. Accordingly, Duff CJ, Cannon, and Davis JJ of the Canadian Supreme Court found in *Reference re Alberta Statutes* [1938] SCR 100[67] that provincial legislatures, but not the central legislature, lacked power to proscribe 'free public opinion and free discussion throughout the nation of all matters affecting the State within the limits set by the criminal code and the common law'.[68] In later decisions, such as in *Switzman v. Elbling* [1957] SCR 285[69] and *OPSEU v. Ontario (Attorney-General)* [1987] 2 SCR 2, there were suggestions that this implication might also restrict the power of the central legislature. In the latter case, Beetz J, on behalf of the majority, said at p. 57 that 'quite apart from *Charter* considerations, the legislative bodies in this country must conform to these basic structural imperatives and can in no way override them'.[70] This view was clearly obiter.

These Canadian decisions are no more than a curious diversion on the path to the Canadian Charter of Rights and Freedoms. While they share some of the common roots of the Australian guarantee, they are also very different, based as they are in the distinct federal system of the Canadian polity. As opposed to the Canadian system, the Australian Constitution does not list the powers of each of the tiers of government, but instead lists only the powers of the Commonwealth, with the residue being left to the state parliaments. This difference means that the Canadian decisions do not provide strong support for the derivation of the implied freedom from the Australian Constitution.[71] The closest that the Canadian Supreme Court comes to breaking away from a freedom squarely based in Canadian federalism is the *obiter dicta* of Beetz J in *OPSEU*.

---

66 See J. Casey, *Constitutional Law in Ireland*, 2nd edn, Sweet & Maxwell, 1992, pp. 314–45; G. Hogan and G. Whyte, *Kelly's The Irish Constitution*, 3rd edn, Butterworths, 1994, pp. 755–89.

67 *Reference re Alberta Statutes* at 132–5 per Duff CJ and Davis J, at 145–6 per Cannon J.

68 *Reference re Alberta Statutes* at 146 per Cannon J. See *Saumur v. City of Quebec* [1953] 2 SCR 299.

69 *Switzman v. Elbling* at 328 per Abbott J.

70 See *RWDSU v. Dolphin Delivery Ltd* [1986] 2 SCR 573 at 584 per McIntyre J. Compare *Attorney-General (Canada) and Dupond v. Montreal* [1978] 2 SCR 770 at 796 per Beetz J.

71 A. Fraser, 'False Hopes: Implied Rights and Popular Sovereignty in the Australian Constitution' (1994) 16 *Sydney Law Review* 213 at 218–19.

In *Australian Capital Television*, Mason CJ overstated the Canadian position in his comment, at p. 141, that:

> It seems that the Supreme Court of Canada has ascertained from the structure of the Constitution granted by the British North America Act and its preamble an implied freedom of speech and expression … the implied freedom of speech and expression in Canada is founded on the view that it is indispensable to the efficacious working of Canadian represen tative parliamentary democracy.

Brennan J's reliance on the Canadian material in *Nationwide News* was more misplaced. He found, at p. 50, that the Australian implied freedom could be derived by 'parity of reasoning' with the approach of Cannon J in *Reference re Alberta Statutes*.

The implied freedom of political communication developed in *Australian Capital Television* and *Nationwide News* is not absolute, but 'is an implication of freedom under the law of an ordered and democratic society'.[72] Different approaches were applied to determine when the freedom might be restricted. Each approach required a balancing of the impact of the relevant law on political communication as against the object of the law in seeking to achieve some other purpose. This balancing process took place within 'the context of the contemporary and relevant political conditions in which the impugned law operates'.[73]

Mason CJ, Deane, Toohey, and McHugh JJ established a two-tier approach under which the level of scrutiny applied to the law differed according to the nature of the law. They found that a restriction, or prohibition, targeting ideas or information should be subjected to greater scrutiny than a restriction, or prohibition, targeting an activity or mode of communication by which ideas or information are transmitted. In *Australian Capital Television*, Mason CJ stated, at p. 143, that where a law targets ideas or information:

> only a compelling justification will warrant the imposition of a burden on free communication by way of restriction and the restriction must be no more than is reasonably necessary to achieve the protection of the competing public interest which is invoked to justify the burden on communication. Generally speaking, it will be extremely difficult to justify restrictions imposed on free communication which operate by reference to the character of the ideas or information.[74]

On the other hand, Mason CJ found, at p. 143, that restrictions imposed on an activity or mode of communication by which ideas or information are transmitted are 'more susceptible of justification'. In this latter case, a law would be valid where:

> the restriction is reasonably necessary to achieve the competing public interest. If the restriction imposes a burden on free communication that is disproportionate to the attainment of the competing public interest, then the existence of the disproportionate burden indicates that the purpose and effect of the restriction is in fact to impair freedom of communication.[75]

A similar distinction was drawn by Deane, Toohey, and McHugh JJ. Similarities can be seen between this two-tier approach and the differing levels of scrutiny applied in United States constitutional law (see Chapter 9).

---

72   *Australian Capital Television* at 169 per Deane and Toohey JJ.
73   *Australian Capital Television* at 158 per Brennan J.
74   See also pp. 233, 234–5 per McHugh J.
75   *Australian Capital Television* at 143–4.

Brennan and Gaudron JJ did not distinguish between different types of laws in applying the implied freedom. Brennan J found, at p. 150, that to escape invalidity 'the restriction must serve some other legitimate interest and it must be proportionate to the interest to be served', while Gaudron J stated, at p. 218, that the restriction must be '"reasonably and appropriately adapted" to achieve some end within the limits of that power'. The scrutiny applied by Brennan and Gaudron JJ was akin to the weaker standard applied by Mason CJ to restrictions imposed on an activity or mode of communication by which ideas or information are transmitted. Brennan J adopted an even weaker approach to the implied freedom, finding that, even where a statute does not meet the reasonable proportionality test, parliament must in some cases be afforded a 'margin of appreciation' and the law be allowed to stand.[76] This extra leeway was one factor that accounted for Brennan J's dissent in *Australian Capital Television*, where he was the only judge who, in addition to recognising the implied freedom of political communication, also found the relevant legislation to be valid.

The expanding freedom

The implied freedom of political communication was applied and developed in three decisions handed down on 12 October 1994: *Theophanous v. Herald & Weekly Times Ltd* (1994) 182 CLR 104, *Stephens v. West Australian Newspapers Ltd* (1994) 182 CLR 211, and *Cunliffe v. Commonwealth* (1994) 182 CLR 272. *Theophanous* arose out of a defamation action brought by Dr Andrew Theophanous, a member of the House of Representatives, chairperson of the Joint Parliamentary Standing Committee on Migration Regulations and chairperson of the Australian Labor Party's Federal Caucus Immigration Committee. In its newspaper the *Sunday Herald Sun*, The Herald & Weekly Times Ltd published a 'letter to the editor' written by Mr Bruce Ruxton. The letter, entitled 'Give Theophanous the shove', accused the plaintiff of 'bias' and 'idiotic antics' in regard to his involvement in immigration matters. The defendant publisher argued that *Nationwide News* and *Australian Capital Television* required that Australian defamation law be modified by the introduction of a 'public figure' defence based on that developed by the United States Supreme Court in *New York Times Co. v. Sullivan* 376 US 254 (1964). In *Sullivan*, the Supreme Court created a defence whereby a statement in a publication is not actionable, even if it is false, unless the plaintiff can prove actual malice or a reckless disregard for truth or falsity on the part of the defendant. In *Theophanous*, Mason CJ, Deane, Toohey, and Gaudron JJ, with Brennan, Dawson, and McHugh JJ dissenting, held that the common law of defamation should be overridden by a new constitutional defence.

The joint judgment of Mason CJ, Toohey, and Gaudron JJ widely defined the scope of the implied freedom of political communication. In describing the implication, they stated, at p. 124:

> For present purposes, it is sufficient to say that 'political discussion' includes discussion of the conduct, policies or fitness for office of government, political parties, public bodies, public officers and those seeking public office. The concept also includes discussion of the political

---

76 *Australian Capital Television* at 159, citing *The Observer and the Guardian v. United Kingdom* (1991) 14 EHRR 153 at 178. See *Theophanous v. Herald & Weekly Times Ltd* (1994) 182 CLR 104 at 156 per Brennam J.

views and public conduct of persons who are engaged in activities that have become the subject of political debate, eg, trade union leaders, Aboriginal political leaders, political and economic commentators.

The width of the freedom was further demonstrated by the adoption of a commentator's statement that '"political speech" refers to all speech relevant to the development of public opinion on the whole range of issues which an intelligent citizen should think about'.[77] Accordingly, the freedom was not limited to matters such as the suitability for office of candidates and their policies, but also extended to matters of public affairs and public opinion. However, it did not extend so far as to protect commercial speech without political content.[78]

The central question in *Theophanous* and *Stephens* was how the implied freedom might affect the common law of defamation, and whether it would intervene to reset the balance, developed by the common law over many years, between reputation and freedom of expression. The South African Constitution provides in s. 39(2) that in 'developing the common law or customary law, every court, tribunal or forum must promote the spirit, purport and objects of the Bill of Rights'.[79] The Australian Constitution makes no such demand. Indeed, this was the first time that such an issue had come before the Court. The paucity of material on the interaction between the Australian Constitution and the common law was demonstrated by the fact that Mason CJ, Toohey, and Gaudron JJ referred only to the extra-judicial writings of Sir Owen Dixon.[80] The joint judgment found that where the Constitution is at variance with the common law, the common law must yield to the Constitution. The common law could, at most, be a guide. The rejection of the common law as a marker of the limits of the freedom meant that the common law had to be recast in line with the content of the implication, rather than vice versa (as had been suggested by Gaudron J in *Australian Capital Television*[81]).

Mason CJ, Toohey, and Gaudron JJ held that the common law of defamation was inconsistent with the implied freedom. They referred to the 'chilling effect' defamation laws have on political communication,[82] and they pointed out the inadequacy of the available defences. This led to the question of how the implication should realign the protection given to reputation and expression. The joint judgment created a new constitutional defence available to a person sued for defamation in respect of comment about a candidate for office. It was held, at p. 137, that where the publisher of the speech can establish the following three conditions, such political communication cannot be attacked by way of a defamation action:

---

77 *Theophanous* at 124, quoting Barendt, p. 152.

78 *Theophanous* at 124–5.

79 See also South African Constitution, s. 8(3).

80 O. Dixon, 'The Common Law as an Ultimate Constitutional Foundation' (1957) 31 *Australian Law Journal* 240.

81 *Australian Capital Television* (1992) 177 CLR 106 at 217 per Gaudron J: 'As the implied freedom is one that depends substantially on the general law, its limits are also marked out by the general law. Thus, in general terms, the laws which have developed to regulate speech, including the laws with respect to defamation, sedition, blasphemy, obscenity and offensive language, will indicate the kind of regulation that is consistent with the freedom of political discourse'.

82 See, as to the existence of the 'chiling effect', E. Barendt, L. Lustgarten, K. Norrie, and H. Stephenson, *Libel and the Media: The Chilling Effect*, Clarendon Press, 1997, pp. 189–94.

- it was unaware of the falsity of the material published *and*
- it did not publish the material recklessly (that is, not caring whether the material was true or false) *and*
- the publication was reasonable in the circumstances.

It was not determined whether this defence could be pleaded whenever a person was sued for defamation in respect of comments that amounted to political communication. In the context of the *Theophanous* decision, the availability of the defence was limited to the situation where a political figure, such as a federal parliamentarian, was the subject of a defamatory imputation. Like the defence created in *Sullivan*, this defence was a constitutional defence. As such, it overrode the common law, as well as any inconsistent legislative or executive action. However, unlike the United States Supreme Court, which does not have the opportunity to develop the common law (that being considered state, as opposed to federal, law), the High Court had the option of instead developing or expanding the common law to bring about a new defence. Such a course might have been preferable on the basis of judicial parsimony.[83]

The defence developed by Mason CJ, Toohey, and Gaudron JJ is a significant departure from that in *Sullivan*. The onus of proof was placed on the defendant publisher rather than on the plaintiff. The standard required of the publisher was also higher: the publisher was unable to claim the defence where it had acted unreasonably, as opposed to the *Sullivan* standard, whereby the defence was available unless actual malice on the part of the publisher could be shown. In these ways the *Theophanous* defence provided weaker protection for political communication, and correspondingly greater protection for a person's reputation, than the *Sullivan* defence. This weakening of the *Sullivan* defence was a response to criticisms of the *Sullivan* defence,[84] criticisms that were recognised by the joint judgment in *Theophanous*. The joint judgment pointed out that the *Sullivan* defence had been extended far beyond its roots to allow criticism of 'public figures' generally, including people not holding official or governmental positions,[85] and that it 'sets too little store by the reputation of the person defamed'.[86] It also stated that the *Sullivan* defence allowed the plaintiff, in an effort to prove actual malice, to subject a defendant publisher to 'intrusive discovery procedures', potentially causing the 'protection of sources to be undermined'.[87]

The judgment of the final member of the majority, Deane J, also reflected strong concerns with the workability of the *Sullivan* defence. However, his response was the converse of that of Mason CJ, Toohey, and Gaudron JJ. While the joint judgment had weakened the *Sullivan* defence, Deane J abandoned any limitation on the availability of the defence to a publisher, finding, at p. 185, that the effect of the implied freedom 'is to

---

83 A. Stone, 'Freedom of Political Communication, the Constitution and the Common Law' (1998) 26 *Federal Law Review* 219.

84 See R. A. Epstein, 'Was *New York Times v. Sullivan* Wrong?' (1986) 53 *University of Chicago Law Review* 782; A. Lewis, '*New York Times v. Sullivan* Reconsidered: Time to Return to "The Central Meaning of the First Amendment"' (1983) 83 *Columbia Law Review* 603; New South Wales Law Reform Commission, *Defamation*, Discussion Paper No. 32, August 1993, pp. 182–4; N. Strossen, 'A Defence of the Aspirations—but not the Achievements—of the US Rules Limiting Defamation Actions by Public Officials or Public Figures' (1986) 15 *Melbourne University Law Review* 419.

85 *Curtis Publishing Co v. Butts* 388 US 130 (1967).

86 *Theophanous* at 134.

87 *Theophanous* at 135.

preclude completely the application of State defamation laws to impose liability in damages on the citizen for the publication of statements about the official conduct or suitability of a member of the Parliament or other holder of high Commonwealth office'. For Deane J, the problem with the *Sullivan* defence was not that it gave too little protection to reputation, but that it did not go far enough in reducing the 'chilling effect' of the law of defamation on political communication. He was particularly concerned, at p. 185, that any protection conferred by a new defence would 'be counter balanced by the increased cost and strain which would be involved in the probing of records and mental processes directed to proof of malice or unreasonableness'. Deane J accordingly took the same position as Black, Douglas, and Goldberg JJ in *Sullivan*, who had found that the First Amendment places an absolute bar on defamation actions by public officials. Deane J, however, achieved this without the benefit of an express guarantee of 'freedom of speech'. In one of his most radical judgments, Deane J based his conclusion, at p. 192, on his vision of the Constitution as '"a living force" representing the will and intentions of all contemporary Australians, both women and men, and not as a lifeless "declaration of the will and intentions of men long since dead"'. Although there was disagreement between the joint judgment and Deane J on the ambit of the protection conferred by the implied freedom, Deane J was prepared to state, at p. 188, that 'the appropriate course for me to follow is to lend my support for the answers which their Honours give to the questions reserved by the stated case'.

The minority in *Theophanous* strongly rejected the majority approach. The difference between majority and minority lay deeper than opposing views on the scope of the freedom. There was a clash both as to the judicial role and as to the respective places of the Constitution and the common law in the Australian legal system. Brennan J retreated into legal formalism with his argument that, unlike in the development of the common law, judicial policy (that is, any consideration external to the text or structure of the Constitution) has no role to play in the interpretation of the Constitution. He argued, at p. 143, that the 'notion of "developing" the law of the Constitution is inconsistent with the judicial power it confers'. Brennan J also argued that no inconsistency could arise between the implied freedom and the common law of defamation. He found, at p. 153, that:

> there is no express inconsistency between the Constitution and those rules of the common law which govern the rights and liabilities of individuals inter se. That is because the Constitution deals not with the rights and liabilities of individuals inter se but with the structure and powers of organs of government, including powers to make laws that deal with those rights and liabilities.

In other words, as the constitutional implication did not purport to affect common law rights and liabilities between individuals, the common law and the Constitution did not overlap. Brennan J also argued that if the implication and the common law of defamation covered the same ground, they would not be inconsistent because, axiomatically, the common law already provided an appropriate balance between free political communication and the protection of reputation.

Dawson J took the notion that extrinsic sources could not be used to imply freedom of political communication from the Constitution even further than Brennan J. In finding that the implied freedom could only have been drawn from an impermissible source, such as by having reference to 'the nature of our society',[88] he drew parallels between the reasoning of the majority in *Theophanous* and that of Murphy J in earlier cases. He concluded, at p. 194: 'To draw an implication from extrinsic sources, which the first defendant's argument necessarily entails, would be to take a gigantic leap away from the *Engineers' Case*, guided only by personal preconceptions of what the Constitution should, rather than does, contain. It would be wrong to make that leap'.[89]

McHugh J also took up the argument that the development of the implied freedom had tarnished the achievement of the *Engineers Case* (see Chapter 4). He charged the majorities in *Nationwide News* and *Australian Capital Television* with unintentionally departing from the method of constitutional interpretation laid down by that decision. He suggested, at p. 197, that this might undermine the 'confidence of the nation' in the High Court as the 'final arbiter of what the Constitution means'.

The decision in *Theophanous* represented the first attempt of the High Court to explore the interaction of the Constitution and the common law. The Canadian Supreme Court has had more opportunities to deal with such issues. The Supreme Court has found that the common law is subject to the Canadian Charter of Rights and Freedoms. This can be manifested in different ways. Where no governmental action is involved, as in an action between private parties, there is a limited role for the Charter to play. This is because s. 32 of the Charter provides that the Charter applies 'to the Parliament and government of Canada' and 'to the legislatures and governments of each province'. Nevertheless, in *RWDSU v. Dolphin Delivery Ltd* [1986] 2 SCR 573 at 603, McIntyre J, delivering the judgment of the majority, held that in such a situation the common law should be developed 'in a manner consistent with the fundamental values enshrined in the Constitution'. Where government action is involved within the meaning of s. 32 and there is a conflict between the common law and the Canadian Charter of Rights and Freedoms, the common law will give way. However, the considerations that arise in such a situation are different from those that arise in the case of statute law—the common law is, after all, a construct of judges rather than a parliament. In *R v. Swain* [1991] 1 SCR 933, it was held that a rule of common law under which a prosecutor could, against the wishes of the accused, adduce evidence as to the insanity of the accused breached s. 7 of the Charter. Section 7 provides that 'Everyone has the right to life, liberty and security of the person and the right not to be deprived thereof except in accordance with the principles of fundamental justice'. However, the decision in *R. v. Swain* indicated that it was inappropriate to find that this rule was invalid. Instead, the Court developed a new rule to replace the old, with the new rule achieving the balance required by the Charter.[90] Importantly, the remedy was to create a new common law rule, rather than to invent a constitutional rule that lay beyond the competence of a parliament to modify. Of course, if a parliament were to pass a statute that replaced the new common law rule with a rule that breached the Charter, that statute would be invalid.

The Canadian Supreme Court has been reluctant to apply the Charter to develop the common law of defamation. In *Hill v. Church of Scientology of Toronto*

---

88   *Theophanous* at 193, quoting *McGraw-Hinds (Aust) Pty Ltd v. Smith* (1979) 144 CLR 633 at 670 per Murphy J.

89   See G. Williams, '*Engineers* is Dead, Long Live the Engineers!' (1995) 17 *Sydney Law Review* 62.

90   See also *R v. Daviault* [1994] 3 SCR 63.

[1995] 2 SCR 1130, a Crown attorney employed by the Attorney General of Ontario sued for defamation in respect of statements made on behalf of the Church of Scientology to the effect that he had misled a judge and had breached orders sealing certain documents. The matter came before the Canadian Supreme Court, where it was argued that 'freedom of expression' as guaranteed by s. 2(b) of the Charter defeated the defamation action. Cory J, delivering the judgment of the Court, recognised that the common law must comply with Charter principles. However, no modification to the common law was necessary in this case, as it was found that the common law struck an appropriate balance between reputation and freedom of expression. There was no 'chilling effect' on expression that made it necessary to change the common law to accord with Charter values. The result in *Hill*, particularly the failure to modify the common law to better protect expression, has been strongly criticised.[91] However, this result might be explained by the fact that it was held that the action for damages by the Crown attorney did not constitute government action within the meaning of s. 32 of the Charter, and thus that the Charter did not apply to the proceedings. If it had fallen within s. 32 the Court may have been more willing to intervene to reshape the common law. As it was, Cory J found, at p. 1188 that 'this appeal does not involve the media or political commentary about government policies' and that, '*in its application to the parties in this action*, the common law of defamation complies with the underlying values of the *Charter*' (emphasis added). It was on this basis that Cory J held, at p. 1188, that 'the issues considered by the High Court of Australia in *Theophanous* … are also not raised in this case and need not be considered'.

Other courts have recognised the 'chilling effect' of defamation law on expression, and have used a common law or constitutional solution to bring about a new balance. *Theophanous* itself was handed down at a time when courts in other countries, notably the United Kingdom[92] and India,[93] were also reshaping defamation law to better foster freedom of expression. In the United Kingdom, the House of Lords found in *Derbyshire County Council v. Times Newspapers* [1993] AC 534, that a local government authority could not maintain an action for defamation. Lord Keith, with whom the rest of the House agreed, stated, at p. 547: 'It is of the highest public importance that a democratically elected governmental body, or indeed any governmental body, should be open to uninhibited public criticism. The threat of civil action for defamation must inevitably have an inhibiting effect on freedom of speech'. *Derbyshire* was applied by the New South Wales Court of Appeal in *Ballina Shire Council v. Ringland* (1994) 33 NSWLR 680.

In other countries, the *Theophanous* defence has proved attractive as a variant on the *Sullivan* 'public figure' test as achieving a more appropriate and workable balance between reputation and expression.[94] It has proved influential in decisions in South

---

91   J. Cameron, 'The Past, Present, and Future of Expressive Freedom under the *Charter*' (1997) 35 *Osgoode Hall Law Journal* 1 at 333–42; J. Ross, 'The Common Law of Defamation Fails to Enter the Age of the *Charter*' (1996) 35 *Alberta Law Review* 117.

92   *Derbyshire County Council v. Times Newspapers* [1993] AC 534. See also the subsequent decision in *Reynolds v. Times Newspapers Ltd* (unreported, English Court of Appeal, 8 July 1998).

93   *R Rajagopal v. State of Tamil Nadu* AIR 1995 SC 264.

94   I. Loveland, '*Sullivan v. The New York Times* Goes Down Under' [1996] *Public Law* 126 at 138–9 praises the *Theophanous* solution in contrast to the approach taken in *Derbyshire*.

Africa[95] and New Zealand.[96] While it might be argued that the reception of the *Theophanous* decision in other countries makes the High Court's subsequent treatment of the case in *Lange v. Australian Broadcasting Corporation* (1997) 189 CLR 520 ironic, the point is not a strong one. What other courts have found useful in *Theophanous* was not its methodology in applying the Constitution to override the common law, but its finding that the common law has a 'chilling effect' on free expression and that a new defence was required to redress this imbalance. It is on this basis that *Theophanous* has been preferred to the decision of the Canadian Supreme Court in *Hill*.

Stephens (1994) 182 CLR 211 was an important case because it demonstrated that the implied freedom of political communication can affect state political matters and state laws.[97] The case arose out of a defamation action brought by six members of the Legislative Council of Western Australia in relation to three articles published in the *West Australian* newspaper. The articles set out statements by another member of the Legislative Council alleging that an interstate and overseas trip undertaken by the plaintiffs was a 'junket of mammoth proportions'. A 4:3 majority of the Court, with the same division of judges as in *Theophanous*, again held that the implied freedom protected the political communication at issue by allowing the newspaper to plead the new *Theophanous* defence. The defence was available in respect of communication about state political matters due to either or both of two bases. The first basis was that the implied freedom of political communication derived from the Australian Constitution extends 'to all political discussion, including discussion of political matters relating to government at State level'.[98] This conclusion was supported by dicta from *Australian Capital Television* (1992) 177 CLR 106,[99] *Nationwide News* (1992) 177 CLR 1[100] and *Theophanous*.[101] For example, Deane and Toohey JJ stated in *Nationwide News* at p. 75:

> The implication of freedom of communication about the government of the Commonwealth most obviously applies in relation to Commonwealth, as distinct from State or other regional, governmental institutions. Under the Australian federal system, however, it is unrealistic to see the three levels of government—Commonwealth, State and Local—as isolated from one another or as operating otherwise than in an overall national context. Indeed, the Constitution's doctrine of representative government is structured on an assumption of representative government within the States and, to a limited extent, an assumption of the co-operation of the governments and Parliaments of the States in the electoral process itself. As a practical matter, taxes levied by the Executive of the Commonwealth under laws made by the Parliament are applied for public purposes through and at all levels of government. Political parties or associations are likely to exist in relation to more

95 *Holomisa v. Argus Newspapers Ltd* 1996 (2) SA 588. See *Du Plessis v. De Klerk* 1996 (3) SA 850 at 883–5 per Kentridge AJ; D. Davis, 'Holomisa v. Argus Newspapers Ltd 1996 (2) SA 588 (W)' (1996) 12 *South African Journal on Human Rights* 328.

96 *Lange v. Atkinson and Australian Consolidated Press NZ Ltd* [1997] 2 NZLR 22; *Lange v. Atkinson* (unreported, New Zealand Court of Appeal, 25 May 1998).

97 See G. Carney, 'The Implied Freedom of Political Discussion—Its Impact on State Constitutions' (1995) 23 *Federal Law Review* 180.

98 *Stephens* at 232 per Mason CJ, Toohey, and Gaudron JJ.

99 *Australian Capital Television* at 142 per Mason CJ, at 168–9 per Deane and Toohey JJ, at 215–17 per Gaudron J.

100 *Nationwide News* at 75–6 per Deane and Toohey JJ.

101 *Theophanous* at 122 per Mason CJ, Toohey and Gaudron JJ, at 164 per Deane J.

than one level of government and political ideas are unlikely to be confined within the sphere of one level of government only. Clearly enough, the relationship and interaction between the different levels of government are such that an implication of freedom of communication about matters relating to the government of the Commonwealth would be unrealistically confined if it applied only to communications in relation to Commonwealth governmental institutions.

The same reasoning might be applied to find that the implied freedom extends down to the level of local government as well.

The second basis on which the defence was available was that a counterpart implication could be derived from the system of representative government created by the Western Australian Constitution. Section 73(2) of the *Constitution Act 1889* (WA) entrenches Western Australian laws, including the Western Australian Constitution itself, against Bills of the several kinds specified in the provision.[102] Such Bills include, in s. 73(2)(c), a Bill that 'expressly or impliedly provides that the Legislative Council or the Legislative Assembly shall be composed of members other than members chosen directly by the people'. In *Stephens*, Brennan J stated, at p. 236, that s. 73(2)(c):

> entrenches in the *Constitution Act* the requirement that the Legislative Council and the Legislative Assembly be composed of members chosen directly by the people. This requirement is drawn in terms similar to those found in ss 7 and 24 of the Australian Constitution from which the implication that effects a constitutional freedom to discuss government, governmental institutions and political matters is substantially derived. By parity of reasoning, a similar implication can be drawn from the *Constitution Act* with respect to the system of government of Western Australia therein prescribed.

The question of which state or territory constitutions, in addition to that of Western Australia, can support such an implication can only be determined on a case-by-case basis.[103]

Where a counterpart implication can be derived from a state constitution, that does not automatically mean that the state parliament is bound by that implication. In seeking to apply the implied freedom to the states via this route, manner–and–form requirements[104] will be a central weapon in the armoury of both sides. Unless a state constitution contains a manner–and–form requirement that entrenches provisions giving rise to a system of representative government, that system might be overridden by an ordinary Act of parliament, thereby destroying the implication. Any implication arising from the state constitution might thus be impliedly amended by a subsequent inconsistent Act of parliament.[105] The lack of an entrenched manner–and–form requirement may be the greatest impediment to the implication of rights and freedoms in state constitutions. For example, the lack of an appropriate manner–and–form requirement in

---

102 Under s. 73(2)(f) and (g), such bills must be passed by an absolute majority of both Houses of the Parliament and be approved by the electors of the state at a referendum.
103 See also Chapter 1.
104 See generally A. R. Blackshield and G. Williams, *Australian Constitutional Law and Theory: Commentary and Materials*, 2nd edn, Federation Press, 1998, ch. 9.
105 *McCawley v. The King* [1920] AC 691.

the *Constitution Act 1934* (Tas) is likely to mean that an implied freedom could not be located in that instrument.[106]

The implied freedom might be extended to the territories in either of the two ways set out above. Under the first method, state laws are bound by the implied freedom at least in part, because under s. 106 of the Australian Constitution the state constitutions continue to operate 'subject to' the Australian Constitution.[107] However, the Commonwealth's territories power in s. 122 of the Constitution lacks this express limitation. This is a weakness in the argument that laws passed for a territory by the Commonwealth are also limited by the implied freedom. McHugh J provided the foundation for such reasoning in *Australian Capital Television* when he held that s. 122 is not restricted by the implied freedom.[108] He expanded on this in *Kruger v. Commonwealth* (1997) 190 CLR 1 at 142–4, where he held that any freedom of movement or association derived from sections 7 and 24 could not apply to the territories. This was because the implied freedom of political communication exists for the protection of 'the people of the State', in regard to the choice of Senators under s. 7, and for 'the people of the Commonwealth', in regard to the choice of the members of the House of Representatives under s. 24. In neither case during the relevant period considered in *Kruger* — that is, 1918–57 — did 'the people' include a resident of a territory. However, this argument is not convincing. It does not account for the freedom applying to the territories because a federal or territory ban on, for example, political communication about native title in the Northern Territory would also impact on the choice to be made by 'the people' in federal elections under sections 7 and 24. This linkage is illustrated by the political organisations and issues common to territory and federal elections. McHugh J was the only judge in *Australian Capital Television* to find that the implied freedom did not apply to the territories. Mason CJ and Gaudron J argued that the implied freedom derived from the Australian Constitution can extend down to territory matters,[109] while Deane and Toohey JJ indicated, at p. 176, that they were 'not presently persuaded' that laws passed under s. 122 were so immune. Deane J went further in *Theophanous* in stating, at p. 164, 'a tentative view that the implication does at least apply to confine the Parliament's legislative powers with respect to internal Territories and accordingly restricts the powers which may be conferred on the organs of government of those Territories'. The most recent decision to deal with, but not resolve, this question was *Kruger*. In that case, Dawson J stated that he agreed with the conclusion of McHugh J in *Australian Capital Television* that s. 122 is not limited by the implied freedom. On the other hand, Toohey and Gaudron JJ found that the implied freedom does apply to the territories power. The issue therefore remains open. In any

---

106 Section 41A of the Tasmanian Constitution Act does provide some degree of entrenchment. However, s. 41A is not itself entrenched. Thus, while s. 41A currently requires that certain amendments be supported by a special majority, s. 41A may itself be amended or repealed by an ordinary Act of Parliament and the entrenchment thereby removed.

107 *Nationwide News* at 76 per Deane and Toohey JJ; *Stephens* at 235 per Brennan J, at 257 per Deane J; *Theophanous* at 122 per Mason CJ, Toohey, and Gaudron JJ, at 155–6 per Brennan J, at 164–6 per Deane J. See Carney; C. Horan, 'Section 122 of the Constitution: A "Disparate and Non-Federal" Power?' (1997) 25 *Federal Law Review* 97 at 123.

108 *Australian Capital Television* at 246: 'nothing in the Constitution suggests to my mind that there is any implied right of freedom of expression or communication within a Territory or any right in a Territory arising from the institutions of representative government and responsible government.'.

109 *Australian Capital Television* at 142 per Mason CJ, at 217 per Gaudron J.

event, under the second method set out above, a counterpart implication might be derived from the relevant territory self-government Act, particularly the *Australian Capital Territory (Self-Government) Act 1988* (Cth) and the *Northern Territory (Self-Government Act) 1978* (Cth).[110] Each of those Acts, like the Commonwealth and Western Australian constitutions, creates a system of representative government. Such an implication could bind the legislature of the relevant territory.

The third of the cases on the implied freedom handed down in 1994 was *Cunliffe* (1994) 182 CLR 272. The *Migration Amendment Act (No 3) 1992* (Cth) introduced into the *Migration Act 1958* (Cth) a new Part 2A ('Migration Agents and Immigration Assistance'). Part 2A established a scheme for the registration of 'migration agents'. It also limited the advice or assistance that could be given to 'entrance applicants' (that is, applicants for visas, entry permits, and refugee status) by persons other than registered 'migration agents'. The plaintiffs, solicitors with an extensive immigration practice, challenged the scheme in the High Court. One basis was that Part 2A infringed the implied freedom. This was rejected by Brennan, Dawson, Toohey, and McHugh JJ, with Mason CJ, Deane, and Gaudron JJ dissenting. As in *Theophanous* and *Stephens*, Brennan, Dawson, and McHugh JJ found that no implication was infringed. They were joined in the result by Toohey J, who held that, even though Part 2A restricted constitutionally protected political communication, the restriction was acceptable. Significantly, four judges (the minority joined on this issue by Toohey J) found that the provision of immigration assistance and the making of immigration representations were constitutionally protected political communication. For example, Deane J stated, at p. 341:

> the freedom of the ordinary citizen of this country to lend support and assistance, by advice, encouragement and representation, to an applicant for admission as a visitor, an ordinary immigrant or a refugee clearly falls within the central area of the freedom of political communication and discussion which the Constitution's implication protects.

He also found, at p. 341, that such communications are 'among the most important of all political communications and political discussions in this country'.

A central issue in *Cunliffe* was whether 'aliens' or 'non-citizens' can claim the benefit of the implied freedom.[111] This issue was not resolved. Mason CJ was the only judge to find that non-citizens are fully entitled to the benefits of the implied freedom. He found, at p. 299, that 'Non-citizens who are actually present within this country, like citizens, are entitled to the protection afforded by the Constitution and the laws of Australia'. On the other hand, Brennan J argued, at p. 328, that non-citizens 'have no constitutional right to participate in or be consulted on matters of government in this country'. Deane J found, at p. 336, that a non-citizen could only receive the benefit of the implied freedom indirectly where the benefit 'flows from the freedom or immunity of those who are citizens'. According to Deane J at p. 336, non-citizens were therefore protected 'to the extent necessary to ensure that the freedom of citizens to engage in discussion and obtain information about political matters is preserved and protected'.

---

110 See G. Williams, 'Freedom of Political Discussion and Australian Electoral Laws' (1997) 4 *Canberra Law Review* 5.

111 See the discussion, in Chapter 8, of *Chu Kheng Lim v. Minister for Immigration, Local Government and Ethnic Affairs* (1992) 176 CLR 1; B. Wells, 'Aliens: The Outsiders in the Constitution' (1996) 19 *University of Queensland Law Journal* 45.

Cunliffe demonstrated the potential reach of the implied freedom of political communication. The freedom might go so far as to extend to the communication involved in every interaction (whether administrative or otherwise) between the people of Australia (including citizens and non-citizens) and government. It is clear from *Theophanous* and *Stephens*, as it was from *Nationwide News* and *Australian Capital Television*, that the origins of the implication lie in the system of representative government laid down by the Constitution. However, in *Cunliffe*, four members of the Court moved beyond the view expressed in *Australian Capital Television* that the 'raison d'être' of the freedom 'is to enhance the political process (which embraces the electoral process and the workings of Parliament), thus making representative government efficacious'.[112] It is difficult to see how a law restricting the giving of immigration assistance and the making of immigration representations is a law trenching on the command in sections 7 and 24 of the Constitution that the federal Parliament is to be 'directly chosen by the people'.[113]

The beginning of the end?

The High Court further examined the implied freedom of political communication in 1996 in *McGinty v. Western Australia* (1996) 186 CLR 140, *Langer v. Commonwealth* (1996) 186 CLR 302, and *Muldowney v. South Australia* (1996) 186 CLR 352.[114] *Muldowney* was a challenge to provisions in the South Australian Electoral Act that made it an offence to encourage voters to fill in or mark their ballot paper other than in accordance with the prescribed method (see pp. 160–1). It was argued that a counterpart implication of freedom of political communication could be derived from the South Australian Constitution. However, the Solicitor-General for South Australia conceded that the South Australian Constitution contains such an implication 'in like manner to the Commonwealth Constitution',[115] meaning that the High Court did not need to decide the issue.[116] In any event, it was held by the Court that the provisions were valid.

In *Langer*, the Court dealt with provisions in the Commonwealth Electoral Act (see pp. 159–60) similar to those in the South Australian Electoral Act. A majority of the Court, with Dawson J dissenting, found that these provisions were valid. It was not strictly necessary for the Court to examine the implied freedom, as the freedom was not relied on by the plaintiff in his oral argument.[117] Nevertheless, in doing so, the majority construed the implied freedom narrowly. The dissent by Dawson J showed just how narrow a construction the majority had adopted. A reluctant advocate of the freedom, Dawson J found, at p. 326, that 'exhortation or encouragement of electors to adopt a particular course in an election is of the very essence of political discussion and it would seem to me that on the view adopted by the majority in the earlier cases, s. 329A must infringe the guarantee which they discern'.

---

112 *Australian Capital Television* at 145 per Mason CJ.

113 Compare Zines, p. 389.

114 The author appeared in this case as counsel for the plaintiff.

115 *Muldowney* at 367 per Dawson J.

116 See *Cameron v. Becker* (1995) 64 SASR 238 at 247, 253, where the Full Court of the Supreme Court of South Australia did not need to decide the issue either. Olsson J did, however, state in *Cameron v. Becker*, at 247: 'I see no conceptual difference between the constitution of Western Australia discussed in *Stephens* and that of this State'.

117 *Langer* at 333 per Toohey and Gaudron JJ.

McGinty was the most significant of the three cases decided in 1996. The plaintiffs argued that just as sections 7 and 24 of the Constitution could support an implied freedom of political communication, so could the sections support a guarantee of voter equality (see pp. 163–5). They argued that this guarantee rendered invalid the electoral boundaries operating in Western Australian state elections. The argument failed. Dawson, McHugh, and Gummow JJ found that a guarantee of voter equality could not be discerned in either the Commonwealth or Western Australian constitutions. Brennan CJ did not decide whether such a guarantee could be derived from the Australian Constitution, finding that such an implication, even if it existed, could not assist the plaintiffs. He did, however, find that an implication of voter equality could not be found in the Western Australian Constitution. Toohey and Gaudron JJ dissented in locating a guarantee of voter equality in the Western Australian Constitution.

The reasoning in *McGinty* reveals much about how the High Court, since the retirements of Mason CJ and Deane J, has viewed the implied freedom of political communication. In prior cases, the freedom was loosely said to be derived from either the system of representative government underlying the Constitution, as recognised by the text and structure of the Constitution, or the text and structure alone. This distinction came to be seen as important in charting the scope of the freedom. If the freedom is derived from the text and structure of the Constitution alone, this would enable the freedom to be narrowly construed as being primarily a freedom of communication as regards the electoral matters set out in sections 7 and 24 of the Constitution. This narrow vision of the freedom was expressed by McHugh J in *Australian Capital Television*, when he stated, at p. 232, that 'the people have a constitutional right to convey and receive opinions, arguments and information concerning matter intended or likely to affect voting in an election for the Senate or the House of Representatives'. It was expressed even more narrowly by Dawson J in *Theophanous*, when he argued, at p. 189, that sections 7 and 24 do no more than confer on electors the ability to make 'a genuine, or informed, choice'. On the other hand, Deane and Toohey JJ viewed the freedom broadly as being based on the system of representative government underlying the Constitution, rather than merely on the bare text of sections 7 and 24. As they stated in *Nationwide News*, at p. 72: 'the doctrine of representative government which the Constitution incorporates is not concerned merely with electoral processes. As has been said, the central thesis of the doctrine is that the powers of government belong to, and are derived from, the governed, that is to say, the people of the Commonwealth'. This broader approach perhaps underlies the finding of four judges in *Cunliffe* that the implied freedom protects the giving of immigration assistance and the making of immigration representations.

The broader view was criticised by the majority in *McGinty*—which consisted of the minority in *Theophanous* and *Stephens*, plus a new appointee, Gummow J—on the basis that the implied freedom would be an implication from the system of representative government, which is itself an implication from the Constitution, including sections 7 and 24.[118] The argument was that such second-order implications are too far

---

118 See N. Aroney, 'A Seductive Plausibility: Freedom of Speech in the Constitution' (1995) 18 *University of Queensland Law Journal* 249; S. Donaghue, 'The Clamour of Silent Constitutional Principles' (1996) 24 *Federal Law Review* 133; J. Goldsworthy, 'Constitutional Implications and Freedom of Political Speech: A Reply to Stephen Donaghue' (1997) 23 *Monash University Law Review* 362; J. Goldsworthy, 'Implications in Language, Law and the Constitution', in G. Lindell (ed.), *Future Directions in Australian Constitutional Law*, Federation Press, 1994, p. 150.

removed from the text of the Constitution to be legitimate inferences. This criticism could in turn be attacked for taking an unduly narrow and semantic view of constitutional interpretation, one that does not take account of the need of the interpreter to rely on context as well as text, such context including the existing structures created by the Constitution and the values underpinning it as they have evolved since federation. It might also be remarked that the connection between the implied freedom of communication and the text of the Constitution is no less tenuous than that of other implications that have been more widely accepted, albeit after a period of time, such as the immunity of the states from Commonwealth laws, and the separation of judicial power (see Chapter 8). The appropriate methodology, if such exists, perhaps lies somewhere in between the two views.

The majority in *McGinty* found that the implied freedom should be seen as being derived from the text and structure of the Constitution alone. They argued that the freedom should not be seen as being shaped by any concept, such as representative democracy, that may underlie the Constitution. Rather, the freedom is to be bounded by 'the text and structure of Pts II and III of Ch I of the Constitution and, in particular, from the provisions of ss 7 and 24'.[119] According to Brennan CJ, at p. 169, 'It is logically impermissible to treat "representative democracy" as though it were contained in the Constitution, to attribute to the term a meaning or content derived from sources extrinsic to the Constitution and then to invalidate a law for inconsistency with the meaning or content so attributed'.

The majority in *McGinty* adopted a narrow view of what implications can be derived from the concept of representative government. Freedoms might only be implied from the core characteristics of the concept, rather than from a wider conception of what might be entailed by representative democracy. Hence, implications may be derived where they are essential to a system in which representatives are 'directly chosen by the people'. This would support freedoms based on the participation of the people in the electoral process to the extent required to enable each person to make a free, genuine, and perhaps informed choice.

Although this refinement of the implied freedom should provide greater certainty in the application of the freedom, the approach of the High Court still requires considerable elaboration. The interpretation of the Constitution now centres on a vision of those characteristics of Australian representative government that are so basic to that system that they cannot be abrogated by Parliament. *McGinty* established that the Court continues to view freedom of political communication as a core characteristic, but not equality of voting power (although a high enough degree of malapportionment might stir the Court into action). While this distinction might be soundly based in the relative importance of these concepts to Australian democracy (freedom of speech has traditionally been well protected, while equality of voting power has often been ignored in the states), other distinctions will not be so clear. There will be an ongoing process of the Court charting whether freedoms such as those of voting, assembly, association, and movement fall within or without its, as yet undisclosed, conception of the basic characteristics of representative government. The challenge for the Court will be to assess these freedoms in a way that promotes a high degree of transparency while avoiding arbitrary distinctions. The *McGinty* approach will not remove the policy choices that are

---

119 *McGinty* at 169 per Brennan CJ.

embedded in any decision-making in the field of constitutional law. This was alluded to by Gummow J in *McGinty*, when he stated, at pp. 269–70:

> To adopt as a norm of constitutional law the conclusion that a constitution embodies a principle or a doctrine of representative democracy or representative government (a more precise and accurate term) is to adopt a category of indeterminate reference. This will allow from time to time a wide range of variable judgment in interpretation and application.[120]

McGinty represents a significant change from the approach of a differently constituted majority in earlier cases. The departure of Mason CJ and Deane J left Toohey and Gaudron JJ from the majority in *Theophanous* as the minority in *McGinty*, while Gummow J joined the minority in *Theophanous* (Brennan, Dawson, and McHugh JJ) to form the majority in *McGinty*. Indeed, *McGinty* cast doubt on the correctness of *Theophanous* and *Stephens*. McHugh J, with some support from Gummow J,[121] vehemently attacked the reasoning employed in earlier decisions on the implied freedom: 'I regard the reasoning in *Nationwide News*, *Australian Capital Television*, *Theophanous* and *Stephens* in so far as it invokes an implied principle of representative democracy as fundamentally wrong and as an alteration of the Constitution without the authority of the people under s. 128 of the Constitution'.[122] As in *Theophanous*, McHugh J argued that the reasoning of earlier cases involved a rejection of the interpretative methods laid down in the *Engineers Case*. Moreover, he suggested at p. 234 that this reasoning was illegitimate in that it relied on representative democracy as if it were a 'free-standing principle, just as if the Constitution contained a Ch IX with a s.129 which read: "Subject to this Constitution, representative democracy is the law of Australia, notwithstanding any law to the contrary"'. This charge was reminiscent of the response to Murphy J's attempt at implications of 'speech and other communications and freedom of movement' in *Miller v. TCN Channel Nine Pty Ltd* (1986) 161 CLR 556 at 581–2. Ironically, it was Mason J in that case who stated, at p. 579, 'It is sufficient to say that I cannot find any basis for implying a new s. 92A into the Constitution'.

The freedom reaffirmed

It did not take long for a challenge to *Theophanous* and *Stephens* to emerge. Controversially, the challenge was initiated by Dawson J, who invited counsel to seek to reopen the decisions during the hearing of *Levy v. Victoria* (1997) 189 CLR 579.[123] The invitation was accepted by the Solicitor-General for Victoria, and the High Court heard argument in *Levy*, which was heard jointly with *Lange v. Australian Broadcasting Corporation* (1997) 189 CLR 520, on whether *Theophanous* and *Stephens* should be overruled.[124] As it turned out, *Lange* rather than *Levy* was the vehicle that the Court used to decide the issue when it handed down judgment in both cases in July 1997. *Lange* was the better vehicle because, unlike *Levy*, it concerned the law of defamation. It was clear from

---

120 See J. Stone, *Legal System and Lawyers' Reasonings*, Maitland Publications, 1964, pp. 263–7.
121 *McGinty* at 291.
122 *McGinty* at 235–6.
123 See Transcript of Argument in *Levy v. Victoria* M42 of 1995 at 89–96. Dawson J also stated at p. 40, 'It would seem that there is now not a majority of the Court which would support those propositions [in *Theophanous* and *Stephens*]'. See *Levy* at 583 per Dawson J (in argument).
124 The author appeared in both cases as counsel for the Media, Entertainment and Arts Alliance.

the hearing of *Levy* and *Lange* that even if the Court had decided to overrule *Theophanous* and *Stephens*, earlier decisions on the implied freedom would continue to stand.

In *Lange*, David Lange, a former prime minister of New Zealand, sued the Australian Broadcasting Corporation (ABC) for alleged defamatory statements made on *Four Corners*, an ABC television program. In response, the ABC sought to rely on the *Theophanous* defence and also on a common law defence of qualified privilege. In *Lange*, the High Court, consisting of Brennan CJ, Dawson, Toohey, Gaudron, McHugh, Gummow, and Kirby JJ, delivered a joint unanimous judgment that at once affirmed the essential features of the implied freedom as developed in *Australian Capital Television* and *McGinty* and recast those principles as they had operated in *Theophanous* and *Stephens*. The Court struck down the reliance on the constitutional defence developed in *Theophanous*, instead crafting an expanded common law defence of qualified privilege on which the ABC could rely. Even though the new defence recognised in *Lange* was firmly a common law conception, it was also profoundly influenced by the Constitution. The content of the new defence was both shaped by the Constitution, notably the implied freedom of political communication, and was protected from repeal by the limitation on legislative power achieved by the implied freedom.

The unanimous judgment in *Lange* conceived the implied freedom in negative terms as an immunity from particular types of governmental action (see Chapters 1 and 3). From this point, applying an approach similar to that of Brennan J in *Theophanous*, the Court held that the constitutional defence could not be pleaded by the ABC because the implied freedom cannot alter the private rights and immunities of individuals or corporate persons *inter se*. It was found at p. 560 that sections 7 and 24 of the Constitution 'do not confer personal rights on individuals. Rather they preclude the curtailment of the protected freedom by the exercise of legislative or executive power'. The implied freedom was thus incapable of intervening in the action between Lange and the ABC to create a new constitutional defence. This conclusion rested on the freedom being seen as a limitation on legislative and executive action, but not as a limitation on judicial power.[125] If it had also been seen as a bar on judicial action, as similar freedoms have been in the USA,[126] the High Court might have held the Australian judiciary incapable of applying the common law of defamation in proceedings between persons *inter se* in a way that conflicted with the implied freedom. This conclusion might have been supported by covering clause 5 of the Constitution, which states that 'This Act, and all laws made by the Parliament of the Commonwealth under the Constitution, shall be binding on the courts, judges, and people of every State and of every part of the Commonwealth'.[127] Covering clause 5 suggests that judicial action, like legislative and executive action, is subject to the Constitution. However, this conclusion must be treated with caution given that covering clause 5 could equally support the conclusion that action of the 'people'—that is, private action—is subject to the Constitution.

---

125 Compare *McGinty* at 291 per Gummow J, who mentions that the implication 'restrains ... the exercise of legislative, executive or judicial power'; G. Kennett, 'The Freedom Ride: Where to Now?' (1998) 9 *Public Law Review* 111 at 115–16.

126 *Shelley v. Kraemer* 334 US 1 (1948). The decision in *Sullivan* can be explained on the basis that the guarantee of 'freedom of speech' in the First Amendment limits the exercise of judicial power.

127 Compare *Lange* at 563–4.

In finding against the existence of any constitutional defence, the High Court over-ruled *Theophanous* and *Stephens*, although the Court did not actually say so. This was the most problematic aspect of *Lange*, and also the strongest evidence of the cost of achieving unanimity. The Court found that as the judgment of Deane J in *Theophanous* went further in its reasoning than the joint judgment of Mason CJ, Toohey, and Gaudron JJ, *Theophanous* contained no majority reasoning demanding observance. Although the reasoning of the joint judgment was clearly the lowest common denominator of those four judges, that was not sufficient to produce a *ratio decidendi*. It only led to a common result, or orders. This allowed the Court in *Lange* to state at p. 556 that 'the appropriate course is to examine the correctness of the defences pleaded in the present case as a matter of principle and not of authority'. This did not sit well with the Court's approach to precedent in other decisions. For many years the Court has agonised over the precedent value of its split decision in *Dennis Hotels Pty Ltd v. Victoria* (1960) 104 CLR 539 on s. 90 of the Constitution. No common majority could be constructed in *Dennis Hotels*, and indeed the result rested on a distinction drawn by only one judge. In contrast to the Court's awkward attempts to conform to precedent in decisions on s. 90,[128] the treatment of *Theophanous* and *Stephens* in *Lange* appears contrived.

The course taken by the Court in dealing with *Theophanous* is understandable. How could the support of Toohey and Gaudron JJ, two of the judges from the *Theophanous* majority, have been gained if *Theophanous* was to be expressly overruled? More funda-mentally, if *Theophanous* had been overturned, this may have had far reaching conse-quences for the Court. Only the composition of the Court had changed since 1994, and this has never been a good reason to overrule a prior decision.[129] If the Court had taken this path, it would have created the impression that new judges could be appointed to override prior controversial decisions. Little could be more detrimental to the respect held for the High Court in Australian society. As Stewart J of the United States Supreme Court stated in *Mitchell v. WT Grant Co.* 416 US 600 at 636 (1974):

> A basic change in the law on a ground no firmer than a change in our membership invites the popular misconception that this institution is little different from the two political branches of the Government. No misconception could do more lasting injury to this Court and to the system of law which it is our abiding mission to serve.

Lange was a decision about methodology.[130] With one hand the Court overruled the *Theophanous* defence, while with the other it developed the common law defence of qualified privilege along the lines suggested by Brennan and McHugh JJ in *Stephens*. The common law defence of qualified privilege was widened to an ambit similar to the constitutional defence developed in *Theophanous*. It was based on the notion that 'this

---

128 See, for example, *Philip Morris Ltd v. Commissioner of Business Franchises (Vic)* (1989) 167 CLR 399.
129 *R v. Commonwealth Court of Conciliation and Arbitration; ex parte Brisbane Tramways Co. Ltd [No 1]* (1914) 18 CLR 54 at 69 per Barton J: 'Changes in the number of appointed Justices can … never of themselves furnish a reason for review' of a previous decision; *Queensland v. Commonwealth (Second Territory Senators Case)* (1977) 139 CLR 585 at 599–600 per Gibbs J, at 603–4 per Stephen J; *Re Tyler; Ex parte Foley* (1994) 181 CLR 18 at 39–40 per McHugh J. Compare *Stevens v. Head* (1993) 176 CLR 433 at 461–2 per Deane J, at 464–5 per Gaudron J; *Re Tyler; Ex parte Foley* at 35 per Gaudron J.
130 For an assessment of the relative merits of the constitutional and common law methodology, see Stone, 'Freedom of Political Communication, the Constitution and the Common Law'.

Court should now declare that each member of the Australian community has an interest in disseminating and receiving information, opinions and arguments concerning government and political matters that affect the people of Australia'.[131] The test to be applied was one of 'reasonableness of conduct':[132] that is, a similar criterion to the third limb of the *Theophanous* defence. As to this test, the Court indicated, at p. 574, that 'as a general rule' this test would not be satisfied:

> unless the defendant had reasonable grounds for believing that the imputation was true, took proper steps, so far as they were reasonably open, to verify the accuracy of the material and did not believe the imputation to be untrue. Furthermore, the defendant's conduct will not be reasonable unless the defendant has sought a response from the person defamed and published the response made (if any) except in cases where the seeking or publication of a response was not practicable or it was unnecessary to give the plaintiff an opportunity to respond.[133]

The Court made it clear that even though this defence is a common law defence, its availability is guaranteed by the Constitution. The Court found, at p. 566, that if a parliament were to abridge the new common law defence this would be unconstitutional because it would infringe the implied freedom of political communication. Accordingly, while *Lange* removed the constitutional defence, at the same time it replaced that defence with a similar common law defence itself guaranteed by the Constitution. While *Lange* did not increase the protection from defamation actions available, as a result of *Theophanous*, to a person wishing to criticise political figures, it is not clear that the decision will reduce this protection. It may be that *Lange* has not brought about any net change.[134] A final assessment will depend on how the 'reasonableness of conduct' test is applied in lower courts. One danger from the perspective of those concerned about the protection of political communication is that a court might adopt the narrow approach that was taken in *Austin v. Mirror Newspapers Ltd* [1986] AC 299 to the concept of 'reasonable care' in the context of s. 22 of the *Defamation Act 1974* (NSW). However, this would seem unlikely.[135] The High Court clearly established the new defence of qualified privilege in a way that is intended to be broadly protective of political communication. This is supported by a comment of McHugh J in *Levy*. In that case he pointed out, at p. 622 (fn. 148), that 'as the decision in *Lange* shows, the scope of that freedom is at least as great as that recognised in the two earlier cases [*Australian Capital Television* and *Theophanous*]'. Indeed, the protection afforded by the *Lange* defence might even turn out to be greater than that granted by *Theophanous*. Unlike the implied freedom, it is clear that 'increasing integration of social, economic and political matters in Australia' means that the new common law defence applies to 'discussion of government or politics at State or Territory level and even at local government level ... whether or not it bears on matters at the federal level'.[136]

---

131 *Lange* at 571.
132 *Lange* at 573.
133 This new defence is examined by S. Walker, '*Lange v. ABC*: The High Court Rethinks the "Constitutionalisation" of Defamation Law' (1998) 6 *Torts Law Journal* 9 at 16–28.
134 M. Chesterman, 'The Common Law Rules in Defamation—OK?' (1998) 6 *Tort Law Review* 9 at 11.
135 Blackshield and Williams, pp. 1130–1; Walker, pp. 25–6. Compare F. A. Trindade, 'Defamation in the Course of Political Discussion—The New Common Law Defence' (1998) 114 *Law Quarterly Review* 1 at 7.
136 *Lange* at 571–2.

The unanimous joint judgment in *Lange* must be seen as a compromise. The implied freedom of political communication was affirmed, but along the lines laid down by the majority in *McGinty*: that is, as an implication based squarely in the text of the Constitution. Nevertheless, the decision swept away any suggestion that the finding in *Australian Capital Television* was itself flawed. The Court may even have gone a little further than the majority in *McGinty*, and perhaps a little further than a strict reading of the text would demand, in stating, at p. 559:

> Freedom of communication on matters of government and politics is an indispensable incident of that system of representative government which the Constitution creates by directing that the members of the House of Representatives and the Senate shall be 'directly chosen by the people' of the Commonwealth and the States, respectively.

The Court also found that the implied freedom extends beyond election periods, and thus beyond the scope suggested in earlier decisions by Dawson and McHugh JJ. The implied freedom was given a wider operation than might be expected on a narrow construction of sections 7 and 24 of the Constitution:

> If the freedom is to effectively serve the purpose of ss 7 and 24 and related sections, it cannot be confined to the election period. Most of the matters necessary to enable 'the people' to make an informed choice will occur during the period between the holding of one, and the calling of the next, election. If the freedom to receive and disseminate information were confined to election periods, the electors would be deprived of the greater part of the information necessary to make an effective choice at the election.[137]

The implied freedom of political communication is now entrenched in Australian constitutional jurisprudence. *Lange* will naturally turn attention away from whether the freedom really exists, to where the implication might be applied and what effect it might have on legislative and executive action, including how the freedom should be balanced against other rights and competing interests. It was thus fortunate that the decision set out more clearly than earlier decisions how the Court will apply the implication to determine whether a law is unconstitutional, and thus where the boundaries of governmental action lie in restricting speech. The Court set out, at pp. 567–8, two questions to be addressed in determining whether a law has breached the implied freedom:

> First, does the law effectively burden freedom of communication about government or political matters either in its terms, operation or effect? Second, if the law effectively burdens that freedom, is the law reasonably appropriate and adapted to serve a legitimate end the fulfilment of which is compatible with the maintenance of the constitutionally prescribed system of representative and responsible government and the procedure prescribed by s. 128 for submitting a proposed amendment of the Constitution to the informed decision of the people … If the first question is answered 'yes' and the second is answered 'no', the law is invalid.

The second of these questions is obviously a proportionality-like test (see Chapter 4). Deane J in *Cunliffe* stated at p. 337 that the outcome of such a test 'will ultimately

---

137 *Lange* at 561.

depend upon an assessment of the character (including purpose), operation and effect of the particular law'. In addressing the first question, difficult issues can arise as to the ambit of political communication. Many issues remain to be resolved, such as when communication about the private life of a public figure is protected, or in what circumstances commercial expression may also be political expression, or to what extent the freedom protects discussion about matters of public concern that are not also current issues of political debate.[138] An area of development is likely to be whether the implied freedom protects protest by unions, such as picketing, or even lock-outs by employers.[139] It is unlikely that actions such as picketing will be constitutionally protected unless they can be seen as containing a political element. Hence, picketing merely as part of an ongoing industrial campaign will be difficult to include within the ambit of the freedom. On the other hand, picketing that is a central component of a campaign against the policies of a government, such as union 'green bans' on particular developments as part of a protest against a government's environmental policies,[140] may amount to protected political communication. The judgment in *Lange* did not comment on the correctness or otherwise of the wide conception of political communication developed in *Theophanous* by Mason CJ, Toohey, and Gaudron JJ, and in *Cunliffe* by four judges. In the absence of such comment, this wide conception must be treated as the current scope of the freedom.[141]

In *Australian Capital Television* and *Nationwide News,* Mason CJ, Deane, Toohey, and McHugh JJ established a two-tier approach to determining whether a law could be justified under the implied freedom. They found that a higher level of scrutiny should be applied to a law that targets ideas or information, as opposed to a law that targets an activity or mode of communication by which ideas or information are transmitted. In *Australian Capital Television*, Mason CJ stated, at p. 143, that a law of the former type could only be valid where it was supported by a 'compelling justification'. This is obviously a harsher test than that set out in *Lange*, which is more akin to the test laid down by Mason CJ for a law that targets an activity or mode of communication by which ideas or information are transmitted. In light of *Lange*, there are two ways of approaching the two-tier approach. Since the decision in *Lange* the test developed in *Australian Capital Television* and *Nationwide News* might not be seen as setting a higher level of scrutiny where a law targets ideas or information. At best, it might merely indicate that such a law will be more difficult to justify as a 'law reasonably appropriate and adapted to serve a legitimate end'.[142] Alternatively, *Lange* might be taken to have set down a general standard that will give way to a higher level of scrutiny in the case of certain laws.

---

138 See *Kruger v. Commonwealth* (1997) 190 CLR 1 at 118 per Gaudron J: 'Freedom of political communication is a freedom which extends to all matters which *may* fall for consideration in the political process' (emphasis added).

139 See S. Bronitt and G. Williams, 'Political Freedom as an Outlaw: Republican Theory and Political Protest' (1996) 18 *Adelaide Law Review* 289 at 299.

140 Kennett, p. 119 gives as further examples 'where industrial action takes the form of refusal to load uranium for export, or where the law protested against is one banning strikes'.

141 *Kruger* at 90–1 per Toohey J. Compare with *Brown v. Classification Review Board* (1998) 154 ALR 67 at 85–6 per Heerey J.

142 *Lange* at 567.

The decision in *Levy* suggests that the latter explanation is the correct one, and that the unanimous judgment in *Lange* may not have clarified the test to be applied as clearly as it seemed.[143] *Levy* showed that the two-tier approach remains attractive to members of the High Court. While giving their support to the *Lange* test, Toohey, Gummow, Gaudron, and Kirby JJ also alluded to the need for a higher standard of review for laws targeting ideas or information.[144] For example, after setting out the *Lange* test, Kirby J stated, at p. 647, that this was not 'a case where the legislation has, by its terms, specifically targeted the idea or message so as to require a "compelling justification"'. *Levy* demonstrates that the *Lange* test is clearly the appropriate starting point for an assessment of the validity of a law under the implied freedom of political communication. However, that test apparently does not tell the whole story, with different levels of justification being applicable depending on the nature of the law.

Symbolic speech

The plaintiff in *Levy*, an animal rights activist, sought to enter an area where ducks were being shot to retrieve dead and injured game birds. He intended to display these birds for the television cameras as a protest against Victorian laws that allowed an annual duck-shooting season. However, the Wildlife (Game) (Hunting Season) Regulations 1994 (Vic) provided that a person could not enter the 'permitted hunting area' unless he or she was the holder of a valid game licence. The plaintiff challenged the Regulations in the High Court on the ground that they infringed an implied freedom of political communication derived either from the Commonwealth or the Victorian Constitution (the *Constitution Act* 1975 (Vic)). The Court accepted that the protest planned for the benefit of the television cameras could fall within the ambit of the implied freedom even though it might not involve verbal communication but a series of images. For example, Brennan CJ stated, at p. 595:

> Televised protests by non-verbal conduct are today a commonplace of political expression. A law which simply denied an opportunity to make such a protest about an issue relevant to the government or politics of the Commonwealth would be as offensive to the constitutionally implied freedom as a law which banned political speech-making on that issue.

Toohey and Gummow JJ found, at p. 613, that even though the television coverage sought by the plaintiff 'would portray or stimulate appeals to emotion rather than to reason', 'The appeal to reason cannot be said to be, or ever to have been, an essential ingredient of political communication or discussion'.

Despite this finding, the challenge was lost after the balancing test set out in *Lange* was applied. Even if constitutionally protected communication was abridged by the Regulations, the Regulations were an appropriate and adapted response to the legitimate concern of protecting safety. This was clear from the effect of the Regulations and by their stated purpose, which as set out in reg. 1(a), was to 'ensure a greater degree of safety of persons in hunting areas during the open season for ducks in 1994'. Even if the challenge had not failed on this basis, the same result would have ensued unless it

143 A. Stone, '*Lange, Levy* and the Direction of the Freedom of Political Communication under the Australian Constitution' (1998) 21 *University of New South Wales Law Journal* 117 at 131–2.

144 *Levy* at 614 per Toohey and Gummow JJ, at 618–19 per Gaudron J.

could have been shown that the implied freedom of political discussion is capable of operating to override a law of the Victorian Parliament (see pp. 179–81).

The significant finding in *Levy* was not that the *Lange* test meant that the Regulations were valid, but that the relevant communication was protected by the implied freedom. *Levy* makes clear that laws may infringe the implied freedom if they prohibit non-verbal political communication, such as, in the context of the electoral process, a candidate shaking the hands of voters or the placement of posters with the picture of a candidate. In achieving this extension to the implied freedom, the Court in *Levy* accepted that the freedom protects what the United States Supreme Court refers to as 'expressive conduct' or 'symbolic speech'. For example, in *Texas v. Johnson* 491 US 397 (1989),[145] the United States Supreme Court held that the burning of the United States flag was protected by the guarantee of 'freedom of speech' in the First Amendment to the United States Constitution. In *United States v. O'Brien* 391 US 367 (1968), in which a person was prosecuted for destroying his draft card, the United States Supreme Court developed a test for determining whether non-verbal communication breached the First Amendment. Warren CJ, delivering the judgment of the Court, found, at pp. 376–7, that 'when "speech" and "nonspeech" elements are combined in the same course of conduct, a sufficiently important governmental interest in regulating the nonspeech element can justify incidental limitations on First Amendment freedoms'.[146] The United States Supreme Court, while recognising non-verbal conduct as a form of 'speech', has drawn a distinction between the two in order to limit the constitutional protection extended to non-verbal conduct. However, there is no basis for such a distinction under the Australian Constitution. A more analogous provision is s. 2(b) of the Canadian Charter of Rights and Freedoms, which protects 'freedom of … expression'. It has been said of that provision that 'Activity is expressive if it attempts to convey meaning',[147] and in relation to this provision, there has been no attempt to distinguish between verbal and non-verbal communication. The freedom of political communication implied from the Australian Constitution is not based on express words protecting 'speech', or even 'expression', but is derived from constitutional text and structure that makes no distinction between speech and non-verbal conduct. It may thus be that the Australian Constitution affords more protection to non-verbal political communication than the United States First Amendment.

Further implications

In delving into the system of representative government created by the Constitution, most attention has focused on the implied freedom of political communication. It is natural that the reaffirmation of that freedom by a unanimous Court in *Lange* will shift attention to whether other freedoms might also be derived. The earlier decision of *McGinty* established a solid foundation for deriving such freedoms. In *McGinty*, the

---

145 Reaffirmed in *United States v. Eichman* 496 US 310 (1990).
146 See, for examples of the application of this test, *Clark v. Community for Creative Non-Violence* 468 US 288 (1984); *Barnes v. Glen Theatre, Inc* 501 US 560 (1991).
147 *Irwin Toy v. Quebec (Attorney-General)* [1989] 1 SCR 927 at 968 per Dickson CJ, Lamer, and Wilson JJ.

majority recognised that the concept of representative government is a shorthand label given to the system created by the structure and text of the Australian Constitution, particularly sections 7 and 24. The system thus defined by the Constitution does not have a separate existence informed by political theory or other extrinsic material. It is not a 'free-standing' principle[148] from which further implications might be derived, but a concept that is itself bounded by the text and structure of the Constitution. From this basis, the Constitution guarantees anything that is necessary for the continued existence of that system: that is, its minimal requirements. The High Court has recognised that freedom of political communication is a basic requirement of the system of representative government created by the Constitution. According to McHugh J in *Australian Capital Television* (1992) 177 CLR 106 at 227:

> When the Constitution is read as a whole and in the light of the history of constitutional government in Great Britain and the Australian colonies before federation, the proper conclusion to be drawn from the terms of sections 7 and 24 of the Constitution is that the people of Australia have constitutional rights of freedom of participation, association and communication in relation to federal elections.[149]

Similarly, Gaudron J found at p. 212 that 'The notion of a free society governed in accordance with the principles of representative parliamentary democracy may entail freedom of movement, freedom of association and, perhaps, freedom of speech generally'.[150]

Further implied freedoms might thus include a freedom of association.[151] It is difficult to see how some version of a freedom to associate could not be implied given the approach in *McGinty* and the existence of a freedom of political communication. The ability to associate for political purposes is obviously a cornerstone of representative government as embodied in the Constitution. How could the people 'directly choose' their representatives if denied the ability to form political associations and to collectively seek political power? The ability to 'choose' must entail the ability to be chosen. Accordingly, a freedom to associate for political purposes may be implied from the Constitution. A law that, for example, prevented persons from forming a political party or banned members of certain political organisations from standing for the federal Parliament would, in the absence of meeting the requirements of a test like that in *Lange*, be unconstitutional.

The *Communist Party Dissolution Act 1950* (Cth) is an example of legislation that might today be held to breach a freedom of association.[152] The Australian Communist Party was a participant in the federal electoral process and stood candidates for election to the Commonwealth Parliament. Section 4 of the Communist Party Dissolution Act declared the Australian Communist Party to be an unlawful association, provided for its

---

148 *McGinty* at 234 per McHugh J.
149 See also pp. 232–3 per McHugh J.
150 See J. Kirk 'Constitutional Implications from Representative Democracy' (1995) 23 *Federal Law Review* 37 at 49–65.
151 Freedom of association is not expressly guaranteed by the United States Constitution. However, it has been implied from that instrument. See *NAACP v. Alabama* 357 US 449 (1958); *Roberts v. United States Jaycees* 468 US 609 (1984).
152 The Communist Party Dissolution Act was held invalid by the High Court in *Australian Communist Party v. Commonwealth* (1951) 83 CLR 1 (see Chapter 8).

dissolution, and enabled the appointment of a receiver to manage its property. Section 7(1) provided that a person would be liable to imprisonment for five years if he or she knowingly committed acts that included continuing to operate as a member or officer of the Party or carrying or displaying anything indicating that he or she was in any way associated with the Party.

Less obviously, sections 7 and 24 might support a freedom of movement. Arguably, such a freedom is a necessary concomitant of representative government as embodied in the Constitution, although a firmer basis would be the federal system created by the Constitution (see Chapter 3), or s. 92 of the Constitution (see Chapter 6). Nevertheless, it is likely that a freedom of movement can be derived to the extent that Australians must be free to access the seat of government and other institutions vital to the system of representative government.[153]

The *Aboriginals Ordinance 1918* (NT) authorised the forced removal and institutional detention of Aboriginal children in the Northern Territory. In *Kruger v. Commonwealth* (1997) 190 CLR 1, a High Court made up of six judges considered whether freedoms of movement and association derived from the Constitution could be applied to strike down the Ordinance. Three judges—Toohey, Gaudron, and McHugh JJ—found that the Constitution gives rise to freedoms of movement and association. Brennan CJ, Dawson J, and Gummow J expressed no view on this question, finding that even if such freedoms existed, they could not apply in the Northern Territory to assist the plaintiffs. Overall, a majority was not prepared to apply either a freedom of movement or association in this case. Only Gaudron J held that the Ordinance was unconstitutional. Toohey J, while he did not feel able to determine the issue—given that no factual material was before the Court—found that there was an argument that should go to trial.

When the possibility of implied freedoms of movement and association was considered in *Kruger*, there were suggestions that such freedoms are merely ancillary to freedom of political communication. For example, Gaudron J stated at p. 115:

> It is clear, and it has been so held, that the fundamental elements of the system of government mandated by the Constitution require that there be freedom of political communication between citizens and their elected representatives and also between citizen and citizen. However, just as communication would be impossible if 'each citizen was an island', so too it is substantially impeded if citizens are held in enclaves, no matter how large the enclave or congenial its composition. Freedom of political communication depends on human contact and entails at least a significant measure of freedom to associate with others. And freedom of association necessarily entails freedom of movement.[154]

McHugh J found at p. 142 that 'the reasons that led to the drawing of the implication of the freedom of communication' also enabled him to find that 'the Constitution also necessarily implies that "the people" must be free from laws that prevent them from associating with other persons, and from travelling, inside and outside Australia'. However, he did not suggest that the latter was merely an incident of the former. The Constitution is capable of supporting implied freedoms of association and movement

---

153 *R v. Smithers; Ex parte Benson* (1912) 16 CLR 99 (see Chapter 3).
154 See also pp. 88–92 per Toohey J.

that are independent of any implied freedom of political communication. While the implications undoubtedly overlap, each should not be seen as limiting the scope of any other freedom, given that each independently arises from sections 7 and 24. The freedom of political communication is not the appropriate source of further freedoms. Such freedoms should be tied back to their source: that is, the text and structure of the Constitution.

In developing freedoms of movement and association, Gaudron J made it clear that such freedoms, like the freedom of political communication, cannot be absolute. Thus, the freedoms cannot restrict 'valid laws of the Commonwealth on topics which clearly comprehend restrictions on movement and association'.[155] She gave as examples the Commonwealth's powers over defence in 51(vi), quarantine in s. 51(ix) and aliens in 51(xix). Rather than applying the *Lange* test to determine the validity of the Ordinance as against the freedoms of movement and association, Gaudron J found at p. 128 that the question to be answered was whether the purpose of the Ordinance was 'to pro- hibit or restrict political communication'. The Commonwealth had claimed that the Ordinance was valid because it was made 'for the purpose of the protection and preser- vation of persons of the Aboriginal race'. Gaudron J rejected this characterisation and held that the Ordinance was invalid.

Conclusion

The system of representative government created by the Constitution, particularly sec- tions 7 and 24, has proved a fertile source of implied rights. The explosion of litigation on the implied freedom of political communication since 1992 shows little sign of abat- ing. Recent decisions such as *Lange*, *Levy*, and *Kruger* show that this and other rights implied from the system of representative government will continue to play an impor- tant role in Australian constitutional jurisprudence. The existence of rights such as free- doms of movement and association, as well as the limits of the rights already discovered (such as the extent to which the implied freedom of political communication might affect parliamentary privilege[156]), is still being explored. This, and the reasoned basis for the existence of such rights, remains a central challenge for the High Court.

Murphy J covered similar terrain in the two decades before the rest of the High Court came to do so. However, there are important differences between the two approaches. As I have argued elsewhere,[157] there is little to indicate that Murphy J's views have been influential in shaping recent developments.[158] Instead, *Australian Capital Television* and subsequent cases should be seen as heralding a fresh start. Nevertheless,

---

155 *Kruger* at 201.
156 *Laurance v. Katter* (1996) 141 ALR 447; *O' Chee v. Rowley* (1997) 150 ALR 199; M. Chesterman, 'Privileges and Freedoms for Defamatory Political Speech' (1997) 19 *Adelaide Law Review* 155; D. O'Brien, 'Parlia- mentary Privilege and the Implied Freedom of Speech' (1995) 25 *Queensland Law Society Journal* 569.
157 G. Williams, 'Lionel Murphy and Democracy and Rights' in M. Coper and G. Williams (eds), *Justice Lionel Murphy: Influential or Merely Prescient?*, Federation Press, 1997, p. 50.
158 Compare L. Campbell, 'Lionel Murphy and the Jurisprudence of the High Court Ten Years On' (1996) 15 *University of Tasmania Law Review* 22; M. Kirby, 'Lionel Murphy and the Power of Ideas' (1993) 18 *Alternative Law Journal* 253 at 256 M. Kirby, 'Lionel Murphy's Legacy', in Coper and Williams (ed.), p. 288.

the implied freedom of political communication, and later freedoms, clearly owe some-thing to the freedom of communication recognised by Murphy J. Even if Murphy J was not influential in the development of the implied freedom, his contribution was per-haps essential for the Court to reach its decision in *Australian Capital Television*. In taking a series of extreme positions, Murphy J broadened the parameters of the playing field. He widened the perceptions of observers of the High Court as to the possible range of approaches on these issues. Before Murphy J, commentators and practitioners could not have reasonably expected that a judge would, for example, find that the Constitution contains a right to freedom from slavery or a freedom from sex discrimination. In broadening the field to include such options (however much they may have been criti-cised), Murphy J succeeded in shifting the middle ground. He created a climate in which the development of the implied freedom of political communication could be perceived to be less radical (and hence more legitimate) than it otherwise might have been. He created an environment in which members of the High Court could seek to protect rights within a framework of more traditional legal reasoning.

EIGHT

Implications from the Separation of Judicial Power

Introduction

Chapter III of the Constitution, most notably s. 71, vests federal judicial power in the High Court and in such other courts as the federal Parliament creates or nominates. Chapters I and II of the Constitution vest legislative and executive power in the Parliament and Queen, respectively. In this way, the structure of the Constitution achieves a separation of powers. In practice, the separation of executive and legislative power has not been rigidly maintained.[1] This is a natural result of the framers' intent to create a Westminster style of government, as reflected in the fact that s. 64 requires 'Ministers of State' to be members of the Parliament. On the other hand, the High Court has strictly enforced the separation of the judiciary from both the executive and the legislature.

The separation of federal judicial power is an important means by which the High Court protects human rights. In *Re Tracey; Ex parte Ryan* (1989) 166 CLR 518 at 580, Deane J suggested that this separation is 'the Constitution's only general guarantee of due process'. Like implications from the system of representative government created by the Constitution (see Chapter 7), implications from the separation of judicial power have been the subject of considerable High Court attention in the 1990s, and offer the promise of a range of implied freedoms. In analysing the system created by the separation of judicial power, judges have been creative in discovering new rights, many of which have yet to be fully explored. Many loose ends remain. For example, it has yet to be seen what aspects of the criminal trial process will be constitutionally entrenched, and to what extent the Constitution guarantees due process in the exercise of judicial power. It is difficult to overstate the potential importance of rights derived from Chapter III of the Constitution. In *Street v. Queensland Bar Association* (1989) 168 CLR 461 at 521, Deane J, in the context of listing a number of constitutional rights, commented that 'The most important of them is the guarantee that the citizen can be subjected to the exercise of Commonwealth judicial power only by the "courts" designated by Ch III (s 71)'.

---

1   *Victorian Stevedoring and General Contracting Co. Pty Ltd and Meakes v. Dignan* (1931) 46 CLR 73.

Judicial review

Judicial review of governmental action is a fundamental protection that the Constitution provides against the infringement of human rights. As Harrison Moore recognised, it offers protection against the exercise of arbitrary power.[2] Judicial review may be implied from Chapter III of the Constitution, particularly sections 75 and 76. These provisions vest 'original jurisdiction' in the High Court. Section 75 establishes certain 'matters' as being within the jurisdiction of the Court, such as matters 'In which a writ of Mandamus or prohibition or an injunction is sought against an officer of the Commonwealth'. Section 76 states that 'The Parliament may make laws conferring original jurisdiction on the High Court' in any of the matters then listed. Strangely, matters 'Arising under this Constitution, or involving its interpretation' is listed under s. 76(i) as a matter that the Parliament may list within the jurisdiction of the Court, rather than in s. 75 as a matter in which the High Court shall have jurisdiction. Despite this, it is clear that the Constitution vests power in the High Court to review legislative and executive action for consistency with the Constitution.[3] Sir Owen Dixon argued that the words of s76(i) 'impliedly acknowledge the function of the courts [to engage in judicial review]'.[4]

In *Marbury v. Madison* 5 US (1 Cranch) 137 (1803), the United States Supreme Court found that it possesses the power to declare legislation to be inconsistent with the United States Constitution and therefore invalid. There is no equivalent single decision in Australia that establishes the authority of the High Court to review legislation for unconstitutionality. The records of the Convention debates indicate that the framers of the Australian Constitution intended, or perhaps assumed, that the High Court would be the ultimate arbiter of constitutional power.[5] In the main, this has been uncritically assumed ever since. The decision in *Australian Communist Party v. Commonwealth* (1951) 83 CLR 1 is the closest that the High Court has come to declaring its role.

In the *Communist Party Case* the High Court heard a challenge to the attempt of the newly elected Menzies coalition Government to suppress Australian communism by banning the Australian Communist Party. Among the more remarkable features of the *Communist Party Dissolution Act 1950* (Cth) were the nine recitals that prefaced the operative sections of the legislation. Recitals four to eight set out Parliament's view of communism and the Communist Party, such as in recital four that the Party 'engages in activities or operations designed to bring about the overthrow or dislocation of the

---

2   W. H. Moore, *The Constitution of the Commonwealth of Australia*, 2nd edn [1910], Legal Books, 1997, pp. 322–4.

3   P. H. Lane, *The Australian Federal System*, 2nd edn, LBC, 1979, pp. 1135–44; G. Lindell, 'The Justiciability of Political Questions: Recent Developments', in H. P. Lee and G. Winterton (eds), *Australian Constitutional Perspectives*, LBC, 1992, pp. 218–29; R. D. Lumb, 'The Judiciary, the Interpretation of the Constitution and the Australian Constitutional Convention' (1983) 57 *Australian Law Journal* 229 at 229.

4   O. Dixon, *Jesting Pilate*, LBC, 1965 at 175. Compare J. A. Thomson, 'Constitutional Authority for Judicial Review: A Contribution from the Framers of the Australian Constitution', in G. Craven (ed.), *The Convention Debates 1891–98: Commentaries, Indices and Guide, 1891–1898*, vol. 6, Legal Books, 1986, p. 200.

5   A. R. Blackshield, 'The Courts and Judicial Review', in S. Encel, D. Horne, and E. Thompson (eds), *Change the Rules! Towards a Democratic Constitution*, Penguin, 1977, p. 132; B. Galligan, 'Judicial Review in the Australian Federal System: Its Origin and Function' (1979) 10 *Federal Law Review* 367; Thomson, p. 186.

established system of government of Australia and the attainment of economic, indus-trial or political ends by force, violence, intimidation or fraudulent practices'. Recital nine stated Parliament's belief that:

> it is necessary, for the security and defence of Australia and for the execution and mainte-nance of the Constitution and of the laws of the Commonwealth, that the Australian Com-munist Party, and bodies of persons affiliated with that party, should be dissolved and their property forfeited to the Commonwealth, and that members and officers of that party or of any of those bodies and other persons who are communists should be disqualified from employment by the Commonwealth and from holding office in an industrial organization a substantial number of whose members are engaged in a vital industry.

The operative provisions of the Act then went on to implement these measures. Section 4 declared the Australian Communist Party to be an unlawful association, provided for its dissolution, and enabled the appointment of a receiver to manage its property. Sec-tion 5 provided the machinery for declarations by the Governor-General that organisa-tions other than the Party were also unlawful. This provision targeted bodies that supported or advocated communism, were affiliated with the Party, or whose policies were substantially shaped by members of the Party or by 'Communists'. Once unlawful, an association would be dissolved under s. 6 and a receiver appointed under s. 8. An organisation could be declared unlawful under s. 5(2) where:

> the Governor-General is satisfied that a body of persons is a body of persons to which this section applies and that the continued existence of that body of persons would be prejudicial to the security and defence of the Commonwealth or to the execution or maintenance of the Constitution or of the laws of the Commonwealth.

Under s. 9(2), the Governor-General could declare any person to be a 'Communist' or member of the Australian Communist Party by applying a similar discretion to that laid out in s. 5(2). 'Communist' was defined by s. 3 to mean 'a person who supports or advo-cates the objectives, policies, teachings, principles or practices of communism, as expounded by Marx and Lenin'. Once declared, s. 10 meant a person could not hold office in the Commonwealth public service or in industries declared by the Governor-General to be vital to the security and defence of Australia. Should a person wish to contest a declaration by the Governor-General, he or she could do so under s. 9(4), although s. 9(5) provided that 'the burden shall be on him to prove that he is not a per-son to whom this section applies'.

The Communist Party Dissolution Act was a draconian attack on several basic lib-erties such as freedom of association and expression. It was an attack that, despite the hysteria of the time, was far out of proportion to any threat posed by the Australian Communist Party to the Australian polity.[6] More subtly, the legislation was also an attack on the position of the High Court. The Parliament had sought to recite itself into power. The recitals amounted to a statement that the Court should take notice that the Parliament believed that its legislation was valid under its implied power to legislate about Australian nationhood or under its defence power in s. 51(vi) of the Constitution.

---

6   G. Williams, 'The Suppression of Communism by Force of Law: Australia in the Early 1950s' (1996) 42 *Aus-tralian Journal of Politics and History* 220.

The recitals were thus a challenge to the High Court's role as the sole arbiter of the scope of Commonwealth power under the Constitution.[7]

The High Court gave a strong reply. With Latham CJ dissenting, the Court held the Communist Party Dissolution Act to be invalid. In argument before the High Court it was forcefully submitted that the Act was invalid due to its derogation of civil liberties and the democratic process.[8] However, the majority reasoning did not find the Act invalid because it breached constitutionally entrenched civil liberties, but because it could not be characterised as law falling within Commonwealth power. This conclusion rested on two findings. First, the Court refused to accept the Parliament's view of the legislation and the Australian Communist Party as expressed in the recitals. The recitals might be of some use in ascertaining the intention of the Parliament in passing the Act, but could play no role in determining whether the Act actually fell within power. That was a decision for the High Court. Second, the Court found that the Act lacked a sufficient connection with a head of power. The Governor-General's power to make declarations under sections 5(2) and 9(2) of the Act were found to be unreviewable by the Court and thus granted an unfettered discretion to determine the scope of Commonwealth power by declaring certain persons or organisations to be 'prejudicial to the security and defence of the Commonwealth'. According to Fullagar J at p. 261, these sections were invalid because they imposed 'legal consequences on a legislative or executive opinion which itself supplies the only link between the power and the legal consequences of the opinion'. Underpinning both of the above findings was the view that responsibility for determining the scope of Commonwealth power lay with the High Court alone. The attempt by the Parliament to determine the scope of its own power breached the maxim that 'a stream cannot rise higher than its source'.[9]

George Winterton has described the decision in the *Communist Party Case* as 'probably the most important ever rendered by the Court'.[10] The decision is important because it held invalid legislation that would have significantly impeded the political liberties of Australians. Argument of counsel on issues of civil liberties did find some voice in the Court's decision. In a departure from the legalism pervading the judgments, Dixon J stated at pp. 187–8:

> History and not only ancient history, shows that in countries where democratic institutions have been unconstitutionally superseded, it has been done not seldom by those holding the executive power. Forms of government may need protection from dangers likely to arise from within the institutions to be protected. In point of constitutional theory the power to legislate for the protection of an existing form of government ought not to be based on a conception, if otherwise adequate, adequate only to assist those holding power to resist or suppress obstruction or opposition or attempts to displace them or the form of government they defend.

---

7   Compare the legislation found to be valid in *Marcus Clark & Co. Ltd v. Commonwealth* (1952) 87 CLR 177.

8   G. Williams, 'Reading the Judicial Mind: Appellate Argument in the *Communist Party Case*' (1993) 15 *Sydney Law Review* 3 at 17–22.

9   *Communist Party Case* at 258 per Fullagar J. See A. R. Blackshield and G. Williams, *Australian Constitutional Law and Theory: Commentary and Materials*, 2nd edn, Federation Press, 1998, p. 671; L. Zines, *The High Court and the Constitution*, 4th edn, Butterworths, 1997, ch. 11.

10 G. Winterton, 'The Significance of the *Communist Party Case*' (1992) 18 *Melbourne University Law Review* 630 at 653.

Despite this and similar[11] rhetoric, the *Communist Party Case* cannot be cast as a decision of great civil libertarian proportions. The Court did strike down a law that infringed basic freedoms, but despite the majority's clear dislike of the Act, the finding of invalidity did not depend on the Act having breached any express or implied constitutional guarantee protective of human rights. Instead, the result flowed from the majority's finding that the Communist Party Dissolution Act could not be characterised as a law falling within a head of Commonwealth power.

The real significance of the *Communist Party Case* lies in the fact that the Court, in striking down the Communist Party Dissolution Act, entrenched its own position as the ultimate arbiter of the Constitution, and thus as an independent check on the power of the legislature and the executive. In particular, the mantra 'a stream cannot rise higher than its source' can be seen as a bulwark against the exercise of arbitrary governmental power. In the *Communist Party Case*, the doctrine of judicial review was emphatically affirmed. As Fullagar J stated at p. 262, 'in our system the principle of *Marbury v. Madison* is accepted as axiomatic'.

The nature of judicial power

Judicial power eludes accurate and precise description. This stems from the imprecise nature and scope of the power and the 'difficulty, if not impossibility, of framing a definition of judicial power that is at once exclusive and exhaustive'.[12] Some powers, such as the power to examine witnesses, or the power to appoint a new trustee, have a 'double aspect': [13] that is, they may be characterised as judicial if conferred on a court, or non-judicial if conferred on a body that is not a court. The classic attempt at a definition of judicial power is that of Griffith CJ in *Huddart, Parker & Co. Pty Ltd v. Moorehead* (1909) 8 CLR 330 at 357:

> I am of the opinion that the words 'judicial power' as used in sec 71 of the Constitution mean the power which every sovereign authority must of necessity have to decide controversies between its subjects, or between itself and its subjects, whether the rights relate to life, liberty or property. The exercise of this power does not begin until some tribunal which has power to give a binding and authoritative decision (whether subject to appeal or not) is called on to take action.

This and similar definitions[14] show that the characteristics and content of judicial power have not proved susceptible to precise definition. Instead, judicial power has a number of indicia: for example, that it is performed in a judicial manner (that is, with judicial fairness and detachment). However, none of these indicia is by itself decisive. Whether a power can be said to be judicial depends on the way in which the indicia apparent in the power are weighed up against those that are absent.

---

11 *Communist Party Case* at 193 per Dixon J ('the rule of law'), at 268 per Fullagar J ('relaxation of a fundamental constitutional rule').
12 *Precision Data Holdings Ltd v. Wills* (1991) 173 CLR 167 at 188 per the Court.
13 *R v. Davison* (1954) 90 CLR 353 at 369 per Dixon CJ and McTiernan J.
14 See *R v. Trade Practices Tribunal; Ex parte Tasmanian Breweries Pty Ltd* (1970) 123 CLR 361, at 372–5 per Kitto J; Blackshield and Williams, pp. 530–8.

The separation of judicial power achieved by Chapter III of the Constitution entails two consequences. As Dixon J recognised in *Victorian Stevedoring and General Contracting Co. Pty Ltd and Meakes v. Dignan* (1931) 46 CLR 73 at 98, 'the Parliament is restrained both from reposing any power essentially judicial in any other organ or body, and from reposing any other than that judicial power in such tribunals'. Hence, the Constitution requires that:

- only Chapter III courts (that is, courts recognised under s. 71 of the Constitution) be conferred with judicial power; *and*
- Chapter III courts not be conferred with power other than judicial power, except where such other power is ancillary or incidental to the exercise of judicial power.[15]

Both limbs were reflected in decisions such as *New South Wales v. Commonwealth (Wheat Case)* (1915) 20 CLR 54 and *Waterside Workers' Federation of Australia v. JW Alexander Ltd* (1918) 25 CLR 434. In the *Wheat Case*, the High Court held that the vesting of judicial power in the Inter-State Commission,[16] which possesses non-judicial power under s. 101 of the Constitution, was unconstitutional. Similarly, in *Waterside Workers' Federation* the High Court found that the conferral of judicial power on the Commonwealth Court of Conciliation and Arbitration, a body also possessing non-judicial power, was invalid. The latter decision culminated in the decisions of the High Court[17] and Privy Council[18] in the *Boilermakers Case*, in which the conferral of judicial power on the Court of Conciliation and Arbitration was found to have breached Chapter III of the Constitution. This meant that the Court had been invalidly constituted for 30 years. Since the *Boilermakers Case*, the Commonwealth has been careful to vest judicial and non-judicial power over industrial matters in separate bodies. In response to the *Boilermakers Case*, the Commonwealth split the Court of Conciliation and Arbitration into a Conciliation and Arbitration Commission (exercising non-judicial power) and a Commonwealth Industrial Court (exercising judicial power). A similar distinction is maintained today by the *Workplace Relations Act 1996* (Cth).

Prior to the *Boilermakers Case* the High Court and the Privy Council considered whether under the *Income Tax Assessment Act 1922* (Cth) the Commonwealth could establish a Board of Review to provide administrative review of taxation decisions. The High Court in *Federal Commissioner of Taxation v Munro* (1926) 38 CLR 153 and the Privy Council in *Shell Co. of Australia v Federal Commissioner of Taxation* [1931] AC 275 held that judicial power had not been conferred by the Act because the Board had merely been given the power of the Commissioner rather than any other powers or functions.[19] As Isaacs J stated at p. 177 in *Federal Commissioner of Taxation v Munro*, he could see no reason why Parliament could not 'entrust successive administrative functionaries to consider and review assessments, making the final decision the governing *factum* fixing the taxpayer's liability'. Starke J found at p. 212 that the functions of the

---

15 These principles have been restated many times. See, for example, *Gould v. Brown* (1998) 151 ALR 395 at 454–5 per Gummow J.

16 See M. Coper, 'The Second Coming of the Fourth Arm: The Role and Functions of the Inter-State Commission' (1989) 63 *Australian Law Journal* 731.

17 *R v. Kirby; Ex parte Boilermakers' Society of Australia* (1956) 94 CLR 254.

18 *Attorney-General (Commonwealth) v. The Queen* [1957] AC 288.

19 Compare the earlier decision of the High Court in *British Imperial Oil Co. v Federal Commissioner of Taxation* (1925) 35 CLR 422, in which it held that a precursor to the Board of Review, the Board of Appeal, had been invalidly conferred with judicial power.

Board were 'in aid of the administrative functions of government'. On appeal, in *Shell Co. of Australia v Federal Commissioner of Taxation*, Lord Sankey (for their Lordships) found at p. 298 that the members of the Board 'are merely in the same position as the Commissioner himself—namely, they are another administrative tribunal which is reviewing the determination of the Commissioner who admittedly is not judicial, but executive'.

There have been suggestions that the strict separation required by the *Boilermakers Case* might be relaxed.[20] In any event, the *Boilermakers Case* has not completely stifled the creation of non-judicial bodies with adjudicative-like power, and the decisions as to the Board of Review remain good law. In cases such as *R v. Trade Practices Tribunal; Ex parte Tasmanian Breweries Pty Ltd* (1970) 123 CLR 361 (as to the Trade Practices Tribunal) and *Precision Data Holdings Ltd v. Wills* (1991) 173 CLR 167 (as to the Corporations and Securities Panel), non-judicial tribunals have been found to be validly constituted on the basis that they exercise administrative rather than judicial power. Nevertheless, it is clear that the *Boilermakers Case* remains good law, and that the vesting of non-judicial tribunals with adjudicative power can be taken too far.

The continuing impact of the *Boilermakers Case* was apparent in the decision of the High Court in *Brandy v. Human Rights and Equal Opportunity Commission* (1995) 183 CLR 245. In *Brandy*, the High Court struck down 1992 and 1993 amendments[21] to the *Racial Discrimination Act 1975* (Cth) that made determinations of a non-judicial body, the Human Rights and Equal Opportunity Commission, enforceable. As amended, s. 25ZAA of the Racial Discrimination Act allowed determinations of the Commission to be registered in the Federal Court. Thereon, under s. 25ZAB, a determination was to have effect 'as if it were an order made by the Federal Court', unless the respondent applied to that Court for review. If the respondent did choose to apply to the Federal Court for review, the Court, under s. 25ZAC, 'may review all issues of fact and law' and 'make such orders as it thinks fit', but 'new evidence' could not be adduced except by leave of the Court. This scheme was unanimously held to be unconstitutional, Mason CJ, Brennan, and Toohey JJ finding, at p. 264, that 'so much of the Act as provides for the registration and enforcement of a determination is invalid'. The basis of the Court's decision was that the power to make enforceable orders, a judicial power, could not be granted to a non-judicial body. The case demonstrated the difficulties for the Commonwealth in seeking to establish non-judicial tribunals as informal, speedy, and cost-effective means of resolving human rights complaints.[22] The Constitution imposes severe limitations on the Commonwealth's capacity to give such tribunals the power to make enforceable determinations. Without such power the effectiveness of such bodies may frequently be compromised.

---

20 *R v. Joske; Ex parte Australian Building Construction Employees & Builders' Labourers' Federation* (1974) 130 CLR 87 at 90 per Barwick CJ, at 102 per Mason J. See P. H. Lane, 'The Decline of the Boilermakers Separation of Powers Doctrine' (1981) 55 *Australian Law Journal* 6.

21 *Sex Discrimination and other Legislation Amendment Act 1992* (Cth); *Law and Justice Legislation Amendment Act 1993* (Cth).

22 See *Fourmile v. Selpam Pty Ltd* (1998) 152 CLR 294; *Wilkinson v. Clerical Administrative & Related Employees Superannuation Pty Ltd* (1998) 152 ALR 332. In *Fourmile* the full Federal Court applied *Brandy* to hold invalid the enforcement mechanism provided for determinations of the National Native Title Tribunal. In *Wilkinson* the Superannuation Complaints Tribunal's power to review the decision of a trustee of a superannuation fund on the basis that such a decision was 'unfair and unreasonable' was struck down by a majority of the Federal Court. See G. Williams, 'The End of the Road for the Superannuation Complaints Tribunal?' (1998) 1 *Journal of Australian Taxation* 31.

The decision in *Brandy* showed that the High Court's recognition of the separation of judicial power may not be sympathetic to the resolution of human rights disputes other than by a court-centred approach. Nevertheless, cases such as the *Boilermakers Case* have provided a framework that has proved capable of supporting the protection of civil liberties. As Gaudron J has remarked extra-judicially, the *Boilermakers Case* was concerned with 'the protection of individual rights and freedoms'.[23] The various freedoms that might be implied from the separation of judicial power are examined below.

Usurpation of judicial power: involuntary detention

The decision of the Privy Council in *Liyanage v. The Queen* [1967] 1 AC 259 arose out of the trial and conviction in the Supreme Court of Ceylon, now Sri Lanka, of 11 people charged with offences committed during an attempted *coup d'état* on 27 January 1962. The Parliament of Ceylon had passed the *Criminal Law (Special Provisions) Act 1962* and the *Criminal Law Act 1962* to redefine the relevant offences and penalties, to modify the laws of evidence, to provide for trial by three judges sitting without a jury, and to validate retrospectively the defendants' arrest without warrant and their detention before trial. The legislation was 'deemed, for all purposes, to have come into operation on January 1, 1962', and was 'limited in its application to any offence against the State alleged to have been committed on or about January 27, 1962'. On appeal in the Privy Council, it was held that the Acts were invalid for inconsistency with the separation of powers contained in the Constitution of Ceylon. Lord Pearce, delivering the judgment of the Privy Council, found at p. 289 that 'there exists a separate power in the judicature which under the Constitution as it stands cannot be usurped or infringed by the executive or the legislature'. Here the Privy Council introduced the idea that a constitution embodying a separation of judicial power prevents the legislature from usurping the exercise of that power.

The separation of judicial power entrenched by the Australian Constitution protects Australians from the usurpation of judicial power in the form of the imposition of involuntary detention of a penal or punitive character by the legislature or executive. *Chu Kheng Lim v. Minister for Immigration, Local Government and Ethnic Affairs* (1992) 176 CLR 1 concerned changes made by the *Migration Amendment Act 1992* (Cth) to the *Migration Act 1958* (Cth). These amendments added a new Div 4B entitled 'Custody of certain non-citizens'. The 'designated persons' to whom Division 4B applied were identified in s. 54K as having 'been on a boat in the territorial sea of Australia after 19 November 1989 and before 1 December 1992'. The amendments were expressed to take effect from the date of assent and provided that, after commencement, 'a designated person must be kept in custody' until he or she left Australia, or was given an entry permit. Section 54R provided, 'A court is not to order the release from custody of a designated person'. In addition, s. 54N(1) provided that 'a designated person ... not in custody immediately after commencement' was liable to be detained without warrant. Section 54N(2) provided that this applied even to 'a designated person ... whose release was ordered by a court'. Two groups of Cambodian 'boat people' challenged this

---

23 M. Gaudron, 'Some Reflections on the Boilermakers Case' (1995) 37 *Journal of Industrial Relations* 306 at 309.

scheme in the High Court, arguing that it amounted to a usurpation of judicial power inconsistent with Chapter III. The Court found that any implication derived from Chapter III protected only Australian citizens and did not extend to protect the non-citizen plaintiffs. The scheme was unanimously upheld, except for s. 54R, which a majority consisting of Brennan, Deane, Dawson, and Gaudron JJ, with Mason CJ, Toohey and McHugh JJ dissenting on this point, found to be invalid.

Brennan, Deane, and Dawson JJ, with whom Gaudron J agreed, held at p. 27 that the effect of Chapter III is to limit the 'adjudgment and punishment of criminal guilt under a law of the Commonwealth' to a Chapter III Court and that this function cannot be vested by the federal Parliament in the federal executive. They found at p. 27 that with some exceptions, 'the involuntary detention of a citizen in custody by the State is penal or punitive in character and, under our system of government, exists only as an incident of the exclusively judicial function of adjudging and punishing criminal guilt'. However, the legislature's inability to empower the executive to impose involuntary detention of a penal or punitive character only applied in respect of Australian citizens, and did not extend to the involuntary detention of non-citizens.[24] Accordingly, if Division 4B had purported to apply to Australian citizens it would have been invalid. As it was, the Commonwealth's power over 'aliens' in s. 51(xix) of the Constitution enabled it to authorise the detention of the non-citizen plaintiffs 'for the purposes of expulsion or deportation'.[25]

The challenge did not entirely fail. Brennan, Deane, Dawson, and Gaudron JJ found that s. 54R was invalid in seeking to deny a court the power to review the detention of a designated person. This breached s. 75(v) of the Constitution, which vests the High Court with the jurisdiction to hear matters 'In which a writ of Mandamus or prohibition or an injunction is sought against an officer of the Commonwealth'. Brennan, Deane, and Dawson JJ added at p. 36 that 'even to the extent that s. 54R is concerned with the exercise of jurisdiction other than this Court's directly vested constitutional jurisdiction, it is inconsistent with Ch III'. On the other hand, Mason CJ, Toohey, and McHugh JJ found s. 54R to be valid, but only on the basis that it could be 'read down' under s. 15A of the *Acts Interpretation Act 1901* (Cth) in such a way that it did not prevent a court from ordering the release of a person held in unlawful custody.

In *Chu Kheng Lim* it was found that involuntary detention of a penal or punitive character of a citizen in custody by the State is essentially a judicial power, and is thus exercisable only by a repository of such power. However, exceptions were recognised whereby the executive might also be vested with the power to bring about involuntary detention. Brennan, Deane, and Dawson JJ mentioned, at p. 28, as exceptions 'the arrest and detention in custody, pursuant to executive warrant, of a person accused of crime to ensure that he or she is available to be dealt with by the courts' and 'Involuntary detention in cases of mental illness or infectious disease'. They left open at p. 28 (fn. 66) 'whether the defence power in times of war will support an executive power to make detention orders'. In the decision of the High Court in *Kable v. Director of Public Prosecutions (NSW)* (1996) 189 CLR 51[26] it was again accepted that, with certain

---

24 See the discussion of *Cunliffe v. Commonwealth* (1994) 182 CLR 272 in Chapter 7; B. Wells, 'Aliens: The Outsiders in the Constitution' (1996) 19 *University of Queensland Law Journal* 45.

25 *Chu Kheng Lim* at 10 per Mason CJ.

26 *Kable* at 87–8 per Dawson J, at 97–8 per Toohey J, at 131 per Gummow J.

exceptions, an order for involuntary detention of a penal or punitive character is an exercise of judicial power.

This issue was further examined by the High Court in *Kruger v. Commonwealth* (1997) 190 CLR 1. Section 16 of the *Aboriginals Ordinance 1918* (NT) empowered the Chief Protector of Aborigines in the Northern Territory to 'cause any aboriginal or half-caste to be kept within the boundaries of any reserve or aboriginal institution'. It was an offence for 'any aboriginal or half-caste' to disobey an order of the Chief Protector. Some people were excepted from this power, such as 'any aboriginal or half-caste ... who is lawfully employed by any person' or 'who is a female lawfully married to and residing with a husband who is substantially of European origin or descent'. The Ordinance was challenged by six plaintiffs, five of whom were Aboriginal Australians who, as children, had been forcibly removed from their families under the Ordinance. The sixth plaintiff was an Aboriginal mother whose child had been taken from her. In each case, involuntary detention had been brought about other than by the exercise of power by a Chapter III court. Accordingly, it was argued that the Ordinance was unconstitutional.

The challenge failed. Brennan CJ, Dawson, and McHugh JJ found that the plaintiffs could not succeed because any protection conferred by Chapter III did not restrict the exercise by the Commonwealth of its power over the territories in s. 122 of the Constitution. The decision in *R v. Bernasconi* (1915) 19 CLR 629 was applied. In that case, the power granted by s. 122 was described by Isaacs J, at p. 637, as being 'an unqualified grant complete in itself'. Gaudron J rejected the approach in *R v. Bernasconi*, and Toohey and Gummow JJ also cast doubt on it. However, they nevertheless found against the plaintiffs. The challenge to the Ordinance did not have the benefit of any evidential material, as it had not gone to trial. The Court was thus left to examine the Ordinance at face value, and the text of the Ordinance expressed a concern for Aboriginal welfare. For example, s. 67 authorised the making of regulations for the effectual carrying out of the Ordinance, in particular by 'providing for the control, care and education of aboriginals or half-castes in aboriginal institutions and for the supervision of such institutions' and by 'prescribing the conditions on which aboriginal and half-caste children may be apprenticed to or placed in the service of suitable people'. Similarly, s. 6(1) empowered the Chief Protector 'to undertake the care, custody, or control of any aboriginal or half-caste, if, in his opinion it is necessary or desirable in the interests of the aboriginal or half-caste for him to do so'. From this perspective, the validity of the Ordinance was assessed against the following statement of principle: 'A power of detention which is punitive in character and not consequent upon adjudgment of criminal guilt by a court cannot be conferred upon the Executive by a law of the Commonwealth'.[27] The fact that the challenge to the legislation was restricted to the effect of the legislation as determined from its text meant that it was not possible to find that the involuntary detention brought about by the Ordinance was 'punitive' and thus an exercise of judicial power. As Gummow J found at p. 162, the powers conferred by the Ordinance on the Chief Protector could be seen as 'reasonably capable of being seen as necessary for a legitimate non-punitive purpose (namely the welfare and protection of those persons) rather than the attainment of any punitive objective'.

---

27 *Kruger* at 161–2 per Gummow J.

Gaudron J viewed the constitutional limitation in a different way to the other members of the Court. She doubted whether a guarantee of freedom from involuntary detention could be derived from Chapter III given the exceptions to any such guarantee recognised in *Chu Kheng Lim* and *Kable*. She stated at p. 110:

> Once exceptions are expressed in terms involving the welfare of the individual or that of the community, it is not possible to say that they are clear or fall within precise and confined categories. More to the point, it is not possible to say that, subject to clear exceptions, the power to authorise detention in custody is necessarily and exclusively judicial power. Accordingly, I adhere to the view that I tentatively expressed in *Lim*, namely, that a law authorising detention in custody is not, of itself, offensive to Ch III.

However, there still existed a limitation on Commonwealth power in respect of involuntary detention. Gaudron J found, at p. 111, that, 'subject to certain exceptions, a law authorising detention in custody, divorced from any breach of the law, is not a law on a topic with respect to which s. 51 confers legislative power'. She therefore argued that any limitation lies not in Chapter III, but arises out of the powers listed in s. 51. This argument is difficult to accept. There is nothing in the language of the powers listed in s. 51 that suggests that they could not be used to legislate for involuntary detention, at least so long as the law is in respect of the particular subject matter. The basis for any limitation on the scope of the Commonwealth's s. 51 powers must lie elsewhere, presumably in Chapter III itself. Gaudron J's argument is reminiscent of the now discredited approaches of Latham CJ in *Melbourne Corporation v. Commonwealth* (1947) 74 CLR 31 and Barwick CJ in *Victoria v. Commonwealth (Payroll Tax Case)* (1971) 122 CLR 353 to the implied immunity of the states from Commonwealth laws. Latham CJ and Barwick CJ argued that the immunity does not have an independent existence and that the protection afforded to the states is merely reflective of the limited nature of the Commonwealth's s. 51 powers. Later cases have shown that s. 51 should not be read in this way and that any limitation on the power of the Commonwealth to legislate to affect the states is to be separately implied from the federal system created by the Constitution (see Chapter 3).[28]

Kruger demonstrates that it will be difficult for a plaintiff to establish an argument based on usurpation of judicial power by way of involuntary detention by a non-judicial body. The exceptions that allow non-judicial officers or bodies to bring about involuntary detention mean that it will only be where it can be shown that the involuntary detention is of a penal or punitive character that constitutional problems will arise. It will be rare that this can be ascertained from the text of legislation, where expedient drafting may express a welfare purpose. As *Kruger* demonstrates, the High Court will be unwilling to look beyond the expressed purpose of legislation without the benefit of evidence or agreed factual material. Nevertheless, the guarantee identified in *Chu Kheng Lim*, *Kable*, and *Kruger* is an extremely significant one. The High Court has found that the Constitution restricts the power of the legislature and executive to order involuntary detention of a penal or punitive character. This guarantee is more than a restriction of the power of the legislature to vest judicial power only in a Chapter III court. It

---

28   See, for example, *Queensland Electricity Commission v. Commonwealth* (1985) 159 CLR 192; *Re Australian Education Union; Ex parte Victoria* (1995) 184 CLR 188.

amounts to a freedom of the individual from certain types of involuntary detention except where imposed by a court of law.

The incompatibility doctrine

The High Court has not always strictly applied the *Boilermakers Case*. It has recognised two broad exceptions. First, in *Harris v. Caladine* (1991) 172 CLR 84 it held that in limited circumstances judicial power could be exercised by court registrars, masters, and other senior administrative officers of Chapter III courts, and not merely by the judges of such courts. Secondly, in *Hilton v. Wells* (1985) 157 CLR 57 and *Grollo v. Palmer* (1995) 184 CLR 348 it held that non-judicial power could be conferred on judges of Chapter III courts if such power is conferred on a judge not as a member of the court, but in his or her personal capacity. This latter exception is known as the *persona designata* rule.

In *Grollo v. Palmer*, a new strand of reasoning was developed as an exception to the *persona designata* rule. Brennan CJ, Deane, Dawson, and Toohey JJ suggested, at p. 365, that the *persona designata* rule was subject to the principle that 'no function can be conferred that is incompatible either with the judge's performance of his or her judicial functions or with the proper discharge by the judiciary of its responsibilities as an institution exercising judicial power ("the incompatibility condition").' They went on, at p. 365:

> Incompatibility might consist in so permanent and complete a commitment to the performance of non-judicial functions by a judge that the further performance of substantial judicial functions by that judge is not practicable. It might consist in the performance of non-judicial functions of such a nature that the capacity of the judge to perform his or her judicial functions with integrity is compromised or impaired. Or it might consist in the performance of non-judicial functions of such a nature that public confidence in the integrity of the judiciary as an institution or in the capacity of the individual judge to perform his or her judicial functions with integrity is diminished.

The Court, with McHugh J dissenting, held that the power to issue a warrant for telephone tapping was compatible with the judicial function, and could thus be conferred on a judge of a Chapter III court in his or her personal capacity.

The incompatibility doctrine was applied in *Wilson v. Minister for Aboriginal and Torres Strait Islander Affairs* (1996) 189 CLR 1. In that case, the High Court held, with Kirby J dissenting, that the appointment of Justice Jane Mathews of the Federal Court to prepare a report for the Commonwealth Minister for Aboriginal and Torres Strait Islander Affairs under s. 10 of the *Aboriginal and Torres Strait Islander Heritage Protection Act 1984* (Cth) was invalid. The report was required in order for the Minister to make a determination for 'the protection and preservation ... from injury or desecration' of areas 'of particular significance to Aboriginals in accordance with Aboriginal tradition'. The High Court majority found that the function of the author of a report under s. 10 was not an independent one, but a 'a position equivalent to that of a ministerial adviser', which 'places the judge firmly in the echelons of administration, liable to removal by the minister before the report is made and shorn of the usual judicial protections'.[29]

---

29 *Wilson v. Minister for Aboriginal and Torres Strait Islander Affairs* at 18–19 per Brennan, CJ, Dawson, Toohey, McHugh, and Gummow JJ.

This breached the incompatibility doctrine in that it undermined 'public confidence in the integrity of the judiciary as an institution or in the capacity of the individual judge to perform his or her judicial functions with integrity'.[30] In a strong dissent, Kirby J argued that the majority decision could not be reconciled with the decision in *Grollo v. Palmer*, which had held that the power to issue a warrant for telephone tapping *was* compatible with the judicial function.[31] He pointed out, at p. 50, that the majority decision marked 'a departure from long-standing practice in Australia in the use of judges, including federal judges' in bodies such as Royal Commissions.

Up until this point the incompatibility doctrine had been applied as a limitation on the ability of the Commonwealth to vest non-judicial power on judges of Chapter III courts. The doctrine took on a very different and expanded aspect in *Kable v. Director of Public Prosecutions (NSW)* (1996) 189 CLR 51. In that case, the doctrine was applied in a way that bore out the statement of Blackmun J of the United States Supreme Court in *Mistretta v. United States* 488 US 361 at 407 (1989) that: 'The legitimacy of the Judicial Branch ultimately depends on its reputation for impartiality and nonpartisanship. That reputation may not be borrowed by the political Branches to cloak their work in the neutral colors of judicial action'.

The *Community Protection Act 1994* (NSW) empowered the Supreme Court of New South Wales to make 'preventive detention orders'. This enabled the Supreme Court to order the imprisonment of a person although that person had not been found guilty of a criminal offence. Under s. 5(1) the Court could order that:

> a specified person be detained in prison for a specified period if it is satisfied, on reasonable grounds: (a) that the person is more likely than not to commit a serious act of violence; and (b) that it is appropriate, for the protection of a particular person or persons or the community generally, that the person be held in custody.

Under s. 5(2), a person could only be detained under such an order for a maximum of six months, although under s. 5(3) more than one order could be applied for in respect of a person. Under s. 15, an order could only be made against a person if the Court was satisfied that the case against that person had been made out 'on the balance of probabilities'. Section 14 provided that proceedings under the Act 'are civil proceedings', and as such were to be conducted according to the rules of evidence applicable to such proceedings. Section 5 mentioned 'a specified person'. However, it was clear that the Act only applied to one person. Section 3(3) provided that 'This Act authorises the making of a detention order against Gregory Wayne Kable and does not authorise the making of a detention order against any other person'. Gregory Wayne Kable was identified in s. 3(4) as 'the person of that name who was convicted in New South Wales on 1 August 1990 of the manslaughter of his wife, Hilary Kable'. The Act was passed because Kable had apparently written letters threatening the safety of his children and his deceased wife's sister.

Two arguments were put to the High Court to suggest that the Community Protection Act was invalid. The first was that the Act infringed the separation of judicial

---

30 *Wilson v. Minister for Aboriginal and Torres Strait Islander Affairs* at 365 per Brennan CJ, Deane, Dawson, and Toohey JJ.

31 See K. Walker, 'Persona Designata, Incompatibility and the Separation of Powers' (1997) 8 *Public Law Review* 153 at 159–60.

power achieved by the *Constitution Act 1902* (NSW). While the Australian Constitution achieves a separation of judicial power, it has been found that the New South Wales Constitution does not. In *Clyne v. East* (1967) 68 SR (NSW) 385 and *Building Construction Employees and Builders' Labourers Federation of New South Wales v. Minister for Industrial Relations* (1986) 7 NSWLR 372, the New South Wales Court of Appeal found that the New South Wales Constitution does not provide for the separation of judicial power. Kirby P stated in the latter case, at p. 401, that:

> far from providing a constitutional protection, separation and entrenchment of the judiciary, with limitation as by the requirement of special majorities for any change in the judiciary or its function, the *Constitution Statute* and the *Constitution Act* both specifically contemplated that, in respect of New South Wales, power would be held by the legislature not just to impinge on courts and the judicial function but even to abolish, alter or vary such courts.

Since this finding, the New South Wales Constitution had been amended to entrench judicial independence and the security of tenure of judges.[32] Nevertheless, the High Court again found in *Kable* that a separation of judicial power was not required by the New South Wales Constitution.

The second argument that the Community Protection Act was invalid was novel. It was submitted that the Act was invalid because it infringed the separation of judicial power achieved by the Australian Constitution. Specifically, it was argued that the Act infringed the incompatibility doctrine first recognised in *Grollo*. A majority of the High Court consisting of Toohey, Gaudron, McHugh, and Gummow JJ, with Brennan CJ and Dawson J dissenting, accepted this, finding that, in the words of McHugh J at p. 109, 'the Act is invalid because it purports to vest functions in the Supreme Court of New South Wales that are incompatible with the exercise of the judicial power of the Commonwealth by the Supreme Court of that State'.

How had an implication of the separation of judicial power in the Australian Constitution come to restrict the functions that could be conferred on a state supreme court by a state parliament? The answer was far from obvious, and involved stretching the incompatibility doctrine far beyond its origins. The clearest explanation was given by McHugh J, who reasoned as follows. First, while the state parliaments possess considerable scope to legislate for the state supreme courts, including the power to vest state supreme courts with non-judicial power, this is not an unlimited power. The Australian Constitution requires, if nothing else, 'the continued existence of a system of State courts with a Supreme Court at the head of the State judicial system'.[33] For example, s. 73, in conferring jurisdiction on the High Court to hear appeals from state supreme courts, implies that the New South Wales Parliament cannot abolish the Supreme Court of New South Wales. This implication is bolstered by other provisions of the Australian Constitution, such as s. 77(iii), which grants the federal Parliament the power to makes laws 'Investing any court of a State with federal jurisdiction'. According to McHugh J at pp. 114–15, the effect of such provisions is that:

---

32 Constitution Act (NSW), s. 7B and Part 9, as amended by the *Constitution (Entrenchment) Amendment Act 1992* (NSW).
33 *Kable* at 110.

Under the Constitution, therefore, the State courts have a status and a role that extends beyond their status and role as part of the State judicial systems. They are part of an integrated system of State and federal courts and organs for the exercise of federal judicial power as well as State judicial power. Moreover, the Constitution contemplates no distinction between the status of State courts invested with federal jurisdiction and those created as federal courts. There are not two grades of federal judicial power.

The second step of McHugh J's argument was to find that this scheme of interlocking state and federal Courts created by Chapter III cannot be undermined by any Australian parliament. A state parliament could not legislate to abrogate the role of state supreme courts as custodians of federal judicial power. To do so would be to infringe on Chapter III. The third step involved the greatest leap. McHugh J found, at p. 116, that 'Given the central role and the status that Ch III gives to State courts invested with federal jurisdiction, it necessarily follows that those courts must also be, and be perceived to be, independent of the legislature and executive government in the exercise of federal jurisdiction'. Any law of a state parliament that compromised this independence would be unconstitutional under Chapter III. (Here the incompatibility doctrine had made its entrance.) Such a law would include any law that conferred non-judicial power on a state supreme court 'of a nature that might lead an ordinary reasonable member of the public to conclude that the Court was not independent of the executive government of the State'.[34] The Community Protection Act was such a law, and was therefore rendered invalid by the Australian Constitution because 'its procedures compromise the institutional impartiality of the Supreme Court'.[35]

There was no common approach by the *Kable* majority, leaving it vulnerable to reassessment by future judges. Gaudron and Gummow JJ reasoned in a similar way to McHugh J, and reached the same result. Toohey J also found the Act to be invalid because it breached the incompatibility doctrine, but applied a different approach in reaching this conclusion. For Toohey J, what was relevant was not that the New South Wales Supreme Court was part of an interlocking scheme of courts exercising federal jurisdiction. Instead, he found that, in *this case*, the New South Wales Supreme Court was exercising federal jurisdiction pursuant to s. 39 of the *Judiciary Act 1903* (Cth) in that it had been argued that the Community Protection Act was invalid by reason of the Australian Constitution. As he stated at p. 96, 'It is not the investing of the Supreme Court with federal jurisdiction that is in issue; it is the exercise of federal jurisdiction by the Supreme Court in the circumstances arising under the Act that is challenged'. The approach of Gaudron, McHugh, and Gummow JJ should be preferred to that of Toohey J. It would be a strange result if the applicability of the incompatibility doctrine were to depend on a plaintiff invoking federal jurisdiction. The consequence would be a scramble to find an argument that would raise an issue of invalidity under the Australian Constitution. The approach is also circular. By invoking an argument that a state Act is inconsistent with the Australian Constitution, a plaintiff might thereby raise an issue of federal jurisdiction that would allow the High Court to determine whether the state Act is in fact inconsistent with the Australian Constitution.

---

34 *Kable* at 117 per McHugh J.
35 *Kable* at 121 per McHugh J.

The dissenting judgments in *Kable* of Brennan CJ and Dawson J attacked the reasoning of the majority. Brennan CJ found, at p. 68, that there was 'no textual or structural foundation' for the application of the incompatibility doctrine to the state Supreme Court. Dawson J argued, at p. 82, that:

> The suggestion that the Act is invalid because it compromises the institutional impartiality of the Supreme Court of New South Wales ignores the fact that the mechanisms for ensuring judicial impartiality and independence—security of tenure and remuneration, and separation from the other arms of government—are not constitutionally prescribed for State courts notwithstanding that they are prescribed for courts created by or under Ch III. It is difficult to conceive of a clearer distinction.

Dawson J also pointed out, at p. 86, that the incompatibility doctrine had been 'raised only to demonstrate that the persona designata doctrine has its limits', and that where there is no constitutionally entrenched separation of judicial power, as in the New South Wales Constitution, issues as to the *persona designata* rule or the incompatibility doctrine cannot arise.

The result and reasoning in *Kable* was remarkable. As McHugh J recognised, it meant that although the separation of judicial power is not entrenched in the New South Wales Constitution, the New South Wales Parliament is constrained by Chapter III of the federal Constitution in the same way as if such a separation did exist. This was underpinned by the incompatibility doctrine, a doctrine that was not developed as a free-standing limit on Commonwealth power, let alone state legislative power, but as an exception to the *persona designata* rule (see Chapter 9).[36] After *Kable* the incompatibility doctrine can no longer be seen as merely an aspect of the *persona designata* rule. Instead, it must be seen as an independent limitation, arising from Chapter III, on the power of the state and federal parliaments to confer power on, or shape, any federal court or state supreme court. This was reinforced by McHugh J in his dissent in *Nicholas v. The Queen* (1998) 151 ALR 312 at 345. In that case (see pp. 218–20), he found, at pp. 346–7, that s. 15X of the *Crimes Act 1914* (Cth) was invalid because it 'direct[s] courts exercising federal jurisdiction to disregard a fact that is critical in exercising a discretion that is necessary to protect the integrity of Ch III courts and to maintain public confidence in the administration of criminal justice'.[37]

Kable leaves many questions unanswered. It is not clear whether the incompatibility doctrine also limits the power of state parliaments to confer non-judicial powers on lower state courts. There is a strong argument that it does. Given that lower courts may also be vested with federal jurisdiction under sections 71 and 77(iii) of the Constitution, and indeed the grant of federal jurisdiction by s. 39 of the Judiciary Act is not limited to state supreme courts, such courts may also be viewed as part of the interlocking scheme of courts exercising federal jurisdiction. The Constitution does not recognise a distinction between the Supreme Court and lower courts of each state in the same way as, for example, the Canadian Constitution does in distinguishing between the 'superior' and 'inferior' courts of each province.[38] The Community Protection Act was an

---

36   See E. Handsley, 'Do Hard Laws Make Bad Cases?—The High Court's Decision in *Kable v. Director of Public Prosecutions (NSW)*' (1997) 25 *Federal Law Review* 171; Walker.

37   See also *Nicholas* at 375, 381–2 per Kirby J.

38   See *Constitution Act 1867* (30 & 31 Vict. Ch. 3), Ch VII; P. Hogg, *Constitutional Law of Canada*, 4th edn, Carswell, 1997, pp. 167–78.

obvious case of legislation that was incompatible with the judicial function. It is not clear how the High Court might apply the incompatibility doctrine in other cases, although *Wilson* suggests that extreme caution should be applied in conferring any non-judicial power on a state court or judge of such a court.[39] Above all, it must be remembered that in *Kable* the High Court applied only one aspect of the incompatibility doctrine recognised in *Grollo*. The impact of the other aspects of the doctrine on state courts remains to be explored.

The trial process

Section 80 of the Constitution guarantees that 'The trial on indictment of any offence against any law of the Commonwealth shall be by jury' (see Chapter 5). However, the provision has been given a limited interpretation that allows the Commonwealth to itself determine when a trial is to be by 'indictment' and thus whether or not there will be a jury. More recent cases have found that where the Commonwealth legislates for a jury trial, it has a limited discretion to determine how such a trial will proceed. The High Court has, held, for example, that majority verdicts are not consistent with a jury trial held under s. 80.[40]

This change of direction in the interpretation of s. 80 coincided with the High Court beginning to explore whether aspects of the trial process might be impliedly entrenched by Chapter III of the Constitution in trials held in federal courts, and perhaps, via the *Kable* mechanism, in state courts. This exploration might ultimately mark a departure from the High Court's earlier decision in *Sorby v. Commonwealth* (1983) 152 CLR 281. In that case it was found that the privilege against self-incrimination is not constitutionally entrenched. Gibbs CJ went further in stating as *obiter dicta* at p. 298 that 'The Parliament can, in relation to a trial by jury, alter the rules of evidence, or the rules relating to the onus of proof'. Subsequent cases have yet to determine whether Gibbs CJ went too far in this statement. For example, a federal law that dramatically lowered the standard of proof in criminal matters heard in Chapter III courts would likely be unconstitutional.[41]

The idea that certain aspects of the trial process cannot be abrogated by legislation was a central issue in the High Court's decision in *Polyukhovich v. Commonwealth (War Crimes Act Case)* (1991) 172 CLR 501. Section 9(1) of the *War Crimes Act 1945* (Cth), as inserted by the *War Crimes Amendment Act 1988* (Cth), provided that an Australian citizen or resident was retrospectively guilty of an indictable offence if he or she had 'committed a war crime' in Europe between 1 September 1939 and 8 May 1945. Ivan Polyukhovich, an Australian citizen, was charged with having committed war crimes in Ukraine when it was under German occupation during the Second World War. He

---

39 See E. Campbell, 'Constitutional Protection of State Courts and Judges' (1997) 23 *Monash University Law Review* 397 at 413–15.
40 *Cheatle v. The Queen* (1993) 177 CLR 541.
41 *Nicholas v. The Queen* (1998) 151 ALR 312 at 321 per Brennan CJ: 'The reversal of an onus of proof affects the manner in which a court approaches the finding of facts but is not open to constitutional objection provided it prescribes a reasonable approach to the assessment of the kind of evidence to which it relates'.

responded by seeking a declaration in the High Court that the War Crimes Amendment Act was invalid. A majority made up of Mason CJ, Dawson, Toohey, and McHugh JJ upheld the legislation. Brennan, Deane, and Gaudron JJ dissented.

The Court, with Brennan J dissenting on this point, held that the Act could be passed under the Commonwealth's power over external affairs in s. 51(xxix) of the Constitution. Brennan J, with whom Toohey J agreed on this point, also considered whether the Act was valid under the defence power in s. 51(vi) of the Constitution. As s. 51(vi) is a purposive power (see Chapter 4), Brennan J examined whether the Act was 'appropriate and adapted' to serve a defence purpose. This allowed him to take into account the abrogation of any fundamental freedoms by the Act. He found at p. 593 that the Act was invalid because it breached 'a principle which is of the highest importance in a free society, namely, that criminal laws should not operate retrospectively'. Brennan J was the only judge who found that the Act was invalid because it could not be supported by a s. 51 power.

Two other judges, Deane and Gaudron JJ, also held the Act to be invalid. Although in their view the Act fell within the Commonwealth's external affairs power, it was nevertheless invalid because it breached Chapter III of the Constitution. They found that the Act was a usurpation of judicial power because it amounted to a legislative judgment of guilt. Deane J summarised the requirements of Chapter III at p. 607, as follows:

> the Parliament cannot, consistently with Ch III of the Constitution, usurp the judicial power of the Commonwealth by itself purporting to exercise judicial power in the form of legislation. Nor can it infringe the vesting of that judicial power in the judicature by requiring that it be exercised in a manner which is inconsistent with the essential requirements of a court or with the nature of judicial power.

This final sentence represented a crucial extension to the implication recognised in earlier decisions. It amounted to a guarantee of due process that has since been accepted in the decisions of other judges, such as that of Brennan, Deane, and Dawson JJ in *Chu Kheng Lim* (1992) 176 CLR 1.[42] For Deane J, Chapter III not only implied that judicial power could only be vested in Chapter III courts, but also that judicial power could only be vested so as to enable such courts to function in accordance 'with the essential requirements of a court'. By this means, Chapter III might also entrench aspects of the trial process. Deane J then went on to find, at p. 610, that the 'whole focus of a criminal trial is the ascertainment of whether it is established that the accused in fact committed a past act which constituted a criminal contravention of the requirements of a valid law *which was applicable to the act at the time the act was done*' (emphasis added). The role of a court vested with judicial power was thus to adjudge guilt according to the law in effect at the time that the alleged acts were done. Accordingly, an attempt by the federal Parliament to require a court to adjudge guilt according to a law not in effect at the time that the alleged acts were committed would breach Chapter III. The War Crimes

---

42   *Chu Kheng Lim* at 27: 'Nor do those grants of legislative power extend to the making of a law which requires or authorizes the courts in which the judicial power of the Commonwealth is exclusively vested to exercise judicial power in a manner which is inconsistent with the essential character of a court or with the nature of judicial power.'

Amendment Act, in seeking to vest jurisdiction in courts to adjudge guilt according to a retrospective criminal law, was therefore invalid.

Gaudron J reached the same result as Deane J, finding that the Act was invalid as it involved a usurpation of judicial power. Her finding at p. 704 also rested on the view that 'the power vested in a court can be exercised only on the basis of the discovered facts and by application of the law which determines the legal consequences attaching to those facts'. She found that the federal Parliament could not vest in a court the jurisdiction to adjudge guilt on criteria set down by a retrospective criminal law.

The Court considered its decision in *R v. Kidman* (1915) 20 CLR 425, in which it held valid the *Crimes Act 1914* (Cth) insofar as it retrospectively established an offence of conspiracy to defraud the Commonwealth. The offence had been added to the Act by an amending Act that had received the royal assent on 7 May 1915, but required that it 'be deemed to have been in force' from 29 October 1914. The defendants had been charged with conspiracy to defraud the Commonwealth by profiteering on supplies to the armed forces in the First World War. It was implicit in the result in *R v. Kidman* that the federal Parliament possessed the power to retrospectively create a criminal offence. Deane and Gaudron JJ found that *R v. Kidman* did not stand in the way of their finding that Chapter III is inconsistent with the enactment of retrospective criminal laws. The case was found to provide only weak authority on this point, as the legislation in that case had not been examined from the perspective of Chapter III.

Mason CJ, Dawson, and McHugh JJ on the other hand found that *R v. Kidman* should be followed and that no implication could be derived from Chapter III to limit the Commonwealth's power to pass retrospective criminal laws. They accordingly rejected the approach of Deane and Gaudron JJ. While Deane and Gaudron JJ found that the War Crimes Amendment Act amounted to a usurpation of judicial power, Mason CJ pointed out, at p. 536, that although the Act was retrospective in operation, it 'leaves it to the courts to determine whether the person charged has engaged in the conduct complained of and whether that conduct is an infringement of the rule prescribed'. There was accordingly no interference with the exercise of judicial power.

The differing approaches in the *War Crimes Act Case* produced no majority finding on whether the Constitution forbids the enactment of retrospective criminal laws. This remains an open question. Deane and Gaudron JJ found such a limitation, while Mason CJ, Dawson, and McHugh JJ rejected this. Toohey J joined Mason CJ, Dawson, and McHugh JJ in finding the Act valid despite expressing support for the reasoning of Deane and Gaudron JJ. Toohey J did not apply the approach of either Deane and Gaudron JJ, as he held, at p. 690, that the Act was not 'retroactive in any offensive way' in that at the time the alleged acts were committed, murder was universally regarded as a crime under Australian law as well as under the law of other nations and the international law of war crimes and crimes against humanity. Even though a majority failed to materialise on the central issue, there was a narrower proposition that attracted majority support. Mason CJ, Deane, Gaudron, and McHugh JJ, with some support from Dawson J, found in obiter that the Commonwealth could not enact a Bill of Attainder or Bill of Pains—that is, a law 'adjudging a specific person or specific persons guilty of an offence constituted by past conduct and imposing punishment in respect of that offence'.[43]

---

43 *War Crimes Act Case* at 535 per Mason CJ.

Such a law would be invalid not because it requires courts to act in a non-judicial manner, but because it would amount to a legislative usurpation of judicial power.

It is not clear whether the approach of Deane and Gaudron JJ in the *War Crimes Act Case* will be further developed.[44] If it is, it offers the means by which the essential components of the criminal trial might be constitutionally set. Their approach rests on the view that Chapter III demands that Chapter III courts can only be vested with judicial power in a way that enables such courts to function according to 'the essential requirements of a court'. If this were accepted by the High Court it would not be such a large step to say that an essential component of the exercise of judicial power is that a court is constrained to giving a defendant a 'fair trial'.[45] After all, it would seem clear that a court could not be required to exercise judicial power so as to oversee an unfair trial. As a minimum, the judicial process might include, as set out by Gaudron J in *Re Nolan; Ex parte Young* (1991) 172 CLR 460 at 496, an:

> open and public enquiry (subject to limited exceptions), the application of the rules of natural justice, the ascertainment of the facts as they are and as they bear on the right or liability in issue and the identification of the applicable law, followed by an application of that law to those facts.[46]

This might enable, for example, the constitutional entrenchment of the presumption of innocence when charged with a criminal offence.[47] If taken to its far reaches, it might mean, as in Canada and the USA, that many of the issues arising out of the criminal justice system, such as the use of certain types of evidence,[48] are determined by constitutional analysis.

The approach of Deane and Gaudron JJ in the *War Crimes Act Case* offers both promise and danger. It promises to add a significant new means of protecting civil liberties by constitutional means. This would add to the minimal protection already afforded by s. 80 of the Constitution. On the other hand, it would take a brave court to begin the process of setting down in constitutional stone the law of criminal procedure. To do so would be to take away power from the federal, and perhaps state, parliaments to shape the justice system in accordance with the perceived interests of the community. The criminal justice system, always a politically charged field, would be moulded according to the vision of individual judges as to the essential characteristics of the judicial process, rather than by elected representatives. Moreover, the Court's intervention would have been achieved by implication from the system created by Chapter III— without the benefit of express guarantees in the Constitution.

Other cases have also explored the possibility of entrenching aspects of the trial process. In *Dietrich v. The Queen* (1992) 177 CLR 292, a majority of the High Court found that the power of a court to order a stay where an unfair trial would result may

---

44   See H. Roberts, 'Retrospective Criminal Laws and the Separation of Judicial Power' (1997) 8 *Public Law Review* 170.

45   L. Zines, 'A Judicially Created Bill of Rights?' (1994) 16 *Sydney Law Review* 166 at 168.

46   See A. Mason, 'A New Perspective on Separation of Powers' (1996) 82 *Canberra Bulletin of Public Administration* 1 at 8.

47   See F. Wheeler, 'The Doctrine of Separation of Powers and Constitutionally Entrenched Due Process in Australia' (1997) 23 *Monash University Law Review* 248 at 263–79.

48   See, for example, *Miranda v. Arizona* 384 US 436 (1966).

be exercised where an accused is charged with a serious offence and, through no fault of his or her own, is unable to obtain legal representation. This was developed by the High Court as an extension of the common law rule governing the right to a fair trial. However, in obiter, Deane and Gaudron JJ suggested that this extension to the rule was 'entrenched by the Constitution's requirement of the observance of judicial process and fairness'.[49] The common law rule expressed in *Dietrich* has yet to be further grounded in constitutional principle. This might occur should the Commonwealth or the states seek to override the rule expressed in *Dietrich* by requiring a court exercising federal judicial power to proceed to hear a matter where an unrepresented accused is charged with a serious criminal offence.

A similar situation arose in *Nicholas v. The Queen* (1998) 151 ALR 312, in which a majority of the High Court exercised restraint in applying the separation of judicial power. The Court's earlier decision in *Ridgeway v. The Queen* (1995) 184 CLR 19 concerned heroin imported into Australia, in breach of the *Customs Act 1901* (Cth), by law enforcement officers who sold it to John Ridgeway in an attempt to entrap him. A majority of the High Court found that evidence of the importation of heroin should not have been admitted because, at common law, a judge has the discretion 'to exclude, on public policy grounds, all evidence of an offence or an element of an offence procured by unlawful conduct on the part of law enforcement officers'.[50] In response to *Ridgeway*, the federal Parliament inserted a new Part 1AB into the Commonwealth Crimes Act.[51] Part 1AB applies to 'controlled operations' in which law enforcement officers engage in what would otherwise be illegal conduct that 'is carried out for the purpose of obtaining evidence that may lead to the prosecution of a person for an offence against section 233B of the *Customs Act 1901* or an associated offence'.[52] The Part works to exempt law enforcement officers from criminal liability, so that the discretion identified in *Ridgeway* is not enlivened. Part 1AB also has a retrospective operation, s. 15X providing that in defined circumstances:

> In determining, for the purposes of a prosecution for an offence against section 233B of the *Customs Act 1901* or an associated offence, whether evidence that narcotic goods were imported into Australia in contravention of the *Customs Act 1901* should be admitted, the fact that a law enforcement officer committed an offence in importing the narcotic goods, or in aiding, abetting, counselling, procuring, or being in any way knowingly concerned in, their importation is to be disregarded.

This section excluded the fact of illegality on the part of law enforcement officers from the consideration of a trial judge in determining whether the *Ridgeway* discretion should be exercised in favour of an accused person. The issue in *Nicholas* was whether s. 15X was invalid for breaching the separation of judicial power achieved by Chapter III of the Constitution.

The High Court delivered seven separate judgments, highlighting the absence of conceptual coherence in this area. A majority of the High Court—Brennan CJ, Toohey,

---

49 *Dietrich* at 326 per Deane J. See also p. 362 per Gaudron J.
50 *Ridgeway* at 33 per Mason CJ, Deane, and Dawson JJ.
51 *Crimes Amendment (Controlled Operations) Act 1996* (Cth).
52 Crimes Act, s. 15H.

Gaudron, Gummow, and Hayne JJ—found that s. 15X was valid. McHugh and Kirby JJ dissented. The accused had made three submissions as to why s. 15X was invalid. First, s. 15X invalidly directs a court to exercise its discretionary power in a way that is inconsistent with the essential character of a court or with the nature of judicial power. Secondly, s. 15X usurps judicial power because it applies to identifiable cases and is directed specifically to the accused in those cases, rather than to the public generally. Thirdly, the attempt to remove the discretion set out in *Ridgeway* invalidly undermines both the integrity of the court's processes and public confidence in the administration of justice. The second argument was rejected by the majority on the basis that s. 15X is concerned with the effect of illegality on the part of law enforcement officers and is not designed to 'secure the conviction of' any persons.[53] In contrast to a law such as a Bill of Attainder, s. 15X could be classified as an 'evidentiary provision'.[54] The third argument failed because the *Ridgeway* discretion was not devised by the High Court to protect the reputation of the courts. Moreover, Chapter III courts were bound to apply s. 15X because 'It is for the parliament to prescribe the law to be applied by a court and, if the law is otherwise valid, the court's opinion as to the justice, propriety or utility of the law is immaterial'.[55]

In relation to the first submission, the majority recognised that the Constitution prevents the Commonwealth from passing a law, such as s. 54R of the Migration Act found invalid in *Chu Kheng Lim*, directing a Chapter III court as to its order or judgment in its exercise of judicial power. However, this left some scope for a parliament to shape the exercise of judicial power by a Chapter III court. As Brennan CJ stated at p. 319, 'a law which merely prescribes a court's practice or procedure does not direct the exercise of the judicial power in finding facts, applying law or exercising an available discretion'. Section 15X was found to be just such a law. It did not impede or otherwise affect the finding of facts, nor did it deal directly with issues of guilt or innocence. Instead, 'it removes the barrier which *Ridgeway* placed against tendering to the jury evidence of an illegal importation of narcotic goods where such an importation had in fact occurred'.[56] Hence, s. 15X was not inconsistent with the separation of judicial power, but was instead conducive to the exercise of such power. Underpinning this conclusion was the finding that the Commonwealth could legislate to direct the exercise of judicial power by manipulating the rules of evidence in the form of s. 15X. Brennan CJ even found at p. 322 that if the Commonwealth had gone further than s. 15X by passing a law declaring that evidence of an illegal importation should be admitted and denying any discretion in the trial judge to exclude such evidence, this would have been valid as 'a mere procedural law assisting in the court's finding of material facts'.

The minority took a different view of s. 15X, finding that it was more than a rule of evidence or procedure. McHugh J found that s. 15X could not be compared with legislation that regulates the exercise of judicial discretion by requiring certain matters to be taken into account. He characterised s. 15X, at p. 348, as 'a direction to a court exercising federal jurisdiction that it cannot have regard to a fact that is relevant and often critical in determining whether the court's processes are being demeaned'. The effect was

---

53 *Nicholas* at 323 per Brennan CJ.
54 *Nicholas* at 330 per Toohey J.
55 *Nicholas* at 326 per Brennan CJ.
56 *Nicholas* at 319 per Brennan CJ.

to 'hamper, and in some cases to prevent, such a court from protecting its processes and thereby maintaining public confidence in courts exercising the judicial power of the Commonwealth'.[57] This offended the separation of judicial power as conceived by McHugh J in *Kable* (see pp. 211–12). Kirby J took a similar approach, finding that the 'high particularity' of the legislation ('Almost certainly, only five individuals are involved') and the 'unrepaired affront of condoning unexcused criminality' invoked 'the unavoidable obligation of the courts' to uphold the 'integrity of the judicial system'.[58]

The dissents of McHugh and Kirby JJ showed that the High Court possesses the tools to constitutionalise much of the criminal trial process. The incompatibility doctrine as developed in *Kable* could have enabled the Court to find that the federal Parliament is incapable of legislating to undermine public confidence in the administration of criminal justice. A pessimistic view of the strength of public confidence would translate into a narrow view of the capacity of a parliament to control the exercise of the judicial process through, for example, changes to the rules of evidence. The majority decision in *Nicholas* demonstrated restraint in not taking this course. This took account of the potential width and uncertain boundaries of the incompatibility doctrine as developed in *Kable*, and the dangers for the Court of seeking to wrest control of the trial process from federal and state parliaments. This restraint still leaves the High Court with a powerful role in this area. While the Court will allow legislatures some leeway in developing rules of procedure and evidence, these might still be struck down where they render a trial by a Chapter III court 'unfair', such as, for example, in the extreme case of a legislature providing that an accused could not call evidence in support of his or her innocence. To require a Chapter III court to conduct an 'unfair' trial may be to require such a court to exercise judicial power in a way that is inconsistent with its nature.

Guarantee of due process, and equality under the law

If the *War Crimes Act Case* conjured up visions of an unfettered court controlling the criminal process, the reasoning of Deane and Toohey JJ in *Leeth v. Commonwealth* (1992) 174 CLR 455 suggested judicial intervention of a far greater order. Pursuant to s. 120 of the Constitution, it has been standard practice for Commonwealth prisoners to be housed in state jails. Until 1989 this practice was regulated by the *Commonwealth Prisoners Act 1967* (Cth). Section 4 of that Act required that after a 'federal offender' was sentenced, the sentencing judge apply the practices and criteria of the relevant state legislation in fixing a minimum non-parole period. This meant that within the one prison, state and Commonwealth prisoners alike would have comparable parole expectations. It also meant that the minimum non-parole periods of Commonwealth prisoners convicted of the same offence varied widely between states. Richard Leeth was convicted under the *Customs Act 1901* (Cth) for importing cannabis in commercial quantities. He argued in the High Court that s. 4 of the Commonwealth Prisoners Act was invalid. The challenge failed by 4:3, with Mason CJ, Brennan, Dawson, and McHugh JJ in the majority, and Deane, Toohey, and Gaudron JJ in dissent.

---

57 *Nicholas* at 349 per McHugh J.
58 *Nicholas* at 378, 381–2.

Isaacs J stated in *Commonwealth v. Kreglinger & Fernau Ltd and Bardsley* (1926) 37 CLR 393 at 411–12 that 'it is the duty of this Court, as the chief judicial organ of the Commonwealth, to take judicial notice, in interpreting the Australian Constitution, of every fundamental constitutional doctrine existing and fully recognized at the time the Constitution was passed'. In *Leeth*, Deane and Toohey JJ quoted this passage, and continued, at p. 485: 'The doctrine of legal equality is in the forefront of those doctrines'. They then sought at p. 486 to tie this principle to a foundation constructed from the common law:

> putting to one side the position of the Crown and some past anomalies, notably, discriminatory treatment of women, the essential or underlying theoretical equality of all persons under the law and before the courts is and has been a fundamental and generally beneficial doctrine of the common law and a basic prescript of the administration of justice under our system of government.

Moreover, it was found that the common law principle of the equality of all persons under the law could be derived by necessary implication from the Constitution and thus existed as a limitation on legislative power. The implication was primarily viewed as arising out of Chapter III. In the *War Crimes Act Case* Deane J had argued that Chapter III prevents the federal Parliament from vesting in a court the power to act other than in accordance with the essential attributes of a court. In *Leeth* these attributes were taken to include 'the duty of a court to extend to the parties before it equal justice, that is to say, to treat them fairly and impartially as equals before the law and to refrain from discrimination on irrelevant or irrational grounds'.[59] This limitation existed as one aspect of the constitutional requirement that the Commonwealth observe the principle of equality under the law.

The implied freedom of equality under the law discovered by Deane and Toohey JJ was not an absolute bar to the federal Parliament enacting laws that discriminated between people or groups. Deane and Toohey JJ found, at p. 488, that 'The doctrine of legal equality is not infringed by a law which discriminates between people on grounds which are reasonably capable of being seen as providing a rational and relevant basis for the discriminatory treatment'. It was found that s. 4 did not meet this standard. It was seen not as a law 'which enabled account to be taken of actual differences in the conditions of imprisonment in different States and Territories' but as a law that 'operated arbitrarily to require a court to treat the State or Territory in which a federal offender was convicted as *the* relevant consideration for determining which of a number of greatly varying legislative schemes should govern the fixing of a non-parole period'.[60]

The reasoning of Deane and Toohey JJ provides a weak basis for a constitutional freedom of equality under the law.[61] The freedom is based on both the common law and the Constitution. However, to find such a freedom in the Constitution is to take a

---

59 *Leeth* at 487 per Deane and Toohey JJ.
60 *Leeth* at 491 (emphasis in original).
61 See J. Goldsworthy, 'Implications in Language, Law and the Constitution', in G. Lindell (ed.), *Future Directions in Australian Constitutional Law*, Federation Press, 1994, pp. 174–8; D. Rose, 'Judicial Reasonings and Responsibilities in Constitutional Cases' (1994) 20 *Monash University Law Review* 195 at 206–9; G. Winterton, 'The Separation of Judicial Power as an Implied Bill of Rights' in Lindell, *Future Directions in Australian Constitutional Law*, pp. 205–7; Wheeler at 282–3; Zines, 'A Judicially Created Bill of Rights?', at 182–4.

great leap from both the text and understandings of the instrument, although this is no greater a leap than was taken by Murphy J in the many cases in which he discovered implied rights (see Chapter 7). Ironically, the implication supported by Deane and Toohey JJ resembles the guarantee of 'the equal protection of the laws' in the Fourteenth Amendment to the United States Constitution. Yet exactly such a provision was rejected by the framers of the Australian Constitution (see Chapter 2).[62] Reliance on the common law is even more problematic. It is one thing to recognise that 'The Commonwealth of Australia was not born into a vacuum. It came into existence within a system of law already established',[63] and therefore to use the common law, as in cases such as *Cheatle v. The Queen* (1993) 177 CLR 541 (see Chapter 5), to explain the content of an existing guarantee. It is another thing entirely to see the common law as a basis for deriving limitations on legislative power. To use the common law in this way is to revive the notion put by Coke CJ in *Dr Bonham's Case* (1610) 8 Co Rep 107a at 118a [77 ER 638] that when 'an Act of Parliament is against common right and reason, or repugnant, or impossible to be performed, the common law will controul it, and adjudge such Act to be void' (see Chapter 1). In any event, even if the common law were an appropriate source of restrictions on legislative power, it is far from obvious that it can, as a matter of history, be seen as generally expressing the notion of equality under the law. The common law has traditionally set different standards for certain members of society, such as married women,[64] which would be unlikely to survive the 'rational and relevant basis' test set down by Deane and Toohey JJ. The dismissal of the historical inequality achieved by the common law ('putting to one side the position of the Crown and some past anomalies, notably, discriminatory treatment of women') is both insensitive and unconvincing.

Gaudron J also found s. 4 to be invalid. However, she did so by applying a guarantee squarely based in Chapter III rather than any constitutional freedom of equality under the law. She found, at p. 502, that 'It is an essential feature of judicial power that it should be exercised in accordance with the judicial process' and that 'the concept of equal justice' is basic to that process. In analysing s. 4, Gaudron J found, at pp. 502–3, that it treated offenders unequally because, in setting minimum non-parole periods according to the state where the offender was convicted rather than the nature of the offence, s. 4 led to 'a failure to treat like offences against the laws of the Commonwealth in a like manner and also a failure to give proper account to genuine differences'. While she reached the same result as Deane and Toohey JJ, her reasoning should be distinguished. Gaudron J's approach can be seen as an extension of her reasoning in the *War Crimes Act Case*. Any concept of equality under the law was, for Gaudron J, rooted in the concept of judicial process and only applied where a court was being asked to exercise a power granted by the federal Parliament. On the other hand, Deane and Toohey JJ did not seek to limit their implication in this way. For them, equality under the law was a guarantee that was not limited to the judicial process but might operate on any law of the Commonwealth.

---

62 See *Kruger v. Commonwealth* (1997) 190 CLR 1 at 61 per Dawson J.
63 *In re Foreman & Sons Pty Ltd; Uther v. Federal Commissioner of Taxation* (1947) 74 CLR 508 at 521 per Latham CJ.
64 See, for example, *Yerkey v. Jones* (1939) 63 CLR 649. Compare *Garcia v. National Australia Bank Ltd* (1998) 155 ALR 614. See also *Kruger v. Commonwealth* (1997) 190 CLR 1 at 66 per Dawson J, at 154–5 per Gummow J.

There is nevertheless a common feature in the approaches of Deane and Toohey JJ, and Gaudron J. Both sets of reasoning bear out the statement of Deane and Toohey JJ at pp. 486–7 that the provisions of Chapter III 'not only identify the possible repositories of Commonwealth judicial power. They also dictate and control the manner of its exercise'. Thus, both sets of reasoning moved beyond the question of *which* powers could be exercised by a Chapter III court into the realm of *how* these powers might be exercised.[65] In this way, these judgments propelled the High Court into the realm of 'substantive due process'.[66] Ironically, this came only a few years after the Court in *Cole v. Whitfield* (1988) 165 CLR 360 recognised the perils of such an approach in the interpretation of s. 92 of the Constitution (see Chapter 6).

The judgments of Deane and Toohey JJ, and Gaudron J, in *Leeth* required examination of the substantive operation of s. 4 so as to determine whether it met the entrenched standard of equality. This illustrates the dangers of such an approach. What is entrenched is a standard of equality perceived by a member of the High Court. There is nothing in the text of the Constitution that provides any guidance in this determination. Ultimately, judges may be increasingly faced with difficult social and political issues similar to those that have faced the United States Supreme Court, such as whether affirmative action programs on the basis of race or gender meet the standard of equality set down in the Constitution.[67] Such judgments dangerously bring judicial political views far into a realm that, in Australia, has traditionally been the sole domain of the political judgment of elected representatives. Moreover, such views must be reached without any firm basis in the Constitution. Even where Constitutions, such as s. 15 of the Canadian Charter of Rights and Freedoms or the Fourteenth Amendment to the United States Constitution, do explicitly provide for a guarantee of equality under the law, this has not meant that courts have avoided becoming embroiled in difficult social and political controversies that may in some cases be insoluble by judicial means.

In their joint judgment in *Leeth*, Mason CJ, Dawson, and McHugh JJ found that there might be some limitations on the way in which a court might be required to exercise its powers. For example, an attempt 'to cause a court to act in a manner contrary to natural justice would impose a non-judicial requirement inconsistent with the exercise of judicial power'.[68] Hence, they accepted that the Constitution does support some form of due process guarantee. However, while Mason CJ, Dawson, and McHugh JJ were prepared to support such a guarantee as operating to limit Commonwealth power as to matters that were 'essentially functional or procedural',[69] they rejected the limitation recognised by Deane and Toohey JJ, which they saw as being substantive. In the context of United States constitutional law, the distinction between procedural and substantive due process has been defined as follows:

> We may view *substantive* due process as referring to the *content* or *subject matter* of a law or an ordinance; that is, whether what it deals with, what it is trying to accomplish, contextually

65 C. Parker, 'Protection of Judicial Process as an Implied Constitutional Principle' (1994) 16 *Adelaide Law Review* 341 at 354.

66 See Winterton, 'The Separation of Judicial Power as an Implied Bill of Rights', pp. 199–207.

67 See generally G. R. Stone, L. M. Seidman, C. R. Sunstein, and M. V. Tushnet, *Constitutional Law*, 3rd edn, Little, Brown & Company, 1996, ch. 5.

68 *Leeth* at 470.

69 *Leeth* at 470.

conforms to due process of law. On the other hand, *procedural due process* … refers to the manner in which a law, ordinance, administrative practice, or judicial task is carried out; that is, whether the procedures employed by those who are charged with the application of the law or ordinance violate *procedural* due process, regardless of the substance of the former.[70]

Even if 'natural justice' is seen as a procedural right, it clearly offers considerable scope to constitutionalise the judicial process.

For Mason CJ, Dawson, and McHugh JJ, the question was whether the effect of s. 4 was to convert the power granted to a court into a power of a non-judicial kind, which could not be vested in a Chapter III court. They found, at p. 471, that there would be no conflict with the exercise of judicial power if, in setting minimum non-parole periods, a court was to 'have regard to those matters to which it would have regard if the law of the State in which the offender was convicted were applicable'. For them, it was an answer to the challenge that there is nothing in the Constitution that requires Commonwealth laws to have a uniform operation throughout Australia.

Brennan J joined Mason CJ, Dawson, and McHugh JJ in upholding the validity of the legislation. However, his approach showed some sympathy for the view that a concept of substantive due process might be implied from the Constitution. He found at p. 475 that the plaintiff would have had a strong argument if s. 4 had prescribed different maximum penalties for the same offence:

> It would be offensive to the constitutional unity of the Australian people 'in one indissoluble Federal Commonwealth', recited in the first preamble to the *Commonwealth of Australia Constitution Act* 1900, to expose offenders against the same law of the Commonwealth to different maximum penalties dependent on the locality of the court by which the offender is convicted and sentenced.

However, Brennan J found, at p. 476, that s. 4 was instead directed to 'the exercise of the executive power to release Commonwealth prisoners from the prisons to which they are respectively sent, which is quite a different thing'. He held, at p. 479, that distinctions between Commonwealth prisoners incarcerated in state prisons according to the law of the relevant State 'is not only a rational ground of discrimination; it is a necessary ground'.

The question of a guarantee of substantive due process was again raised in *Kruger v. Commonwealth* (1997) 190 CLR 1. As outlined above (pp. 207–8), the Court examined whether the Aboriginals Ordinance (NT) was valid insofar as it authorised the forced removal of Aboriginal children from their families and communities. It was argued that the Ordinance was invalid because the treatment of Aboriginal children was discriminatory and unequal and therefore breached the concept of legal equality developed in *Leeth*. The argument unanimously failed.

Kruger provided an opportunity for the High Court to reexamine the doctrine of equality under the law developed by Deane and Toohey JJ in *Leeth*. Toohey J was the only judge to support the view he and Deane J had taken, although even he did not find for the plaintiffs as there was no evidence before the Court that could make out

---

70   H. J. Abraham and B. A. Perry, *Freedom and the Court: Civil Rights and Liberties in the United States*, 6th edn, Oxford University Press, 1994, p. 95 (emphasis in original).

the argument that the Ordinance did anything other than discriminate on 'a rational and relevant basis'.[71] In *Kruger*, Brennan CJ held, at p. 44, that no requirement of 'substantive equality' could assist the plaintiffs, but he expressed no opinion as to the existence of such a requirement. He rejected the plaintiffs' argument on the basis that even if any such requirement existed, it could not limit the Commonwealth's power over the territories under s. 122 of the Constitution. Gaudron J adhered to the view she had taken in *Leeth* that 'Ch III operates to preclude the conferral on courts of discretionary powers which are conditioned in such a way that they must be exercised in a discriminatory manner'.[72] She then determined at p. 113 that there was no scope to derive any broader guarantee: 'the constitutional provisions which sanction and those which operate to prevent discriminatory laws so combine, in my view, that there is no room for any implication of a constitutional right of equality beyond that deriving from Ch III'. Dawson J, with whom McHugh J agreed, strongly attacked the reasoning of Deane and Toohey JJ in *Leeth*. He found that it was not possible to imply a guarantee of equality under the law from either the Constitution or the common law, and that even if such a doctrine were recognised by the common law, there was no reason why it should fetter the exercise of legislative power. Dawson J was not prepared to go further than he had in *Leeth* in his joint judgment with Mason CJ and McHugh J; he was prepared only to find at p. 63 that the separation of judicial power might afford 'a measure of due process, but it is due process of a procedural rather than substantive kind'. His view was thus narrower than that of Gaudron J, which, although based in Chapter III, did recognise that the Constitution guarantees substantive due process, at least in regard to the exercise of judicial power by Chapter III courts.

The result of *Kruger* was that the approach of Deane and Toohey JJ in *Leeth* was clearly rejected by a High Court majority composed of Dawson, Gaudron, McHugh, and Gummow JJ. It was held that no general guarantee of equality under the law could be derived from the Constitution or the common law. However, it was also established that some form of due process is guaranteed by Chapter III in relation to the exercise of judicial power by Chapter III courts. *Kruger* showed that guarantees of individual liberty will continue to be explored in the context of Chapter III in determining what form of judicial process is required by the Constitution. The question that remains is whether this guarantee is of a purely procedural nature, or whether, as has been maintained by Gaudron J, it might also operate as a substantive limitation on Commonwealth power. Of course, this question assumes that a distinction can be adequately maintained between procedural and substantive limitations.

Conclusion

The separation of judicial power has provided a fertile source of implied rights. A clear vision of the scope and range of such rights has yet to be articulated by the High Court. The rights derived from the judicial process have not been subjected to the same doubt, scrutiny, and reassessment that has characterised the implied freedom of political

---

71 *Kruger* at 96.
72 *Kruger* at 112. See *Nicholas v. The Queen* (1998) 151 ALR 312 at 335–6 per Gaudron J.

communication, and guarantees derived from the system of representative government generally (see Chapter 7). This is perhaps one reason why, unlike the implied freedom of political communication, implications from the separation of judicial power have yet to be firmly linked to the text of the Constitution (see Chapter 9). It is perhaps also why guarantees from Chapter III are emerging as more rigid restrictions on parliament's ability to shape the judicial process and to use judges in non-judicial capacities. This may also be a consequence of judges being more confident of their own view of the judicial process than they are of the democratic process.

Such rigidity in the judicial process is dangerous and may ultimately prove counterproductive. It is important that the Court does not develop the separation of judicial power so as to constitutionalise its own vision of the judicial process to the exclusion of any other vision held by an elected parliament. Apart from leading to legitimate cries for increased judicial accountability, and thereby perhaps a weakening of judicial independence, this would be to fall into the same error that beset the High Court in its interpretation of s. 92 until 1988 and the United States Supreme Court in its recognition of a concept of 'substantive due process' in *Lochner v. New York* 198 US 45 (1905) (see Chapter 6). That error would be to leave too little leeway for legitimate change to the judicial process through, for example, new rules of evidence or procedure, requiring instead that the judicial process adhere to fixed characteristics determined by the judges of the High Court.[73]

Other nations, such as Canada, have constitutionalised important parts of their criminal process. However, in countries such as Canada this may be traced directly to the text of the Constitution, rather than being a mere implication from the creation of a judicial system by the constitutional instrument.[74] For example, s. 11 of the Canadian Charter of Rights and Freedoms explicitly constitutionalises aspects of the criminal process, such as, under s. 11(d), that a 'person charged with an offence has the right … to be presumed innocent until proven guilty according to law in a fair and public hearing by an independent and impartial tribunal'. In Australia, in the absence of such a constitutional mandate, it is one thing to foster civil liberties by requiring that judicial power be exercised by a Chapter III court, it is another thing entirely to entrench a complete vision of the criminal justice system.

---

73   Compare *Dietrich v. The Queen* (1992) 177 CLR 292 at 328 per Deane J: 'the practical content of the requirement that a criminal trial be fair may vary with changing social standards and circumstances'.
74   See Hogg, chs 38, 47–51.

Double Standards and Unarticulated Premises

Introduction

Against what criteria should we measure High Court decisions? Michael Coper has suggested two: doctrinal clarity (or coherence and consistency) and conformity with constitutional purpose.[1] This Chapter is primarily concerned with whether the High Court has met the former criterion in its interpretation of constitutional rights. The Court should seek to develop a constitutional jurisprudence that achieves coherence and consistency between rights of the same class, such as civil and political rights, as well as between rights of different classes, such as between implications derived from the separation of judicial power and implications derived from the system of representative government. On occasions the Court will need to depart from a coherent and consistent approach, such as where it gives overriding weight to the second criterion of conformity with constitutional purpose. However, such departures can only be justified where they are sufficiently explained and supported by the reasons of the Court.

As a whole, High Court decisions on the express and implied rights in the Australian Constitution have been neither consistent nor coherent. The Court's lack of consistency or coherence is due in part to the limited opportunities that the Court has had to deal with these issues over the course of the century. In the case of several of the express rights, there have only been a few occasions where any one judge, or group of judges, have had the chance to develop an approach over a series of cases (although this is partly a consequence of the narrow interpretations reached by such judges on these few occasions). This explanation does not hold true in recent times. In the 1990s the High Court has heard many cases on constitutional rights, but it has yet to develop a consistent approach. While battles have been waged over the place of rights within the interpretative scheme, and over issues such as the consistency of developments (such as the implied freedom of political communication) with the

---

1   M. Coper, 'Interpreting the Constitution: A Handbook for Judges and Commentators', in A. R. Blackshield, (ed.), *Legal Change: Essays in Honour of Julius Stone*, Butterworths, 1983, p. 53.

approach in *Amalgamated Society of Engineers v. Adelaide Steamship Co. Ltd (Engineers Case)* (1920) 28 CLR 129 (see Chapters 4 and 7), the Court has yet to resolve these debates in a way that presents a coherent understanding of the place of constitutional rights in Australian law. It is not surprising that many of the new rights being developed by the High Court, such as the right to due process in the exercise of judicial power (see Chapter 8), are fraught with uncertainty.

The discussion and analysis in Chapters 5 to 8 demonstrates that there are deep influences at work that have contributed to the unsatisfactory nature of High Court interpretation of the express and implied freedoms in the Constitution. The interpretation of the Constitution and the rights therein will always be shaped by visions of the Constitution and the perceived role of the High Court. This is an inevitable component of constitutional interpretation by judges. What is unsatisfactory is that such influences have rarely been explicit. As a result, the field of express and implied rights is replete with double standards and unarticulated premises.

The failure to articulate the deep doctrines that have shaped the interpretation of constitutional rights is an unfortunate consequence of the legalism that has pervaded constitutional interpretation for much of this century. Legalism appeals to the desire of the judiciary for controversy-free adjudication (see Chapter 4). Hence Sir Owen Dixon's statement on becoming Chief Justice of the High Court in 1952 that 'There is no other safe guide to judicial decisions in great conflicts than a strict and complete legalism'.[2] However, where the Court of the 1990s has adopted a legalistic or black-letter approach, as in decisions such as *Wik Peoples v. Queensland* (1996) 187 CLR 1, this has not insulated the Court from public controversy. Instead, the Court, in its decisions on rights and on topics such as native title,[3] has been subjected to more intense criticism and political attack than at any time since its creation in 1903. Beset by criticism and failing to achieve a consistent or coherent vision of constitutional rights, the Court must move beyond legalism to an approach that identifies the forces at work in the interpretation of constitutional freedoms (see Chapter 10). The Court has begun this process, but it has a long way to go. This process must continue. Confidence in the Court and the legitimacy of its constitutional jurisprudence depend on it.

Rights versus powers

The High Court has adopted one approach for construing the Commonwealth powers listed in s. 51 of the Constitution and another, almost opposite, approach for interpreting express civil and political rights (see Chapters 4 and 5). Grants of power have been consistently given a broad operation, in part because the Court has applied the dicta of O'Connor J in *Jumbunna Coal Mine NL v. Victorian Coal Miners' Association* (1908) 6 CLR 309 at 367–8, in which it was argued that in the event of ambiguity the Court should adopt a broad, over a narrow, interpretation of a power. Of course, the spare words of the Constitution make ambiguity the norm and thus render the dicta of O'Connor J very powerful. O'Connor J's approach influenced a unanimous Court in

---

2   'Swearing in of Sir Owen Dixon as Chief Justice' (1951) 85 CLR xi at xiv.
3   See *Mabo v. Queensland (No. 2)* (1992) 175 CLR 1.

R v. Public Vehicles Licensing Appeal Tribunal (Tas); Ex parte Australian National Airways Pty Ltd (1964) 113 CLR 207 at 225 to state that s. 51 powers 'should be construed with all the generality which the words used admit'. In the 1980s and 1990s, such reasoning underpinned the wide scope given to the Commonwealth's corporations and external affairs powers in s. 51(xx) and 51(xxix) of the Constitution respectively.[4]

On the other hand, where the scope of an express civil and political right has been ambiguous, the Court has leant towards a narrow, literal interpretation. This has rarely been made explicit. An exception was in the interpretation of s. 116, which guarantees a measure of freedom of religion, by Gibbs, Mason, and Wilson JJ in *Attorney-General (Vict); Ex rel Black v. Commonwealth (DOGS Case)* (1981) 146 CLR 559[5] (see Chapter 5). Wilson J, for example, found at p. 653, that while grants of power should be broadly construed 'the same is not true of a provision which proscribes power'. Menzies J took a similar approach in *King v. Jones* (1972) 128 CLR 221, in finding that the word 'adult' in s. 41 does not include a person of 18 years of age. He found, at p. 246, that:

> It has often been said that the Constitution must be construed generously to meet changes in circumstances in so far as its language permits. This, as a general proposition, I fully accept but it is based on principles which have little influence when what has to be construed are words of limitation.

Even where the tendency to interpret express civil and political rights narrowly was not made explicit, the decisions examined in Chapter 5 show that such an approach was clearly evident. In many of those cases, as the dissents in several of them demonstrate, while a broad construction of the limitation on power was available, a majority of the Court nevertheless interpreted the right so narrowly as to make it almost meaningless.

The doctrine of parliamentary sovereignty—that is, the notion expressed by A. V. Dicey that a parliament has 'the right to make or unmake any law whatever'[6]—might provide a consistent and principled basis for the different approach to powers and express civil and political rights. Parliamentary sovereignty generally favours interpretations supportive of a wide ambit of governmental power, over those that would restrict such power. Hence, a limitation on power might be narrowly construed, while grants of power are broadly construed. However, the broad interpretation of some limitations on Commonwealth power undermines any explanation based on parliamentary sovereignty. The doctrine is at odds with the High Court's generous construction of the express economic rights in the Constitution, such as the requirement of just-terms compensation for the taking of property in s. 51(xxxi), and the guarantee that 'trade, commerce, and intercourse among the States … shall be absolutely free' in s. 92 (see Chapter 6). Parliamentary sovereignty provides no basis for a regime whereby some

---

4   See, for example, *Commonwealth v. Tasmania (Tasmanian Dam Case)* (1983) 158 CLR 1; *Re Dingjan; Ex parte Wagner* (1995) 183 CLR 323; *Victoria v. Commonwealth (Industrial Relations Act Case)* (1996) 187 CLR 416.

5   *DOGS Case* at 603 per Gibbs J, at 614–15 per Mason J, 652–3 per Wilson J. Compare p. 577 per Barwick CJ.

6   A. V. Dicey, *Introduction to the Study of the Law of the Constitution*, 10th edn [1st edn, 1885], Macmillan, 1959, p. 40. See *R v. Public Vehicles Licensing Appeal Tribunal (Tas); Ex parte Australian National Airways Pty Ltd* at 226 per the Court: 'The will of a Parliament is expressed in a statute or Act of Parliament and it is the general conception of law that what Parliament may enact it may repeal'; *Kartinyeri v. Commonwealth* (1998) 152 ALR 540.

limitations are broadly interpreted while others are narrowly construed. On the other hand, the High Court's discovery of an implied immunity of the states from federal law[7] is not inconsistent with the notion of parliamentary sovereignty. This implication can be seen as protective of parliamentary sovereignty, although it is protective of the sovereignty vested in state parliaments rather than that of the federal Parliament. It recognises that Australia's constitutional structure embodies an irreducible level of sovereignty for the state Parliaments that is guaranteed, via constitutional means, against, at the very least, destruction by a law of the federal Parliament.

Even if the doctrine of parliamentary sovereignty were put forward as a basis for restricting the scope of rights-based limitations on power, it should not be uncritically applied. While it may have been persuasive for much of this century, it must now be set against the emerging doctrine of popular sovereignty (see Chapter 4). The notion of popular sovereignty can be applied either to reinforce the effect of parliamentary sovereignty as a limiting factor on constitutionally protected rights, or as a powerful new catalyst capable of supporting substantive interpretations of rights thus far given little or no scope. In the former guise, it can be argued that the sovereignty of the people is exercised in accordance with the Constitution by the people's representatives in Parliament, who in this capacity should be given the maximum scope to implement the wishes of the people as they see them. The people, of course, retain the ability to change their representatives at the periodic election provided for by the Constitution. Under this approach, the ability of Parliament to implement its mandate is to be preferred to the judicial review exercised by the unelected and unaccountable High Court.

On the other hand, in the latter guise the doctrine of popular sovereignty might support a role for the High Court as a buffer between governmental power and the people. The doctrine suggests that the Court has a role to play in ensuring that the people remain sovereign and in resisting any exercise of government power that would, for example, undermine the electoral process by which the people exercise this sovereignty.[8] In this way, popular sovereignty can serve as an effective counterpoint to the view that the Constitution should be applied to maximise the power of a parliament. Popular sovereignty might support the High Court as a check on the exercise of arbitrary power by the people's representatives. Strong arguments that this view should be preferred are that the ballot box does not amount to an effective obstacle to the exercise of arbitrary governmental power, and that the ballot box, with its in-built preference for majoritarianism, does not adequately protect the interests of those sections of the community with little electoral power.

This conception of popular sovereignty is supported by Philip Pettit's republican vision of liberty as 'freedom as non-domination'[9] (see Chapter 1). His analysis is based on the idea that a person is only truly free when he or she is not under the arbitrary sway of another or subject to the arbitrary interference of another. A central danger in

---

7   *Melbourne Corporation v. Commonwealth* (1947) 74 CLR 31; *Queensland Electricity Commission v. Commonwealth* (1985) 159 CLR 192; *Re Australian Education Union; Ex parte Victoria* (1995) 184 CLR 188. Compare the implied immunity of the Commonwealth from state law recognised in *Commonwealth v. Cigamatic Pty Ltd (In Liquidation)* (1962) 108 CLR 372; *Re Residential Tenancies Tribunal (NSW); Ex parte Defence Housing Authority (Henderson's Case)* (1997) 190 CLR 410.

8   See *Nationwide News Pty Ltd v. Wills* (1992) 177 CLR 1 at 72 per Deane and Toohey JJ.

9   P. Pettit, *Republicanism: A Theory of Freedom and Government*, Oxford University Press, 1997, p. 51.

modern democratic systems is that minorities may fall under the domination of the majority through the majority's control of the parliament. Hence, a model of governance that is based on maximising the power of the parliament, or of parliamentary sovereignty, should not be preferred. Instead, the system should be designed such that there is 'as little room as possible for the exercise of arbitrary power'; it should be 'maximally non-manipulable'.[10] For example, the danger of control of the parliament by majorities, and the resulting domination of minorities, should be resisted by the imposition of counter-majoritarian checks and balances—such as judicial review of legislative action by the courts. The courts are appropriate repositories of such power. They are less susceptible to majority control through the electoral process, and thus to being used to abrogate the rights and freedoms of those in the minority. It has been said that courts such as the High Court:

> will always be the least dangerous to the political rights of the Constitution; because it will be least in capacity to annoy or injure them … The judiciary … has no influence over either the sword or the purse; no direction either of the strength or of the wealth of the society, and can take no active resolution whatever. It may truly be said to have neither FORCE nor WILL, but merely judgment.[11]

If the doctrine of parliamentary sovereignty does not explain the High Court's approach to express civil and political rights in the Constitution, what does? The answer lies in the High Court's long-standing antipathy to the view that the Constitution, and thus the Court, has a role to play in fostering human rights in Australia. While for most of this century High Court judges have been confident and creative in determining the scope of Commonwealth power or in deriving implications from Australia's federal structure, they have been ill at ease in applying the document as a source of protection of individual liberty (even where the document itself expressly takes this position—for example, the protection of rights of out-of-state residents in s. 117). The lack of a Bill of Rights in the Constitution and the limited role seen for constitutional rights by the instrument's framers (see Chapter 2) have influenced the judges of the High Court to the extent that they, with few exceptions, have seen almost no role for the Constitution to protect civil and political rights. The approach of the High Court is best summed up by the following statement of Knox CJ, Isaacs, Rich, and Starke JJ, which railed against the derivation from the Constitution of implications protective of rights:

> If it be conceivable that the representatives of the people of Australia as a whole would ever proceed to use their national powers to injure the people of Australia considered sectionally, it is certainly within the power of the people themselves to resent and reverse what may be done. No protection of this Court in such a case is necessary or proper.[12]

Even if later judges did not hold to this view, it nevertheless exercised a powerful force. The legalistic approach to interpretation applied by judges for much of this century limited their ability to apply doctrine or material that might suggest a different approach. As Sir Anthony Mason has suggested, 'Legalism, when coupled with the

---

10 Pettit, p. 173.
11 J. Madison, A. Hamilton, and J. Jay, *The Federalist Papers*, Penguin Books, 1987, p. 437 (No. 78).
12 *Engineers Case* at 151–2.

doctrine of *stare decisis*, has a subtle and formidable conservative influence'.[13] Where legalism masks the original values underpinning a decision, that decision may be reproduced even where those values no longer hold true. It is by this means that the approach set out in the *Engineers Case* has been fortified by many of the decisions on express civil and political rights. As decisions such as *Street v. Queensland Bar Association* (1989) 168 CLR 461 show (see Chapter 5), it can take a united Court to oust such values.

Whether it is due to the doctrine of parliamentary sovereignty or merely an antipathy to protecting certain rights via constitutional means, the High Court has given only narrow and grudging scope to the Constitution's express civil and political rights, at least until recent times. In the 1990s there are strong indications that the narrow approach to certain rights in the Constitution may be reversed. This began with the unanimous decision in *Street*, in which a substantive interpretation was given to s. 117. The result in the *DOGS Case* had rested on a narrow view of the role of constitutional rights. *Street* rested on the opposite, finding that such rights can play a prominent part in constitutional jurisprudence. In stark contrast to the approach articulated by Wilson J in the *DOGS Case*, Deane and Toohey JJ cited decisions such as *Jumbunna Coal Mine* and *R v. Public Vehicles Licensing Appeal Tribunal* to argue for a broad construction of rights-based limitations on governmental power. Such sentiments have been echoed by other judges since *Street* (see Chapter 4)—for example, by Gaudron J in *Kruger v. Commonwealth* (1997) 190 CLR 1 at 123 and 131—and played an important part in dissents by Murphy J in earlier cases.[14] Most powerfully, in arguing that s. 51(xxxi) applies to laws passed by the Commonwealth for the territories under s. 122 of the Constitution, Kirby J stated in *Newcrest Mining (WA) Ltd v. Commonwealth* (1997) 147 ALR 42 at 147, 'There is one final consideration which reinforces the view to which I am driven by the foregoing reasons. Where the Constitution is ambiguous, this Court should adopt that meaning which conforms to the principles of fundamental rights rather than an interpretation which would involve a departure from such rights'.

Such statements represent a doctrinal change in the approach of the Court to constitutional rights, particularly express civil and political rights. However, apart from the decision in *Street*, it has yet to make an impact on such express rights. While *Street* showed that there had been a fundamental shift, it is not clear how far this will be carried. Decisions such as *Kruger* (see Chapter 5) show that there is still considerable judicial reluctance to apply the Constitution in a way that recognises an interventionist role in protecting individual liberty.

Why has the jurisprudence of the Court shifted so that some of its members are now finding that rights, like Commonwealth powers, should be broadly construed where a choice exists between a broad and a narrow construction? Part of the answer lies in the focus and business of the Court shifting from issues concerning Australian federalism to issues involving constitutional rights. Many of the large questions in Australian federalism, such as the ambit of the Commonwealth's external affairs power in

---

13 A. Mason, 'The Role of a Constitutional Court in a Federation: A Comparison of the Australian and the United States Experience' (1986) 16 *Federal Law Review* 1 at 5.
14 See, for example, *R v. Pearson; Ex parte Sipka* (1983) 152 CLR 254 at 268, 274.

s. 51(xxix), have been resolved or demand less of the Court's time than they did in previous decades.[15] In addition, since the Second World War it has become increasingly recognised in international law and in the domestic law of other nations that the judiciary does have a central role to play in protecting rights. Such developments naturally seep into the High Court's work on Australian law through the use of precedent from other nations, and less formally, through the involvement of its judges, such as Kirby J, in international judicial colloquia.[16] Kirby J has been more supportive of this process, particularly in regard to the use of international law in constitutional interpretation, than any other High Court judge (see Chapter 1).[17] In *Newcrest* he found, at p. 148, that 'international law is a legitimate and important influence on the development of the common law and constitutional law, especially when international law declares the existence of universal and fundamental rights'. It remains to be seen whether this dictum gains general acceptance, and thus allows instruments such as the *International Covenant on Civil and Political Rights 1966* and the *International Covenant on Economic, Social and Cultural Rights 1966* (see Chapter 1) to directly impact on the interpretation of the Constitution. Even in the absence of such an approach gaining wider support on the High Court, it is clear that the High Court's development of constitutional rights in the 1980s and 1990s is broadly reflective of, and undoubtedly influenced by, international developments.

Another factor that has dissolved the antipathy of the modern High Court to the protection of individual freedoms by constitutional means is the Court's increasing reliance on the decisions of courts in other constitutional systems. Despite the warning issued in the *Engineers Case* ('we conceive that American authorities, however illustrious the tribunals may be, are not a secure basis on which to build fundamentally with respect to our own Constitution'[18]), Australian judges have increasingly turned to decisions of nations such as the USA and Canada, where constitutional law plays an important role in the protection of human rights. Indeed, the contemporary constitutional jurisprudence of such nations is pervaded with the objective of protecting the individual from arbitrary governmental interference. The differences between these systems and the Australian Constitution has not meant that the High Court has applied such decisions uncritically.[19] Nevertheless, in developing the implied freedom of political

---

15 See, in relation to s. 51(xxix), *Victoria v. Commonwealth (Industrial Relations Act Case)* (1996) 187 CLR 416 at 480–9 per Brennan CJ, Toohey, Gaudron, McHugh, and Gummow JJ.

16 See M. Kirby, 'The Australian Use of International Human Rights Norms: From Bangalore to Balliol—A View from the Antipodes' (1993) 16 *University of New South Wales Law Journal* 363; M. Kirby, 'The Role of International Standards in Australian Courts', in P. Alston and M. Chiam (eds), *Treaty-Making and Australia: Globalisation versus Sovereignty*, Federation Press, 1995, p. 81.

17 Compare, for example, the use of international law by Gummow and Hayne JJ, and Kirby J in *Kartinyeri v. Commonwealth* (1998) 152 ALR 540 at 571–3 and 598–600 respectively.

18 *Engineers Case* at 146 per Knox CJ, Isaacs, Rich, and Starke JJ. See *West v. Commissioner of Taxation (NSW)* (1937) 56 CLR 657 at 679 per Dixon J in which the use of Canadian precedents is also cautioned against. See generally, on the use made of United States precedents, P. E. von Nessen, 'The Use of American Precedents by the High Court of Australia, 1901–1987' (1992) 14 *Adelaide Law Review* 181.

19 See the use of *New York Times Co. v. Sullivan* 376 US 254 (1964) by the High Court in *Theophanous v. Herald & Weekly Times Ltd* (1994) 182 CLR 104. Compare the citation of Canadian decisions such as *Switzman v. Elbling* [1957] SCR 285 and *Reference re Alberta Statutes* [1938] SCR 100 by Brennan J in *Nationwide News Pty Ltd v. Wills* (1992) 177 CLR 1 and Mason CJ in *Australian Capital Television Pty Ltd v. Commonwealth* (1992) 177 CLR 106 (see Chapter 7). Compare also with the conclusions of G. N. Rosenberg and J. M. Williams, 'Do Not Go Gently into that Good Right: The First Amendment in the High Court of Australia' (1997) 11 *Supreme Court Review* 439.

communication in decisions such as *Australian Capital Television Pty Ltd v. Commonwealth* (1992) 177 CLR 106 and *Theophanous v. Herald & Weekly Times Ltd* (1994) 182 CLR 104, such precedent has played an important role in enabling the High Court to explore the boundaries of the Australian Constitution.

Underpinning the narrow construction given to express civil and political rights was the High Court's long-running preoccupation with such provisions as limitations on Commonwealth power.[20] Thus, in *Australian Communist Party v. Commonwealth* (1951) 83 CLR 1 the High Court struck down the *Communist Party Dissolution Act 1950* (Cth) not because it infringed a fundamental freedom implied from the Constitution, but because the law could not be characterised as falling within a head of Commonwealth power (see Chapter 8). As has been suggested extra-judicially by Toohey J, the 'preservation of liberty' achieved by the decision in the *Communist Party Case* 'may be only a fortuitous by-product of that power-dividing process'.[21] The change in the approach of the Court has meant that provisions such as s. 117 are now being seen as more than mere limitations on governmental power. This is particularly appropriate in the case of s. 117, which is expressed as a personal right. In *Street*, s. 117 was viewed not only as a restriction on what the Commonwealth can do, but also a guarantee, or commitment, to individual liberty.[22] Such provisions are more easily given a substantive interpretation when they are viewed other than merely in relation to the power that they limit.

Civil and political rights versus economic rights

In *Adelaide Company of Jehovah's Witnesses Inc. v. Commonwealth (Jehovah's Witnesses Case)* (1943) 67 CLR 116 at 136, Latham CJ suggested that 'The rights of property, however important they may be, have never been held in the courts to be as sacred as the right of personal liberty'. In fact, the experience of the High Court in the interpretation of the Constitution has been to the opposite effect. Until the High Court reinterpreted s. 117 in *Street* in 1989, none of the express civil and political rights in the Constitution protective of personal liberty (sections 41, 80, 116, and 117) had been successfully invoked by a plaintiff to strike down a state or federal law (see Chapter 5). On the few occasions that the Court had interpreted these provisions, it had chosen an approach that rendered the relevant provision largely meaningless. On the other hand, when similar opportunities arose to interpret the express economic rights in the Constitution (sections 51(xxiiiA), 51(xxxi), and 92) the Court revealed a willingness to apply the provisions to invalidate state and federal legislation (see Chapter 6). These latter rights, such as the guarantee of 'just terms' for the 'acquisition of property' in s. 51(xxxi), were vigorously interpreted as substantial and effective limitations on governmental power.

A clear difference in approach can be identified between the pre-1989 case law on civil and political rights, and case law on economic rights (excluding decisions on s. 92

---

20   See S. McLeish, 'Making Sense of Religion and the Constitution: A Fresh Start for Section 116' (1992) 18 *Monash University Law Review* 207.

21   J. Toohey, 'A Government of Laws, and Not of Men?' (1993) 4 *Public Law Review* 158 at 169.

22   See M. Coper, *Encounters with the Australian Constitution*, CCH, 1987, p. 372.

from the 1988 decision in *Cole v. Whitfield* onwards). In the pre-1989 case law on civil and political rights, the High Court developed strained and overly narrow interpretations. In the case law on economic rights, the Court strained the text of the Constitution in an opposite direction to develop significant protection of economic interests, using sections that, apart from s. 51(xxiiiA), were not originally conceived as rights-based provisions at all. Thus, while s. 117 was clearly expressed as an individual guarantee, the guarantee of freedom of interstate trade in s. 92 was remade into a guarantee of the rights of the individual trader. Similarly, s. 51(xxxi) was not primarily intended as a general guarantee of property rights but was inserted to ensure that the Commonwealth possessed the power to effect compulsory acquisitions. Yet, in contrast to the limited scope given to provisions such as s. 80, s. 51(xxxi) was interpreted as a general limitation on the Commonwealth's power to acquire property.

Even individual justices adopted different approaches to the different classes of rights. For example, Barwick CJ was prepared to interpret s. 92 so as to strike down laws that had the real and practical effect of burdening interstate trade. This substantive approach can be contrasted with his interpretation of s. 116 in the *DOGS Case*, in which he found that a law would be struck down only where the law has a purpose prohibited by s. 116 as 'its express and, as I think, single purpose'.[23] This purpose was to be gleaned from the law at the time of its making, and not from the operation or administration of the law. In another example, Mason J stated in the *DOGS Case* that while a grant of legislative power might be applied over time to new things and events, the same was not true of limitations. These, he argued at p. 615, must be applied according to their meaning as at 1900, as there was 'no reason for enlarging its scope of operation beyond the mischief to which it was directed'. On the other hand, in *Permewan Wright Consolidated Pty Ltd v. Trewhitt* (1979) 145 CLR 1 at 35, Mason J found 'no compelling reason why we should interpret s. 92 by reference to doctrines which were current at the end of the nineteenth century'. He accepted that while the connotation, or core characteristics, of the words used in s. 92 remain fixed, he held at p. 35 that as to the denotation or application of those words, 'it is incorrect to confine the application of the language of a constitutional provision by reference to the meaning which it had in 1900'. He also found at p. 35 that quite apart from this method of expanding the scope of s. 92, it should be recognised 'that the organized society which s. 92 assumes is not the society of 1900 but the Australian community as it evolves and develops from time to time'.

The basis for this fundamental difference in approach has not been articulated. The Court's great interest in s. 92 might be explained by its vision of the Constitution as a document more about federalism than human rights, while its willingness to give substantive interpretations to sections 51(xxiiiA) and 51(xxxi) might lie in its fascination with the construction of s. 51 powers. However, neither basis offers an adequate explanation for the Court's approach. There have obviously been reasons given for why *particular* civil and political rights have been narrowly construed, and why certain economic rights have been broadly constructed, but never more. One reason given for the conclusion that s. 51(xxxi) applies to all acquisitions effected under a law of the Commonwealth—that is, whether by the Commonwealth itself or by some other body

---

23 *DOGS Case* (1981) 146 CLR 559 at 579.

or person—was that if s. 51(xxxi) only applied to acquisitions by the Commonwealth there would be a 'serious gap in the constitutional safeguard'.[24] Yet why was such reasoning not applied in several of the cases on civil and political rights? For example, why in *Davies and Jones v. Western Australia* (1904) 2 CLR 29 did the Court find that the protection of residence in s. 117 did not extend to the analogous and overlapping concept of domicile? Surely to find that a law could impose a disability or discrimination on the basis of domicile would be to recognise a 'serious gap in the constitutional safeguard'.

An irony in the distinction drawn between civil and political rights, on the one hand, and economic rights, on the other, is that the broad interpretation given to provisions protecting economic rights has in one instance allowed a civil and political right to be equally protected. Despite the guarantee of freedom of interstate 'intercourse' in s. 92 being of a different character to the protection afforded to interstate trade and commerce, the former guarantee had been widely construed (see Chapter 6). As an aspect of s. 92, interstate 'intercourse' was strongly protected even before the High Court's change of approach to s. 92 in *Cole v. Whitfield*. Isaacs and Higgins JJ in *R v. Smithers; Ex parte Benson* (1912) 16 CLR 99, and the whole Court in *Gratwick v. Johnson* (1945) 70 CLR 1, applied s. 92 to invalidate laws that restricted interstate movement. The guarantee of civil and political rights in s. 92, in the form of interstate movement, escaped the narrow and pedantic interpretation given to other express civil and political rights, perhaps only because it existed as an adjunct of the economic right located in s. 92.

The different interpretative approaches of the High Court to classes of rights reveals a double standard that has spanned the decision-making of generations of High Court judges. At least until the late 1980s the High Court preferred to implement economic over civil and political rights. This double standard was never expressly set down by any member of the Court but is an obvious inference from the pattern of decisions. This is not to suggest that it was the intent or design of members of the High Court to discriminate between economic and civil and political rights. It is simply that such a standard is apparent over the course of decisions.

This double standard reflects a similar pattern of decisions in the USA in the first part of the twentieth century. In decisions such as *Lochner v. New York* 198 US 45 (1905), the United States Supreme Court developed the concept of 'substantive due process' to protect a range of economic rights such as freedom of contract (see Chapter 6). The origins of the concept of 'substantive due process' can be traced back to the infamous decision of *Dred Scott v. Sandford* 60 US (19 Howard) 393 (1857), in which the personal rights of slaves were subordinated to the property rights of their masters. In general, economic rights were seen to be more deserving of protection than civil and political rights. The intervention of the United States Supreme Court in the field of economic regulation came to a head in the 1930s, when the Court struck down aspects of President Roosevelt's 'New Deal', a set of policies aimed at revitalising the United States economy (see Chapter 6). In *West Coast Hotel Co. v. Parrish* 300 US 379 (1937), the Court overruled *Lochner* and indicated that its preference for economic rights was at an

---

24   *Trade Practices Commission v. Tooth & Co. Ltd* (1979) 142 CLR 397 at 452 per Aickin J. A similar line of reasoning is employed in *Australian Tape Manufacturers Association Ltd v. Commonwealth* (1993) 176 CLR 480 at 510 per Mason CJ, Brennan, Deane, and Gaudron JJ ('reduced to a hollow facade').

end and that constitutional rights would thereafter not be applied to impede governmental regulation of the economy. Under this approach, the Court was prepared to find
that 'a state is free to adopt whatever economic policy may reasonably be deemed to
promote public welfare' so long as its laws 'have a reasonable relation to a proper legislative purpose'.[25]

The demise of *Lochner* did not stop the United States Supreme Court applying a
double standard. The Court simply reversed the standard to foster civil and political
rights over economic rights. While the decline of economic rights in *West Coast Hotel
Co. v. Parrish* marked the change, the shift in direction was not left to be discerned from
the course of decision-making thereafter. Instead, an approach based on preferring civil
and political freedoms was heralded by the famous 'footnote four' in the judgment of
Stone J in *United States v. Carolene Products Co.* 304 US 144 (1938).[26] In that footnote,
Stone J foreshadowed that the Court might apply a 'more searching judicial inquiry' to
certain civil and political rights, such as where the constitutional issues require a 'review
of statutes directed at particular religious ... or national ... or racial minorities'.[27]
Moreover, 'prejudice against discrete and insular minorities may be a special condition,
which tends seriously to curtail the operation of those political processes ordinarily to
be relied on to protect minorities, and which may call for a correspondingly more
searching judicial inquiry'.[28] This came to stand for the principle that the Court will
prefer certain freedoms or interests, which it will police vigilantly, while infringements
on other freedoms or interests, such as the right to contract, will not be subjected to the
same level of scrutiny.[29]

The development of the idea that some rights have a 'preferred position'[30] over
other rights led to a period of intense creativity on the United States Supreme Court.
In implementing the civil and political rights in the United States Bill of Rights the
Court constitutionalised key aspects of the criminal process[31] and even found itself at
the forefront of debates over desegregation and abortion, in decisions such as *Brown v.
Board of Education* 347 US 483 (1954) and *Roe v. Wade* 410 US 113 (1973) respectively.
The period of creativity culminated in the intensely controversial decision of *Roe v.
Wade*, in which the Court held by 7:2 that a woman's choice to have an abortion was
an interest protected by the Fourteenth Amendment to the United States Constitution.
Such a decision would have been unthinkable in the first part of the twentieth century.
The decision gave United States women total autonomy over pregnancy during the
first trimester, and set out different levels of possible state intervention for the second

---

25 *Nebbia v. New York* 291 US 502 at 537 (1934).
26 See L. Lusky, *By What Right? A Commentary on the Supreme Court's Power to Revise the Constitution*, Michie,
    1975; L. Lusky, *Our Nine Tribunes: The Supreme Court in Modern America*, Praeger, 1993, ch. 7. Compare B. A.
    Ackerman, 'Beyond Carolene Products' (1985) 98 *Harvard Law Review* 713.
27 *United States v. Carolene Products Co.* at 152, fn. 4.
28 *United States v. Carolene Products Co.* at 152, fn. 4.
29 See H. J. Abraham and B. A. Perry, *Freedom and the Court*, 6th edn, Oxford University Press, 1994, ch. 2; J. D.
    Hyman and W. J. Newhouse, 'Standards for Preferred Freedoms: Beyond the First' (1965) 60 *Northwestern
    University Law Review* 1; P. A. Freund, *The Supreme Court of the United States: Its Business, Purposes and Per-
    formance*, World Publishing Company, 1967, pp. 81–3. Compare L. Hand, 'Chief Justice Stone's Conception
    of the Judicial Function' (1946) 46 *Columbia Law Review* 696 at 698.
30 *Jones v. Opelika* 316 US 584 at 608 (1942) per Stone CJ.
31 See, for example, *Miranda v. Arizona* 384 US 436 (1966).

and third trimesters.[32] The freedom to choose to have an abortion was not expressly contained in the United States Constitution but was an aspect of the right to privacy in the marital relationship implied in *Griswold v. Connecticut* 381 US 479 at 484–5 (1965) from 'penumbras' to the Bill of Rights (see Chapter 7). The application of the implied right to privacy in decisions such as *Roe v. Wade* has been seen as a revival of the concept of 'substantive due process', applied in *Lochner* to protect economic rights, but in the second half of the century applied to foster civil and political rights instead.[33] Most recently, it has been argued that the concept might support a constitutionally protected 'right to die'.[34]

'Footnote four' in *Carolene Products* established one double standard. It also foreshadowed another. The Supreme Court has applied the suggestion that certain types of legislation ('statutes directed at particular religious ... or national ... or racial minorities') might be subjected to a 'more searching judicial inquiry' by identifying certain interests or classifications that are to be accorded greater protection. Legislation that breaches a 'suspect' classification, such as a statute that discriminates on the basis of race,[35] will be subject to 'strict judicial scrutiny' under which it will be valid only where the legislature or the executive is able to affirmatively show that the classification can be justified by a 'compelling state interest'. By contrast, legislation not breaching a 'suspect' classification is accorded a lower standard under which it will be upheld where the Supreme Court can identify a reasonable, rational, or relevant basis for the distinction brought about by the legislation. In more recent times, the Supreme Court has also developed an intermediate standard of review for classification on the basis of gender, finding that 'classifications by gender must serve important governmental objectives and must be substantially related to achievement of those objectives'.[36]

The United States Supreme Court has been explicit in developing the idea that some rights are to be preferred over others, although under Rehnquist CJ the United States Supreme Court has been struggling with the idea of giving greater recognition to economic rights.[37] Whether or not a preferred freedom approach is the correct one, it is at least an open statement of policy by the Court, as opposed to a policy or preference that can only be discerned over time from the course of decisions. The approach

---

32 There have been many attempts to overrule *Roe v. Wade*. The most recent attempt was in *Planned Parenthood of Southeastern Pennsylvania v. Casey* 505 US 833 (1992). In that case a plurality opinion of O'Connor, Kennedy, and Souter JJ found, at p. 846, that the doctrine of *stare decisis* should be followed at least to the extent that the 'essential holding' of *Roe v. Wade* should be retained: that is, they retained the right of a woman to an abortion but rejected the trimester framework established by *Roe v. Wade*. These three judges made up the majority along with Blackmun and Stevens JJ. Blackmun J, the author of the opinion in *Roe v. Wade*, stated at pp. 943 and 923 respectively: 'I am 83 years old. I cannot remain on this Court forever' and 'I fear for the darkness as four Justices anxiously await the single vote necessary to extinguish the light.' Rehnquist CJ, White, Scalia, and Thomas JJ strongly dissented.

33 J. H. Ely, 'The Wages of Crying Wolf: A Comment on *Roe v. Wade*' (1973) 82 *Yale Law Journal* 920; G. Gunther, *Constitutional Law*, 12th edn, Foundation Press, 1991, ch. 8.

34 *Cruzan v. Director, Missouri Department of Health* 497 US 261 (1990); *Washington v. Glucksberg* 138 L Ed 2d 772 (1997).

35 See, for example, *Loving v. Virginia* 388 US 1 (1967).

36 *Craig v. Boren* 429 US 190 at 197 (1976) per Brennan J.

37 See R. A. Epstein, 'Property, Speech, and the Politics of Distrust', in G. R. Stone, R. A. Epstein, and C. R. Sunstein, *The Bill of Rights in the Modern State*, University of Chicago Press, 1992, p. 41; D. A. Schultz and C. E. Smith, *The Jurisprudential Vision of Justice Antonin Scalia*, Rowman & Littlefield, 1996, ch. 1.

of the High Court has also embodied a double standard, or preferred freedoms, but not in a way that can be discerned from any clear statement of principle. However, it is important to note that the USA developed an explicit policy only after overturning its first double standard in the 1930s, and it did so in response to the need to move away from a preferred freedom based on economic rights to one based on civil and political rights. The Australian High Court has never been confronted with a crisis of the sort that faced the United States Supreme Court in the 1930s, because the economic rights in the Australian Constitution have not impeded governmental regulation to the same extent as the United States concept of 'substantive due process'. If the High Court had faced such a crisis, perhaps as a consequence of its interpretation of s. 92, it may have been prompted to explicitly shift direction.

The Australian preference for economic rights was informed by the *laissez-faire* view taken by many High Court judges in interpreting s. 92. This reliance can be traced to the leanings of the drafters in framing the Constitution (it has been said that the drafters 'wanted a Constitution that would make capitalist society hum'[38]) and to the fact that the Court's earliest attempts to interpret constitutional rights coincided with United States Supreme Court decisions such as *Lochner*. The fact that both United States and Australian courts applied a double standard that gave preference to economic rights may not be a coincidence when it is recalled that early judges of the High Court such as Isaacs J[39] had a strong knowledge of United States constitutional law. However, while the United States Supreme Court came to reverse its double standard, the Australian High Court continued to apply it.

Murphy J attacked the High Court's preference for economic rights over civil and political rights. While he advocated a creative and progressive approach to the protection of rights such as trial by jury in s. 80 of the Constitution (see Chapters 5 and 7), he repudiated the same approach in the interpretation of s. 92. Accordingly, in *Uebergang v. Australian Wheat Board* (1980) 145 CLR 266 at 309 he narrowly construed s. 92 to avoid the Court taking on 'a super-legislative role' as regards interstate trade and commerce. Yet in the same case he made it clear, at p. 308, that 'in human rights and other non-economic areas, courts have applied tests of due process, natural justice, reasonableness and fairness': that is, courts could appropriately have recourse to 'public policy tests'. Murphy J's approach was reminiscent of the preferred freedoms doctrine applied by the United States Supreme Court after 1937, as exemplified by 'footnote four' in *United States v. Carolene Products Co.*

The High Court did not develop Murphy J's scheme of preferred freedoms while he was a member of the Court. Indeed, Murphy J found himself in persistent dissent in arguing for a broad construction of express and implied civil and political rights. However, since Murphy J's death in 1986 the Court has dramatically shifted its approach to such rights. The beginnings of a new double standard akin to that applied by the United States Supreme Court since 1937, and advocated by Murphy J, have been evident in recent High Court decisions. First, the Court has restricted the scope for economic rights under s. 92 by rejecting the 'individual rights theory' of that section in

---

38   M. Clark, 'The People and the Constitution', in S. Encel, D. Horne, and E. Thompson (eds), *Change the Rules! Towards a Democratic Constitution*, Penguin, 1977, p. 18.

39   J. A. La Nauze, *The Making of the Australian Constitution*, Melbourne University Press, 1972, p. 232.

1988 in *Cole v. Whitfield*. Secondly, it is arguable that in five 1994 cases[40] the Court cut back the protection offered by s. 51(xxxi) to individuals whose property was subject to acquisition under Commonwealth legislation, although this was tempered by the broad interpretation given to s. 51(xxxi) in 1997 in *Newcrest*. Thirdly, the shift may be shown by the reversal of the interpretation of s. 117 in *Street* in 1989. Fourthly, recent decisions have encompassed the development of implied rights from both the system of representative government (see Chapter 7) and the separation of judicial power (see Chapter 8).

These four developments represent the rumblings of a deep change of approach by the Court. The emergence of a range of implied rights, such as a freedom of political communication (see Chapter 7) and a freedom from involuntary detention (see Chapter 8), is the strongest indication that the Court has departed from the double standard under which it held back from developing civil and political rights. Although it seems that the scheme of preferred freedoms apparent in many of the Court's decisions over this century has been overthrown, it is too early to tell if this, as in the USA, indicates a shift to a new set of preferred freedoms based on creatively developing civil and political rights and avoiding the application of economic rights. Such a revised double standard would seem unlikely. While antipathy to civil and political rights has been eroded, and s. 92 has lost much of its impact, s. 51(xxxi) continues to be strongly applied by the Court. The extension of s. 51(xxxi) by the Court in *Newcrest* to apply to laws passed by the Commonwealth under its territories power in s. 122 of the Constitution indicates that s. 51(xxxi) will continue to be positively developed. Indeed, while the United States experience and the direction taken by nations such as Canada on economic rights (see Chapter 6) suggests that the Court should not develop any limitation of 'substantive due process' to protect economic rights, there is no compelling reason why the High Court should not continue to apply the level of protection currently afforded to such rights. Sections such as 51(xxxi) and 92 have an ongoing role to play. Nevertheless, after many decades of inactivity it can be expected that much of the High Court's energy in the field of constitutional rights, and even in constitutional law generally, will be expended in constructing viable civil and political rights from the text and structure of the Constitution.

Representative government versus the separation of judicial power

The implied freedom of political communication, an implication from the system of representative government embodied in the Constitution, has been carefully and critically scrutinised by the High Court over several cases (see Chapter 7). Indeed, the significance of one recent decision on the implied freedom, *Lange v. Australian Broadcasting Corporation* (1997) 189 CLR 520, lies in its development of the interpretative

---

40 *Mutual Pools & Staff Pty Ltd v. Commonwealth* (1994) 179 CLR 155; *Health Insurance Commission v. Peverill* (1994) 179 CLR 226; *Re Director of Public Prosecutions; Ex parte Lawler* (1994) 179 CLR 270; *Georgiadis v. Australian and Overseas Telecommunications Corporation* (1994) 179 CLR 297; *Nintendo Co. Ltd v. Centronics Systems Pty Ltd* (1994) 181 CLR 134.

methodology underlying the freedom, rather than in any expansion or contraction of the right. Earlier cases had also been concerned to ensure that the implied freedom was constitutionally viable. Thus, in *McGinty v. Western Australia* (1996) 186 CLR 140, the High Court sought to tie the freedom developed in *Nationwide News Pty Ltd v. Wills* (1992) 177 CLR 1 and *Australian Capital Television* (1992) 177 CLR 106 more precisely to the text and structure of the Constitution.

Decisions such as *McGinty* emphasised the need for any implication of rights to be fully attributable to the language of the Constitution. In *McGinty* at p. 234, McHugh J was critical of the idea that the implied freedom might be drawn from the system of representative democracy as if that system were a 'free-standing principle'. By this, he was concerned to honour the commitment made by the majority in the *Engineers Case* that the Court would not derive implications from sources extrinsic to the Constitution (see Chapter 4). As Brennan J stated in *Queensland Electricity Commission v. Commonwealth* (1985) 159 CLR 192 at 231: 'Any implication affecting the specific powers granted by the Constitution must be drawn from the Constitution itself. It is impermissible to construe the terms of the Constitution by importing an implication from extrinsic sources'. Accordingly, the scope of the implied freedom of political communication must be determined and bounded by the extent to which it is given recognition by the text of the Constitution. If it exists beyond that provided for by the text, the ambit of the implication will be uncertain and the legitimacy of the freedom called into question. As a consequence of the Court recognising this, the implied freedom of political communication, as well as other freedoms that can be derived from the system of representative government, can now be clearly seen to be delineated by the Constitution itself, particularly sections 7 and 24. These sections require, respectively, that the members of the Senate and the House of Representatives be 'directly chosen by the people'.

The implication of rights from the separation of judicial power achieved by Chapter III of the Constitution (see Chapter 8) has not been subjected to the same interpretive rigour as have implications from the system of representative government. The fidelity of modern judges to the interpretative scheme laid down in the *Engineers Case* has been a constant theme in cases on the implied freedom of political communication, such as in *Theophanous v. Herald & Weekly Times Ltd* (1994) 182 CLR 104. On the other hand, this has not emerged as a concern in the derivation of rights from Chapter III. This is a strange omission. The debate over the place of the *Engineers Case* is at least as relevant in that context.

The High Court has not yet soundly based rights derived from Chapter III in the text and structure of the Constitution. One reason for this is that the Court has not focused, as it has in the field of representative government, on one possible implied freedom, but has ranged over a number of possible implications. Several of these implications, such as the possibility that the federal Parliament cannot enact a retrospective criminal law,[41] have yet to be resolved. Another example is the controversial suggestion in decisions such as *Leeth v. Commonwealth* (1992) 174 CLR 455 and *Kruger v. Commonwealth* (1997) 190 CLR 1 that the Constitution contains a guarantee that would require

---

41   See *Polyukhovich v. Commonwealth (War Crimes Act Case)* (1991) 172 CLR 501.

substantive, or perhaps only procedural, due process in the exercise of judicial power. By contrast, the High Court quickly recognised the existence of the implied freedom of political communication in *Nationwide News* and *Australian Capital Television*. It was then able to largely concentrate on the legitimacy and scope of the freedom rather than on whether the freedom even existed.

In *Kable v. Director of Public Prosecutions (NSW)* (1996) 189 CLR 51, an implication from the separation of judicial power did gain majority support (see Chapter 8). However, the implication in that case was not squarely based in the Constitution. The *Community Protection Act 1994* (NSW) empowered the Supreme Court of New South Wales to make 'preventive detention orders' against Gregory Wayne Kable, who had apparently written letters threatening the safety of his children and his deceased wife's sister. Such orders would have enabled Kable to be imprisoned, even though he had not been found guilty of a criminal offence. A majority of the High Court consisting of Toohey, Gaudron, McHugh, and Gummow JJ, with Brennan CJ and Dawson J dissenting, found that the Act was invalid because it infringed the separation of judicial power achieved by the Australian Constitution. The Act was invalid because 'it purports to vest functions in the Supreme Court of New South Wales that are incompatible with the exercise of the judicial power of the Commonwealth by the Supreme Court of that State'.[42]

A key element of the reasoning of the majority in *Kable* was that the incompatibility doctrine should be applied to determine whether the power to make 'preventive detention orders' could be vested in the State Supreme Court. That doctrine was applied to find that such a power was incompatible with the judicial function because the power 'compromise[d] the institutional impartiality of the Supreme Court'.[43] The incompatibility doctrine had been developed as an exception to the *persona designata* rule:[44] that is, the rule that a non-judicial power can be conferred on judges of Chapter III courts by the federal Parliament if such power is conferred on a judge not as a member of the court but in his or her personal capacity. In this context, there was nothing to suggest that the incompatibility doctrine might operate as a limit on the power of state parliaments to legislate for state supreme courts. Why then was the doctrine applied in *Kable*? It was one thing to find that the Australian Constitution might limit the power of a state parliament to abolish the Supreme Court of that state (this clearly being an implication from provisions such as sections 73 and 77(iii)). It was another thing altogether to import the incompatibility doctrine as a general limitation on the power, not only of the Commonwealth to vest judicial power under Chapter III, but also on the capacity of the New South Wales Parliament to vest judicial power under the state constitution. Significantly, the result in *Kable* could not be based on the New South Wales Constitution because it had been found in *Kable* and in earlier decisions[45] that the *Constitution Act 1902* (NSW) did not embody a separation of judicial power. This gave the application of the incompatibility doctrine from the Australian Constitution the appearance of being contrived.

---

42 *Kable* at 109 per McHugh J.
43 *Kable* at 121 per McHugh J.
44 See *Grollo v. Palmer* (1995) 184 CLR 348.
45 *Clyne v. East* (1967) 68 SR (NSW) 385; *Building Construction Employees and Builders' Labourers Federation of New South Wales v. Minister for Industrial Relations* (1986) 7 NSWLR 372.

The use of the incompatibility doctrine in *Kable*, and in *Nicholas v. The Queen* (1998) 151 ALR 312 by McHugh and Kirby JJ, does not sit well with the strong position taken by judges such as McHugh J in *McGinty*. In *McGinty* McHugh J spoke strongly against the notion of guarantees based on a 'free-standing principle'. Yet it is hard to describe the use of the incompatibility doctrine in *Kable*, by judges including McHugh J, as anything else. The doctrine was taken out of the context in which it was developed, that is, the *persona designata* rule, and was applied as a broad-based limitation on state and federal power. This was achieved without adequately grounding the doctrine in the text and structure of the Australian Constitution.

The majority in *McGinty* found that the implied freedom of political communication must be directly implied from the text and structure of the Constitution. They criticised the idea that the freedom could be seen as an implication from an implication: that is, that the freedom could be seen as an implication from the system of representative government, which is itself an implication from the Constitution, including sections 7 and 24. The argument was that such second-order implications are too far removed from the text of the Constitution to be legitimate inferences. The incompatibility doctrine, as applied in *Kable*, is an implication of at least the second order. It cannot, or at least thus far has not, been persuasively shown to be based in Chapter III of the Constitution. Rather, it exists as an implication from the fact that the Constitution in some ways limits the power of the states to legislate for and about their supreme courts, which is in turn clearly an implication from Chapter III, particularly sections 73 and 77(iii). If the Court is to rely on the notion that implications cannot be drawn from implications in the field of representative government, this should be equally applied in analysing freedoms drawn from Chapter III of the Constitution.

The High Court has been concerned to construct a tight analytical framework for the derivation of rights from the system of representative government created by the Constitution. The reasoning applied in describing implications from Chapter III lacks this. It is important that the Court remedy this discrepancy by reexamining the basis on which it has approached freedoms derived from the separation of judicial power. Unless it does this, the development of notions such as due process in the exercise of judicial power may extend beyond the proper limits imposed by the Constitution, and at the same time may undermine the persuasiveness of High Court decision-making in this area. There are also greater dangers. As Kirby J remarked in *Kartinyeri v. Commonwealth* (1998) 152 ALR 540 at 584, 'judicial interpretation of the Constitution risks the loss of legitimacy if it shifts its ultimate focus of attention away from the text and structure of the document'.

Conclusion

There is no formula or rule that can be applied by the High Court in interpreting constitutional rights. The struggle to define an interpretative method will be an ongoing one that will parallel the process of giving meaning to the rights themselves. However, there are criteria against which High Court decisions can be examined. It is important that the High Court develop a coherent and consistent approach to the interpretation of the Australian Constitution, including to the construction of constitutional rights.

This is a necessary foundation for the long-term development of the express and implied rights in the Australian Constitution, lest such rights remain vulnerable to the changing composition of the High Court. Where the Court applies some other approach, or draws distinctions between otherwise similar provisions (or classes of rights) or between rights and powers, the Court must articulate the basis for this. This is necessary as part of the court giving reasons for its decisions, which in turn is necessary for both an acceptable level of certainty in constitutional interpretation and for meaningful scrutiny of the decisions of the Court.

For much of this century, the Court's approach to express constitutional rights has been characterised by a marked preference for the application of economic rights over civil and political rights. Recent decisions have shown that this preference has shifted and is no longer maintained. However, it is unclear whether the Court will adopt the course of the United States Supreme Court of reversing the preference. While this would seem unlikely, it is a direction open to the Court. It can be expected that interpretation in this area will remain in a state of flux until such issues are worked through and determined. Such issues are not as clear cut in Australia as they have been in the USA (where there was an upheaval in constitutional interpretation in the 1930s) or in Canada (where the Charter of Rights and Freedoms explicitly builds in a preference for civil and political rights over economic rights—see Chapter 6).

The High Court has also yet to develop a sustainable approach to the interpretation of implied civil and political rights. While decisions such as *McGinty* and *Lange* have gone a long way towards constructing a solid foundation for the implied freedom of political communication, the Court has yet to do the same for implications derived from the separation of judicial power. As a result, the ambit and nature of implications drawn from the latter source remain unclear and extremely uncertain. Developments in the 1990s have left the High Court with much work to do. In pushing the frontiers of Chapter III of the Constitution, the Court has outpaced its own development of constitutional methodology. This also occurred, for a time, in the development of the implied freedom of political communication. As has been the case in relation to that freedom, the Court must now establish a sound approach to underpin new concepts such as due process and the incompatibility doctrine, in order to retain the legitimacy of the High Court's decision-making. Decisions on concepts such as the incompatibility doctrine have yet to develop into a stable and predictable jurisprudence that is clearly founded in the text and structure of the Constitution.

The Future of Human Rights under the Australian Constitution

Introduction

The High Court's interpretation of constitutional rights presents a complex picture. Certainly, the Australian Constitution was not drafted to contain a Bill of Rights, yet for much of this century the High Court has failed to give a meaningful operation to those few civil and political rights that are expressed in the Constitution (see Chapter 5). The absence of the former seemingly overwhelmed the presence of the latter. It was not until the decision in *Street v. Queensland Bar Association* (1989) 168 CLR 461 that a plaintiff was successful in having the High Court apply an express civil and political right to strike down a law. Yet, during the same period that civil and political rights were narrowly interpreted, the Court applied, and generously construed, the economic rights in the Constitution (see Chapter 6). This double standard showed that the Court was not averse to applying rights to strike down Commonwealth and state legislation, just that it preferred to foster economic interests and a *laissez-faire* economy over civil and political freedoms (see Chapter 9). The jurisprudential methodology developed by the High Court in and since *Amalgamated Society of Engineers v. Adelaide Steamship Co. Ltd (Engineers Case)* (1920) 28 CLR 129, particularly its deference to the doctrines of legalism and literalism, enabled the Court to apply these different approaches and to maintain the value-neutral appearance of its work. Such an approach also underpinned the Court's overriding concern with issues involving the construction of Commonwealth power and Australian federalism (see Chapter 4).

This picture has shifted in the last decade. For many years, the legalistic approach applied by the High Court allowed it to cloak the policy preferences implicit in its decision-making.[1] This has begun to crumble as it has become increasingly apparent that the Court cannot make its decisions in a policy-neutral fashion. Constitutional methodology centred around legalism and literalism has been slowly abandoned by the Court as it has opened its decision-making to the influences of international law and

---

1   B. Galligan, *Politics of the High Court*, University of Queensland Press, 1987, pp. 30–41.

international norms (see Chapters 1 and 9). In this post-legalist era, judges have appealed to other sources such as community values,[2] and even to the Constitution as a 'living force'.[3] A key factor in this process of exposing the policy underpinnings of the Court's decision-making has been its new-found concern for human rights, and for the Constitution as a means of protecting such rights. This presents a striking contrast to the approach of an earlier Court. The judgment of Knox CJ, Isaacs, Rich, and Starke JJ in the *Engineers Case* argued against the Court implying rights from the Constitution to protect Australians from the abuse of power by their governments, stating at pp. 151–2:

> If it be conceivable that the representatives of the people of Australia as a whole would ever proceed to use their national powers to injure the people of Australia considered sectionally, it is certainly within the power of the people themselves to resent and reverse what may be done. No protection of this Court in such a case is necessary or proper.

How far the Court has come. Australians are increasingly turning to the High Court rather than the ballot box to protect their liberty. This is particularly true for Australians with little political power, such as Australia's indigenous peoples.[4] Time will tell whether such reliance will ultimately prove misguided. Nevertheless, by its decisions in cases such as *Kable v. Director of Public Prosecutions (NSW)* (1996) 189 CLR 51, in which it struck down an attempt by the New South Wales Parliament to enable a person to be imprisoned without having been found guilty of a criminal offence (see Chapter 8), the Court has shown itself willing to apply the Constitution creatively to protect fundamental freedoms. The Court has firmly thrust itself between the people and their elected governments, as a bulwark against the expression of arbitrary governmental power.

Some judges have pushed further than the rest of the Court. In particular, Murphy and Deane JJ have sought to achieve results that depend on a vision of the Constitution as intimately concerned with fostering individual freedom. They have given a glimpse of the Constitution as a document embodying many rights, indeed almost an implied Bill of Rights. While Murphy and Deane JJ might be applauded for their sympathy for human rights, their reasoning also presents great dangers. The Constitution offers much to the protection of civil liberties, but this should not be taken too far. The instrument was not designed to provide a general scheme of protection for fundamental freedoms. To interpret the Constitution as containing an implied Bill of Rights, or rights that amount to 'substantive due process' (see Chapters 6 and 8), would be to compromise the legitimacy of the High Court as the arbiter and interpreter of the Constitution. It would also compromise the role of the Australian people as the only body able to sanction basic constitutional reform. As Kirby P stated in *Building Construction Employees and Builders' Labourers Federation of New South Wales v. Minister for Industrial Relations* (1986) 7 NSWLR 372 at 405 of fundamental rights derived not from the Constitution but from the common law: 'Such extra-constitutional notions must be viewed with reservation not only because they lack the legitimacy that attaches to the enactments ultimately

---

2 A. Mason, 'The Role of a Constitutional Court in a Federation: A Comparison of the Australian and the United States Experience' (1986) 16 *Federal Law Review* 1 at 5 (see Chapter 4).
3 *Theophanous v. Herald & Weekly Times Ltd* (1994) 182 CLR 104 at 173 per Deane J.
4 See, for example, *Kruger v. Commonwealth* (1997) 190 CLR 1 (see Chapters 5, 7, and 8).

sanctioned by the people. But also because, once allowed, there is no logical limit to their ambit'.[5] The course charted by Murphy and Deane JJ would intrude the Court far into the legislative realm without an adequate constitutional mandate. Despite this author having heralded its demise,[6] the *Engineers Case* and its demand for a rigorous linkage between all constitutional doctrine and the text of the instrument still has a role to play in the field of constitutional rights.

Future directions in constitutional interpretation

Two factors have been primarily responsible for the narrow ambit given to many of the civil and political rights in the Constitution, at least up until 1989. First, the limited role seen for such rights in the 1890s Convention debates (see Chapter 2) has constrained the interpretation given to such rights by later judges. Even though it was not permissible for the High Court to have reference to such debates until the decision of the Court in *Cole v. Whitfield* (1988) 165 CLR 360, the narrow scope given to the express civil and political rights has had an uncanny propensity to reflect the limited aspirations of the framers. This was particularly evident in the Court's interpretations of sections 41 and 80, which deal respectively with the right to vote and trial by jury (see Chapter 5).

A second factor in the Court's narrow approach to certain rights has been the legalistic methodology of the High Court in its interpretation of the Constitution (see Chapter 4). However, legalism was not the cause of these narrow constructions. Legalism does not suggest results, just the methodology by which results can be achieved. As in the interpretation of the Commonwealth's s. 51 powers, legalism does not necessarily entail a broad or a narrow scope for constitutional rights. It merely allows the Court to cloak its own policy preferences in its construction of the Constitution. This is clearly demonstrated by the legalistic formulae developed by the Dixon Court in its application of the guarantee of freedom of interstate 'trade, commerce, and intercourse' in s. 92 (see Chapter 6), which gave an apparently neutral facade to a policy-charged area of the law.[7] Legalism, therefore, is the means by which the Court has hidden its preferences for some rights over others, notably economic rights over civil and political rights (see Chapter 9). It has also enabled the Court to implement its vision of the Constitution as a document concerned centrally with the granting of Commonwealth power and the interaction of the Commonwealth and the states.

As the High Court continues to play a role in the field of human rights, both the aspirations of the framers and legalism must be carefully scrutinised. Neither should be applied to restrict the derivation and application of constitutional rights. The Convention debates provide evidence of the strong policy objective of many, but by no means all, of the framers to create an instrument that was not sympathetic to fostering human rights. However, this should not be used to rule out the meaning that might otherwise

---

5   See G. Winterton, 'Extra-Constitutional Notions in Australian Constitutional Law' (1986) 16 *Federal Law Review* 223 at 239: 'Once the realm of extra-constitutional power has been entered, there is no logical limit to its ambit'.

6   G. Williams, '*Engineers* is Dead, Long Live the Engineers!' (1995) 17 *Sydney Law Review* 62.

7   L. Zines, *The High Court and the Constitution*, 4th edn, Butterworths, 1997, pp. 124–9.

be given to the express and implied rights recognised by the text of the Constitution. To do so would be to allow the framers' desire to permit the states to pass racially discriminatory laws to override the meaning that could otherwise be derived from the Constitution (see Chapters 2 and 4). Such a result could only be justified on a strongly originalist approach to interpretation that left little or no room for the Constitution to be revised or re-imagined in light of the changing values of the Australian people.[8] The failure to give weight to the views of the framers where such views are fundamentally inconsistent with the values held by Australians today or where another meaning is supported by the text of the Constitution, is not to abandon the Constitution. It is instead to recognise the role of the High Court of every generation to give meaning to the text of the Constitution in a developing legal and political landscape.

The High Court must also continue to re-evaluate legalism as an appropriate method of constitutional interpretation. One aspect of this process has been the recourse some judges, including Mason CJ, have had to notions such as 'community values' (see Chapter 4). The decisions of judges such as Murphy and Deane JJ amount to a challenge to legalism. Murphy J conceived the Constitution as 'a Constitution for a free society',[9] while Deane J implemented his vision of the Constitution as a 'living force'.[10] Both are radical departures from Dixonian 'strict and complete legalism'.[11] The policy-, or perhaps results-oriented nature of some of the decisions of Murphy and Deane JJ in the field of constitutional rights is diametrically at odds with legalism and its preoccupation with close analysis of the text of the instrument and authoritative legal sources. The challenge posed by such non-legalistic reasoning has yet to be resolved. However, it has become clear, in the words of Stephen Gageler, that legalism simply cannot 'achieve the level of objectivity on which its legitimacy depends'.[12] Murphy and Deane JJ have exposed the failure of legalism to remove the need for policy choices. The power of legalism instead lies in its ability to render decision-making by the Court apparently neutral. This has enabled the Court to apply the double standards and unarticulated premises that have formed the backbone of much of the High Court's work in the area of constitutional rights over this century (see Chapter 9).

The formidable task before the High Court in this post-legalist era is to articulate the relevant policy considerations as well as the choices inevitably involved in its interpretation of the Constitution. The Court is moving slowly in this direction. In doing so it is beginning the process of setting down a constitutional methodology that is more explicit and open. This is particularly apparent where the Court has recognised that the text of the Constitution is not determinative, but ambiguous. In such cases, the judges of the High Court have shown an increasing tendency to indicate the policy or other factors that have shaped their decision. A good example is the judgment of Kirby J in *Newcrest Mining (WA) Ltd v. Commonwealth* (1997) 147 ALR 42. In that decision, Kirby J

---

8   That such a process may be necessary is shown, in the Canadian context, by Webber, J, *Reimagining Canada: Language, Culture, Community, and the Canadian Constitution*, McGill-Queen's University Press, 1994.

9   *R v. Director-General of Social Welfare (Vic); Ex parte Henry* (1975) 133 CLR 369 at 388.

10 *Theophanous v. Herald & Weekly Times Ltd* (1994) 182 CLR 104 at 173.

11 'Swearing in of Sir Owen Dixon as Chief Justice' (1951) 85 CLR xi at xiv.

12 S. Gageler, 'Foundations of Australian Federalism and the Role of Judicial Review' (1987) 17 *Federal Law Review* 162 at 181.

argued strongly for the role of international norms in shaping the interpretation of the Constitution (see Chapter 1). He also set out the following statement of principle at p. 147: 'Where the Constitution is ambiguous, this court should adopt that meaning which conforms to the principles of fundamental rights rather than an interpretation which would involve a departure from such rights'.[13] In time, this statement may come to be as powerful a dictum in favour of a broad construction of constitutional rights as the statement of O'Connor J in *Jumbunna Coal Mine NL v. Victorian Coal Miners' Association* (1908) 6 CLR 309 at 367–8, which favours a broad scope being given to Commonwealth powers.

Much of the Court's struggle to create a post-legalist approach to constitutional interpretation will continue to lie in its derivation of implications from the separation of judicial power (see Chapter 8) and the system of representative government created by the Constitution (see Chapter 7). In decisions such as *McGinty v. Western Australia* (1996) 186 CLR 140 and *Lange v. Australian Broadcasting Corporation* (1997) 189 CLR 520, the Court went a long way towards erecting a solid foundation for rights derived from the system of representative government. On the other hand, it has much further to go with regard to rights implied from the separation of judicial power. Thus far, the reasoning of the Court on freedoms from the separation of judicial power has failed to coalesce into a persuasive and stable jurisprudence (see Chapter 9). This is disturbing given evidence that rights taken from this latter source, such as a guarantee of due process, have the potential to support widespread judicial intervention in social and political issues thus far considered to be the domain of Australian legislatures.

The future is promising for the development of constitutional rights. The text of the Constitution is capable of supporting significant protection for fundamental freedoms. However, it is critical that this future is not seen as an unbounded one. The development and growth of constitutional rights is limited by the lack of any Bill of Rights in the Constitution, something that has not always been apparent in judgments by Murphy and Deane JJ, particularly those decisions where recourse was had to common law concepts lying outside the Constitution. Unless the judges of the High Court are to follow the path of Murphy J and derive rights from their perceptions of the Constitution as 'a Constitution for a free society'[14] or Deane and Toohey JJ in *Leeth v. Commonwealth* (1992) 174 CLR 455, and find a right to equality under the law implicit in both the common law and the Constitution, there will be little or no scope for the High Court to guarantee rights such as a freedom from sexual, or racial, discrimination, or indeed many of the rights listed in instruments such as the *International Covenant on Civil and Political Rights 1966* and the *International Covenant on Economic, Social and Cultural Rights 1966* (see Chapter 1). Such rights may be a 'good thing', but they cannot be justified unless they are supported by an adequate constitutional foundation. To retain the confidence of the Australian people as the interpreter of the Constitution and the protector of their rights, the Court must be seen to be limited in its role. If it exercises an unfettered discretion or travels beyond what the text and structure of the Constitution can reasonably support, the Court will have committed the same error as any institution of government that has exercised arbitrary power. As McHugh J stated in

---

13 Kirby J again set out this approach in *Kartinyeri v. Commonwealth* (1998) 152 ALR 540 at 598.
14 *R v. Director-General of Social Welfare (Vic); Ex parte Henry* (1975) 133 CLR 369 at 388.

Theophanous v. Herald & Weekly Times Ltd (1994) 182 CLR 104 at 197: 'If this Court is to retain the confidence of the nation as the final arbiter of what the Constitution means, no interpretation of the Constitution by the Court can depart from the text of the Constitution and what is implied by the text and the structure of the Constitution'.

Much can be achieved with the Constitution that Australia already has. However, there is also much that cannot be achieved. For example, the Court has been able to protect political communication by applying an implication drawn from the system of representative government created by the Constitution. However, the Constitution is unable to support a general freedom of expression, and thus artistic expression containing no political comment lacks constitutional protection. This demonstrates that to protect basic rights such as a general freedom of expression there is a need for legal reform. Constitutional or statutory reform should be the long-term goal of any attempt to protect civil liberties in Australia. Ironically, any move by the High Court to recognise an implied Bill of Rights may undermine attempts to bring about such reform. If the Constitution is seen to protect the full spectrum of fundamental rights, why embark on the exhaustive process of drafting a Bill of Rights?

A Bill of Rights for Australia?

Proposals for change

Several states and territories have made faltering steps towards enacting a Bill of Rights. Despite several reports advocating a Bill of Rights,[15] and even the introduction of such Bills into state parliaments,[16] the necessary state and territory legislation has yet to be passed. At best, state and territory statutes have recognised rights on an ad hoc basis, such as the right of peaceful assembly in the *Peaceful Assembly Act 1992* (Qld). This has left much of the focus for change at the federal level. At that level there has been advocacy for both a statutory Bill of Rights and a constitutional Bill of Rights.

Amendment of the Australian Constitution is provided for by means of a referendum under s. 128. This is the only way that the text of the Constitution can be altered, s. 128 providing that 'This Constitution shall not be altered except' in the manner set out in that section. A referendum proposal under s. 128 must be passed by an absolute majority of both houses of the federal Parliament, or by one House twice,[17] and then by a majority of the people and by a majority of the people in a majority of the states—that is, in at least four of the six states. Under s. 45 of the

---

15 Australian Capital Territory Attorney-General's Department, *A Bill of Rights for the ACT?*, Australian Capital Territory, 1993; Constitutional Committee of the Victorian Parliament, *Report on the Desirability or Otherwise of Legislation Defining and Protecting Human Rights*, Victorian Government Printer, 1987; Electoral and Administrative Review Commission (Qld), *Report on Review of the Preservation and Enhancement of Individuals' Rights and Freedoms*, Electoral and Administrative Review Commission (Qld), August 1993; Sessional Committee on Constitutional Development (NT), *Final Draft Constitution for the Northern Territory*, Legislative Assembly of the Northern Territory, August 1996. See S. Gibb and K. Eastman, 'Why are we Talking About a Bill of Rights?' (1995) 33(7) *Law Society Journal* 49.

16 Constitution (Declaration of Rights) Bill 1959 (Qld); Constitution (Declaration of Rights and Freedoms) Bill 1988 (Vic). See Australian Capital Territory Attorney-General's Department, pp. 91–3; Electoral and Administrative Review Commission (Qld), pp. 51–3.

17 However, by convention, should a referendum proposal be passed twice by the Senate against the wishes of the government, it still need not be submitted to the people unless the Governor-General is instructed by the executive to do so.

Referendum (Machinery Provisions) Act 1984 (Cth), voting in a referendum is compulsory. Forty-two proposals have been put to the Australian people under s. 128. Of these, only eight have succeeded.[18]

The reasons put forward for the failure of over 80 per cent of the proposals put to the people are many, ranging from an in-built reluctance of the Australian people to vote for any change to the Constitution, to inadequate political management that has meant that few proposals have gained the support of each of the major political parties.[19] On the other hand, it has been argued that the reluctance of the Australian people to vote 'Yes' demonstrates the 'innate good sense of the voters who have said "No" so often and often so loudly'.[20] This latter argument is difficult to reconcile with the ignorance of the Australian people about their Constitution. The 1994 report on citizenship by the Civics Expert Group[21] found that only 18 per cent of Australians have some understanding of what their Constitution contains, while only 40 per cent could correctly name both Houses of the Federal Parliament. More than a quarter of those surveyed nominated the Supreme Court, rather than the High Court, as the 'top' court in Australia.[22]

The need for a double majority in a referendum held under s. 128 (that is, a national majority as well as state majorities in at least four states) has not proved to be a significant impediment to constitutional change. Only in three instances, two referendums held on 28 September 1946 (on the exclusion of cooperative marketing schemes from s. 92 and an additional Commonwealth power over industrial employment) and one on 21 May 1977 (on simultaneous elections for both Houses of the Federal Parliament), would the removal of the requirement for a state majority in at least four states have enabled the referendum to be carried. The evidence instead suggests that to be successful a referendum must gain support across Australia. In every case where a referendum was carried, with the exception of the referendum of 13 April 1910 that amended s. 105, a national majority was accompanied by a majority voting 'Yes' in every state.

There have been several attempts to bring about an Australian Bill of Rights or to amend the Constitution to incorporate new fundamental rights.[23] In 1942 it was

---

18 For the results of each referendum, see A. R. Blackshield and G. Williams, *Australian Constitutional Law and Theory: Commentary and Materials*, 2nd edn, Federation Press, 1998, pp. 1183–8. See generally E. Campbell, 'Changing the Constitution—Past and Future' (1989) 17 *Melbourne University Law Review* 1; M. Coper, *Encounters With the Australian Constitution*, CCH, 1988, ch. 9; J. Crawford 'Amendment of the Constitution' in G. Craven (ed.), *Australian Federation: Towards the Second Century*, Melbourne University Press, 1992, p. 177; B. Galligan, *A Federal Republic: Australia's Constitutional System of Government*, Cambridge University Press, 1995, ch. 5; House of Representatives Standing Committee on Legal and Constitutional Affairs, Parliament of Australia, *Constitutional Change: Select Sources on Constitutional Change in Australia 1901–1997*, AGPS, 1997.

19 M. Coper, *Encounters with the Australian Constitution*, CCH, 1988, ch. 9; J. McMillan, 'Constitutional Reform in Australia', in *One People, One Destiny*, Papers on Parliament, No. 13, Department of the Senate, November 1991, p. 63.

20 J. C. Finemore, 'Commentary' in G Evans (ed.), *Labor and the Constitution 1972–1975*, Heinemann Educational, 1977, p. 94.

21 Civics Expert Group, *Whereas the People: Civics and Citizenship Education*, AGPS, 1994, p. 133.

22 Civics Expert Group, p. 133.

23 See P. Bailey, *Human Rights: Australia in an International Context*, Butterworths, 1990, pp. 51–5; H. Charlesworth, 'The Australian Reluctance About Rights' (1993) 31 *Osgoode Hall Law Journal* 195 at 205–10; B. Galligan, 'Australia's Rejection of a Bill of Rights' (1990) 28 *Journal of Commonwealth and Comparative Politics* 344; P. Hanks, 'Constitutional Guarantees', in H. P. Lee and G. Winterton (eds), *Australian Constitutional Perspectives*, 1992, pp. 123–6; N. O'Neill and R. Handley, *Retreat from Injustice: Human Rights in Australian Law*, Federation Press, 1994, pp. 79–83.

proposed at the Constitutional Convention held in Canberra that the Commonwealth be given a series of new powers. Such powers were to include the power to make laws with respect to: 'carrying into effect the guarantee of the four freedoms, that is to say— (i) freedom of speech and expression; (ii) religious freedom; (iii) freedom from want; and (iv) freedom from fear'.[24] This proposal would not have amounted to new guarantees of rights, but would have given the Commonwealth the power to legislate to guarantee such rights from abrogation by state legislation. Under s. 109 of the Constitution, inconsistent state legislation would have been rendered inoperative (see Chapter 1). This provision did not emerge in the proposal that went to the people in a referendum held on 19 August 1944. Instead the referendum proposal put to the people was that the Constitution be amended to grant the Commonwealth 14 new heads of power over post-war reconstruction. The proposal also sought to insert guarantees of speech and expression, as well as extend the guarantee of religious freedom in s. 116 (see Chapter 5) to the states.[25] These powers and guarantees would only have operated for a period of five years. The referendum was lost with a 45.39 per cent 'Yes' vote to a 53.30 per cent 'No' vote.

The referendum that has received the highest 'Yes' vote was a proposal put to the people on 27 May 1967.[26] That referendum gained the support of 89.34 per cent of voters and was carried overwhelmingly in every state.[27] Previously, s. 51(xxvi) of the Constitution had empowered the Parliament to make laws with respect to 'The people of any race, *other than the aboriginal race in any State,* for whom it is deemed necessary to make special laws' (emphasis added). The 1967 referendum deleted the words in italics. It also repealed s. 127 of the Constitution, which had provided, 'In reckoning the numbers of the people of the Commonwealth, or of a State or other part of the Commonwealth, aboriginal natives shall not be counted'. Although these changes to the Constitution have been popularly seen as granting Aboriginal people 'equal rights' and in particular the right to vote,[28] this is not correct. The right to vote in federal elections had been denied to Aboriginal people by s. 4 of the *Commonwealth Franchise Act 1902* (Cth). This was reversed and the franchise extended to Aboriginal people by amendments to the *Commonwealth Electoral Act 1918* (Cth) made in 1962.[29] Although the 1967 changes to the text of the Constitution gave recognition to Aboriginal people and repealed the discriminatory s. 127, they did not actually grant Aboriginal people any rights. Indeed, it remains unclear whether the extension of the races power in s. 51(xxvi) to Aboriginal people gave the federal Parliament the power to legislate for the benefit *as well as the detriment* of Aboriginal people.[30] This point was argued before the

---

24 *Post-war Reconstruction: A Case for Greater Commonwealth Powers*, Government Printer, 1942, p. 116.
25 Constitutional Alteration (Post-War Reconstruction and Democratic Rights) Bill 1944 (Cth).
26 See B. Attwood and A. Markus, *The 1967 Referendum, or When Aborigines Didn't Get the Vote*, Aboriginal Studies Press, 1997.
27 The 'Yes' vote is sometimes cited as being 90.77 per cent. However, this figure excludes the fact that 1.58 per cent of votes cast were informal.
28 See Attwood and Markus, ch. 5.
29 *Commonwealth Electoral Act* 1962 (Cth).
30 See Blackshield and Williams, pp. 164–76; M. J. Detmold, 'Original Intentions and the Race Power' (1997) 8 *Public Law Review* 244; N. Pengelley, 'The Hindmarsh Island Bridge Act. Must Laws Based on the Race Power be for the "Benefit" of Aborigines and Torres Strait Islanders? And What Has Bridge Building Got to Do with the Race Power Anyway?' (1998) 20 *Sydney Law Review* 144; J. Williams and J. Bradsen, 'The Perils of Inclusion: The Constitution and the Race Power' (1997) 19 *Adelaide Law Review* 95.

High Court in *Kartinyeri v. Commonwealth* (1998) 152 ALR 540.[31] However, the Court failed to resolve the issue; Gummow and Hayne JJ suggested that the power could be used to impose a detriment on Aboriginal people, Gaudron and Kirby JJ found that this would not be constitutionally permissible, and Brennan CJ and McHugh J did not decide the question. The case was heard by only six judges, Callinan J having disqualified himself from deciding the matter.

Despite the success of the 1967 referendum, the next two attempts to bring about greater protection for fundamental rights came in the form of statutory Bills of Rights. In 1973 Lionel Murphy, as Attorney-General in the Whitlam Labor Government, introduced the Human Rights Bill 1973 (Cth) into the federal Parliament. The Bill sought to implement the *International Covenant on Civil and Political Rights 1966* (see Chapter 1) in Australia and would have protected a range of rights such as freedom of expression, freedom of movement, the right to marry and found a family, and individual privacy.[32] It even sought to prohibit 'Any propaganda for war'.[33] Murphy promoted the Bill on the basis that the Constitution provides scant protection for rights, arguing that 'although we believe these rights to be basic to our democratic society, they now receive remarkably little legal protection in Australia'.[34] He stated:

> What protection is given by the Australian Constitution is minimal and does not touch the most significant of these rights ... Ideally, in my view, a Bill of Rights should be written into the Australian Constitution ... [T]he enactment of this legislation will be a significant milestone in the political maturity of Australia. It will help to make Australian society more free and more just.[35]

Under s. 109 of the Constitution, the rights listed in the Bill would have overridden inconsistent state legislation. The Bill provided that Commonwealth legislation would also be ineffective if it breached any of the rights listed in the Bill, unless the Commonwealth statute expressly provided that it was to operate notwithstanding the Bill (see pp. 266–9).[36] It also went further than subsequent attempts at statutory Bills of Rights in one critical respect. The rights listed could be enforced not only against governmental action, but also against private action.[37] The Human Rights Bill met strong opposition and was never enacted, lapsing with the prorogation of Parliament in early 1974. Murphy was appointed soon after to the High Court, where he broadly interpreted the express rights in the Constitution (see Chapter 5) and discovered that a number of other rights could be implied by the instrument (see Chapter 7).

The failure of the Human Rights Bill did not end attempts to bring about rights protection by Commonwealth implementation of international instruments. The Whitlam Government, for example, was successful in enacting the *Racial Discrimination Act 1975* (Cth), while the Hawke Labor Government enacted the *Sex Discrimination Act 1984* (Cth). Senator Gareth Evans, as Attorney-General in the Hawke Labor Government sought to take up where Murphy had left off in promoting a statutory Bill of

---

31 The author appeared in this case as counsel for the plaintiffs.
32 Human Rights Bill, sections 11, 16, 18, 19.
33 Human Rights Bill, s. 12.
34 Australia, Senate, November 1973, *Debates*, vol. 58, p. 1972.
35 Australia, Senate, November 1973, *Debates*, vol. 58, pp. 1972–4.
36 Human Rights Bill, s. 5(3).
37 Human Rights Bill, s. 40.

Rights. In 1983 he oversaw the drafting of a Bill of Rights Bill that, like its 1973 predecessor, would have implemented international rights instruments. However, the 1983 model was weaker than its 1973 predecessor in several ways[38]—most significantly in that it would only have applied to governmental action, whereas the Murphy Bill would have applied to any action that infringed the protected rights. Although the Evans Bill was given Cabinet support, it was not introduced into Parliament. Lionel Bowen replaced Evans as Attorney-General after the December 1984 federal election. After being redrafted and its operation watered down,[39] the Bill was introduced into the federal Parliament in November 1985 as the Australian Human Rights Bill 1985 (Cth). It was passed by the House of Representatives, but failed to gain majority support in the Senate. Encountering strong opposition, the Bill was finally withdrawn in November 1986.[40]

The Bills promoted by Murphy, Evans, and Bowen sought to enact a statutory Bill of Rights. In the wake of the failure of the Bowen Bill, the Government changed tack. It established the Constitutional Commission in December 1985 to report on the revision of the Australian Constitution in order, among other things, to 'ensure that democratic rights are guaranteed'.[41] The Commission was assisted by an Advisory Committee on Individual and Democratic Rights under the Constitution. This Committee reported in 1987.[42] It did not recommend a Bill of Rights as such, but instead recommended the insertion of several new rights to be scattered throughout the Constitution. Overall, the proposal was a relatively modest one. While it proposed new rights such as 'a right to a speedy trial'[43] and a right to vote, rather than suggesting that the Constitution should guarantee freedom of expression generally, the Committee found that it should only protect expression 'concerning government, public policy, and administration, and politics'.[44] Moreover, it recommended that under a new s. 117A, a Commonwealth or state parliament should be able to abrogate the rights listed in the Constitution by passing legislation expressly stating a statute was to 'operate notwithstanding' the constitutional guarantee.[45]

The Constitutional Commission responded in an interim report in April 1987,[46] in which it made recommendations to expand the scope of the express rights already in the Constitution, but also foreshadowed the need for wider change. For example, it was recommended that the protection of religious freedom in s. 116 of the Constitution be extended to laws passed by the states and territories. The Commission's final report was

---

38 Charlesworth, at 208–9.
39 Charlesworth, at 209; O'Neill and Handley, *Retreat from Injustice: Human Rights in Australian Law*, Federation Press, 1994, pp. 81–2.
40 The government was, however, successful in enacting the *Human Rights and Equal Opportunity Commission Act 1986* (Cth).
41 Constitutional Commission, *Final Report of the Constitutional Commission*, AGPS, 1988, vol. 1, p. 1.
42 Constitutional Commission, *Report of the Advisory Committee on Individual & Democratic Rights under the Constitution*, AGPS, 1987.
43 Constitutional Commission, *Report of the Advisory Committee on Individual & Democratic Rights under the Constitution*, p. 49.
44 Constitutional Commission, *Report of the Advisory Committee on Individual & Democratic Rights under the Constitution*, p. 55.
45 Constitutional Commission, *Report of the Advisory Committee on Individual & Democratic Rights under the Constitution*, p. 38.
46 Constitutional Commission, *First Report of the Constitutional Commission*, 2 vols, AGPS, 1988.

provided in June 1988,[47] and was far more ambitious. It proposed significantly greater protection for rights by constitutional means than had the Advisory Committee. The Commission recommended that a new Chapter ('Chapter VIA—Rights and Freedoms'[48]) containing a wide range of fundamental rights, drawn heavily from the Canadian Charter of Rights and Freedoms, should be inserted into the Constitution.[49] It also recommended that a person whose rights were breached should be able to gain an appropriate remedy in the courts. The Commission rejected the limited guarantee of expression proposed by its Advisory Committee, and instead recommended a freedom of expression not limited as to content.[50] The Commission also rejected the insertion of a provision that would allow the Commonwealth or the states to pass legislation 'notwithstanding' a guarantee in the Constitution. A majority of the Commission found that a power to 'opt-out' or override constitutional guarantees 'is inconsistent with the whole process of entrenching rights in the Constitution'.[51]

Bowen had requested that the Commission provide an interim report so that a referendum to amend the Constitution could be held in 1988, the bicentenary of White settlement of Australia. Accordingly, after the interim report had been provided, but before the Commission had completed its final report, the Hawke Government announced that it would initiate constitutional change. Legislation was introduced to this effect on 10 May 1988 and four proposals were put to the Australian people on 3 September 1988. The proposals were derived, with some variations,[52] from the recommendations of the Constitutional Commission in its interim report. The first and third proposals concerned four-year maximum terms for the federal Parliament and recognition of local government, respectively. The second proposal sought to guarantee 'one vote one value' by requiring that the population count in each electorate not deviate by more than 10 per cent. This proposal would also have inserted a right to vote into the Constitution.[53] The fourth proposal also sought to guarantee basic freedoms, but only by extending the operation of existing guarantees in the Constitution.[54] Section 80 would have been repealed and replaced with a provision guaranteeing trial by jury for offences under Commonwealth, state, and territory laws 'where the accused is liable to imprisonment for more than two years or any form of corporal punishment'. New sections 115A and 115B would have extended the guarantee of 'just terms' for any 'acquisition of property' to state laws and laws made in respect of the territories by the Commonwealth under s. 122 of the Constitution. Finally, s. 116 would have been deleted and replaced with a section guaranteeing the religious freedom already spelt out in s. 116 not just in regard to Commonwealth laws but also in respect of laws passed by a state or territory.

All four proposals were defeated. The results were dismal. The highest national 'Yes' vote for any of the proposals was 37.10 per cent, which was in respect of the proposal on 'one vote one value'. The fourth proposal received an astonishingly low vote, the

---

47 Constitutional Commission, *Final Report of the Constitutional Commission*, 2 vols.
48 Constitutional Commission, *Final Report of the Constitutional Commission*, vol. 1, p. 476.
49 See G. Ferguson, 'The Impact of an Entrenched Bill of Rights: The Canadian Experience' (1990) 16 *Monash University Law Review* 211 at 216–17.
50 Constitutional Commission, *Final Report of the Constitutional Commission*, vol. 1, p. 508.
51 Constitutional Commission, *Final Report of the Constitutional Commission*, vol. 1, p. 492.
52 See Hanks, pp. 125–6.
53 Constitution Alteration (Fair Elections) Bill 1988 (Cth).
54 Constitution Alteration (Rights and Freedoms) Bill 1988 (Cth).

lowest of any of the proposals. Nationally, 30.33 per cent of voters registered a 'Yes' vote, while 68.19 per cent voted 'No'. This was the lowest 'Yes' vote ever recorded in any referendum. In South Australia, the 'Yes' vote was only 25.53 per cent, while in Tasmania it was 25.10 per cent. The failure of the 1988 referendum undermined any suggestions that an attempt should be made to insert other rights into the Constitution or to implement the final report of the Constitutional Commission.

The 1988 referendum showed the difficulty in gaining the popular vote for constitutional change.[55] It demonstrated that bipartisan support for a proposal will be essential for successful constitutional change and that the support of the Australian people cannot be assumed, even for a proposal that is designed to protect the rights of Australians as against government. Lack of bipartisan support leaves open the prospect of a determined opposition misrepresenting the effects of constitutional change through use of the media for its own political purposes. To achieve reform in the area of constitutional rights it will be necessary to build a broad political and popular base for change, underpinned by real understanding of the issues and proposals. The result in 1967, as well as a recent successful referendum in New South Wales that entrenched judicial independence and the security of tenure of judges in the *Constitution Act 1902* (NSW),[56] shows that it is possible to harness the will of the Australian people in favour of changing the Constitution to protect human rights. However, the 1988 result shows that this is by no means easy and that any attempt to insert new rights into the Constitution should be carefully considered and prepared.

The failure of the 1988 proposals was a factor in the lack of headway made by rights issues at the 1998 Constitutional Convention.[57] That Convention was called by the federal government to debate an Australian republic. It was based on the assumption that Australia would be a republic once there is an Australian as Head of State, a narrow view of what it means to be a republic. The focus of the Convention was on change to the symbols and traditions of the Constitution, and not on deeper issues such as federalism and the financial problems of the states, or the need to protect human rights. It was even deemed to be beyond the scope of the Convention to discuss the Australian flag or the Australian coat of arms. Although some delegates were elected to the Convention on the basis that Australia could not be said to be a republic unless the Constitution were to protect fundamental freedoms, there was little support for the canvassing of rights issues at the Convention. This was because Prime Minister John Howard had limited the agenda of the Convention to issues concerning whether, when and how Australia might make the transition to a republic. It was also due to the belief of many republicans at the Convention, who might otherwise have supported a Bill of Rights, that to concurrently consider the republic and a Bill of Rights would be to load the republican option with a millstone at any subsequent referendum.

There was, however, some recognition at the 1998 Convention of the need to protect basic rights. The Communique of the Convention[58] recognised the need to incor-

55 See B. Galligan and J. R. Nethercote, *The Constitutional Commission and the 1988 Referendums*, Centre for Research on Federal Financial Relations, Australian National University, 1989.
56 *Constitution Act 1902* (NSW), s. 7B and Part 9, as amended by the *Constitution (Entrenchment) Amendment Act 1992* (NSW).
57 See, on the Convention, G. Williams, 'The People's Convention?' (1998) 23 *Alternative Law Journal* 2.
58 *Report of the Constitutional Convention*, vol. 1, *Report of Proceedings*, Commonwealth of Australia, 1998, pp. 42–50.

porate a new preamble to the Constitution in the event of a shift to a republic. It was agreed that this preamble should include, among other things, affirmation of the rule of law and acknowledgment of the original occupancy and custodianship of Australia by Aboriginal peoples and Torres Strait Islanders. The Convention left open whether the following should also be recognised: affirmation of the equality of all people before the law, recognition of gender equality, and recognition that Aboriginal people and Torres Strait islanders have continuing rights by virtue of their status as Australia's indigenous peoples. Any force such provisions might have had as an aid to constitutional interpretation was muted by the decision of the Convention that the preamble should be of symbolic relevance only, and should not have any legal effect. To this end, it was resolved that Chapter III of the Constitution should be amended to state that the preamble could not be used to interpret other provisions of the Constitution. Ironically, this would prevent the High Court from applying the values and aspirations entrenched in the preamble to the Constitution by popular vote, leaving it instead to develop its own conception of 'community values' (see Chapter 4).

The Convention delegates also supported an ongoing constitutional review process. The Convention resolved that, if a republican system of government should be introduced by referendum, at a date being not less than three years or more than five years thereafter, the Commonwealth government should convene a further Constitutional Convention. This Convention would review the operation and effectiveness of the republican system of government introduced by a constitutional referendum, as well as address any other matter related to the operation of the Australian system of government under republican arrangements, including the rights and responsibilities of citizenship and constitutional aspects of indigenous reconciliation. If the Australian people support a republic at a referendum, this ongoing constitutional review process might be an appropriate forum in which to debate the merits of an Australian Bill of Rights.

For and against

There are strong arguments for and against a Bill of Rights for Australia. The most significant arguments are set out below.[59]

The main arguments for a Bill of Rights

- Australian law affords inadequate protection to fundamental freedoms.
- It would give recognition to certain universal rights.
- It would give power of action to Australians who are otherwise powerless.
- It would bring Australia into line with the rest of the world
- It would meet Australia's international obligations.
- It would enhance Australian democracy by protecting the rights of minorities.
- It would put rights above politics.
- It would improve government policy-making and administrative decision-making.

---

59 Adapted from Bailey, pp. 62–76; Constitutional Commission, *Report of the Advisory Committee on Individual and Democratic Rights under the Constitution*, chs 3 and 4; M. Kirby, 'The Bill of Rights Debate' (1994) 29(11) *Australian Lawyer* 16; Legal, Constitutional and Administrative Review Committee (Qld), *The Preservation and Enhancement of Individuals' Rights and Freedoms: Should Queensland Adopt a Bill of Rights?*, Legislative Assembly of Queensland, Issues Paper No. 3, September 1997, pp. 8–9; M. A. Zander, *A Bill of Rights?*, 4th edn, Sweet & Maxwell, 1997.

- It would serve an important educative function.
- It would promote tolerance and understanding in the community.

The main arguments against a Bill of Rights

- Rights are already well protected in Australia.
- The political system itself is the best protection of rights in Australia.
- It would be undemocratic to give unelected judges the power to override the judgment of a parliament.
- It would politicise the Australian judiciary.
- It would be very expensive given the amount of litigation it would be likely to generate.
- It would be alien to the Westminster tradition of parliamentary sovereignty.
- It would actually restrict rights because to define a right is to limit it.
- It would ignore legitimate differences between different regions of Australia.
- Rights listed in constitutions or statutes actually make little or no difference to the protection of fundamental freedoms.
- It would be unnecessary, as the High Court is already protecting rights through its interpretation of the Constitution and its development of the common law.
- It would be unable to take account of changing conceptions of rights and would protect some rights (for example, the right to bear arms) that might not be so important to future generations.

A Bill of Rights has many weaknesses and limitations (see Chapter 3). Some of these are apparent in the Canadian Charter of Rights and Freedoms and, perhaps more clearly, in the United States Bill of Rights. However, this does not negate the importance of such an instrument. Overall, the importance of protecting fundamental rights against the exercise of arbitrary government power makes the case for a Bill of Rights compelling. An Australian Bill of Rights would have the potential to make a positive and lasting contribution to the liberty of Australians. The statement made 30 years ago, without overdue exaggeration, that 'the rights of individuals in Australia are as adequately protected as they are in any other country in the world',[60] could not be repeated with conviction today. Sir Anthony Mason, former Chief Justice of the High Court, has become a strong proponent of a Bill of Rights.[61] He has remarked:

> the common law system, supplemented as it presently is by statutes designed to protect particular rights, does not protect fundamental rights as comprehensively as do constitutional guarantees and conventions on human rights ... The common law is not as invincible a safeguard against violations of fundamental rights as it was once thought to be.[62]

The correctness of this statement has even been recognised in the United Kingdom, where the Human Rights Bill 1998 has been introduced into the British Parliament.[63]

---

60 R. Menzies, *Central Power in the Australian Commonwealth*, Cassell, 1967, p. 54.
61 See A. Mason, 'A Bill of Rights for Australia?' (1989) 5 *Australian Bar Review* 79. Compare H. Gibbs, 'The Constitutional Protection of Human Rights' (1982) 9 *Monash University Law Review* 1.
62 Mason, 'The Role of a Constitutional Court in a Federation: A Comparison of the Australian and the United States Experience' (1986) 16 *Federal Law Review* 1 at 12. See J. Toohey, 'A Government of Laws, and Not of Men?' (1993) 4 *Public Law Review* 158 at 163.
63 See Lord Irvine of Lairg, 'The Development of Human Rights in Britain under an Incorporated Convention on Human Rights' [1998] *Public Law* 221.

The failure of the several attempts to bring about statutory or constitutional change to better protect human rights in Australia demonstrates that a rights regime cannot be imposed on the Australian people. Neither should it be. An imposed regime would not achieve the aims of an Australian Bill of Rights. Rights are meaningless unless they are respected within an appropriate legal and cultural environment. What is necessary is change that engenders a culture of rights protection, including a tolerance and respect for rights, built on the fundamental values held by the Australian people.[64] Accordingly, any scheme that is designed to better protect civil liberties by way of constitutional or statutory change must be judged according to its potential not only to change the text of the law but to also bring about a culture of rights protection in Australia. This has been a notable success of the Canadian Charter, which has been praised for its 'success in enhancing the "culture of liberty" in Canada'.[65] It was also an area in which the failed 1988 referendum to change the Australian Constitution was conspicuously lacking.

Philip Pettit has developed a conception of republican theory that views 'freedom as non-domination':[66] that is, that individual liberty exists where a person is independent from the dominion of another. One precondition of non-domination is that rights are known by the person entitled to the right and are a matter of common knowledge in the rest of the community.[67] In essence, rights are only effective, and individuals are only free from domination, within a community permeated by a culture of rights protection. Rights that exist as a matter of shared knowledge can be located within a social and political context, and not merely as legal phenomena. Otherwise, rights are merely text on a page and thereby suffer from many of the criticisms that have been levelled at them as part of the critique of rights debate (see Chapter 3).

This exposes the inadequacies of any system of rights protection based on the High Court implying a Bill of Rights from the Constitution. It also suggests a weakness of the rights already implied by the Court from the separation of judicial power and the system of representative government created by the Constitution (see Chapters 8 and 7 respectively). Implied rights are unlikely to become matters of common knowledge and invocation if they are created by the High Court, even if they are soundly based in the text of the Constitution. They lack the community participation involved in the process of bringing about either a statutory or constitutional Bill of Rights. While judicial leadership on rights is better than no leadership at all, it is a poor substitute for political and popular leadership. It will be extremely difficult to bring about a rights culture in Australia except where rights are founded on the commitment of the Australian people or their elected representatives. The social and political background to rights created in this way may also assist the High Court in its role by giving it the context necessary to balance rights against other community interests. This would not necessarily resolve the issue of how a right should be interpreted but it would assist a court in ascertaining the appropriate limits of a right and where it might draw the line between the judicial and

---

64   See J. Braithwaite, 'Community Values and Australian Jurisprudence' (1995) 17 *Sydney Law Review* 351.

65   R. Penner, 'The Canadian Experience with the Charter of Rights: Are there Lessons for the United Kingdom?' [1996] *Public Law* 104 at 123.

66   P. Pettit, *Republicanism: A Theory of Freedom and Government*, Oxford University Press, 1997, p. 51.

67   J. Braithwaite and P. Pettit, *Not Just Deserts: A Republican Theory of Criminal Justice*, Clarendon Press, 1990, p. 65.

political process. This line-drawing may be more difficult where rights are essentially judicial, as opposed to popular, creations.

The role of the judiciary

The judiciary is central to the arguments for and against a Bill of Rights. A Bill of Rights would grant the judiciary a key role in enhancing the protection of human rights in Australian law. However, the judiciary would not itself be unaffected by this and the impact of a Bill of Rights on the judiciary should not be underestimated. The introduction of the Canadian Charter of Rights and Freedoms in 1982 has been described as 'the most significant legal development in Canada since Confederation [in 1867]'.[68] From 1982 to 1990, over 4000 reported Charter cases were decided by the Canadian judiciary, with the Canadian Supreme Court deciding over 100 of these, and with the number expanding by 500 to 1000 reported cases each year.[69] The invocation of constitutional rights to strike down legislation will necessarily involve the judiciary in difficult policy questions that will inevitably contribute to its politicisation and to strong popular interest in the institution and its members.[70] If the judiciary is seen to be performing a role placed on it by the Parliament and the people, this high profile need not undermine the independence and integrity of the judiciary in the eyes of the Australian community. Although a Bill of Rights would involve a transfer of power from the executive and the legislature to the judiciary, this is a consequence of any expansion of the scope for judicial review. Nevertheless, some judges will be reticent in developing a rights jurisprudence. Indeed, it has been said of the Canadian Supreme Court that:

> after an initial flurry of activity, increasingly over time, and as new justices took their seats on the Bench, the Court adopted a highly deferential, even submissive posture towards the other two branches of government. Caution, restraint, and a very attenuated standard of review are widely acknowledged to be the leitmotif of Canadian constitutional law.[71]

While this perhaps understates the generous interpretation of some rights achieved by the Canadian Supreme Court,[72] it could be expected that the Australian judiciary, with its similar traditions to that of the Canadian judiciary, would be generally circumspect in applying a Bill of Rights.

The Chief Justice of the High Court, Sir Gerard Brennan, has argued that 'It is clear that the Australian judiciary could not perform a role under a Bill of Rights unless the Australian people consciously casts that role on them'.[73] Conversely, a scheme of rights protection that has been forged in a 'democratic crucible',[74] or has traversed the

---

68 Ferguson, at 212.
69 Ferguson at 217–19. See F. L. Morton, P. H. Russell, and M. J. Withey, 'The Supreme Court's First One Hundred Charter of Rights Decisions: A Statistical Analysis' (1992) 30 *Osgoode Hall Law Journal* 1.
70 P. Hanks, 'Moving Towards the Legalisation of Politics' (1988) 6 *Law in Context* 80.
71 D. Beatty, 'The Canadian Charter of Rights: Lessons and Laments' (1997) 60 *Modern Law Review* 481 at 494.
72 J. Webber, 'Tales of the Unexpected: Intended and Unintended Consequences of the Canadian Charter of Rights and Freedoms' (1993) 5 *Canterbury Law Review* 207 at 232.
73 G. Brennan, 'The Impact of a Bill of Rights on the Role of the Judiciary: An Australian Response', in P. Alston (ed.), *Towards an Australian Bill of Rights*, Centre for International and Public Law, ANU, 1994, pp. 183–4.
74 Penner at 107.

Australian political process by gaining a majority of the popular vote at a referendum, is likely to be given judicial support. In a sense, the High Court would have been granted a limited mandate to apply legal norms to override parliamentary judgment. The experience of guarantees of civil and political rights in the Constitution shows that an unenthusiastic judiciary can undermine even express protection (see Chapter 5). On the other hand, a judiciary willing to play a full role in protecting human rights can transform even apparently weak protection into an impenetrable barrier. The Canadian judiciary, despite strong criticisms of the effectiveness of the Canadian Charter of Rights and Freedoms by 'Charter skeptics',[75] has been a willing, although cautious, participant in the application of constitutional rights.[76]

The New Zealand model is an even stronger example of where judicial enthusiasm can lead. The *New Zealand Bill of Rights Act 1990* (NZ) apparently offers little in the way of rights protection. It is an ordinary unentrenched Act of the New Zealand Parliament. The Act recognises a number of rights, ranging from the freedoms of expression (s. 14) and association (s. 17), to the 'right not to be subjected to medical or scientific experimentation without that person's consent' (s. 10). The protection afforded to such rights by the statute is limited. Section 2 states that 'The rights and freedoms contained in this Bill of Rights are affirmed' and s. 3 that the Act applies to acts done by the legislative, executive, or judicial branches or by a person or body in the performance of a public function carried out under law. Under s. 5, the listed rights 'may be subject only to such reasonable limits prescribed by law as can be demonstrably justified in a free and democratic society'. However, under s. 4:

> No court shall, in relation to any enactment (whether passed or made before or after the commencement of this Bill of Rights), —
>
> (a) Hold any provision of the enactment to be impliedly repealed or revoked, or to be in any way invalid or ineffective; or
>
> (b) Decline to apply any provision of the enactment—
>
> by reason only that the provision is inconsistent with any provision of this Bill of Rights.

At best, the statute allows the judiciary, under s. 6, to interpret an enactment of the New Zealand Parliament so as to prefer 'a meaning that is consistent with the rights and freedoms contained in this Bill of Rights'. While the meaning of each of sections 4, 5, and 6 is clear, they produce a difficult and confusing interaction.[77] For example, it is not easy to reconcile the protection afforded to the rights listed in the Act by s. 5 with the limits placed by s. 4 on the power of a Court to actually protect such rights. Despite the apparently limited protection granted by s. 6 to the rights listed in the New Zealand Bill of Rights Act, creative judicial application has meant that the Act

---

75 See, for example, J. Bakan, *Just Words: Constitutional Rights and Social Wrongs*, University of Toronto Press, 1997; J. Fudge, and H. Glasbeek, 'The Politics of Rights: A Politics with Little Class' (1992) 1 *Social and Legal Studies* 45; A. Hutchinson and A. Petter, 'Private Rights/Public Wrongs: The Liberal Lie of the Charter' (1988) 38 *University of Toronto Law Journal* 278; T. Ison, 'A Constitutional Bill of Rights—The Canadian Experience' (1997) 60 *Modern Law Review* 499; M. Mandel, *The Charter of Rights and the Legalization of Politics in Canada*, Thomson Educational, 1994.

76 Compare the interpretation of the *Canadian Bill of Rights 1960* by the Canadian judiciary: P. Hogg, *Constitutional Law of Canada*, 4th edn, Carswell, 1997, pp. 796–7.

77 A. S. Butler, 'The Bill of Rights Debate: Why the New Zealand Bill of Rights Act 1990 is a Bad Model for Britain' (1997) 17 *Oxford Journal of Legal Studies* 323.

has played a prominent, and unexpected, role in fostering civil liberties.[78] The former President of the New Zealand Court of Appeal, Sir Robin Cooke, in a moment of hyperbole described s. 6 as a 'key and strong section' that is 'a weapon of justice' for the judiciary.[79] Generally, the Act has been 'regarded by judges as a fundamental constitutional document' which must be given what has been called a purposive interpretation'.[80] For example, even though the Act does not expressly confer any remedies, it has been interpreted to provide for the recovery of damages on the basis that it must be implied that effective remedies would be available for a breach of the Act.[81] This finding was reached despite the clear intention of the Parliament expressed in the second reading speech to the legislation that the New Zealand Bill of Rights Act not bring about any new remedies.[82]

A gradual path

The experience of the New Zealand Bill of Rights Act demonstrates the potential effectiveness of a statutory Bill of Rights and the value, at least initially, of protecting rights via this means. In the United Kingdom, the Human Rights Bill 1998, which has been introduced into the British Parliament, follows this model in giving statutory force to the requirement that British courts interpret legislation in accordance with the *European Convention for the Protection of Human Rights and Fundamental Freedoms*.[83] Indeed, if the goal is to bring about an effective scheme of rights protection in Australia, there should not be any immediate move to insert a Bill of Rights in the Constitution. The 1988 referendum and the lack of basic knowledge of Australians about their constitutional system repudiates such a course. A recent survey also found a 'deep partisan divide among legislators over a bill of rights', and concluded from this that 'any possibility of constitutional entrenchment by means of referendum is out of the question'.[84] Instead, a more gradual course should be adopted that seeks to build and marshal both community support and understanding, so as to effect social and political change that might ultimately emerge as significant constitutional amendment. Parliament must play a central role in this process. A good first step would be to convene a joint parliamentary committee or a special commission consisting of both parliamentary and non-parliamenty members to examine publicly the level of protection afforded to fundamental freedoms in Australia, and, if appropriate, to suggest means of enhancing this. This might produce support for a statutory Bill of Rights containing fundamental freedoms such as the right to free expression and a right of peaceful assembly. Until the

---

78 P. A. Joseph, 'The New Zealand Bill of Rights' (1996) 7 *Public Law Review* 162.

79 R. Cooke, 'A Sketch from the Blue Train: Non-Discrimination and Freedom of Expression: The New Zealand Contribution' [1994] *New Zealand Law Journal* 10 at 10.

80 J. Elkind, 'New Zealand's Experience with a Non-Entrenched Bill of Rights', in Alston, p. 252.

81 *Simpson v. Attorney-General (Baigent's Case)* [1994] 3 NZLR 667.

82 E. Campbell, 'The Citizen and the State in the Courts', in P. D. Finn (ed.), *Essays on Law and Government*, vol. 2, *The Citizen and the State in the Courts*, LBC, 1996, p. 21.

83 See M. Taggart, 'Tugging on Superman's Cape: Lessons from Experience with the New Zealand Bill of Rights Act 1990' [1998] *Public Law* 266.

84 B. Galligan and I. McAllister, 'Citizen and Elite Attitudes Towards an Australian Bill of Rights' in B. Galligan and C. Sampford (eds), *Rethinking Human Rights*, Federation Press, 1997, pp. 145–6. The same conclusions were reached by Senate Standing Committee on Constitutional and Legal Affairs, *A Bill of Rights for Australia? An Exposure Report for the Consideration of Senators*, AGPS, 1985, p. 35.

Australian Parliament is able to enact such a bill, the prospects for any change to the Constitution to protect a range of rights is virtually non-existent. The experience of many failed referendums is that a united Parliament is a necessary precondition for constitutional change.

The operation of a Commonwealth statutory Bill of Rights could usefully be supplemented by the establishment of a joint standing committee of the federal Parliament, or of standing committees of both the Senate and the House of Representatives, charged with examining legislation for the purpose of ascertaining compliance with the statute. Alternatively, the mandate of the existing Senate Standing Committee for the Scrutiny of Bills might be extended. Both the *Canadian Bill of Rights 1960* and the New Zealand Bill of Rights Act contain a similar non-judicial means to securing compliance. Under s. 3 of the Canadian Bill of Rights and s. 7 of the New Zealand Bill of Rights Act the federal Minister of Justice and the Attorney-General, respectively, are required to examine legislation introduced into parliament with a view to reporting any inconsistencies with protected rights. An obligation is also imposed on the Minister for Justice in respect of the Canadian Charter of Rights and Freedoms. Section 4.1(1) of the *Department of Justice Act 1985* requires the Minister to examine regulations and Bills for inconsistency with the Charter, and any inconsistency must be reported to the House of Commons 'at the first convenient opportunity'.[85] The weakness in the Canadian and New Zealand approach is that it entrusts the responsibility for detecting breaches of these rights instruments in the government that has proposed the legislation and that may suffer political damage if the legislation it has sponsored is found to breach civil liberties. A Canadian commentator has suggested that 'To put real teeth into such a provision, a standing committee of the House of Commons would have to be established'.[86] The creation of a committee in the Commonwealth Parliament would serve two purposes. It would allow the vetting of legislation before enactment so as to reduce the likelihood of Commonwealth legislation being found invalid.[87] It would also incorporate parliamentarians into the rights protection process by building on the already robust parliamentary committee system. This latter aspect should contribute to a greater understanding of rights issues by representatives and, through media coverage of committee deliberations and submissions, by the Australian people.

It is difficult to see that any proposal for a Bill of Rights in the Constitution could succeed without some process of familiarisation for both the players in the political process and the community. Over time, a statutory Bill of Rights enacted by the federal government, perhaps supplemented or even preceded by statutory Bills of Rights enacted by state and territory governments,[88] would contribute positively to a rights

---

85   See also *Statutory Instruments Act 1985* (Canada), s. 3; Human Rights Bill 1998 (United Kingdom), s. 19.

86   P. H. Russell, 'A Democratic Approach to Civil Liberties' (1969) 19 *University of Toronto Law Journal* 109 at 126. See J. L. Hiebert, 'A Hybrid Approach to Protect Rights? An Argument in Favour of Supplementing Canadian Judicial Review with Australia's Model of Parliamentary Scrutiny' (1998) 26 *Federal Law Review* 115; D. Kinley, *The European Convention on Human Rights: Compliance without Incorporation*, Dartmouth, 1993.

87   Committees of the Federal Parliament already play this role. See, for example, Senate Legal and Constitutional Legislation Committee, *Constitutional Aspects of the Native Title Amendment Bill 1997*, Senate Printing Unit, November 1997.

88   Following the enactment of the Canadian Bill of Rights, statutory Bills of Rights were also enacted by Alberta (*Alberta Bill of Rights 1972* (Alberta)) and Quebec (*Quebec Charter of Human Rights and Freedoms 1975* (Quebec)).

culture within Australian society. The process should also help to establish which rights are deserving of protection and which are not. In the longer term, those rights that are generally accepted might be incorporated into the Constitution via a referendum under s. 128. Even then, it may be appropriate in the case of some rights to allow the Parliament to override a right by passing legislation expressly indicating an intent to change the law notwithstanding the constitutional position, or by requiring that the Parliament achieve a specified majority. Alternatively, such an override might be permitted where it is supported by the Australian people voting at a referendum.[89] However, this latter override sets too high a standard. It would achieve little given that a referendum is sufficient to amend the Constitution to expunge the right. A final decision on whether an override clause would be appropriate would depend on the operation of a like clause within the statutory Bill of Rights.

In protecting rights by statutory means or by constitutional entrenchment, difficult decisions must be made about which rights should be protected. Again this would best be determined over time, step by step. Before seeking to protect a wide range of rights, the Parliament might move to protect a few core rights that are obviously regarded as basic and fundamental to Australian democracy. This would *not* include rights such as 'due process of law' in the Fifth Amendment to the United States Constitution, which has a highly developed meaning in the United States context but no resonance in Australia.[90] Core rights might include freedom of expression and freedom from discrimination on the basis of race and sex, or even collective rights such as the cultural rights of Australia's indigenous peoples.[91] In each case such rights should be carefully defined and limited. The success of legislation such as the Racial Discrimination Act may mean that it will not be too long before it will be possible to gain popular and political support for inserting a guarantee of freedom from discrimination on the basis of race in the Australian Constitution. Otherwise, a good place to start would be to examine the rights favoured by the Constitutional Commission in its 1988 report[92] or by the Queensland Electoral and Administrative Review Commission in its 1993 report.[93] Other rights, such as many of the rights listed in the *International Covenant on Civil and Political Rights*, might be examined once a culture of rights protection by way of statutory or constitutional means has begun to emerge.

Difficult issues arise as to whether the Constitution should ultimately guarantee rights as between citizens rather than merely as between citizen and government. Traditionally, constitutional rights in Australia have conferred protection from government

---

89 M. R. Wilcox, *An Australian Charter of Rights?*, LBC, 1993, pp. 265–6.
90 F. Brennan, 'An Australian Convert from a Constitutional Bill of Rights' (1996) 7 *Public Law Review* 132; F. Brennan, 'Thirty Years On, Do We Need a Bill of Rights?' (1996) 18 *Adelaide Law Review* 123.
91 See F. Brennan, 'The Indigenous People', in P. D. Finn (ed.), *Essays on Law and Government*, vol. 1, *Principles and Values*, LBC, 1995, p. 33; F. Brennan, *Securing a Bountiful Place for Aborigines and Torres Strait Islanders in a Modern, Free, and Tolerant Australia*, Constitutional Centenary Foundation, 1994; Constitutional Commission, *Report of the Advisory Committee on Individual and Democratic Rights under the Constitution*, ch. 10; Sessional Committee on Constitutional Development (NT).
92 Constitutional Commission, *Final Report of the Constitutional Commission.* See Wilcox, pp. 252–61.
93 Electoral and Administrative Review Commission (Qld). For a table comparing the rights recommended in this report as against the rights put forward in the 1988 report of the Constitutional Commission and the rights listed in the Australian Human Rights Bill 1985 (Cth) and the Constitution (Declaration of Rights and Freedoms) Bill 1988 (Vic), see Legal, Constitutional and Administrative Review Committee (Qld), pp. 10–12.

action, rather than as between private actors (such as between landlord and tenant, or employer and employee—see Chapter 3). With the exception of Murphy's Human Rights Bill 1973 (Cth) (see p. 253), where there has been the desire to protect rights in the latter context this has not been achieved by constitutional means, but by statute, such as the Sex Discrimination Act. This delineation needs to be reassessed. Today, it is the exercise of private rather than public power that poses the greater threat to the basic rights of Australians.[94] The increasing privatisation of government and the correspond-ing exercise of what had been considered to be public power by large corporations means that it may be appropriate to constitutionally guarantee rights as against non-governmental action. For example, the right to privacy is arguably in greater danger of abrogation by secret surveillance undertaken by large corporations than by the actions of government. Given also that some Australian prisoners are held in private rather than public prisons[95] and that there are now more private than public police in Australia,[96] it may no longer be appropriate to limit the protection conferred by the Constitution to protection from governmental action.

This incremental approach of protecting rights by statutory means before constitu-tional means, and of protecting certain rights before others, is a pragmatic and potentially achievable means of bolstering rights protection in Australia. This approach also max-imises the chances of achieving a workable balance between, on the one hand, enabling the judiciary to protect the rights of Australians, and on the other, the need to avoid placing too much faith in the High Court's ability to solve Australia's pressing social, moral, and political concerns. Constitutional rights have an important role to play in increasing individual liberty, but they are 'blunt tools for redressing social injustice'.[97]

Entrenching a statutory Bill of Rights

The Constitution is obviously the most effective legal means of limiting governmental power in Australia. However, a statutory Bill of Rights could also be effective in limit-ing the scope of Australian law-makers to abrogate fundamental rights.[98] A federal statu-tory Bill of Rights, like legislation such as the Racial Discrimination Act, would, as a consequence of s. 109 of the Constitution, prevent both the states and the territories from abrogating the listed rights (see Chapter 1).[99] If this aspect of a statutory Bill of Rights were politically inexpedient, perhaps because it would raise concerns as to 'states' rights' and the centralisation of power in the Commonwealth, the bill might only be made applicable to federal legislation.[100] The states and territories might then be encouraged to enact their own Bills of Rights.

It is clear that a state can legislate to entrench a statutory Bill of Rights against abroga-tion by a subsequent legislature, by, for example, providing that a Bill of Rights can only

---

94 See Bakan, ch. 4; J. Braithwaite, 'On Speaking Softly and Carrying Big Sticks: Neglected Dimensions of a Republican Separation of Powers' (1997) 47 *University of Toronto Law Journal* 305 at 307.
95 See, for example, *Corrections Act 1986* (Vic).
96 C. D. Shearing and P. C. Stenning (eds), *Private Policing*, Sage, 1987.
97 Bakan, p. 152.
98 Compare C. Sampford, 'The Four Dimensions of Rights' in Galligan and Sampford, pp. 67–9.
99 See, for example, *Mabo v. Queensland (No 1)* (1988) 166 CLR 186.
100 This could be achieved by the federal legislation clearly indicating an intention not to 'cover the field' with respect to state and territory laws (see Chapter 1).

be amended with the support of the people of the state at a referendum.[101] The notion that a parliament can lay down procedural restrictions in its Constitution that might bind its successors has its origins in s. 5 of the *Colonial Laws Validity Act 1865* (28 & 29 Vict. Ch. 63). After granting to colonial legislatures 'full Power to make Laws respecting the Constitution, Powers, and Procedure of such Legislature', s. 5 states that such power may only be exercised 'provided that such Laws shall have been passed in such Manner and Form as may from Time to Time be required'. The efficacy of manner-and-form requirements in the Australian states now depends on s. 6 of the *Australia Act 1986* (Cth)[102] or alternatively on the principle outlined in *Bribery Commissioner v. Ranasinghe* [1965] AC 172.

On the other hand, neither s. 5 of the Colonial Laws Validity Act, nor s. 6 of the Australia Act, applies to Commonwealth laws, making the ability of a statutory Bill of Rights to limit the future exercise of legislative power by the federal Parliament more problematic. A basic facet of the doctrine of parliamentary supremacy is that the Commonwealth Parliament has 'the right to make or unmake any law whatever'.[103] However, in doing so the Commonwealth must comply with the procedures laid down for the lawmaking process. As Dixon J remarked somewhat cryptically in *Attorney-General (NSW) v. Trethowan* (1931) 44 CLR 395 at 426, 'the Courts might be called on to consider whether the supreme legislative power in respect of the matter had in truth been exercised in the manner required for its authentic expression and by the elements in which it had come to reside'. As George Winterton has shown,[104] and despite contrary dicta by members of the High Court in *Kartinyeri v. Commonwealth* (1998) 152 ALR 540,[105] this means that the Commonwealth Parliament would also need to comply with a manner-and-form requirement set out in a statutory Bill of Rights. Such a requirement might be in the form of a 'notwithstanding clause': that is, a requirement that in order to abrogate a right listed in the statutory Bill of Rights a later statute must expressly state an intention to breach this right notwithstanding the fact that the right is protected by the statutory Bill of Rights. If a later statute infringes a protected right without expressing the necessary intention, that statute would be invalid. On the other hand, a statutory Bill of Rights could not be entrenched by requiring for its amendment a special majority, say two-thirds, of either House of the federal Parliament. This is precluded by sections 23 and 40 of the Constitution, which provide, respectively, that questions arising in the Senate and the House of Representatives are to be resolved by a simple majority.[106]

Some doubt is cast on the potential effectiveness of a 'notwithstanding' clause requirement in a statutory Bill of Rights by the decision of the High Court in *South-Eastern Drainage Board (SA) v. Savings Bank of South Australia* (1939) 62 CLR 603.[107] In that case,

---

101 *Attorney-General (NSW) v. Trethowan* (1931) 44 CLR 395. See Blackshield and Williams, pp. 386–96.
102 Section 6 of the Australia Act states that 'a law made after the commencement of this Act by the Parliament of a State respecting the constitution, powers or procedure of the Parliament of the State shall be of no force or effect unless it is made in such manner and form as may from time to time be required by a law made by that Parliament, whether made before or after the commencement of this Act'.
103 A. V. Dicey, *Introduction to the Study of the Law of the Constitution*, 10th edn [1st edn, 1885], Macmillan, 1959, p. 40.
104 G. Winterton, 'Can the Commonwealth Parliament Enact Manner and Form Legislation?' (1980) 11 *Federal Law Review* 167.
105 *Kartinyeri* at 549 per Brennan CJ and McHugh J, at 560 per Gaudron J.
106 Gibbs, at 10; Winterton, 'Can the Commonwealth Parliament Enact Manner and Form Legislation?', at 191.
107 See *Ellen Street Estates Ltd v. Minister of Health* [1934] 1 KB 590 at 597 per Maugham LJ: 'The Legislature cannot, according to our [British] constitution, bind itself as to the form of subsequent legislation'.

the High Court held that a mere requirement of a special declaratory form of words was not a manner-and-form requirement capable of limiting the future exercise of legislative power under s. 5 of the Colonial Laws Validity Act. Section 6 of the *Real Property Act 1886* (SA) stated that 'No law, so far as inconsistent with this Act, shall apply to land subject to the provisions of this Act, nor shall any future law, so far as inconsistent with this Act, so apply unless it shall be expressly enacted that it shall so apply "notwithstanding the provisions of *The Real Property Act 1886*"'. The *South-Eastern Drainage Amendment Act 1900* (SA) was inconsistent with the Real Property Act in that it detracted from the security of title given by that Act. Despite this, the South-Eastern Drainage Amendment Act did not contain a 'notwithstanding' clause as required by the Real Property Act.

The High Court held that s. 6 of the Real Property Act did not contain a manner-and-form requirement capable of binding later legislatures and that, accordingly, the absence of the 'notwithstanding' clause in the South-Eastern Drainage Amendment Act did not prevent that Act from overriding the former Act to the extent of any inconsistency. The result in *South-Eastern Drainage Board* might be taken to mean that the Commonwealth or a state cannot limit its power by way of a 'notwithstanding' clause in a statutory Bill of Rights. There are two reasons why this is unlikely to be correct.[108] First, the analysis in the case is flawed.[109] Except for Evatt J, the High Court incorrectly reached its conclusion by asking whether s. 6 of the Real Property Act was a law 'respecting the Constitution, Powers, and Procedure of such Legislature' within the meaning of s. 5 of the Colonial Laws Validity Act. Instead, what s. 5 of the Colonial Laws Validity Act required the Court to ask is whether the law that is later in time is such a law. Hence, it should have asked whether the South-Eastern Drainage Amendment Act was a law 'respecting the Constitution, Powers, and Procedure of such Legislature', which it clearly was not. If the Court had asked the correct question, the issue of whether s. 6 of the Real Property Act contained an effective manner-and-form requirement would never have arisen.

Second, subsequent cases suggest that the conclusion in *South-Eastern Drainage Board* might in any event have been incorrect, at least in relation to human rights statutes. The Canadian experience is particularly relevant.[110] Three decades before the Canadian Charter of Rights and Freedoms was enacted, the Canadian Parliament passed the *Canadian Bill of Rights 1960*. This Act continues to guarantee a wide range of rights such as 'freedom of religion' (s. 1), 'freedom of speech' (s. 1), and 'freedom from cruel and unusual treatment or punishment' (s. 2). Section 2 also provides that laws passed by the federal legislature should, 'unless it is expressly declared by an Act of the Parliament of Canada that it shall operate notwithstanding the Canadian Bill of Rights', be construed and applied so as not to abrogate any of the rights listed in the Canadian Bill of Rights. In *R v. Drybones* [1970] SCR 282, the Supreme Court of Canada considered the effect of s. 2. It was held, at p. 294, that s. 2 was effective in rendering 'inoperative' federal legislation inconsistent with any of the rights listed in the Canadian Bill of Rights. This can be explained by viewing s. 2 as a manner-and-form limitation on the law-making process of the Canadian Parliament.[111] *R v. Drybones* suggests that, at least in the

---

108 See Winterton, at 187–8.
109 Blackshield and Williams, pp. 391–2.
110 See W. S. Tarnopolsky, *The Canadian Bill of Rights*, 2nd edn, McClelland & Stewart, 1975, ch. 3.
111 Hogg, p. 794.

field of human rights, a 'notwithstanding' limitation has the potential to bind a legislature. The decision of the House of Lords in the litigation in *R v. Secretary of State for Transport; Ex parte Factortame Ltd* [1990] 2 AC 85; [1991] 1 AC 603 suggests that this is not limited to the field of human rights but applies more generally.

A federal statutory Bill of Rights could act as an absolute bar to the abrogation of certain rights by state or territory parliaments. A manner-and-form requirement in a federal statutory Bill of Rights would not give the same level of protection as against Commonwealth laws. The Commonwealth Parliament would be able to breach a right if the Parliament complied with the manner-and-form requirement set down. However, the political difficulties involved in complying with a manner-and-form requirement mean that a statutory Bill of Rights may put rights beyond the scope of Commonwealth legislation as well. The long story of the Howard Coalition Government's enactment of a response to the High Court's decision in *Wik Peoples v. Queensland* (1996) 187 CLR 1 demonstrates the political difficulties of amending or lessening the protection offered by the Racial Discrimination Act.[112] It has proved extremely difficult for any government to gain sufficient political support to override a statutory guarantee of a basic human right granted to, and popularly known by, the Australian people.

The Canadian experience is again instructive. Section 33(1) of the Canadian Charter of Rights and Freedoms provides that 'Parliament or the legislature of a province may expressly declare in an Act of Parliament or of the legislature, as the case may be, that the Act or a provision thereof shall operate notwithstanding a provision included in section 2 or sections 7 to 15 of this Charter'. A declaration made under s. 33(1) has, under s. 33(3), an operation of five years, after which time the declaration may be reenacted. It is important to note that the 'notwithstanding' clause requirement in s. 33(1) does not apply to all of the rights listed in the Charter, just to the rights listed in sections 2 and 7–15. This means that a legislature can abrogate rights such as 'the right not to be arbitrarily detained or imprisoned' (s. 9), the rights to equality under the law and freedom from discrimination on the basis of race (s. 15), and even the fundamental freedoms listed in s. 2 (which include 'freedom of thought, belief, opinion and expression, including freedom of the press and other media of communication'). On the other hand, other rights such as the right to vote in federal elections (s. 3) and the right to 'enter, remain in and leave Canada' (s. 6(1)) are beyond the reach of a notwithstanding clause.

Quebec did not give its approval to the Canadian Charter of Rights and Freedoms. It argued that a federal Charter is unnecessary in Quebec given the *Quebec Charter of Human Rights and Freedoms 1975*. Much of Quebec's use of s. 33(1) came as a protest against the imposition of the Charter of Rights and Freedoms. Soon after the Charter came into effect, the Quebec Parliament passed *An Act Respecting the Constitution Act 1982*, which added a standard-form 'notwithstanding' clause to every statute then in force in Quebec.[113] Each new piece of legislation was also drafted to include the 'notwithstanding' clause. This latter practice stopped with a change of government in Quebec in December 1985. When, under s. 33(3) of the Charter, the 1982 Act

---

112 See *Native Title Amendment Act 1998* (Cth) and s. 7 (as amended) of the *Native Title Act 1993* (Cth).
113 This legislation was upheld in *Ford v. Quebec (Attorney-General)* [1988] 2 SCR 712.

ceased to operate after five years in 1987, the new Parliament also failed to re-enact the 'blanket override' in the Act.[114] This government did, however, apply the notwithstanding clause in five pieces of legislation, including in *An Act to Amend the Charter of the French Language 1988*, which prohibited the use of the English language on outside commercial signs. Quebec's willingness to take advantage of s. 33(1) of the Charter has not been repeated in other parts of Canada. The only other province to take advantage of s. 33(1) has been Saskatchewan, and even this exercise of s. 33(1) ultimately proved unnecessary when the Supreme Court of Canada held that the Saskatchewan law did not breach the Charter.[115] No other province or the federal legislature has passed legislation applying s. 33(1). The political price to be paid in invoking s. 33(1) has been too high. A government desiring, for example, to override the 'right not to be subjected to any cruel and unusual treatment or punishment' in s. 13 of the Charter must be prepared to meet strong and organised resistance from many sections of the community.[116] This does not mean that s. 33(1) has been a failure. It offers an escape valve should the interpretation of the Charter by the Canadian judiciary ever stand in the way of overriding public policy objectives. Section 33(1) may operate to maintain the independence and integrity of the judiciary. It offers an alternative to threats such as the one issued by President Roosevelt in the 1930s to 'pack' the United States Supreme Court (see Chapter 6).

Conclusion

Ismail Mahomed, Deputy President of the Constitutional Court of South Africa, has said:

> A skillful and committed Constitutional Court is only a *necessary* condition for an enduring and defensible constitutional future. It is not a *sufficient* condition. It will fail in its objectives if it is not underpinned by a vigorous *culture* of human rights and constitutionalism, sedulously disseminated by non-governmental structures of civil society, permeating the schools, the universities, the electronic media, the free press, the trade unions and village communes, alerted and conscientised by activists of integrity operating at all levels, with infrastructures adequately endowed. If the *culture* of human rights and constitutionalism does not become part of the national ethos internalised within the psyche of its citizens, the scholarship and integrity of the Constitutional Court will remain forever vulnerable.[117]

These words apply equally in Australia. The protection of human rights under the Australian Constitution will not be effective unless this occurs within a culture of rights protection. The High Court of the 1990s has already begun to advance such a culture in its constitutional decisions. However, it must pass on the baton if Australia is ever to embrace a general scheme of rights protection. The Constitution is incapable of supporting an implied Bill of Rights. To imply this would be to damage the legitimacy of the High Court and to undermine the ability of the Court to act as a bulwark between the Australian people and their governments.

---

114 Hogg, p. 909.
115 *RWDSU v. Saskatchewan* [1987] 1 SCR 460.
116 Hogg, p. 914.
117 I. Mahomed, 'Constitutional Court of South Africa', in C. Saunders (ed.), *Courts of Final Jurisdiction: The Mason Court in Australia*, Federation Press, 1996, p. 173 (emphasis in original).

A rights culture cannot be created overnight. The history of constitutional reform in Australia shows the need for a gradual approach involving popular participation as well as political leadership. The Australian landscape is littered with failed attempts at constitutional reform. The 1988 referendum, in which an attempt to increase the coverage of basic rights in the Constitution failed, shows that the road to an Australian Bill of Rights will not be an easy one. A statutory Bill of Rights would build political support for rights protection as well as provide a real defence for civil liberties. In due course, a government could seek the support of the people for constitutional entrenchment of those rights that have operated successfully in a statutory form. It is difficult to see any other process gaining the necessary support to pass the referendum requirement set down by s. 128 of the Constitution. In any event, Australia needs more than just a change to the text of the Constitution. It needs to continue to develop a culture of liberty.

The Australian Constitution

Commonwealth of Australia Constitution Act 1900

with alterations to the Constitution made by

CONSTITUTION ALTERATION (SENATE ELECTIONS) 1906
(No 1 of 1907)

CONSTITUTION ALTERATION (STATE DEBTS) 1909
(No 3 of 1910)

CONSTITUTION ALTERATION (STATE DEBTS) 1928
(No 1 of 1929)

CONSTITUTION ALTERATION (SOCIAL SERVICES) 1946
(No 81 of 1946)

CONSTITUTION ALTERATION (ABORIGINALS) 1967
(No 55 of 1967)

CONSTITUTION ALTERATION (SENATE CASUAL VACANCIES) 1977
(No 82 of 1977)

CONSTITUTION ALTERATION (RETIREMENT OF JUDGES) 1977
(No 83 of 1977)

CONSTITUTION ALTERATION (REFERENDUMS) 1977
(No 84 of 1977)

Commonwealth of Australia Constitution Act

(63 & 64 VICTORIA, CHAPTER 12)

An Act to constitute the Commonwealth of Australia.

[9th July 1900]

WHEREAS the people of New South Wales, Victoria, South Australia, Queensland, and Tasmania, humbly relying on the blessing of Almighty God, have agreed to unite in one indissoluble Federal Commonwealth under the Crown of the United Kingdom of Great Britain and Ireland, and under the Constitution hereby established:

And whereas it is expedient to provide for the admission into the Commonwealth of other Australasian Colonies and possessions of the Queen:

Be it therefore enacted by the Queen's most Excellent Majesty, by and with the advice and consent of the Lords Spiritual and Temporal, and Commons, in this present Parliament assembled, and by the authority of the same, as follows:—

1. Short title This Act may be cited as the Commonwealth of Australia Constitution Act.

2. Act to extend to the Queen's successors The provisions of this Act referring to the Queen shall extend to Her Majesty's heirs and successors in the sovereignty of the United Kingdom.

3. Proclamation of Commonwealth It shall be lawful for the Queen, with the advice of the Privy Council, to declare by proclamation that, on and after a day therein appointed, not being later than one year after the passing of this Act, the people of New South Wales, Victoria, South Australia, Queensland, and Tasmania, and also, if Her Majesty is satisfied that the people of Western Australia have agreed thereto, of Western Australia, shall be united in a Federal Commonwealth under the name of the Commonwealth of Australia. But the Queen may, at any time after the proclamation, appoint a Governor-General for the Commonwealth.

4. Commencement of Act The Commonwealth shall be established, and the Constitution of the Commonwealth shall take effect, on and after the day so appointed. But the Parliaments of the several colonies may at any time after the passing of this Act make any such laws, to come into operation on the day so appointed, as they might have made if the Constitution had taken effect at the passing of this Act.

5. Operation of the constitution and laws This Act, and all laws made by the Parliament of the Commonwealth under the Constitution, shall be binding on the courts, judges, and people of every State and of every part of the Commonwealth, notwithstanding anything in the laws of any State; and the laws of the Commonwealth shall be in force on all British ships, the Queen's ships of war excepted, whose first port of clearance and whose port of destination are in the Commonwealth.

6. Definitions "The Commonwealth" shall mean the Commonwealth of Australia as established under this Act.

"The States" shall mean such of the colonies of New South Wales, New Zealand, Queensland, Tasmania, Victoria, Western Australia, and South Australia, including the northern territory of South Australia, as for the time being are parts of the Commonwealth, and such colonies or territories as may be admitted into or established by the Commonwealth as States; and each of such parts of the Commonwealth shall be called "a State."

"Original States" shall mean such States as are parts of the Commonwealth at its establishment.

7. Repeal of Federal Council Act 48 & 49 Vict c 60 The Federal Council of Australasia Act, 1885, is hereby repealed, but so as not to affect any laws passed by the Federal Council of Australasia and in force at the establishment of the Commonwealth.

Any such law may be repealed as to any State by the Parliament of the Commonwealth, or as to any colony not being a State by the Parliament thereof.

8. Application of Colonial Boundaries Act 58 & 59 Vict c 34 After the passing of this Act the Colonial Boundaries Act, 1895, shall not apply to any colony which becomes a State of the Commonwealth; but the Commonwealth shall be taken to be a self-governing colony for the purposes of that Act.

9. Constitution The Constitution of the Commonwealth shall be as follows:—

THE CONSTITUTION.

This Constitution is divided as follows

CHAPTER I.

THE PARLIAMENT.

PART I—GENERAL.

1. Legislative Power The legislative power of the Commonwealth shall be vested in a Federal Parliament, which shall consist of the Queen, a Senate, and a House of Representatives, and which is herein-after called "The Parliament," or "The Parliament of the Commonwealth."

2. Governor-General A Governor-General appointed by the Queen shall be Her Majesty's representative in the Commonwealth, and shall have and may exercise in the Commonwealth during the Queen's pleasure, but subject to this Constitution, such powers and functions of the Queen as Her Majesty may be pleased to assign to him.

3. Salary of Governor-General There shall be payable to the Queen out of the Consolidated Revenue fund of the Commonwealth, for the salary of the Governor-General, an annual sum which, until the Parliament otherwise provides, shall be ten thousand pounds.

The salary of a Governor-General shall not be altered during his continuance in office.

4. Provisions relating to Governor-General The provisions of this Constitution relating to the Governor-General extend and apply to the Governor-General for the time being, or such person as the Queen may appoint to administer the Government of the Commonwealth; but no such person shall be entitled to receive any salary from the Commonwealth in respect of any other office during his administration of the Government of the Commonwealth.

5. Sessions of Parliament. Prorogation and dissolution The Governor-General may appoint such times for holding the sessions of the Parliament as he thinks fit, and may also from time to time, by Proclamation or otherwise, prorogue the Parliament, and may in like manner dissolve the House of Representatives.

After any general election the Parliament shall be summoned to meet not later than thirty days after the day appointed for the return of the writs.

The Parliament shall be summoned to meet not later than six months after the establishment of the Commonwealth.

6. Yearly session of Parliament There shall be a session of the Parliament once at least in every year, so that twelve months shall not intervene between the last sitting of the Parliament in one session and its first sitting in the next session.

PART II—THE SENATE.

7. The Senate The Senate shall be composed of senators for each State, directly chosen by the people of the State, voting, until the Parliament otherwise provides, as one electorate.

But until the Parliament of the Commonwealth otherwise provides, the Parliament of the State of Queensland, if that State be an Original State, may make laws dividing the State into divisions and determining the number of senators to be chosen for each division, and in the absence of such provision the State shall be one electorate.

Until the Parliament otherwise provides there shall be six senators for each Original State. The Parliament may make laws increasing or diminishing the number of senators for each State, but so that equal representation of the several Original States shall be maintained and that no Original State shall have less than six senators.

The senators shall be chosen for a term of six years, and the names of the senators chosen for each State shall be certified by the Governor to the Governor-General.

8. Qualification of electors The qualification of electors of senators shall be in each State that which is prescribed by this Constitution, or by the Parliament, as the qualification for electors of members of the House of Representatives; but in the choosing of senators each elector shall vote only once.

9. Method of election of senators The Parliament of the Commonwealth may make laws prescribing the method of choosing senators, but so that the method shall be uniform for all States. Subject to any such law, the Parliament of each State may make laws prescribing the method of choosing the senators for that State.

Times and places The Parliament of a State may make laws for determining the times and places of elections of senators for the State.

10. Application of State laws Until the Parliament otherwise provides, but subject to this Constitution, the laws in force in each State, for the time being, relating to elections for the more numerous House of the Parliament of the State shall, as nearly as practicable, apply to elections of senators for the State.

11. Failure to choose senators The Senate may proceed to the despatch of business, notwithstanding the failure of any State to provide for its representation in the Senate.

12. Issue of writs The Governor of any State may cause writs to be issued for elections of senators for the State. In case of the dissolution of the Senate the writs shall be issued within ten days from the proclamation of such dissolution.

13. Rotation of senators [altered by No 1, 1907, s 2] As soon as may be after the Senate first meets, and after each first meeting of the Senate following a dissolution thereof, the Senate shall divide the senators chosen for each State into two classes, as nearly equal in number as practicable; and the places of the senators of the first class shall become vacant at the expiration of ~~the third year~~ **three years,** and the places of those of the second class at the expiration of ~~the sixth year~~ **six years,** from the beginning of their term of service; and afterwards the places of senators shall become vacant at the expiration of six years from the beginning of their term of service.

The election to fill vacant places shall be made ~~in the year at the expiration of which~~ **within one year before** the places are to become vacant.

For the purposes of this section the term of service of a senator shall be taken to begin on the first day of ~~January~~ **July** following the day of his election, except in the cases of the first election and of the election next after any dissolution of the Senate, when it shall be taken to begin on the first day of ~~January~~ **July** preceding the day of his election.

14. Further provision for rotation Whenever the number of senators for a State is increased or diminished, the Parliament of the Commonwealth may make such provision for the vacating of the places of senators for the State as it deems necessary to maintain regularity in the rotation.

15. Casual vacancies [substituted by No 82, 1977, s 2] If the place of a senator becomes vacant before the expiration of his term of service, the Houses of Parliament of the State for which he was chosen, sitting and voting together, or, if there is only one House of that Parliament, that House, shall choose a person to hold the place until the expiration of the term. But if the Parliament of the State is not in session when the vacancy is notified, the Governor of the State, with the advice of the Executive Council thereof, may appoint a person to hold the place until the expiration of fourteen days from the beginning of the next session of the Parliament of the State or the expiration of the term, whichever first happens.

Where a vacancy has at any time occurred in the place of a senator chosen by the people of a State and, at the time when he was so chosen, he was publicly recognized by a particular political party as being an endorsed candidate of that party and publicly represented himself to be such a candidate, a person chosen or appointed under this section in consequence of that vacancy, or in consequence of that vacancy and a subsequent vacancy or vacancies, shall, unless there is no member of that party available to be chosen or appointed, be a member of that party.

Where—

(a) in accordance with the last preceding paragraph, a member of a particular political party is chosen or appointed to hold the place of a senator whose place had become vacant; and

(b) before taking his seat he ceases to be a member of that party (otherwise than by reason of the party having ceased to exist),

he shall be deemed not to have been so chosen or appointed and the vacancy shall be again notified in accordance with section twenty-one of this Constitution.

The name of any senator chosen or appointed under this section shall be certified by the Governor of the State to the Governor-General.

If the place of a senator chosen by the people of a State at the election of senators last held before the commencement of the *Constitution Alteration (Senate Casual Vacancies) 1977* became vacant before that commencement and, at that commencement, no person chosen by the House or Houses of Parliament of the State, or appointed by the Governor of the State, in consequence of that vacancy, or in consequence of that vacancy and a subsequent vacancy or vacancies, held office, this section applies as if the place of the senator chosen by the people of the State had become vacant after that commencement.

A senator holding office at the commencement of the *Constitution Alteration (Senate Casual Vacancies) 1977*, being a senator appointed by the Governor of a State in consequence of a vacancy that had at any time occurred in the place of a senator chosen by the people of the State, shall be deemed to have been appointed to hold the place until the expiration of fourteen days after the beginning of the next session of the Parliament of the State that commenced or commences after he was appointed and further action under this section shall be taken as if the vacancy in the place of the senator chosen by the people of the State had occurred after that commencement.

Subject to the next succeeding paragraph, a senator holding office at the commencement of the *Constitution Alteration (Senate Casual Vacancies) 1977* who was chosen by the House or Houses of Parliament of a State in consequence of a vacancy that had at any time occurred in the place of a senator chosen by the people of the State shall be deemed to have been chosen to hold office until the expiration of the term of service of the senator elected by the people of the State.

If, at or before the commencement of the *Constitution Alteration (Senate Casual Vacancies) 1977*, a law to alter the Constitution entitled "*Constitution Alteration (Simultaneous Elections) 1977*" came into operation, a senator holding office at the commencement of that law who was chosen by the House or Houses of Parliament of a State in consequence of a vacancy that had at any time occurred in the place of a Senator chosen by the people of the State shall be deemed to have been chosen to hold office—

(a) if the senator elected by the people of the State had a term of service expiring on the thirtieth day of June, One thousand nine hundred and seventy-eight—until the expiration or dissolution of the first House of

Representatives to expire or be dissolved after that law came into operation; or

(b) if the senator elected by the people of the State had a term of service expiring on the thirtieth day of June, One thousand nine hundred and eighty-one—until the expiration or dissolution of the second House of Representatives to expire or be dissolved after that law came into operation or, if there is an earlier dissolution of the Senate, until that dissolution.

16. Qualifications of senator The qualifications of a senator shall be the same as those of a member of the House of Representatives.

17. Election of President The Senate shall, before proceeding to the despatch of any other business, choose a senator to be the President of the Senate; and as often as the office of President becomes vacant the Senate shall again choose a senator to be the President.

The President shall cease to hold his office if he ceases to be a senator. He may be removed from office by a vote of the Senate, or he may resign his office or his seat by writing addressed to the Governor-General.

18. Absence of President Before or during any absence of the President, the Senate may choose a senator to perform his duties in his absence.

19. Resignation of senator A senator may, by writing addressed to the President, or to the Governor-General if there is no President or if the President is absent from the Commonwealth, resign his place, which thereupon shall become vacant.

20. Vacancy by absence The place of a senator shall become vacant if for two consecutive months of any session of the Parliament he, without the permission of the Senate, fails to attend the Senate.

21. Vacancy to be notified Whenever a vacancy happens in the Senate, the President, or if there is no President or if the President is absent from the Commonwealth the Governor-General, shall notify the same to the Governor of the State in the representation of which the vacancy has happened.

22. Quorum Until the Parliament otherwise provides, the presence of at least one-third of the whole number of the senators shall be necessary to constitute a meeting of the Senate for the exercise of its powers.

23. Voting in the Senate Questions arising in the Senate shall be determined by a majority of votes, and each senator shall have one vote. The President shall in all cases be entitled to a vote; and when the votes are equal the question shall pass in the negative.

PART III—THE HOUSE OF REPRESENTATIVES.

24. Constitution of House of Representatives The House of Representatives shall be composed of members directly chosen by the people of the Commonwealth, and the number of such members shall be, as nearly as practicable, twice the number of the senators.

The number of members chosen in the several States shall be in proportion to the respective numbers of their people, and shall, until the Parliament otherwise provides, be determined, whenever necessary, in the following manner: —

(i) A quota shall be ascertained by dividing the number of the people of the Commonwealth, as shown by the latest statistics of the Commonwealth, by twice the number of the senators:

(ii) The number of members to be chosen in each State shall be determined by dividing the number of the people of the State, as shown by the latest statistics of the Commonwealth, by the quota; and if on such division there is a remainder greater than one-half of the quota, one more member shall be chosen in the State.

But notwithstanding anything in this section, five members at least shall be chosen in each Original State.

25. Provision as to races disqualified from voting For the purposes of the last section, if by the law of any State all persons of any race are disqualified from voting at elections for the more numerous House of the Parliament of the State, then, in reckoning the number of the people of the State or of the Commonwealth, persons of that race resident in that State shall not be counted.

26. Representatives in first Parliament Notwithstanding anything in section twenty-four, the number of members to be chosen in each State at the first election shall be as follows: —

New South Wales	twenty-three;
Victoria	twenty;
Queensland	eight;
South Australia	six;
Tasmania	five;

Provided that if Western Australia is an Original State, the numbers shall be as follows:—

New South Wales	twenty-six;
Victoria	twenty-three;
Queensland	nine;
South Australia	seven;
Western Australia	five;
Tasmania	five;

27. Alteration of number of members Subject to this Constitution, the Parliament may make laws for increasing or diminishing the number of the members of the House of Representatives.

28. Duration of House of Representatives Every House of Representatives shall continue for three years from the first meeting of the House, and no longer, but may be sooner dissolved by the Governor-General.

29. Electoral divisions Until the Parliament of the Commonwealth otherwise provides, the Parliament of any State may make laws for determining the divisions in each State for which members of the House of Representatives may be chosen, and the number of members to be chosen for each division. A division shall not be formed out of parts of different States.

In the absence of other provision, each State shall be one electorate.

30. Qualification of electors Until the Parliament otherwise provides, the qualification of electors of members of the House of Representatives shall be in each State that which is prescribed by the law of the State as the qualification of electors of the more numerous House of Parliament of the State; but in the choosing of members each elector shall vote only once.

31. Application of State laws Until the Parliament otherwise provides, but subject to this Constitution, the laws in force in each State for the time being relating to elections for the more numerous House of the Parliament of the State shall, as nearly as practicable, apply to elections in the State of members of the House of Representatives.

32. Writs for general election The Governor-General in Council may cause writs to be issued for general elections of members of the House of Representatives.

After the first general election, the writs shall be issued within ten days from the expiry of a House of Representatives or from the proclamation of a dissolution thereof.

33. Writs for vacancies Whenever a vacancy happens in the House of Representatives, the Speaker shall issue his writ for the election of a new member, or if there is no Speaker or if he is absent from the Commonwealth the Governor-General in Council may issue the writ.

34. Qualifications of members Until the Parliament otherwise provides, the qualifications of a member of the House of Representatives shall be as follows:—

    (i) He must be of the full age of twenty-one years, and must be an elector entitled to vote at the election of members of the House of Representatives, or a person qualified to become such elector, and must have been for three years at the least a resident within the limits of the Commonwealth as existing at the time when he is chosen;

    (ii) He must be a subject of the Queen, either natural-born or for at least five years naturalized under a law of the United Kingdom, or of a Colony which has become or becomes a State, or of the Commonwealth, or of a State.

35. Election of speaker The House of Representatives shall, before proceeding to the despatch of any other business, choose a member to be the Speaker of the House, and as often as the office of Speaker becomes vacant the House shall again choose a member to be the Speaker.

The Speaker shall cease to hold his office if he ceases to be a member. He may be removed from office by a vote of the House, or he may resign his office or his seat by writing addressed to the Governor-General.

36. Absence of Speaker Before or during any absence of the Speaker, the House of Representatives may choose a member to perform his duties in his absence.

37. Resignation of member A member may by writing addressed to the Speaker, or to the Governor-General if there is no Speaker or if the Speaker is absent from the Commonwealth, resign his place, which thereupon shall become vacant.

38. Vacancy by absence The place of a member shall become vacant if for two consecutive months of any session of the Parliament he, without the permission of the House, fails to attend the House.

39. Quorum Until the Parliament otherwise provides, the presence of at least one-third of the whole number of the members of the House of Representatives shall be necessary to constitute a meeting of the House for the exercise of its powers.

40. Voting in House of Representatives Questions arising in the House of Representatives shall be determined by a majority of votes other than that of the Speaker. The Speaker shall not vote unless the numbers are equal, and then he shall have a casting vote.

PART IV—BOTH HOUSES OF THE PARLIAMENT.

41. Right of electors of States No adult person who has or acquires a right to vote at elections for the more numerous House of the Parliament of a State shall, while the right continues, be prevented by any law of the Commonwealth from voting at elections for either House of the Parliament of the Commonwealth.

42. Oath or affirmation of allegiance Every senator and every member of the House of Representatives shall before taking his seat make and subscribe before the Governor-General, or some person authorised by him, an oath or affirmation of allegiance in the form set forth in the schedule to this Constitution.

43. Member of one House ineligible for other A member of either House of the Parliament shall be incapable of being chosen or of sitting as a member of the other House.

44. Disqualification Any person who—

(i) Is under any acknowledgment of allegiance, obedience, or adherence to a foreign power, or is a subject or a citizen or entitled to the rights or privileges of a subject or a citizen of a foreign power: or

(ii) Is attainted of treason, or has been convicted and is under sentence, or subject to be sentenced, for any offence punishable under the law of the Commonwealth or of a State by imprisonment for one year or longer: or

(iii) Is an undischarged bankrupt or insolvent: or

(iv) Holds any office of profit under the Crown, or any pension payable during the pleasure of the Crown out of any of the revenues of the Commonwealth: or

(v) Has any direct or indirect pecuniary interest in any agreement with the Public Service of the Commonwealth otherwise than as a member and in common with the other members of an incorporated company consisting of more than twenty-five persons:

shall be incapable of being chosen or of sitting as a senator or a member of the House of Representatives.

But sub-section iv does not apply to the office of any of the Queen's Ministers of State for the Commonwealth, or of any of the Queen's Ministers for a State, or to the receipt of pay, half pay, or a pension, by any person as an officer or member of the Queen's navy or army, or to the receipt of pay as an officer or member of the naval or military forces of the Commonwealth by any person whose services are not wholly employed by the Commonwealth.

45. Vacancy on happening of disqualification If a senator or member of the House of Representatives—

(i) Becomes subject to any of the disabilities mentioned in the last preceding section: or

(ii) Takes the benefit, whether by assignment, composition, or otherwise, of any law relating to bankrupt or insolvent debtors: or

(iii) Directly or indirectly takes or agrees to take any fee or honorarium for services rendered to the Commonwealth, or for services rendered in the Parliament to any person or State:

his place shall thereupon become vacant.

46. Penalty for sitting when disqualified Until the Parliament otherwise provides, any person declared by this Constitution to be incapable of sitting as a senator or as a member of the House of Representatives shall, for every day on which he so sits, be liable to pay the sum of one hundred pounds to any person who sues for it in any court of competent jurisdiction.

47. Disputed elections Until the Parliament otherwise provides, any question respecting the qualification of a senator or of a member of the House of Representatives, or respecting a vacancy in either House of the Parliament, and any question of a disputed election to either House, shall be determined by the House in which the question arises.

48. Allowance to members Until the Parliament otherwise provides, each senator and each member of the House of Representatives shall receive an allowance of four hundred pounds a year, to be reckoned from the day on which he takes his seat.

49. Privileges, &c of Houses The powers, privileges, and immunities of the Senate and of the House of Representatives, and of the members and the committees of each House, shall be such as are declared by the Parliament, and until declared shall be those of the Commons House of Parliament of the United Kingdom, and of its members and committees, at the establishment of the Commonwealth.

50. Rules and orders Each House of the Parliament may make rules and orders with respect to—

(i) The mode in which its powers, privileges, and immunities may be exercised and upheld:

(ii) The order and conduct of its business and proceedings either separately or jointly with the other House.

PART V—POWERS OF THE PARLIAMENT.

51. Legislative powers of the Parliament The Parliament shall, subject to this Constitution, have power to make laws for the peace, order, and good government of the Commonwealth with respect to:—

(i) Trade and commerce with other countries, and among the States:

(ii) Taxation; but so as not to discriminate between States or parts of States:

(iii) Bounties on the production or export of goods, but so that such bounties shall be uniform throughout the Commonwealth:

(iv) Borrowing money on the public credit of the Commonwealth:

(v) Postal, telegraphic, telephonic, and other like services:

(vi) The naval and military defence of the Commonwealth and of the several States, and the control of the forces to execute and maintain the laws of the Commonwealth:

(vii) Lighthouses, lightships, beacons and buoys:

(viii) Astronomical and meteorological observations:

(ix) Quarantine:

(x) Fisheries in Australian waters beyond territorial limits:

(xi) Census and statistics:

(xii) Currency, coinage, and legal tender:

(xiii)   Banking, other than State banking; also State banking extending beyond the limits of the State concerned, the incorporation of banks, and the issue of paper money:

(xiv)   Insurance, other than State insurance; also State insurance extending beyond the limits of the State concerned:

(xv)   Weights and measures:

(xvi)   Bills of exchange and promissory notes:

(xvii)   Bankruptcy and insolvency:

(xviii)   Copyrights, patents of inventions and designs, and trade marks:

(xix)   Naturalization and aliens:

(xx)   Foreign corporations, and trading or financial corporations formed within the limits of the Commonwealth:

(xxi)   Marriage;

(xxii)   Divorce and matrimonial causes; and in relation thereto, parental rights, and the custody and guardianship of infants:

(xxiii)   Invalid and old-age pensions:

(xxiiiA)   **[inserted by No 81, 1946, s 2]** The provision of maternity allowances, widows' pensions, child endowment, unemployment, pharmaceutical, sickness and hospital benefits, medical and dental services (but not so as to authorize any form of civil conscription), benefits to students and family allowances:

(xxiv)   The service and execution throughout the Commonwealth of the civil and criminal process and the judgments of the courts of the States:

(xxv)   The recognition throughout the Commonwealth of the laws, the public Acts and records, and the judicial proceedings of the States:

(xxvi)   **[altered by No 55, 1967, s 2]** The people of any race~~, other than the aboriginal race in any State,~~ for whom it is deemed necessary to make special laws:

(xxvii)   Immigration and emigration:

(xxviii)   The influx of criminals:

(xxix)   External affairs:

(xxx)   The relations of the Commonwealth with the islands of the Pacific:

(xxxi)   The acquisition of property on just terms from any State or person for any purpose in respect of which the Parliament has power to make laws:

(xxxii)   The control of railways with respect to transport for the naval and military purposes of the Commonwealth:

(xxxiii)   The acquisition, with the consent of a State, of any railways of the State on terms arranged between the Commonwealth and the State:

(xxxiv)   Railway construction and extension in any State with the consent of that State:

(xxxv)   Conciliation and arbitration for the prevention and settlement of industrial disputes extending beyond the limits of any one State:

(xxxvi)   Matters in respect of which this Constitution makes provision until the Parliament otherwise provides:

(xxxvii)   Matters referred to the Parliament of the Commonwealth by the Parliament or Parliaments of any State or States, but so that the law shall extend only to States by whose Parliaments the matter is referred, or which afterwards adopt the law:

(xxxviii) The exercise within the Commonwealth, at the request or with the concurrence of the Parliaments of all the States directly concerned, of any power which can at the establishment of this Constitution be exercised only by the Parliament of the United Kingdom or by the Federal Council of Australasia:

(xxxix) Matters incidental to the execution of any power vested by this Constitution in the Parliament or in either House thereof, or in the Government of the Commonwealth, or in the Federal Judicature, or in any department or officer of the Commonwealth.

52. Exclusive powers of the Parliament The Parliament shall, subject to this Constitution, have exclusive power to make laws for the peace, order, and good government of the Commonwealth with respect to—

(i) The seat of government of the Commonwealth, and all places acquired by the Commonwealth for public purposes:

(ii) Matters relating to any department of the public service the control of which is by this Constitution transferred to the Executive Government of the Commonwealth:

(iii) Other matters declared by this Constitution to be within the exclusive power of the Parliament.

53. Powers of the Houses in respect of legislation Proposed laws appropriating revenue or moneys, or imposing taxation, shall not originate in the Senate. But a proposed law shall not be taken to appropriate revenue or moneys, or to impose taxation, by reason only of its containing provisions for the imposition or appropriation of fines or other pecuniary penalties, or for the demand or payment or appropriation of fees for licences, or fees for services under the proposed law.

The Senate may not amend proposed laws imposing taxation, or proposed laws appropriating revenue or moneys for the ordinary annual services of the Government.

The Senate may not amend any proposed law so as to increase any proposed charge or burden on the people.

The Senate may at any stage return to the House of Representatives any proposed law which the Senate may not amend, requesting, by message, the omission or amendment of any items or provisions therein. And the House of Representatives may, if it thinks fit, make any of such omissions or amendments, with or without modifications.

Except as provided in this section, the Senate shall have equal power with the House of Representatives in respect of all proposed laws.

54. Appropriation Bills The proposed law which appropriates revenue or moneys for the ordinary annual services of the Government shall deal only with such appropriation.

55. Tax Bill Laws imposing taxation shall deal only with the imposition of taxation, and any provision therein dealing with any other matter shall be of no effect.

Laws imposing taxation, except laws imposing duties of customs or of excise, shall deal with one subject of taxation only; but laws imposing duties of customs shall deal with duties of customs only, and laws imposing duties of excise shall deal with duties of excise only.

56. Recommendation of money votes A vote, resolution, or proposed law for the appropriation of revenue or moneys shall not be passed unless the purpose of the appropriation has in the same session been recommended by message of the Governor-General to the House in which the proposal originated.

57. Disagreement between the Houses If the House of Representatives passes any proposed law, and the Senate rejects or fails to pass it, or passes it with amendments to which the House of Representatives will not agree, and if after an interval of three months the House of Representatives, in the same or the next session, again passes the proposed law with or without any amendments which have been made, suggested, or agreed to by the Senate, and the Senate rejects or fails to pass it, or passes it with amendments to which the House of Representatives will not agree, the Governor-General may dissolve the Senate and the House of Representatives simultaneously. But such dissolution shall not take place within six months before the date of the expiry of the House of Representatives by effluxion of time.

If after such dissolution the House of Representatives again passes the proposed law, with or without any amendments which have been made, suggested, or agreed to by the Senate, and the Senate rejects or fails to pass it, or passes it with amendments to which the House of Representatives will not agree, the Governor-General may convene a joint sitting of the members of the Senate and of the House of Representatives.

The members present at the joint sitting may deliberate and shall vote together upon the proposed law as last proposed by the House of Representatives, and upon amendments, if any, which have been made therein by one House and not agreed to by the other, and any such amendments which are affirmed by an absolute majority of the total number of the members of the Senate and House of Representatives shall be taken to have been carried, and if the proposed law, with the amendments, if any, so carried is affirmed by an absolute majority of the total number of the members of the Senate and House of Representatives, it shall be taken to have been duly passed by both Houses of the Parliament, and shall be presented to the Governor-General for the Queen's assent.

58. Royal assent to Bills When a proposed law passed by both Houses of the Parliament is presented to the Governor-General for the Queen's assent, he shall declare, according to his discretion, but subject to this Constitution, that he assents in the Queen's name, or that he withholds assent, or that he reserves the law for the Queen's pleasure.

Recommendations by Governor-General The Governor-General may return to the house in which it originated any proposed law so presented to him, and may transmit therewith any amendments which he may recommend, and the Houses may deal with the recommendation.

59. Disallowance by the Queen The Queen may disallow any law within one year from the Governor-General's assent, and such disallowance on being made known by the Governor-General by speech or message to each of the Houses of the Parliament, or by Proclamation, shall annul the law from the day when the disallowance is so made known.

60. Signification of Queen's pleasure on Bills reserved A proposed law reserved for the Queen's pleasure shall not have any force unless and until within two years from the day on which it was presented to the Governor-General for the Queen's assent the Governor-General makes known, by speech or message to each of the Houses of the Parliament, or by Proclamation, that it has received the Queen's assent.

CHAPTER II.

THE EXECUTIVE GOVERNMENT.

61. Executive power The executive power of the Commonwealth is vested in the Queen and is exercisable by the Governor-General as the Queen's representative, and extends to the execution and maintenance of this Constitution, and of the laws of the Commonwealth.

62. Federal Executive Council There shall be a Federal Executive Council to advise the Governor-General in the government of the Commonwealth, and the members of the Council shall be chosen and summoned by the Governor-General and sworn as Executive Councillors, and shall hold office during his pleasure.

63. Provisions referring to Governor-General The provisions of this Constitution referring to the Governor-General in Council shall be construed as referring to the Governor-General acting with the advice of the Federal Executive Council.

64. Ministers of State The Governor-General may appoint officers to administer such departments of State of the Commonwealth as the Governor-General in Council may establish.

Such officers shall hold office during the pleasure of the Governor-General. They shall be members of the Federal Executive Council, and shall be the Queen's Ministers of State for the Commonwealth.

Ministers to sit in Parliament After the first general election no Minister of State shall hold office for a longer period than three months unless he is or becomes a senator or a member of the House of Representatives.

65. Number of Ministers Until the Parliament otherwise provides, the Ministers of State shall not exceed seven in number, and shall hold such offices as the Parliament prescribes, or, in the absence of provision, as the Governor-General directs.

66. Salaries of Ministers There shall be payable to the Queen, out of the Consolidated Revenue Fund of the Commonwealth, for the salaries of the Ministers of State, an annual sum which, until the Parliament otherwise provides, shall not exceed twelve thousand pounds a year.

67. Appointment of civil servants Until the Parliament otherwise provides, the appointment and removal of all other officers of the Executive Government of the Commonwealth shall be vested in the Governor-General in Council, unless the appointment is delegated by the Governor-General in Council or by a law of the Commonwealth to some other authority.

68. Command of naval and military forces The command in chief of the naval and military forces of the Commonwealth is vested in the Governor-General as the Queen's representative.

69. Transfer of certain departments On a date or dates to be proclaimed by the Governor-General after the establishment of the Commonwealth the following departments of the public service in each State shall become transferred to the Commonwealth:—

Posts, telegraphs, and telephones:

Naval and military defence:

Lighthouses, lightships, beacons, and buoys:

Quarantine.

But the departments of customs and of excise in each State shall become transferred to the Commonwealth on its establishment.

70. Certain powers of Governors to vest in Governor-General In respect of matters which, under this Constitution, pass to the Executive Government of the Commonwealth, all powers and functions which at the establishment of the Commonwealth are vested in the Governor of a Colony, or in the Governor of a Colony with the advice of his Executive Council, or in any authority of a Colony, shall vest in the Governor-General, or in the Governor-General in Council, or in the authority exercising similar powers under the Commonwealth, as the case requires.

CHAPTER III.

THE JUDICATURE.

71. Judicial power and Courts The judicial power of the Commonwealth shall be vested in a Federal Supreme Court, to be called the High Court of Australia, and in such other federal courts as the Parliament creates, and in such other courts as it invests with federal jurisdiction. The High Court shall consist of a Chief Justice, and so many other Justices, not less than two, as the Parliament prescribes.

72. Judges' appointment, tenure and remuneration The Justices of the High Court and of the other courts created by the Parliament—

    (i) Shall be appointed by the Governor-General in Council:

    (ii) Shall not be removed except by the Governor-General in Council, on an address from both Houses of the Parliament in the same session, praying for such removal on the ground of proved misbehaviour or incapacity:

    (iii) Shall receive such remuneration as the Parliament may fix; but the remuneration shall not be diminished during their continuance in office.

[this and the following paragraphs added by No 83, 1977, s 2] The appointment of a Justice of the High Court shall be for a term expiring upon his attaining the age of seventy years, and a person shall not be appointed as a Justice of the High Court if he has attained that age.

The appointment of a Justice of a court created by the Parliament shall be for a term expiring upon his attaining the age that is, at the time of his appointment, the maximum age for Justices of that court and a person shall not be appointed as a Justice of such a court if he has attained the age that is for the time being the maximum age for Justices of that court.

Subject to this section, the maximum age for Justices of any court created by the Parliament is seventy years.

The Parliament may make a law fixing an age that is less than seventy years as the maximum age for Justices of a court created by the Parliament and may at any time repeal or amend such a law, but any such repeal or amendment does not affect the term of office of a Justice under an appointment made before the repeal or amendment.

A Justice of the High Court or of a court created by the Parliament may resign his office by writing under his hand delivered to the Governor-General.

Nothing in the provisions added to this section by the *Constitution Alteration (Retirement of Judges)* 1977 affects the continuance of a person in office as a Justice of a court under an appointment made before the commencement of those provisions.

A reference in this section to the appointment of a Justice of the High Court or of a court created by the Parliament shall be read as including a reference to the appointment of a person who holds office as a Justice of the High Court or of a court created by the Parliament to another office of Justice of the same court having a different status or designation.

73. Appellate jurisdiction of High Court The High Court shall have jurisdiction, with such exceptions and subject to such regulations as the Parliament prescribes, to hear and determine appeals from all judgments, decrees, orders, and sentences—

> (i) Of any Justice or Justices exercising the original jurisdiction of the High Court:
>
> (ii) Of any other federal court, or court exercising federal jurisdiction; or of the Supreme Court of any State, or of any other court of any State from which at the establishment of the Commonwealth an appeal lies to the Queen in Council:
>
> (iii) Of the Inter-State Commission, but as to questions of law only:

and the judgment of the High Court in all such cases shall be final and conclusive.

But no exception or regulation prescribed by the Parliament shall prevent the High Court from hearing and determining any appeal from the Supreme Court of a State in any matter in which at the establishment of the Commonwealth an appeal lies from such Supreme Court to the Queen in Council.

Until the Parliament otherwise provides, the conditions of and restrictions on appeals to the Queen in Council from the Supreme Courts of the several States shall be applicable to appeals from them to the High Court.

74. Appeal to Queen in Council No appeal shall be permitted to the Queen in Council from a decision of the High Court upon any question, howsoever arising, as to the limits inter se of the Constitutional powers of the Commonwealth and those of any State or States, or as to the limits inter se of the Constitutional powers of any two or more States, unless the High Court shall certify that the question is one which ought to be determined by Her Majesty in Council.

The High Court may so certify if satisfied that for any special reason the certificate should be granted, and thereupon an appeal shall lie to Her Majesty in Council on the question without further leave.

Except as provided in this section, this Constitution shall not impair any right which the Queen may be pleased to exercise by virtue of Her Royal prerogative to grant special leave of appeal from the High Court to Her Majesty in Council. The Parliament may make laws limiting the matters in which such leave may be asked, but proposed laws containing any such limitation shall be reserved by the Governor-General for Her Majesty's pleasure.

75. Original jurisdiction of High Court in all matters—

    (i) Arising under any treaty:

    (ii) Affecting consuls or other representatives of other countries:

    (iii) In which the Commonwealth, or a person suing or being sued on behalf of the Commonwealth, is a party:

    (iv) Between States, or between residents of different States, or between a State and a resident of another State:

    (v) In which a writ of Mandamus or prohibition or an injunction is sought against an officer of the Commonwealth:

the High Court shall have original jurisdiction.

76. Additional original jurisdiction The Parliament may make laws conferring original jurisdiction on the High Court in any matter—

    (i) Arising under this Constitution, or involving its interpretation:

    (ii) Arising under any laws made by the Parliament:

    (iii) Of Admiralty and maritime jurisdiction:

    (iv) Relating to the same subject-matter claimed under the laws of different States.

77. Power to define jurisdiction With respect to any of the matters mentioned in the last two sections the Parliament may make laws—

    (i) Defining the jurisdiction of any federal court other than the High Court:

    (ii) Defining the extent to which the jurisdiction of any federal court shall be exclusive of that which belongs to or is invested in the courts of the States:

    (iii) Investing any court of a State with federal jurisdiction.

78. Proceedings against Commonwealth or State The Parliament may make laws conferring rights to proceed against the Commonwealth or a State in respect of matters within the limits of the judicial power.

79. Number of judges The federal jurisdiction of any court may be exercised by such number of judges as the Parliament prescribes.

80. Trial by jury The trial on indictment of any offence against any law of the Commonwealth shall be by jury, and every such trial shall be held in the State where the offence was committed, and if the offence was not committed within any State the trial shall be held at such place or places as the Parliament prescribes.

CHAPTER IV.

FINANCE AND TRADE.

81. Consolidated Revenue Fund All revenue or moneys raised or received by the Executive Government of the Commonwealth shall form one Consolidated Revenue Fund, to be appropriated for the purposes of the Commonwealth in the manner and subject to the charges and liabilities imposed by this Constitution.

82. Expenditure charged thereon The costs, charges, and expenses incident to the collection, management, and receipt of the Consolidated Revenue Fund shall form the first charge thereon; and the revenue of the Commonwealth shall in the first instance be applied to the payment of the expenditure of the Commonwealth.

83. Money to be appropriated by law No money shall be drawn from the Treasury of the Commonwealth except under appropriation made by law.

But until the expiration of one month after the first meeting of the Parliament the Governor-General in Council may draw from the Treasury and expend such moneys as may be necessary for the maintenance of any department transferred to the Commonwealth and for the holding of the first elections for the Parliament.

84. Transfer of officers When any department of the public service of a State becomes transferred to the Commonwealth, all officers of the department shall become subject to the control of the Executive Government of the Commonwealth.

Any such officer who is not retained in the service of the Commonwealth shall, unless he is appointed to some other office of equal emolument in the public service of the State, be entitled to receive from the State any pension, gratuity, or other compensation, payable under the law of the State on the abolition of his office.

Any such officer who is retained in the service of the Commonwealth shall preserve all his existing and accruing rights, and shall be entitled to retire from office at the time, and on the pension or retiring allowance, which would be permitted by the law of the State if his service with the Commonwealth were a continuation of his service with the State. Such pension or retiring allowance shall be paid to him by the Commonwealth; but the State shall pay to the Commonwealth a part thereof, to be calculated on the proportion which his term of service with the State bears to his whole term of service, and for the purpose of the calculation his salary shall be taken to be that paid to him by the State at the time of the transfer.

Any officer who is, at the establishment of the Commonwealth, in the public service of a State, and who is, by consent of the Governor of the State with the advice of the Executive Council thereof, transferred to the public service of the Commonwealth, shall have the same rights as if he had been an officer of a department transferred to the Commonwealth and were retained in the service of the Commonwealth.

85. Transfer of property of State When any department of the public service of a State is transferred to the Commonwealth—

(i) All property of the State of any kind, used exclusively in connexion with the department, shall become vested in the Commonwealth; but, in the case of the departments controlling customs and excise and bounties, for such time only as the Governor-General in Council may declare to be necessary:

(ii) The Commonwealth may acquire any property of the State, of any kind used, but not exclusively used in connexion with the department; the value thereof shall, if no agreement can be made, be ascertained in, as nearly as may be, the manner in which the value of land, or of an interest in land, taken by the State for public purposes is ascertained under the law of the State in force at the establishment of the Commonwealth:

(iii) The Commonwealth shall compensate the State for the value of any property passing to the Commonwealth under this section; if no agreement can be made as to the mode of compensation, it shall be determined under laws to be made by the Parliament:

(iv) The Commonwealth shall, at the date of the transfer, assume the current obligations of the State in respect of the department transferred.

86. On the establishment of the Commonwealth, the collection and control of duties of customs and of excise, and the control of the payment of bounties, shall pass to the Executive Government of the Commonwealth.

87. During a period of ten years after the establishment of the Commonwealth and thereafter until the Parliament otherwise provides, of the net revenue of the Commonwealth from duties of customs and of excise not more than one-fourth shall be applied annually by the Commonwealth towards its expenditure.

The balance shall, in accordance with this Constitution, be paid to the several States, or applied towards the payment of interest on debts of the several States taken over by the Commonwealth.

88. Uniform duties of customs Uniform duties of customs shall be imposed within two years after the establishment of the Commonwealth.

89. Payment to States before uniform duties Until the imposition of uniform duties of customs—

    (i) The Commonwealth shall credit to each State the revenues collected therein by the Commonwealth.

    (ii) The Commonwealth shall debit to each State —

        (*a*) The expenditure therein of the Commonwealth incurred solely for the maintenance or continuance, as at the time of transfer, of any department transferred from the State to the Commonwealth;

        (*b*) The proportion of the State, according to the number of its people, in the other expenditure of the Commonwealth.

    (iii) The Commonwealth shall pay to each State month by month the balance (if any) in favour of the State.

90. Exclusive power over customs, excise, and bounties On the imposition of uniform duties of customs the power of the Parliament to impose duties of customs and of excise, and to grant bounties on the production or export of goods, shall become exclusive.

On the imposition of uniform duties of customs all laws of the several States imposing duties of customs or of excise, or offering bounties on the production or export of goods, shall cease to have effect, but any grant of or agreement for any such bounty lawfully made by or under the authority of the Government of any State shall be taken to be good if made before the thirtieth day of June, one thousand eight hundred and ninety-eight, and not otherwise.

91. Exceptions as to bounties Nothing in this Constitution prohibits a State from granting any aid to or bounty on mining for gold, silver, or other metals, nor from granting, with the consent of both Houses of the Parliament of the Commonwealth expressed by resolution, any aid to or bounty on the production or export of goods.

92. Trade within the Commonwealth to be free On the imposition of uniform duties of customs, trade, commerce, and intercourse among the States, whether by means of internal carriage or ocean navigation, shall be absolutely free.

But notwithstanding anything in this Constitution, goods imported before the imposition of uniform duties of customs into any State, or into any Colony which, whilst the goods remain therein, becomes a State, shall, on thence passing into another State within two years after the imposition of such duties, be liable to any duty chargeable on the importation of such goods into the Commonwealth, less any duty paid in respect of the goods on their importation.

93. Payment to States for five years after uniform tariffs During the first five years after the imposition of uniform duties of customs, and thereafter until the Parliament otherwise provides—

    (i)   The duties of customs chargeable on goods imported into a State and afterwards passing into another State for consumption, and the duties of excise paid on goods produced or manufactured in a State and afterwards passing into another State for consumption, shall be taken to have been collected not in the former but in the latter State:

    (ii) Subject to the last subsection, the Commonwealth shall credit revenue, debit expenditure, and pay balances to the several States as prescribed for the period preceding the imposition of uniform duties of customs.

94. Distribution of surplus After five years from the imposition of uniform duties of customs, the Parliament may provide, on such basis as it deems fair, for the monthly payment to the several States of all surplus revenue of the Commonwealth.

95. Customs duties of Western Australia Notwithstanding anything in this Constitution, the Parliament of the State of Western Australia, if that State be an Original State, may, during the first five years after the imposition of uniform duties of customs, impose duties of customs on goods passing into that State and not originally imported from beyond the limits of the Commonwealth; and such duties shall be collected by the Commonwealth.

But any duty so imposed on any goods shall not exceed during the first of such years the duty chargeable on the goods under the law of Western Australia in force at the imposition of uniform duties, and shall not exceed during the second, third, fourth, and fifth of such years respectively, four-fifths, three-fifths, two-fifths, and one-fifth of such latter duty, and all duties imposed under this section shall cease at the expiration of the fifth year after the imposition of uniform duties.

If at any time during the five years the duty on any goods under this section is higher than the duty imposed by the Commonwealth on the importation of the like goods, then such higher duty shall be collected on the goods when imported into Western Australia from beyond the limits of the Commonwealth.

96. Financial assistance to States During a period of ten years after the establishment of the Commonwealth and thereafter until the Parliament otherwise provides, the Parliament may grant financial assistance to any State on such terms and conditions as the Parliament thinks fit.

97. Audit Until the Parliament otherwise provides, the laws in force in any Colony which has become or becomes a State with respect to the receipt of revenue and the expenditure of money on account of the Government of the Colony, and the review and audit of such receipt and expenditure, shall apply to the receipt of revenue and the expenditure of money on account of the Commonwealth in the State in the same manner as if the Commonwealth, or the Government or an officer of the Commonwealth, were mentioned whenever the Colony, or the Government or an officer of the Colony, is mentioned.

98. Trade and commerce includes navigation and State railways The power of the Parliament to make laws with respect to trade and commerce extends to navigation and shipping, and to railways the property of any State.

99. Commonwealth not to give preference The Commonwealth shall not, by any law or regulation of trade, commerce, or revenue, give preference to one State or any part thereof over another State or any part thereof.

100. Nor abridge right to use water The Commonwealth shall not, by any law or regulation of trade or commerce, abridge the right of a State or of the residents therein to the reasonable use of the waters of rivers for conservation or irrigation.

101. Inter-State Commission There shall be an Inter-State Commission, with such powers of adjudication and administration as the Parliament deems necessary for the execution and maintenance, within the Commonwealth, of the provisions of this Constitution relating to trade and commerce, and of all laws made thereunder.

102. Parliament may forbid preferences by State The Parliament may by any law with respect to trade or commerce forbid, as to railways, any preference or discrimination by any State, or by any authority constituted under a State, if such preference or discrimination is undue and unreasonable, or unjust to any State; due regard being had to the financial responsibilities incurred by any State in connexion with the construction and maintenance of its railways. But no preference or discrimination shall, within the meaning of this section, be taken to be undue and unreasonable, or unjust to any State, unless so adjudged by the Inter-State Commission.

103. Commissioners' appointment, tenure, and remuneration The members of the Inter-State Commission—

    (i) Shall be appointed by the Governor-General in Council:

    (ii) Shall hold office for seven years, but may be removed within that time by the Governor-General in Council, on an address from both Houses of the Parliament in the same session praying for such removal on the ground of proved misbehaviour or incapacity:

    (iii) Shall receive such remuncration as the Parliament may fix; but such remuneration shall not be diminished during their continuance in office.

104. Saving of certain rates Nothing in this Constitution shall render unlawful any rate for the carriage of goods upon a railway, the property of a State, if the rate is deemed by the Inter-State Commission to be necessary for the development of the territory of the State, and if the rate applies equally to goods within the State and to goods passing into the State from other States.

105. Taking over public debts of States [altered by No 3, 1910, s 2] The Parliament may take over from the States their public debts ~~as existing at the establishment of the Commonwealth,~~ or a proportion thereof according to the respective numbers of their people as shown by the latest statistics of the Commonwealth, and may convert, renew, or consolidate such debts, or any part thereof; and the States shall indemnify the Commonwealth in respect of the debts taken over, and thereafter the interest payable in respect of the debts shall be deducted and retained from the portions of the surplus revenue of the Commonwealth payable to the several States, or if such surplus is insufficient, or if there is no surplus, then the deficiency or the whole amount shall be paid by the several States.

105A. Agreements with respect to State debts [inserted by No 1, 1929, s 2]—

    (1) The Commonwealth may make agreements with the States with respect to the public debts of the States, including—

        (*a*) the taking over of such debts by the Commonwealth;

        (*b*) the management of such debts;

(c) the payment of interest and the provision and management of sinking funds in respect of such debts;

(d) the consolidation, renewal, conversion, and redemption of such debts;

(e) the indemnification of the Commonwealth by the States in respect of debts taken over by the Commonwealth; and

(f) the borrowing of money by the States or by the Commonwealth, or by the Commonwealth for the States.

(2) The Parliament may make laws for validating any such agreement made before the commencement of this section.

(3) The Parliament may make laws for the carrying out by the parties thereto of any such agreement.

(4) Any such agreement may be varied or rescinded by the parties thereto.

(5) Every such agreement and any such variation thereof shall be binding upon the Commonwealth and the States parties thereto notwithstanding anything contained in this Constitution or the Constitution of the several States or in any law of the Parliament of the Commonwealth or of any State.

(6) The powers conferred by this section shall not be construed as being limited in any way by the provisions of section one hundred and five of this Constitution.

CHAPTER V.

THE STATES.

106. Saving of Constitutions The Constitution of each State of the Commonwealth shall, subject to this Constitution, continue as at the establishment of the Commonwealth, or as at the admission or establishment of the State, as the case may be, until altered in accordance with the Constitution of the State.

107. Saving of Power of State Parliaments Every power of the Parliament of a Colony which has become or becomes a State, shall, unless it is by this Constitution exclusively vested in the Parliament of the Commonwealth or withdrawn from the Parliament of the State, continue as at the establishment of the Commonwealth, or as at the admission or establishment of the State, as the case may be.

108. Saving of State laws Every law in force in a Colony which has become or becomes a State, and relating to any matter within the powers of the Parliament of the Commonwealth, shall, subject to this Constitution, continue in force in the State; and, until provision is made in that behalf by the Parliament of the Commonwealth, the Parliament of the State shall have such powers of alteration and of repeal in respect of any such law as the Parliament of the Colony had until the Colony became a State.

109. Inconsistency of laws When a law of a State is inconsistent with a law of the Commonwealth, the latter shall prevail, and the former shall, to the extent of the inconsistency, be invalid.

110. Provisions referring to Governor The provisions of this Constitution relating to the Governor of a State extend and apply to the Governor for the time being of the State, or other chief executive officer or administrator of the government of the State.

111. States may surrender territory The Parliament of a State may surrender any part of the State to the Commonwealth; and upon such surrender, and the acceptance thereof by the Commonwealth, such part of the State shall become subject to the exclusive jurisdiction of the Commonwealth.

112. States may levy charges for inspection laws After uniform duties of customs have been imposed, a State may levy on imports or exports, or on goods passing into or out of the State, such charges as may be necessary for executing the inspection laws of the State; but the net produce of all charges so levied shall be for the use of the Commonwealth; and any such inspection laws may be annulled by the Parliament of the Commonwealth.

113. Intoxicating liquids All fermented, distilled, or other intoxicating liquids passing into any State or remaining therein for use, consumption, sale, or storage, shall be subject to the laws of the State as if such liquids had been produced in the State.

114. States may not raise forces. Taxation of property of Commonwealth or State A State shall not, without the consent of the Parliament of the Commonwealth, raise or maintain any naval or military force, or impose any tax on property of any kind belonging to the Commonwealth, nor shall the Commonwealth impose any tax on property of any kind belonging to a State.

115. States not to coin money A State shall not coin money, nor make anything but gold and silver coin a legal tender in payment of debts.

116. Commonwealth not to legislate in respect of religion The Commonwealth shall not make any law for establishing any religion, or for imposing any religious observance, or for prohibiting the free exercise of any religion, and no religious test shall be required as a qualification for any office or public trust under the Commonwealth.

117. Rights of residents in States A subject of the Queen, resident in any State, shall not be subject in any other State to any disability or discrimination which would not be equally applicable to him if he were a subject of the Queen resident in such other State.

118. Recognition of laws, &c of States Full faith and credit shall be given, throughout the Commonwealth to the laws, the public Acts and records, and the judicial proceedings of every State.

119. Protection of States from invasion and violence The Commonwealth shall protect every State against invasion and, on the application of the Executive Government of the State, against domestic violence.

120. Custody of offenders against laws of the Commonwealth Every State shall make provision for the detention in its prisons of persons accused or convicted of offences against the laws of the Commonwealth, and for the punishment of persons convicted of such offences, and the Parliament of the Commonwealth may make laws to give effect to this provision.

CHAPTER VI.

NEW STATES.

121. New States may be admitted or established The Parliament may admit to the Commonwealth or establish new States, and may upon such admission or establishment make or impose such terms and conditions, including the extent of representation in either House of the Parliament, as it thinks fit.

122. Government of territories The Parliament may make laws for the government of any territory surrendered by any State to and accepted by the Commonwealth, or of any territory placed by the Queen under the authority of and accepted by the Commonwealth, or otherwise acquired by the Commonwealth, and may allow the representation of such territory in either House of the Parliament to the extent and on the terms which it thinks fit.

123. Alteration of limits of States The Parliament of the Commonwealth may, with the consent of the Parliament of a State, and the approval of the majority of the electors of the State voting upon the question, increase, diminish, or otherwise alter the limits of the State, upon such terms and conditions as may be agreed on, and may with the like consent, make provision respecting the effect and operation of any increase or diminution or alteration of territory in relation to any State affected.

124. Formation of new States A new State may be formed by separation of territory from a State, but only with the consent of the Parliament thereof, and a new State may be formed by the union of two or more States or parts of States, but only with the consent of the Parliaments of the States affected.

CHAPTER VII.

MISCELLANEOUS.

125. Seat of Government The seat of Government of the Commonwealth shall be determined by the Parliament, and shall be within territory which shall have been granted to or acquired by the Commonwealth, and shall be vested in and belong to the Commonwealth, and shall be in the State of New South Wales, and be distant not less than one hundred miles from Sydney.

Such territory shall contain an area of not less than one hundred square miles, and such portion thereof as shall consist of Crown lands shall be granted to the Commonwealth without any payment therefor.

The Parliament shall sit at Melbourne until it meet at the seat of Government.

126. Power to Her Majesty to authorise Governor-General to appoint deputies The Queen may authorise the Governor-General to appoint any person, or any persons jointly or severally, to be his deputy or deputies within any part of the Commonwealth, and in that capacity to exercise during the pleasure of the Governor-General such powers and functions of the Governor-General as he thinks fit to assign to such deputy or deputies, subject to any limitations expressed or directions given by the Queen; but the appointment of such deputy or deputies shall not affect the exercise by the Governor-General himself of any power or function.

127. [repealed by No 55, 1967, s 3]

CHAPTER VIII.

ALTERATION OF THE CONSTITUTION.

128. Mode of altering the Constitution This Constitution shall not be altered except in the following manner:—

[this paragraph altered by No 84, 1977, s 2] The proposed law for the alteration thereof must be passed by an absolute majority of each House of the Parliament, and not less than two nor more than six months after its passage through both Houses the proposed law shall be submitted in each State **and Territory** to the electors qualified to vote for the election of members of the House of Representatives.

[this paragraph altered by No 84, 1977, s 2] But if either House passes any such proposed law by an absolute majority, and the other House rejects or fails to pass it, or passes it with any amendment to which the first-mentioned House will not agree, and if after an interval of three months the first-mentioned House in the same or the next session again passes the proposed law by an absolute majority with or without any amendment which has been made or agreed to by the other House, and such other House rejects or fails to pass it or passes it with any amendment to which the first-mentioned House will not agree, the Governor-General may submit the proposed law as last proposed by the first-mentioned House, and either with or without any amendments subsequently agreed to by both Houses, to the electors in each State **and Territory** qualified to vote for the election of the House of Representatives.

When a proposed law is submitted to the electors the vote shall be taken in such manner as the Parliament prescribes. But until the qualification of electors of members of the House of Representatives becomes uniform throughout the Commonwealth, only one-half the electors voting for and against the proposed law shall be counted in any State in which adult suffrage prevails.

And if in a majority of the States a majority of the electors voting approve the proposed law, and if a majority of all the electors voting also approve the proposed law, it shall be presented to the Governor-General for the Queen's assent.

No alteration diminishing the proportionate representation of any State in either House of the Parliament, or the minimum number of representatives of a State in the

House of Representatives, or increasing, diminishing, or otherwise altering the limits of the State, or in any manner affecting the provisions of the Constitution in relation thereto, shall become law unless the majority of the electors voting in that State approve the proposed law.

[this paragraph added by No 84, 1977, s 2] In this section, "Territory" means any territory referred to in section one hundred and twenty-two of this Constitution in respect of which there is in force a law allowing its representation in the House of Representatives.

SCHEDULE.

OATH.

I, *A.B.*, do swear that I will be faithful and bear true allegiance to Her Majesty Queen Victoria, Her heirs and successors according to law. SO HELP ME GOD!

AFFIRMATION.

I, *A.B.*, do solemnly and sincerely affirm and declare that I will be faithful and bear true allegiance to Her Majesty Queen Victoria, Her heirs and successors according to law.

(NOTE.—*The name of the King or Queen of the United Kingdom of Great Britain and Ireland for the time being is to be substituted from time to time.*)

Select Bibliography on the Constitutional Protection of Rights in Australia

Allan, J. and Cullen, R., 'A Bill of Rights Odyssey for Australia: The Sirens are Calling' (1997) 19 *University of Queensland Law Journal* 171.

Alston, P. (ed.), *Towards an Australian Bill of Rights*, Centre for International and Public Law, Australian National University, Canberra, 1994.

Anderson, G. W., 'Corporations, Democracy and the Implied Freedom of Political Communication: Towards a Pluralistic Analysis of Constitutional Law' (1998) 22 *Melbourne University Law Review* 1.

Aroney, N., 'Representative Democracy Eclipsed? The *Langer*, *Muldowney* and *McGinty* Decisions' (1996) 19 *University of Queensland Law Journal* 75.

——, 'A Seductive Plausibility: Freedom of Speech in the Constitution' (1995) 18 *University of Queensland Law Journal* 249.

Ball, D., 'The Lion that Squeaked: Representative Government and the High Court: *McGinty & Ors v The State of Western Australia*' (1996) 18 *Sydney Law Review* 372.

Bailey, P., *Human Rights: Australia in an International Context*, Butterworths, Sydney, 1990.

——, ' "Righting" the Constitution without a Bill of Rights' (1995) 23 *Federal Law Review* 1.

Baker, R. W., 'The Compulsory Acquisition Powers of the Commonwealth', in Else-Mitchell, R. (ed.), *Essays on the Australian Constitution*, 2nd edn, LBC, Sydney, 1961, p. 193.

Barendt, E., 'Election Broadcasts in Australia' (1993) 109 *Law Quarterly Review* 168.

——, 'Free Speech in Australia: A Comparative Perspective' (1994) 16 *Sydney Law Review* 149.

Beasley, F. R., 'The Commonwealth Constitution: Section 92—Its History in the Federal Conventions' (1948–1950) 1 *University of Western Australia Annual Law Review* 97, 273, 433.

Behrendt, J., 'So Long, and Thanks for all the Fish … ' (1995) 3(72) *Aboriginal Law Bulletin* 11.

Bell, A., 'Section 92, Factual Discrimination and the High Court' (1991) 20 *Federal Law Review* 240.

Bell, D., Bendall, S., Dang, M. K., Dowling, S., Stiel, M., and Wu, P., 'Implying Guarantees of Freedom into the Constitution: *Nationwide News* and *Australian Capital Television*' (1994) 16 *Sydney Law Review* 288.

Bickovskii, P., 'No Deliberate Innovators: Mr Justice Murphy and the Australian Constitution' (1977) 8 *Federal Law Review* 460.

Blackford, R., 'Judicial Power, Political Liberty and the Post-Industrial State' (1997) 71 *Australian Law Journal* 267.

Blackshield, A. R., 'The Implied Freedom of Communication', in Lindell, G. (ed.), *Future Directions in Australian Constitutional Law*, Federation Press, Sydney, 1994, p. 232.

——, 'Reinterpreting the Constitution', in Brett, J., Gillespie, J., and Goot, M. (eds), *Developments in Australian Politics*, Macmillan, Melbourne, 1994, p. 23.

Blackshield, A. R., Brown, D., Coper, M., and Krever, R. (eds), *The Judgments of Justice Lionel Murphy*, Primavera Press, Sydney, 1986.

Blackshield, A. R. and Williams, G., *Australian Constitutional Law and Theory: Commentary and Materials*, 2nd edn, Federation Press, Sydney, 1998, chs 24–7.

Boas, G., '*Dietrich*, the High Court and Unfair Trials Legislation: A Constitutional Guarantee?' (1993) 19 *Monash Law Review* 256.

Bogen, D. S., 'Comparing Implied and Express Constitutional Freedoms' (1995) 2 *James Cook University Law Review* 190.

——, 'The Religion Clauses and Freedom of Speech in Australia and the United States: Incidental Restrictions and Generally Applicable Laws' (1997) 46 *Drake Law Review* 53.

——, 'Telling the Truth and Paying for It: A Comparison of Two Cases—Restrictions on Political Speech in Australia and Commercial Speech in the United States' (1996) 7 *Indiana International and Comparative Law Review* 111.

Booker, K., Glass, A., and Watt, R., *Federal Constitutional Law: An Introduction*, 2nd edn, Butterworths, Sydney, 1998, ch. 10.

Brennan, F., 'An Australian Convert from a Constitutional Bill of Rights' (1996) 7 *Public Law Review* 132.

——, *Legislating Liberty: A Bill of Rights for Australia?*, University of Queensland Press, Brisbane, 1998.

——, *Securing a Bountiful Place for Aborigines and Torres Strait Islanders in a Modern, Free and Tolerant Australia*, Constitutional Centenary Foundation, Melbourne, 1994.

——, 'Thirty Years On, Do We Need a Bill of Rights?' (1996) 18 *Adelaide Law Review* 123.

Brennan, G., 'Courts, Democracy and the Law' (1991) 65 *Australian Law Journal* 32.

Bronitt, S. and Williams, G., 'Political Freedom as an Outlaw: Republican Theory and Political Protest' (1996) 18 *Adelaide Law Review* 289.

Brooks, A., 'A Paragon of Democratic Virtues? The Development of the Commonwealth Franchise' (1993) 12 *University of Tasmania Law Review* 208.

Byers, M., 'The Kruger Case' (1997) 8 *Public Law Review* 224.

Campbell, L., 'Lionel Murphy and the Jurisprudence of the High Court Ten Years On' (1996) 15 *University of Tasmania Law Review* 22.

Campbell, T., 'Democracy, Human Rights, and Positive Law' (1994) 16 *Sydney Law Review* 195.

Campbell, T. and Sadurski, W. (eds), *Freedom of Communication*, Dartmouth, Aldershot, United Kingdom, 1994.

Carne, G., 'Representing Democracy or Reinforcing Equality?: Electoral Distribution and *McGinty v Western Australia*' (1997) 25 *Federal Law Review* 351.

Carney, G., 'Freedom of Political Discussion—A New Restriction on State Power' (1995) 6 *Public Law Review* 147.

——, 'The Implied Freedom of Political Discussion—Its Impact on State Constitutions' (1995) 23 *Federal Law Review* 180.

——, 'The Re-interpretation of Section 92: The Decline of Free Enterprise and the Rise of Free Trade' (1991) 3 *Bond Law Review* 149.

Cass, D. Z., 'Through the Looking Glass: The High Court and the Right to Speech' (1993) 4 *Public Law Review* 229.

Cass, D. Z. and Rubenstein, K., 'Representation/s of Women in the Australian Constitutional System' (1995) 17 *Adelaide Law Review* 3.

Cassimatis, A. E., 'Defamation—The Constitutional Public Officer Defence' (1996) 4 *Tort Law Review* 27.

——, 'The Law of Defamation in Queensland—The Defence of Fair Comment and the Constitutional Public Officer Defence' (1996) 16 *Queensland Lawyer* 159.

——, '*Theophanous*—A Review of Recent Defamation Decisions' (1997) 5 *Torts Law Journal* 27.

Charlesworth, H., 'The Australian Reluctance About Rights' (1993) *Osgoode Hall Law Journal* 195.

——, 'The Australian Reluctance about Rights', in Alston, P. (ed.), *Towards an Australian Bill of Rights*, Centre for International and Public Law, Australian National University, Canberra, 1994, p. 21.

——, A Constitutional Bill of Rights: North American Experience and Australian Prospect, SJD thesis, Harvard University, 1985.

——, 'Individual Rights and the Australian High Court' (1986) 4 *Law in Context* 52.

Chesterman, M., 'The Common Law Rules in Defamation—OK?' (1998) 6 *Tort Law Review* 9.

——, 'The Money or the Truth: Defamation Reform in Australia and the USA' (1995) 18 *University of New South Wales Law Journal* 300.

——, 'Privileges and Freedoms for Defamatory Political Speech' (1997) 19 *Adelaide Law Review* 155.

Civics Expert Group, *Whereas the People: Civics and Citizenship Education*, AGPS, Canberra, 1994

Clark, A. I., *Studies in Australian Constitutional Law*, 1901 edn, Legal Books, Sydney, 1997.

Claus, L., 'Implication and the Concept of a Constitution' (1995) 69 *Australian Law Journal* 887.

Comans, C. K., 'The Jury in Federal Jurisdiction—Constitutional Aspects' (1968) 3 *Federal Law Review* 51.

Connolly, P. D., 'Cole v Whitfield—The Repeal of Section 92 of the Constitution?' (1991) 16 *University of Queensland Law Journal* 290.

Constitutional Commission, *Final Report of the Constitutional Commission*, 2 vols, AGPS, Canberra, 1988.

Constitutional Commission, *First Report of the Constitutionl Commission*, 2 vols, AGPS, 1988.

Constitutional Commission, *Report of the Advisory Committee on Individual & Democratic Rights under the Constitution*, AGPS, 1987.

Coper, M., *Encounters with the Australian Constitution*, CCH, Sydney, 1988 (deluxe edn, 1987).

——, *Freedom of Interstate Trade under the Australian Constitution*, Butterworths, Sydney, 1983.

——, 'The High Court and Free Speech: Visions of Democracy or Delusions of Grandeur?' (1994) 16 *Sydney Law Review* 185.

——, 'Section 92 and the Impressionistic Approach' (1984) 58 *Australian Law Journal* 92.

——, 'Speak Easy' (1992) 3 *Polemic* 156.

Coper, M. and Williams, G. (eds), *The Cauldron of Constitutional Change*, Centre for International and Public Law, Australian National University, Canberra, 1997.

—— (eds), *Power, Parliament and the People*, Federation Press, Sydney, 1997.

—— (eds), *Justice Lionel Murphy: Influential or Merely Prescient?*, Federation Press, Sydney, 1997.

Cowen, Z., 'A Comparison of the Constitutions of Australia and the United States' (1955) 4 *Buffalo Law Review* 155.

Creighton, P, 'Apportioning Electoral Districts in a Representative Democracy' (1994) 24 *Western Australian Law Review* 78.

——, 'Defectively Representing Representative Democracy—A Reply' (1995) 25 *University of Western Australia Law Review* 85.

——, 'The Implied Guarantee of Free Political Communication' (1993) 23 *University of Western Australia Law Review* 163.

Cumbrae-Stewart, F. D., 'Section 116 of the Constitution' (1946) 20 *Australian Law Journal* 207.

Detmold, M. J., 'Australian Constitutional Equality: The Common Law Foundation' (1996) 7 *Public Law Review* 33.

——, 'The New Constitutional Law' (1994) 16 *Sydney Law Review* 228.

Dixon, O. *Jesting Pilate*, LBC, Sydney, 1965.

Donaghue, S, 'The Clamour of Silent Constitutional Principles' (1996) 24 *Federal Law Review* 133.

Douglas, N. F., 'Freedom of Expression Under the Australian Constitution' (1993) 16 *University of New South Wales Law Journal* 315.

Ebbeck, G., 'The Future for Section 117 as a Constitutional Guarantee' (1993) 4 *Public Law Review* 89.

——, 'Section 117: The Obscure Provision' (1991) 13 *Adelaide Law Review* 23.

Ely, R, *Unto God and Caesar: Religious Issues in the Emerging Commonwealth*, 1891–1906, Melbourne University Press, Melbourne, 1976.

Evans, G, 'Benign Discrimination and the Right to Equality' (1974) 6 *Federal Law Review* 26.

Ewing, K. D., 'The Legal Regulation of Electoral Campaign Financing in Australia: A Preliminary Study' (1992) 22 *University of Western Australia Law Review* 239.

——, 'New Constitutional Constraints in Australia' [1993] *Public Law* 256.

Finn, P. D. (ed.), *Essays on Law and Government*, vol. 1, *Principles and Values*, LBC, Sydney, 1995.

—— (ed.), *Essays on Law and Government*, vol. 2, *The Citizen and the State in the Courts*, LBC, Sydney, 1996.

Fitzgerald, B. F., 'Proportionality and Australian Constitutionalism' (1993) 12 *University of Tasmania Law Review* 263.

Fraser, A., 'False Hopes: Implied Rights and Popular Sovereignty in the Australian Constitution' (1994) 16 *Sydney Law Review* 213.

Fricke, G., 'Constitutional Implications—A Misty and Uncertain Light' (1996) 3 *Deakin Law Review* 129.

Galligan, B., *A Federal Republic: Australia's Constitutional System of Government*, Cambridge University Press, Melbourne, 1995, ch. 6.

——, 'Parliamentary Responsible Government and the Protection of Rights' (1993) 4 *Public Law Review* 100.

——, *Politics of the High Court*, University of Queensland Press, Brisbane, 1987.

Galligan, B. and Sampford, C. (eds), *Rethinking Human Rights*, Federation Press, Sydney, 1997.

Gaze, B. and Jones, M., *Law, Liberty and Australian Democracy*, LBC, Sydney, 1990.

Gibbs, H., 'The Constitutional Protection of Human Rights' (1982) 9 *Monash University Law Review* 1.

Gibbs, H. T., 'Section 116 of the Constitution and the Territories of the Commonwealth' (1947) 20 *Australian Law Journal* 375.

Glass, A., '*Australian Capital Television* and the Application of Constitutional Rights' (1995) 17 *Sydney Law Review* 29.

Goldsworthy, J., 'Constitutional Implications and Freedom of Political Speech: A Reply to Stephen Donaghue' (1997) 23 *Monash University Law Review* 362.

——, 'The Constitutional Protection of Rights in Australia', in Craven, G. (ed.), *Australian Federation: Towards the Second Century*, Melbourne University Press, Melbourne, 1992, p. 151.

——, 'The High Court, Implied Rights and Constitutional Change' (March 1995) *Quadrant*, 46.

——, 'Implications in Language, Law and the Constitution', in Lindell, G. (ed.), *Future Directions in Australian Constitutional Law*, Federation Press, Sydney, 1994, p. 150.

——, 'Originalism in Constitutional Interpretation' (1997) 25 *Federal Law Review* 1.

Hamilton, R. L., 'Some Aspects of the Acquisition Power of the Commonwealth' (1973) 5 *Federal Law Review* 265.

Handsley, E., 'Do Hard Laws Make Bad Cases?—The High Court's Decision in *Kable v Director of Public Prosecutions (NSW)*' (1997) 25 *Federal Law Review* 171.

——, 'Public Confidence in the Judiciary: A Red Herring for the Separation of Judicial Power' (1998) 20 *Sydney Law Review* 183.

Hanks, P., 'Adjusting Medicare Benefits: Acquisition of Property?' (1992) 14 *Sydney Law Review* 495.

——, 'The Australian Legal Foundation', in *Laws of Australia*, vol. 21, *Human Rights*, LBC, Sydney, 1995.

——, 'Constitutional Guarantees', in Lee, H. P. and Winterton, G. (eds), *Australian Constitutional Perspectives*, LBC, Sydney, 1992, p. 92.

——, *Constitutional Law in Australia*, 2nd edn, Butterworths, Sydney, 1996, ch. 14.

——, 'Moving Towards the Legalisation of Politics' (1988) 6 *Law in Context* 80.

Hogan, M., 'Separation of Church and State: Section 116 of the Australian Constitution' (Winter 1981) *Australian Quarterly* 214.

Hope, J., 'A Constitutional Right to a Fair Trial? Implications for the Reform of the Australian Criminal Justice System' (1996) 24 *Federal Law Review* 173.

Hughes, A., 'The High Court and Implied Constitutional Rights: Exploring Freedom of Communication' (1994) 1 *Deakin Law Review* 173.

Irving, H. (ed.), *A Woman's Constitution*, Hale & Iremonger, Sydney, 1996.

Johnston, P. and Hardcastle, R., 'State Courts: The Limits of Kable' (1998) 20 *Sydney Law Review* 216.

Jones, M., 'Free Speech Revisited: The Implications of Lange and Levy' (1997) 4 *Australian Journal of Human Rights* 188.

Jones, T. H., 'Freedom of Political Communication in Australia' (1996) 45 *International and Comparative Law Quarterly* 392.

——, 'Legal Protection for Fundamental Rights and Freedoms: European Lessons for Australia?' (1994) 22 *Federal Law Review* 57.

Kainthaje, P., 'Strict Construction Meets Deconstruction: A Constructive Defence of Implied Rights' (1996) 12 *Australian Journal of Law and Society* 1.

Kennett, G., 'The Freedom Ride: Where to Now?' (1998) 9 *Public Law Review* 111.

——, 'Individual Rights, the High Court and the Constitution' (1994) 19 *Melbourne University Law Review* 581.

Keyzer, P., *Constitutional Law*, Butterworths, Sydney, 1998, chs 8, 11, 13, 14.

Kirby, M., 'Deakin: Popular Sovereignty and the True Foundation of the Australian Constitution' (1996) 3 *Deakin Law Review* 129.

——, 'Constitutional Protections for Free Speech' (1992) 66 *Australian Law Journal* 775.

——, 'Lionel Murphy and the Power of Ideas' (1993) 18 *Alternative Law Journal* 253.

Kirk, J., 'Constitutional Guarantees, Characterisation and the Concept of Proportionality' (1997) 21 *Melbourne University Law Review* 1.

——, 'Constitutional Implications from Representative Democracy' (1995) 23 *Federal Law Review* 37.

La Nauze, J. A., 'A Little Bit of Lawyers' Language: The History of "Absolutely Free", 1890–1900', in Martin, A. W. (ed.), *Essays in Australian Federation*, Melbourne University Press, Melbourne, 1969, p. 57.

——, *The Making of the Australian Constitution*, Melbourne University Press, 1972.

Lane, P. H., *Lane's Commentary on the Australian Constitution*, 2nd edn, LBC, Sydney, 1997, ch. 2.

——, 'The Present Test for Invalidity Under Section 92 of the Constitution' (1988) 62 *Australian Law Journal* 604.

Lee, H. P., 'The Australian High Court and Implied Fundamental Guarantees' [1993] *Public Law* 606.

Lindell, G. (ed.), *Future Directions in Australian Constitutional Law*, Federation Press, Sydney, 1994.

——, 'Theophanous and Stephens Revisited' (1997) 20 *University of New South Wales Law Journal* 195.

Lloyd, S. B., 'Constitutional Guarantees of Rights', *Laws of Australia*, vol. 19, *Government*, LBC, Sydney, 1995.

Loveland, I., 'Privacy and Political Speech: An Agenda for the "Constitutionalisation" of the Law of Libel', in Birks, P. (ed.), *Privacy and Loyalty*, Clarendon Press, Oxford, 1997, p. 51.

——, '*Sullivan v The New York Times* Goes Down Under' [1996] *Public Law* 126.

Lumb, R. D. and Moens, G. A., *The Constitution of the Commonwealth of Australia Annotated*, 5th edn, Butterworths, Sydney, 1995.

Lynch, A., 'Unanimity in a Time of Uncertainty: The High Court Settles its Differences in *Lange v. Australian Broadcasting Corporation*' (1997) 6 *Griffith Law Review* 211.

McDonald, L., 'The Denizens of Democracy: The High Court and the "Free Speech" Cases' (1994) 5 *Public Law Review* 160.

McLachlan, J., 'Constitutional Validity of Orders for Divestiture of Property under the Trade Practices Act' (1990) 1 *Public Law Review* 120.

McLeish, S., 'Making Sense of Religion and the Constitution: A Fresh Start for Section 116' (1992) 18 *Monash University Law Review* 207.

McMillan, J., Evans, G., and Storey, H., *Australia's Constitution: Time for Change?*, Allen & Unwin, Sydney, 1983.

McNamara, L. and Solomon, T., 'The Commonwealth *Racial Hatred Act* 1995: Achievement or Disappointment?' (1996) 18 *Adelaide Law Review* 259.

Maher, L. W., 'Defamation, Free Speech and Local Government Politics' (1995) 3 *Torts Law Journal* 116.

Mason, A., 'A Bill of Rights for Australia?' (1989) 5 *Australian Bar Review* 79.

——, 'A New Perspective on Separation of Powers' (1996) 82 *Canberra Bulletin of Public Administration* 1.

Mason, K., 'Citizenship', in C. Saunders (ed.), *Courts of Final Jurisdiction: The Mason Court in Australia*, Federation Press, Sydney, 1996, p. 35.

Meagher, R. P., 'Civil Rights: Some Reflections' (1998) 72 *Australian Law Journal* 47.

Mendelson, W., 'Foreign Reactions to American Experience with "Due Process of Law"' (1955) 41 *Virginia Law Review* 493.

Miller, J., 'The End of Freedom, Method in *Theophanous*' (1996) 1 *Newcastle Law Review* 39.

Moffat, R. C. L., 'Philosophical Foundations of the Australian Constitutional Tradition' (1965) 5 *Sydney Law Review* 59.

Moore, T. and Maddox, G., 'Rights, Jurisdiction and Responsible Government—The Spectre of *Capital Television*' (1995) 33 *Journal of Commonwealth and Comparative Politics* 400.

Moore, W. H., *The Constitution of the Commonwealth of Australia*, 2nd edn [1910], Legal Books, Sydney, 1997.

Mortensen, R., 'Blasphemy in a Secular State: A Pardonable Sin?' (1994) 17 *University of New South Wales Law Journal* 409.

Neasey, J. M., 'Andrew Inglis Clark Senior and Australian Federation' (1969) 15(2) *Australian Journal of Politics and History* 1.

O'Brien, B., 'Inchoate Rights to Interstate Communications Under Section 92' (1982) 13 *Melbourne University Law Review* 198.

O'Brien, D., 'Parliamentary Privilege and the Implied Freedom of Speech' (1995) 25 *Queensland Law Society Journal* 569.

Official Record of the Debates of the Australasian Federal Convention, 1891–1898, 5 vols, Legal Books, Sydney, 1986.

Omar, I., 'Towards a Meaningful Discourse on Rights in Australia' (1996) 1 *Newcastle Law Review* 15.

O'Meara, S., '*Theophanous* and *Stephens*: The Constitutional Freedom of Communication and Defamation Law' (1995) 3 *Torts Law Journal* 105.

O'Neill, N., 'Blue-eyed Babies May be Murdered: Dicey's First Principle Upheld in the Court of Appeal' (1987) 12 *Legal Service Bulletin* 2.

——, 'Constitutional Human Rights in Australia' (1987) 17 *Federal Law Review* 85.

O'Neill, N. and Handley, R., *Retreat from Injustice: Human Rights in Australian Law*, Federation Press, Sydney, 1994.

O'Neil, R. M., 'Freedom of Expression and Public Affairs in Australia and the United States: Does a Written Bill of Rights Really Matter?' (1994) 22 *Federal Law Review* 1.

Orr, G., 'The Choice Not to Choose: Commonwealth Electoral Law and the Withholding of Preferences' (1997) 23 *Monash University Law Review* 285.

Pannam, C. L., 'Discrimination on the Basis of State Residence in Australia and the United States' (1967) 6 *Melbourne University Law Review* 105.

——, 'Section 116 and the Federal Territories' (1961) 35 *Australian Law Journal* 209.

——, 'Travelling Section 116 with a US Road Map' (1963) 4 *Melbourne University Law Review* 41.

——, 'Trial by Jury and Section 80 of the Australian Constitution' (1968) 6 *Sydney Law Review* 1.

Parker, C., 'Protection of Judicial Process as an Implied Constitutional Principle' (1994) 16 *Adelaide Law Review* 341.

Patapan, H., 'Competing Visions of Liberalism: Theoretical Underpinnings of the Bill of Rights Debate in Australia' (1997) 21 *Melbourne University Law Review* 497.

——, 'The Dead Hands of the Founders? Original Intent and the Constitutional Protection of Rights and Freedoms in Australia' (1997) 25 *Federal Law Review* 211.

——, 'Rewriting Australian Liberalism: The High Court's Juriprudence of Rights' (1996) 31 *Australian Journal of Political Science* 225.

Potter, R., 'The Development of Freedom of Speech Defences to Defamation in Australia and Other Common Law Jurisdictions' (1998) 3 *Media and Arts Law Review* 82.

Puls, J., 'The Wall of Separation: Section 116, the First Amendment and Constitutional Religious Guarantees' (1998) 26 *Federal Law Review* 139.

Quick, J. and Garran, R., *The Annotated Constitution of the Australian Commonwealth*, 1901 edn, Legal Books, Sydney, 1995.

Rares, S., 'Free Speech and the Law' (1995) 13 *Australian Bar Review* 209.

Reynolds, J., 'A. I. Clark's American Sympathies and his Influence on Australian Federation' (1958) 32 *Australian Law Journal* 62.

Rich, W., 'Approaches to Constitutional Interpretation in Australia: An American Perspective' (1993) 12 *University of Tasmania Law Review* 150.

——, 'Converging Constitutions: A Comparative Analysis of Constitutional Law in the United States and Australia' (1993) 21 *Federal Law Review* 202.

Richardson, M., 'Constitutional Freedom of Political Speech in Defamation Law: Some Insights from a Utilitarian-Economic Perspective' (1996) 4 *Torts Law Journal* 242.

——, 'Freedom of Political Discussion and Intellectual Property Law in Australia' (1997) 11 *European Intellectual Property Review* 631.

Roberts, H., 'Retrospective Criminal Laws and the Separation of Judicial Power' (1997) 8 *Public Law Review* 170.

Rose, D., 'Discrimination, Uniformity and Preference', in Zines, L. (ed.), *Commentaries on the Australian Constitution*, Butterworths, Sydney, 1977, p. 191.

——, 'Judicial Reasonings and Responsibilities in Constitutional Cases' (1994) 20 *Melbourne University Law Review* 195.

Rosenberg, G. N. and Williams, J. M., 'Do Not Go Gently into that Good Right: The First Amendment in the High Court of Australia' (1997) 11 *Supreme Court Review* 439.

Sackville, R., 'Continuity and Judicial Creativity—Some Observations' (1997) 20 *University of New South Wales Law Journal* 145.

Sadurski, W., 'Neutrality of Law Towards Religion' (1990) 12 *Sydney Law Review* 420.

——, 'On Legal Definitions of "Religion" ' (1989) 63 *Australian Law Journal* 834.

Sampford, C. and Preston, K. (eds), *Interpreting Constitutions: Theories, Principles and Institutions*, Federation Press, Sydney, 1996.

Santow, G. F. K., 'Aspects of Judicial Restraint' (1995) 13 *Australian Bar Review* 116.

Saunders, C., 'Concepts of Equality in the Australian Constitution', in Lindell, G. (ed.), *Future Directions in Australian Constitutional Law*, Federation Press, 1994, p. 209.

—— (ed.), *Courts of Final Jurisdiction: The Mason Court in Australia*, Federation Press, Sydney, 1996.

Sawer, G., 'The Australian Constitution and the Australian Aborigine' (1966) 2 *Federal Law Review* 17.

——, 'The Separation of Powers in Australian Federalism' (1961) 35 *Australian Law Journal* 177.

Scutt, J. A. (ed.), *Lionel Murphy: A Radical Judge*, McCulloch Publishing, Melbourne, 1987.

Smallbone, D. A., 'Recent Suggestions of an Implied "Bill of Rights" in the Constitution, Considered as Part of a General Trend in Constitution Interpretation' (1993) 21 *Federal Law Review* 254.

Sonter, D., 'Intention or Effect? Commonwealth and State Legislation after Cole v Whitfield' (1995) 69 *Australian Law Journal* 332.

Speagle, D., '*Australian Capital Television Pty Ltd v Commonwealth*' (1992) 18 *Melbourne University Law Review* 938.

Stokes, M., 'Constitutional Commitments not Original Intentions: Interpretation in the Freedom of Speech Cases' (1994) 16 *Sydney Law Review* 250.

Stone, A., 'Freedom of Political Communication, the Constitution and the Common Law' (1998) 26 *Federal Law Review* 219.

——, 'Incomplete Theorizing in the High Court' (1998) 26 *Federal Law Review* 195.

——, '*Lange, Levy* and the Direction of the Freedom of Political Communication under the Australian Constitution' (1998) 21 *University of New South Wales Law Journal* 117.

Stow, F. L., 'Section 117 of the Constitution' (1906) 3 *Commonwealth Law Review* 97.

Temby, I., ' "In this Labyrinth There is No Golden Thread": Section 92 and the Impressionistic Approach' (1984) 58 *Australian Law Journal* 86.

Thomson, J. A., 'An Australian Bill of Rights: Glorious Promises, Concealed Dangers' (1994) 19 *Melbourne University Law Review* 1020.

——, 'Constitutional Authority for Judicial Review: A Contribution from the Framers of the Australian Constitution', in G. Craven (ed.), *The Convention Debates 1891–1898: Commentaries, Indices and Guide*, vol. 6, Legal Books, Sydney, 1986, p. 173.

——, 'Slouching Towards Tenterfield: The Constitutionalization of Tort Law in Australia' (1995) 3 *Tort Law Review* 81.

Toohey, J., 'A Government of Laws, and Not of Men?' (1993) 4 *Public Law Review* 158.

——, 'A Matter of Justice: Human Rights in Australian Law' (1998) 27 *Western Australian Law Review* 129.

Trindade, F. A, 'Defamation in the Course of Political Discussion—The New Common Law Defence' (1998) 114 *Law Quarterly Review* 1.

——, ' "Political Discussion" and the Law of Defamation' (1995) 111 *Law Quarterly Review* 199.

Tucker, D., 'Representation-Reinforcing Review: Arguments about Political Advertising in Australia and the United States' (1994) 16 *Sydney Law Review* 274.

Turello, A., 'Extinguishment of Native Title and the Constitutional Requirement of Just Terms' (1993) 3(62) *Aboriginal Law Bulletin* 11.

Twomey, A., 'Dead Ducks and Endangered Political Communication—*Levy v State of Victoria* and *Lange v Australian Broadcasting Corporation*' (1997) 19 *Sydney Law Review* 76.

——, 'Free to Choose or Compelled to Lie?—The Rights of Voters after *Langer v The Commonwealth*' (1996) 24 *Federal Law Review* 201.

——, 'Theophanous v Herald & Weekly Times Ltd; Stephens v West Australian Newspapers Ltd' (1994) 19 *Melbourne University Law Review* 1104.

Walker, B., 'Has Lange Really Settled the Common Law?' (1997) 8 *Public Law Review* 216.

de Q Walker, G., 'The Constitutional Protection of Property Rights: Economic and Legal Aspects', in James, M. (ed.), *The Constitutional Challenge*, Centre for Independent Studies, Sydney, 1982, p. 135.

Walker, K., 'Persona Designata, Incompatibility and the Separation of Powers' (1997) 8 *Public Law Review* 153.

——, 'Who's the Boss? The Judiciary, the Executive, the Parliament and the Protection of Human Rights' (1995) 25 *University of Western Australia Law Review* 238.

Walker, K. and Dunn, K., 'Mr Langer is not Entitled to be Agitator: *Albert Langer v Commonwealth*' (1996) 20 *Melbourne University Law Review* 909.

Walker, S., 'The Impact of the High Court's Free Speech Cases on Defamation Law' (1995) 17 *Sydney Law Review* 43.

——, '*Lange v. ABC*: The High Court Rethinks the "Constitutionalisation" of Defamation Law' (1998) 6 *Torts Law Journal* 9.

Wells, B., 'Aliens: The Outsiders in the Constitution' (1996) 19 *University of Queensland Law Journal* 45.

Wheeler, F., 'The Doctrine of Separation of Powers and Constitutionally Entrenched Due Process in Australia' (1997) 23 *Monash University Law Review* 248.

Wilcox, M. R., *An Australian Charter of Rights?*, LBC, Sydney, 1993.

Williams, G., 'Civil Liberties and the Constitution—A Question of Interpretation' (1994) 5 *Public Law Review* 82.

——, '*Engineers* and Implied Rights', in Coper, M. and Williams, G. (eds), *How Many Cheers for Engineers?*, Federation Press, 1997, p. 105.

——, '*Engineers* is Dead, Long Live the Engineers!' (1995) 17 *Sydney Law Review* 62.

——, 'Freedom of Political Discussion and Australian Electoral Laws' (1997) 4 *Canberra Law Review* 5.

——, 'The High Court and the People', in Selby, H. (ed.), *Tomorrow's Law*, Federation Press, 1995, Sydney, p. 271.

——, 'Lionel Murphy and Democracy and Rights', in Coper, M. and Williams, G. (eds), *Justice Lionel Murphy: Influential or Merely Prescient?*, Federation Press, Sydney, 1997, p. 50.

——, 'Reading the Judicial Mind: Appellate Argument in the *Communist Party Case*' (1993) 15 *Sydney Law Review* 3.

——, 'Sounding the Core of Representative Democracy: Implied Rights and Electoral Reform' (1996) 20 *Melbourne University Law Review* 848.

——, 'The Suppression of Communism by Force of Law: Australia in the Early 1950s' (1996) 42 *Australian Journal of Politics and History* 220.

Williams, G. and Darke, M., 'Euthanasia Laws and the Australian Constitution' (1997) 20 *University of New South Wales Law Journal* 647.

Williams, J. M., 'In Search of the Federal Citizen: Andrew Inglis Clark and the "14th Amendment" ', Discussion Paper No. 30, Federalism Research Centre, Australian National University, November 1995.

——, 'Race, Citizenship and the Formation of the Australian Constitution: Andrew Inglis Clark and the "14th Amendment" ' (1996) 42 *Australian Journal of Politics and History* 10.

——, 'Revitalising the Republic: Lionel Murphy and the Protection of Individual Rights' (1996) 8 *Public Law Review* 27.

——, ' "With Eyes Open": Andrew Inglis Clark and our Republican Tradition' (1995) 23 *Federal Law Review* 149.

Winterton, G., 'Extra-Constitutional Notions in Australian Constitutional Law' (1986) 16 *Federal Law Review* 223.

——, 'Murphy: A Maverick Reconsidered' (1997) 20 *University of New South Wales Law Journal* 204.

——, 'Popular Sovereignty and Constitutional Continuity' (1998) 26 *Federal Law Review* 1.

——, 'The Separation of Judicial Power as an Implied Bill of Rights', in Lindell, G. (ed.), *Future Directions in Australian Constitutional Law*, Federation Press, 1994, p. 185.

——, 'The Significance of the *Communist Party Case*' (1992) 18 *Melbourne University Law Review* 630.

Wiseman, D., 'Defectively Representing Representative Democracy' (1995) 25 *University of Western Australia Law Review* 77.

Wright, H. G. A., 'Sovereignty of the People—The New Constitutional *Grundnorm*?' (1998) 26 *Federal Law Review* 165.

Zines, L., *Constitutional Change in the Commonwealth*, Cambridge University Press, 1991.

——, 'Constitutionally Protected Individual Rights', in Finn, P. D. (ed.), *Essays on Law and Government*, vol. 2, *The Citizen and the State in the Courts*, LBC, Sydney, 1996, p. 136.

——, *The High Court and the Constitution*, 4th edn, Butterworths, Sydney, 1997.

——, 'A Judicially Created Bill of Rights?' (1994) 16 *Sydney Law Review* 166.

Zines, L. and Lindell, G. J., 'Form and Substance: "Discrimination" in Modern Constitutional Law' (1992) 21 *Federal Law Review* 136.

Index